# THE
# CAMPAIGN OF 1866
## IN
# GERMANY

COMPILED BY

## THE DEPARTMENT OF MILITARY HISTORY
## OF THE PRUSSIAN STAFF

TRANSLATED INTO ENGLISH BY

## COLONEL VON WRIGHT
CHIEF OF THE STAFF VIII. THE PRUSSIAN CORPS AND

## CAPTAIN HENRY M. HOZIER,
ASSISTANT CONTROLLER

PREPARED AT

## THE TOPOGRAPHICAL AND STATISTICAL DEPARTMENT
## OF THE WAR OFFICE

**The Naval & Military Press Ltd**

Reproduced by kind permission of the Central Library,
Royal Military Academy, Sandhurst

Published by

**The Naval & Military Press Ltd**

Unit 10, Ridgewood Industrial Park,

Uckfield, East Sussex,

TN22 5QE England

Tel: +44 (0) 1825 749494

Fax: +44 (0) 1825 765701

**www.naval‑military‑press.com**

© The Naval & Military Press Ltd 2005

Printed and bound by Antony Rowe Ltd, Eastbourne

# CONTENTS.

## BOOK THE FIRST.

## BOOK THE SECOND.

## BOOK THE THIRD.

# BOOK THE FIRST.

## CHAPTER I.

### DIPLOMATIC PRELIMINARIES AND PREPARATION.

THE war of 1866 between Prussia and Austria was a necessity of the history of the world; it must have sooner or later broken out. The German nation could not for ever exist in the political weakness into which it had sunk between the Latin West and the Slavonian East, since the early and glorious age of Germanic Emperors. During the centuries in which, with the exception of Italy, all the neighbouring States consolidated themselves, broke the power of their vassals, and firmly knitted together the forces of often heterogeneous races, an independence of the different parts sprung up in Germany, which condemned the whole to a state of impotence. The experiment of installing some thirty sovereignties as the constituent members of a Confederation which should take its place as an European Power, was successful neither as regarded its internal or external relations. A deep inclination towards unity was current in the whole German nation, but for the sake of unity neither were the princes prepared to sacrifice their rights nor the people their peculiarities. The experience of fifty years had shown that the goal of unity was not to be attained by means of moral advancement, but that to achieve it a physical compulsion on the part of some German Power was necessary. The gradual development of events had now left only two great European Powers in Germany, each too strong to submit to the other; on the equal balance of power of both existed the minor States in the fatherland. Germany's importance in the European world, whenever Austria and Prussia followed a mutual external policy, has always been proved by the results obtained by their alliances, but in Germany itself their interests were irreconcileable. In Germany there was not room for both, one or the other must succumb. Austria had an existence foreign from Germany. Prussia could not give up her Germanic situation without being annihilated.

During a century's apparent peace between Prussia and Austria this antagonism of the two States had never died. One of the links in the chain of contest for the leadership of Germany was the strife for the Elbe Duchies, but this was only a single symptom of the deep-seated contest which the Campaign of 1866 brought to a decision.

The United success of the Prussian and Austrian arms against Denmark in 1866 had led to the Peace of Vienna, by which King Christian IX. surrendered all his rights over the duchies of the Elbe to the King of Prussia and the Emperor of Austria. Further arrangements depended upon the accord of these two sovereigns without the power of interference on the part of any third. The territory thus acquired lay entirely within the sphere of Prussia's power. Austria could claim as little title to participation therein as if Prussia and Austria together in Italy had acquired Modena and Tuscany. The expedient of a cession of the Austrian right to the Elbe Duchies in return for some other indemnity did not appear impossible, and was even sought for. The Emperor Francis Joseph was unwilling to cede his claims without a concomitant cession of territory to Austria on the part of Prussia, and against any such cession King William had openly expressed his views, so that the Duchies remained under the common administration of the two Powers. Such a system soon conduced to not only great disadvantages for the territory itself, but also to an increasing discord between the Cabinets of Vienna and Berlin.

Once more the Convention of Gastein, framed in August, 1865, caused a momentary understanding : by the terms of this Convention, Lauenburg, in return for the payment of one and a-half millions of thalers, passed into the sole possession of the King of Prussia, while in future Prussia alone was to carry on the administration of Schleswig, and Austria that of Holstein ; but this arrangement was only a postponement, not a definite settlement, of the question at issue.

To prevent the increase of power of her neighbour in the north, Austria strove to create a minor State of the Duchies, although she, equally with Prussia, had ever combated against the development of minor States, and brought forward as Pretender to the crown of this minor State a Pretender whom she had hitherto never recognized. This pretender was supported by a political party which Austria, no less than Prussia, had always opposed at home. The creation of a new minor State on the Eider must involve Prussia in another war ; for besides that financial ruin must be the lot of a sovereign Schleswig-Holstein, its military power would never have sufficed to hold its own against Denmark, and the protection due to it from the German Confederation must always come from Prussia.

Austria had full right to expect compensation if she consented to yield her rights to Prussia ; but as long as the territory was held in common, it was a breach of existing conventions that the Austrian Administration of Holstein permitted such public meetings as took place in Altona in the commencement of 1866, the direct aim of which was to transfer Holstein, which was co-possessed by Prussia, to Duke Frederic. At these meetings South German democrats encouraged the people to refuse the payment of taxes, made, with the concurring sanction of one, the most invidious attacks against the other possessor of the Duchy, and planted revolutionary ideas in an essentially conservative and loyal population.

26th January.   In a note of the 26th January, the President of the Prussian Ministry protested against such a breach of the principle of sovereignty, under the protection of the double eagle, and demanded the maintenance of the common rule of the Duchies in *statu quo*, asserting at the same time that no infringement of it would be permitted. He desired no diminution of the Austrian rights, but solely the maintenance of the rights of both Powers. He added that if the Imperial Government returned a negative or evasive answer it would be evident that it was no longer willing to act side by side with Prussia, in which case the latter would regain her full political liberty of action, and must avail herself of it in her own interest.

An answer did not come from Count Mensdorff until the 8th February, in which it was pointed out that it was Prussia's 8th February. own fault that no arrangement had as yet been made with regard to the Duchies, that the Austrian administration of Holstein depended on Austrian ideas alone, but the reply was silent on the main point adduced by Prussia that this administration affected perniciously the rights of Prussia. No answer was sent to Vienna, and it appeared as if the relations between the two Cabinets would have been broken off.

In the meantime agitation continued in Holstein, and matters arrived at a crisis which might easily lead to either peace or war. It was necessary to consider whether a lasting and sincere friendship with Austria might be obtained by further concession, not in this special case alone, but in the whole Holstein question, or whether it was the policy of Vienna here, as elsewhere, to suppress Prussia, and to prevent her free development in Germany by means of the press, the elements of revolution, the power of the Confederation, overtures for an alliance with France; in fact by every possible means.

On the 28th February a council was held in Berlin, under the presidency of the King, to which, among others, the Governor of Schleswig and the Chief of the Staff of the Army were called, because, there being the possibility of a rupture, military consequences must be considered.

It is said that on this occasion everybody agreed in the view that no retraction was possible in the matter of the Elbe Duchies without a humiliation of the honour of the country, and a wounding of national feeling, and that it was necessary to proceed in the way hitherto pursued, even at the risk of a war. No warlike preparation was at this time decreed, for practically the matured organization of the army insured a proper display of military force at any time, if it were required for the defence of the fatherland, and the King's feelings were averse to an offensive war.

In Vienna also, on the 10th March, there was held a Council 10th March. of General Officers, to which General Benedek was summoned; immediately afterwards an increased activity was manifested both in the political and military departments.

On the 16th March the Cabinet of Vienna despatched to 16th March. several German Courts a secret circular note which, though at first denied, ultimately became known, holding out a prospect

of the Schleswig-Holstein question being eventually settled by
the Confederation, but expressing the expectation that the VIIth,
VIIIth, IXth, and Xth Corps of the Federal Army would be
prepared for war and would co-operate with the Austrian forces.

All this was proposed "in case that Prussia should cause an
open breach," and " with reference to Prussia's preparations
for war."

The Austrian Government thus overrode the stipulations
of the Conventions of Vienna and Gastein, as well as the
normal relations of the Germanic Confederation, on the supposition of warlike preparations, which notoriously had not
been made in Prussia, while at that time in Austria reserves
had already been called in, troops had been transported from
Moravia, Galicia, and Hungary to Bohemia, and the fortresses
nearest the Prussian frontier had been repaired.

The distribution of the Austrian troops in the middle of
March was known, it was—

|  | Field Battalions. | 4th Battalions. | Squadrons. | Batteries. |
|---|---|---|---|---|
| In Bohemia :— |  |  |  |  |
| Infantry | 18 | 10 | 10 | 19 |
| Jägers | 3 | .. | .. | .. |
|  |  |  |  |  |
| In Moravia :— |  |  |  |  |
| Infantry | 12 | 4 | 12 | 10 |
| Jägers | 2 | .. | .. | .. |
|  |  |  |  |  |
| In Western Galicia :— |  |  |  |  |
| Infantry | 6 | 4 | 12 | 4 |
| Jägers | 1 | .. | .. | .. |
|  |  |  |  |  |
| Total | 42 | 18 | 34 | 33 |

By the 28th March these were reinforced by—
In Bohemia—

The Brigade Ringelsheim from Cracow, namely—

> The " King of Hanover " Regiment, No. 42 ;
> The Würtenberg Regiment, No. 73 ;
> Jäger Battalion, No. 26 ;
> Besides the Constantine Regiment, No. 18, from Pesth;
> The Regiment of Radetsky Hussars, No. 5 ;
> The Regiment of Hesse Cassel Hussars, No. 8, from
> Upper Austria.

In Galicia the seven battalions which had been moved were
replaced by three field battalions which had formerly been
quartered further eastwards, and three 4th battalions augmented
to a war strength.

The 30th Jäger Battalion came to Teschen.

The troops in Bohemia were thus reinforced by ten battalions and ten squadrons.

Besides, there were twenty squadrons, namely,—

The Uhlans* of Archduke Charles, No. 3;
The Uhlans of the Emperor Francis Joseph, No. 6;
The Uhlans of the Archduke Charles Louis, No. 7;
The Uhlans of Count Mensdorff, No. 9;

on the march from Hungary and Siebenbürgen to Bohemia; two other regiments of Cavalry had already reached Moravia from Galicia.

All these measures could hardly be considered as solely a distribution for peace. Some, indeed, of the regiments moved to Bohemia were thus quartered in the vicinity of their recruiting districts, but on the other hand, those whose recruiting districts lay in other provinces were not removed from Bohemia. The Jewish† riots did not afford a sufficient motive either, as the troops were for the most part quartered near the Prussian frontier where such broils had never occurred. The Austrian press was cautioned to publish nothing concerning movements of troops, and this secrecy, and official denials of preparatives for war, increased distrust.

On the 28th March, a Council of State was held in Berlin, 28th March. in which, before everything else, the military situation was considered. Without reckoning the troops on the march there were now, as shown above, in the Austrian territories bordering on Silesia, 71 battalions, 44 squadrons, and 33 batteries. The Cavalry was fully prepared for war, the Artillery mustered 240 horsed pieces, and it wanted only the calling in and the very easy transport of the Reserves of the Infantry to form in those parts within a few days an army of 80,000 men. In Silesia, to face these, there were 38 battalions, 29 squadrons, 18 batteries, about 25,000 men, scattered in the garrisons ordinarily occupied in time of peace. Men on furlough and soldiers of the Reserve had not been called in, and the complement of horses of the Artillery and Cavalry was only on a peace footing.

If Prussia had had a breach with Austria in view the pretext 29th March. was thus given. But the King, rejecting all proposals for more extensive preparation, limited himself to purely defensive measures.

As Austria in peace held nine-tenths of her guns horsed and Prussia only five-eighths, the following Decrees were issued on the 29th and 31st March. The regiments of the Field Artillery of the Guard, of the IIIrd, IVth, and VIth Corps, and the 1st and Horse Division of the Vth Corps, were to be placed on a war strength by calling up the junior men on furlough and have their depôts formed. The necessary horses were to be bought.

The battalions of regiments in the provinces immediately threatened—that is to say, those of the 12th, 11th, 9th, 5th, and 7th Divisions, as well as those of the four new regiments

---

* Lancers.
† Some riots took place in Prague during the early part of 1866, caused by the antagonism of the Christian population towards the Jews.

of the Guard, and of the 72nd Regiment in garrison at Torgau, were to be placed on the same peace strength as the Guard, —686 men.

The Infantry and Artillery of the VIth Corps, quartered in the Elbe Duchies, were similarly strengthened; three ammunition columns were forwarded thither by railway, and there horsed.

The fortresses of Cosel, Neisse, Glatz, Torgau, and Wittenberg, received their full war garrisons of Artillery and Pioneers, as well as the guns still necessary for their armament, while in Glogau, Spandau and Magdeburg the above-mentioned troops were raised to the strength fixed for the first mobilization period. In Cosel, Neisse, and Glatz, the batteries for sallies were horsed.

When now the Austrian Government declared that an attack upon Prussia was far removed from the ideas of the Kaiser, and expressed the hope that the Prussian Cabinet would also clearly express its disinclination for a breach of the peace, the latter could be given with a clear conscience, but it was coupled with the remark that the measures taken by Prussia had only been called forth by Austria's previous military preparations; the priority of armaments, however, the Austrian 7th April. note of the 7th April steadily disputed. "No considerable "concentration, no unusual purchase of horses, no recall of "men on furlough to any amount worthy of notice had taken "place." On the contrary, Count Mensdorff complained of measures for the preparation of "mobilization in Prussia."

It was easy to perceive the purely defensive extent of the preparations undertaken, so transparent is the organization of the Prussian Army, and so full the freedom of the Prussian press. Not a single body of troops had really been mobilized, the battalions could not leave the fortresses because no Depôt and Landwehr battalions were disposable for their relief, and all that had been decreed made only a single division available for the defence of the frontier. On the other hand, it was difficult to discern what went on in Austria. It is true that the reports of preparations there may have been manifoldly exaggerated, but there were no means afforded to test their veracity. All assertions coincided in stating that men on furlough had been called in, that numerous military trains had been despatched to the north, and that at the least the 4th Battalions had been placed on a war footing.

As the Austrian note of the 7th April regretted that no news had been received that in consequence of the peaceable declarations of the Kaiser the Prussian "order for mobiliza-tion" of the 28th March had not been put into execution, the 15th April. Prussian Cabinet, on the 15th April, sent a message to say that first the distribution of troops acknowledged by Austria and similar measures undertaken before any preparation was made on the Prussian side should be repealed.

18th April. On the 18th April, in reply, Count Mensdorff declared that, in order to afford satisfactory results to the exchange of friendly declarations on either side, His Majesty the Kaiser was prepared to repeal the distribution as yet ordered, and such measures as had been taken towards preparing the army for war, by an order of the 25th of that month, provided that the Court of Berlin would promise to issue on the same or the following day an order to place all its forces on a peace footing.

The Prussian Cabinet entered into this proposal. It promised on the 21st April to cancel any preparations undertaken 21st April. in the same proportion as the Austrian Court did the measures which had caused them. As the disarmaments went on communication was requested, so as to allow matters on the Prussian side to proceed in equal degrees. The expectation was also expressed that the other German States should cancel their preparations. So for a time it appeared as if the threatening danger of war was to pass over, but this episode did not long endure.

Even before the arrival of the Prussian answer in Vienna the *Abendpost* announced: "The Imperial Government will " under all circumstances adhere to the programme which " will lead to a solution of pending questions on the basis of " the national interest and the necessities of the German " people." These ambiguous phrases were explained by a despatch from Count Mensdorff, dated the 26th April, which proposed, in consideration of certain advantages to Prussia, to yield the Elbe Duchies to the pretender to them who could show the best title, and that the Germanic Confederation should decide upon who this should be. Such a decision could only be valid if both possessors consented thereto. Not the less Austria declared her intention alone to pursue this policy in default of a common agreement. A fresh despatch ensued in relation to the question of disarmament after the term fixed for its commencement had elapsed.

His Majesty the Emperor, as Count Mensdorff wrote on the 26th April. same 26th April, was fully ready to cancel the order for the reinforcement of the garrisons of Bohemia, but it appeared from the latest intelligence from Italy that the latter State contemplated an attack on Venetia. It was therefore necessary to increase the means of defence of the empire in another direction, and to place the Austrian Army in Italy on a war footing, which could not be done without considerable movement of troops in the interior of the empire, which, however, would not prevent the Prussian Government from reducing its mobilized corps. If these two despatches were placed side by side, the result would be that while Prussia disarmed, the middle German States, under Austria's presidency, and influenced by the democratic current of feeling in favour of the Prince of Augustenberg, would decide on Prussia's right to the Duchies, and Austria would have time and leisure to put as much of her army as she liked on a war footing undisturbedly. It was immaterial whether this was done in Bohemia, as was hitherto the case, or in Hungary or Illyria, in either case a strong army would be quickly assembled on the Lower Po or the Upper Elbe. In the latter case the Prussian Army had not only to make the necessary march, but to be previously mobilized, and must necessarily arrive too late for the occasion.

It could hardly have been believed in Vienna that the Prussian Cabinet would agree to such a proposition. There arose in Berlin a deep and general distrust of the neighbouring Power, the more so as it was well known that Italy was at that time by no means prepared for war. The less security Prussia found in the German Confederation the more was she compelled to seek for an ally elsewhere. Such a one was Italy, either with or without an express treaty of alliance. War between the two German Powers offered to King Victor Emmanuel the opportunity which he could not well slip if he wished ever to make good his claims to Venetia. Prussia indeed naturally wished that Italy should be prepared to act in case of war against such a formidable enemy as Austria, but could not expect that she would arm only in case of an eventuality. The Cabinet of Florence must naturally in its own interest be assured that the armies of both States were at the same time prepared for war, for this Prussia could fix no given period, because she did not contemplate an attack on Austria. Under these circumstances it is manifest that hitherto only general stipulations could be discussed with General Govone, the Italian envoy to Berlin. The despatches of the 26th April gave a new energy to these negotiations, in which full care was taken of the interests of Germany, and as Austria had caused the first preparations on the part of Prussia, so she now called those of Italy into action.

In his answer to the Austrian despatch, Count Bismarck expressed his opinion that according to the ideas of the Prussian Government Austria had no cause to prepare for war to defend herself against Italy, and that Prussia could not enter into the impending, so important, negotiations with the Imperial Government, unless a perfectly equal footing were maintained in the war preparation of both powers.

30th April. On the 30th April, Count Mensdorff declared that in consequence of this declaration the Austrian Cabinet must regard the negotiations for a *pari passu* disarmament as void of effect.

It is now necessary to cast a glance on the attitude of the other German Powers.

Prussia had, in a circular despatch of the 24th March, asked the German Courts what assistance she might expect from them in case of being attacked by Austria, and at the same time had pointed out the necessity of a reform of the Germanic Confederation. The answers thereto were evasive and referred, with regard to the desired assistance, to the 11th Article of the Constitution of the Confederation: Herr Von Beust,* especially in a note of the 6th April, expressed the view

---

* At this time Herr Von Beust was Prime Minister of Saxony.

that, to remove the threatening dangers, the application of the existing laws of the Bund alone was necessary.

According to this article, Austria and Prussia should bring their disputes before the Diet, which should endeavour to mediate by means of a committee, and if that failed the matter in dispute should be decided by the Confederation, which should compel the obedience of the disputing parties.

The paragraph referred to leaves nothing to be desired with regard to clearness, but does not state what is to be done if, as was here the case, the two conflicting parties—here two European Powers—could not be compelled to obedience.

It is hardly credible that statesmen could have expected that the course of affairs would rest quiescent until a well-ordered Committee of the Confederation had declared its decree. The result was much more calculated to demonstrate how rotten was the whole constitution of the Confederation unless it were supported by the common action of Austria and Prussia.

The present moment was not considered convenient for a reform of this constitution; but no other opportunity had ever been found which appeared to the various Courts suitable. Prussia reverted, in a further despatch of the 11th April, to the question of reform. After giving the outlines of the proposed reform she recommended an immediate assembly of a common Parliament as the sole still remaining means of preserving peace.

Among the Middle States, Würtemberg, and particularly Saxony, had lately assumed a hostile attitude towards Prussia. In that State recruits had been called in as early as March, and the purchase of horses had been ordered.

If it had been possible for Saxony to maintain neutrality it would willingly have been accepted by Prussia, as the Marks and Berlin would thereby have been covered from every attack. But the case to be considered was rather that if Saxony desired to remain neutral, whether her neutrality would be respected. The Saxon arms could insure the security of that country neither against Austria nor against Prussia, they rather compelled her to assume the cause of one or the other side. It must be conceded that the Saxon Government lay in a very difficult position between the two contending Powers. But it was the grossest political error to foment their quarrel. The Middle States could hardly doubt that their separate existence, at least in their present independent state, was seriously threatened if a breach of the peace occurred, and perhaps not least if Austria gained the upper hand.

When the Cabinet of Berlin now threatened Saxony with corresponding measures on account of her preparations, Herr Von Beust appealed to the Confederation, in order through it to demand a promise from Prussia that would accommodate herself to the 11th Article.

On the 9th May ten votes, among which was Hanover, declared themselves in favour of the motion.

What could be the result of such a step? All the Governments had solemnly declared that they contemplated no attack; but all armed, even those who declared that, from the theoretical view of the German Confederation, a war was impossible, and whose armaments were consequently a breach of the Confederation. Prussia notoriously only armed unwillingly and *pari passu* with the other armaments. Notwithstanding, the majority of the members of the Confederation called, not upon Austria and Saxony, but upon Prussia to abstain from violating the peace. This declaration showed what Prussia had to expect from the Middle States, and how she must, with all energy, take precautions for her own safety.

As far as Cabinets foreign from Germany were composed, there were no signs that they would not hold themselves apart from any stuggle between Austria and Prussia.

Denmark had not armed, and from France, at least, immediately, a well-meaning friendly neutrality might be anticipated.

Strengthening of Prussia to the extent that apprehension of her western neighbour would no longer induce her to lean unconditionally towards Russia or Austria was not antagonistic to the interests of France.

The establishment of a fleet of the second class would be pleasing to France, as it would aid in the balance of the command of the sea against the existing monopoly of England.

Napoleon's policy, since the commencement of his reign, had been friendly towards Prussia; but it was necessary to expect that in the course of events he could not remain an impartial spectator, and the prospect of his ultimate interference was a danger not to Prussia individually, but to Germany universally, if the latter were not first united.

To this reflection, and to the decided aversion of the King to wage war except for the honour and safety of Prussia, it must be ascribed that from March to May, no further defensive measures were undertaken.

In the meantime the Austrian armaments had uninterruptedly continued.

The Infantry regiments quartered in Bohemia, Moravia, and Western Galicia, as well as the greatest part of the 4th Battalions, had been augmented to a war strength; the carriages of the former had been horsed, and the depôts (200 men in strength) had been formed.

Two regiments of Hussars from Galicia, and three regiments of Uhlans from Hungary and Transylvania had been moved into Bohemia and Moravia. The ammunition wagons of the Artillery had also been horsed.

Theresienstadt and Josephstadt had been armed, and a strained activity had been apparent in the strengthening of Cracow and Königgrätz.

Troops had been assembled in Pesth, Vienna, and Laybach.

The border regiments had, by being placed on a war footing, supplied an available reserve of 40 battalions.

The recall of men on furlough of all arms, as well as of the Transport Train, caused the Austrian armaments, in the beginning of May, to appear nearly complete; they had already thus an advantage of five weeks, and Silesia and the Marks lay defenceless.

Such was the condition of affairs when the two despatches already mentioned (the 26th of April) reached Berlin.

The Councillors of the Crown now expressed their opinion that immediate measures should be taken to guard the honour, security, and independence of Prussia. The mobilization of the Prussian Army is a measure which interferes with all civil, as well as military, relations, and makes a deep impression both on public and private life, both on the palace and the cottage. But it is so fully prepared in peace, and organized in the minutest detail, that a superior order alone is necessary to cause it to be fully completed in a quite regulated period.

A partial or successive mobilization is more complicated and difficult for the executive authorities; it necessitates special regulations, which must differ from those already laid down.

A General Order from the Cabinet, on the 3rd May, ordered a preparation for war of the whole of the Cavalry of the Line, and of the Artillery, but of the Infantry only in the territories immediately menaced—that is to say, in the VIth, Vth, IIIrd, and IVth Corps d'Armée. In these, as well as in the corps of the Guards, the battalions of Infantry, Jägers, and pioneers were augmented to a complete war strength, and the necessary depôts were formed. It was only in the districts occupied by the Vth and VIth Corps that the Landwehr were called upon, and then only in small numbers, to furnish the necessary garrisons of the fortresses.

Of old it was possible to prepare the Prussian Army for war without actually calling it into action. This can hardly ever now be the case. In 1866, certainly, everyone was convinced that if the Army in its entirety was once called out it could not be dismissed without a struggle. The mobilization of the Army was then in fact war, and for that very reason every possible delay was made in speaking the decisive word, for even in May the hope that hostilities might still with honour be avoided had not been entirely abandoned.

It cannot be doubted that the decided declarations of both the Emperor Francis Joseph and King William were intended to be honestly acted up to. But Austria could well foster the hope that, by her political and military display of strength, Prussia, as in 1850, might be forced into compliance with her demands. The handing over of the question of the Elbe Duchies to the Confederation won popular opinion, led by democracy, in the small and Middle States; and the Princes, fearing a diminution of their power from Berlin, hung towards Vienna. None of the members of the Confederation had as yet declared for Prussia. The

latter stood totally isolated in Germany among estranged or
neutral neighbours. Internal affairs also appeared to throw
great difficulties in the way of the Prussian Government. The
re-organization of the Army had been carried out in opposition
to the majority of the House of Deputies, which also refused
the financial means for carrying on a war. Representatives of
the Prussian people, in public speeches, advanced the cause of
the Augustenburg Pretender. Public meetings passed resolu-
tions hostile to the Government, and petitions came in from
different parts of the kingdom, which begged the King, very
unnecessarily, to preserve peace.

But Austria deceived herself concerning the military strength
of Prussia, which afterwards showed itself a match for all its
enemies. Austria deceived herself concerning the real opinion
of the Prussian people, which had not been expressed in party
speeches. Men of the Reserve and Landwehr joined the
ranks, it is true, without enthusiasm for a war the cause
of which they did not comprehend, but obediently and with a
calm resolve. The Austrian preparations had convinced the
multitude that the measures adopted were unavoidable; and
the personality of the King was a warrant that the country
would not, except in case of the most urgent necessity, be
exposed to the costs of war. Austria also deceived herself in
the firmness of the King and his Councils, whom neither the
threat nor the actual danger of war would ever have induced
to allow Prussia to be thrust back into her former position, in
which she played the second part in Germany, and no part at
all in Europe.

But although an offensive war may have never been
originally contemplated by either one side or the other, the
preparations of the one compelled new gradations in those of
the other, until both reached a pitch which must infallibly lead
to a breach.

The order of the Cabinet of the 3rd May was quickly followed
5th to 12th by others of the 5th, 7th, 8th, 10th, and 12th May, the general
May. result of which was to call out the whole Field Army.

The troops of all branches of the Service were filled up to
war strength by the youngest men of the Reserve, the Depôts
were formed, and as far as necessary completed by the intro-
duction of recruits.

The regiments in the Elbe Duchies, and in the fortresses on
the Rhine were also mobilized, but no transgression of the
garrison arranged by Treaty for the federal fortresses was
allowed, as the number of battalions were there either corre-
spondingly diminished, or the men required for their augmentation were held back.

Finally, the pontoon trains of the Guard, of the IInd, IIIrd,
Vth and VIth Corps d'Armée were mobilized, as well as six
light field bridge trains, and four field telegraph divisions.

Of the Landwehr in Silesia and Posen, at first, only *cadres*
of 300 men had been called up. These 24 battalions were

increased to an individual strength of 806 men, and besides, for the defence of the threatened frontier, four regiments of Landwehr Cavalry, the 2nd and the 6th Landwehr Hussars, and the 1st and 2nd Regiments of Landwehr Uhlans were mobilized.

As in the majority of the fortresses only the ordinary peace garrison duty had to be performed, it was deemed admissible to employ part of the Landwehr for other purposes. There were, therefore, in the territory of the IInd Corps, the 9th and 21st Landwehr Regiments; in that of the VIIth Corps, the 13th and 15th Landwehr Regiments, as well as the 12 Battalions of the Landwehr of the Guard—in all 24 battalions,—raised to the strength of 806 men, mobilized and armed with needle-guns. Besides, the 7th Regiment of Landwehr Heavy Cavalry, the 2nd Regiment of Landwehr Dragoons, the 1st, 5th, and 10th Regiments of Landwehr Hussars, and the 3rd, 4th, and 8th Regiments of Landwehr Uhlans; altogether 32 squadrons of Landwehr were mobilized; the 16th and 17th Regiments of Landwehr were increased to 806 men, but without being mobilized.

All other battalions of Landwehr intended for the garrisons of fortresses were formed of a strength of only 500 men, and were armed with Minié rifles.

The full power of the country, especially in Cavalry, was not yet exerted.

Besides the fortresses of Cosel, Neisse, Glatz, Torgau and Wittenberg, Magdeburg and Spandau were also armed against a *coup de main*, and provided with a full complement of artillerymen and pioneers. The batteries for sallies were horsed, and the detachments of garrison cavalry formed.

Glogau, Coblenz, Cologne, Wesel, Stettin, and Dantzig, as well as Sonderburg, received the first augmentation of garrison gunners and pioneers. Glogau was afterwards armed against a *coup de main*. The maritime station of Kiel was also strengthened, and the marine battalion increased to a war strength.

*Pari passu* with the Prussian preparations, those in Austria, Saxony, Bavaria, Würtemberg, and Hanover had gone forward. From the last State a distinct declaration of their purpose was demanded, as a hostile action on the part of Hanover could have severed the communications between the two halves of the Prussian monarchy.

On the 20th May eight of the Middle States, of which two had armed, proposed a general disarmament. This motion, however, naturally had no effect on the course of affairs. More important was the proposition made by France, Great Britain, and Russia, on the 27th May, to Austria, Prussia, Italy, and the Germanic Confederation, to take part in negotiations at Paris for the preservation of peace.

Prussia consented to this proposition without reserve; Austria coupled her possible compliance therewith with the condition that every combination should be set aside from discussion which might lead to the increase of the territorial power of any State which took part in the negotiations—a condition which, to be satisfied, required that everything 2nd June. should remain in the existing state of suspense. Austria besides declared that she could make no alteration in the attitude she had assumed towards the Government of Victor Emanuel, and demanded further that the Papal Government should be represented in negotiations concerning the "Italian question." The endeavours of foreign Powers for the pre-servation of peace could after this be only regarded as of no avail.

Although Austria, by the 1st June, had already placed the entire decision of the question of the Elbe Duchies in the hands of the Confederation, and so withdrawn from the Convention of Gastein, she still on the 5th ordered her Commissioner in Holstein to assemble the Estates of that Duchy on the 11th. In con-sequence of the exercise of this one-sided act of sovereignty Prussia declared that she now considered the Convention of Gastein as cancelled, that she returned to the basis of the Treaty 5th June. of Vienna, and had entrusted the guardianship of her common rights to the Governor of the Duchy of Schleswig.

The strife hitherto carried on in the form of negotiations appeared now to be immediately trenching on the field of active hostilities.

Not less urgent were affairs in the Federal fortresses which were occupied in common. The troops on both sides, in those places, preserved chivalrously an outwardly friendly atti-tude; but most bloody and tragical conflicts must necessarily ensue between the equally strong contingents if matters came to an open breach between the two Governments, and this was possible at any moment. A shot fired in Holstein would suffice for this.

It must then be considered as a fortunate solution of this difficulty that a motion proposed by Prussia, and seconded by Bavaria, was accepted by the Confederation. The result of this motion was that the Prussian as well as the Austrian troops were withdrawn from Mayence, Frankfort, and Rastadt, and replaced by troops belonging to other States of the Confedera-tion. Mayence was to be guarded by Bavaria, Weimar, Meiningen, Anhalt, Schwarzburg, Lieppe, and Detmold; Rastadt by Baden, Altenburg, Gotha, Waldeck, and Reuss; and in Frankfort one Bavarian battalion was to remain. In Rends-burg and Kiel also, the friendly relations which were preserved to the last moment between the Governor of Schleswig and the Commissioner of Holstein prevented collisions between the troops on either side, which might have easily occurred, and which could be of no use.

In the meantime the political situation had entered upon a stage which left no hope of a peaceful issue. On the 5th June (the day on which the last trains of Prussian troops reached the frontiers of the Marks and Saxony, and of Silesia and Bohemia,

and so eight and a half corps ready for action were there
assembled) the order was issued by which Lieut. Field-Marshal
Von Gablenz, by desire of the Emperor of Austria, summoned
the Estates of the Duchy of Holstein to meet on the 11th at
Itzehoe. No more unfortunate instant could have been selected.
On the following day General Van Manteuffel, in accordance
with his instructions, declared this one-sided summons to be
an encroachment on the rights of the King of Prussia, and
requested the Austrian Commissioner to recail it. He at the
same time communicated to him, that, in execution of the
revived right of Prussia to a share in the occupation of
Holstein, he would occupy some places in that Duchy not held
by garrisons, and would next morning enter Holstein for that
purpose.

It was requested that the authorities of those places should
be furnished with the necessary instructions, in order to avoid
conflicts; and it was enunciated that this step was one of a
purely defensive character.

In his answer, which was sent by return of post, Lieut. Field-
Marshal Von Gablenz declined to withdraw the summons for
the assembly of the Estates which had been issued by order of
the Emperor; protested against the contemplated inroad, which
he on his side declared to be a violation of the Convention of
Gastein; and at the same time indicated that he would remove
the seat of the Government of the district to Altona.

In the meantime General Von Manteuffel had concentrated
his troops opposite Rendsburg. This fortress had a Prussian
Commandant, and the Prussian garrison therein was superior to
the Austrian; consequently the passage of the Eider at that
point, which afforded immense advantages by being the key of
the road and railway communication with Itzehoe and Altona,
was assured under all circumstances; orders had also already
been issued for the most rapid assembly of troops possible on
that point. On the evening of the 6th, the corps (which
mustered 12,000 men, including the garrison of the fortress,
and consisted of 11 battalions, 6 squadrons, and 4 batteries)
stood *écheloned* on the road between Schleswig and Rendsburg. Only one battalion remained in garrison at Sonderburg,
which was provisioned for three months for 8,000 men and
600 horses. Two squadrons were in Lauenburg.

In Holstein there was of Austrian troops only the Kalik
brigade, which mustered about 4,800 men, viz., two regiments
of Infantry, one battalion of Rifles, two squadrons, and one
battery.

Lieut. Field-Marshal Von Gablenz was therefore not in a
position to oppose the inroad of General Von Manteuffel with
a much superior force of troops. He could reckon on no support
from Austrian reinforcements, and the artificially excited
enthusiasm of the Holsteiners for the Duke was far removed
from such intensity as to provoke an effective action on the part
of the population. Lieut. Field-Marshal Von Gablenz therefore

pursued the only course that the situation in which his Government had placed him allowed, and immediately withdrew all his troops in the direction of Altona.

7th June.     At daybreak on the 7th June, the Austrian garrison, conducted by the Prussian officers, quitted Rendsburg, and a few hours later General Manteuffel crossed the Eider. The head of his column advanced to Brinjahe, two German miles further on the road to Itzehoe. The troops were ordered not to disturb places occupied by the Austrians, and to avoid any conflict.

8th and 9th June.     On the 8th the advanced guard reached Neuenkrug, and on the 9th Grönland. The main body occupied Itzehoe.

Since the protest against the assembly of the Estates by Austria had remained disregarded, Prussia now assumed the administration of the government of Holstein also. The Government of the Duchies which had hitherto existed was dissolved, and Baron Von Scheel-Plessen was entrusted, as President, with the administration of both Duchies.

10th June.     On the 10th June the troops rested. In the course of this day the Estates of Holstein assembled at Itzehoe, and were collected in considerable numbers.

General Van Manteuffel had orders to prevent their meeting. The most considerate method of doing so appeared to be the removal of the Imperial Commissioner, who was to open the assembly on the following day. He was accordingly compelled to withdraw to Rendsburg during the night, and to remain there for the next few days.

11th June.     The Deputies, in consequence, quitted Itzehoe on the 11th, without any open breach of the peace. The population remained altogether passive. The same day General Von Manteuffel pursued his march on Altona, reached Borstell and Thimen, and occupied Pinneberg. On the approach of the Prussians the Austrians, who were quartered round Altona, withdrew all their troops into the interior of this town. In the meantime the 16th and 17th Regiments of Prussian Landwehr, which were destined as depôt troops for the Duchy of Schleswig, and had been moved into Lauenberg, had there united with the two squadrons of the 6th Regiment of Magdeburg Dragoons, and had been set in motion on Altona, so that, mustering 5,000 men, they had already reached the vicinity of New Balsdorf, one march from Altona.

The position of Lieut. Field-Marshal Von Gablenz had become extremely difficult. Circumstances threatened that at any time there might be a conflict. On the Elbe, near Altona, there lay the Prussian armour-plated ship " Arminius," and several gunboats. If war were declared, the Brigade Kalik stood opposite to three times its strength, without any possible retreat.

Under these circumstances Lieut. Field-Marshal Von Gablenz made a speedy resolve and crossed in the night between the 12th June. 11th and 12th with his troops to Harburg, whence in the next few days they were transported by railway to Southern Germany.

General Von Manteuffel on the 12th entered Altona; the detachment coming from Lauenburg occupied Wandsbeck.

The operations of General Manteuffel were so arranged and conducted with so large a force that they relieved the weak Austrian brigade from the necessity of a conflict for the honour of its arms, and it was a fortunate solution that no bloodshed ensued between Austrians and Prussians on the same ground that they had occupied as friends and allies.

As Austria was thus compelled to relinquish the Duchies without a struggle, it was the more certain that she would enforce her claims on another field. A more decisive step was now made. The Austrian Cabinet declared that Prussia by the invasion of Holstein had broken the peace of the Confederation, and on these grounds proposed to the Bund on the 11th the mobilization within fourteen days of all federal corps which did not appertain to Prussia. This was the virtual dissolution of the Confederation, since one portion thereof declared war against another.

This motion which, according to the constitution of the Bund, was untenable, and against the rapid entertainment of which the Prussian envoy energetically protested, was put to the vote in the memorable sitting of the 14th June. Prussia took no part, and there was no vote for Holstein Lauenburg. <sub>14th June.</sub>

There voted with Austria, Bavaria, Saxony, Hanover, Würtemberg, the two Hesses, the 13th and the 16th Curiæ.

With regard to the last the voting Deputy declared that he had not sufficient instructions, but, nevertheless, gave a vote against Prussia. It was immediately disavowed by his Government, but the President of the Diet had decided that the motion was carried by nine votes against six.

The Prussian envoy left the assembly after declaring that his Government considered the Germanic Confederation as dissolved, but still adhered to the unity of the German nation, and was ready to conclude a new Confederation on the basis of the proposal for reform of the 10th June, with such Governments as were inclined to enter into it.

The majority of the Middle and minor States had pronounced their own judgment. Countries, especially such as lay intruded between the two halves of the Prussian State, could not possibly deceive themselves on the consequences of a hostile attitude towards Prussia.

In consequence of the entrance of the Prussian troops into Holstein, on the 12th June, the Imperial Ambassador was recalled from the Court of Berlin; the Prussian quitted Vienna a few days later, and diplomatic intercourse between the two Powers was broken off. On the 15th June, the day after voting in the Diet, the Prussian ambassadors at Dresden, Hanover, and Cassel, delivered similar notes, in which the neutrality of their territories and a guarantee of the sovereign rights of the Princes were offered to both Kings, and to the Elector, if they would agree to the proposal of reform of the

10th June. The period allowed for the replies to these notes was till the evening of the same day.

The Saxon Government immediately declined the proposal, and as no peaceful answers were received by midnight from the two other Powers, the three ambassadors declared war against Saxony, Hanover, and Electoral Hesse.

## CHAPTER II.

### CONCENTRATION AND FIRST MOVEMENTS OF THE ARMIES.

THE Prussian Staff had estimated the probable strength of the Austrian Army of the North at 240,000 men, a calculation which afterwards proved very near the truth.

It could be easily foreseen that in the approaching war Austria would make every exertion to enter into the struggle as strong as possible in Germany.

Supported in Italy on the Quadrilateral, she was able, by making short offensive movements, to act on the defensive for a long time with but comparatively trifling forces. The Italians could hardly be suspected capable of difficult or lengthy sieges. They could less reckon on directly acquiring Venetia by the power of their own arms than on gaining the possession thereof, if the general operations of the war compelled Austria to resign it.

The decisive blows, however, which could alone induce her to do so, must, in all probability, be struck not south of the Alps, but north of the Danube.

It was known that the Austrian Army was formed in ten Corps d'Armée, of which the Vth, VIIth, and IXth were being concentrated against Italy.

• As far as very defective intelligence could be relied upon, towards the middle of May there were stationed—

> The Austrian Ist Corps in Northern Bohemia, along the frontiers of Saxony and Silesia, from Komothau to Wildenschwerdt.
>
> The IInd Corps in Moravia and Austrian Silesia, from Wildenschwerdt to Oswiecim.
>
> The IVth Corps in Western Galicia.

The mobilization of all other parts of the Army in their stationary quarters was so far advanced that it might almost be regarded as completed. The formation of the staff of each Corps d'Armée, as well as of the head-quarters, was complete, and Feldzeugmeister Benedek had come to Vienna on the 12th May after he had given over the command of the Southern Army to the Archduke Albrecht. All preparations for the movement by railway of the masses of troops which had been assembled at Pesth, Vienna, and Laibach had been made, and the systematical transport of soldiery had commenced on the 11th May. By means of much exertion, a considerable number of men, both of Infantry, Cavalry, Artillery, and Transport Corps could, by the expiration of the month, be assembled, both on the Saxon and the Silesian frontier. The Cavalry for some time had been marching in these directions. On the side of Prussia at the same time, the middle of May, the orders for mobilization had only just been issued. The troops were quartered in their ordinary peace garrisons, and were awaiting their reinforcements of men and horses. The transport of one Corps d'Armée with its appurtenances (whether for a long or a short time) repuires from nine to twelve days if all ordinary traffic is not suspended, and if a few trains of the Intendance were allowed daily to pass along the line. Thus it could be precisely calculated that the arrival of the Corps d'Armée from the different parts of the monarchy on the frontier could not be accomplished earlier than the first week in June.

This result even could only be achieved if all through lines of rail were used, and if none of them transported more than one Corps d'Armée, since each successive Corps would cause a delay of from nine to twelve days.

The corps of which the mobilization had been first decreed were ordered to assemble on the 8th May as follows:—

> The VIth at Neisse,
> „ Vth at Schweidnitz,
> „ VIIIth at Coblenz,
> „ IIIrd and IVth between Torgau and Cottbus.

Of the last Corps the 8th Division remained at Erfurt until the armament of that place had been accomplished, and the 32nd Brigade of Infantry was concentrated at Wetzlar.

The Corps of the Guards was to assemble at Berlin, the 13th Division of the VIIth Corps at Minden and Bielefeld, and the 14th Division at Münster and Hamm.

As a general rule such concentrations of large bodies of troops previous to their transport are not advisable. They practically make the future transport more difficult than if the troops are marched direct from their garrison to the suitable points of embarkation. But under existing circumstances the first strategical positions of the army could not yet be fixed. It was as yet hardly known who in the approaching conflict would be friend or foe. It was still hoped that Southern Germany, led by Bavaria, would assume a favourable, or at least a neutral attitude towards Prussia, and negotiations still pended with Hanover and Hesse Cassel likewise.

As was shown in the previous sketch, circumstances became even more serious in the course of the month. Prussia had to recognize that in the war which threatened she must be all alone and dependent solely upon herself, and would have, besides Austria, all the States of the Confederation against her.

Under these circumstances there could be assembled by—

North Germany about    ..    ..    36,000 men.

Southern Germany about ..    ..    100,000 ,,

The Austrians and Saxons..    ..    264,000 ,,

These three hostile groups had a very different value. Hanover and Electoral Hesse could be in the highest degree inconvenient, if they were left unobserved in rear, as they severed all communications with the Rhine and with the Elbe Duchies. Still it was open to question whether these would commit themselves to the chance of open hostilities, in any case it was tolerably certain that their possible concentration could be prevented, and accordingly, the actual loss of time which might thereby be occasioned was all that was to be considered.

The Southern Germans were, notwithstanding all the preparations which had taken place in Würtemberg, Bavaria, and Hesse Darmstadt, a not very formidable foe. It was known how little in peace they were prepared for war. The want of a single guidance and organization bespoke little results from those troops, which were good in themselves, and it was to be expected that they would only commence their action late and dissevered. In this direction the most secure action was an offensive one, which should employ them in their own territories.

The third group, however, stood a strong well-organized Army already prepared for battle.

There lay the key of the whole question. A victory over the Austrian Army must paralyze all other enemies, but the seven corps of the eastern monarchy did not suffice to assemble the forces necessary thereto. If the two western corps were drawn to the main decision, the Rhine provinces would remain palpably undefended; and it would be possible to oppose only a very inferior strength to the Southern Germans.

Nevertheless, His Majesty the King came to this difficult decision, which was, however, crowned with fortunate results, by which alone it was afterwards possible to enter in sufficient might on the spot where the main question was to be decided, and even to approach the hostile capital. The strong fortresses of the Rhine provinces, sufficiently garrisoned by Landwehr, could not indeed prevent an invasion of that territory, but could prevent an enemy from there firmly establishing himself. If victory could be won in the east, it would be easy to regain anything that had been lost in the west.

In order to prevent, as far as possible, a hostile invasion of this territory, a special army was formed out of a portion of the troops in Schleswig-Holstein, and from the regiments destined for the defence of the fortresses, to which the 13th Division of Infantry was attached as a nucleus. The latter could in a very short time be assembled from its cantonments around Minden, in the immediate neighbourhood of the Hanoverian capital.

It could be calculated that if Hanover and Hesse Cassel were disarmed, this army could proceed against Bavaria. This improvised army had a twofold superiority against it, and must by energy and rapidity retrieve its want in strength.

The next consideration was now to determine where the important strength of troops destined for the eastern theatre of war should be assembled, and whither they should be transported.

The outposts of the first Austrian Army were placed near Tetschen, Reichenberg, and Trautenau. Under cover of these, on one of these three points, 60,000 to 80,000 could, by aid of the existing railways be assembled; this force would not suffice to carry out a real offensive war against Prussia, but could seriously threaten either Berlin or Breslau. In the one direction stood the Saxon Army as a powerful advanced guard only six or seven marches distant from the Prussian capital, which is protected against the south by no considerable vantage ground; in the other Breslau could the more easily be reached in five marches, because, trusting to the former federal compact with Austria, Schweidnitz had been given up as a fortress.

Nothing was to be more desired than that the whole Prussian forces should have found a position which at once would have covered Berlin and Breslau, even if they could not for the moment protect the territory on the left of the Elbe and on the Upper Oder. The most favourable point for this was Görlitz.

The difficulties of supplying with food a quarter of a million of men could have been overcome if an immediate advance had been contemplated; but they were insuperable if an assembly of so great a number was to be anticipated for a totally undetermined time. The concentration of the whole Army on one point, whether at Görlitz or in Upper Silesia, demanded a considerable expense of time. If the whole force would have to be transported by few and ultimately by only one line of railway, the arrival of all would be delayed for several weeks. The Marks and silesia required, however, an immediate defence, and the preparation of two separate armies was consequently necessary.

That a concentrated Austrian army could throw itself on the half of the Prussian was clear, but whatever arrangement was determined upon, none could alter either the geographical circumstances of the theatre of war or the fact that an enemy stationed in Bohemia intervened between Lusatia and Silesia.

There was only one way of anticipating this inconvenience, which was that the Prussians themselves should invade Bohemia.

In any case, the Corps d'Armée must in the first instance be brought as near the frontier as the railway transport would allow.

If it had not been necessary to respect the Saxon territory, the lines leading from the Rhenish provinces, Westphalia, Pomerania, and the Marks, could have been used to assemble a formidable army at Dresden. But practically for the Prussian transport these lines ended at Zeitz, Halle, Herzberg, Görlitz, Schweidnitz, and Neisse. At these points, which formed a theatre of war of 300 miles in length, it was necessary to relinquish railway transport, and to march. This was palpably not the real strategical march of the army for concentration, but only the first step thereto. Whether the further marches of the still separate parts of the force should be made towards different points of this periphery, or towards the centre, depended whether it was decided to assume the offensive or the defensive.

In accordance with orders already issued, the 11th Division of the VIth Corps d'Armée had been assembled at Frankenstein, the 12th at Neisse, the reserve brigade of Cavalry, and the Artillery at Münsterberg. The 51st Regiment and the 6th Battalion of Jägers had been pushed forward to Glatz and Silberberg, the 10th Regiment and one battery remained in Schweidnitz until the Vth Corps, which was already marching in that direction, should enter that place.

There were besides, for the protection of the frontier of Upper Silesia, posted under General Von Knobelsdorff between Leobschütz and Oderburg, the 62nd Regiment of Infantry, the 2nd Regiment of Uhlans, and one battery. Besides, there was formed there, under General the Count of Stolberg, a special detachment consisting of the 6th Brigade of Landwehr Cavalry and six Landwehr battalions of the second levy.

On the 24th May it was ordered that the VIth Corps d'Armée should take up cantonments round Waldenburg and the Vth round Landshut. The reserve Cavalry of the two Corps was united in one division at Striegau. All these divisions were under the command of His Royal Highness the Crown Prince, to form the second or Silesian Army.

Similarly, in accordance with the orders issued, the IIIrd and IVth Corps d'Armée were assembled in Lower Lusatia between Torgau and Cottbus. Their advanced posts were on the Black Elster, at a short distance from the Saxon frontier. The 8th Division, which had hitherto been retained at Erfurt, was now moved up, and on the 16th May the second Corps d'Armée was ordered to move, per rail, from the province of Pomerania by way of Berlin, to Herzberg. The Corps of the Guards, after completing its mobilization, was to march to cantonments between Baruth and Luckau.

The four divisions of the IIIrd and IVth Corps d'Armée were not retained in their corps, but were individually placed under the command of His Royal Highness the Prince Federic Charles of Prussia; to them the IInd Corps d'Armée and the Guards were to be added. A special Cavalry corps was to be formed out of the reserve Cavalry of these four corps, and the whole, under the command of the above-mentioned Prince, was to form the 1st Army. Also, on the 16th May, the Ist Corps d'Armée was warned to *échelon* its troops along the railway between Königsberg and Kreuz, to be transported to Görlitz. The corps was then to preserve the communication between the Ist and IInd Army, and stood available to strenghten either the one or the other, as circumstances demanded.

The earlier arrangements for the VIIIth Corps d'Armée were altered, inasmuch as the 15th Division was to be assembled at Cologne, the 16th at Coblenz, and thence to be transported by rail by way of Hanover to cantonments round Halle.

Of the VIIth Corps, the 13th Division remained in its usual quarters, the rest was to be moved by rail by way of Paderborn and Cassel, into cantonments round Zeitz, and with the VIIIth Corps to form a third army, or Army of the Elbe, the command of which was given to General Herwarth Von Bittenfeld.

The Brigade Beyer of the VIIIth Corps, which had already been moved to Wetzlar, and which, by the addition of a portion of the garrisons of the fortresses that had become available had attained the strength of a strong division, remained there. To it were added—

From Mayence, the 32nd Regiment;
  „   Luxemburg, the 20th Regiment;
  „   Coblenz and Cologne, the 19th and the 39th Regiments.

The 9th Regiment of Hussars and three batteries were attached to this new Division Beyer, so that it attained a strength of 18 battalions, 5 squadrons, and 18 guns.

Finally, on the 19th May, the formation of a Reserve Corps was ordered at Berlin, which was formed of 24 battalions, and of 24 squadrons of Landwehr, which then were mobilized, and to them a newly-formed reserve regiment of artillery was added. This corps was intended to occupy the posts in rear of the Field Army, but was sufficiently prepared to be able to take its place in the line of battle at any moment. The command of this corps was given to General Von der Mülbe.

Thus, under the command of the King, who assumed in person the chief command, there stood at that time—

The Ist Army in Lusatia;
  „   IInd Army (Silesian) in Lower Silesia;
  „   Elbe Army in Thuringia;
  „   Ist Corps d'Armée at Görlitz;
  „   Reserve Corps at Berlin;

and the Army of the Maine, which was, as operations proceeded, formed of the 13th Division, the Division Beyer, and the troops of General Von Manteuffel.

It was expressly stated, however, that no union of armies was to be considered as definitive, since His Majesty reserved to himself the right to transfer corps or divisions of one army to another according to the course of circumstances.

The details of the Staff and the special disposition of the troops can be found in the Appendix. Order of Battle. Appendix II.

In consequence of the orders issued on the 15th and 16th May, and after the necessary preparations on the main lines of railway, the transport of the troops was effected between the

16th May and the 5th June. The marches by road were so arranged as to be accomplished in the same time.

The whole of the marches and of the railway movements were so arranged by the General Staff in harmony with the railway department that in their execution, in which both the military and civil powers were concerned, no impediments or delays could occur.

The result of these arrangements was, that in the 21 days allowed, 197,000 men, 55,000 horses, 5,300 wagons were transported for distances varying between 120 to 300 miles, without any failure, and in such a manner that they attained the required spots at the very hour requisite.

Details of Transport Appendix I. The details can be found in the Appendix.

In preparation, Austria had gained an important advantage. This was, however, counteracted in the transport of the troops, since she could only use the one railway which, from Vienna to Lundenburg has two lines, but beyond that point in the direction of Olmütz and Brünn, has only one line. In Prussia, on the other hand, there were five through lines of railway, with their several branches, available.

The Prussian frontier was more or less in danger during the month of May, but soon a time arrived when forces superior to those of the adversary were assembled there.

All military reasons urged that the campaign should be commenced by Prussia on the 6th June. It is necessary, however, to recollect that it was only on the 11th June that Austria introduced her motion to the Diet. At the beginning of this month it was still possible to hope for a peaceful solution of the pending differences, and under these circumstances King William would never have decided to take steps towards causing a war, the consequences of which for Germany it was impossible to foresee.

When, on the 14th June, the hostile motion was adopted by the Diet, the Prussian Government, as shown above, could not postpone energetic steps, but by this time the transport of the Austrian troops was also practically concluded.

While still the main portion of the corps were being moved by railway, the necessary orders were issued to move the IInd, IIIrd, and IVth Corps nearer to the IInd Army in Silesia.

This could only be accomplished if the troops marched along the frontier, through a comparatively poor country, in great heat, and along sandy lanes. The cantoned troops must also keep before their eyes that at any moment a concentration might be necessary. Besides, such a transverse movement always throws great difficulties in the way of sustenance. This march towards the left was, however, ordered on the 30th May, and could be completed by the 8th June in such a manner that the IIIrd Corps d'Armée closed up to the Ist at Görlitz, the IVth Corps d'Armée arrived at the neighbourhood of Hoyerswerda, and the IInd reached Senftenberg. Behind these the Guards were collected in cantonments round Cottbus.

On the 6th June, the last *échelons* of the Ist Corps d'Armée entered Görlitz, and on the 7th that corps commenced its march in the direction of Hirschberg.

At the same time as this movement towards the left was made, the three divisions of the Army of the Elbe were moved from Zeitz and Halle to the Elbe.

Thus the width of the forces available for action was reduced by nearly one-half.

The Army of the Elbe took up cantonments on both sides of that stream, between Mulde and Elster. On the right bank the advanced guard was posted at Mühlberg; the 16th Division and the Reserve Cavalry at Liebenwerda ; the Reserve Artillery near Torgau. On the left bank, the 15th Division was posted at Belgern, and the 14th at Schildau and Düben. The permanent bridge at Torgau, and a pontoon bridge thrown near Belgern, made it possible to assemble the Army within 48 hours on either bank of the stream.

The first certain intelligence of the situation of the Austrian Army was received in Berlin on the 11th June by means of the "Order of Battle," which was then made known. Thus it was found that the principal Austrian force was not stationed, as had been hitherto supposed, in Bohemia, but that of seven Corps d'Armée five were still in Moravia.

The "Austrian Military Journal" states as a reason for such a withdrawn position "that the Army had indeed con-"cluded its concentration on the 10th June, but that it was "numerically too weak for an aggressive advance against the "Prussians."

It may perhaps be asserted that the concentration was indeed not yet finished, because the brigades of Abele (formerly of Kalik), and of Prohaska had not yet come up, as well as a part of the Artillery Reserve, but that the forces already available, including the Saxons, were numerically about equal to the enemy, as a reckoning which we shall give later will show.

It was besides announced that " the position at Olmütz held " Prussia in doubt, and had compelled her to divide her force." We shall see that, as soon as the position near Olmütz was known, every doubt vanished. An invasion of Prussian territory could only be directed against Silesia ; corresponding measures were taken, and no care was hereafter requisite for the security of Berlin.

It appears that at Vienna people believed in earlier and more extensive preparations on the part of Prussia than had really occurred through the defensive measures of the 29th March, that, therefore, alarm was felt in case of a disturbance out of their own concentration, and that it was desired to make it more certain by a considerable distance, and by the shelter of the fortresses. Also the protection of the railways contingent to the Silesian frontier had to be considered.

Added to this the corps were, it is true, with the above-mentioned exceptions, complete as to the number of their troops, but it is acknowledged that there was still much to be done by the " Intendance."

The Austrian Army was really not fully prepared to enter upon operations. Time was required to complete its preparations, and its allies also required time.

Council was held in Ölmütz, in the middle of June, with these allies, on the subject of the general operations. The Bavarian Army, which consisted of from 40,000 to 50,000 men, was to form an independent corps under Prince Charles of Bavaria, under whose command also were placed the contingents of Würtemberg, Baden, Hesse, and Nassau. The Prince was to conduct his operations in accordance with directions given to him from the Imperial Commander-in-Chief. Since a concentration of all the armies of Southern Germany in Bohemia could not be accomplished, the protection of the territory of the different States engaged in the struggle was to be united with the most practicable service of the combatants in respect to the main object. Austria engaged to conclude no independent peace; and in case that territorial alterations should result from the war, to protect Bavaria from any loss, and to take care that the latter should be indemified for any sacrifices. The 5th Article of this Treaty of the 14th June says, " The " Bavarian Army shall by the middle of June have taken up " a position in Franconia, and in the vicinity of the railways." Such a concentration would have been the most advantageous for Saxony and for Austria.

If then the Prussians advanced through Saxony into Bohemia, the Saxon Army would move off in the direction of Plauen, thus avoiding their superior forces. If the Army of the Elbe followed, it would be separated entirely from the 1st Army; if it pushed forward into Bohemia, the Saxons united with the Bavarians, and forming a force of from 60,000 to 70,000 men, could well hope to reoccupy their country, and seriously to threaten the communications of the Prussian Army.

The collection of magazines in Annaberg and Schneeberg, of which news reached Berlin, seemed to show that at Dresden this plan was willingly entertained; but it was a great exaction from Bavaria that her battalions should fight in Saxony or Bohemia for Austria, while her own territory was threatened from the Rhine. Würtemberg and Baden, still more so Darmstadt and Nassau, remained then entirely dependent on their own strength.

In any case, neither on the 15th, nor even within the next few days, could a formidable force be assembled in Upper Franconia, for the Bavarian troops still stood upon the Danube and the Maine, without being ready to march.

In consequence of all these circumstances, it is said that on the 30th June, it was finally determined that Bavaria should first unite her Army with the VIIIth Federal Corps, and then assume the offensive in a north-westerly direction. There remained now to the Saxon Army no prospect except quitting its own territory to fight as an auxiliary force in Bohemia—a lamentable situation into which the ruler of the Saxon policy had drawn a brave and patriotic army.

What was expected from an offensive movement in a north-westerly direction, which at a great distance could only lead to Coblenz or Cologne, it is difficult to see. If the support of Hanover was contemplated, an immediate and powerful aid could have been afforded to that power by means of the Brigade Kalik. It would have formed the nucleus to which the Hanoverian and perhaps the Electoral troops of Hesse might have attached themselves; but this brigade, as indeed every available force, was drawn to the Northern Army. The Brigade Hahn alone, formed of the garrisons drawn from the Federal fortresses, was attached to the VIIIth Federal Corps. No other sacrifices did Austria make for her allies.

As soon as the distribution of the Austrian Army was known at Berlin, it was recognized that the enemy's march was a threatening, not against Berlin nor west of the county of Glatz, but in the east, not by way of Schweidnitz, where the Silesian Army was posted, but by way of Neisse; and that some five or six corps could in about eight days be concentrated on the line between Grulich and Troppau.

The Commander of the IInd Army had already requested permission to march towards the Neisse. A position behind this river covered the greatest part of Silesia. It also prevented the Austrians from operating against Breslau, and forced them to attack it, if they were not willing utterly to sacrifice their communications, The fortress of Neisse supported the left wing, and in an attack on the right the assailant would have had Glatz and the mountains in rear. The proposed measure appeared therefore in itself advantageous, but had the disadvantage that by means of it the distance between the Ist and IInd Army was still further increased by about five or six marches, and that two Corps d'Armée, even in a strong position, could not have resisted such superiority of strength as threatened them. His Majesty the King accordingly permitted the advance of the IInd Army, but ordered at the same time that it should be reinforced, and that the Ist Army should continue its move to the left.

The Ist Corps, after it had been relieved in Görlitz by the IIIrd, had already been placed under the command of the Crown Prince, and stationed in Hirschberg, Warmbrunn, and Schönau. It had to watch the roads leading over the mountains from Friedland and Reichenbach, as well as that from Trautenau. The Guards Corps was also now attached to the IInd Army. Nine battalions of this corps were still in Berlin and Potsdam; these were at once put in movement to Brieg, on the railway which now became free by way of Frankfort and Breslau. The rest of the troops of this corps were placed in cantonments east of Cottbus towards Sorau and Sommerfeld, where they could be successively placed in the railway.

The Guard arrived in this manner on the left wing of the position which the IInd Army purposed to take up on the Neisse.

The Ist Army received orders to concentrate, from its cantonments in Lower Lusatia, in such a manner round Görlitz that it stood ready as well for operations in Silesia as for an advance into Saxon Upper Lusatia.

In case a closer concentration was not ordered, the new cantonments were to extend from Niesky to Hirschberg, so as to make as many roads as possible available for that advance.

According to these orders there marched, of the IInd Army—

    The VIth Corps, by Reichenbach, Frankenstein, and Ottmachau, to Steinau;

    The Vth Corps, by Schweidnitz, and Lauterbach, to Grottkau;

    The Ist Corps, by Kupferberg, Schweidnitz, and Nimptsch, to Münsterberg;

    The Cavalry, by Metkau and Jordansmühl, to Strehlen.

The columns arrived at their destinations respectively on the 16th, 17th, and 18th, by which time also the greater portion of the Guard had already reached Brieg.

Of the Ist Corps a detachment of six battalions, two regiments of Cavalry, and four batteries, had remained at Waldenburg, to watch the passes from Landshut to Charlottenbrunn.

As a summons from Austria was every day to be expected, all preparations were made for a rapid concentration of the IInd Army.

Of the Ist Army there marched—

    The IIIrd Corps to the vicinity of Löwenberg, Friedeberg, and Wiegandsthal;

    The IVth Corps to the district of Lauban and Greiffenberg;

    The IInd Corps to the country between Niesky, Reichenbach, Görlitz, and Seidenberg;

    The Corps of Cavalry to quarters on both sides of the Bober, round Löwenberg.

The roads leading through the mountains to Löbau, Zittau, Friedland, and Reichenberg were occupied and guarded; for a similar purpose a detachment of three battalions, one squadron, and one battery was pushed forward to Warmbrunn. All these marches of the Ist Army were accomplished in the same time as those of the IInd Army—that is, by the 18th June. On the other hand, the Army of the Elbe still remained in the cantonments which it had taken up on the 8th. With regard to Saxony, it was impossible that it could follow the movements of the two former.

General Von Herwarth had charge over 38 battalions, five regiments of Cavalry, 28 batteries.

If the Saxons remained without foreign aid, they had only the choice either to fight against twice their number or to quit their land without a blow.

If they withdrew into Bohemia they could reinforce the Austrian Army, but then the whole Army of the Elbe could follow them thither. If they moved to Bavaria it was necessary that a Prussian corps should follow to watch them. Under all circumstances a powerful force was wanted on the Elbe.

It was hardly to be supposed that the Austrians would leave their most zealous allies without any support. It was rather expected that at least the Ist Austrian Corps would be told off to unite with the Saxons. The huge materials of land and water transport assembled at Bodenbach appeared to be collected for this purpose.

The Saxons had concentrated near Dresden on the left bank of the Elbe; only a few detachments were pushed forward on the right bank as far as Grossenhayn; but the corps could at any moment cross the Elbe. If united with an Austrian corps it assumed one of the strong positions for the defence of Dresden which the country affords in plenty, this could not, even with much superior strength, be assailed from the opposite bank with chance of success. Also, it was impossible to march past such a strength of troops as could debouch from Dresden in rear of the movement.

It was thus unavoidable that the Army of the Elbe should remain in the position assigned to it, which allowed it as requisite to act on the one or the other bank.

If the corps of Count Clam joined the Saxons, their total force, without the brigade Abele (Kalik), would be increased to 48 battalions, 10 regiments of Cavalry, and 23 batteries, then the Army of the Elbe would not be strong enough to repulse them. It was therefore determined that the Reserve Corps which was being assembled at Berlin and Brandenburg should be despatched immediately in the direction of Torgau.

The arrival of this corps brought the strength of the Army of the Elbe up to 62 battalions, 9 regiments of Cavalry, and 44 batteries. Berlin and the Marches were still sufficiently covered.

It would have been possible to push the march of the Ist Army closer to the IInd, but we know that at this time the hostile decisions had already been passed by the Bund, which made war unavoidable, and released Prussia from all former obligations with regard to procuring peace. Diplomatic proceedings henceforth sank into the back-ground, and the purely military developed their whole importance.

The Prussian main armies at this time stood in three groups at Torgau, Görlitz, and Neisse, which were distant from each other from 100 to 125 miles. The most rapid concentration was to the front, and lay in the enemy's territory.

The advance into Saxony was necessary, not on political

D

grounds alone, but also because it made the strategical advance of the Ist Army, and of the Army of the Elbe,—*i.e.*, their concentration,—possible on the line between Dresden and Bautzen by means of numerous and converging roads in few marches. Then the Prussian force formed two armies, the conduct of which so as ultimately to insure their mutual co-operation in the decisive moment was the difficult but soluble problem placed before its leaders. Armies of over 100,000 men are tolerably independent, and the Austrians could not develop their whole force against the one as they must resist with detachments the other. The shortest road to their junction lay forwards, and to clear it the hostile opposition must be broken down.

From the moment when the Decree of the Bund of the 14th June was passed, the King determined to wage an offensive war. There was now no more talk of defensive flank marches; it was determined to seek the enemy on his own soil.

As we now pass to the account of the operations themselves, it is necessary to cast a glance over the strength of the troops which were brought into operation. In reckoning these, we can naturally have recourse to States alone. These are a sure guide as far as regards the Prussian Army, as all the troops included therein were complete. If on the other side the effective strength did not come up to the strength on paper, the true information can only be obtained from those concerned; it may, however, be correctly assumed that, after a long preparation, the differences are not sufficient to cause a very practical diminution. Casualties in sick, men on command, &c., must be considered on both sides, and those on either side would be about equal.

The details of the "Order of Battle" of the armies of all the States allied against Prussia are given in Appendix.

### I. *Austrian Army of the North.*

| | Combatants. |
|---|---|
| Ist Corps, with its four brigades, in Teplitz, Prague, Theresienstadt, and Josephstadt, and 1st division of Light Cavalry posted from Königinhof to Reichenberg, in Northern Bohemia, mustered | 36,000 |
| IInd Corps, in Wildenschwerdt, Böhmisch Trübau, Zwittau, Brüssau | 31,000 |
| IVth Corps, on the right of the above, in Sternberg, Zittau, Troppau, and Teschen | 31,000 |
| VIth Corps, in rear round Olmütz and Leipnick | 30,850 |
| IIIrd Corps, with three Brigades, at and south of Brünn | 23,750 |
| Xth Corps, in Brünn and Meseritsch | 30,250 |
| VIIIth Corps (furthest to the rear) in Auspiz, Austerlitz, Selowitz, and Paulowitz | 31,000 |
| 2nd division of Light Cavalry on the Silesian frontier east of the county of Glatz | 3,350 |
| Carried forward | 217,200 |

|  | Combatants. |
|---|---|
| Brought forward .. .. .. .. | 217,200 |
| Ist Division of Reserve Cavalry at Prossnitz .. | 4,270 |
| IInd ,, ,, Kremsier .. | 4,270 |
| IIIrd ,, ,, Wischau .. | 4,270 |
| Reserve Artillery of the Army .. .. .. | 3,000 |
| By the arrival of the brigades of Kalik and Prohaska | 14,000 |
| In Moravia and Austrian Silesia .. .. .. | 211,000 |
| Austrian Army of the North, including 1st Corps .. | 247,000 |
| Saxon Army at Dresden .. .. .. .. | 24,000 |
|  | 271,000 |

## II. *The Forces of Southern Germany.*

### Bavarian Army.

| | |
|---|---|
| One division at Schweinfurt, detachments at Frankfort and in the Palatinate .. .. .. .. | 11,450 |
| One division at Bamberg .. .. .. .. | 11,450 |
| One division on the Lechfeld.. .. .. .. | 11,450 |
| One brigade on the railway from Regensburg to Amberg .. .. .. .. .. .. | 5,700 |
| One brigade at Munich .. .. .. .. | 5,700 |
| The Reserve of Cavalry and Artillery south of the Upper Maine.. .. .. .. .. .. | 6,200 |
| Total of Bavarian Army.. .. .. | 52,000 |

(About 10,000 more were in Bavaria, but not with the Field Army.)

| | | |
|---|---|---|
| Wurtemberg Contingent, the troops still in their ordinary garrison .. .. .. .. .. | | 16,250 |
| Baden Contingent .. .. mobilized troops | | 10,850 |
| Grand Duchy of Hesse .. ,, | | 9,400 |
| Nassau .. .. .. .. ,, | | 5,400 |
| South German troops not yet concentrated, *circa* | | 94,000 |

## III. *The Contingents of North Germany.*

| | |
|---|---|
| Hanover .. .. .. effective strength | 18,400 |
| Electoral Hesse .. .. ,, | 7,000 |
| In their garrisons .. .. .. | 25,000 |
| Austria and Saxony .. .. .. .. .. | 271,000 |
| Southern Germany .. .. .. .. .. | 94,000 |
| North Germany .. .. .. .. .. | 25,000 |
|  | 390,000 |

### IV. *Prussian Army.*

Combatants.

IInd (Silesian) Army :—
The Guard, Ist, Vth, and VIth Corps, and a division
of Cavalry in Cantonments on the Neisse, between
Brieg and Patschkau; detachments at Waldenburg
and in Upper Silesia    ..    ..    ..    ..    115,000

Ist Army :—
IInd, IIIrd, and IVth Corps, and Corps of Cavalry.
near Görlitz, between Niesky, Bunzlau, and Wie-
gandsthal; a detachment in Warmbrunn..    ..    93,000

The Army of the Elbe :—
VIIIth Corps and 14th Division in Cantonments
round Torgau, between Düben and Elsterwerda ..    46,000

Reserve Corps :—
At Berlin (still in the course of formation)    ..    24,300
13th Division round Minden    ..    ..    ..    14,300
Manteuffel's Corps at Hamburg    ..    ..    ..    14,100
Beyer's Division at Wetzlar    ..    ..    ..    19,600

326,000

Against total of enemies.    ..    390,000

Of which in the east of the monarchy, Prussia    ..    278,600
Against Austrians and Saxons    ..    ..    ..    271,000
In the west, Psussia ..    ..    ..    ..    ..    48,000
Against the former Federal Contingents    ..    ..    119,000

Thus, in the east, Prussia was stronger by about 7,600 combatants; in the west, weaker by about 71,000 combatants than
her enemies.

On both sides the combatants only of the Infantry, Cavalry,
and Artillery are reckoned, and given in round numbers.
Naturally, the troops are not counted in the Field Armies, which
remained as garrisons for fortresses, or to assure the tranquility
of districts.

To the latter category belonged the detachments in Upper
Silesia :—

Men.

General Von Knobelsdorff    ..    ..    ..    ..    3,844
General Count Von Stolberg ..    ..    ..    ..    5,358

9,202

On the Prussian side, Mülber Reserve Corps of 24,000 men
is reckoned, which was formed and in reality only employed as
such, but was so organized as to act as field troops. On the
Austrian side, the fourth battalions are not balanced against
this, although they actually were brought into action. It is
easy by subtraction of the Reserve Corps, which was formed

of Landwehr, and never came into action, to perceive that the remaining 255,000 Prussian combatants in the east opposed 271,000 hostile combatants.

We can then discard all the assertions which were designed to attribute the success of Prussia in the eastern theatre of war solely to numerical superiority.

---

# CHAPTER III.

### THE OPERATIONS AGAINST HANOVER AND ELECTORAL HESSE.

THE result of the Federal vote of the 14th June was known the same evening to General Von Manteuffel, who, as shown above, since the 12th had been with his corps in and round Altona. The outbreak of hostilities with Hanover, which had declared against Prussia, was to be expected; and it was necessary to secure the important passage of the Elbe at Harburg. The vessels stationed on the Elbe were placed under the command of General Von Manteuffel. Harburg was without a garrison. The place could, however, be occupied from the fortress of Stade, which lay near, and which lately had received a stronger garrison: thus rapid action was necessary.

At the time of the transport of the Kalik Brigade through Hanover, the Prussian Government requested, and after some delays obtained, permission for the passage of its troops in Holstein in the direction of Minden. On the ground of this, the advanced guard of General Von Manteuffel on the 15th 15th June. moved to Harburg, and on the 16th the remainder of the corps 16th June. followed.

The passage was very quickly accomplished, as the troops moved partly by means of the Hamburg steam-ferry and by the island of Wilhelmsburg, and partly were transported by the Prussian gunboats and private steamers. The heads of the columns, on the 16th, advanced about ten miles on the roads to Lüneburg and Celle. The Generals Von Falckenstein and Von Beyer, in accordance with their instructions, also commenced their operations on the 16th June. War was formally declared, and the advance therefore fully justified.

The former advanced with Goeben's Division from Minden towards Hanover as far as Stadthagen; the latter from Wetzlar, in the direction of Cassel, to the neighbourhood of Bellnhausen.

Neither in Hanover nor Hesse Cassel does it appear to have been sufficiently clearly perceived what consequences would necessarily ensue from their hostile attitude towards their neighbour State, they seem rather to have believed that they could still restrain Prussia by diplomatic negotiations. It can only so be explained that the declaration of war found both these countries fully unprepared in military circumstances.

In Hanover, indeed, the spring manœuvres which usually took place only among the Cavalry and Artillery, were extended to the whole Army. The different regiments had been assembled for drill for some time, and in the next few days combined brigades were to be assembled at various points for exercises with all arms. The regiments were already partly on the march for that purpose.

The troops also, by the calling in of men on furlough, had been placed on the highest strength for manœuvre; the battalions mustered 560 men, exclusive of recruits; the squadrons 80 to 90 horses; but no preparation had been made for a mobilization, and especially no purchase of horses had been made.

In Hesse Cassel the troops were entirely on a peace footing. The rapid action on the part of Prussia caused the imbecility of these states to become apparent. It was impossible for them to think of defending their territories, and no possibility of resistance lay except in the most rapid retreat on the contingents of Southern Germany.

The King of Hanover, on this account, at noon on the 15th, immediately after the arrival of the news of the occupation of Harburg, resolved to concentrate his army at Göttingen. The telegraph forwarded the necessary orders through the whole country, and on the same afternoon the troops everywhere put themselves in motion. The whole of the Infantry, some batteries, and much material, were forwarded by the railways, on which the trains were moved uninterruptedly till the 17th June; the remainder marched.

The Hessian troops which garrisoned Cassel and Hofgeismar, six battalions, ten squadrons, and four batteries (4,200 men, 800 horses, 16 guns), were, on the news of the advance of General Von Beyer, also immediately set in motion towards the southern part of the country. They went by rail to Hünfeld, and then, as may be mentioned prematurely, by way of Fulda to Hanau, where they arrived on the 22nd June; and being reinforced by the four battalions which garrisoned the two last-named places, remained there till further orders.

The unexpectedly rapid occupation of Holstein by the Prussians, the energetic measures connected therewith, the retreat of the Austrians without resistance, and the hasty flight of the Prince of Augustenburg, did not fail to make a deep impression in the Duchies. In Schleswig, a careful and provident administration had already for some time awakened the sound sense of the people, and shattered the democratic and Augustenburg intrigues; but also in Holstein the political agitation of late times quickly yielded to the sober presence of mind natural to the character of the people. The Prussian troops had everywhere been received with the greatest friendship, and nowhere was any trace of hostile feeling exhibited.

Under such circumstances, not only was it possible to detach the whole of Manteuffel's Corps for future operations in Ger-

many, but it appeared also admissible to diminish the garrison
troops which at the beginning had been determined upon for
the Duchies. Of the latter, the 4th Westphalian Landwehr
Regiment, No. 17, was first handed over to General Von
Manteuffel, who also brought forward the two battalions of the
line left in Sonderburg and Rendsburg. Some days later the
10th Regiment of Landwehr Hussars, which had gone to Altona,
advanced into Hanover. There remained then only the 3rd
Westphalian Landwehr Regiment, No. 16, the depôt battalions
of the 11th and 25th Regiments, one company of garrison
Artillery, the 7th Regiment of heavy Landwehr Cavalry, which
had come from Halberstadt, and the Marine Battalion,
about 5,000 men in all, under the command of the Commandant of Rendsburg, General Von Kaphengst, in Schleswig-
Holstein.

The functions of Governor, during the absence of General
Von Manteuffel, were handed over to President Von Scheel-
Plessen.

General Von Manteuffel, on the 17th, advanced from Har- 17th and 18th
burg towards Hanover. One column, under General Von Korth June.
(8 battalions, 4 squadrons, 2 batteries), marched in the direction
of Lüneburg; the other, under General Von Flies (6 battalions,
4 squadrons, 2 batteries), on the direct road to Celle. The
former reached Lüneburg, the latter Heber, on the 18th. The
railway could not be used, as all the material had been carried
away by the Hanoverians.

It had been ascertained that a quantity of material of war
lay in Stade, and that a great part of the garrison of that place
had marched in the direction of Bremen. The fortress could
therefore only be occupied by a small strength, and it was
determined to take it by a *coup de main*.

To gain information of the locality, during the night between the 16th and 17th, Captain Werner, with the ironclad
"Arminius," and the gunboats "Tiger" and "Cyclops," had
made a reconnaissance from the Elbe, by which the Hanoverian
coast battery at Brunshausen had been spiked.

Late in the evening of the 17th, Lieutenant-Colonel Von
Cranach started from Harburg with the Fusilier battalion of the
1st Rhenish Infantry Regiment, No. 25, in the "Loreley," the
"Cyclops," and a private steamer. About 1 A.M. on the 18th
he reached Twidenfleth, where the troops disembarked, and
began their march to Stade, which was about five miles distant.

A Cavalry outpost, quickly retreating, alarmed the garrison,
but Colonel Von Cranach succeeded, after bursting open the
gate, in entering the town before any opposition could be
offered. First, in the vicinity of the market-place, in the
middle of the town, a close detachment with charged bayonets
attacked the Prussians, and some shots were exchanged; but
further conflict was prevented by an officer who hurried up
with the declaration that the Commandant was inclined to
negotiate.

Soon a capitulation was agreed upon, by which the fortress was given up. The Hanoverian officers were allowed to depart free with their arms; the men, about 500, partly undrilled recruits, were dismissed to their homes.

Rich material of war fell into the hands of the Prussians. Among others, a 6-pounder rifled battery, fully equipped with everything except horses; eight rifled 12-pounders, seven rifled 24-pounders, many other guns, 14,000 new rifled arms, 2,000 cwt. of powder, 1,000,000 cartridges, 11,000 woollen blankets, &c.

The occupation of the Hanoverian coast batteries on the Ems and the Weser, by the Prussian ships, followed in the few next days after the capitulation of Stade, by which a large number of heavy guns were taken. The garrison of Emden capitulated on the same conditions as that of Stade.

In the meantime General Von Falckenstein, on the evening of the 17th, after a twelve hours' march, entered Hanover with Goeben's Division.

The rich stores which were found here were used to complete much that was wanting, and especially to organize a light field bridge train and a light field hospital. Also horses were demanded, partly to complete the necessities of the troops, partly for the formation of a horse dopôt. General Von Falckenstein immediately assumed the administration of the country. A Prussian civil Commissioner was placed at the head of the Government, but in other respects all Hanoverian officials continued their functions, so that all stagnation of business was avoided.

General Von Beyer marched on the 17th to Kirchhain and Neustadt. He also could not make use of the railway, because the rails in places had been torn up, and the material had been carried away for the transport of the Hessian troops to Cassel.

The General, on his side, had the railway to Frankfort entirely destroyed, in order to secure his rear against the assembling Federal troops there. In a northerly direction, the line was again laid down by officials detached for that purpose.

It was ascertained that the Electoral Hessian troops stationed at Cassel had left, and at the same time that considerable war material still remained there. In order to prevent its removal it was necessary to destroy the railway to Bebra as soon as possible.

For this purpose, at Marburg, a small train was put together of some carriages found there, which carried a company to Gensungen; thence it marched to Melsungen on the Frederic-William Railway, where this object was effected without hindrance.

By a lucky chance, at that station there was a considerable train of empty wagons, of which possession was taken, and by means of which it advanced to Guntershausen. A detachment of Hessian troops stationed there were taken prisoners and the existing railway material seized. Early on the 18th, the company moved with two strong trains towards the division which in the meantime had advanced to the vicinity of Gilserberg.

General Von Beyer now directed a great part of his troops on Zimmersrode, whence the railway transport to Guntershausen began.

By noon on the 19th, five battalions, half a squadron, and one battery were there assembled; and on the same evening, General Von Beyer at their head, entered Cassel. On the 20th the remainder of the division followed, partly by rail, partly by marching by way of Fritzlar. 19th and 20th June.

As in Hanover, also in Cassel, a Prussian Government was established, and the Hessian Ministers alone removed from their functions. The Elector himself, who had not left Wilhelmshöhe, remained there: but was afterwards, when he again refused to accede to the Prussian reform of the Confederation, removed to Minden, and later to Stettin.

The stores found in Cassel were particularly welcome to the corps of General Von Beyer, which in peace had formed no organic band of troops, but, as already shown, formed at the last moment from single regiments, wanted much in the material of equipment. The field equipages of the regiments were completed; a hospital, a provision column, an intendance detachment, and a depôt of horses were formed.

General Von Falckenstein had received orders above all things to force the Hanoverian Army out of the field, and as far as possible to disarm it, in order to have his troops afterwards available for other operations. If it were desirable, in consequence, to push forward with Goeben's Division as rapidly as possible to Göttingen, Hanover could not be left without a garrison. The troops of General Manteuffel, who had been placed under Falckenstein's command, were accordingly drawn in that direction.

In the course of the 18th it was possible to get some railway material together, and send it to Lüneburg. Two locomotives of the Berlin-Hamburg Railway were also transported across the Elbe at Lauenburg on the steamers lying there; and on the night of the 19th the transport of Korth's Detachment at Lüneburg was commenced to Hanover. Goeben's Division, on the 19th, consequently began its march on Göttingen, reached the line Nordstemmen, Hildesheim, and on the 20th as far as Alfeld.

The railways leading to Göttingen were so thoroughly destroyed that their restoration required several days. The transport of Korth's Detachment was continued on the 19th, his troops halted on the 20th at Hanover. General Flies marched on the 19th to Bergen, on the 20th to Celle.

On the Hanoverian side it had been possible, by great exertions, to assemble all the troops of the contingent, with the exception of small detachments at Göttingen, on the 18th. The Hanoverian force had consequently gained a considerable start, and could count upon several days' rest. The mobilization of the Hanoverian Army was first ordered on the 17th, and now was the opportunity to make it fit to undertake operations as far as means would allow. The march southwards had been made with the greatest haste, and the troops consequently were in general badly provided with field equipment. Before the arrival of the Prussians it had been possible to despatch considerable supplies of clothing, equipment, arms, and ammunition from the magazines of Hanover by rail to Göttingen. Here it was then possible to make the troops to some extent fit to take the field, especially the recruits and furlough men called to the colours in consequence of the decree of the Bund of the 14th June, of whom about 3 000 joined the Army at Göttingen, without arms and without clothing. It was attempted to complete the want of horses by purchase and requisitions, so that all the field batteries and the guns of reserve were horsed up to a peace footing. The ammunition columns, the pontoon train, the field hospital, and all the regimental carriages, were dependent on relay horses.

By the 20th the Army was placed in a tolerable state of preparation for operations or battle. The battalions averaged 700 men, the squadrons about 90 horses. The total strength of the Army mustered 15,000 Infantry (inclusive of 2,000 not yet drilled recruits), 2,000 horses, 42 guns (of which 22 were rifled 6-pounders), besides 10 guns of reserve. It was divided into four Infantry brigades, to which the necessary Artillery and Cavalry were attached, with the reserve Cavalry and reserve Artillery. Details are given in the order of battle, Appendix II.

As long as the Army was being organized, it was necessary to remain on the defensive at Göttengen. Measures were therefore taken both to throw difficulties in the way of the enemy's advance, and to oppose with advantage any casual attack.

One brigade was pushed forward on each of the roads leading to Hanover, Münden, and Witzenhausen; the rest of the troops were cantoned at Göttingen. On the news of the occupation of Cassel, the railway leading thither was rendered impassable, the passage of the Werra at Münden placed in a state of defence, further back in the valley of the Schede earthworks were thrown up, and an advantageous position south of Dransfeld entrenched. Also, on the road to Witzenhausen, troops advanced to the Leine, and occupied its passages. Against the enemy marching from Hanover, a position was selected near Nörten, and entrenchments begun therein. Opinions had from the first differed as to the next operations; but as the troops became more ready for battle, the voices of those who advocated a march southwards to unite with the Bavarians, began to preponderate in the counsels of the King, and on the 20th the order was given to break up the position on the following day. It was wished, at first, to take the most direct road by Witzennausen, Allendorff, and

Eschwege. But, as it might be expected, there to come upon the troops of General Beyer and then to be engaged in the difficult defiles of the Werra and Meizner under circumstances extremely unfavourable for action, at the last moment the direction of Heiligenstadt was adopted.

On the 21st June accordingly the army marched and, with- 21st June. out any encounter, reached the village of Heiligenstadt. The advanced guard was pushed forward towards Mühlhausen as far as Helmsdorf. The rear-guard, which all day occupied Nördheim, in the evening moved to Geismar, two miles south of Göttingen.

It had been anticipated at Berlin that the Hanoverians would attempt to move through the Eichsfeld, and measures had been provided accordingly.

On the 20th June, General Von Schack, at Magdeburg, received notice thereof. He, on the 21st, sent two battalions of the 20th Landwehr Regiment (Brandenburg), and the Depôt Squadron of the 10th Magdeburg Hussars, under General Von Seckendorf, by rail to Nordhausen, whence they marched, the same evening, to Bleicherode. The battalions mustered 400 men, the squadron about 100 horses.

The Commandant of Erfurt also received orders to send from his garrison three Landwehr battalions, one squadron, and a sally-battery to Eisenach. As the Duke of Coburg-Gotha had declared for Prussia, his regiment of Fusiliers which had been assembled at Gotha, was also sent to Eisenach.

Thus, on the 21st, there were at Eisenach 5 battalions, 1 squadron, 1 battery; together 2,250 men, 75 horses, 4 guns. The command of these was given to Colonel Von Fabeck, Commander of the Regiment of Gotha. The Prussian Landwehr battalions mustered on the average, only 350, the Gotha battalions hardly 650, since the regiment had not completed its mobilization, and the reservists were only partly clothed.

General Beyer, who was warned from Berlin of the sending of this detachment, despatched on the afternoon of the 20th, under the command of General Von Glümer, a mixed detachment of 1 battalion, 1 squadron, and 2 guns, to watch the roads leading from Göttingen southwards by Witzenhausen and Allendorf. The Infantry was placed in wagons, and next morning the detachment reached Reichensachsen. The remaining troops of Glümer's Brigade followed in the same direction, and, on the evening of the 21st, there were 8 battalions, 2 squadrons, and 1 battery in the triangle Lichtenau, Allendorf, Reichensachsen.

As, by reports coming in early on the 21st, Münden was occupied by the enemy General Beyer despatched General Von Schachtmeyer with 4 battalions, 1 squadron, and 1 battery in this direction. The town, which had been in the meanwhile abandoned by the Hanoverians, was occupied in the evening by the Prussians.

General Beyer himself remained with the dechment of Colonel Selchow, six battalions, two squadrons, one battery, in Cassel.

The direction which the Hanoverians might have determined to take to break through into Southern Germany was not known, and the orders on the Prussian side could only have the object of observing all roads leading there. The detachment of troops was consequently unavoidable. It was requisite first to face the enemy wherever he might appear, to sustain a first opposition, and then to assemble decisive forces. General Falckenstein, on the 21st, began his march from the north to Göttingen. Goeben's division advanced to Einbeck and Gandersheim. Of Manteuffel's troops, early in the morning the transport of Korth's detachment commenced on the restored Hanover-Brunswick Railway to Seesen, whence the advanced guard marched to Echte. Flies's detachment halted at Celle.

Since Goeben's advanced troops came upon the Hanoverians' rear-guard near Nordheim, the hostile army was expected to be at Göttingen, Falckenstein determined to advance thither on the 22nd, and attack on the 23rd. He sent a warning to Beyer, who was placed under his orders, to waylay the retreat of the enemy southwards.

The most different and contradictory reports of the movements of the Hanoverians had reached Cassel. According to intelligence from Berlin, they were said to have taken the direction of Mülhausen; but there the outposts had reported nothing; General Beyer, therefore, determined to approach Göttingen, and so to concentrate more closely his separated 22nd June. divisions. For this purpose, Glümer was to concentrate along the Werra, between Allendorf and Witzenhausen, Schachtmeyer was to move to Dransfeld, and Selchow to Münden. Late in the evening of the 21st, to Falkenstein also, the advance of the Hanoverians on Mühlhausen was communicated from Berlin, and the proposition was made to send troops circuitously by way of Magdeburg to Gotha, and so to hinder the retreat of the enemy through the Thuringian forest.

Still, after the experiences as yet derived from the use of the railways in Hanover, it was doubted whether the detachment could arrive in time at its destination. The troops were not sent, and no alteration was made in the existing dispositions.

But when, on the morning of the 22nd, the retreat of the enemy from Göttingen was also confirmed by General Goeben, orders were sent to Beyer to advance to Ottmanshausen.

The latter, by this time, had received indubitable intelligence of the march of the Hanoverians on Mühlhausen. The order to concentrate at Ottmanshausen was immediately published; but reached the troops already in motion so late that only Selchow could be moved back to Kauffungen.

Goeben's division marched to Göttengen, Manteuffel, with Korth's detachment, to Nordheim; Flies's detachment went by rail from Celle by Brunswick to Seesen, and thence advanced to Nordheim. The head-quarters were moved to Göttingen and the South Hanover Railway could thus, for the first time, be made use of as far as Salzderhelden.

For the occupation of Hanover there remained two battalions of the 17th Landwehr Regiment and the 10th Landwehr Hussars which were drawn from Altona. The 3rd battalion of the 17th Regiment returned to Harburg and Stade, and, in exchange, General Manteuffel drew forward the Fusilier Battalion of the 25th Regiment, which had remained there.

Colonel Fabeck, on the report that the enemy was advancing against the defiles of the Werra, had moved with his detachment from Eisenach to Mihla, but, when he found this news to be untrue, had returned in the evening to Eisenach.

The Hanoverians had, on the 22nd, made their march from Heiligenstadt to the neighbourhood of Mühlhausen. A detachment had been sent to Wanfried. But when it was found that, on the 21st, Prussian troops had already appeared in the Eschweg, and therefore on this day all passages over the Werra might be expected to be occupied, this detachment was withdrawn to Mühlhausen. On all grounds, a difficult contest in the defiles of the Werra was to be avoided, and it could not be supposed in the Hanoverian head-quarters, that Beyer's movement to the left had for the moment left them open.

The road by Mühlhausen had the advantage that by it the Werra was altogether turned, and it passed far from Cassel, whence, at the moment, the greatest danger threatened.

The results of the movements of the 22nd were particularly favourable to the Hanoverians.

Beyer's division was from two to three severe marches distant, and was therefore as much as the main body of Falckenstein in no position to overtake within the next few days the retiring enemy, who had only the weak detachment of Fabeck in front of him.

On the 23rd June no alterations of any importance occurred 23rd June. in the situation.

Goeben's division, after four severe marches, had to halt at Göttingen. Manteuffel's corps, the last troops of which— Flies's detachment—in the course of the day reached Nordheim from Celle, by way of Seesen, remained in the cantonments of the previous day.

The arrival of the Hanoverians at Mühlhausen was telegraphed from Berlin, and troops were ordered to be sent thither by way of Cassel. This could not be done by rail, since the line was broken up; orders were, therefore, given to General Beyer to march to Eisenach.

In the afternoon Glümer reported from Witzenhausen that, after an unsuccessful contest, the enemy had retired to Heiligenstadt; consequently, General Von Wrangel was, in the night, pushed forward to Siemerode with three battalions, two squadrons, and one battery.

Of Beyer's troops two battalions had remained as a garrison

in Cassel. Selchow, with four battalions, two squadrons, and one battery, in pursuance of orders, reached Ottmanshausen. Glümer, in accordance with the earlier order, had already reached Friedland when the countermand reached him. He could only reach his former quarters, between Witzenhausen and Allendorf. On the assumption that the Hanoverians had returned to Heiligenstadt, he occupied, with a few battalions, an advantageous position near Hohengandern, where, in the evening, Schachtmeyer, coming from Dransfeld, bivouacked.

Fabeck's troops, early in the morning, moved by rail from Eisenach to Gotha, as it was supposed that the Hanoverians would take their way thither.

At Berlin it was considered urgently necessary to occupy the Thuringian Forest in greater force. As the despatch of troops from Hanover had not taken place, two battalions of the 4th Regiment of the Guard received orders to start by railway from Berlin. The first arrived in the afternoon, the second about midnight at Eisenach. Besides, in the course of the day, the detachments already ordered arrived at Gotha, namely, the depôt battalion of the 3rd Thuringian Regiment of Infantry, No. 71, and a squadron of Landwehr Dragoons from Erfurt, and two batteries of Horse Artillery from Dresden.

The Hanoverians actually advanced in the direction of Gotha, and in the evening, their main body tolerably concentrated, was between Gross-Gottern, Langensalza, and Oster-Behringen. Their advanced troops were pushed forward as far as Henningsleben and Gross-Behringen, on the roads to Gotha and Eisenach. The rear-guard occupied Mühlhausen.

The original intention had been to march by Eisenach; but the news that the enemy's troops had been seen on the road thither, led it to be feared that opposition might be met with in the roads of wooded Hainich, in themselves sufficiently difficult, so the straight road to the south was abandoned, and the critical circuit by Langensalza undertaken.

This starting back before every difficulty allows it to be presumed that the determination to cut a way to South Germany was already practically abandoned. But, nevertheless, when advanced patrols of Cavalry, on the 23rd at midday, found Eisenach unoccupied, it was decided to attempt to break through there. Early on the 24th, the troops were already paraded at Oster-Behringen and Langensalza ready for the march, when the order came to return to cantonments.

24th and 25th June.

Colonel Fabeck had received orders from Berlin to propose to the Hanoverian Commander to lay down his arms, as he was surrounded on all sides. This proposal, sent by an officer on the 23rd, was rejected; but the Hanoverians took the opportunity to make counter proposals, with which a *parlementaire* was sent to Gotha. He asked a free passage for the Hanoverians to the south, on condition that for a year they did not fight against Prussia. As no answer to this had come from Berlin early on the 24th, and that *parlementaire* announced that stronger forces of the enemy were already in Gotha and Eisenach, the movement against those places was for the time stopped.

The Hanoverian Colonel Bülow, stationed at Behringen, had learned during the night that Eisenach was again occupied, but only by two battalions. He thought right, under these circumstances, to depart from the order to return to camp, and advanced with his brigade direct on Eisenach to Lupnitz and Stockhausen. At the same time, one battalion, a detachment of Pioneers, a squadron, and two guns, the first in wagons, were sent to Mechterstädt to destroy the railway, and prevent the passage of any train from Gotha to Eisenach.

The report of this, and a request for further orders, was sent to head-quarters at Langensalza, and, since an answer might be expected about 3 P.M., the Prussian Colonel Osten, commanding in Eisenach was told to surrender the town of his own accord, or threatened with bombardment.

The King of Hanover not only approved of the measures of Colonel Bülow, but also ordered the negotiations at Gotha to be broken off, and the march of the whole Army on Eisenach that afternoon. Colonel Osten had no intention to quit the town, and the troops sent to Mechterstädt came upon Prussian Infantry on the other side of the place. A combat of skirmishers had commenced, when, on the Hanoverian side, a telegraphic despatch came, to avoid hostilities, as the Prussians had agreed to the proposals made. The action was broken off, and a truce upon both sides provisionally agreed to.

The totally impracticable proposals of King George had not been, indeed, agreed to at Berlin; but negotiations had been entered into. It was hoped that, during these, the Prussian detachments arriving from all points would be assembled in such superior strength that the Hanoverians would be relieved of the duty of engaging in a totally hopeless battle, solely for the honour of their arms.

King William was determined, above all things, to render the Hanoverian Army harmless, but was induced, under the sad condition in which it was, to grant it generous conditions.

The Hanoverian *parlementaire* still in Gotha had on his side considered that he ought not, without further orders, to break off negotiations, and asked for new instructions. He now sent to General Bülow, whose orders were known to him, the despatch above-mentioned, in order to avoid useless bloodshed.

The latter was about to attack the town, but now concluded, in order to give his tired troops rest at least over the night, an armistice till 8 in the morning.

King George was willing to enter into negotiations with a Prussian Plenipotentiary, in order, as his letter says, " to avoid bloodshed and the injury of the inhabitants," but would not suspend the operations against Eisenach under the conditions proposed to him.

The Army accordingly advanced. The Hanoverian General

in command learned late in the evening that, in consequence of the interference from Gotha, Eisenach was not taken by Bülow's brigade. The armistice, however, was agreed upon, and night came on. The army remained between Stockhausen, Mechterstedt, and Reichenbach; one brigade only, as a precaution, was placed in the direction of Gotha at Henningsleben; and Langensalza was occupied by a weak rear-guard. The Hanoverian head-quarters were at Gross-Behringen.

There next day it was discovered that the enemy during the night had seriously strengthened himself at Eisenach. The opportune moment for an operation in this direction thus appeared passed. The Prussian Plenipotentiary also was expected, and consequently a day of rest was given to the Army on the 25th.

In the morning, General Von Alvensleben came from Berlin to Gross-Behringen. The King of Hanover desired a space of 24 hours to decide on his proposals; this was agreed to, and a further armistice was concluded.

In the meantime, at Berlin, continuous efforts had been made to strengthen the military power at Gotha and Eisenach, and General Von Falckenstein had received positive orders to send troops to Gotha, by way of Magdeburg, from Göttingen.

With regard to further operations by way of Cassel, Goeben's division went there early on the morning of the 24th on the railway which was repaired as far as Münden, and Manteuffel's corps marched to Göttingen, whither also General Wrangel returned from his reconnaissance at Siemerode.

General Falckenstein now sent five battalions of Infantry and one rifled 4-pounder of Manteuffel's corps, under the command of General Flies, by way of Magdeburg and Halle, to Gotha, and desired General Goeben to march as quickly as possible with all available troops from Münden to Cassel, in order thence to be able to detach by railway to Eisenach. Besides this order, an urgent request came direct from Colonel Osten, at Eisenach, to General Goeben for support, since, as we know, the Hanoverians were before the town and threatened it with bombardment. The General on this account accelerated his movements as much as possible, and towards evening the first battalions reached Cassel, whence they were forwarded by railway to Eisenach. During the night and next morning the transport continued uninterruptedly, and by mid-day on the 25th, 5 battalions, 2 squadrons, and 3½ batteries were at Eisenach, under General Von Kummer. The rest of the division, which General Wrangel also joined on the 25th, remained at Cassel.

Of Manteuffel's corps, on the 25th, 4 battalions, 6 squadrons, 2 batteries, went to Münden; 3 battalions, 2 squadrons, 1 battery, held Göttingen.

General Falckenstein himself, since the Göttingen-Cassel Railway was again practicable went to Eisenach on the 25th. General Beyer was requested also from that place to furnish support, and received orders from Berlin to move as quickly as possible. He had allowed his troops to rest on this day, but now moved with Selchow's detachment, which was at Ottmanshausen, to Kreuzburg, where he arrived about midnight, and on the morning of the 25th moved to Eisenach.

General Glümer also, on the evening of the 24th, moved from his cantonments at Allendorf and Witzenhausen, and at mid-day on the 25th reached Kreutzburg and Treffurt. General Schachtmeyer, on the 25th, reached Frieda, on the right bank of the Werra, between Eschwege and Wanfried. Colonel Fabeck remained on the 24th and 25th at Gotha, and was reinforced by General Seckendorf, who marched there during the preceding days from Bleichenrode, by way of Ebeleden.

On the evening of the 25th the first troops of Flies's detachment, the march of which had been somewhat delayed by want of transport, entered Gotha from Göttingen. The remainder followed during the night.

At the distance of one march there now stood, in a semi-circle round Langensalza,—

At Gotha, General Flies, with 13 battalions, 3 squadrons, and 4 batteries, about 8,150 men, 225 horses, 22 guns.

At Eisenach, 12 battalions, 4 squadrons, 4½ batteries, altogether 12,000 men, 550 horses, 28 guns. Here General Goeben assumed the command.

At Krouzburg and Treffurt, General Von Glümer, with 8 battalions, 2 squadrons, 1 battery, 8,000 men, 250 horses, 6 guns.

Thus the result could be assured with sufficient strength.

On the afternoon of the 25th the King of Hanover had sent an officer with his definitive answer to the proposals of General Von Alvensleben.

This envoy took the road to Berlin, by way of Eisenach. General Von Falckenstein, who had shortly before reached that place, and who knew nothing officially of the conclusion of an armistice, did not permit his further journey, and the officer returned to the Hanoverian head-quarters. From various observations at Eisenach, he believed that precautions should be taken against an attack, and for this reason in the evening Bülow's brigade was drawn back to a position round Gross-Behringen; and at the earliest dawn of the 26th the remainder 26th June. of the Army, with the exception of the Brigade Knesebeck, which remained at Henningsleben, was concentrated between Gross- and Oster-Behringen. Here news was received that General Von Falckenstein had learnt of the armistice, and would respect it, whereon the Army marched to Langensalza, to take up wider cantonments for purposes of supply. The head-quarters of the King were removed to this town.

The conviction had been arrived at that escape was not possible, but it was not wished to capitulate without a contest.

The moment that diplomatic negotiations were entered upon

E

at the Hanoverian head-quarters, the fate of the army was decided. From that point we meet with repeated vacillations between determination for decisive military movements and the inclination for amicable interposition.

On the afternoon of the 23rd the Hanoverians opened negotiations with Berlin, but broke them off in the evening to break through at Eisenach the next day. The troops already assembled were next morning sent back to their cantonments, because first they wanted to await the answer from Berlin; but before this arrived a fresh determination was formed to commence operations against Eisenach, and the troops, who had hardly reached their quarters, were again ordered to advance. They declared then to wish to break off all diplomatic negotiations, but were ready to receive the expected Prussian Plenipotentiary to avoid bloodshed. Thus they went only half-way in either direction; they wanted to capitulate, but would make no concessions; they wanted to break through the hostile lines, but wanted to avoid an action.

We shall not err if we attribute the causes of this to the different influences of the opposing parties at head-quarters. The war party, if we may so call it, had triumphed at Göttingen, and the march to the south prevailed, but the many difficulties which its execution entailed—the great heat, scanty provisions, deficient equipment, &c., brought forward again the views of the opposition, that the battles which must be expected, and the march across the Thuringian forest, which would be especially difficult, on account of want of provisions and through scanty transport, would cause a disproportionately great loss, and that it appeared questionable whether the Army could reach Southern Germany in a position sufficiently ready for battle.

Now, in addition, the aid expected thence had not arrived. From Hanover and Göttingen trusted persons had been sent to solicit the support of the South Germans, but they were not in a condition to afford such. The 8th Federal Corps was at Frankfort, employed in its formation, and could therefore undertake nothing; and the Bavarian troops were being transported to the Maine when the Hanoverian envoy, on the 19th, met Prince Karl at Schweinfurt. The latter declared himself ready to move his army as quickly as possible towards the Hanoverians, and on the 22nd began to move on Fulda.

This direction was, however, altered, as on the following day intelligence came in that the Hanoverians, on account of the occupation of Cassel, would march through the Prussians on Eisenbach, and on this day, the 26th June, the main body of the Bavarian Army was still south of the Franconian Saale, between Neustadt, Münnerstadt, Lauringen, and Königshofen; the reserves at Schweinfurt, one Infantry Brigade was, as an advanced guard, pushed forward to between Unsleben and Mellrichstadt, and had weakly occupied Fladungen and Tann. The Light Cavalry Brigade, late in the eveing, reached Meiningen.

In this position a halt was made, as later intelligence did not arrive from the Hanoverians.

Rumours of the advance of the Bavarians were brought to General Von Falckenstein on the 25th, at Eisenach, which made it urgently desirable to finish the operations against the Hanoverians as soon as possible. The attack was accordingly ordered for 4 o'clock on the morning of the 26th, and the necessary dispositions taken.

The armistice concluded by General Von Alvensleben necessitated, however, the postponement of this undertaking.

In the afternoon the Prussian Colonel Von Döring appeared at Langensalza, to again propose an alliance on the basis of the conditions of the 14th June. The King of Hanover most decidedly refused this, whereupon Colonel Von Döring gave notice of the termination of the armistice.

In consequence. the Hanoverian Army, after a new idea to break through at Gotha had been abandoned, on account of the great fatigue of the troops on the night before the 27th, took up a defensive position on the left bank of the Unstrut, between Thamsbrück and Negelstädt, where a possible attack might be awaited. Langensalza remained occupied.

At Berlin a telegram had arrived on the night of the 26th, by which the Hanoverians were said to have drawn off in a northerly direction by way of Mühlhausen, already on the previous evening.

This news, which was afterwards found to be false, awoke the fear that the Hanoverian Army might attempt to return to its own home, whereby Falckenstein's Army for a longer time would be distracted from the special object of its operations—the Army of Southern Germany.

General Falckenstein received orders to immediately follow the enemy. The troops not required were alone to watch the Bavarians at Eisenach. General Von Manteuffel was to march from Göttingen against the Hanoverians.

General Von Falckenstein took this occasion to send the two battalions of the Guard from Eisenach by railway to Göttingen, to strengthen General Von Manteuffel, to whom also the troops of Goeben's division, remaining at Cassel, were given over.

General Von Flies received orders from Gotha to follow the Hanoverians, while General Von Schachtmeyer was charged to march parallel to this line of march and occupy the defiles of the Werra, to prevent escape in that direction. He moved at once to the vicinity of Eschwege.

The detachments of Von Glümer and Von Selchow were placed in cantonments round Gerstungen, to rest for further operations, and of the troops of General Von Goeben, a strong detachment of three battalions, $1\frac{1}{2}$ squadrons, went towards Vacha to get further intelligence of the Bavarians. Three battalions—half a squadron, three and a half batteries—remained at Eisenbach.

General Von Flies, who had advanced at 6 in the morning,

from Gotha on Langensalza, soon discovered the falsehood of the intelligence. His patrols came upon the Hanoverians marching from Behringsdörfer to Langensalza, and he accordingly took up a position between Bollstedt and Hochheim, but retreated in the evening to a bivouac at Warza.

General Von Falbkenstein heard this in the course of the forenoon. As the Hanoverians had left the position which they had occupied opposite to him, and had withdrawn to Langensalza, it was desirable to await the result of the mission of Colonel Von Döring, as a preliminary measure no alterations were made in the arrangements already settled, except that General Von Flies was ordered not to attack the Hanoverians as long as they remained at Langensalza, but to remain close on their heels.

After the proposals of Colonel Von Döring had not been accepted, late in the evening orders came from Berlin to concentrate all available strength, and to force a capitulation, as it was feared that the enemy still might retreat by way of Tennstedt.

27th June.    The troops of General Goeben and Beyer's division remained on the 27th in their cantonments; only the detachment sent to Vacht returned to Gerstungen, as nothing had been seen of the Bavarians. General Falckenstein himself went on the 27th on administrative business to Cassel.

The news of the retreat of the Hanoverians still prevailed on the night of the 26th-27th June. General Flies determined, in accordance with his orders, "to remain close upon the enemy," to advance from Warza to Langensalza on the morning of the 27th June, at half-past seven o'clock.

## BATTLE OF LANGENSALZA.

The almost improvised detachment of General Flies, of which the greater part was not intented for service in the field, and still less equipped with that view, numbered 8,150 Infantry, Appendix IV. 225 Cavalry, and 24 guns, of which six only were rifled.[*]

On the same night, between the 26th and 27th, the Hano-
Appendix V. verian Army, 20,500 men strong, with 52 guns,[†] had left the cantonments hitherto occupied, and taken up a defensive position on the left bank of the Unstrut. At daybreak, Bülow's brigade was, with the reserve Artillery at Thamsbrück, Vaux's brigade at Merxleben and Knesebeck's brigade in rear of it; at Nägelstedt was Bothmer's brigade, and the Reserve Cavalry

---

[*] The battalions numbered about 900 men each, the Coburg-Gotha regiment, in two battalions, 1,300; the Landwehr and Depôt Battalions between 300 and 400 men per battalion. Besides, the Landwehr were equipped only with Minié arms, and the Sally batteries with limber ammunition.

[†] Of these 16,177 men and 42 guns took part in the action of Langensalza.

was at Sundhausen. The detachments had outposts on the
right bank of the Unstrut. Three-and-a-half-squadrons were
pushed forwards on the road to Gotha, as far as Henningsleben,
and to support them Langensalza was occupied by one battalion
of Vaux's brigade. To protect the right flank, some earthworks had been commenced half-way between Thamsbrück
and Merxleben by the two companies of pioneers and 400 men
of Bülow's brigade.

The head of the Prussian advanced guard, watched by the
retreating Hanoverian Cavalry, appeared about 11 A.M. before 11 A.M.
Langensalza, where it was received with Infantry fire. After a
short skirmish, the 1st company of the Coburg-Gotha Regiment
pushed into the town; the enemy evacuated it, but sought to
prevent the *débouché* on the north-eastern exit. Here, driven back
by the 1st, 2nd, and 5th companies, he retreated on Merxleben.
On the Hanoverian side the advance of the Prussian troops had
been regarded only as a strong reconnaissance, and, in order
to prevent Langensalza, an important support of the army,
from falling into the hands of the enemy, Knesebeck's brigade
was ordered to advance. Bothmer's brigade was also instructed,
in case of a further advance of the enemy, to fall on the
latter's right flank. Not far from Callenberg's Mill the head of
Knesebeck's brigade came upon the retreating advanced troops;
at the same time it encountered Artillery fire from Blottnitz's
battery, which had unlimbered near the Siechenhof, while
detachments of Prussian Infantry appeared on the Judenhügel.
Made aware of the greater strength of the advancing enemy,
General Knesebeck covered the retreating troops with both
battalions of the Leib Regiment, and then followed with the
latter to the left bank of the Unstrut. The regiment of the
Guards remained on the west of Merxleben, while the rest
of the brigade retired to the reserve position intended for it,
2,000 paces north of that place.

Of the Prussian advanced guard, four companies of the 11.30 A.M.
Coburg-Gotha Regiment occupied the Judenhügel, the remainder of the regiment the northern exits of the town. The
main body and the reserve had meanwhile formed line; the
former was directed on the south-eastern corner of Langensalza,
towards the Judenhügel, the latter to the Siechenof. The
advance was made under the fire of the enemy's batteries,
which were in position on the further side of the Unstrut. The
horse batteries of the Prussian Artillery developed themselves
on the Judenhügel, but difficult ground prevented them from
appearing, except one after the other. A little later the eight
guns of the advanced guard came up on their left. Two companies of the 1st battalion of the 25th Regiment and three
squadrons of Cavalry covered the Artillery.

A hot fire was now opened at a range of about 2,000 paces.
The enemy had 15 guns (12 rifled 6-pounders and three
12-pounders) on the Kirchberg, and six rifled 6-pounders
(Egger's battery) in position on the west of Merxleben; he

was, besides, soon reinforced by four rifled 6-pounders, and four horsed guns of Bothmer's brigade (Müller's and Merten's batteries), which, west of Nägelstadt, at a distance of 1,700 paces flanked the position of the Prussian guns. Bothmer's and Bülow's brigades, directly after the commencement of the action, had approached the centre; the former moved from Nägelstedt halfway to Merxleben; the latter came on the north-west of this place, near Knesebeck's brigade, whither the reserve Cavalry also moved. In this strong and concentrated portion it was easy to remain till the enemy, not half so strong, attacked.

12 o'clock. Of General Flies's detachment, the 8th Company of the 11th Regiment, and a troop of the Merseburg squadron, were sent to cover the left flank towards Thamsbrück, whither somewhat later the 6th and 7th Companies of the Coburg-Gotha Regiment also followed. The place was found unoccupied; on the further side two squadrons of the Crown Prince's Dragoons and one battalion of the 4th Hanoverian Regiment showed themselves, with which a skirmish at a far distance was for some time maintained.

In the front, Colonel Hanstein pushed forward the 2nd Battalion of the 25th Regiment, on the road towards Merxleben, to which the 3rd Company of the Coburg-Gotha Regiment closed up. In columns of separate companies, these detachments extended from Gräser's Fabrik, by the Callenberg Mill, to the Bad Plantation. The left wing succeeded in crossing the Salza, and in opening fire upon the enemy's columns posted at Merxleben. An attempt of the 7th Company from Callenberg's Mill to cross the bridges of the Unstrut failed at first, but when the 2nd and 3rd Companies of the regiment entered into the action of the 2nd Battalion, and the 1st and 4th Companies advanced beyond the Bad Plantation, some detachments of skirmishers succeeded in wading through the Unstrut, and establishing themselves on the further side. The near fire of the skirmishers caused the three 12-pounders on the Kirchberg to retire, and some of the enemy's detachments, which in close order, assumed the offensive, were repulsed by file firing.

12.30 o'clock. At half-past 12 o'clock, the Fusilier Battalion of the 11th Regiment also engaged in the fight; the 9th and 12th Companies occupied Callenberg's Mill, the 10th reinforced the line of riflemen in the left of the high-road; the 11th Company remained on the left of it. Three companies of the 25th Regiment drew towards the Bad Plantation, into which the 1st Battalion of the 11th Regiment had already entered, and whither later also the 2nd Company of the Depôt Battalion, as well as the Potsdam Landwehr Battalion were sent from the Reserve.

It appeared now necessary for the protection of the right flank also to occupy the Erbsberg, as Bothmer's Brigade was making preparations to cross the Unstrut in its neighbourhood. The 1st Company of the Depôt Battalion which was then sent there succeeded, although its leader and only officer was severely wounded, in driving off Müller's battery. About one o'clock, Major-General Seckendroff followed hither with the first line of the Reserve, the 3rd Company of the Depôt Battalion, and two 6-pounder guns of the Sally Battery. The 10th and 11th Companies of the Aschersleben Battalion, and the 11th Company of the Naumburg Battalion drove back the enemy's detachments (of the 1st Battalion of the 7th Regiment), which had waded through the river, the guns took post on the hill, and fired upon Bothmer's Brigade with canister.

Somewhat later the last detachment of the Prussian Reserve, the Landwehr Battalion of Treuenbrietzen, was brought here, and carried on a musketry action with the Hanoverians in the valley of the Unstrut, while the Torgau Landwehr Battalion, from the main body, maintained the communication between the Erbsberg and the Bad Plantation.

Under these circumstances it was not possible for Bothmer's Brigade, the Jäger Battalion of which was engaged opposite the Bad Plantation, to cross the river.

While thus the Infantry battle on the Unstrut was more and 1 o'clock. more developed, about one o'clock the force of the Artillery fire somewhat slackened. On the Prussian side two howitzers had to retire behind Langensalza. They were provided only with limber ammunition, and had fired this away except two rounds. Blottnitz's battery was also compelled, in order to engage Müller's hostile battery, to take post at Siechenhof for a time. On the Hanoverian side the three 12-pounders on the Kirchberg had been compelled to retire; of the two 6-pounder rifled batteries one retired to complete its ammunition; the other, through a misunderstanding. Müller's battery had also been compelled to sacrifice its flanking position.

General Arentschild had, at Merxleben, eight battalions and opposite the Erbsberg four battalions engaged, there remained still eight fresh battalions of Bülow's and Knesebeck's brigades. From the hill of Merxleben the General had scrutinized the strength and dispositions of his adversary. When then it was reported to him, about one o'clock, that General Bothmer contemplated crossing the Unstrut, he considered the moment favourable for assuming the offensive generally, and sent orders to Bülow's and Knesebecks Brigades to cross the Unstrut, and attack the Prussian left wing.

General Flies had only three intact companies of the 2nd Battalion of the 11th Regiment to oppose to this offensive attack made with fresh forces. On the Erbsberg indeed the Prussian troops succeeded in repelling all attemps of the four battalions of Bothmer's Brigade to cross the river, so that General Bothmer, after a loss of 14 officers and 119 men, gave up these attempts and withdrew his troops out of the valley of the Unstrut to a more covered position on the hills in rear. On the other hand, the few Prussian companies which for a long time had been engaged on the left wing, and had no support worthy of the name behind them, were not in a position to repulse the attack made upon them by seven Hanoverian battalions.

While in the front the artillery fire grew hotter as the rifled 6-pounders, and the battery of 24-pounder howitzers of the Hanoverian Reserve Artillery drove up on the Kirchberg, and 1.30 o'clock. were anew joined by the battery of Vaux's Brigade, Bülow's Brigade, about half-past one o'clock, reached the Unstrut. It succeeded, in conjunction with the Regiment of Guards, in crossing the river west of Merxleben, and forcing the Prussian skirmishers behind the Salza. One battalion, as well as the battery of the brigade, and the regiment of Crown Prince's Dragoons, had taken up a covering position towards Thamsbrück, but the battalion soon followed across the Unstrut.

In the centre the advance of the Jäger Battalion of Bothmer's Brigade dislodged the Prussian skirmishers, who had already established themselves on the left bank. A similar attempt of the Jäger Battalion of Vaux's Brigade to advance from the 2 o'clock. heights of Merxleben had been frustrated. After two o'clock, Colonel Vaux, in person, succeeded in leading this battalion, as well as the 1st Battalion of the 2nd Regiment, down to the Unstrut, and, in company with the 3rd Jäger Battalion, in pushing over the river east of the bridges. The bridges and the bed of the Unstrut were occupied by portions of Vaux's Brigade. The defenders were confined to Callenberg's Mill, the avenue leading to Bad, and the Bad Plantation.

To further strengthen the attack, the Jäger Battalion of Guards, and the 2nd Battalion of the Leib Regiment of Knesebeck's Brigade advanced over the Kirchberg; the latter, however, here suffered such serious loss—in a few moments six officers and about 50 men—that it had to draw back. The battery of Knesebeck's Brigade also again took part in the fight; its first division which came up directed its 12-pounders on Callenberg's Mill, and compelled its defenders to evacuate it. As, however, their retreat was rendered impossible by the fire of the Hanoverian detachments, which had already crossed the Unstrut and Salza, they again established themselves in the mill, and laid down their arms here to the hostile companies which came to storm it.

Considering the serious superiority of the adversary, a further prosecution of the fight did not appear advisable to General Flies; besides, the object of the action—the detention of the Hanoverian army—had been fully accomplished, and indeed too much had already been done for the purpose. The retreat was ordered.

Of the three companies of the 11th Regiment still in reserve, the 7th was sent forward in the direction of Gräser's Fabrik, to support the left wing, which was ever gradually losing more ground, Colonel Zglinitzki led the 5th and 6th Companies to the churchyard, at the Erfurt Gate, where the 8th Company of the Coburg-Gotha Regiment joined them. Colonel Fabeck received orders to hold the Judenhügel with four companies of the latter regiment, until the Artillery and the troops engaged in front had withdrawn.

General Seckendorff was also directed to retire the right wing from the Erbsberg in the direction of Siechenhof.

The left wing strove with all its strength to detain the advance of Bülow's Brigade and the Guards, but one after another all the points outside of the town, Gräser's Fabrik, the Rasen Mill, the brick-field (Ziegelei), and the hospital (Lazareth), fell into the hands of the assailants. Under a hot fire, the retreat was commenced through Langensalza, on the Gotha road. It was not long before the detachments at the Erfurt Gate and on the Judenhügel received fire in flank and rear from the enemy's Infantry, which was spreading out in the town, and were also compelled to retreat after Major Petzel had withdrawn the batteries to a covering position south of Langensalza. In this position the 3rd 4-pounder battery, which was standing without protection on the east of the road, was suddenly attacked in rear by a hostile squadron. Captain Blottnitz reversed his guns while loading, repulsed the attack with canister, and then resumed his fire in the original direction. South of the town General Flies, about 4 o'clock, assembled 4 o'clock. his detachments, returning singly from the fray. General Seckendorff also moved here with the battalions from the Erbsberg; he had conducted his march along the Klinggraben unmolested by the hostile Infantry; only three squadrons of the Cambridge Dragoons, who had crossed earlier by Nägelstedt, showed themselves on his right flank. One of these squadrons attacked the two guns of the Sally Battery, which were marching with the 3rd Company of the Depôt Battalion, now numbering only 30 men, in the middle Illeben Road. Notwithstanding canister fire and two salvos from the Infantry, several Dragoons, with the squadron leader Captain Einem at their head, burst into the artillery division, but were for the most part either killed or taken. The remainder fled, pursued by the garrison squadron of the 12th Hussars. The draught horses were however frightened, bolted, and fell in a hollow road immediately in rear, out of which it was impossible to get them. In vain several detachments of Infantry manned the guns. As no means of dragging them out could be sent, they were obliged to be left lying, and were so found by the Hanoverians. By desire of the Duke of Saxe Coburg-Gotha, who came upon the field later, indeed some relay horses were sent with the Stendal squadron for them, but found the guns already removed.

The situation of these troops, which formed the garrison of the Bad Plantation, and had not followed the main body at the same time, had become peculiarly difficult. There were here, besides the 1st Battalion of the 11th Regiment, several companies of the 25th Regiment, the Potsdam Landwehr Battalion, and two companies of the Depôt Battalion. After the Judenhügel had also been abandoned by the Prussian troops, the greatest part of the enemy's artillery concentrated its fire on the Bad Plantation. This was, however, although attacked on three sides by Vaux's brigade, the available battalions of Knesebeck's brigade and the 3rd Jäger Battalion, for a long time held, and the retreat was commenced very late.

Now the Hanoverian Cavalry also advanced. Some time before two squadrons of the Queen's Hussars had crossed the bridges of the Unstrut, but had found themselves compelled in column of fours, to seek shelter north of Callenberg's Mill, in the narrow defile between the Salza and the *chaussée*. The two other squadrons of the regiment which somewhat later tried to follow from Merxleben, came unexpectedly upon the column halted in the defile, and a portion of them were forced, through want of room, to go back again. Some horsemen were thereby forced into the Salza and Unstrut. So the reserve Cavalry now ordered forward came upon the Hussars, and the delay thus caused, and accompanied with loss, was taken advantage of by its battery to unlimber on the bank, and to fire some rounds of canister against the Bad. When, immediately after this, the Bad Plantation was abandoned on the receipt of the first order which had arrived for retreat, and the Prussian Infantry in loose order after several hours of a musketry action, were entering open ground, the Queen's Hussars burst forth.

Several detachments, before they had time to form squares, were ridden down, others scattered, while the Infantry remaining behind in the plantation fell into the hands of the attacking hostile Infantry. It was, however, possible to unite the supports and the best part of the retiring skirmishers into two columns, which commenced their retreat by way of the Siechenhof, and here picked up a few detachments.

First, in the middle and upper Illeben Weg, east of the Klinggraben, were these columns reached by the hostile reserve Cavalry, while the Cambridge Dragoons, at the same time, sought to waylay their further march. The two columns were separated about 700 paces from each other, south of the Klinggraben. The western, under the command of Captain Rosenberg, of the 11th Grenadier Regiment, formed of men of the 3rd Company of this regiment, and the remains of the 9th and 12th Companies of the Potsdam Landwehr Battalion, and detachments of different troops, was on the upper Illeben Weg, first attacked by the Garde-du-Corps. The attack, made with two squadrons in the first and one in the second line, did not succeed. In passing, the squadron received fire from both flanks, and lost 2 officers, 16 men, and 42 horses.

Almost at the same time the second column, on the middle Illeben road, came in contact with the hostile Cavalry. Under the command of Lieutenant-Colonel des Barres, the column, composed of the main portion of the 1st Battalion of the 11th Grenadiers, the remains of the 10th and 11th Companies of the Potsdam Landwehr Battalion, and scattered men of different troops, had already, not far from the Bed Plantation, repulsed the attack of the Hussars of the Guard; its further march had been accompanied by hostile Artillery fire. On the rise of the middle Illeben road, Cavalry was seen, towards which Colonel des Barres, as he thought it Prussian, rode. It happened, however, this was the three squadrons of Cambridge Dragoons: their leader approached Colonel des Barres, and requested him to surrender. This proposal was declined, but, almost at the same time, the head of the quickly formed squares was attacked from the centre by the Cuirassier Regiment of the Guard which came up from the north; this advanced with two squadrons in the first line, while the third followed as a reserve, and a fourth was further in rear as escort to the horse battery. The attack was repulsed, also a second which the Cambridge Dragoons made against the rear of the column, and a third which the two Cuirassier squadrons, when again rallied, made. Some horsemen, as well as riderless horses, forced into the squares at each of these attacks, and men were thrown and wounded; the Infantry had reclosed its ranks with undisturbed coolness. In the presence of the strong hostile Cavalry to which now were added the Hussars of the Guard who had come from Nägelstedt, and which now mustered 16¾ squadrons, and under the enemy's artillery fire, the retreat was conducted in the direction of Henningsleben, and a junction was there effected with the remaining portions of the 6.30 o'clock. detachment of General Flies, who in the meantime had marched off along the Gotha road.

The enemy's infantry brigades assembled in and near Langensalza. Some squadrons resumed the positions held by the outposts in the morning.

General Flies continued his retreat from Henningsleben to Warza. Here also came, on the morning of the 28th June, the left flanking detachment, which, on the afternoon of the 27th, soon after 4 o'clock, had learned at Thamsbruck the result of the fight. Its march, accompanied by hostile Cavalry and Artillery, and molested by some shells, had been by Ufhofen and Grumbach.

The losses in the battle of Langensalza were, on both sides, under the circumstances, very considerable.

The Prussian loss in killed and wounded was 41 officers and 805 men.

|  | Killed. | | Wounded. | | Missing. |
|---|---|---|---|---|---|
|  | Officers. | Men. | Officers. | Men. | Men. |
| Coburg-Gotha Regiment .. .. .. | 2 | 11 | 3 | 44 | 1 |
| 25th Infantry     „     .. .. .. | 4 | 59 | 11 | 191 | 20 |
| 11th Grenad'er   „     .. .. .. | 3 | 56 | 9 | 253 | 9 |
| Depôt Battalion, 71st Regiment .. .. | .. | 3 | 2 | 16 | .. |
| Landwehr Battalions, Torgau and Naumburg .. .. .. .. .. | .. | 5 | 1 | 13 | .. |
| Landwehr Battalion, Aschersleben .. | .. | 8 | 2 | 29 | 3 |
| Landwehr Battalions, Potsdam and Treuenbrietzen .. .. .. .. .. | 1 | 11 | 2 | 41 | .. |
| 12th Hussars, Depôt Squadron .. .. | .. | .. | .. | 6 | .. |
| 3rd 4-pr. Battery, 6th Artillery Regiment | .. | 1 | .. | 5 | .. |
| 3rd Horse Battery, 7th   „      „ | .. | 1 | .. | 8 | .. |
| 4th    „     „     „    „ | 1 | 2 | .. | 2 | .. |
| Sally Battery, 4th Artillery Regiment .. | .. | 2 | .. | 5 | .. |
| Total.. .. .. .. | 11 | 159 | 30 | 613 | 33 |

Lieutenants-Colonel Von Westenhagen and Von Oettinger were among the wounded; the former died of his wound. Colonel Fabeck and Major Busse had horses shot under them.

The extraordinary heat of the 27th June, as well as the hot fight, had taxed the strength of the men to the utmost. For example, in the 1st Battalion 11th Regiment, when it had advanced into the Bad Plantation, already 50 to 60 men had sunk exhausted; consequently a not inconsiderable number of wearied men fell into the hands of the enemy during the retreat. On the Prussian side, the number of men taken prisoners was not ascertained, as they, on the 28th, again returned to their regiments; according to Hanoverian reckoning, it was said to have been 10 officers and 897 men. The Hanoverian loss amounted to 102 officers and 1,327 men killed and wounded, of whom 10 were Staff Officers. Vaux's brigade suffered most, as its Infantry and Jägers lost 24 officers, 492 men; while the Cambridge Dragoons attached to it lost 5 officers and 51 men. On the night after the battle, from the Hanoverian side, an armistice for several days was requested from General Flies, and, at the same time, a free passage to the south was requested on condition of not fighting against Prussia for two months; these proposals were declined.

As soon as the result of the battle of Langensalza was known in Berlin, positive orders were sent to General Falckenstein and direct to the divisions, to advance against the Hanoverians without any regard to the probable approach of the Bavarians with all forces disposable, and to accomplish their disarmament. This order reached Cassel at midnight, whence General Falckenstein immediately went to Eisenach after he had telegraphed the necessary orders.

Before receiving them, General Goeben during the night

moved the troops stationed nearest the railway from Eisenach and Gerstungen to Gotha, so that General Flies early on the 28th was reinforced at Warza by several battalions and two batteries.

All the rest, except the troops of General Schachtmeyer, which only reached Kreuzburg, were assembled in the course of the forenoon at Eisenach, whence Generals Goeben and Beyer in the afternoon, with 11 battalions, 6 squadrons, and 4 batteries advanced on Langensalza. Not less also General Manteuffel pushed forward against the Hanoverians. His movements from Göttingen were as follows :—

On the very early morning of the 26th he received intelligence from Berlin of the retreat of the enemy through Mühlhausen with orders to advance against him. The northerly direction which the Hanoverian Army was said to have taken led him to push forward the troops stationed at Göttingen, under General Korth, as an advanced guard to Duderstadt. The detachment sent on the previous day to Münden, and General Wrangel with four battalions and one battery of Goeben's division from Cassel, were drawn to Göttingen by rail, which they entered together towards evening and marched successively to the vicinity of Beyenrode. Two battalions of the Guard which had been sent from Eisenach to Göttingen arriving late in the evening remained there for the night. Also a rifled 6-pounder battery, the material for which was found in Stade, and which General Manteuffel had horsed and provided with men, came up to-day as a reinforcement to the corps. In the course of the day the march of the Hanoverians was not corroborated, and the Cavalry patrols, pushed forward to Bodungen, Worbis, and Kreuzeber heard nothing of the enemy. For this reason a more southerly direction of march was taken on the 27th.

By midday on the 27th General Korth reached Worbis—the other troops, Dingelstedt and Heiligenstadt. Here six squadrons of reserve Cavalry of Goeben's division, with a horse battery from Cassel, joined Manteuffel.

The latter, in the afternoon, heard of the battle of Langensalza, and at the same time the certain announcement that the Hanoverians had again taken up their position at Merxleben. He determined to attack them there next day, and in the evening drew the troops from Heiligenstedt to Dingelstedt. whither Korth was also to move.

The latter had received a report that the enemy was drawing off on the road to Sondershausen, and had moved in this direction as far as Elende. Thus no disposition could be made with this detachment, and there remained to General Manteuffel only about 8,000 men, with whom he marched to Mühlhausen early on the 28th.

There it was learned that the support of General Goeben, which had been requested by telegraph, could not that day be depended upon, and as the enemy showed no sign of quitting his position, the attack was put off till the following day. The troops advanced in the afternoon to the line between Gross-

Gottern and Welsbach. General Korth in the evening entered Kircheilingen.

The enemy's outposts on the approach of the Prussians withdrew rapidly to Langensalza.

Thus, on the evening of the 28th, at last the circle was completed, and the Hanoverians were surrounded by more than 40,000 men. The wavering decisions of the Hanoverian head-quarters, the frequent false reports of the movements of the Army had hitherto much hindered and delayed this.

The assurance now of being surrounded by such a serious superiority of strength, the exhaustion of the troops, the want of ammunition and provisions, and the losses in the battle, convinced the King of Hanover that a further contest could only lead to useless bloodshed.

Unconditional submission was accordingly determined upon, and a messenger was to take the notice thereof to Berlin.

General Flies, to whom he was first sent to request a pre-liminary armistice, and to declare that the Hanoverian troops had orders to make no further resistance, could not, on account of the instructions he had received, allow him to proceed, but reported to Berlin and to General Falckenstein at Eisenach.

A second *parlementaire* in the neighbourhood of the Behringen villages, fell in with Generals Goeben and Beyer, who, under existing circumstances, halted. It seemed useless to march the tired troops further; they bivouacked round Hütscherode, and the advanced guard occupied Behringsdörfer.

In regard to the brave resistance which the Hanoverian Army had offered, the King of Prussia was inclined to grant such conditions as would for all futurity remove the sting of a grievous remembrance. General Manteuffel was specially com-missioned to arrange this matter.

29th June. When he for this object, on the forenoon of the 29th, reached Langensalza, he found an unconditional capitulation which had been already concluded between Generals Falkenstein and Arentschildt. Nevertheless, the milder stipulations granted by Appendix IV. His Majesty, which are in the Appendix, were added to the original capitulation, and a clear stipulation made for the return of the Hanoverian troops to their homes.

They remained on the 29th in cantonments round Langen-salza, and in the course of the 30th June and 1st July moved from Gotha by railway through Magdeburg to Celle and Hilde-sheim, whence the men were dismissed to their homes.

The Prussian troops on the 29th took up wider cantonments in the districts they occupied, and halted on the 30th June.

# CHAPTER IV.

## INVASION OF BOHEMIA AND SAXONY.

WHILE in North-Western Germany, by the occupation of Hesse Cassel, and the capitulation of the Hanoverian Army, the imminent danger of a separation of the two halves of the Prussian Monarchy was fortunately avoided, the main armies had not remained inactive. The army of the Elbe stood ready at Torgau for the invasion of Saxony, with the same object the reserve corps concentrated at Berlin had been put in motion by marches and railway, besides, the first army was moved close to the Elbe with its right wing through Upper Lusatia.

Warned by the Chief of the Staff that the advance would probably take place on the 16th June, General Von Herwarth received his latest orders to move direct on Dresden, where it was hoped that he would fall in with the enemy.

The advanced guard, General Von Schöler, stood at Fichtenberg, close to the frontier, Etzel's division directly in rear of it; both concentrated on the right bank of the Elbe. A bridge was at once thrown at Lösnig by the pontooners of the IInd Corps, to carry these detachments to the other bank. There Canstein's division was assembled between Auszig and Staritz, and Münster's division at Schildau and Sitzenroda.

It had been anticipated that the large railway bridge at Riesa was prepared to be burnt, and was occupied by a detachment of pioneers. To prevent, if possible, the unnecessary destruction of such a costly erection, the first battalion of the 34th Regiment was placed on the proposed evening in the quick train going to Dresden with orders to move direct on Riesa, but before the battalion arrived the bridge was seen in flames. The Saxon post at Lösnig had been alarmed by the defile of the advanced guard over the pontoon bridge at Lösnig, and the work of destruction was at once begun at Riesa, by which a considerable loss of material, without any military advantage, was caused to the Saxons.

The Prussian advanced guard reached Riesa in the night, and the restoration of the bridge at the cost of the country was at once ordered. The detached battalion closed up to the 16th Division from Burxdorf by way of Lösnig.

One battalion of the 12th Division had occupied the bridge of the Mulde at Wurzen.

Only the first echelons or the reserve corps had, as yet, reached Roederau, and there was no intelligence whether the Saxons at Dresden had been reinforced by the Austrian Ist Corps. Nevertheless, on the 16th June, General Herwarth, 16th June. early in the evening, crossed the frontier in three columns; the advanced guard pushed its outposts to Johannishausen, Etzel's division reached Riesa, Canstein's division, Seehausen, and Münster's division, Zöschau.

It was now ascertained that Dresden was abandoned by its garrison, the Saxon troops were marching on Pirna, and that King John had gone there.

Horn's division of the Ist Army had, on this day, entered Löbau.

17th June. On the 17th June the Elbe Army pursued its advance, the advanced guard to Bockwen, Etzel's division to Meissen, Canstein's division to Canitz and Seehausen, Münster's division to Leippau and Eula, and a detachment of the latter of all arms was pushed to cover the right flank to Ostrau and Döbeln.

On this day Horn's division occupied Bautzen. At Meissen, the bridge over the Elbe had been found destroyed; the pioneers with the pontoons of the IIIrd Corps d'Armée had already placed a bridge on this day at Riesa.

18th June. On the 18th June, General Von Schöler advanced through Dresden, and Etzel's division followed him into the town. The people were quiet and conciliatory. Refreshments were willingly brought to the soldier's, and no difficulty was experienced in providing quarters for them.

Canstein's division marched to Kesselsdorf, and pushed its advanced guard to Tharand and Potschappel; Münster's division reached Leinbach and Tannenberg, its advanced troops Herzogswalde.

The Pontoon column of the IInd Corps this day placed a bridge at Meissen, after it had removed that at Lösnig on the afternoon of the 16th.

The Commander of the Ist Army had pushed the 4th Regiment of Uhlans and the 5th Hussars under Major-General Count Bismarck to Bischofswerder. After severe marching, this detachment, on the following day, reached Dresden, and so took up the communication between the Ist and the Elbe Army. The latter halted on the 19th. The advanced guard occupied the line Pillnitz, Nieder-Zedlitz, and Lockwitz with its outposts.

The Saxon Army had received no support from the Austrian. In the face of tremendous odds it could only evacuate its territory which lay open to the Prussian invasion, supported as it was by strong reinforcements.

But more was to be done than only to occupy Saxony. The Elbe Army had become available for operations against Austria, its distance from the Ist Army shortened by one half, had even the communication from Dresden to Bohemia on the right bank of the Elbe. This must be protected, and Dresden held, as the whole country on the left of the Elbe might be lost if a Bavarian reinforcement supported an advance of the Saxon Army. Measures were immediately taken to fortify Dresden against an attack form the west, the main body of the Prussian Army defended its presence from the east. The occupation of this important point was entrusted to the 2nd Division of the Reserve Corps, which was sent by rail to Herzberg, and thence by way of Riesa and Meissen entered Dresden on the 22nd.

To immediately occupy the most important points of the country on the 18th, a battalion of the 4th Regiment of Guards and a weak detachment of Cavalry had already, on the 18th, been ordered to Leipzig. Unmobilized Landwehr battalions from Stralsund and Stettin also arrived there on the 30th.

General Mülbe was appointed Military Governor of Saxony. With the small means at his disposal it appeared necessary to throw obstacles in the way of a Bavarian advance, and, therefore, the railway leading to Hof was broken up on the further side of Werdau. Colonel Mertens was entrusted with the fortifying of Dresden. After all had been done for the security of Saxony, which immediate circumstances demanded, all other mobilized troops which had entered that country were intended for the decisive main movement in Bohemia.

By a royal order of the 19th June, the Elbe Army was united with the Ist Army, and General Herwarth placed under command of His Royal Highness Prince Frederick Charles.

The 1st Division of the Reserve Corps was transported to Bittenfeld by rail; it marched by Eilenburg, Wurzen, and Döbeln, and entered Meissen on the 21st. This division—12 battalions, with 2 Cavalry Regiments, and 2 batteries—was placed under the direct orders of General Herwarth.

The intelligence of the position ot the Austrian Army was various and partly false. It all tended to say that the Ist Corps which had been nearest the frontier on both banks of the Elbe had been reinforced by the IInd Corps, and that even the Saxon Corps had been added.

Further, that the IIIrd Corps was marching on Pardubitz, the VIIIth on Brünn, and the IVth moving in a westerly direction. The manifesto of the Emperor Francis Joseph allowed a speedy commencement of hostilities to be anticipated, and it was at least not improbable that the Austrian main Army proposed a concentration in Northern Bohemia, where it would have stood united on an interior line between the Prussian Armies. Such a situation could not be disregarded, but the assembly of the Prussian forces had to be undertaken to counteract it. Appendix VII.

Austria had taken the initiative in arming; it was not desirable to yield up to her that of action. The advance into Bohemia was ordered.

On the 18th June, King William published a proclamation to his people. Appendix VIII.

On the same day Austrian Hussars crossed the frontier of Upper Silesia at Klingbeutel, and fired on Prussian patrols.

A special declaration of war against Austria did not

follow, because, by the Federal Decree of the 14th June, war against Prussia had already been announced; on the morning of the 23rd June, Prussian *parlementaires* took to the enemy's outposts the message, "that through the bearing of Austria " at Frankfort, the state of war had practically broken out, " and that the Prussian troops had instructions to act accord- " ingly."

How far a concentration of the main force of the enemy had proceeded in Northern Bohemia was not known. Care had to be taken that the Ist Army in advancing was sufficiently strengthened, the more so as the strong defiles of the Iser and the Upper Elbe lay before it. As before told, the Elbe Army was, therefore, fo close to the right wing of the Ist Army. With its left the latter was to hold on to the mountains, and the nearest division of the IInd Army—the Ist Corps—was ordered by telegraph on the 19th June immediately to march in the direction of Landshut, in order, if it were requisite, to be able to push up to the Ist Army by the hill road of Schreibershau.

For a concentration of the whole strength for decisive action in Bohemia it did not suffice that the Ist Army should advance from the north, but the IInd also must be drawn to it from the east. Still, however, as there was no security that an inroad might not still be made into Silesia, the Guards and the Vth Corps were only concentrated on the line between Camenz and Silberberg. To cover their march the VIth Corps still remained on the Neisse to mask it, and thence to make demonstrations against the frontier.

It was desirable, as long as possible, to maintain the power either with the IInd Army to meet a hostile invasion on the Neisse, or by an offensive movement from the county of Glatz to disturb the march of the enemy, or to be able for the sake of union with the Ist Army to break up. But since, on the termination of this first movement, there was no indication of an Austrian concentration against Upper Silesia, on the 22nd of June this telegram was sent to the head-quarters of the Ist and IInd Armies:

" His Majesty commands that both armies shall advance " into Bohemia, and endeavour to concentrate in the direction " of Gitschin."

The details were explained by a letter of the same date from the Chie of the Stafff of the Army, in which was said:— " The direction of Gitschin, with regard to the concentration " of both armies has been pointed out in the cypher telegram " sent to-day in reference to distances, road communiations, " and railways. It is naturally not intended that this point " must be reached under all circumstances, the concentration " hangs much more in the course of circumstances. According " to all intelligence that has arrived here it is improbable that " the main Army of Austria can, within the next few days, be " concentrated in Northern Bohemia. The initiative assumed by

Nº 1.

PROPOSED ADVANCE OF 2ᴺᴰ ARMY FROM 25ᵀᴴ TO 28ᵀᴴ JUNE.

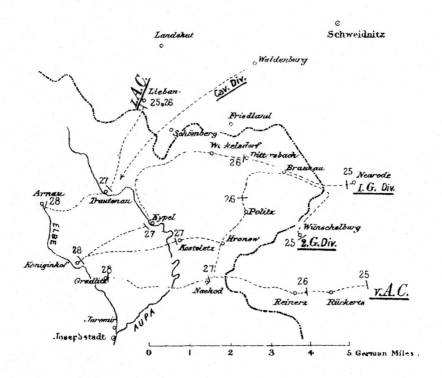

Weller & Graham. Lᵗᵈ Litho London

" us may give an easy opportunity to attack the enemy while
" still separated with superior force, and to follow up the
" victory in another direction. Then the concentration of all
" the forces for the principal decision must be kept in view.
" The Commanders of the Armies are, from the moment when
" they advance against the enemy, to act according to their
" necessities and exigencies, but to have regard to the circum-
" stances of the neighbouring army. By an arranged under-
" standing between each other the common support is to be
" facilitated."

To the Commander of the Ist Army it was added, " Since
" the difficult task of debouching from the mountains falls on
" the IInd weaker Army, so, as soon as the junction with
" Herwarth's corps is effected, the Ist Army must, by its rapid
" advance, shorten the crisis."

According to the dispositions of the Crown Prince the
several corps on the 24th June were to make a halt, which was
necessary after the previous marches, and to prepare for the
approaching exertion. These were then afterwards to march—

> The Ist Corps by way of Liebau and Trautenau to
> Arnau.
> The Guards by way of Neurode, Braunau, Eypel to
> Königinhof.
> The Vth Corps by Glatz, Reinerz, Nachod to
> Gradlitz ; and
> The Division of Cavalry was to follow the Guards
> from Waldenburg by Schömberg and Trautenau.

The VIth Corps had carried out the demonstration laid
down for it, as it had advanced to Freywaldau, and there had a
small skirmish, in which the 9th Company of the 10th Regiment repulsed an attack of Austrian Hussars. It then followed
the Army into the county of Glatz.

The projected advance to the Upper Elbe was, according *Vide* Plan 1.
to purpose, to be accomplished on the 28th June. The
Crown Prince did not overlook the great difficulties which
the country might oppose to him in this advance, if it
were rightly used by the enemy; he hoped, however, with
good ground, even if unfortunate, to hold fast an important
part of the enemy's forces, and to keep them away from the
Ist Army, the arrival of which must quickly accomplish the
union.

With whatever impatience in the Ist Army the moment to
cross the frontier was awaited, it was necessary first to await
the approach of the Elbe Army, in order to debouch at the
same time with it from the Lusatian mountains.

On the left bank no road leads along the Elbe; the sand-
stone mountains of Schandau, which are totally impassable
in a transversal direction, compel the circuit by Rumburg and
Schönlinde in order to reach Bohemia.

Thus the Elbe Army could only use the one road from Dresden by Stolpen, while the Guard division of the Reserve Corps could use the road from Meissen, and as far as Bischofswerder partly the railway.

On the former the advanced guard of the Elbe Army began its march on the 20th of June to Stolpen, on the 21st pursued it to Burkersdorf, on the 22nd to Schluckenau, on the 23rd to Rumburg, on the 24th to Gross-Mergenthal, and on the 25th reached the country south of Gabel. Etzel's, Canstein's, and Count Münster's division followed it in *échelon* on the same road. Thus this march of about 65 miles, in mountainous country, in great heat, and under circumstances very unfavourable for supplies, could only be accomplished in six days; but altogether the Elbe Army had from the 16th June, therefore, in ten days traversed the 115 miles from Torgau to Gabel.

The Ist Army concentrated itself on the 22nd June in Saxon Upper Lusatia, with—

The 8th and 7th Divisions respectively west and east of the Neisse, round Zittau.

The 3rd Division at Herrenhut, the 4th at Hirschfelde in Silesia, with—

The 5th Division at Seidenberg.

The 6th Division at Marklissa.

The Cavalry Corps in rear of these two.

*Vide* Plan 2. From this position the march for union could be made by each division on a separate road on the 23rd and 24th June.

On the 25th the Ist Army remained concentrated closely round Reichenberg; the Elbe Army reached Gabel and its vicinity; the division of Landwehr of the Guard moved to Georgenthal and Rumburg.

Hitherto Cavalry patrols alone were in front, which watched the march, and from which some prisoners were taken. A somewhat serious skirmish occurred on the 24th, when the 4th Squadron of the 6th Regiment of Uhlans, at the head of Horn's division, came upon the Regiment of Liechtenstein Hussars at Langenbrück. Two of the enemy's squadrons attacked it, both lines broke through each other in the charge, and then wheeled about against each other. The approach of the Prussian Infantry terminated the contest. On the Prussian side the squadron leader, Major Guretzki, Lieutenant Kiselbach, and eleven men were wounded and one man killed. On the Austrian side four men and ten horses were taken.

The reason that the débouché from the Lusatian hills met with no serious opposition must be sought in the Austrian orders.

Nothing certain is yet known of General Benedek's plan of campaign. It must be concluded from what appeared in the military journals that he intended to concentrate his main force on the right bank of the Upper Elbe, in the neighbourhood of Josephstadt and Königinhof. The Austrian Army would

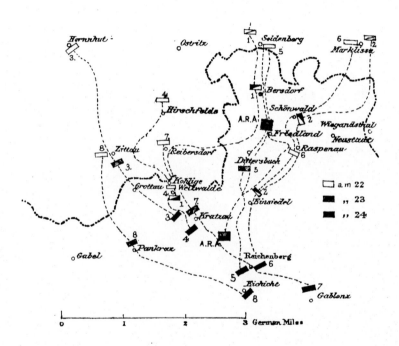

N⁰ 2.

1ˢᵀ ARMY ON 22ᴺᴰ, 23ᴿᴰ & 24ᵀᴴ JUNE.

there have been on the inner line of operation between the two Prussian Armies. It could then, with a weak detachment, hold the strong defiles of the Iser or the Elbe if it wished to throw its whole strength on either the Crown Prince or Prince Frederic Karl.

It appears now that the general held this view, in itself right, with the unalterable determination which is one of the finest qualities of a great captain. It remains, however, open to question whether this view was still correct, when it was necessary to execute it when the Prussian Armies were in full march.

To reap the advantages of an inner line of operations it is necessary that one enemy should be attacked while several marches distant from the other. If this distance is seriously diminished the danger arises that it may be necessary to deal with both at once. An army attacked in front and flank while in the battle-field also stands on an inner line of operations, but the strategical advantage is eliminated by the tactical disadvantage. If the Prussians were allowed to advance to the Elbe and the Iser, and if a few of the defiles fell into their hands, it was very doubtful if it were possible to push in between the two armies. The danger arose that while the one was attacked the other would at the same time attack the assailant in rear.

It has been already shown that General Benedek, by the want of proper equipment for his troops, was compelled with his forces already assembled on the 10th June to remain till the 17th in Moravia.

On the 20th June, the Prussian Armies were at Dresden, Görlitz, and Neisse; to Gitschin they had not a greater distance to traverse than the Austrians from the Moravian frontier. The time within which General Benedek could hope to operate against separated armies was very small.

Now that all is over, any one may say that the best plan would have been to have fallen with all force on the IInd Army debouching from the mountains. But the march of the Crown Prince behind the county of Glatz was not even known, and could hardly have been known except at the moment that his Army was already issuing from the defiles. Bespeaking quarters for 100,000 men in Upper Silesia, and the small action at Zuckmantel may have contributed to conceal the knowledge of the real purpose.

After, on the 10th to 12th June, the brigades of the IVth Austrian Corps, hitherto posted at Troppau and Teschen, had been withdrawn by railway, and the Intendance was to a certain extent ready, General Benedek, on the 17th and 18th June, commenced to march to Bohemia. To cover the right flank the IInd Corps and 2nd Light Cavalry Division were arrayed against the county of Glatz.

In the first line there marched on the right, the Xth Corps with the 1st Division of Reserve Cavalry; in the centre, the

IIIrd Corps; on the left the 2nd Division of Reserve Cavalry. These Infantry Corps had been brought from the neighbourhood of Brünn, the Cavalry Divisions from Prosnitz and Kremsier respectively. These were followed by, on the right, the IVth Corps from Olmütz, in the centre the VIIIth from Brünn, and on the left the Reserve Artillery of the Army. The VIIIth Corps left Rothkirch's brigade and the 7th Regiment of Uhlans, which had been detached from the 3rd Division of Reserve Cavalry at Wildenschwerdt, to secure the important railway junction there, to which the southern spurs of the county of Glatz approached with a dangerous proximity. Then followed, in the third line on the right, the IVth Corps from the neighbourhood of Olmütz, and in the middle column the 3rd Cavalry Division from Wischau.

The Xth Corps in the first line on the 25th reached Jaromir, the IIIrd on the 26th the Elbe at Königgrätz, while the 1st Division of Reserve Cavalry had already, on the 24th, entered Skalitz, and at first was left there. Of the remainder the VIth Corps was on the 26th at Opocno, the VIIIth Corps at Tynist; the 3rd Division of Reserve Cavalry this day reached Wildenschwerdt, and the Reserve Artillery of the Army, Leitomischl. Thus the contemplated rendezvous of the whole Army on the Upper Elbe could hardly be expected before the 2nd July.

Let us now turn to the situation of the Ist Austrian Corps.

It is correct that Count Clam was warned "that he was " to seek to facilitate the approach of the Saxons to the main " body of the Austrians, and to keep in view his own approach " thereto."

He was further recommended, "for the attainment of both " objects, to take up a position between Jung Bunzlau and " Münchengrätz."

It may be truly said that he acted, not according to circumstances, but strictly according to his instructions.

In these the union of all the forces was laid down as the main object, but not shown that to attain this the Prussian advance from Saxony and Lusatia should be checked.

Count Clam accordingly purposed only to hold his position on the Iser until the Saxons reached the neighbourhood of Chemnitz, Bela, and Bohdanetz, and then, if possible, without sustaining a check, to retire on the main body of the Army.

The Saxons had, on the 18th June, crossed the Bohemian frontier and marched to Theresienstadt and Lowositz. Ringelsheim's brigade had immediately supported them, while the remaining brigades of the Corps, Poschacher's, Leiningen's, Piret's and Abele's (formerly Kalik's) brigade attached to it, assembled at Jung Bunzlau.

For the utmost rapidity the Saxon Infantry, Artillery, and trains were taken by rail to the neighbourhood of Chlumetz and Pardubitz, the Cavalry with Ringelsheim's brigade withdrew, by forced marches to Jung Bunzlau.

Nº 3

POSITION OF BOTH ARMIES ON THE EVENING OF THE 25ᵀᴴ JUNE

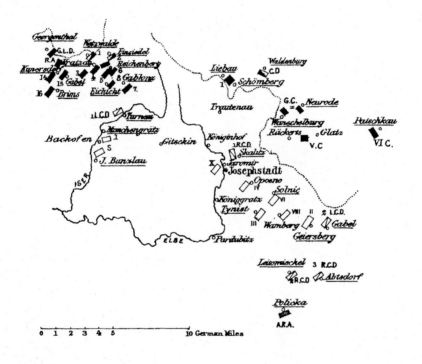

On the 21st of June, when the greatest part of the Saxon Corps had arrived at Pardubitz, Count Clam received an order from the Commander-in Chief of the Army saying that "the "Ist Corps and the Saxons were to take up a position at "Jung Bunzlau."

Surely, it would have been more desirable and requisite that the Commander of the Ist Corps should have received some explanation of the intentions of the Commander-in-Chief how to carry this out, than only an order, which tied all freedom of action, to take up a position the object of which was by no means explained. It must be presumed that the Commander-in-Chief on the 21st still expected with his main body to reach the Iser before Prince Frederic Karl.

Count Clam followed also his new orders literally. The railway transport of the Saxons was stopped, the detachment which had been already sent was sent back, eight battalions and four batteries which were still in Theresienstadt were drawn to Jung Bunzlau.

On the 25th of June, the Ist Austrian Corps stood round Münchengrätz fronting the north, Ringelsheim's brigade with the Saxons still on the march had reached Backofen.

It is of interest to review the positions of the different corps on the 25th June, as here the combats commenced which, in quick succession, led up to the decisive battle. With the exception of unimportant details that position is shown on the Plan No. 2. annexed plan.

It may be seen that the Ist Austrian Corps and the Saxons stood opposed to the whole power of Prince Frederic Karl, and that six Austrian Corps could, within a few days, be assembled against the Crown Prince if his advance were known.

On the Prussian side it was expected to find a strong opposition behind the Iser, as it was erroneously accepted that the IInd Austrian Corps was also there. It appeared, therefore, necessary to allow the Elbe Army to come nearer to the Ist before an advance was made against that strong defile.

------

# CHAPTER V.

### THE BATTLES IN BOHEMIA UP TO THE BATTLE OF KÖNIGGRÄTZ.

The Elbe Army was ordered to make Niemes and Oschitz its objects of march on the 26th. General Herwarth ordered that the advanced guard should march beyond the former place as far as Plauschnitz, and should push forward detachments towards Hühnerwasser and Hirschberg. The 15th and 16th Divisions were to follow to Niemes and Barzdorf, while the 14th Division on the left was directed on Oschitz.

Combat of
Hühnerwasser

At 6 A.M., General Schöler moved from his bivouac at Postrum with the advanced guard—four battalions of Infantry, one battalion of Jägers, five squadrons and 12 guns. Beyond Niemes the 3rd squadron of the King's Hussars, which marched at the head of the column, came upon patrols of the enemy's Cavalry, which withdrew into the wood in front of Hühnerwasser. Captain Goltz pursued and drove back the Infantry patrols showing themselves there. When the advanced division, under Lieutenant Count Moltke, was debouching from the wood it received Infantry fire, but trotted on in front of Hühnerwasser, while the squadron in column of divisions followed along the road. Near to the town a squadron of Nicolaus Hussars, which had been drawn up in concealment, suddenly attacked the advanced division; Captain Goltz threw himself immediately on the flank and rear of the pursuing enemy, who lost three officers and thirty men. After the rally was sounded the squadron found itself exposed to a heavy Infantry fire, so that only one dismounted trumpeter and eight captured horses could be carried off.

The report of this skirmish of Hussars showed General Schöler that he could not halt at Plauschnitz as long as the neighbouring wood was held by the enemy. When the Infantry came up, at 11 A.M., he formed it in column of companies, advanced it, and drove the enemy's detachments towards Hühnerwasser. Then two 4-pounders came up, and after a few shots two companies of the 33rd Regiment took the nearest farm. Supported by Gaza's company of Jägers, Colonel Marshall pushed with his battalion into the place, drove out the Haugwitz battalion and pursued it into the wood lying in rear.

General Herwarth, who had arrived on the battlefield at 1 o'clock, ordered the advanced guard to remain in Hühnerwasser, and to occupy the ground gained. In consequence of its advanced position in a very wooded country, it was supported by two battalions of the 40th Regiment, and the 15th Division was brought to the defile of Plauschnitz.

The Infantry of the Guard took up alarm-quarters in Hühnerwasser, the Cavalry, Artillery, and Pioneers bivouacked in rear of and near the place. As outposts, one battalion was posted towards Weiszwasser, a second towards Münchengrätz, and a third towards Gablonz, in the wood.

Lieutenant Count Moltke, severely wounded, was taken by the enemy.

The loss of the enemy could not be ascertained. One officer was found dead on the field, 82 Austrians were taken, among whom were one officer, but only 13 wounded.

At 6 P.M., the advanced posts were alarmed from Münchengrätz; it was the 32nd Jäger Battalion, which was making a reconnaissance. A sharp fight in the wood developed itself, in which the supports being brought up joined. The Austrians were attacked by an overwhelming superiority, and driven back with serious loss. In vain an Infantry detachment posted on the heights of Gruppay attempted to support the Austrian Jägers, and the fall of night terminated the fight at the defile of the Teper Brook. The troops returned to their bivouacs.

The loss in the two combats at Hühnerwasser was as follows:—

|  | Killed. | | Wounded. | |
| --- | --- | --- | --- | --- |
|  | Officers. | Men. | Officers. | Men. |
| East Prussian Fusilier Regiment, No. 33 .. | .. | 2 | 1 | 14 |
| Hohenzollern Fusilier Regiment, No. 40 .. | 1 | 1 | .. | 1 |
| 7th Rhine Infantry Regiment, No. 69 .. | .. | 1 | 1 | 15 |
| Rhenish Jäger Battalion, No. 8 .. .. | .. | 2 | .. | 5 |
| King's Hussars, No. 7.. .. .. .. | .. | .. | .. | 5 |
| Total .. .. .. | 1 | 6 | 3 | 40 |

The Austrian loss must, by the number of dead on the field, have been much more considerable. In the evening five officers and 24 Jägers were taken prisoners, of whom four officers and 46 men were wounded.

This day the Austrian troops engaged belonged to Leiningen's brigade, and it was ascertained from the prisoners that the Saxons were on the left wing of the Austrians.

As it was proposed, on this day, that the 1st Army should halt to await the arrival of the right wing, Horn's division received orders to make a reconnaissance on Liebenau.

The advanced guard of the division was formed of two battalions of the 72nd Regiment, the 1st squadron of the 6th Uhlans, and the 3rd 4-pounder battery. This was followed by a Cavalry division under General Hann, formed of the Cavalry regiments of the 5th, 6th, 7th, and 8th divisions.

As the advanced guard, soon after 7 A.M., was debouching from Liebenau, it was fired upon from a plantation 800 paces from the east of the town, which was occupied by Austrian Dragoons. The 1st battalion of the 72nd advanced in column of companies; an abatis on the road was cleared away, and the Infantry came under the fire of a hostile battery, distant about 2,000 paces. The battery of the advanced guard opened upon this, but the Artillery combat did not last long, as the approach of the Prussian skirmishers made the enemy retire.

By midday Goldenstern was occupied by the Infantry, and when the Cavalry debouched from the place it was fired upon by an Austrian battery on the height near Dauby, which was masked by several squadrons. The Prussian Cavalry in consequence took ground here to the left, on the height of Sichrow, behind a hill on the east of the Chaussée. After the Artillery of the division came up three batteries opened, but the cannonade was ineffective, and to obtain a result six companies of the advanced guard, concealed by the ground, moved against the Austrian guns, which now withdrew upon Turnau with the Hussars and Dragoons of Edelsheim's division. Prince Friederic Karl, who was present, had already ordered the advance of the remaining divisions, in order that day to seize the important defiles of Turnau.

With this object the 7th and 8th divisions were to advance to Preper, the latter was to push its outposts to Podol.

The 5th Division was ordered to Gablonz, the 6th to Liebenau, the IInd Corps was to march to Reichenberg.

General Fransecky, on his arrival in the afternoon, found Turnau unoccupied. He immediately threw a pontoon bridge over the Iser, and had the partly destroyed bridge restored so as to be available for Infantry. It was learned that Edelsheim's Cavalry division had in the morning crossed the river here to join the IInd Corps at Münchengrätz. Two squadrons of Hussars which had been at Eisenbrod, and a company of Jägers from Wurzelsdorf, had withdrawn, in the direction of Gitschin, by way of Lomnitz.

In the afternoon, between 2 and 3 o'clock, an order from the Commander-in-Chief reached the Austrian-Saxon Head-Quarters, which especially prescribed "to hold Turnau and "Münchengrätz at all cost."

In the evident difficulty of still solving this problem, Count Clam considered it judicious not to separate his forces, but, giving up the defence of Münchengrätz, to concentrate them towards Turnau. As this point, however, was not, on account of its locality, advantageous for strictly defensive action, it was determined to advance against it, attack it, and, passing by, to take up on the following day, the 27th, north of Sichrow, a position at Gilloway, the better to accomplish the charge received.

In the meantime, news came that Turnau was already occupied by the Prussians, but only in small force. The proposed operation was in consequence to be carried out the same evening, by surprising Turnau and occupying the hills on the further side of Podol, at Swiegan, in order there also to make the debouch for the next day secure. These proposals were reported to Josephstadt.

As circumstances have been narrated, it can easily be seen that time was not now available for execution. If even it had been possible to win the defiles, the Austrians in advancing on Gilloway would have had the Prussian Ist Army in front, the Elbe Army on their flank, and the Iser in rear.

After the 8th Division had cooked at Sichrow, it marched, at 6 P.M., to Preper. In this village the advanced guard halted. A reconnaissance told that Podol was occupied by the enemy, and General Schmidt ordered "a company of the Magdeburg "Jägers, No. 4, to advance, take Podol, and secure the passages "of the river there."

## ACTION OF PODOL.

The 4th Company, under Captain Michalowski, was fired upon in the middle of the village, from a barricade, and took it by a resolute attack. During the fight in the village, round three other barricades, Captain Mertens, with the 2nd Company, who had swept the hill of Swigan of the enemy, entered from the western side. The garrison of this place, a company of the Martini Regiment, retired, and in rapid pursuit the Jägers pressed over all four bridges; on the far side of the last they were, however, met with a hot fire from the ditches along the road, and a single standing house. Captain Michalowski fell, and his company retired behind the bridge of the Iser. At half-past eight o'clock, the 10th and 11th Companies of the 72nd Regiment arrived, which had been sent in support. Major Flotow led them over the bridge, and drove the enemy out of the single house. The two Fusilier Companies remained there till half-past nine o'clock. Two companies of the 71st Regiment, which were advancing, were sent back by the Divisional Commander. As the fire in Podol ceased, the action could be regarded as over.

On the Austrian side, Poschacher's brigade had been intended to occupy the height of Swigan. The Martini Regiment and the 18th Jäger Battalion were now assembled, and advanced to a comprehensive attack, which drove again the 10th and 11th Companies over the bridge. An advance of the 9th was repulsed, but the fire of the skirmishers prevented the enemy's pursuit. On the report that an enemy's battalion was advancing against the village, and on account of the difficulty of conducting the action in the dark, and in unknown ground, Major Flotow determined, at 11 o'clock, to abandon the village.

In the bivouac at Preper at Swerzin, $2\frac{1}{2}$ miles distant, General Bose remarked, about 10 o'clock, the increase of the firing, and hastened forward with the two second battalions of the 31st and 71st Regiments, the total strength of which hardly amounted to 1,300 men, since the return of the men sent to fetch water was not awaited. Helmets and knapsacks were laid aside. From the retiring detachments the considerable strength which the enemy had developed in front of Podol was ascertained. But on the reflection that this important passage must in any case be won, and would probably later cause a great sacrifice, General Bose determined on an immediate attack. The 2nd Battalion of the 71st Regiment advanced from the west against the bridge. Its 5th company was fired upon from the nearest houses, and soon an enemy's column advanced to the attack. The battalion halted, the two leading ranks knelt down, so as to receive the enemy advancing in close formation with a salvo from four ranks. When the enemy's column, at 30 paces off, could be clearly seen in the bright moonlight, the fire was delivered in full effect, and an immediate attack with the bayonet made. Leaving a large number of dead, the Austrian column retired, but established itself behind the barricade, which had been carried at first, but only partly destroyed. Several bugle calls caused a new attack to be expected. It was made, and was now, by the 7th company, repulsed in the same way. In the meantime, on the other side, the 2nd Battalion of the 71st Regiment had pushed into the village. The enemy evacuated a part of the village, and thereby lost, in a large farm, a great number of prisoners. All his attempts again to occupy it failed. Soon after 11 o'clock the two Fusilier Battalions of the 31st and 71st Regiments arrived at the northern entrance of Podol. The first was pushed forward to storm the bridges, General Bose and Colonel Drygalski placed themselves at its head; firing was forbidden. When the column had approached within 60 paces of the bridge, it was received by a salvo, and a flanking fire from the railway embankment; it hesitated, and began to return the fire. The endeavours of the officers soon, however, succeeded in setting the battalion in motion. General Bose himself seized a musket, and marched forward with it. A regular hand-to-hand fight ensued, in which the enemy was driven back. Since Colonel Drygalski was mortally wounded by many bullets, General Bose led the battalion in person over the bridge, and with three companies took up a position in front of it; the 4th was posted on the right, on the railway embankment.* In rear the Fusilier Battalion of the 71st Regiment occupied the road and the railway bridge, each with one company.

Count Clam, who was on the spot, had brought up parts of Piret's and Abele's brigades, among them the Ramming Regiment, No. 72, and made fresh attempts, which, however, had no success.

The action ended at 1 o'clock in the night.

To secure his position General Bose rode back to the quarters of the Divisional Staff at Preper, and returned again to Podal before daybreak, with the 3rd 6-pounder battery given to him for this object.

During his absence, in the expectation of a general attack, the detachments pushed beyond the bridge had retired behind it; the attack was not, however, made.

General Bose had correctly recognized the whole importance of the passage of the Iser won by him. It opened the shortest line to Gitschin, and threatened the communication of the Saxon-Austrian Corps with the main army. The projected offensive movement of Count Clam on Turnau also was prevented.

Not less fortunate than the strategical was the material result of this hard fought night action.

---

* It must be borne in mind that the Prussian battalion consists of four companies only, the regiment of three battalions (the companies are numbered in the regiment from 1 to 12). Each company musters 250 combatants.

The loss on the Prussian side was—

| | Killed. | | Wounded. | | Missing. |
|---|---|---|---|---|---|
| | Officers. | Men. | Officers. | Men. | Men. |
| 2nd Company, 4th Jäger Battalion .. | 1 | 1 | .. | 2 | .. |
| Fusilier Battalion, 72nd Regiment .. | .. | 4 | 3 | 9 | 15 |
| 2nd Battalion, 31st Regiment .. | .. | 8 | 3 | 21 | .. |
| Fusilier Battalion, 31st Regiment .. | 1 | 14 | 3 | 32 | 2 |
| 2nd Battalion, 71st Regiment .. | .. | 3 | 1 | 7 | .. |
| Total .. .. | 2 | 30 | 10 | 71 | 17 |

The other troops suffered no loss.

The following was believed to be the Austrian loss :—

| | Killed. | | Wounded. | | Prisoners. | |
|---|---|---|---|---|---|---|
| | Officers. | Men. | Officers. | Men. | Officers. | Men. |
| On the 27th, by the Prussians, were buried .. .. .. .. | 3 | 107 | .. | .. | .. | .. |
| Removed .. .. .. .. | 1 | .. | .. | .. | .. | .. |
| There fell prisoners into Prussian hands .. .. .. .. | .. | .. | 2 | 240 | 5 | 504 |
| According to the report of a parlementaire the Austrians took away with them .. .. .. .. | .. | .. | .. | 190 | .. | .. |
| Total .. .. | 4 | 107 | 2 | 430 | 5 | 504 |

While in this manner, on the 26th June, the Elbe Army opened its road to Münchengrätz, by the action of Hühnerwasser, the Ist Army gained the passage of Podol, and occupied that at Turnau, the Army of Silesia also made a further step forward towards the proposed junction.

The Ist Corps d'Armée stood ready at Liebau and Schömberg to cross the frontier. Patrol skirmishes had here already, on the 24th, occurred against detachments of the Windischgrätz Dragoons, who had been detached from the 1st Light Cavalry Division, towards Trautenau. The passage of the Guards across the frontier had already been effected. The 1st Division was marched to Dittersbach, the 2nd to Pickau; the advanced guards were pushed forward to Weckelsdorf and Politz.

The Vth Corps had reached Reinertz, the Cavalry division Waldenburg. The VIth Corps had arrived at Landeck and Glatz. Of the latter, the 8th Regiment of Dragoons, and two batteries, by order of the Crown Prince, were placed under the command of the Vth Corps to cover its flank and rear. These troops, on the 26th, reached Alt-Heyde and Neu-Wilmsdorf, and in the evening, by command of General Steinmetz, the 8th Dragoons joined the main body of the Vth Corps.

The Guards thus stood in the centre between the two points, separate only 20 miles from each other, where the 1st and Vth Corps had to cross the mountain frontier, and could support the debouch of either the one or the other.

In the course of this day, the Austrian Cavalry outposts reported to Josephstadt the advance of the Army of Silesia, and that it had already, at several points, crossed the frontier. Hitherto there had been only insignificant skirmishes. A part of the 3rd Regiment of Uhlans of the Guard had come upon detachments of the Windischgrätz Dragoons and Mexico Uhlans, and brought in some prisoners and captured horses.

The advanced guard of the Vth Corps had reached Jürcker, and pushed its leading sections to Gellenau. It was, in the afternoon, to move to the Metau, the frontier.

As it was reported that detachments of the enemy were in Nachod, Major-General Loewenfeld personally rode forward to reconnoitre. The bridge of the Metau was broken, the toll-house occupied; some shells were thrown against the General and his Staff, but the enemy evacuated Nachod after a few shots from the first division of the 5th 4-pounder battery, which was brought up. His strength was only 70 Infantry, $2\frac{1}{2}$ squadrons, and 2 guns. The Cavalry belonged to the reserve division of the Prince of Holstein, which was with Schindlöcker's brigade, at Dolan, and Prince John's brigade, at Skalitz, and had pushed forward some squadrons to Dobruska, Neustadt, Nachod, and Kosteletz.

The bridge of the Metau was made practicable by the Infantry pioneers. The 3rd Battalion of the 37th Regiment, as well as two Jäger companies, crossed, and were afterwards followed by the 2nd Battalion of the same regiment. Colonel Below took up with his troops the following:—

The two Jäger companies occupied Nachod; behind them stood Braun's half-battalion in support; on the neighbouring heights, north of the town, Bogan's half-battalion; on the south, Kurowski's half-battalion; while Schimonski's half-battalion remained at the toll-house.

The 2nd Company of Pioneers proceeded at once to restore the bridge, and prepared two new passages near it, which were finished by three in the morning.

The main body of the advanced guard was withdrawn to the heights of Schlaney; one of its battalions occupied the passage of the Metau.

The position of the armies on both sides is shown on the Sketch No. 4. annexed sketch. It appears thence that the two Prussian Armies were still separated by about 50 miles; but were con-

N.º 4.

POSITION OF BOTH ARMIES ON THE EVENING OF THE 26ᵀᴴ JUNE.

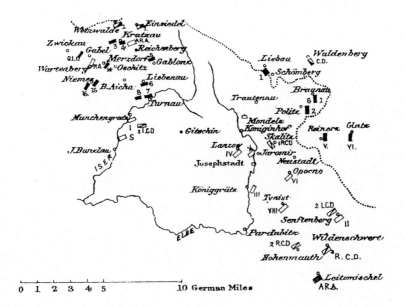

0 1 2 3 4 5       10 German Miles

Weller & Graham, Lᵗᵈ Litho. London.

*1123.*

centrated in themselves, while the main corps of the Austrian force were also separated by about 50 miles.

On the 27th June, the advanced guard of the Elbe Army, which had been pushed forward above five miles. halted at Hühnerwasser. The 15th Division remained at Plauschuitz; the 14th advanced from Merzdorf to Böhmisch Aicha; the 16th Division concentrated at Barzdorf, while the Landwehr Division of the Guard was close behind it at Wartenberg and Grünau. On the right flank the passages over the Polzen river were watched by detachments.

In the 1st Army also the 7th and 8th Divisions remained on the Iser, near Turnau. The 6th Division pushed close up to them to Luzan, followed by the Cavalry brigade of the Duke of Mecklenburg, by way of Liebenau. The head of the IInd Corps reached this place, and the Cavalry Corps Reichenberg. The 5th Division was advanced on the left from Gablonz to Eisenbrod.

On the Iser there was, therefore, only an advance with regard to a closer concentration of force.

According to the reports brought to the Commander of the 1st Army, the brigade Abele, Edelsheim's Cavalry division, and the Saxon corps were still at Münchengrätz; entrenchments there showed that Count Clam wished to stand there and await reinforcements, notwithstanding the probable risk to his communications by way of Gitschin, and although the nearest corps still on the Elbe were from two to three marches distant.

The Austrian Main Army, however, had had enough to do on account of the debouch of the Silesian Army from the mountains, which threatened the right flank of any advance against the Iser.

A telegram from the Feldzeugmeister reached Münchengrätz at midday, which left to the discretion of the Crown Prince of Saxony whether the operation contemplated on the previous day, by way of Turnau, was still prudent, and it was determined to march off at least on the following day. To secure the retreat the brigade of Ringelsheim was immediately directed on Podkost.

We have now to turn to the orders which Feldzeugmeister Benedek gave to stave off the advance of the IInd Army.

To oppose it stood, the nearest available, the reserve Cavalry division of Prince Holstein, at Dolan and Skalitz;

The Xth Corps, Lieutenant Field-Marshal Baron Gablenz, at Josephstadt and Schurz, which had pushed forward Mondl's brigade to Prausnitz, Keile, and Weiberkränke, half way to Trautenau; and

The VIth Corps, Lieutenant Field-Marshal Ramming, at Opocno, of which the brigades Hertweck and Jonak had quarters at Neustadt, near the frontier of Glatz.

The IVth Corps stood at Lanzow, west of Jaromir; the IIIrd and VIIIth Corps at Königgrätz and Tynist; the remaining detachments of the army still more than a march in rear.

On account of the intelligence received, it was ordered that the Xth Corps, with the 9th Uhlan Regiment of the IIIrd Corps attached to it, should, at 8 A M. on the 27th, advance on Trautenau, calling in Mondl's brigade, and pushing forward an advance-guard, take up a position against Trautenau, and attack with all energy the enemy already reported to be advancing, but not pursue too far.

The VIth Corps was ordered on the same day, at 3 A.M., instead of the march already ordered from Opocno to Josephstadt, to advance to Skalitz, there to take up a position, and to push an advance-guard against Nachod. The 1st Reserve Cavalry Division was placed under the orders of General Ramming.

" The combination has the object of covering the march of " the Army, not yet completed, on Josephstadt; but this will " not prevent the enemy from being attacked with all energy " wherever he may show himself. The pursuit of the enemy " must, however, be stayed within the frontier, and not carried " too far. Of the strength of the enemy opposed to the VIth " and Xth Corps I expect speedy information."

The VIIIth Corps, which was disposed from Tynist through Königgrätz to Wsestar, was ordered to move directly by way of Josephstadt to the quarters vacated by the Xth Corps round Schurz, an order which, in the morning of the 27th, while the corps was marching, was altered by the following direction :—

" Journal, No. 846.

" The Xth Corps, arriving to-day at Josephstadt, is not " to take up the position of the Xth Corps, but to march by " Jaromir to Czaslawek and Dolan, and there to occupy a " position with the object of eventually supporting the VIth " Corps."

(Signed) " BENEDEK."

Further, the IVth Corps d'Armée, which had already crossed the Elbe and reached Lanzow, was ordered back to Jaromir, while the IIIrd Corps d'Armée, which had reached Königgrätz, marched on Miletin.

The portions of the Army further in rear received orders to hasten their advance. The 3rd Reserve Cavalry Division was not to halt at Wamberg on its march from Wildenschwerdt, but was to push on to Hohenbruck; so the IInd Corps and the 2nd Light Cavalry Division, instead of moving on the 27th from Senftenberg to Reichenau, were to advance to Solnitz.

Of the Prussian IInd Army, according to the orders of the Crown Prince for the march through the mountains on this day, the 1st Corps was to advance by Trautenau, and its advanced guard, if possible, to reach Arnau, the main body of the Vth Corps was directed on Nachod. To each of these corps a division of the Guards was to serve as reserve, and consequently the 1st Division of the Guards was to advance by Braunau and Weckelsdorf, the 2nd by Hronow, and move respectively on Eypel and Kosteletz, in case the corps on the wings accomplished the debouch through the mountains without hindrance.

---

## BATTLE OF TRAUTENAU.

The first Corps d'Armée started at 4 A.M., in the order of battle shown in the Appendix, formed in two columns, from Königshann, south of Liebau, and from Schömberg to Trautenau. A detachment on the right flank was directed by Schatzlar on Ober-Altstadt. The two main columns were ordered, after passing through the mountains, to unite at Parchnitz, and there rest for two hours under protection of the advanced guard which was to occupy Trautenau.

Appendix XI.

The left column, at 8 A.M., reached Parschnitz, and there awaited the arrival of the right. The march of the latter had been materially impeded, and as the advanced guard had been provided by it, Trautenau remained for two hours unoccupied. When at last, about 10 o'clock, the head of the advanced guard approached the town, the bridge over the Aupa was found barricaded, but occupied only by dismounted dragoons of the Windischgrätz Regiment, who withdrew on the approach of the Infantry.

The 3rd and 5th Squadrons of the Lithuanian Dragoons followed through Trautenau. Debouching from the south-western exit from the town, they perceived on their right front Austrian Cavalry deployed; but at the same time also three divisions of Rittmeister Hagen, which had been pushed forward from the flank detachment, and had passed the Aupa, at Ober-Altstadt. The latter at once threw themselves upon the former, who mustered one and a-half squadrons, and, although received with a salvo from carbines, broke in upon them.

At the same time, Major Jastrzembski attacked with the 3rd Squadron, while the 5th Squadron, following *en échelon* under Rittmeister Oettinger, moved against several hostile squadrons which showed themselves on the flank. The whole regiment of Windischgrätz Dragoons, and a detachment of the Mensdorf Ulhans were here united. A sharp hand-to-hand combat ensued, which only ceased when Prussian Infantry, hurrying up, and Austrian Jägers also, fired into it. The Prussian Cavalry rallied and took post near the 1st 4-pounder battery, which unlimbered in the west of the town, on the right bank of the Aupa.

The brink of the Aupa meets here with the steep spurs of the Kapellen and Galgen Hills, south and east of Trautenau, close to the town. Deep and steep sunken roads alone lead to the plateau.

If these were once occupied by the enemy, it must be extremely difficult to obtain possession of them, and the brigade of Mondl, of the Xth Corps, was already hurrying there. West of the great road to Hohenbruck a battery was opening fire on the Prussian advanced guard, and the Infantry was on the

G

point of entering the town, when it was prevented by General Gablenz, who had hurried forward from his corps.

Colonel Beeren, now employed five companies of the Crown Prince's regiment against the heights, while one company occupied the edge of the town, and two companies were held in reserve. The detachment of Pioneers engaged in the action, and some shots were delivered from the houses, which were repeated later in the action. Now, for first time, the main body of the Prussian advanced guard moved forward. Its three Jäger companies reinforced partly the line of skirmishers, partly the garrison of the houses ; the Fusilier battalions of the Crown Prince's Regiment remained on the near side of the Aupa, not far from the bridge, and hence pushed two companies into the hollow road leading to Krieblitz, while the Fusilier battalion of the 41st Regiment, which had advanced into the town, maintained the communication with the vanguard by four divisions of skirmishers. The ten guns which were with the main body of the advanced guard unlimbered 300 paces north-east of the town, on both sides of the chaussée, and enfiladed the enemy's position; on their right marched the remainder of the Dragoon regiment and the East Prussian Uhlans.

The position on the heights was hardly to be faced in front; the Tirailleur action had also assumed a very serious character, without succeeding in gaining any advantage, when about 11 o'clock the right flanking detachment approached on the chaussée from Ober-Altstadt. Colonel Koblinski moved with it at once into the town, while his two guns drew near to the 1st 4-pounder battery. Only the 3rd Company of the 41st Regiment, which had covered the right flank of the march, moved without the town against the Galgenberg. As soon as the Colonel had set himself right on the condition of the action, he reinforced the attack on the Kapellenberg by two companies and one division of Jägers, and the flanking movement of the 3rd Company, by degrees, with three more companies. Two companies and the rest of the Jägers remained in reserve.

However important this support was, yet, for the moment, it had no decisive result. When General Boin, at half-past 11, recognized how strongly the opposite heights were held, he ordered the main body, which at this time was yet beyond Parschnitz, to detach three battalions, and soon afterwards three more battalions in the direction of Hohenbruck-Alt-Rognitz against the right flank of the enemy. The advanced guard was informed of this, and ordered to do all to take the heights. The three batteries already in action were besides withdrawn to the hill north of Trautenau, in order there, supported by one battalion, and the Cavalry regiment of the main body, to support the advanced guard in an eventual retreat, or to oppose a possible attack from the direction of Arnau. The three squadrons which were on the right bank of the Aupa, retired to the reserve.

Lieutenant-General Clausewitz ordered the 44th and 45th Regiments, with Böhnke's Battery, to carry out the flank attack, and gave the command to Major-General Buddenbrock. The 45th Regiment crossed the Aupa, about 500 paces above Parschnitz, the 44th Regiment within the village. The further advance led, however, into extraordinarily difficult ground. The steep banks could only be climbed in open order, the wooded ridges could only be passed in single file. The mounted officers were forced to leave their horses behind. To overcome these difficulties, it not only taxed the strength of the men to a high degree, but also caused much loss of time; and before it was possible for General Buddenbrock to come into action, the renewed exertions of the advanced guard succeeded in gaining the heights so obstinately defended. The left wing of the enemy had succumbed to the concentrated attack of the 2nd and 3rd Companies of the 41st Regiment, and the 1st Company following them.

The companies climbed up the Galgenberg, and flanked the Austrian detachments which were on the hill of the Chapel of St. John, which now also were losing ground before the attack directed against their front. Slowly, and fighting, the brigade of Mondl left its position and the plantations lying west of it in the direction of Hohenbruck. Sixteen guns from a position south of the Kapellenberg covered this retreat, which a portion only of the wearied Prussian Infantry followed. The Crown Prince's Regiment, and the 9th and 12th Companies of the Fusilier Battalion of the 41st Regiment, were assembled in and near Trautenau, Colonel Koblinski alone, with the Musqueteer Battalion of the Regiment, and Captain Buddenbrock, with the 10th and 11th Companies, as well as Major Sommerfeld, with the Jägers, pushed further forwards. The action came soon to a standstill, and only was pushed forward when, after 1 o'clock, the battalions of General Bruddenbrock joined in it. The 44th Regiment passed Kriblitz and the wood lying to the south of that place; the 45th Regiment left the village on its right, and moved with its left wing on the north-west angle of Alt-Rognitz, while Böhnke's Battery, covered by two companies, ascended the hill south-west of the suburb of Kriblitz, and replied to the fire of a hostile battery which had come up to the south-west of Hohenbruck, and which had been pushed forward with the Mensdorf Regiment of Uhlans of Grivicics' brigade. At this time also there took part in the fight the 1st Battalion of the 4th Regiment and the Fusilier Battalion of the 5th Regiment. Both had been ordered forward from the main body, had waded through the Aupa, and had drawn up on the left wing of the advanced guard, whereby portions of the 44th Regiment pushed between them. Besides, from the advanced guard, two and a-half companies of the Fusilier Battalion of the Crown Prince's Regiment were pushed forward to relieve the Jägers.

At this time, 1 o'clock, the 1st Division of the Infantry of the Guard, which, in consequence of the cannonade, had hurried its march to the utmost, had entered Parschnitz. Its support was, however, declined, as the battle went forward, and only one Austrian Brigade was known to be in front. Besides, the Commanding-General did not wish to hinder it from attaining its prescribed object to reach Eypel this day. In the meantime, the division of the Guard rested for two hours at Parschnitz.

About half-past 2 o'clock, Major Noak had placed the 3rd 6-pounder Battery in position on the Galgenberg, and the 3rd 4-pounder Battery on the Hopfenberg, and thus had diverted the fire of the 24 hostile guns, which had already compelled Böhnke's Battery to retire, from the Infantry. The 3rd 12-pounder Battery remained at the western exit of Trautenau in reserve.

The enemy now retired to the line Alt-Rognitz, Hohenbruck; his left flank was covered by the Windischgrätz Regiment. A signal, made in Trautenau, " the general assembly," caused, on the Prussian side, the part of the advanced guard in action, with the exception of the 5th and 10th Company of the 41st Regiment, and one division of Jägers, to retire into the town. Still the battalions of the main body and the remaining battalions of the advanced guard compelled the enemy to retire from his lost position, and to retreat in a southerly direction. The Prussian right wing established itself in Hohenbruck, the left in Alt-Rognitz. A further pursuit was impossible with the weary troops. Their fatigue was the greater, since the 43rd Regiment, on the previous night, had been on outpost duty, and the 44th, on the previous evening, had only returned at 10 o'clock from a reconnaissance, but all the troops had been paraded at 3 o'clock in the morning.

Firing ceased along the whole line. Lieutenant-General Clausewitz re-established, as far as possible, the communication of the different detachments, as on the broken ground the company columns were separated by 3,000 paces. He then awaited further orders from the Commanding-General. The latter had ordered the Reserve Infantry to Kriblitz; the battle seemed finished, and the division of the Guard commenced its march to Eypel. About half-past 3, reports from various quarters announced that the enemy had received reinforcements, and was advancing to attack. It was Grivicics' brigade which was coming on the field. General Gablenz directed it against the left Prussian wing, while Mondl's brigade again attacked in front.

General Bonin consequently caused the three still disposable battalions of Lieutenant-General Grossman to occupy Trautenau, as a support, and caused the artillery on the north of the town to be reinforced by two battalions from the reserve. The advanced guard and the eight battalions which had already been engaged were ordered to advance to attack the enemy, but by a misunderstanding this order did not reach the advanced guard. The exhausted battalions of the main body, which were in the first line, at first defended themselves with success. A hostile Jäger battalion, which advanced against the front, retired much shaken. On the left wing, west of Alt-Rognitz, the 2nd and Fusilier Battalions of the 45th Regiment also repulsed the general attack of the first line of Grivicics' brigade. Through the want of any support they could not, however, await its renewal, since the regiment of Mensdorff Uhlans, accompanied by guns, appeared on their left flank. Between 4 and 5 o'clock they began to retire on Parschnitz; the remaining battalions followed. The two batteries on the heights south of Trautenau were also compelled to evacuate their position. The enemy at first pushed straight on, but was repulsed by the fire of nine companies, and detachments of the Fusilier Battalion of the 44th Regiment held still for some time the plantation south of Kriblitz. The 41st Regiment, which had taken up a supporting position north of Hohenbruck, also retired with the Fusilier Battalion on Parschnitz.

The further advance of the enemy was, however, hindered by the Reserve Infantry, and it also enabled the battalions of the main body unmolested to reach the left bank of the Aupa.

As a support Major-General Barnekow had occupied the plantation at the Kapelle and the heights south of it, with the 1st and Fusilier Battalions of the 43rd Regiment, while two and a-half battalions of the 3rd Regiment had taken up a position further in rear with five companies on the edge of the wood north of Kriblitz, and had pushed forward the 2nd Battalion on the north of the village, and the 9th Company into the wood at the south end of the village.

The enemy meanwhile had reinforced himself with Wimpffen's brigade, which had come up; the battery of which, as well as an 8-pounder battery of the reserve, unlimbered southeast of Kaltenhof. Trautenau and the position occupied by the Prussian Infantry was now assailed by a very heavy fire from 40 Austrian guns. The idea of debouching from Trautenau with the Prussian Reserve Cavalry, with which the 1st Regiment of Hussars and two squadrons of East Prussian Uhlans were united, had under these circumstances to be abandoned. Still the two battalions of the 43rd Regiment, under Colonel Treskow, succeeded in repelling the attack of several detachments of Wimpffen's brigade by salvos and a bayonet assault. The losses on both sides were very heavy. The first battalion, under Major Hüllesheim, who fell here, alone lost in an action of one and a-half hour's duration 8 officers and 238 men.

The case of these battalions appeared still more dangerous, when the brigades of Mondl and Grivicics continued advancing against Trautenau and east of Kriblitz; and Knebel's brigade also appeared on the field. Their retreat was then began about half-past 6 o'clock, under cover of the 3rd Regiment, on Parschnitz.

The enemy's attack was now turned against the latter regiment. Knebel's brigade also advanced against it as soon as it perceived the repulse of Wimpffen's brigade. About 7 o'clock the 2nd Battalion of the 3rd Regiment was attacked by three columns, while heavy swarms of skirmishers attempted through the ravine of Kriblitz, to turn its left wing. This attack was, however, repulsed by an offensive movement of the battalion in conjunction with two companies of the first battalion. In the same manner failed the attacks of detachments of Grivicics' brigade against the company posted north-east of Kriblitz. As, in the meantime, Trautenau had been evacuated by the East Prussian troops, the task of the 3rd Regiment appeared accomplished; about half-past 7 o'clock the 2nd Battalion retired on Parschnitz, and at 8 o'clock the remaining six companies followed, covered by the Jäger Battalion, which, in the meantime, had been withdrawn to the wooded hill south of Parschnitz. The attempt of the enemy to follow on the main road from Trautenau was repulsed by the Fusilier Battalion of the 4th Regiment, posted on the western bridge over the Aupa, and later failed before the fire of two batteries, placed north-west of Parschnitz. On the right bank of the Aupa also the Jäger Battalion prevented the further advance of the enemy, and held its position till 9 o'clock, when, unmolested by the enemy, it joined the retreat of the corps.

The 1st Corps d'Armée was, during the whole day, thus held in a disadvantageous position, because, at the commencement, Trautenau and the heights commanding it had not been immediately occupied, and the debouché of the main body thus secured.

Its early superiority thus remained without influence.

While the main body remained on the near side of the Aupa only detachments were engaged on the further side, which were indeed successively supported, but had to succumb before the steadily increasing force of the enemy, so long as the whole body was not in position to oppose him.

The Infantry fought almost alone; it had little support from the Cavalry, and the greatest part of the Artillery remained in positions whence it could have little effect on the important field of action. The Austrians, with full freedom of movement, used all their arms against the Prussian Infantry, and could bring the whole superiority of their fire to advantage.

The proximity of the 1st Division of the Guard, at 2 o'clock in the afternoon, which could have, by a close advance on the enemy's right flank, decided the issue, was not taken advantage of. The division marched away at the very moment when the enemy had concentrated his force, and advanced to the renewed attack.

Battalions detached from all brigades, and some companies, made the most desperate resistance. The enemy was also exhausted by actions, in which he suffered much. The late arrival of his main body in the afternoon showed that he too had made a march. On the near side of the Aupa could all the forces be assembled; the debouché from Trautenau be rendered extraordinarily difficult, in which case the Cavalry, for the most part intact, and the reserve position of the Artillery, could be taken advantage of.

If it was possible during the night to occupy in front the defiles of the Riesengebirg, the advance of the remaining corps must disengage the first corps. The Commanding General had perceived this; he wished to take up a position north of Trautenau, and near Parschnitz, whither the trains were already ordered. But the detachments which retreated from the latter point, had marched on the high road. Therefore, the idea of further resistance had to be abandoned, and the corps, very much exhausted, reached, between 1 and 3 o'clock in the night, the bivouacs, which it had quitted on the previous morning, on the far side of the hills.

The Austrians, on the day of the battle of Trautenau, did not advance over the Aupa. The 10th Company of the 41st Regiment and two companies of the 43rd Regiment remained till 3.30 A.M. on the 28th right in front of the eastern exit of Parschnitz, on the road to Schömberg.

General Gablenz had attained the object of preventing the advance of his enemy on one main road.

The Xth Corps remained with the brigades of Wimpffen and Grivicics in the south of Trautenau, as well as on the heights south of Parschnitz, while General Gablenz bivouacked, with the brigades of Mondl and Knebel, further to the rear, near Neu-Rognitz.

The loss of the Ist Prussian Corps in this action of Trautenau amounted to—

|       |       |       |          |
|-------|-------|-------|----------|
| 15 Officers | 229 Men | killed. |  |
| 41 „ | 967 „ | wounded. |  |
|  | 86 „ | missing. |  |
| 56 | 1,282 Men, besides 78 horses. |  |  |

The loss of the Xth Austrian Corps was returned as 196 officers, 5,586 men, and 185 horses.

---

## BATTLE OF NACHOD.

In consequence of the order, which we have already mentioned, of the Austrian Commander-in-Chief, which directed the VIth Corps on Skalitz instead of on Josephstadt, General Ramming marched his troops in the following manner:— The brigade of Hertweck, from Dobruska, by Neustadt and Wrchowin, to Wysokow, as advanced guard. Jonak's brigade, from Krowitz and Waly, also by Neustadt and Wrchowin, but thence by Prowodow to Kleny. Rosenzweig's brigade, from Bohuslawitz, by Cernoitz and Spitta, to Skalitz, and thither also Waldstatten's brigade from Mezric, by Robenitz, Slawetin, Nauzin, Mestec, and Jesenitz, followed by the Reserve Artillery, which was directed on Rzikow.

The Commandant of the Corps advanced with the last-named brigade.

Jonak's brigade was to march off at 3.30 A.M., the other brigades at 3 A.M., but the march was delayed by about half-an-hour.

That the Prussians had occupied Nachod had not been reported to General Ramming; still their proximity was known to him, as already, in the afternoon of the 26th, Prussian officers, making requisitions, had alarmed the brigades of Hertweck and Jonak.

General Steinmetz was to reach Nachod on the 27th. His corps began its march thither at 5 A.M., the advanced guard at 6 A.M. Soon after 8 A.M., the Commanding General, with Prince Adalbert, had reached Nachod, and here received the report that the advanced guard had, without encountering the enemy, reached the point where the road divides to Joseph-stadt and Neustadt, It received orders to bivouac on the plateau, and to push outposts towards Neustadt and Skalitz. Bivouacs were also ordered for the remaining portions of the corps, and a communication made to the second division of the Guard that possession had been taken of Nachod without opposition, and that on this day its support was not required.

Major-General Löwenfeld pushed forward a squadron of the 4th Dragoon Regiment, to reconnoitre on each of the roads to Neustadt and Skalitz, and had occupied Wysokow with a company of Jägers. While he was still occupied in arranging the places for the bivouacs, the approach of strong hostile columns of all arms—as was later discovered, the brigade of Hertweck, followed by that of Jonak—was reported to him. The head of the first had already reached Prowodow. As the vicinity of the enemy was here apparent by the appearance of Prussian Dragoons, Major-General Hertweck here formed his brigade, and led it forward in the direction of the plateau north of Wenzels-berg. The 25th Feldjäger Battalion occupied the church of Wenzel. The main body, with three battalions of Kellner in the first line, and two battalions of Gorizutti in the second line, advanced, followed by a battery in the east of the village, while the 3rd Battalion of Gorizutti, and one of Kellner's companies, in the plantations on the Neustadt road, covered the right flank.

On the first report of the advance of the Austrians, Major-General Von Löwenfeld had ordered the leading troops to ascend the plateau, and to move against the enemy. At the same time, the main body of the advanced guard was ordered to advance from Altstadt over the hills lying to the south of that place.

Bojan's half-battalion, which had furnished the outposts,

had not yet rejoined the advanced guard. Major Von Plötz was detached from the advanced guard, with Kurowski's half-battalion, and 1½ companies of Jägers as a cover towards Skalitz, and posted at the eastern entrance of Wysokow. Colonel Von Below moved on to the plateau the remaining 4½ companies, 3 squadrons, and 1 battery.

The 5th 4-pounder Battery, covered by the regiment of Dragoons, to which the squadron sent along the Neustadt road again united, at once opened fire on the advancing enemy, and forced the battery of Hertweck's Brigade to retire to the heights south-west of Schonow, where it joined the battery of Jonak's brigade. The Austrian Artillery was now further reinforced by two batteries; the Prussian by 1st 4-pounder Battery. Major Meiszner held his own with 12 guns during the whole of the advanced guard's battle against a considerable superiority, even when the Infantry fire of the enemy reached his batteries, and forced them to make several changes of position.

The Jägers pushed into the plantation north of Wenzelsberg, whither Winterfeld's and Schreiner's half-battalions of the main body of the advanced guard also later moved. From the edge of the wood a musketry action was begun with the Austrian Jägers, who held the church of Wenzel.

The 2nd Battalion of the 37th Regiment divided into two half battalions, and separated by some distance from each other, pushed from the Neustadt road in the direction of Wenzelsberg, and here encountered the advancing main body of the hostile brigade. The attack of both its lines was repulsed by the salvoes of the deployed half battalions, and the enemy was pursued a short way by skirmishers. The battalion then engaged in a musketry action against the church of Wenzel, while Major-General Hertweck assembled his main body south of Wenzelsberg.

The detachments of the main body of the advanced guard, which had advanced further to the left, had already joined the right flanking detachment of Hertweck's brigade on the Neustadt road. Here only four half battalions were available after leaving Suchodoletz's half-battalion in Altstadt, and both companies of Jägers in a supporting position on the left bank of the Metau. Major Von Lemmers moved with one half-battalion of the 37th Regiment of these, and soon met in the ravine leading to Brazetz detachments of the Gorizutti battalion, which were repulsed partly in a hand-to-hand contest. Captain Vogelsang, in advance of his men, was here killed. The half-battalion crossed the road and moved against the plantations lying in the west of the road, which at the same time were attacked from the north by Colonel Von François with the half-battalion of Gfug, and carried at the first assault. The half-battalion of the 58th Regiment occupied then the remaining plantations in front, where about half an hour later the half-battalions of Wernecke and Gronefeld entered into the fight. Sochors, as well as the 10 A.M. copse, was taken, the hostile flanking detachments driven back on Wrchowin. The first attack of the Austrians was thus, at 10 o'clock, completely repulsed.

Although Major-General Hertweck had led into action the 1st Battalion of Gorizutti, and the 3rd Battalion of Kellner to cover his right flank, and the brigade of Jonak, which had in the meantime marched up, now attacked, still the six companies of the 58th Regiment, under Colonel Von François, succeeded, after a hot fight, in holding possession of the woods and plantations. Major-General Von Ollech was here severely wounded. On reaching Domkow at 9 o'clock, Colonel Jonak had formed his brigade in line, with the battery and the Uhlan Regiment on the left wing.

Advancing, after a short halt at Prowodow, in the direction of Wenzelberg, he had supported the battle in the wood without achieving a result.

Behind Jonak's brigade, the brigade of Rosenzweig arriving, took up a position so that it rested on Prowodow and Schonow.

Field-Marshal Lieutenant Ramming had already, at a quarter past 8 o'clock, arrived at Skalitz with the head of Waldstätten's brigade, and had gone hence to the battle-field soon after the beginning of the action. Thither were directed soon the Cavalry Brigade of Prince Solms, which was at Kleny, and, at 10 o'clock, also the brigade of Waldstätten, the latter in the direction of Wysokow. At 11 o'clock followed the Reserve Artillery of the corps, which had entered Skalitz, as well as the Cavalry Brigade of Schindlöcker, coming from Dolan.

11 A.M.   Till 11 o'clock, a musketry action alone was maintained along the whole line; on the Prussian side the concentration of formidable hostile forces had at this time been remarked, and their attack was expected. General Steinmetz, arriving on the battle-field, had sent orders to the main body of the corps to hasten its march as much as possible, and was especially anxious to bring up artillery quickly. At this time, Wnuck's Cavalry brigade had alone arrived of the main body, which, on the first report of the approach of the enemy, had been ordered to reinforce the advanced guard. It had trotted over 7,000 paces of stony and in part hilly road, and took up a covered position south of the Branka. Its battery took part at once in the Artillery engagement.

At half-past 11 o'clock came the expected principal attack of the enemy. Rosenzweig's brigade advanced east of Wenzelsberg against the plantation, supported by the Gondrecourt Regiment in the first, Deutschmeister in the second line. The left flank of the brigade was covered by Prince Solm's Cuirassiers, of which the regiment of the Emperor Ferdinand and one squadron of the Prince Hesse Regiment were in position, while a second squadron of the latter regiment, which was attached to Jonak's Infantry brigade, was near. East of Wenzelsberg, Jonak's brigade closed the attack; in the first line was the regiment of the Crown Prince of Prussia, which the Wasa Regiment followed.

The four Prussian companies and two subdivisions of Jägers, which were in the wood north of the Wenzel church, were forced to evacuate it, and retired to the Neustadt road, where they took up a position covered by Wnuck's brigade. Here the half-battalions of Bojan and Suchodoletz came up on the left from Altstadt.

After having received the fire of the 3rd Company of the 58th Regiment from the direction of the Ranger's house on their right flank, the battalions of Colonel Jonak's first line were repulsed by the fire of the two 4-pounder batteries westward of the high road, and by the rapid file fire of the half-battalions Braun and Schimonski. Nevertheless, Lieutenant-Colonel Von Eberstein was also forced to fill back to the Neustadt road, when the regiment 'Deutschmeister" advanced against his right wing from the wood to the north of the Wenzelskirche. All pursuit on the part of the Austrians was checked by the valour of the Fusiliers, who repeatedly turned to face the enemy during their retreat.

The turn which affairs had thus taken in the centre was necessarily felt by the left wing also. The two batteries that had hitherto kept the enemy's advance under fire, and the 4th Dragoon Regiment, were obliged to be withdrawn to the Neustadt road as soon as the slope of the hill sheltered the advancing enemy from the fire of the former, and Colonel Von François was at last forced to follow with the four half-battalions of the extreme left. They fell back as far as the ravine leading to Brazetz.

General Loewenfeld was now in a very critical position. Pressed back to the utmost edge of the plateau and to the wooded hillside at Brazetz, his troops stood in one single line 3,000 paces long and without reserves.

Still this unfavourable position must be held against the enemy's superior forces, to enable the remainder of the corps to debouch.

The fire of the 2nd Battalion of the 37th Regiment and of the two batteries repulsed the attack of the enemy's right wing.. The 4th Dragoons dashed forward to charge the retreating Austrians, but found the ground too broken for further pursuit.

In the centre large bodies of Austrian Infantry—the main body of General Rosenzweig's brigade—now issued from the wood on the north of the "Wenzelskirche" and proceeded to attack the Prussian centre. Received by the fire of the half-battalions Winterfeld and Schreiner, and of two divisions of rifles under Captain Von Klass in front, and attacked by the half-battalions Bojan and Suchodoletz in their right flank, they fell back with great loss.

On the right wing the engagement had taken an equally favourable turn. General Wnuck's Cavalry Brigade was drawn up near Wysokow, under shelter of the brow of the hill; the 1st Lancer Regiment on the right and the 8th

Dragoons on the left. The squadrons were formed in contiguous columns of divisions to the right. Soon after the loss of the wood Prince Solm's Cuirassiers appeared. The first line was met by the 1st Prussian Lancers which advanced to the charge in direct *échelon* of squadrons. As the left flank of the Lancers was threatened by the squadron of "Hesse" Cuirassiers attached to General Rosenzweig's Brigade, General Wnuck led the 8th Dragoons forward to their support. As soon as Lieutenant-Colonel Von Wichmann's squadrons had taken sufficient ground to the left for the regiment to deploy, the line was formed at a gallop, and the Dragoons charged the right flank of the Austrian line with loud cheers, reckless of the infantry fire they received from the wood. The full force of the shock fell on the right flank and partly on the rear of the Cuirassiers. The Prussian Lancers had been charged in front by the Austrian line, whilst, at the same time, a squadron of "Ferdinand" Cuirassiers burst forth from Wysokow and fell on their right flank. This last movement of the Cuirassiers was, however, parried by the 2nd squadron of the Prussian 4th Dragoon Regiment, under Lieutenant Count Roedern, which had been watching the Skalitz road, but now dashed past the south side of Wysokow and joined in the *mêlée* with great effect. Along the whole front both sides broke through their adversary's ranks and then intermingled in a desperate *mêlée*. The struggle did not last long, for the charge of the 8th Dragoons had so effectively turned the enemy's flank that the Cuirassiers wavered and fell back, at first slowly, towards Wysokow, but soon they fled in total disorder and at full speed, past the south side of the village, closely pursued by a confused mass of Dragoons and Lancers. At the moment when the Cuirassiers were being pressed back on Wysokow and their rout was already evident, Captain Kurowski's half-battalion of the 37th Regiment, which had meanwhile entered the village, stepped out beyond the outskirts and fired on the mass of Cuirassiers that was dashing on towards it. The Austrian brigade attempted to rally near the western end of Wysokow, but was prevented doing so by the rapid fire which two divisions of rifles, under Captain Von Sobbe, poured into its ranks. These rifle companies had passed through the village from the opposite side and established themselves in the southern outskirts. This unexpected rifle fire impressed General Wnuck with the idea that the village was occupied by the enemy, and induced him to check the pursuit and rally his brigade.

In the *mêlée* both standards of the Austrian Regiment, "Ferdinand" fell into the hands of the Prussians after a desperate struggle. All three Commanders of the Prussian Cavalry. General Wnuck, Lieutenant-Colonel Wichmann, and Colonel Tresckow, as well as 12 officers were wounded, the two former, however, so slightly that they did not leave the field.

The Prussian brigade was rallied near Wysokow under a

severe shelling from the enemy. Whilst the regiments were
still in the act of re-forming, the Austrian infantry was seen
retreating to the Wenzelsberg wood after its unsuccessful
attack on General Loewenfeld's line. General Wnuck immediately gave Major Von Paczensky leave to charge with the
first divisions of Dragoons, which were re-formed. The latter
threw himself on the left flank of the Austrain infantry,
which Lieutenant-Colonel Wichmann charged in front with
the remainder of the Dragoons. The square of a battalion of
Rifles and several groups of infantry were run down and dispersed, and the colours of the infantry battalion captured.
Major Von Natzmer, Commander of the 3rd Squadron was
killed in the charge; Lieutenant Von Pogrell, who first broke
into the square, and two other officers were wounded, the
former mortally. On the whole the losses of the Dragoons
were by no means slight, as several of them penetrated into
the wood in pursuit of the flying infantry.

For three full hours had General Loewenfeld thus held his
ground on the plateau with five and a half battalions against
twenty-one battalions available on the Austrian side.

By the time, 12 o'clock, the Crown Prince had arrived on 12 o'clock.
the field from Braunau, and in the last period of the engagement
the heads of the 10th Division had begun to reach the scene of
action, after a march of thirteen miles and a half.

The 46th Regiment immediately formed in two lines and
swept the enemy from the plateau, in company with the half-
battalions Bojan and Suchodoletz, of the advanced guard.
The wood northward of the "Wenzelskirche" was retaken
and the Austrian regiment "Gondrecourt," which was on the
east of the wood, put to flight. Its Commander, Oldofredi,
was wounded and taken prisoner. Wenzelskirche and Wenzelsberg were then stormed by the half-battalions Priebsch and
Gallwitz.

The Austrian brigades now retreated at all points under
cover of their Artillery. In the meantime the Reserve
Artillery of the Corps had arrived from Skalitz, accompanied
by the 3rd Battalion of the 9th Regiment (Hartmann). These
five batteries took up a position on the brow of the hill, eastward of Kleny, and the main body of the Prussian Corps had
to form its line under the fire of 80 pieces of artillery.

The batteries of the Prussian 10th Division were unable
alone to sustain so unequal a combat. The 3rd 4-pounder
battery came on the field at the time when the advanced guard
was forced to quit the wood and had been involved in its
retreat. The 4th 4-pounder battery was held back in reserve
to the west of Altstadt. The two other batteries had, it is
true, crossed the Metau on the temporary bridges that the
Pioneers had built, but only eight of their guns could get over
the meadows, in which four 12-pounders and all the caissons
stuck fast.

Under these circumstances the Artillery could only be

brought forward by single batteries, and was unable to hold its ground between Wysokow and the wood. Within the short space of half-an-hour Captain Ohnesorge's horse artillery battery, sent forward from the Reserve, lost twenty-one killed and thirty-two wounded horses in the attempt to do so. The batteries either sought whatever shelter the ground afforded, or withdrew to the east of Wenzelsberg, where the 3rd 6-pounder and 3rd 12-pounder batteries again opened fire. The two batteries of the advanced guard which had been in fire so long were now withdrawn to refit.

At this period of the action the position of the Prussian advanced guard was as follows:—One half-battalion and half a company of Rifles were in Wysokow, two half-battalions eastward of Wenzelsberg; all the rest were still on the ground where they had repulsed the enemy's attacks.

The Infantry of the main body could only reach the plateau very gradually. It found the greatest difficulty in getting through the defile, which was stopped up in many places by ammunition wagons and ambulances. As it successively came up, strong detachments were thrown into Wysokow, Wenzelsberg, and the wood between the two villages. The remainder drew up between these three points of appui. Lieutenant-General Von Kirchbach took the command at Wysokow, Major-General Von Tiedemann at the wood.

The enemy's artillery fire still commanded the whole of the plateau and caused considerable losses.

The Austrian brigades that had been engaged were drawing near Kleny from the west, and General Waldstatten had reached this village with the last brigade that was still intact. General Ramming now ordered forward the 2nd Battalion of the 9th Regiment (Hartmann) and the 3rd Battalion of 1 P.M. the 79th Regiment (Frank) for a fresh attack; they advanced on the south of the Skalitz road against the west angle of the wood, whilst the other battalions of the brigade were being formed for the purpose of attacking Wysokow. Some detachments of General Rosenzweig's brigade still at Prowodow, joined in the attack on the wood.

1 P.M. As the Austrian columns approached the wood, the half-battalion Heugel and the skirmishers of the Fusilier battalion of the 6th Regiment quitted the cover of the wood and advanced to meet the attack. The were followed by Lieut.-Colonel Von Gottberg with the remainder of the battalion. At the same time the half-battalions Priebsch and Gallwitz fell on the enemy's right flank from Wenzelsberg. The Austrians retreated after suffering severe losses and left 200 prisoners in the hands of the Prussians. Shortly after this repulse the remainder of General Waldstatten's brigade advanced from the direction of Starkoc and proceeded to attack Wysokow. The eastern part of this village was garrisoned by the Prussians, but the western part, which lies in a hollow, was as

yet unoccupied. This attack was supported by the fire of three light batteries of the Reserve Artillery posted on the heights north and south-west of Starkoc. At the same time Prince Holstein led a Regiment of Cuirassiers and some guns through the " Buchwald " towards " Shotkerhof," and tried to turn the Prussian right flank.

The leading battalions of the regiments " Frank " and " Hartmann," and two companies of the 6th Rifle Battalion passed through the unoccupied part of Wysokow, but soon became involved in a fierce struggle for some houses held by the Prussians, which ultimately resulted in the Austrians being driven out of the village by Major Von Plötz's Riflemen, and the half-battalions Bronikowsky and Runckel.

During this combat the northern side of the centre of the village was attacked by the two other companies of the 6th Rifle Battalion, the 2nd battalion of the 79th Regiment (Frank) and the brigade battery. General Kirchbach had perceived this flank movement of the enemy and proposed to meet it by sending Generals Wittich and Wnuck to the north side of Wysokow, with two battalions which had been hitherto kept in reserve, and the Cavalry brigade. Before these troops came up, the attack on the village had been repulsed by the fire of the half-battalions Webern and Thadden from the out-skirts, and by half-battalion Bendler, which dashed out of the village and fell upon the enemy's flank. General Wittich's battalions reached the spot in time to take part in the further course of the action.

He formed his troops in two lines of half-battalions and reached the northern side of the village just as Prince Holstein's Artillery issued from the wood southward of Shotkerhof, under cover of two squadrons of Cuirassiers.

The half-battalions of the right flank column formed line to the right to meet the Cuirassiers in case they should charge, then wheeled in section to the left, and continued their advance against the Austrian Infantry, in company with the left flank column.

The fire of half-battalion Tschirschky was directed on the enemy's left flank, that of Captain Vietinghof's half-battalion on the brigade battery and its coverers. The engagement ended with the retreat of the enemy, which was effected in such disorder that one gun fell into the hands of Major Bendler's skirmishers, and a second one was taken by Captain Von Sobbe's Riflemen, who burst forth from the village ; three other guns stuck fast in the low ground, where they were afterwards found.

The Fusilier Battalion of the 47th Regiment, Major Von Brandenstein, now turned against the Austrian Cuirassiers on his right flank, but before he reached them they had already fallen back before two squadrons of the Prussian 1st Lancers. On his way with General Kirchbach's orders, that the Cavalry brigade should advance northwards of Wysokow, Captain

Haenisch (Aide-de-Camp of the division) remarked that the Austrian guns to the south of Shotkerhof were in a very exposed position. In the hope of capturing them he led the 3rd and 4th Squadrons of the 1st Lancers through a farm-yard of Wysokow towards the hill, on which the guns were planted. Both squadrons first tried to turn the enemy's left flank under cover of the hill, but dashed on the battery on seeing that the guns were beginning to limber up. The Austrian Cuirassiers did not wait for the shock, and two guns of the Austrian 4-pounder battery No. 5, and the horse artillery battery No. 7, were captured.

After great exertions the Prussian Artillery at last succeeded in bringing a greater number of guns into action, and in somewhat subduing the Austrian fire. The first batteries brought up from the Reserve Infantry were the 1st 6-pounder, and the 4th 12-pounder. Of these the former was not able to hold its ground on the plateau, and was forced to withdraw, but the latter managed to take up a position on the Neustadt road, and fired on the retreating columns of the enemy. Now, however, the Reserve Artillery of the Corps arrived on the field, and drew up between Wysokow and the Wenzelsberg wood. The leading battery (Captain Treuenfels) lost 16 men and 18 horses before it unlimbered, but nevertheless opened fire immediately. The remaining field batteries of the Reserve and the 1st and 5th 4-pounder batteries of the advanced guard took post on Captain Treuenfel's left. From this spot 42 rifled guns were now brought to bear on the enemy's columns which were retreating towards Kleny, and which were, at the same time, suffering from the fire of the two horse artillery batteries northwards of Wysokow.

General Ramming could make no further attack, and all his brigades continued their retreat towards Skalitz.

During the last period of the action the Fusilier battalion of the 52nd and the three battalions of the 6th Regiment had arrived on the field. The former and one battalion of the latter were sent as reserve to Wysokow, the two others were partly employed to cover the line of Artillery, and partly posted in the wood, to the south of which and near Wysokow they skirmished with the retreating enemy. Thirty men of the 1st Battalion of the 6th Regiment entered Prowodow, and captured 70 prisoners.

General Wnuck's Cavalry brigade, and the Fusilier battalion of the 52nd Regiment, followed the enemy almost to Kleny, where General Schindlöcker's brigade was drawn up in line, but the extreme fatigue of men and horses compelled the Prussian troops to confine themselves to merely watching the enemy.

5 P.M.  The Vth Corps d'Armée having far exceeded its day's task, which was originally only to reach Nachod, went into bivouac on the battle-field at 5 o'clock; the 9th Division to the north of Altstadt; the 10th to the east of Wysokow, on both sides of the Skalitz road, the Reserve Artillery and the Pioneers further

to the rear. The 1st Battalion of the 37th Regiment occupied Nachod; the 8th Dragoons bivouacked behind the Neustadt road. The line of outposts extended on the right wing from Kramolna to Wysokow, with a detached post in the wood towards Starkoc; the picquets of the Fusilier battalion 52nd Regiment reached from Wysokow to the extreme left on the Neustadt road. The Fusilier battalion of the 47th Regiment was posted behind a burning house at the western outlet of Wysokow.

The two latter regiments were to have been relieved by General Von Hoffman's brigade which had reached Schlaney, but this was not effected before daybreak of the 28th, as the brigade only arrived on the field at 11 o'clock P.M., and then bivouacked behind the 10th Division.

General Ramming retreated as far as Skalitz, but still held Kleny and Dubno with his rear guard.

The losses of the Austrian VIth Corps amounted to 227 officers, 7,145 men, and 137 horses. Prince Holstein's Cavalry Division is said to have lost 8 officers, 130 men, and 142 horses, making a total of 235 officers and 7,275 men, of whom about 2,500 were taken prisoners.

One flag, two standards, and seven guns fell into the hands of the victors.

The Prussian Vth Corps lost 62 officers, 1,060 men, and 222 horses, viz. :—

H

| | Killed. | | Wounded. | | Missing. | | Total. | | Horses. |
|---|---|---|---|---|---|---|---|---|---|
| | Officers. | Men. | Officers. | Men. | Officers. | Men. | Officers. | Men. | |
| Head-Quarters of the Vth Corps | .. | .. | 1 | .. | .. | .. | 1 | .. | .. |
| „ the 10th Division | .. | 1 | .. | .. | .. | .. | .. | 1 | 2 |
| „ the 17th Brigade | .. | .. | 1 | .. | .. | .. | 1 | .. | .. |
| 87th Regiment | 2 | 52 | 7 | 184 | .. | 1 | 9 | 187 | 4 |
| 58th „ | 1 | 40 | 3 | 65 | .. | 2 | 4 | 107 | 2 |
| 7th „ | 2 | 22 | 2 | 59 | .. | .. | 4 | 81 | 1 |
| 5th Battalion of Rifles | .. | 4 | .. | 15 | .. | .. | .. | 19 | .. |
| 6th Regiment | 2 | 51 | 6 | 81 | .. | 2 | 8 | 134 | .. |
| 46th Regiment | 4 | 20 | 4 | 43 | .. | 2 | 8 | 65 | 2 |
| 47th „ | .. | 25 | 2 | 93 | .. | 2 | 2 | 120 | .. |
| 52nd „ | 4 | 23 | 1 | 80 | .. | 1 | 5 | 104 | .. |
| 1st Regiment of Lancers | .. | 2 | 6 | 71 | .. | .. | 6 | 73 | 42 |
| 4th „ Dragoons | 1 | 3 | 4 | 28 | .. | .. | 5 | 31 | 17 |
| 8th „ „ | 3 | 8 | 6 | 33 | .. | 4 | 9 | 45 | 60 |
| 5th Regiment of Field Artillery | .. | 13 | .. | 80 | .. | .. | .. | 93 | 92 |
| Total .. .. | 19 | 264 | 43 | 782 | .. | 14 | 62 | 1,060 | 222 |

Nº 5.

POSITION OF BOTH ARMIES ON THE EVENING OF THE 27ᵀᴴ JUNE.

Weller & Graham, Lᵗᵈ  Litho. London.

His Royal Highness the Crown Prince remained on the field until the action was over, and then returned to Hronow, after promising General Von Steinmetz the support of the 2nd Division of Guards for the next day.

The 1st Division of Guards had, in the meantime, arrived at Eypel. After a fatiguing march of more than 24 miles, it pushed an advanced guard over the Aupa, and occupied Raatsch. The 2nd Division of Guards reached Kosteletz, and sent its advanced guard on towards Skalitz as far as Miletin; from here the 2nd and half of the 4th Squadron of the 3rd Guard-Lancers went forward, under command of Colonel Mirus, to reconnoitre the country towards Czerwenahora; the 3rd and 1st Squadrons of the Regiment followed as Reserve. When near Czerwenahora it was reported to Colonel Mirus that a line of the enemy's Cavalry was drawn up beyond the village, upon which he immediately led forward a squadron and a half that were nearest at hand. The Lancers could only debouch from the village by a road bordered by trees and with a deep ditch on either side, so that their line was not yet formed when two squadrons of the 8th Regiment of Austrian Lancers (Emperor of Mexico) advanced to the charge in close order, but at a gentle pace. As many of the Prussian Lancers as had formed line dashed forward at full speed to meet the enemy, the remainder followed as fast as they could get out of the village. The Austrians received the shock with a volley of pistols, but were immediately broken. A desperate struggle ensued, in which two fresh Austrian divisions and the 3rd Squadron of the Prussian Lancers joined, the 1st Squadron of the latter followed close behind. The combat waved to and fro for about ten minutes, after which the enemy retreated, leaving 3 officers and 22 men, of whom some were severely wounded, on the field; besides these, 9 men and 13 horses were captured. The Prussian loss amounted to 2 men and 22 horses killed, 1 officer and 10 men severely, and 2 officers and 21 men slightly, wounded. The Commander of the Regiment was among the latter.

As considerable bodies of the enemy's Cavalry appeared in the distance, the pursuit was not followed up further, and the Regiment rejoined the advanced guard near Msestin.

The Heavy Cavalry Brigade of the Guards reached Starckstadt on this day, the Reserve Artillery, Dittersbach.

The VIth Corps d'Armée was sent by the Commander-in-Chief in the direction of Habelschwerdt, on account of a report of the arrival of Austrian troops at Bobinkau. As was afterwards proved, the latter had already retreated from the place.

The 11th Division reached Habelschwerdt to-day, the 12th Division, Ebersdorf.

The accompanying sketch shows the positions of the armies Sketch No. 5. on either side after the actions of the 27th of June.

## ACTION OF OSWIECIM.

The 27th of June was marked by a serious encounter on another part of the theatre of war, on the frontier of Upper Silesia, where hitherto nothing but trifling skirmishing had taken place. At the commencement of hostilities, the railway bridges at Oderberg, Neu-Berun, and Myslowitz, had been blown up; the viaduct at Prochna, and the railway bridges at Zawada and Schönbrunn were destroyed by small detachments of Count Stolberg's and General Von Knobelsdorff's troops. The defence of West Gallicia was entrusted to the Austrian brigade of Major-General Trentinaglia, who posted the main body of his brigade, consisting of four battalions, the 1st Lancer Regiment (Count Grünne), and a rifled 4-pounder battery of 4th Artillery Regiment, along the frontier from Myslowitz to Oswiecim. The troops at the latter place were commanded by Colonel Von Ziegler.

The best way of protecting Upper Silesia was by entering the enemy's country, and General Count Stolberg had already made all preparations for so doing, when he received a letter from the Commander-in-Chief, on the 26th, recommending the same line of action.

The execution of this project was fixed for tke 27th, and the 10th and 11th Companies of the 62nd Regiment, and two guns of the 1st Battery, of the 6th Field Artillery Regiment, belonging to General Von Knobelsdorff's detachment, were brought up to take part in the expedition; they were for the present replaced, in General Knobelsdorff's Corps, by three squadrons of the Landwehr Hussar Regiment. The main object of the expedition was to attack Oswiecim, whilst Major du Caillat's Battalion advanced from Myslowitz towards the Przemsza to attract the enemy's attention in that direction.

3 A.M.  By 3 o'clock A.M. the main body of the detachment was assembled on the Sedlin road, about three miles and a half from the frontier; it mustered four and a half battalions, one company of rifles, four squadrons, and two guns,* and started at 4 A.M.

4 A.M.  The advanced guard and the Lancer Regiment crossed the Vistula at Jablunka, and took the route Plawy-Oswiecim; the main body crossed at Jedlin, and marched on Oswiecim by way of Brzczinka.

The Infantry of the Reserve was left as support at the Vistula and at Plawy. A detachment which, for some time past, had been stationed on outpost duty at Berun (one battalion and one squadron) advanced on the high road towards Zabrzez.

On fording the Vistula, the leading company of the main body (the 10th Company of the 62nd Regiment) fell in with

---

* *Vide* Order of Battle of the detachment in Appendix XIII.

the enemy's skirmishers, and found Brcczinka occupied. With assistance of Major Von Busse's companies, the outlying buildings of the village were soon taken, but an Austrian Company coming up to relieve the outposts, considerable resistance was then met with. Four of the enemy's guns opened fire from the north of the railway station.

The two guns of the advanced guard had been delayed in crossing, first, the Vistula, and then a wet ditch; they now joined the main body, and took up a position to the north of the village, from whence they opened fire on the Austrian Artillery. About the same time, the advanced guard itself began to arrive on the field, and the 11th Company of the 62nd Regiment was pushed forward to the railway embankment, from whence it fired on the enemy's Cavalry beyond. Thereupon the Austrian Infantry quitted Brzczinka, and the main body and advanced guard followed through the village, and proceeded to attack the railway station, which was defended by the 4th Battalion of the 57th Regiment (Meklenburg-Schwerin). After a severe struggle, all the buildings were taken, except one that was occupied in great force. A heavy Infantry fire now ensued, which lasted some time, and cost the Prussians a number of men. In the meantime, Major Von Busse advanced on Lazy with the Regiment of Lancers. He first met half a squadron of Austrian Lancers, who retreated through the village by the Oswiecim road, and fell back on two or three squadrons, which were drawn up in line in a corn field 2,000 paces north-eastward of the village.

As soon as the Landwehr Lancers debouched from Lazy, and before the 1st and 2nd squadrons were formed, the enemy's Cavalry wheeled in divisions to the left, in order to turn their flank, then wheeled into line and charged. Major Von Busse hastened forward with two squadrons to meet them; the 3rd and 4th squadrons followed by degrees, as they got out of the village. The Austrian leader, Captain Baron Lehmann, galloped past Major Von Busse, then turned sharp round, and aimed a cut at his shoulder, but was immediately cut down himself. A mêlée then ensued, which ended with the flight of the Austrians. The 4th Dragoons followed in pursuit, but were checked by the appearance of fresh Austrian Cavalry near Oswiecim; the Prussian regiment was then rallied on the spot where the charge had taken place. It had lost four men killed, one officer and 24 men wounded, and 31 horses. One Austrian officer and 37 men were taken prisoners.

The repeated attempts of the Prussian Infantry to gain possession of the whole of the railway station failed, and a general retreat was commenced at half-past eight o'clock, under cover of the two companies of the Line, and of the Lancer Regiment. The Vistula was crossed by a bridge thrown over by Lieutenant Priem's self-organized train. The enemy did not pursue, and the troops, having retreated as far as Urbanowitz, were dismissed to their cantonments towards evening.

Major Von Caillat's Detachment had a slight skirmish, first with the enemy's outposts, and then with three companies and a squadron, after which it fell back to Amalien-Hütte, near Myslowitz, with a loss of ten men wounded and one missing.

The Prussian losses at Oswiecim amounted to six officers, 166 men, and 36 horses. The Austrians state theirs to have been—

|  | Killed. | Wounded. | Missing. |
|---|---|---|---|
| 57th Regiment .. .. .. .. | 12 | 28 | 4 |
| 1st Lancers .. .. .. .. | 7 | 32 | 8 |
| Total .. .. .. | 19 | 60 | 12 |

The inaccuracy of this statement is proved by the fact that in the Cavalry engagement alone one officer and 27 men were taken prisoners.

## THE 28TH OF JUNE.

June 28th. Prince Frederick Charles had, on the 27th, already determined to attack the position in and near Münchengrätz on the following day, in the hope that the enemy would thereby be induced to accept a general engagement. Reports had been received that the IInd Austrian Corps had already joined Count Clam's Army, it seemed, therefore, advisable to have sufficient forces at hand in case the enemy should offer obstinate resistance in his strong position.

The Prince's dispositions were as follows:—

"According to reports which have come in, it seems proba-"ble that the enemy will accept battle near Münchengrätz. "I intend to dislodge him from this position to-morrow. For "this purpose I have requested General Von Herwarth so to "regulate his march from Niemes with the VIIIth Corps "d'Armée, as to be able to attack the position at München-"grätz by 9 o'clock A.M.

"In support of this attack General Count Münster will move "forward with the 14th Infantry Division, and will cross the "Iser at Mohelnic by 9 A.M.

"The following are my orders for the Ist Army for to-"morrow:—

"1. General Von Horn's Division will stand near Podol by "half-past 7 A.M, in readiness to march on Brezina and Mün-"chengrätz, and will there await further orders for starting, "which will probably be given as soon as General Herwarth's "fire becomes audible. The bridge over the Iser at Podol "must be rebuilt at daybreak.

"2. General Von Fransecky's Division will stand, at half-past

" 7 A.M., between Mokry and Wschen, where it will await
" further orders. The Division is informed that the enemy
" still occupies Wschen to-day, and must therefore, first of all,
" be dislodged to-morrow morning. One battalion of the
" division will occupy Turnau.

" 3. General Von Manstein's Division, and the two field
" divisions of the Reserve Artillery of the Army will be
" between Preper and Stwerzin at 7.30 A.M., in order to follow
" the advance of General Horn's Division.

" 4. The horse divisions of the Reserve Artillery of the
" Army will be eastward of Wohrasenitz by 9 A.M. One Horse
" Battery of the Brandenburg Reserve Artillery, No. 3, will
" follow Lieutenant-Colonel Heinichen's advance.

" 5. General Von Tümpling's Division will so time its
" departure from Eisenbrod and Semil, that its main body will
" be westward of Rowensko by 8 A.M., on the Turnau-
" Gitschin road; it will have the position at this spot before its
" front. The advanced guard of the position will be pushed
" forward beyond Ktowa, towards Gitschin, where it will serve
" as support for Lieutenant-Colonel Heinichen.

" 6. Two squadrons of the 3rd Regiment of Lancers, two
" of the 10th Hussars, two of the 2nd Dragoons, and a Horse
" Artillery battery of the Brandenburg Reserve Artillery, No. 3,
" under command of Lieutenant-Colonel Heinichen, will be at
" Ktowa, behind General Tümpling's advanced guard, by 8 A.M.,
" from whence Lieutenant-Colonel Heinichen will advance to
" reconnoitre the country towards Gitschin.

" The divisions that furnish these troops will take care
" that the latter reach Ktowa in proper time,

" 7. The Cavalry Corps is hereby instructed to despatch the
" two brigades, Von der Goltz and Von Groeben, of General
" Von Horn's Division, with their respective batteries of Horse
" Artillery, so that they reach Liebenau, if possible, by 7 A.M.

" From this place they will advance in company with Duke
" William of Mecklenburg's bridade, under command of General
" Von Horn, and will take post between Luzan and Danby.

" Duke William's brigade will be in the appointed position
" by 8 A.M. General Von Horn and Duke William have been
" already made acquainted with these orders. The whole
" Cavalry Division of General Von Horn will be accompanied
" by its provision trains, as no supplies can be provided for it
" from here. These trains will park at Liebenau until they can
" be brought up to their division; but they must on no account
" leave Reichenberg before the last troops of the IInd Corps
" have passed the town.

" The remainder of the Cavalry Corps will march to-morrow
" to the line Liebenau-Reichenau, to the north of which they
" will take up cantonments as far as Langenbrück.

" 8. The IInd Corps will stand, by 9 o'clock A.M., with one
" division at Sichrow-Husa, with the other by Pacerice.
" Reichenberg will remain occupied by one or two companies.

" 9. I shall myself be to-morrow on the heights eastward of
" Podol, in the vicinity of the reserve of the 1st Army.

" 10. All baggage and trains of the 6th, 7th, and 8th Infantry
" divisions will remain in their bivouacs of to-day ; those of the
" 2nd Cavalry division will be left on the right bank of the
" Iser.

" As soon as the engagement at Münchengrätz is over, the
" divisions will make arrangements for bringing up their
" trains.

(Signed)    " FREDERICK CHARLES,
" *General of Cavalry.*"

## ACTION OF MÜNCHENGRÄTZ.

### 28TH OF JUNE.

In accordance with this disposition, General Von Herwarth
gave orders to General Von Schoeler's advanced guard to start
from Hühnerwasser at half-past 4 A.M., and proceed to Münchengrätz; it was to be followed first by the 15th Division, then
by the Reserve Artillery, and lastly by the 16th Division. The
division of Guard-Landwehr was instructed to push forward on
Hühnerwasser.

The vanguard of the advanced guard, consisting of half a
division of the 7th Hussars and the 8th Rifle Battalion, debouched from the wood at half-past 6. The Austrian outposts
6.30 A.M. left Nieder-Gruppay and Unter-Rokitas, and fell back on Weisslein. As soon as the heads of the Prussian columns appeared
8.30 A.M. on the Schuster-Berg at half-past 8, the Austrian Artillery
opened fire on them, and was answered by the two batteries of
the advanced guard, which took position *à cheval* of the road.
Colonel Von Gerstein did not wait for the results of this fire,
but proceeded to attack the enemy's position with the Fusilier
Battalion of the 33rd Regiment, and the 1st and 2nd Companies
of the 8th Rifle Battalions.

Colonel Zimmermann followed with the 2nd and 3rd Battalions of the 40th Regiment as reserve. The outskirts were
carried at the first onset, the enemy left the village at half-
9.30 A.M. past 9, after a short fight, and fell back to Haber. As soon,
however, as the Prussian battalions debouched from Weisslein,
they were exposed to the fire of the enemy's artillery, which
had established itself on the heights to the south of Kloster,
and at the Jewish cemetery on the right bank of the Iser.

General Von Herwarth, who was on the spot, reinforced the
Artillery of the advanced guard by two rifled batteries of the
main body ; these guns soon brought their whole fire to bear
on the Austrian guns at the cemetery, as the battery at Kloster
withdrew from its position. This was the result of a flank
movement on the part of the 7th Hussar Regiment, the 2nd
Battalion (two companies) of the 33rd, and the Fusilier Bat-

talion of the 69th Regiment. This detachment had advanced by Ober-Bukovina, and crossed the Zabrtitz at this spot, after leaving two companies on the right bank of the stream to keep up communications with their corps. A similar diversion was made on the right wing, where the 1st Battalion of the 40th Regiment and the 3rd and 4th Companies of the Rifles were sent through the wood towards Mankowitz. It was thus intended to attack Haber in the front, and to turn both flanks at the same time, so as to enter Kloster from both sides. As soon as the Infantry had formed for action under cover of the Artillery, the two battalions of the 40th Regiment advanced in two lines against Haber, and entered the village without meeting any serious resistance. About 100 men of Count Leiningen's brigade were taken prisoners.

The Fusilier Battalion of the 28th Regiment advanced on the right of the high road to keep connection with the right flank detachment. It was met by an Austrian battalion and a squadron of Cavalry, which soon retired as the Prussians continued to advance.

The troops that had taken Haber crossed the stream which separates this village from Kloster, at 10 o'clock, and found the 10 A.M. latter place already in possession of detachments from the left flank column. No serious resistance had been offered on the part of the enemy, whose departure was no doubt hastened by the heavy firing which became audible from the direction of the "Muskey-Berg." As it was, part of the troops that occupied a large building and the adjacent hop-fields could not affect their retreat in time, and 240 of them were taken prisoners.

As soon as the Austrians had left Kloster, their batteries at the Jewish cemetery began playing on the village; this fire was returned by Captain Wolf's battery. The advanced guard pressed close on the retiring enemy, but found the bridge over the Iser in flames. A ford was found somewhat below the bridge, but the swift current and a quantity of floating timber rendered it almost impracticable. Nevertheless the troops crossed; the leading files reached Münchengrätz at half-past 11, and found three companies of the Fusilier Battalions of the 11.30 A.M. 56th Regiment, under Lieutenant-Colonel Von Busse, already in possession of the place. This detachment belonged to the 14th Division, which had started from Boehmisch-Aicha and Liebitsch at 5 o'clock, but had been somewhat delayed at Podhara, by having to repair the bridge before being able to cross the Mohelka. The advanced guard of the division reached Mohelnic by 8 o'clock, and found the bridge over the Iser at this place totally destroyed. Nevertheless, the three companies of the 56th Regiment succeeded in fording the river at a spot where the stream was only three feet deep; they then dislodged the skirmishers of the Austrian 32nd Rifle Battalion, from Count Waldstein's park, northward of Münchengrätz. After a short struggle they entered the town, and penetrated as far as the market-place, taking 185 men prisoners.

By degrees the remainder of the advanced guard of the 14th Division crossed the ford after suffering some loss through the enemy's batteries on the Muskey-Berg.

Before the main body of the Army of the Elbe could cross, tressle bridges had to be built at Mohelnitz, and 1,200 paces below Münchengrätz. Captain Bliesner commenced this work 11.30 A.M. at the latter spot at half-past 11. A battery of the enemy, posted on the Horka-Berg, tried to disturb the work, whereupon the Prussian 2nd and 4th 6-pounder batteries were brought into action on the heights behind Klein-Pteinow, and 1 P.M. the troops began to cross at 1 o'clock. The bridge was 120 feet long.

Count Leiningen's brigade evidently only defended Münchengrätz in order to cover the retreat of the Austrian Corps, which seems to have begun even before the action commenced at 9 o'clock. The Saxons had started as early as 5 o'clock, and the resistance offered by the brigades of General Piret and Colonel Abele was also but slight.

8 A.M. At 8 o'clock the sound of firing beyond the Iser announced that the Army of the Elbe had commenced its attack on Münchengrätz, and orders were despatched for the advance of General Horn's and General Fransecky's divisions, the former by way of Brezina, the latter by Wschen and Zdiar.

This soon brought them within range of the Austrian batteries on the Muskey-Berg, which played upon them with great effect. Although three Prussian batteries were brought into action between Brezina and Housob, and one eastwards of Zdiar, still the enemy had so dominant a position, and the distance was so great, that their fire made but little impression. The enemy's fire, however, in no way checked General Fransecky's advance. As his troops reached Zdiar, he detached the 2nd and Fusilier Battalions of the 27th Regiment to Przihwas, with instructions to climb up a narrow and wooded gorge that leads up to the plateau at this place. Somewhat later, on reaching Walschina, he gave similar orders to the 2nd and Fusilier Battalions of the 66th Regiment, and then proceeded to attack Dneboch with the two 1st Battalions of these regiments. The village was occupied by part of the 72nd Austrian Regiment (Ramming) that very soon retired.

The battalions that were sent to attack the position on the Muskey-Berg drove the enemy's skirmishers before them through the road, and reached the summit at 11 o'clock, after a toilsome 11 A.M. ascent across narrow rocky gullies, and through dense brushwood. The Austrian troops on the plateau, detachments of the 45th Regiment (Archduke Sigismund), and of the 29th Rifle Battalion, were dislodged, and their Artillery forced to withdraw in great haste. The Prussian battalions then descended the slope towards Zasadka, where they were joined by these troops that had advanced by way of Dneboch, and that now proceeded to attack Bossin.

A few shots from the 1st 4-pounder Battery soon set the

village on fire, whereupon the Austrian troops, consisting of part of the 35th Regiment (Khevenhüller), and some Riflemen, retreated in the direction of Fürstenbrück, and covered their retreat by a battery of 16 guns, posted southwards of Boissin. It was now 1 o'clock; the Prussian 1st 4-pounder and 1st 6-pounder Batteries took up a position on a hill by Lhotitz; the Austrian guns withdrew in about 25 minutes, and the action ceased. 1 P.M.

On the Prussian side 14 battalions had been engaged. Their losses were—

| | Killed. | | Wounded. | | Missing. | | Total. |
|---|---|---|---|---|---|---|---|
| | Officers. | Men. | Officers. | Men. | Officers. | Men. | |
| Advanced Guard (General Von Schöler) | .. | 13 | 6 | 139 | .. | 9 | 167 |
| 7th Division .. | .. | 19 | 2 | 75 | .. | 1 | 97 |
| 8th „ | .. | 12 | .. | 49 | .. | 6 | 67 |
| 14th „ | .. | 2 | .. | 8 | .. | .. | 10 |
| Total .. .. | .. | 46 | 8 | 271 | .. | 16 | 341 |

The Austrians and Saxons had commenced their retreat to Sobotka and Unter Bautzen sufficiently early to avoid a serious catastrophe. The losses of the former may, without exaggeration, be estimated at more than 2,000, for General Schoeler's advanced guard captured 3 officers and 502 men, General Fransecky's division 700, and Count Münster's 185 men, making a total of 1,390 in prisoners alone.

The 7th Division bivouacked at Bossin, the 8th reached Dobrawoda without fighting; the 6th halted at Brezina, General Von Horn's Cavalry Division at Hrdetz. The 14th Division was brought up to Münchengrätz, the 15th assembled to the south of the town, near Wesela, and the 16th halted at Haber. The IInd Corps had moved forward on the Podol-Gitschin road, as far as Zehrow and Daubrow, the main body of the Cavalry Corps bivouacked behind it. Thus, eight divisions of Infantry, mustering, with the Cavalry together, upwards of 100,000 men, were concentrated in an area of 20 square miles. The villages were forsaken by their inhabitants, who had blocked up the wells and removed all provisions, so that the troops were but scantily fed, more especially as only a part of the provision trains reached the bivouacs.

The 5th Division had advanced on the Turnau-Gitschin road, and bivouacked near Rowensko, its advanced guard in a position at Ktowa.

Lieutenant-Colonel Heinichen's detachment, six squadrons and one battery, marched from Ktowa to Gitschin, where it was fired on from the nearest houses. A company of Austrian Rifles that had fallen back from Wurzelsdorf, occupied the town and checked any further progress of Colonel Heinichen's detachment, which only consisted of Cavalry. A squadron was sent round the west side of the town to reconnoitre, and found the two Austrian squadrons that had retreated from Turnau to Gitschin on the day before drawn up there; this battery opened fire, which the Prussian battery returned from a position near Rybnicek. It was not long before heavy clouds of dust on the Sobotka road announced the approach of a considerable body of troops, at the head of which marched General Edelsheim's Cavalry Division.

As soon as the arrival of a Prussian detachment at Rowensko was reported at Austrian head-quarters, General Poschacher's brigade received orders to occupy Gitschin the same evening. It was followed by the greater part of General Piret's Brigade.

Under these circumstances Lieutenant-Colonel Heinichen returned to Ktowa, and the Austrian Hussars watched his march from a distance.

The Prussian Army now concentrated between München-grätz and Podol had only two roads by which it could march on Gitschin, the one leading by way of Fürstenbrück, the other by Podkost; it was therefore necessary to march in several *échelons*. Both these roads meet at Sobotka, the Podkost road forming a strong rocky and wooded defile.

---

## ACTION OF PODKOST.

The 3rd Division received orders at Zehrow, on the 28th, to push forward a detachment to Podkost the same evening, in order to open this defile for the advance of the army on the following day. Accordingly, Colonel Von Stahr started at

10 P.M. 10 P.M. with the 1st and Fusilier Battalions of the 14th Regiment, the 1st and 3rd Companies of the 2nd Rifle Battalion,

11 P.M. one division of Hussars and 100 Pioneers. An hour later he came upon the outposts of General Ringelsheim's brigade and found a detachment of the Austrian 26th Rifle Battalion posted behind a barricade which blocked up the road.

The moon shone bright, and Major Von Garrelts spread out his rifle companies as well as the broken nature of the ground permitted, carried the barricade, and had it cleared away by the Pioneers. At an opening in the road fresh resistance was met

29th of June. with. It was now one o'clock in the morning, the country

1 P.M. perfectly unknown and so complicated that no clear view of the neighbourhood could be obtained; it was therefore deemed advisable to wait for daybreak, before proceeding any further.

3 A.M. At the first dawn of day, at 3 o'clock, a brisk skirmishing commenced, Major Garrelts dislodged the enemy from a second barricade, but met four companies of Austrian Rifles posted

*à cheval* of the high road, on a rise in the ground about a mile
on this side of Kost. Colonel Von Stahr reinforced the Rifles
by two companies of Infantry and then pressed forwards on
Podkost. A struggle of some duration ensued in a deep ravine
near the village. On the other side of this defile a large
mansion perfectly bars the high road which passes through the
castle gates. This spot was held in force by the Austrians,
who were posted on both sides, and opened fire with four guns.
Under these circumstances Colonel Von Stahr merely watched
the enemy's movements with the two companies of Infantry,
and posted the remainder of his detachment in a position,
where it was sheltered from the enemy's fire. He had lost
18 men.

About 8 o'clock A.M. the Austrians fell back to Podkost of 8 A.M.
their own accord, having attained their object, namely, the
covering the retreat of the Saxon and Austrian brigades from
Münchengrätz and Backofen.

Whilst these actions were being fought by the Ist Army, on
the 28th of June, the Corps of Guards and the Vth Corps
d'Armée had continued their advance towards the Upper
Elbe.

## ACTION OF SOOR, 28TH OF JUNE.*

The Crown Prince received the first intelligence of the issue
of the action of Trautenau at 1 o'clock A.M. of the 28th in his
head-quarters at Hronow; it was brought by an officer of his
own Staff. This news precluded all idea of sending the 2nd
Division of Guards to the assistance of General Von Steinmetz,
at least for the present. It was unavoidably necessary to disengage the Ist Corps, and to open the defile of Trautenau;
for this purpose the united forces of both divisions were indispensable.

Under the impression that the Ist Corps would renew its
attempt to debouch on the 28th, and not knowing that it had
retreated as far as Liebau and Schömberg, the Crown
Prince issued the following orders to the Corps of Guards
at 2 o'clock A.M. :—

"As the issue of the action of the Ist Corps d'Armée
"at Trautenau is undecided, the Corps of Guards will
"continue its march in the direction already ordered as
"far as Keile; if the action at Trautenau be still going
"on, it will then march on the latter place and engage
"the enemy immediately. The Corps will set off as
"early as possible.
(Signed) "FREDERICK WILLIAM,
"*Crown Prince.*"

---

* The order of battle of the Corps of Guards in this action is given in Appendix XV.

General Prince of Würtemberg issued the necessary orders at Kosteletz without delay. General Von Plonski's Division, which was posted there, was turned out by sounding the alarm 4.30 A.M. at half past four, and started for Eypel, where it arrived behind 7.45 A.M. the 1st Brigade of Guards at a quarter before eight. At this time the 2nd Brigade of Guards and the advanced guard were marching on Ober-Raatsch.

General Von Gablentz had sent his report on the measures he had taken after the action of Trautenau, to the Feld-zeugmeister at Josephstadt, by half-past 9 P.M. of the 27th. Conceiving well-founded apprehensions for the safety of his right flank, he requested that a detachment might be sent to 6 A.M. Prausnitz-Keile for its protection. At 6 A.M. of the 28th he received the answer that four battalions of the IVth Corps would immediately occupy Prausnitz-Keile and Eypel. This measure was, however, not carried out, because the detach-ment of Colonel Fleischhacker's brigade, that was despatched for this purpose, marched by mistake to Ober-Prausnitz, four and a half miles westward ot Königinhof, an error of which, moreover, General Von Gablentz was not informed.

About an hour later, however, the danger of the situation seems to have been felt at the Austrian head-quarters, for at 7 A.M. 7 o'clock orders were sent to General Gablentz to quit Trautenau and to hasten to Prausnitz, where he was to take up a position fronting eastward, as heavy Prussian columns were marching in that direction. The Corps commenced its march immediately. The baggage and ammunition trains were first set in motion, they were followed by the Reserve Artillery, and then successively by the brigades of General Knebel, Colonel Mondl, and General Wimpfen. To cover this retreat Colonel Grivicic's brigade was to march from its position southwards of Parschnitz by way of Alt-Rognitz, and was to hold the heights of Rudersdorf until further orders.

Whilst the Prussian advanced guard was marching on Ober-Raatsch, two squadrons of the Guard Hussars recon-noitred the country in the direction of Burkersdorf, and reported that columns of the enemy were marching on the high road from Königinhof to Trautenau. Similar information arrived of an advance of the enemy on Eypel.

In consequence of these reports General Von Hiller's Division received orders to wait for further information in a suitable position. It was thought that such a one could only be found behind the Aupa, and the main body of the division set off in this direction, whilst the advanced guard took post on the heights to the west of Raatsch to cover this movement, which was a difficult one amongst the mountainous defiles.

The troops had already commenced this retrograde move-ment, when the former reports were proved to be false, as long lines of Austrian baggage-wagons were seen marching on the high road from Trautenau to Königinhof. Some stragglers and wagons were brought in by the Prussian patrols. It was now

9 o'clock, and, under the impression that the 1st Corps would co-operate, Prince Von Wurtemberg resolved to press forward with the Guards in a direction that must be most fatal to the enemy. He gave orders to the advanced guard to pass through Staudenz, and to march towards the high road in the direction of Burkersdorf; the main body of the 1st Division of Guards was to follow to the last-named village.

In the meantime General Gablenz had ordered the trains to turn off from the high road, and to proceed in the direction of Pilnikan and Neustadt. When the Prussian advanced guard debouched from Staudenz, at half-past 9, the Austrian Reserve Artillery had arrived at Burkersdorf. An 8-pounder battery went into position immediately, and General Gablenz's personal escort, a company of the the 8th Regiment (Gerstner), was thrown into the neighbouring woods to cover it. Battery after battery of the Austrian Reserve Artillery now came up and increased the line of fire, to answer which the Prussians brought first the 1st 4-pounder and then the 6th 6-pounder battery into action, the former eastward, the latter westward of Staudenz.

The 11th and 12th Companies of the 3rd Regiment of Guards were despatched to Marschau to cover the left flank, and the Infantry of the advanced guard then formed for action, and proceeded to attack the patches of wood westward of Staudenz, which had in the meantime been occupied by General Knebel's brigade. Only five battalions of the brigade (about 3,500 men) were on the spot; their line fronted eastwards; the brigade battery was on the left wing. One Battalion of the 3rd Regiment (Archduke Charles), two companies of the 1st Regiment (Kaiser Franz Joseph), and the greater part of the 28th Battalion of Rifles were detached as covering guard for the Reserve Artillery and as garrison of Trautenau.

The undulating ground and the high-standing corn both sheltered and favoured the advance of the Prussian Infantry, so that in spite of a very severe fire, especially from the enemy's artillery, the intervening space was crossed, often at a quick run, and the three groups of wood eastward of the Kaile-Neu-Kognitz road were carried; in like manner the 10th and 12th Companies of the 1st Regiment of Guards gained possession of the wood close to a disused stone quarry (Alter-Steinbruch), and the enemy was thus forced back into Burkersdorf and the woods to the south of the village.

Colonel Von Kessel halted his troops on reaching the west border of the woods they had taken, in order to wait for the arrival of the main body, and only kept up a skirmishing fire for the present. The Cavalry of the advanced guard was behind his left wing, the batteries were forward as far as the old stone quarry.

In the meantime the main body of the 1st Division of Guards continued its march and debouched from Staudenz at

**11 A.M.**  11 o'clock.  At this time the 2nd Division was still crossing the Aupa, its head having as yet only reached Unter-Raatsch.

On the Austrian side, General Knebel's brigade had established itself again at Burkersdorf, Colonel Mondel's brigade had reached the wood to the south of Neu-Rognitz, which it occupied with its foremost troops.  General Wimpfen's brigade had swerved to the right, and was marching on Ober-Altenbach, in the rear of the two former brigades, Colonel Grivicic's brigade was drawing near Rudersdorf.

**11.30 A.M.**  As soon as the latter movement was reported, at half-past 11, the leading battalion of the 2nd Division of Guards (2nd Battalion of the 2nd Regiment of Guard-Grenadiers, Emperor Francis) was ordered to march on Rudersdorf likewise.

When the main body of the 1st Division of Guards had passed Staudenz, the 4-pounder battery of the advanced guard was relieved by the 5th 4-pounder battery, and the Infantry of the main body moved up to the line on which the advanced guard was already engaged.

**11.30 A.M.**  At half-past 11 Colonel Von Pape gave the signal to advance quickly, and seven companies advanced against Burkersdorf, viz., on the right three companies of the Fusilier battalion of the 2nd, in the centre the 9th and 10th Companies of the 3rd, and on the left the 9th and 11th Companies of the 1st Foot Guards.  At the same time the 1st and 2nd Battalions of the 2nd Foot Guards, under Lieutenant-Colonel Von Neumann, the 1st Battalion of the Guard-Fusiliers, and some detachments of the advanced guard, followed by the 1st Battalion of the 3rd Foot Guards, which had come up in the meantime, advanced against the the wood to the south of Burkersdorf.  The wooded hillocks and the village were carried by the Prussian Infantry at the first onset, and General Knebel's brigade fell back, partly on Soor and partly on Altenbach.  An Austrian battery, posted to the south of Hainwiese, attempted to cover the retreat of the brigade, upon which Captain Eltester's battery took up a position between Burkersdorf and the wood which had just been taken.  During the fire of these batteries the 1st Company of the 2nd Foot Guards, which was pursuing the enemy towards Hainwiese, got within 300 paces of another Austrian battery and its covering squadron, and forced it to retreat precipitately with a loss of three guns and three caissons.  The 2nd and 3rd Companies of the 2nd Foot Guards continued their pursuit of the enemy as far as the farm Hainwiese also, whilst the 2nd Battalion of the 3rd Foot Guards advanced northwards of Burkersdorf, towards Altenback, and dislodged a detachment of Austrian Rifles from the Graner-Koppel.

On the right wing of the line of attack the 2nd Battalion of the Guard-Fusiliers lost its touch to the left, in consequence of the broken ground, and got into the direction of Neu-Rognitz.  It found the wood to the south of the village occupied by detachments of Colonel Mondel's brigade, attacked them immediately, drove the enemy back into the village, and then kept up a skirmishing fire from the skirts of the wood. Parties of skirmishers that left the cover of the wood were prevented from advancing any further by detachments of Windischgrätz Dragoons, but an Austrian battery planted close to the village was forced to withdraw as Captain Von Schickfuss led the 5th Company along the border of the wood northwards, and then advanced against the east side of the village. Two companies of the 10th Regiment (Mazzuchelli) left the place after slight resistance. Soon after, however, two divisions (four companies) of the 24th Regiment (Parma) came out of the wood on the north-west, and rushing on the village, drove the Fusilier company out; on advancing still further they turned the right of the Prussian line. This attack, and an announcement on the part of General Hiller that the battalion could not reckon on any support, induced Lieutenant-Colonel Von der Knesebeck to draw the companies out of action, more particularly so as Austrian columns were advancing on Rudersdorf, and a sharp engagement commencing at this place. The enemy did not follow.

Numerous prisoners and quantities of the enemy's baggage fell into the hands of the Prussians during these engagements. Three brigades of the Austrian Xth Corps were forced back in so westerly a direction that their junction with the Austrian main forces became very doubtful. The fatigue of the Prussian troops, who had marched above 27 miles over very hilly ground the day before, was very great, and a pause now ensued in the action on this part of the field, whilst the engagement burst forth in fresh force on the opposite wing. The 4th Austrian brigade was there placed in a most unfortunate position. The orders that General Gablenz despatched, as soon as he became fully aware of the danger of his situation, did not reach the brigade, and Colonel Grivicic was completely cut off from his corps.

At the moment, it is true, only one single Prussian battalion was opposed to him, namely, the 2nd Battalion of the 2nd Guard-Grenadiers (Emperor Francis). This battalion ascended the heights of Rudersdorf at half-past 11, and then proceeded 11.30 A.M. to attack the buildings on the south side of the ravine. The 5th and 8th Companies, with skirmishers thrown out in front, formed the first, the 6th and 7th Companies the second line; the latter were united in one half-battalion. The buildings were taken, although the Commander of the battalion, Lieutenant-Colonel Von Gaudy fell mortally wounded whilst leading the charge. The companies of the second line advanced against the wood eastward of the village, which they carried in spite of the enemy's heavy fire. Captain Von Witzleben, who had taken the command of the battalion fell here, and the battalion suffered severely, almost all its officers were killed or wounded.

During the struggle for the possession of the wood, the

I

Austrians advanced against the buildings with very superior forces, and retook them from the Prussians, who held their ground in the wooded ravine and the quarries south-eastward of the village until Major Von Boehn, who had been sent to their assistance with the 1st Battalion of the Regiment, came 12.30 P.M. up about half-past 12 o'clock.

Major Boehn immediately proceeded to attack the enemy with the 1st half-battalion, supported by the 8th Company, drove him from the heights into the village, and seized on the southernmost buildings. The second half-battalion advanced against the copse in the hollow, westward of the stone cross, drove the Austrian detachments that were posted there back over the heights towards Alt-Rognitz, and then took up a position westward of Rudersdorf.

He now desisted from further attack until reinforcements, that he had asked for from the Commanding-General, should have arrived, and merely kept up the fire on the line he had gained. In the meantime the 2nd Division of Guards had passed the ravine at Raatsch and ascended the heights to the west of the village.

In the course of their march towards Kaile, on arriving at Staudenz, they received orders to proceed in the direction of Trautenau. Eight companies of the 3rd Guard-Grenadiers had been already sent from Ober-Raatsch towards Alt-Rognitz and arrived westwards of Rudersdorf at 3 o'clock.

In order to gain possession of the whole village Major Boehn now renewed his attack with six companies. The Austrians retreated to Alt-Rognitz and left 3 officers and 222 men in the hands of the Prussians.

The 3rd Guard-Grenadiers advanced to the left of Rudersdorf, and Major Von Zaluskowsky attacked those detachments of Colonel Grivicic's brigade that were posted in the neighbouring patches of wood with the 1st half-battalion of the regiment, captured the colours of the 2nd Austrian Regiment (Alexander) and pursued the enemy towards Alt-Rognitz.

The 9th and 12th Companies of the Regiment now came up and attacked the centre of the village. They drove a detachment of the 16th Rifle Battalion out of the cemetery on the hill, and forced it back into the wood behind the village with considerable loss. The 1st and 3rd Companies captured three officers and 108 men in one of the buildings of Alt-Rognitz and 100 in the village itself; 200 more fell into the hands of the 2nd Battalions, which advanced on the west side of the place.

Thus, 16 companies of the 2nd and 3rd Guard-Grenadier Regiments now met in Alt-Rognitz, where they were re-formed by Colonel Von Pritzelwitz.

Almost simultaneously with these engagements, Lieutenant-Colonel Von der Knesebeck renewed his attack of Neu-Rognitz with three companies of the Guard-Fusiliers. The village was taken after a short resistance from detachments of Rifles and of the 56th Regiment (Stephan), for the greater part of

Colonel Moudel's brigade was already retreating towards Alten-bach and Pilnikau. One officer and 60 men were taken prisoners.

The 2nd, 9th, and 11th Companies of the Guard-Fusiliers and the 4th Squadron of the Guard-Hussars, that had been at last sent to support Lieutenant-Colonel Von der Knesebeck, did not arrive until the action at Neu-Rognitz was over.

Colonel Grivicic's brigade was now completely dispersed, its commander wounded and a prisoner. Part of the brigade succeeding in escaping for the moment in a northerly direction, but was captured the next day; another part endeavoured to reach Trautenau, but fell in with the main body of General Von Plonski's division, which was marching on the town, and lost numerous prisoners. Only a few scattered detachments escaped to Pilnikau.

In order to cause the enemy as much loss as possible, the 1st Battalion of the 4th Guard-Grenadiers was sent to the " Grabenhaeuser," whilst the remainder of the division pursued its march on Trautenau.

The 5th, 6th, 8th, and 12th Companies of the 2nd Guard-Grenadiers drove the enemy's detachments out of Hohenbruck and ultimately dislodged the Austrians from Trautenau, Weigelsdorf and Kaltenhof, in company with the 3rd Battalion of the 4th Guard-Grenadiers. Numerous prisoners were taken at all of these places. Colonel Von Fabeck's brigade* followed and picked up numerous Austrian stragglers; the Colonel sent the 2nd Battalion of the 1st Guard-Grenadiers westward of Trautenau to Nieder-Alstadt, where it took four officers and 40 men of the 2nd Austrian Regiment (Alexander) prisoners. A detachment that was retreating from Trautenau, was overtaken by the 4th Squadron of the 3rd Guard-Lancers and nine Austrian officers with 400 men laid down their arms.

The pursuit did not end until half-past 5 in the evening.

General Von Plonski's division bivouacked in and by 5.30 P.M. Trautenau, Alt- and Neu-Rognitz; General Von Hiller's in and southward of Burkersdorf with a line of outposts towards Ober-Soor; the latter village was held by the Austrians during the night. The Reserve Artillery accompanied by the 2nd Battalion of the 1st Guards had left Braunau and Dittersbach in the morning; it marched by way of Kronau and Kosteletz, and went into bivouack between Ober-Raatsch and Staudenz after 10 o'clock at night.

The head-quarters of the Corps of Guards were moved to 10 P.M. Trautenau and communications opened with the 1st Corps the same evening. The latter remained for the day in Liebau and Schömberg to re-form, and pushed the Cavalry Division on to Grunau.

Between 6 and 8 o'clock in the evening the main body of General Gablenz's Corps was assembled in a bivouac near Neustadt and Neu-Schloss.

---

* *Vide* Appendix XV.

I 2

The losses of the Corps of Guards in the action of Soor (Trautenau, Alt-Rognitz) were:—

| | Killed. | | Wounded. | | Missing. | | Total. | |
|---|---|---|---|---|---|---|---|---|
| | Officers. | Men. | Officers. | Men. | Officers. | Men. | Officers. | Men. |
| 1st Division of Guard-Infantry: | | | | | | | | |
| 1st Regiment of Guards | 1 | 15 | 5 | 42 | .. | .. | 6 | 57 |
| 3rd Regiment of Guards | .. | 6 | 3 | 53 | .. | .. | 3 | 59 |
| 2nd Regiment of Guards | .. | 16 | 4 | 104 | .. | .. | 4 | 120 |
| Guard - Fusilier Regiment .. .. .. | 4 | 55 | 1 | 147 | .. | .. | 5 | 202 |
| Guard-Rifle Battalion .. | .. | .. | .. | 14 | .. | .. | .. | 14 |
| Guard - Hussar Regiment .. .. .. | .. | 1 | .. | 2 | .. | .. | .. | 3 |
| 2nd Division of Guard-Infantry: | | | | | | | | |
| 3rd Regiment of Guard-Grenadiers .. .. | .. | .. | .. | 2 | .. | .. | .. | 2 |
| 2nd Regiment of Guard-Grenadiers .. .. | 4 | 46 | 6 | 154 | .. | .. | 10 | 200 |
| 4th Regiment of Guard-Grenadiers .. .. | .. | .. | .. | 2 | .. | 1 | .. | 3 |
| 3rd Regiment of Guard-Lancers .. .. | .. | .. | .. | 1 | .. | 1 | .. | 2 |
| Artillery .. .. | .. | 7 | .. | 16 | .. | .. | .. | 23 |
| Total .. .. | 9 | 146 | 19 | 537 | .. | 2 | 28 | 685 |

The Austrian losses cannot be given in detail; their own accounts state them to have been 102 officers, 3,572 men and 22 horses.

The trophies which fell into the hands of the Corps of Guards in this brilliant action were about 3,000 prisoners (among them one commander of brigade, Colonel Grivicic and two commanders of regiments), one flag, eight guns, and a military chest containing about 10,000 florins.

This engagement had re-opened the road for the advance of the Ist Corps, but the Vth Corps had been again left without support, and solely dependent on its own resources.

We may here anticipate the events of the next day, and mention, that at 3 o'clock the next morning a detachment of the Austrian 23rd Regiment (Airoldi) tried to cut its way through the Prussian lines, among the bushes eastward of Burkersdorf. It fell in with a picket of the 1st Foot Guards which fired on it, whereupon the 6th and 8th Companies of the 3rd Foot Guards and the 2nd Squadron of the Guard-Hussars hastened to the support of the picket, and barred the road of the Austrians, whilst, at the same time, the 7th Company of the 3rd Guard-Grenadiers came up in their rear. The Austrian Commander, 15 officers, and 394 men surrendered after a short resistance. The Prussian troops engaged lost four men wounded of the 3rd Guard-Grenadiers, one man killed and one missing of the 3rd Foot Guards.

---

## ACTION OF SKALITZ, 28TH OF JUNE.

During the night of the 27th reports came in from the out-posts of the Vth Corps that railway trains were continually passing through Skalitz. It was possible that they had brought up reinforcements, but more probable that they had been employed in removing the wounded. Austrian outposts were seen in Domkow and Kleny, and Infantry detachments at Dubno.

When General Ramming sent his reports on the action of the 27th at Nachod to the Austrian Head-Quarters in Joseph-stadt, he asked for reinforcements, as an attack on his position at Skalitz might be expected on the 28th. The same evening the answer was returned that Archduke Leopold had been instructed to move the VIIIth Corps forwards to Czaslawek and Dolan to support him, and that he (General Ramming) was to put himself in communication with the Archduke, and follow his orders.

The VIIIth Corps had a long way to march from Tynist, and reached Dolan late on the 27th, where it received the following orders:—

> " *Head-Quarters, Josephstadt, June 27th, 1866.*
> " *Six o'clock p.m.*
>
> " If an action takes place at Skalitz to-morrow, the
> " VIIIth Corps will move up into the foremost line;
> " the VIth Corps will form the reserve, and both Corps
> " will be under the command of His Royal Highness
> " Lieutenant Field Marshal Archduke Leopold.
> (Signed) " BENEDEK."

Besides these orders, the following letter, which afterwards fell into the hands of the Prussians, reached Dolan; it shows the state of the VIth Corps after the action of Nachod:—

> " *The Commanding-General of the VIth Corps d'Armée to*
> " *the Commanding-General of the VIIIth Corps d'Armée*
> " *at Dolan.*
>
> " According to an announcement which I have
> " received to-day from the Commander-in-Chief, the
> " VIIIth Corps d'Armée will encamp at Dolan, and is
> " destined as support to the VIth Corps. After the long
> " and serious action in which my troops were
> " engaged to-day, they are exhausted, and not in a

" condition successfully to repulse an attack, which may
" be expected early to-morrow; I therefore request the
" assistance of two brigades, which must, however,
" move into the first line of my troops to-day.

" Head-Quarters, Skalitz, June 27th, 1866, 6 P.M.
(Signed)  " VON RAMMING,
" *Lieutenant Field-Marshal.*"

During the night of the 27th, the VIth Austrian Corps
remained on the heights eastward of Skalitz; its line extended
as far as Zlitsch, to the north, and half-way to Spitta, on the
south. One brigade was held back in reserve. The outposts
of General Waldstätten's brigade held the wood eastward of
Dubno in force, Kleny but slightly. Cavalry watched the
front of the position from Zlitsch to Domkow, and a strong
detachment was posted on the road to Nachod.

Towards morning the VIIIth Corps came up to relieve the
VIth, and the IVth Corps was moved up to Dolan in the course
of the morning, so that on the 28th of June three Austrian
Corps, mustering about 70,000 men, with 200 guns, were
echeloned on the road between Skalitz and Jaromir, in a depth
of only four and a half miles. If it, however, be true, as
Austrian Military Journals affirm, that Archduke Leopold was
instructed only to wait till two o'clock in the afternoon, in case
a hostile attack should ensue, and otherwise to return to
Josephstadt, then these considerable forces cannot have been
concentrated for any offensive purpose. Anyhow, the Archduke only had two Corps d'Armée at his disposal. When he
crossed the Aupa with the VIIIth Corps, the Prussian outposts
took this movement for the commencement of an attack. The
VIth Corps, however, was withdrawn and posted as a reserve
to the rear of Zagezd, probably in consideration of its shattered
condition. This change between the two corps was effected
by 7 o'clock A.M. Thus only the VIIIth Corps and General
Schindlöcker's Cavalry brigade came into action on the left
bank of the Aupa. General Rothkirch's brigade of the VIIIth
Corps was left to guard the railway at Wildenschwerdt, but
two 4th battalions of the regiments Creneville and Degenfeldt,
that formed part of the garrison of Josephstadt, joined the
corps. It mustered on the whole 23 battalions, 17 squadrons,
and 88 guns.

The order of battle of the Prussian troops on the 28th of
June,* fixes the strength of General Von Steinmetz's force on
this day at 29 battalions, 13 squadrons, 102 guns. Among
these are included a Pioneer battalion, and General Hoffmann's
brigade of the VIth Corps. In the course of the ensuing
engagement a heavy brigade of the Guard-Cavalry drew near
the field, but only its battery came into action.

The Archduke occupied the position in front of the Aupa,
as follows: On the extreme left General Fragnern's Brigade

---

* *Vide* Appendix XVI.

was posted on the heights northward of Skalitz, and occupied Zlitsch; on the right wing, General Schulz's brigade extended from the railway station to Spitta, Colonel Kreyssern's brigade was stationed as reserve between both, à cheval of the high road. General Schindlöcker's brigade of the 1st Reserve Cavalry Division was on the left wing at Zlitsch, the squadrons of the 3rd Regiment of Lancers (Archduke Charles), that were originally attached to the brigades, and a regiment of Cuirassiers stood on the right wing.

The Prussians sent scouting parties out early in the morning, but gained no further insight into the enemy's intentions. The 8th Dragoons went forward so far as Neustadt without meeting with the enemy. A squadron was left to watch the high road, and the regiment returned to its bivouac at 7 A.M. 7 A.M. The 4th Dragoons were likewise sent beyond the outposts, in the direction of Skalitz, but only met with small detachments of the enemy that fell back on their supports. The advanced guard detached two companies of rifles into the "Buchwald" on this side of Skalitz, and posted Captain Von Kamptz's half battalion as support behind it, and Captain Von Unruhe's half battalion on its right flank, at "Shotker-Hof."

General Von Steinmetz arrived on the heights of Wysokow, from whence the enemy's position could be in a measure overlooked, at 7 o'clock. His corps had received orders to march to Gradlitz, and had been promised the support of the 2nd Division of Guards. Wishing to give this division time to come up, the Commanding-General sent General Von Loewenfeldt with a right flank detachment to Studnitz to open communication with the Guards.

The latter General started at 7 o'clock. The head of his 7 A.M. column consisted of two companies of Rifles, which were successively followed by the 37th Regiment, two batteries, the 58th Regiment, and a third battery. In order to strike the road to Studnitz, the column passed close by Nachod. A squadron of Dragoons examined the country in advance, and to the right of the column, the light baggage and their ammunition trains followed to Studnitz, the remainder of the trains and the pontoons were sent to Kosteletz.

The advanced guard (Colonel Von Voigts-Rhetz) was at the same time ordered to proceed to Starkoc. In expectation of an attack, the Infantry marched in two lines, with the Artillery in front, and the Dragoons on the right rear.

As soon as the patrols reported that they were in communication with the 2nd Guard Division, Captain Unruhe's half battalion joined the advanced guard. The main body (10th Division, General Von Kirchbach) left its bivouacs an hour later, at 8 o'clock, and advanced on the Skalitz road. The 19th Brigade was at the head of the column, then followed first the 20th Brigade, and then the Reserve Artillery. The division halted at Wysokow.

General Von Hoffmann's Brigade remained between the

Wenzelsberg wood and Wysokow; the 8th Dragoons and the 1st Lancers were stationed on its left flank.

General Von Steinmetz's arrangements were perfectly adapted to the situation. During its march on Gradlitz the Vth Corps might well expect to meet with serious resistance in its front, and at the same time to be attacked by the enemy on its left flank. If, as was probable, the enemy was met at the Aupa, the 9th Division and the 2nd Guard Division would materially assist the attack which the 10th Division would make in the front; if, on the other hand, as was also very possible, the enemy advanced with superior forces from the south, the 10th Division would form a strong advanced guard, which would fall back on the two other divisions.

It was thus not possible that the Vth Corps could be thrown back into the defiles of Nachod, and be separated from the other corps; even at the worst, it would only be forced back upon the main body of the IInd Army, the junction of which would then be effected.

At half-past eight an officer was sent to Kosteletz to direct the march of the 2nd Guard Division on Studnitz. Verbal orders, given on the plateau of Wysokow, instructed General Von Loewenfeld to attack the enemy from the last named village as soon as the Guards should have come up. Colonel Von Voigts-Rhetz and General Von Kirchbach were to support this attack as left flank echelons.

General Von Hoffmann was instructed to remain in his position, but it was at the same time left to his discretion to join in the action as circumstances might demand, or as he himself might deem advisable. General Von Steinmetz then went to Studnitz, and gave orders to the column debouching from the village to deploy, with four half battalions of the 37th Regiment in first and four half battalions of the 58th Regiment in second line. The remainder of both regiments stopped in the rear to guard the ammunition train and the baggage.

As soon as the woods to the south of Studnitz were passed, General Schindlöcker's Heavy Cavalry Brigahe was seen marching from Zernow to Zlitsch. The Prussian Artillery unlimbered, but had scarcely began to fire on the Cavalry when it was opened upon by, apparently, five batteries posted to the north of Skalitz. The Austrian Cuirassiers retired through Zlitsch, crossed the Aupa, and marched on the right bank towards Ratiboritz. On the heights by Zernow another body of Cavalry appeared, which proved to be the Prussian brigade of Prince Albrecht.

The Prussian 12-pounder batteries on the Schafberg were withdrawn as the enemy's batteries were 3,500 paces distant, and after half an hour, the 4-pounders also ceased firing, because the Austrian guns were well sheltered, and the numerous trees at the road sides prevented the former from observing the effect of their fire.

At a quarter before 11, an officer from the Staff of the

Crown Prince informed General Steinmetz that, in consequence of the action of Trautenau, the 2nd Guard Division had been otherwise disposed of, and that the heavy brigade of the Guard-Cavalry was the only assistance that could be sent to the Vth Corps.

This removed all the reasons that had hitherto induced the General to wait, and he now ordered General Loewenfeldt to advance from the Schafberg, to take the barricaded farm houses at Dubno, and to gain possession of the oak wood behind them.

As soon as the fire from the Schafberg commenced, General Von Hoffmann availed himself of the permission granted to him, and sent Colonel Von Witzleben forwards with the 1st and 2nd Battalions of the 38th Regiment in the direction of the railway, in order to assist in the attack on the Dubno wood. The second 4-pounder battery moved forward towards Kleny.

A deep ravine eastward of Dubno afforded the two battalions some shelter from the enemy's shells, which had much incommoded them while crossing the open country. A company was thrown into the orchards on the left towards Kleny, where the battery had already opened fire.

Colonel Von Voigts-Rhetz had been instructed to advance with his left wing by the side of the high road, and to keep his right wing in connection with General Loewenfeld's troops. He advanced towards Kleny under a heavy fire from Skalitz, during which the battalions of the 38th Regiment got ahead of him.

The Dubno wood was now attacked on all sides; on the right by General Loewenfeld, with eight half battalions of the 37th and 58th Regiments; on the left by Colonel Von Witzleben, with four half battalions of the 38th Regiment; the latter were followed by Colonel Von Voigts-Rhetz, with six half battalions of the 7th Regiment.

As Austrian Infantry was seen advancing from Zblow, the 3rd Battalion of the 37th Regiment occupied the farm houses at Dubno, and put the buildings into a state of defence, whilst the 1st battalion and Captain Braun's half-battalion pushed on, on both sides, past Dubno, and drove the enemy's skirmishers before them. A half battalion of the regiment that had been brought up from Studnitz, covered this movement towards Zblow, and repulsed an attack of one of General Fragnern's battalions by its fire.

The 1st Battalion of the 58th Regiment, followed by half of the 2nd Battalion, now advanced from the Schafberg, and proceeded to attack the northern skirts of the wood with one half-battalion. The 4th 12-pounder battery unlimbered, and had an opportunity of firing on the Austrian Infantry without exposing itself to the enemy's Artillery fire. The other half of the 1st battalion advanced towards the southern skirts of the wood; it was followed by the 1st and 5th 4-pounder batteries that could not find good positions for rifled guns further northward. This half-battalion got behind Conenel Von Witzleben's two battalions that were already advancing with a cloud of skirmishers against the enclosed part of the wood (Fasanerie). The 1st, 4th and 5th companies were received with a fire of skirmishers at about 150 paces, but overcame the enemy's resistance at the first outset. The 1st battalion followed in the direction of the ranger's house, the 2nd along the skirts of the wood, the 8th company along the Skalitz road. Though severely shelled, this company repulsed an attack of Austrian rifles by its rapid fire.

The advanced Guard (Colonel Von Voigts-Rhetz) crossed the railway, and followed Colonel Von Witzleben's battalions into the Dubno wood. Captain Von der Mülbe's half-battalion had to stop in the open country under the enemy's Artillery fire, to cover the Prussian batteries which now came up by degrees, as fast as they could get over the broken ground. The battalions specially belonging to the advanced guard had stopped behind at Wysokow. The first one that arrived was Captain Manteuffel's Horse Artillery Battery, which was attached to the 4th Dragoon Regiment, but the distance was too great for smooth-bores, and the battery rejoined the regiment, which was sheltered from the fire in a dip in the ground southwards of Kleny.

12 A.M. At 12 o'clock the 1st 6-pounder battery of the 5th and the 2nd 4-pounder battery of the six Field Artillery Regiments came into action, to do so the latter battery had to pass through a flank fire of the enemy's Artillery in single file.

These two batteries were exposed to the fire of a formidable Artillery, which was posted 2,500 paces off, north and south of Skalitz in two lines; one line at the railway embankment, and the other on the heights behind it.

In the meantime the Prussian Infantry had gained ground in the Dubno wood, which was defended by the 4th Battalion of the Creneville Regiment and the 5th Rifle Battalion. In advancing through the wood the troops got so intermingled that all guidance of the action ceased. The concentrated fire that the enemy poured into the wood caused considerable losses, but the different detachments still pressed forward, and made many prisoners. The first serious check they met with was at the ranger's house, which was held by a company of Austrian Rifles. At this spot, however, the 1st Battalion of the 38th Regiment, and Captain Loewenstein's half-battalion united for a joint attack. The skirmishers rushed forward with cheers, the supports followed close behind them in compact order across the clearing, and they carried the buildings, and ultimately the whole of the western skirts of the wood. The enemy was now soon dislodged from some detached patches of wood, from which he had hitherto kept up a lively flank fire. One Battalion of the 15th Austrian Regiment (Nassau) fled in complete disorder towards the north-west. In like manner, the hill immediately on the left of the road, leading from the ranger's house to Zlitsch, was next taken. In vain did the Austrian 5th Rifle Battalion strive to its utmost to hold its ground here; it was thrown back towards Zlitsch with heavy loss, and then pursued by Captain Unruhe's half-battalion of the 7th Regiment, which came up at the moment, and after firing a few volleys, dashed at full speed on the southern entrance of the village; 70 Austrians were taken prisoners in the first house. Three companies of the Prussian 5th Rifle Battalion that came up from Studnitz and Starkoc, also shared in the attack on Zlitsch, and followed the enemy over the Aupa.

In order to secure the advantages gained on the right wing, Colonel Von Below rallied the 37th Regiment as much as possible on and behind the hillocks at the side of the Zlitsch road, and had the men's knapsacks brought up from the rear.

The skirmishing parties of the 38th Regiment were approaching the Zlitsch-Skalitz road, under cover of several ditches in this part of the field, when an Austrian battery was seen in the act of unlimbering on the road. Lieutenant-Colonel Von Knobelsdorff immediately ordered a rapid file fire to be poured on the horses of the battery, whilst the skirmishers rushed forward. Only one gun managed to fire, but this single discharge of grape cost the 6th company its Captain and 16 men. When the skirmishers were within 150 paces of the battery, its covering party, half a company of the 15th Austrian Regiment (Nassau) advanced to its defence, but the Prussian skirmishers rushed into the battery, and captured five guns and two caissons. Two Austrian companies hurried up from the Aupa, and two others along the Skalitz road, to rescue the battery, but in vain, they were repulsed with heavy loss.

Captain Von Unruhe's half-battalion joined the right wing, where the skirmishing fire had become stationary. The Austrian 24th Rifle Battalion was posted in a sheltered position on a wooded hill close to the left bank of the Aupa valley, and kept up a well directed fire, which caused much loss. It was at this spot that Prince Adalbert's Aide-de-Camp, Lieutenant Von Saint Paul, fell.

In the meantime the troops on the left wing were in a very difficult position. It was some time before the Prussian Artillery, which only came up to Kleny by degrees could draw the fire of the enemy's batteries at Skalitz off from the Infantry. As soon as the battalions left the south border of the wood they were met not only by the fire of the Austrian batteries, but also by that of the skirmishers of the 77th Regiment (Salvator) that were ensconced under shelter of the railway embankment. It was above all things necessary to gain possession of the latter. This was done, but as soon as two half-battalions of the 38th and 58th Regiments advanced in line towards the high-road beyond it, they were met by a shower of shell and grape. Lieutenant-Colonel Von Wenkstern fell mortally wounded, and the companies were forced to fall back again behind the embankment. In a few minutes the attempt was renewed. A half-battalion of the 58th and three of the 7th Regiment had come up, and the high-road was gained. The losses which the enemy's Artillery and Rifle fire from the distant heights caused were very severe; the 2nd Battalion of the 7th Regiment suffered especially. Colonel Von Witzleben, who had taken such a prominent part in the action with the two battalions of the 58th Regiment, was shot through the shoulder.

At this moment Colonel Kreyssern's whole brigade, formed in two lines, advanced from Skalitz to the attack; the 32nd Regiment (Este) on the right, the 21st Regiment (Reischach) on the left of the high-road, a squadron of Lancers behind the right wing and extending somewhat beyond it.

Three Prussian battalions (six half-battalions) were all that were at hand to meet this shock; the other troops were still too far to the rear to be of any assistance. In order not to be outflanked on the left it was necessary to extend the line. The right wing rested on the railway embankment, from there to the left the half-battalions, Natzmer, Kaisenberg, Horst, Schroetter, and Schreiner were deployed in one line, behind which the half-battalion, Necker, arrived in time to serve as reserve.

The Prussian line awaited the attack on the spot, and met it by destructive volleys and file-firing at the most effective range. The left wing of the Austrians pressed on to within 50 paces of the detachments of the 7th Regiment. Here, however, their columns halted and faced about. The losses were very heavy on both sides, in many places the skirmishers met hand-to-hand, and used the bayonet freely in the *melée*. The right flank battalion of the Austrian line encountered Captain Schreiner's half-battalion, which, deducting the skirmishers, scarcely mustered more than 100 men. At a distance of 100 paces the Austrian battalion wavered and halted. In vain the officers attempted to induce their men to advance further; they stood two or three more volleys and then fled to the railway station, pursued by the fire of the Prussian skirmishers, who followed them. In like manner the fire of the other half-battalion repulsed the enemy's attack, and a charge of the Lancers failed totally. The Prussian loss was considerable, particularly that of the 7th Regiment. General Von Steinmetz greeted the thinned ranks on the spot, where their steady behaviour had just beaten off the attack of such superior numbers. The brave leader of the Austrian troops, Colonel Kreyssern, was killed.

As yet the engagement had been sustained by the flank detachment and the advanced guard; the Prussian Artillery had only come into action by degrees. Now, however, the main body and the Reserve Artillery arrived on the field.

As soon as the advanced guard had started in the morning, the 10th Division debouched from two outlets of Wysokow, and then formed for action beyond the village, the 6th Regiment was thrown forward as advanced-guard, the 47th and 52nd Regiments formed the main body and the 46th Regiment the reserve. The Lancer Regiment stopped on the south of the high-road, and afterwards joined the 8th Dragoons on the extreme left wing, where both regiments and Captain Manteuffel's battery were united under General Von Wnuck's command. The division then advanced past Starkoc towards the Schafberg.

The nature of the ground, especially at the deep gully southward of Starkoc, rendered an advance in line-of-battle order very difficult. The division deployed on the range of hills to the south of Zblow, under a severe shelling from the enemy's batteries.

The 6th Regiment rested its right wing on the village, on its left a gap was left for the 46th Regiment, and still further off the 52nd and 47th Regiments moved into the alignment. The line thus faced the Dubno wood, and the whole ground in its front was occupied by the troops of the 9th Division.

For this reason General Von Tiedemann resumed the flank march to the right with the 19th Brigade. When his men had laid down their knapsacks, he led the 6th Regiment through Zblow towards Zlitsch, which was already occupied by Prussian troops, and then formed the brigade in two lines at the southernmost outlet of the village. The 46th Regiment was brought to the same spot, straight across country. In the rear of the brigade Prince Albrecht's brigade of Cuirassiers was stationed, whose battery of Horse Artillery was firing on the enemy beyond the Aupa.

Before coming into action, the 20th Brigade now had to pass the wood. The men laid down their knapsacks. the battalions increased their intervals, and threw out a line of skirmishers, which General Wittich led forward in the direction of the ranger's house. General Steinmetz ordered the 52nd Regiment to support the attack on the enemy's left wing, whilst the 47th Regiment was directed against his right.

The Reserve Artillery had been blocked up in the street of Wysokow until past 11 o'clock. As soon as the advance of the Infantry left the passage free, Lieutenant-Colonel Von Kameke sent the rifled batteries ahead of the Horse Artillery batteries that had hitherto been in the front, and reached 12.30 P.M. Kleny at half-past 12 o'clock, where they took up a position with the two 4-pounder and two 6-pounder batteries of the 2nd Field Artillery Division (Abtheilung) on the east side of the village. It has already been mentioned that two rifled batteries, originally attached to General Loewenfeld's command, had moved round the south side of Dubno, on their march from Starkoc. They now took up a position between this place and Kleney, and the 6-pounder battery behind the latter village.

The Austrian line of Artillery near Skalitz was still above 3,000 paces distant. The Prussian Horse Artillery batteries were, therefore, left en *échelon* further to the rear. In front of Kleny, as has been stated already, the batteries of Captain Troilo and Wahlen-Jürgass (the 1st 6-pounder and 2nd 4-pounder batteries) had for some time sustained an unequal combat against the Austrian guns.

A fierce field of Artillery now commenced on either side. In spite of the great distance, the Austrian 8-pounders fired with great accuracy. Numerous shells fell among the Prussian batteries and their ammunition wagons, but being fired at a great elevation, they sank deep into the soft ground, very often without bursting. Kleny took fire, and when the two batteries were afterwards obliged to withdraw further to the rear, they had to pass the blazing village at a gallop. There were now nine Prussian batteries assembled at the spot, and their fire was so effective that the Austrian batteries on the north of Skalitz were soon silenced, and the fire of those on the south of the town perceptibly subdued.

Three Austrian battalions (probably part of General Schultz's brigade) issued from the wood south of Skalitz, and essayed another attack on the Prussian left wing, but did not get within range of the Infantry; they were beaten back by the fire of the batteries of Kleny, which kept up their fire until two o'clock.

About this time the Austrians seem to have renounced all hope of holding their position on the left bank of the Aupa. Though with diminished forces, but with all the more obstinacy, they still disputed every inch of ground to cover their retreat. Much now depended on gaining possession of Skalitz itself.

The massive buildings of the railway station in front of the town formed a very strong position, which was occupied by General Fragnern's brigade and the 31st Battalion of Rifles. A breastwork of beams and railway sleepers had been constructed on the embankment, and afforded admirable shelter to the Austrian skirmishers.

The same troops that had repulsed the attack of Colonel Kreyssern's brigade had gained ground immediately afterwards. The 6th and 7th companies of the 38th Regiment were within 500 paces of the railway station, where a ditch afforded them some shelter from the Austrian fire. The 8th Company filled up the gap between these companies and Captain Schreiner's half-battalion, which advanced further to the left; the other half battalions had also pushed forward, with the exception of Captain Necker's, which General Steinmetz held back in order to have some reserve in case of a repulse. The losses at this spot were not inconsiderable, but the whole intervening space between the high-road and the railway was cleared of the enemy.

As the 3rd 6-pounder battery had already advanced from the Artillery position behind Kleny, Colonel Von Voigts-Rhetz requested Captain Aust to aid him in the attack he proposed making. Immediately acceding to this request, the battery moved to the extreme left, under cover of the 4th Dragoon Regiment, which was just then trotting past towards Spitta, and took up a position to the north of the Rowensko pond. Captain Von der Mülbe's half-battalion covered the battery, which opened fire with shell at 1,600 paces distance, on a battery posted on the heights southward of Skalitz, that had hitherto harassed the Infantry during its advance.

General Wittich now personally led forward the 47th Regiment, which was as yet wholly intact. He issued out of the wood and reached the high road at the spot where Colonel Kreyssern's attack had shortly before been beaten off. The regiment crossed the open country in two lines, with skirmishers in front, and with its band playing. The movement was executed with the greatest order, and us steadily as if on parade. All the troops that had hitherto been fighting in detached groups joined in the attack, among others the 1st Company of the Rifle Battalion that had come up from the extreme right. One half-battalion was sent towards Spitta. The fire was murderous; 30 paces from the enemy the whole colour-guard party of the 47th Regiment was struck down. Captain Vellay seized the colours, and the railway embankment was carried on all points almost at the same moment; but a fierce struggle still raged among the buildings of the railway station, from the windows of which the Austrian riflemen kept up a deadly fire. Attack and defence were equally obstinate, but at last the Austrians succumbed. Only seven officers and 150 men fell living into the hands of the victors. General Fragnern lost his life.

In the moment when the Prussian left wing reached the viaduct, a squadron of Austrian Lancers charged over the railway with great bravery, but the Infantry and the Rifle company delivered their fire so steadily, and with such effect, that the daring Lancers only got within 30 paces of them. The squadron retreated with severe loss.

The 38th Regiment took an active part in this engagement, by storming the massive buildings further to the right, where the high road crosses the railway, as well as the custom-house, in which 150 men were made prisoners.

Simultaneously with the attack on the railway station, the 6th Regiment advanced from Zlitsch, It has been already mentioned that the 24th Austrian Rifle Battalion had established itself among bushes and iu rifle pits on the heights between the Zlitsch-Skalitz road and the Aupa, on the right bank of which other Austrian detachments were stationed. In face of the fire of these troops, and the battery near Skalitz, Lieutenant-Colonel Scheffler led his regiment against this position, Captain Unruhe's half-battalion of the 7th Regiment joined in the attack. The skirmishers advanced to within 30 paces of the enemy, who seemed inclined to hold his ground, but then suddenly fled to the Aupa, leaving one officer and 90 men in the hands of the Prussians.

As the further advance towards Skalitz was much harassed by the enemy's flank fire from the other bank of the Aupa, strong bodies of skirmishers were sent down to the river side. The march on Skalitz was then resumed. The 52nd Regiment came out of the wood, and joined the left wing of the 6th Regiment, the 46th followed as reserve.

The fire of the great Prussian battery at Kleny was much hindered by the smoke of the burning village, and was masked by the advancing troops, besides which the enemy's fire had almost ceased to be directed upon this spot. Lieutenant-Colonel Von Kameke, therefore, had already moved his battery further forward, when he was ordered by General Steinmetz to shell Skalitz. The two Horse Artillery batteries took post on the heights to the north of Skalitz, and opened fire on the town; they were joined by several rifled batteries. One battery went more to the left, to the south-west of the station, where it could harass the enemy's retreat.

3 P.M. It may have been about three o'clock when General Steinmetz proceeded to storm Skalitz. On the north-east side of the town the 6th and 52nd Regiments advanced; along the high road half-battalions of the 37th, 7th, and 58th Regiments; from the railway station the 47th Regiment, all the rest followed.

It is very difficult to say which of so many troops first entered the town. The 6th Regiment and Captain Unruhe's half-battalion stormed the mills on the Aupa. They were fired on by two guns from the other side of the river; of these Captain Von Plötz and Lieutenant Von Brun captured one, the other escaped. The houses in the town were still obstinately defended, they had to be stormed singly, in which the pioneers were of great service. Numerous prisoners fell into the hands of the victors. General Wittich put himself at the head of the 1st and 4th Companies of the 47th Regiment, and was the first to reach the market place, where the companies were met by a volley of Infantry, and were, moreover, under the fire of their own artillery, they therefore turned towards the bridge over the Aupa, which they crossed, and then pushed on to the western outlet of the town. The companies of the 5th Rifle Battalion, which had also advanced on the right bank of the river, met at the cemetery of the town. They followed the enemy as far as Zagezd, where he again attempted to make stand in the last buildings of the village, but was dislodged with a loss of several prisoners. Lieutenant-Colonel Von Kameke followed up the enemy's retreat by the fire of 48 rifled guns, which he brought up in place of the Horse Artillery batteries. The Austrian Artillery returned the fire from a position 3,000 paces north-westward of Skalitz, but the firing very soon died away on both sides, the action was at an end, and the troops were drawn out of the town to be re-formed.

The Vth Corps bivouacked south-eastward of Skalitz. General Von Hoffmann, who had brought up his brigade as soon as his position near Wysokow became unnecessary, threw out a line of outposts towards Josephstadt, but had first to dislodge the Austrian 31st Rifle Battalion from Rzikow. By eight o'clock the 7th Company of the 51st Regiment occupied the village and bridge over the Aupa; the pickets of the 11th and 12th companies were advanced as far as Zesenitz.

To cover the rear of the corps towards Neustadt, the 2nd Battalion of the 47th Regiment, and two squadrons of the 4th Dragoons were sent back to Kleny, where they posted pickets beyond the village.

On the right bank of the Aupa Lieutenant-Colonel Von Blumenthal guarded the country towards Jaromir with the 52nd Regiment, the 1st Lancers, and one battery. The factory on the Aupa south of the town was held by the 5th, Zagezd by the 6th and 8th, and the cemetery in Klein-Skalitz by the 7th companies. At night the 2nd company was doubled in between the two latter points. Pickets were posted on all the roads, and extended in a semicircle, both flanks leaning on the Aupa, above and below the town.

The head-quarters of the corps were established in Skalitz, which was occupied by the 7th Regiment. Prince Albrecht's brigade returned to Kosteletz.

In the course of the afternoon and the evening the VIth Austrian Corps retreated to Lanzow, the VIIIth to Salney, beyond the Elbe; only the IVth Corps and the 1st Reserve Cavalry Division still remained on the left bank of the river in their bivouac at Dolan; the IIIrd Corps was at Miletin. The IInd Corps and the 2nd Light Cavalry Division reached the neighbourhood of Josephstadt, the 2nd Reserve Cavalry Division Holohlaw, the 3rd Smiritz.

The day had cost some of the troops very heavy losses. The greatest had been suffered by the 2nd Battalion of the 7th Regiment, which lost 14 officers and 292 men; more than 33 per cent. of its whole strength were killed or wounded. Next in the list comes the 1st Battalion of the 38th Regiment, with four officers and 174 men, or 20 per cent. The four companies of the 58th Regiment, the only ones that were engaged in a hand-to-hand combat, lost 11 officers, and 154 men, i.e., 25 per cent.

The following is a detail list of the casualties:—

| | Killed. | | Wounded. | | Missing. | | Total. | |
|---|---|---|---|---|---|---|---|---|
| | Officers. | Men. | Officers. | Men. | Officers. | Men. | Officers. | Men. |
| Vth Corps d'Armée : | | | | | | | | |
| 9th Division— | | | | | | | | |
| Staff .. .. .. | .. | .. | 1 | .. | .. | .. | 1 | .. |
| 37th Regiment .. .. | 1 | 31 | 4 | 99 | .. | .. | 5 | 130 |
| 58th ,, .. .. | 3 | 32 | 8 | 113 | .. | 1 | 11 | 146 |
| 7th ,, .. .. | 6 | 92 | 17 | 336 | .. | 5 | 23 | 463 |
| 5th Rifle Battalion .. | .. | 3 | .. | 6 | .. | .. | .. | 9 |
| 10th Division— | | | | | | | | |
| Staff of 20th Infantry | | | | | | | | |
| Brigade .. .. | .. | .. | 1 | .. | .. | .. | 1 | .. |
| 6th Regiment .. .. | 1 | 17 | 3 | 63 | .. | .. | 4 | 80 |
| 46th ,, .. .. | .. | 1 | .. | 4 | .. | .. | .. | 5 |
| 47th ,, .. .. | 1 | 25 | 3 | 74 | .. | 3 | 4 | 102 |
| 52nd ,, .. .. | .. | 6 | 2 | 30 | .. | 2 | 2 | 38 |
| 5th Field Artillery | | | | | | | | |
| Regiment .. .. | .. | .. | .. | 5 | .. | 5 | .. | 5 |
| General Hoffmann's | | | | | | | | |
| Brigade— | | | | | | | | |
| 38th Regiment .. .. | 5 | 72 | 6 | 251 | .. | 2 | 11 | 325 |
| Total .. .. | 17 | 279 | 45 | 981 | .. | 18 | 62 | 1,303 |

Among the wounded was the Commander of the 38th Regiment.

The Austrian losses are shown in the accounts published by their military journals. Two Commanders of Brigades, General Von Fragnern and Colonel Von Kreyssern, were killed.

The following casualties among the officers are known :—

| | Killed. | Wounded or Missing. |
|---|---|---|
| 21st Regiment (Reischach) .. | 4 | 29 |
| 32nd ,, (d'Este) .. .. | 6 | 19 |
| 15th ,, (Nassau) .. .. | 13 | 17 |
| 77th ,, (Salvator) | 13 | 29 |
| 5th Field Rifle Battalion.. .. | 4 | 15 |
| 24th ,, ,, .. .. | 1 | 9 |
| 31st ,, ,, .. .. | .. | 6 |
| 9th Field Artillery Regiment .. | .. | 2 |
| 3rd Lancer Regiment .. .. | .. | 2 |
| Total .. .. .. | 41 | 128 |

Corresponding accounts of the other regiments have not been made known.

The losses of rank and file are stated in Hirtenfeld's calendar as follows :—

N.º 6.

POSITION OF BOTH ARMIES ON THE EVENING OF THE 28.ᵀᴴ JUNE.

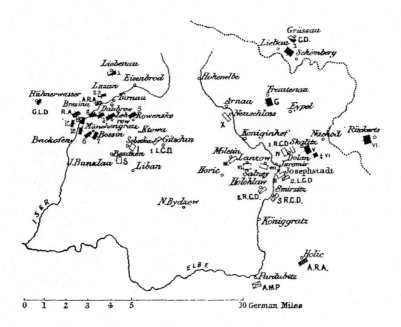

|  | Killed. | Wounded. | Missing. | Total. |
|---|---|---|---|---|
|  | Men. | Men. | Men. | Men. |
| Brigade Fragnern— |  |  |  |  |
| 5th Rifle Battalion .. .. | 119 | 113 | 285 | 517 |
| 15th Regiment.. .. .. | 329 | 141 | 372 | 842 |
| 77th ,, .. .. | 376 | 366 | 721 | 1,463 |
| Brigade Schulz— |  |  |  |  |
| 31st Rifle Battalion .. .. | 15 | 40 | 13 | 68 |
| 8th Regiment .. .. .. | 1 | 10 | 7 | 18 |
| 74th ,, .. .. | 2 | 13 | 25 | 40 |
| Brigade Von Kreyssern— |  |  |  |  |
| 24th Rifle Battalion .. .. | 109 | 7 | 318 | 464 |
| 21st Regiment.. .. .. | 151 | 380 | 647 | 1,178 |
| 32nd ,, .. .. | 92 | 252 | 335 | 79 |
| 4th Battalion 36th Regiment (Deg- |  |  |  |  |
| enfeld) .. .. .. .. | 12 | 31 | 40 | 83 |
| 4th Battalion 75th Regiment |  |  |  |  |
| (Creneville) .. .. | 17 | 19 | 66 | 402 |
| Archduke Charles' Lancers .. | 11 | .. | 30 | 41 |
| Artillery .. .. .. .. | 16 | 57 | 31 | 104 |
| Total.. .. .. | 1,250 | 1,429 | 3,220 | 5,899 |

2,500 of these were made prisoners. The trophies of the day were seven guns, of which five were captured by the 1st battalion, in company with a skirmishing party of the 2nd Battalion of the 38th Regiment, and a peloton of the 7th Regiment, the sixth gun by detachments of the 6th and 7th Regiments, the seventh was found on the field.

The Crown Prince had gone early in the morning from Hronow to the heights of Kosteletz, where the Reserve Artillery of the Corps of Guards was stationed; after the action he moved his head-quarters to Eypel, but went himself in the course of the night to Trautenau. Whilst he was still at Kosteletz, orders were despatched at 11 o'clock A.M. to the VIth Corps, which was to reach Rückerts and Alt Heyde in the course of the day, to push on towards Nachod, in order to reinforce the Vth Corps, and to cover the left flank of the Army. The corps was now placed under the command of General Von Steinmetz.

The positions of all corps of both armies is shown in the accompanying sketch. Sketch No. 6.

## The 29th of June.

The information received at his Majesty's head-quarters proved beyond doubt that the bulk of the Austrian forces could not have reached the Iser. The actions in which the IInd Army had been engaged plainly showed that the Xth, IVth, VIth, and VIIIth Corps were opposed to it, the IInd Corps was known to be still further to the rear, so that the IIIrd Corps, the position of which was not yet known, was the only one that could have joined Count Clam.

These facts, as well as accounts of the Crown Prince's progress, were telegraphed to the head-quarters of the Ist Army at noon of the 28th and early on the 29th.

The heads of both armies in Ktowa and Burkersdorf were only 27 miles apart; still it would have been highly dangerous for the IInd Army to cross the Elbe as long as such considerable hostile forces were in its front and flank, besides which the Ist and VIth Corps were still as far back as Liebau and Lewin. It was, therefore, deemed imperative that the Ist Army should proceed beyond the originally appointed rendezvous, and the following telegram was despatched from Berlin on the 29th:—

> "His Majesty expects that a speedy advance of the Ist "Army will disengage the IInd Army, which, notwith- "standing a series of successful actions, is still mo- "mentarily in a precarious situation."

Prince Frederick Charles had already resolved to push the 5th Division and part of the IInd Corps forward beyond Gitschin to Aulibitz on the 29th. The command of these troops was given to Lieutenant-General Von Schmidt; the other divisions were to follow as soon as possible.

The dispositions for this march were as follows :—

> "1. General Von Schmidt will move forward with the 3rd "Division (Von Werder), will take Podkost and "Sobotka, and march on Gitschin, which will probably "be already in the hands of General Tümpling's "Division. Gitschin must be occupied to-day without "fail. General Von Herwarth's Division will also march "on Gitschin, by way of Libun, and General Alvens- "leben's Cavalry Division will proceed in the same "direction. One battalion must be left in Turnau, "where it will relieve the battalion of General Fran- "secky's Division, which will then rejoin its division.

> "2. General Von Tümpling's Division is hereby instructed "to start immediately and to seize on Gitschin, where "it will establish itself, and push forward an advanced "guard. General Von Werder's Division of the IInd "Corps will set off at 12 o'clock, and march by Sobotka "on Gitschin, where it will arrive in the course of the "day. General Von Fransecky's Division will follow "General Von Werder, and will, if possible, reach "Podhrad. General Von Herwarth's Division and the "Cavalry Division of Von Alvensleben will both follow "General Von Tümpling, by way of Turnau, in the "course of the day.

> "3. General Von Manstein's Division will give the men a "meal in their present bivouacs, and will then so time "its march as to reach Ober-Bautzen by half-past 8 "o'clock; it will push forward an advanced guard "towards Jung-Bunzlau. The division will guard the

"reserve artillery of the IIIrd and IVth Corps, which "remains between Solletz and Bratritz (westwards of "Ober-Bautzen).

"4. General Von Fransecky's Division will march by way "of Ober-Bautzen and Sobotka, and will attempt to "cut off all troops of the enemy retreating by way of "Podkost; the division will eventually assist General "Von Werder's attack, and will follow the division "towards Gitschin, if possible, as far as Podhrad.

"5. General Von Horn's Division will set off this evening, "so that its last troops reach Unter Bautzen by "8 o'clock, in order that General Von Manstein's "Division, which is to reach Ober-Bautzen at half-"past 8, may find the roads leading thither perfectly "free. The division will provide for its own security "towards the south and Jung-Bunzlau.

"6. The Cavalry Corps will detach the Division Von Alvens-"leben to follow General Von Herwarth's Division by "way of Turnau—Gitschin. General Von Hann's "Division will follow General Von Manstein's Division "in the course of the day; the latter will be ordered "to march on Ober-Bautzen.

"7. The Reserve Artillery of the Army will set off this "evening, and join General Von Manstein's Division; "it will remain on the Fürstenbrück-Ober-Bautzen road "between Solletz and Bratritz.

"8. Head-quarters will move to Ober-Bautzen.
                    (Signed)      "FREDERICK CHARLES."
" Münchengrätz, June 29, 1866, 9 a.m.

In accordance with these orders, the leading divisions of the Army started at mid-day and made a long march, thus enabling the other divisions to follow in the evening on the same roads. On the other hand, no space was left for the Army of the Elbe to follow immediately, it was therefore obliged to make a detour to the right; but, as reports arrived, stating the enemy to have fallen back from Jung-Bunzlau to Gitschin during the night, the 15th Division only marched on the left bank of the Iser as far as Backofen on the evening of the 29th; the 16th on the right bank to Kleina-Wiesel, where it crossed the river. The 14th Division and General Von Schöler's advanced guard stopped at Münchengrätz; the Division of Guard-Landwehr moved up to Kloster.

On this day it became evident with what great difficulty the moving of large masses of troops is attended when they are once assembled. It is obvious how important it is to keep an army in separate columns as long as possible. The narrower the front of an army becomes, the more the number of roads available for its march diminishes, whilst not only does the number of the *échelons* marching on them increase, but the length of the different columns also, until they take up the ground of whole days' marches. The timely concentration of an army for decisive action depends as much on its depth as on the breadth of its front.

The orders issued by Feldzeugmeister Benedek on the 29th of June seem to have been founded on the supposition that he would be able to assemble his main forces in front of Joseph-stadt by the 30th, and that they would then be available for an offensive movement northwards. Under this presumption the IIIrd Austrian Corps was to advance to Gitschin on the 29th; the 3rd Reserve Cavalry Division to Horsitz; four other corps probably the IInd, VIth, VIIIth, and Xth, were to follow on the 30th, in the direction of Lomnitz and Turnau.

*One single corps* on the Upper Elbe must have been deemed sufficient to cover the right flank of this offensive movement, and the engagements of Trautenau, Nachod, and Skalitz do not yet seem to have convinced the Feldzeugmeister that it was the advance of a whole army that must there be checked. The first, but serious, reverses of the Austrian arms as yet produced no change in this plan of operation. The Commander-in-Chief is said to have telegraphed to Vienna as late as the 28th that he was only opposed to inconsiderable forces, and should continue the intended offensive movement of his main forces against Prince Frederick Charles.

Corresponding orders had been issued, and were being carried out. We shall soon see, however, what a different view of the situation dire necessity forced the Austrian head-quarters to take in the course of the morning of the 29th.

## ACTION OF GITSCHIN.

### 29TH JUNE.

On the 29th the Ist Austrian Corps and General Edel-sheim's Cavalry Division resumed their march to join the main army. They reached the neighbourhood of Gitschin at 9 A.M., and took up a position $2\frac{1}{2}$ miles northwards of the town. *à cheval* of the Turnau road.

On the heights of Brada, which reach close up to the west side of the road, Colonel Poschacher's Brigade was posted; General Leiningen's Brigade was behind it. General Piret's Brigade was stationed on the right, at Markt-Eisenstädt; Colonel Abele's on the left, at Prachow; whilst General Ringelsheim's Brigade, reinforced by the 2nd Regiment of Hussars (Nicolaus) and three squadrons of the 3rd Saxon "Reiter" Regiment, held the Sobotka-Gitschin road, near Lochow, about two miles farther west. General Edelsheim's Cavalry Division and the Reserve Artillery of the Corps stood at Diletz, between the two Brigades Poschacher and Piret, and pushed forward detachments towards Libun.

The Saxon Army had started from the neighbourhood of Unter Bautzen at 3 A.M.: General Schimpff's Division marched to Jicinowes (4½ miles southward of Gitschin); General Stieglitz's Division and the Reserve Artillery arrived at Podhrad in the course of the morning, and then bivouacked south-westward of Gitschin at Brezina and Wolkschitz. The " Reiter " Division marched with the Austrian Corps from Sobotka to Gitschin, and bivouacked to the south of the town, at Staremjesto.

The troops were excessively fatigued, both with the shortness of their night's rest and the heat of the day. The Crown Prince went into Gitschin in the course of the morning to confer with Count Clam Gallas. Whilst there, Feldzeugmeister Benedek's despatch arrived, announcing the approaching arrival of the IIIrd Corps d'Armée in the course of the 29th and the offensive movement of the main army on Turnau, the idea of which had, however, at that moment been already relinquished. It was, in consequence, resolved to accept battle if the enemy advanced still further to-day. In case an attack took place on the Turnau road, a Saxon brigade of Infantry was to advance to Diletz, and a second one take post behind it as reserve.

At half-past one o'clock General Von Tümpling left Rovensko. His line of march brought him opposite to the enemy's main force, with which he came in contact shortly after 3 o'clock. General Von Werder's Division left Zehrow as early as 12, but did not meet with the enemy until half-past 5.

The wooded rocks of Prywicin separate the roads leading from Turnau and Sobotka to Gitschin, so that two perfectly isolated actions were fought, in which no mutual assistance was possible; indeed, each of the two Prussian Divisions thought itself to be the only one engaged on this day.

The other divisions of the Ist Army were too far distant to take any part in the action.

---

## 1. ACTION OF THE 5th DIVISION.

### (LIEUTENANT-GENERAL VON TÜMPLING).*

THE Advanced Guard of the 5th Division reached Ober-Knisnitz at half-past 3 o'clock, after having previously driven an Austrian squadron back from Libun. An Austrian battery was seen beyond the village, and the Fusilier Battalion of the Prussian 8th Regiment advanced through the two other battalions of the regiment northwards of the place. The enemy opened a sharp fire of shells, which set fire to the village. Lieutenant-General Von Tümpling rode forward to reconnoitre the Austrian position, whereby his orderly officer was killed at his side. Several Austrian batteries were visible westward of Diletz, and others further to the right, on the slope of the

---

* *Vide* Order of Battle, Appendix XVII.

Prywicin, as well as a rocket battery on the heights of Brada; Podulsch and Klein-Ginolitz seemed to be occupied by Infantry.

The 4-pounder battery, No. 5, of the Advanced Guard galloped through the burning village, and unlimbered 200 paces to the south-east, in spite of the enemy's fire. At 4 o'clock, the other battery of the Advanced Guard (the 1st 4-pounder) came up to the same spot.

The 9th and 10th Companies of the 8th Regiment continued their march on the high-road and entered Ginolitz, from whence they kept up a skirmishing fire with detachments of the 30th Austrian Regiment (Martini), which were posted on the other side of the meadows in Klein-Ginolitz and in the skirts of the wood beyond.

The left wing of the Austrian position was almost inaccessible from the nature of the rocky and wooded mountains. In the centre four Horse Artillery batteries were in position westward of Diletz, a rocket battery on the Brada-Berg, and an 8-pounder battery on the slope of the hill on a clearing behind Podulsch. The fire of these batteries swept the whole country in front of the line, and commanded all approaches in this direction. With a correct *coup d'œil*, General Tümpling determined to attack the enemy's right wing—a movement which at the same time most effectually threatened the communications of the Austrian Ist Corps with its main army. He issued the following orders on the spot :—

> " The church steeple of Gitschin will be taken as " general *point de vue* and ultimate rendezvous of all the " troops. The artillery of the main body will move for- " ward at a trot, and join the artillery of the advanced " guard, which is already engaged. The Fusilier bat- " talions of the 12th and 48th Regiments will march " along the valley of the Cydlina, by Zames and Diletz. " The 9th Infantry Brigade and the 3rd Regiment of " Lancers will follow. The 18th Regiment will follow " the Fusilier companies of the 8th Regiment in the " direction of the wood. The 12th Regiment will march " to Ober-Kniznitz and form the reserve."

The artillery of the main body, that was sent forwards to the head of the division, came up there about half-past 4 o'clock. The first 6-pounder battery opened fire immediately, but the distance was too great for the fourth 12-pounder battery : it was therefore for the present kept back in a sheltered position eastwards of Kniznitz.

At first only three companies of the two Fusilier battalions could commence the march on Zames, for Austrian Cavalry appeared near Podulsch, and made it necessary to retain the other companies on the plateau as covering for the artillery. The former three companies were commanded by Major des Barres. In the meantime General Schimmelmann's Brigade had turned off from the high road at Libun and marched to Cydlina. On arriving there the 1st Battalion of the 48th Regiment relieved the Fusilier companies on the plateau, which now followed Major des Barres.

About the same time General Kamiensky's Brigade reached Libun, but its further progress was much impeded by the fire of the Austrian Artillery. The 8-pounder battery on the Brada-Berg had indeed been silenced, but the enemy unmasked a 4-pounder battery in an entrenchment on the heights, by the side of the rocket battery, where it had hitherto been concealed by stems of trees. In like manner still more batteries opened fire from the hills to the south of Diletz. It was necessary to dislodge the enemy from Podulsch before the Prussian Artillery could get within effective range of the Austrian line. General Tümpling therefore gave orders to the 1st Battalion of the 48th Regiment, which was guarding the Artillery, to seize on the village.

Major des Barres had already reached Zames. Some companies of the Austrian 45th Regiment (Sigismund) advanced from the direction of Eisenstadtl, and attempted to retake the village, but they were too late, and were beaten off with loss, as was also the charge of a squadron of Lancers.

In spite of the enemy's fire, which was very severe on this wing (Cydlina and Bresca* were set on fire by it), the other Fusilier companies succeeded in rejoining Major des Barres in Zames; their march was in some degree sheltered by the valley of the stream. They were soon followed by the 2nd Battalion of the 48th Regiment, the 5th Company of which now took part in the attack on Podulsch.

This village was held by a company of the Austrian 34th Regiment (King of Prussia), and a company of the 18th Rifle Battalion, both belonging to General Poschacher's Brigade. The village itself was carried by the first assault, not so however a group of detached buildings to the south-west of the high road, which here crossed some swampy meadows at the foot of the mountain. Major Spieker was obliged to confine himself to keeping up a skirmishing fire, which cost the five companies of the 48th Regiment considerable loss. The 1st and 2nd Battalions of the 48th Regiment took post to the north of Podulsch.

In the meantime General Von Kamiensky had detached a battalion of the 18th Regiment from Libun towards Jawornitz, where the enemy occupied the wooded slopes behind the village: thus by half-past 5 the division was engaged at Zames, Podulsch, Ginolitz, and Jawornitz.

After a slight struggle the 1st Battalion of the 18th Regiment gained possession of the last-named village and the hill beyond it; but then came upon a swampy strip of meadow land on this side of the rocky plateau, which was held by the

---

* There are two villages of the same name on the battle-field; one in the Cydlina valley, the other southwards of Libun; it is the former that is meant here.

enemy's skirmishers in force. To avoid this obstacle Colonel Von Kettler led the 2nd Battalion and three companies of the Fusilier Battalion still further to the right, to Bresca, and from there towards Prachow. This gave the whole line of attack the considerable breadth of 6,000 paces.

Colonel Abele's Brigade threw forward considerable forces to meet Colonel Kettler's threatening flank attack, and a very sharp engagement ensued amidst the rocks and trees, in which the 18th Regiment could gain ground but very slowly. Wishing to break through the enemy's strong mountain position in some part or other, General Kamiensky at last sent the two battalions of the 12th Regiment, that were destined as reserve, to Klein-Ginolitz, under the impression that these battalions were at his disposal: thus at 6 o'clock two Grenadier Battalions of the 8th Regiment were the sole reserves of the division, and this at a moment when the enemy was bringing up two fresh brigades from Gitschin.

As soon as the action began to assume greater dimensions General Stieglitz's Division at Brezina received orders to move forwards with the Saxon Reserve Artillery. This division had been in readiness at Gitschin since 6 o'clock, and reached Diletz at half-past 6.

On the part of the Prussians, nine Fusilier companies, under Lieut.-Colonel Von Gaudy, had advanced on Diletz from Zames, and two divisions of skirmishers had already entered the village. The battalions themselves were spread out in columns of companies, and had sought shelter from the enemy's fire in the undulations of the ground. In so doing they had somewhat got out of their original direction, and were not sufficiently near at hand to support the skirmishers, so that the latter were driven out of Diletz by the Saxon Brigade Crown Prince.

The latter now occupied the village with the 1st, 2nd, and 4th Battalions. The 3rd Battalion was posted behind; the 1st Battalion of Rifles to the north of the place; a rifled battery was planted on the heights northwards of Kbelnitz. The Prussian Fusilier Companies and the 11th Company of the 8th Regiment now received orders to retake the village. The 2nd Battalion of the latter regiment followed as support. The near neighbourhood of the Prussian skirmishers had already compelled the Austrian batteries near Diletz to withdraw to a position further to the rear; and Major Rüstow was now ordered by General Tümpling to move his three batteries forward, under cover of the 3rd Lancers, to a very advantageous position at the edge of the valley of the Cydlina, close to the Zames-Podulsch road. From here he could bring his fire to bear upon Diletz, and upon the enemy's artillery on the Eisen and Zehin Hills.

The assault of Diletz was preceded by a rapid fire of the Prussian Infantry. As soon as Major Von Zglinitzki gave the signal to charge on the right wing, the skirmishers, closely followed by the companies themselves, rushed upon the western

and northern skirts of the village, and entered it at the first
onset. At the same time Lieut.-Colonel Von Wulffen advanced
with the 7th and 8th Companies of the 48th Regiment from the
direction of Zames, against the Saxon Rifle Battalion outside of
the village. He was met by a galling fire from the enemy's
battalion; a shell passed through the colours of the battalion,
and both the Lieut.-Colonel and his Adjutant lost their horses.
The Saxons, who were by mistake fired on in the rear by an
Austrian Battalion on the other side of the Cydlina, were
obliged to give way.

In the village itself a protracted and fierce hand-to-hand
struggle ensued, in which the Saxons were ultimately driven
out.

During this combat Colonel Von Berger made a circuit round
the village with the 2nd Battalion of the 8th Regiment, and
dislodged the Saxon reserves behind it. Whilst he was still
engaged in this pursuit six squadrons of General Edelsheim's
Cavalry Division appeared on the high road almost in his rear.
A subdivision of the 8th Company faced about, the 6th Company wheeled to the right, the skirmishers closed up on its
flank, and the whole line opened a rapid file fire. An attempt
of the Hussars to charge in two divisions failed, with a loss of
50 men and many horses. At half-past 7 Diletz was in the
hands of the Prussians, and their fire compelled the Saxons to
fall back beyond the Cydlina with considerable loss. Their
Commander, Colonel Von Boxberg, was taken prisoner severely
wounded.

In the meantime the two Grenadier Battalions of the 12th
Regiment had taken Klein-Ginolitz, which the 1st Company
stormed at the point of the bayonet. The detachments of the
30th Austrian regiment (Martini) still held their ground, however, at the meadows beyond the village, and by degrees six
companies were brought forward against them. The latter
tried to open communication with the 18th Regiment, whose
attempt to force their way to Prachow has been already mentioned. The ground in this part of the field was very rugged,
and all view of the country shut out, so that on climbing the
rocks that opposed their progress the skirmishers frequently
found themselves face to face with their adversaries, and many
a desperate hand-to-hand fight ensued.

One of the patrols of the 18th Regiment that had been
thrown out on the right flank met men of the 14th Regiment
belonging to General Werder's Division. Although Colonel
Abele had already been obliged to detach troops against the
latter, yet his position was so strong that he could still continue to reinforce his line on the front, which was engaged with
Colonel Von Kettler.

The whole forces of the brigades of Colonel Abele and
General Poschacher had not yet been brought into action,
besides which the enemy still had his whole Cavalry and nineteen intact battalions at his disposal. For this reason General

Tümpling gave most positive orders that the engagement at Klein-Ginolitz, which had been commenced against his intention, should be broken off; and he brought up the two Grenadier Battalions of the 12th Regiment to the centre of his line, in order to form a stronger reserve, as well as to be able to strike a decisive blow on the key of the enemy's position at Brada.

The enemy, however, was not able to make further use of his reserves, partly because the engagement on the Sobotka road had taken a turn that seriously threatened his line of retreat, and partly on account of a despatch from Feldzeugmeister Benedek, which had been received by the Crown Prince during the fight at Diletz.

As the day wore on all hopes of seeing the IIIrd Austrian Corps appear on the field, as was promised in the morning, had by degrees more and more vanished. At half-past 7 Major Count Sternberg arrived from head-quarters with instructions "to avoid any encounter with superior forces of the enemy, and "to effect a junction with the main army by Horsitz and "Miletin, the four other corps having in the meanwhile been "otherwise disposed of."

In accordance with these instructions, first the Saxon and then the Austrian Brigade of the right wing commenced their retreat.

On the extreme right the batteries on the Zehin and Eisenberg seemed in such danger, now that Diletz was in the hands of the Prussians, that General Piret determined to ensure their retreat by an offensive movement, the direction of which bid fair to render all previous successes of the 5th Division very doubtful.

Shortly after half-past 7 he debouched from Eisenstadtl with six battalions of his brigade; the 2nd and 3rd Battalions of the 18th Regiment (Grossfürst Constantin), followed by the 3rd Battalion of the 45th Regiment (Sigismund), crossed the Cydlina at the Walcha Mill, and advanced towards the north-eastern corner of Diletz; a fourth battalion with a squadron on Zames, whilst two battalions attempted to reach the latter village on the left bank of the stream.

Colonel Von Diringshofen first saw, from Diletz, the three Austrian battalions crossing at the Walcha Mill, and posted the 6th and 7th Companies of the 48th Regiment, under Lieut.-Colonel Von Wulffen, in the orchards at the north-eastern outlet of the village. As soon as the enemy had reached the brow of the hill he advanced in two lines with the band playing, and preceded by a line of skirmishers. The Prussian companies deployed in line, delivered their first volley at 350 paces, and then commenced file-firing, in which the 11th Company of the 12th Regiment, and the skirmishers of the 9th and 10th Companies of the 48th Regiment, joined. The Austrian battalions continued to advance for 200 paces farther, but their ranks thinned rapidly, and at last they fled at full speed behind the brow of the hill, pursued by Lieut.-Colonel Wulffen's two companies.

General Tümpling had also perceived the enemy's advance from Eisenstadtl, and felt obliged to send forward the last intact battalion that was at hand (the 1st Battalion of the 8th Regiment) from Lunacek to check it. Major Von Rheinbaben attempted to strike the road leading from Zames along the crest of the hill to Eisenstadtl, but fell mortally wounded; Captain Von Wussow took the command. On reaching the road the battalion was suddenly fired on in its left flank. Skirmishers of the Austrian battalion, that was marching in the hollow of the valley, had crept up the slope, but were driven back immediately. The enemy's battalion tried to establish itself in the meadows, and a squadron of Lichtenstein Hussars aided their attempt by a charge, which was repulsed by the 1st and 3rd Companies and their skirmishers, the latter remaining lying down in skirmishing order during the charge.

During this encounter the two last battalions of General Piret's brigade were seen advancing against Zames on the left bank of the Cydlina. The 4th Company and the supports of the 2nd Company went forward to meet them. At a distance of 250 paces a rapid file-fire was opened on the enemy, who wavered and fell back, which brought him within range of a subdivision of the 8th Company of the 48th Regiment, that had been sent by way of Dabrowitz to cover the left flank of the division. Whatever Austrians attempted to gain a footing at the Cydlina were driven back by the 2nd and 4th Companies.

Shortly after 8 o'clock General Piret's attack was beaten off at all points. The Saxon Division (Stieglitz) took up a fresh position at the Zehin-Berg, but the Brigade Crown Prince very soon resumed its march to Gitschin. Six batteries were planted between Kbelnitz and Rybnicek, under cover of General Edelsheim's Division, and under the protection of this position the Austrian Brigade of the left wing fell back on Gitschin.

Colonel Abele gained time for his retreat by an energetic offensive movement, which for the moment checked the troops that were pressing on him from the north. The 18th Prussian Regiment, however, soon followed through the wood, as fast as the nature of the ground and the fatigue of the men permitted, and the meadows at Klein-Ginolitz were crossed at last. The critical task of breaking off a serious and sanguinary engagement had been performed by the two Grenadier battalions of the 12th Regiment with exemplary order and steadiness. After passing Ginolitz they reached the high road by half-past 8, and General Tümpling now proceeded to attack the position of Brada-Podulsch, which, as well as the outbuildings of the latter village, was still occupied by the enemy in force, and obstinately defended. At this spot, namely, nine companies of the Austrian 34th Regiment (König Von Preussen) resolutely held their ground, as no order to retreat had reached them, when the west part of the Austrian position was evacuated. Without further delay General Tümpling now personally led the two wearied battalions, that had just come up, against this position, which he attacked from the north-east, whilst Major Spicker advanced from the north against the detached farms of Podulsch and Brada, and parts of the 18th Regiment pushed on to Brada from the west, as soon as they had gained the summit of the Prywicin. The Austrian companies were driven back, and the summit of the Brada hill gained. General Tümpling was severely wounded by a musket-shot; and General Kamiensky, who had hitherto directed the engagement of the right wing, took command of the division.

He arrived in the centre of the line about 10 o'clock, and ordered a still further advance in accordance with General Tümpling's instructions, not to rest until he had gained possession of Gitschin.

The nearest troops available for this purpose were the 1st Battalion and the 10th Company of the 18th, the two Grenadier Battalions of the 12th, the 5th Company of the 48th, and the 9th and 10th Companies of the 8th Regiment. At half-past 10 these troops set off towards Gitschin, partly by the high road and partly by way of Rybnicek. By order of General Von Schimmelmann, Lieut.-Colonel Von Gaudy advanced at the same time with the Fusilier Battalions of the 12th and 48th, and the 2nd Battalion and the 11th Company of the 8th Regiment from Diletz by way of Kbelnitz to the left bank of the Cydlina against the eastern entrance of the town. Before these troops reached Gitschin the 3rd Division had already approached the town.

## 2. ENGAGEMENT OF THE 3RD DIVISION.

### (GENERAL VON WERDER).*

About 4 o'clock, during its march from Zdiar past Sobotka, General Werder's Division heard heavy firing in a north-westerly direction; but it ceased again, so that there seemed but little hope of encountering the enemy to-day.

As soon, however, as the head of the division had passed Woharsitz, about half-past 5, it was suddenly met by a fire of shell from a battery planted about 1,000 paces to the west of Ober-Lochow; and almost at the same time reports came in from the " Spitz-Bergen," stating that the enemy's Cavalry and Infantry were in force at Unter-Lochow.

It was General Ringelsheim's Brigade and the Cavalry attached to it. These troops had reached the plateau of Woharsitz about 5 o'clock, and had taken up a position there after throwing out skirmishers beyond the meadows on the west and Unter-Lochow. Ober-Lochow was occupied by detachments of Colonel Abele's Brigade, that was stationed at Prachow. Besides the above-mentioned battery on the west side of the

---

* Order of Battle, Appendix XVIII.

village there were two others on the east side, which opened fire also as soon as General Von Werder brought the battery of the advanced guard into action at the high road in front of Woharsitz. A few rounds of Captain Gallus's battery sufficed to induce the foremost of the enemy's batteries to fall back beyond Ober-Lochow.

In the meantime the Infantry of the advanced guard formed for action opposite to the wooded hills that enclose the road between Woharsitz and Lochow, whilst the Brigade Januschowsky deployed to the south of Woharsitz.

The 7th Company of the 14th and the 11th Company of the 42nd Regiment advanced on the north side of the high road, and drove the enemy's skirmishers in the wood back to Ober-Lochow; but the village itself was occupied in such force that the companies could for the present only keep up a skirmishing fire from the skirts of the wood. The battery of Captain Gallus followed them, and took post under shelter of a projecting angle of the wood northwards of the road, from whence he fired on the hostile columns that appeared on the plateau of Wokawec.

The remaining Infantry of the advanced guard pushed forwards on the south side of the high-road. The 6th Company of the 14th Regiment dislodged the enemy from the copses in its front, then drove him out of Unter-Lochow, in company with detachments of the 42nd Regiments, and occupied the village.

The two Rifle Companies moved more to the right over the "Housa Berg," towards the St. Anna Chapel, which they reached without encountering the enemy. Somewhat later, the 1st Battalion of the 42nd Regiment, belonging to General Januschowsky's Brigade and Captain Ekensteen's Battery, which had been for a short time in action with Captain Gallus's Battery, advanced in the same direction. The battery unlimbered and opened fire on the enemy's Artillery.

In this position the troops were still separated from the enemy by a broad strip of meadow land. The slope of the plateau on the other side of this meadow was held by a strong line of the enemy's skirmishers. Repeated attempts on the part of single subdivisions to break forth from the skirts of the village were frustrated by the enemy's superior numbers. Their losses were considerable. Major Von Malotki and seven officers were killed or wounded—among them three commanders of companies.

The advanced guard was not strong enough to make any further progress, and a personal reconnaissance of Unter-Lochow convinced General Werder that it would cost a heavy sacrifice to storm the enemy's position in the front.

He therefore determined only to hold his ground at Unter-Lochow, where he reinforced the troops already engaged by the 2nd Battalion of the 2nd Regiment, and gave orders to General Januschowsky to turn the enemy's left flank by way of Wostruschno with the three other battalions of his brigade,

Captain Dewitz's Battery, and the Hussar Regiment of the Division.

7 P.M. General Von Winterfeld's Brigade reached Woharitz at 7 o'clock, and deployed on the south-west side of the village as reserve.

The right flank column could make but slow progress on account of the nature of the ground, during which time the troops that were engaged with the enemy had a hard time of it.

On the left wing, an offensive movement made by two battalions of the Austrian 35th Regiment (Khevenhüller), and about two companies of Rifles forced the two Prussian companies in front of Lochow back towards Woharsitz, and Captain Gallus was obliged to withdraw his battery to its former position.

It was originally intended that the 54th Regiment of General Winterfeld's Brigade should join the right flank detachment; but the whole brigade was now needed at this spot, and took up a position at the small wood eastward of Woharsitz.

As the enemy, however, did not push his advance any farther, General Werder ordered the two regiments to move forward on both sides of the high-road.

7.15 P.M. In the centre of the line Major Von der Osten reached Unter-Lochow at a quarter past 7, with the 2nd Battalion of the 2nd Regiment, and debouched from the north-east corner of the village in column of attack.

The fire of the enemy's artillery and skirmishers was immediately concentrated on the battalion, which suffered severely, and got into some confusion. Major Von der Osten was wounded, but Captain Von Kayserlingk succeeded in rallying the battalion on the spot and under the enemy's fire, and thus surmounted the dangerous crisis. As the ground offered no shelter whatever, the battalion lay down, and its leading ranks and skirmishers that were thrown out on both flanks, returned the enemy's fire with great coolness. A charge of Cavalry, coming from Ober-Lochow, was repulsed at a distance of 200 paces, as was also an attack of a battalion of the Austrian 42nd Regiment (König Von Hannover) and Captain Von Kayserlingk took advantage of the moment to improve his position by following the enemy. He led the battalion across the meadows up to the brow of the Wohawec plateau, and drove swarms of the enemy's skirmishers before him. By these means the battalion found at least some shelter; two subdivisions covered the left flank on the bridge on the high-road, and one was spread out in skirmishing order on the edge of the plateau, which was also reached by three other companies of the advanced guard.

8 P.M. Affairs remained in this state until 8 o'clock, when General Januschowsky arrived at Wostruschno and Captain Von Reibnitz's Rifle Company at the dyke which crosses the meadows in a northerly direction. A subdivision of the 1st Battalion of the 2nd Regiment joined the Rifles. Advancing still farther,

the latter had the opportunity of firing on a Cavalry brigade of the enemy, and forcing it to retire behind Wohawec. Almost immediately afterwards, however, whilst passing a hollow way, they were themselves driven by detachments of the Austrian 26th Rifle Battalion that appeared on the edge of the ravine above them. At the same time, Ringelsheim brought the Austrian 73rd Regiment König Von Würtemberg) into the foremost line, and advanced upon Unter-Lochow. Captain Von Kayserlingk immediately ascended the summit of the plateau, threw himself upon the two right flank battalions of the enemy, and drove them back by the file fire of his battalion. The left flank column was crushed by the fire of the other detachments that were established on the edge of the plateau; at the same time Captain Von Reibnitz's Riflemen faced to the front again on the southern edge of the plateau, and forced the Austrian Rifle Battalion to retreat.

In all probability this offensive movement of the enemy, 9 P.M. which ended with heavy loss, was only undertaken to gain time for his retreat, which was already determined upon.

Capt. Kayserlingk followed without delay towards Wohawec, and again repulsed a charge of Cavalry, but was now compelled to give his utterly exhausted battalion some rest.

Wohawec was set on fire by Captain Ekensteen's Battery, and then soon taken by the 1st Battalion of the 2nd Regiment, after which it was occupied by the 2nd Battalion of the 42nd Regiment. The Fusilier battalion of the regiment was posted in the hollow way to the east of the village. Captain Dewitz's Battery exchanged a few shots with the Artillery that covered the enemy's retreat, but could not reach his Infantry. Large bodies of Cavalry were seen near Gitschin, but kept out of range.

About 9 o'clock, General Winterfeld also arrived at Wohawec. The enemy's skirmishers that opposed his march northwards of the high-road were driven back, and Ober-Lochow occupied by the skirmishers of the 11th and 12th Companies of the 54th Regiment. The 1st Battalion of the 14th Regiment advanced on the extreme left of the Brigade; near Prachow its four companies came within range of some of Colonel Abele's Brigade during the retreat of the latter.

All the troops were much fatigued, and darkness had set in, so that the enemy was not pursued any further; but, as there was no water in the immediate neighbourhood, Lieutenant-General Schmidt determined to push on to Gitschin.

At half-past 9, therefore, the march was resumed on the 9.30 P.M. high-road, the 1st Squadron of the Hussars and the 2nd Battalion of the 2nd and 52nd Regiments forming the advanced guard.

General Schmidt himself accompanied the leading files and was fired on from a detached building on this side of the town. A considerable body of the 33rd Austrian Regiment (Count Giulay), just then retiring from Holin, surrendered to Major

L

Voss's Battalion after a few shots. Short as it was, this encounter caused some delay, so that the head of the division 10.30 P.M. did not reach Gitschin till half-past 10 o'clock.

---

### 3. OCCUPATION OF GITSCHIN.

As soon as the advance of the 3rd Prussian Division forced General Ringelsheim's Brigade to retreat, the Austrian and Saxon position northward of Gitschin became untenable. All troops that were still on the right bank of the Cydlina were forced to retreat, and the Saxon "Leib Brigade" were ordered to occupy Gitschin as rear-guard. The head-quarters of the corps also remained in the town. The Saxon "Reiter Brigade" was moved from Staremjesto close up to the town, and the "Weisse-Mühle," was occupied by a battalion of the 36th Regiment (Khevenhüller), in order to cover the retreat of two battalions of the 33rd Regiment (Giulay) that were still to the rear.

In the meantime, both Prussian divisions were drawing near Gitschin on the Turnau and Sobotka roads. On reaching the west entrance of the town at half-past 10, General Werder's advanced guard found the town still unoccupied, but at the same moment the Saxon "Leib Brigade" arrived from the "Zehin Berg" at the northern entrance on the other side of the Cydlina, and Major Stölting's Battalion encountered the 14th Saxon Battalion on the spacious market-place. The Prussian Battalion was at the same time fired upon from the houses, and compelled to retreat to the bridge at the entrance of the town. In order to disengage any men that might have been cut off, the battalion once more pressed forward towards the market-place, but the heavy fire that was kept up from the houses proved that the town was occupied in force, and General Werder recalled the battalion. By orders of General Schmidt the division bivouacked 1,000 paces westward of the town; it was covered by Major Voss's Battalion, which was spread out in columns of companies.

At the same moment when Major Stölting's Battalion must entered the town the head of the 5th Division was drawing near Kbelnitz, where the 1st Battalion of the 18th Regiment surprised and captured a picket of the enemy. Numerous stragglers of the 33rd Regiment (Giulay) fell into the hands of the battalion in the swampy meadows which extend from the Cydlina to the high-road. On reaching the entrance of the town, however, the Prussians were met by the fire of the Saxon troops.

Seeing the 3rd Division in bivouac before the west entrance of Gitschin, General Von Kamiensky also refrained from attacking the town until the flank movement of Lieutenant-Colonel Von Gaudy should have come into play. The latter crossed the Cydlina near the "Weisse Mühle," where the 9th Company of the 48th Regiment came upon the above-mentioned Austrian battalion of the Khevenhüller Regiment. The 10th Company of the Prussian 48th and the 11th of the 8th Regiment came up, and all three companies charged the Austrians with the bayonet, and drove them back. The "Khevenhüller" Battalion got entangled in a swamp, and 1 Lieutenant-Colonel, 6 officers, and 478 men were taken prisoners, after a few shots.

The Fusilier Battalion of the 12th Regiment now reached the "Jesuiten Kloster" an extensive building at the entrance of the town, without meeting any further resistance. On emerging from these buildings it only encountered the rear-guard of the "Leib Brigade," the 4th Saxon Rifle Battalion; the brigade itself had left the town already.

All outlets of the town were immediately occupied, and six companies stationed in the market-place as reserve. On searching the town several officers and about 300 Austrians and Saxons, besides 4,500 wounded, were made prisoners.

As soon as General Kamiensky was informed of the occupation of Gitschin, the main body of the 5th Division bivouacked between Podulsch and Kbelnitz. Some parts of both divisions still remained on the spots where they were at the end of the engagement.

The entrance of the Prussians into Gitschin after midnight was a serious affair for the enemy, as his head-quarters were disturbed in despatching the orders for the next day; the troops in consequence, received them either too late, or not at all; many Commanders retreated at their own discretion, and those troops that were south-west of Gitschin could no longer reach the Miletin road. Order was not re-established among the troops of the Austrian Ist Corps until the 2nd of July, in front of Königgrätz, whereas the Saxons succeeded in keeping together and preserving their order and readiness for action even under the trying circumstances of this nocturnal retreat.

How great the exertions of this day were is shown by the fact that two Prussian officers fell dead from sheer exhaustion during the action.

The Prussian losses on the 29th were—

1. Of the 5th Division.

| | Killed. | | Wounded. | | Missing. | | Total. | |
|---|---|---|---|---|---|---|---|---|
| | Officers. | Men. | Officers. | Men. | Officers. | Men. | Officers. | Men. |
| Staff of the Division .. .. | .. | .. | 1 | 1 | .. | .. | 1 | 1 |
| 48th Regiment .. .. .. | 4 | 86 | 8 | 267 | .. | .. | 12 | 353 |
| 8th „ .. .. .. .. | 1 | 31 | 2 | 133 | .. | .. | 3 | 164 |
| 18th „ .. .. .. .. | 3 | 32 | 8 | 140 | .. | .. | 11 | 172 |
| 12th „ .. .. .. .. | 2 | 53 | 11 | 225 | .. | .. | 13 | 278 |
| 3rd Lancer Regiment .. | 1 | 1 | .. | 12 | .. | .. | 1 | 13 |
| 3rd Field Artillery Regiment .. | .. | 3 | 2 | 32 | .. | .. | 2 | 35 |
| Total losses of the 5th Division.. | 11 | 206 | 32 | 810 | .. | .. | 43 | 1,016 |

2. Of the 3rd Division.

| | Killed. | | Wounded. | | Missing. | | Total. | |
|---|---|---|---|---|---|---|---|---|
| | Officers. | Men. | Officers. | Men. | Officers. | Men. | Officers. | Men. |
| 42nd Regiment .. .. .. | 3 | 31 | 4 | 101 | .. | 6 | 7 | 138 |
| 2nd „ .. .. .. .. | 6 | 52 | 10 | 174 | .. | 3 | 16 | 229 |
| 54th „ .. .. .. .. | .. | 1 | 1 | 7 | .. | 1 | 1 | 9 |
| 14th „ .. .. .. .. | .. | 9 | 1 | 38 | .. | 2 | 1 | 49 |
| 2nd Rifle Battalion .. .. .. | .. | 6 | .. | 21 | .. | .. | .. | 27 |
| 5th Hussar Regiment .. .. | .. | 1 | 1 | .. | .. | .. | 1 | 1 |
| 2nd Field Artillery Regiment .. | 1 | 2 | 1 | 11 | .. | .. | 2 | 13 |
| Total losses of the 3rd Division.. | 10 | 102 | 18 | 352 | .. | 12 | 28 | 466 |
| The total losses of both Divisions were .. .. .. .. | 21 | 102 | 50 | 1,162 | .. | 12 | 71 | 1,482 |

The Commander of the 5th Division, Lieutenant-General Von Tümpling, was among the wounded.

"Hirtefeld's Military Calendar" states the Austrian losses at 383 killed, 520 wounded, and 1,681 missing—together 2,593; a figure that is evidently much too small. The prisoners that were made amounted alone to—

　　　21 Officers and 1,403 Men by the 3rd Division.
　　　39　　„　　1,893　　„　　5th　　„

　Total　..　60　　„　　3,296 Men.

A special list of killed, wounded, and missing officers gives the following number :—

| | | | | | Officers. |
|---|---|---|---|---|---|
| General Poschacher's Brigade | .. | .. | .. | | 11 |
| „ Leiningen's „ | .. | .. | .. | | 20 |
| „ Ringelsheim's „ | .. | .. | .. | | 44 |
| „ Piret's „ | .. | .. | .. | | 43 |
| Colonel Abele's „ | .. | .. | .. | | 27 |
| Cavalry .. .. | .. | .. | .. | | 8 |
| Total.. .. .. | .. | .. | .. | | 153 |

Colonel Count Pejacsevich, Commander of the Lichtenstein Hussars was wounded and taken prisoner.

The Saxon losses were :—

|  | Officers. | Men. |
|---|---|---|
| Killed .. .. .. .. | 5 .. .. | 83 |
| Wounded .. .. .. | 21 .. .. | 329 |
| Missing .. .. .. .. | 1 .. | 154 |
| Total .. .. .. | 27 | 566 |

Among the wounded were Colonel Von Boxberg, Commander of the 1st Infantry Brigade, who died of his wounds, and Colonel Von Ludwiger, Commander of the 3rd "Reiter" Regiment.

The total losses of the enemy may well be estimated at 7,000.

We have seen that five brigades of the Austrian Ist Corps and Generel Edelsheim's Division of Cavalry, *minus* the Windischgrätz Dragoon Regiment, together with the Saxon Corps were concentrated between Eisenstadt, Ober-Lochow, and Jicinowes on the forenoon of the 29th of June.

These troops mustered when complete :—

|  | Men. |
|---|---|
| Five Austrian Brigades and the Cavalry Division .. | 42,000 |
| The Saxon Corps .. .. .. .. .. | 24,000 |
| Total .. .. .. .. | 66,000 |

Of these probably only four Austrian and two Saxon Brigades, with part of the Cavalry, were actually engaged; at all events, 42,000 men.

On the Prussian side, two divisions, mustering, when complete, 26,000 men, came into action, but were separated from each other by the wooded hills of Brada. No co-operation was possible before reaching Gitschin or its immediate neighbourhood.

It is evident that the Allies could have operated with great numerical superiority, either *offensively* on one road, or *defensively* at the junction of both roads near Gitschin. With the bulk of their force, however, they took up a defensive position in front of Gitschin, on the northern road. The position they selected extended from Eisenstadt to Brada, and was about 2¼ miles in breadth, but the strong *points d'appui* on which both wings rested, the villages and meadows before the front, and particulary the favourable Artillery positions, gave it a high degree of strength.

On this day the Austrians also had the advantage that is inherent to defensive operations, of being able to bring their numerous and admirable Artillery into full play at the very commencement of the action, whereas that of their adversaries had first to be brought forward.

In this position 12,000 men of the 5th Division attacked two Austrian and two Saxon brigades, 24,000 men, in addition to which Count Leiningen's Brigade was close at hand as a support.

In spite of all this numerical superiority, the defence of the Austrian position on the northern road necessarily depended on the degree of resistance that General Ringelsheim's Brigade could oppose to the 3rd Division.

The position at Diletz must anyhow have been given up as soon as General Januschowcky's Brigade reached Wostruschno at 8 o'clock, even if the orders from the head-quarters of the Austrian Army had not, as it was, made it necessary to do so.

The other divisions of the Prussian 1st Army all reached their appointed destinations.

The 7th Division heard the firing from Gitschin at its rendezvous by Sobotka, set off again, in consequence, at 6 o'clock in the evening, and reached Woharsitz.

The IInd Army was to reach the Elbe to-day. The Ist Corps d'Armée moved up by the way of Trautenau, and bivouacked round about Pilnikau; the Cavalry Division followed, and reached Praussnitz-Kaile, where the Crown Prince had established his head-quarters. The Corps of Guards and the Vth Corps were, however, not to reach their appointed destinations without fresh combats.

All the corps which the Feldzeugmeister had pushed forward to cover the formation of the Austrian Army on the heights of Dubenec, and which had encountered the columns of the IInd Prussian Army on the left bank of the Elbe, were thrown back to the right bank of the river by the engagements of the preceding days; the IVth Corps alone remained on the other side of the stream. Königinhof was occupied by the 6th Regiment (Coronini) of General Fleischhacker's Brigade; the three other brigades of the corps were at Dolan.

We may assume that the Austrian head-quarters had now become fully convinced of the imminent danger resulting from the advance of the Silesian Army. All idea of the proposed advance on the Iser must now be relinquished. The troops already on the march thither—namely, the IIIrd Corps and the 3rd Reserve Cavalry Division, that were already en route for Gitschin and Horsitz—received counter orders.

The instructions sent to the Ist Corps and the Saxons have been already mentioned. Their main object was now to be to unite with the main army by way of Horsitz and Miletin. The IIIrd Corps was directed to remain at the latter place.

All other detachments of the army were to be concentrated in a position on the plateau of Dubenec against the army of the Crown Prince.

According to the orders issued in the course of the forenoon, the IVth Corps was still to remain at Dolan for the present. It was to avoid any engagement with superior forces of the enemy, but rather to fall back on Salney, and go into position on the neighbouring heights between the church and the 1st

Reserve Cavalry Division, where the latter was already stationed, facing eastwards, with the 2nd Light Cavalry Division on its right rear.

The IInd Corps was instructed to occupy the heights at Salney and Kukus, and to hold itself in readiness to meet an attack as well from the east as from the north-west.

As the nearest reserves of this corps, two brigades of the VIIIth Corps, were to take post between Kasow and the Salney-Litic road, they were to face eastwards, with their right wing half-way between Westetz and Litic. The 3rd Brigade of the corps was to form line westwards of Kasow, fronting northwards; on its left, first the VIth Corps and then the 3rd Reserve Cavalry Division were to follow; the 2nd Reserve Cavalry Division was to form the extreme left wing at Silberleit.

The Xth Corps was destined as reserve for this wing, and moved into a position between Stern and Liebthal.

The Artillery Reserve of the Army was to remain at Gross-Bürglitz, under cover of the 2nd Lancer Regiment. The headquarters of the Army were moved to Dubenec, and earthworks for the artillery commenced.

The narrative of the ensuing actions will show that the IVth Corps crossed the Elbe in the course of the day, and that all the troops had therefore taken up their appointed positions by the afternoon and evening; only the 3rd Reserve Cavalry Division remained at Daubrawitz.

The Austrian Army was therefore prepared to meet an attack of the Silesian Army in this position on the 30th of June. Five corps d'armée and four Cavalry divisions were concentrated in a line $5\frac{1}{2}$ miles long. Although from the nature of the country the interior communications of the position were insufficient, still it derived great strength from the Elbe and the considerable heights on the north and west. On the other hand, the Trautenau-Königinhof road to Gitschin was almost entirely given up; and it was just in this direction, and still further up the Elbe, that the columns of the Prussian Corps of Guards and Ist Corps were advancing.

---

## ACTION OF KÖNIGINHOF.

### 29TH JUNE.

Detachments of the Xth Austrian Corps still held Ober-Soor in front of the Corps of Guards during the night of the 28th, but retired towards Königinhof in the morning of the 29th. General Von Hiller's Division was ordered to seize the latter town; General Von Plonski's Division and the Reserve Artillery were to follow. The 4th Squadron of the Guard Hussars was detached to open communications with the Vth Corps, whilst the 2nd Squadron of the regiment performed the same service with regard to the 1st Corps, towards Ketzelsdorf and Pilnikau.

The brigade of the advanced guard left its bivouac near Burkersdorf at noon ; and the leading troops, under command of Lieut.-Colonel Count Waldersee, came upon a small Austrian detachment at Bettendorf, which fell back upon Königinhof.

As was afterwards proved, the garrison of the later place consisted of ten companies of the 6th Austrian Regiment (Coronini) and half a squadron of Hussars, under command of Colonel Stocklin. They had orders to defend the town until a brigade arrived for their support.

As the head of the Prussian advanced guard reached the spot where the high-road makes a sudden bend to the west, it was fired on from the nearest buildings. The two batteries of the advanced guard were brought up, and covered by their fire two companies of the Guard Rifle Battalion, and the 3rd Battalion of the Guard Fusiliers formed for action.

The Austrians soon quitted the foremost buildings, but offered serious resistance somewhat further back in the "ziegelei"* and the neighbouring houses. The 11th Company of the Fusiliers, asisted by the fire of the Rifles, carried the "zeigelei" and an adjoining massive house, which was obstinately defended, and where numerous prisoners were taken. Colonel Stocklin himself was wounded. After an attempt of the enemy to advance again had been repulsed, the 10th Company proceeded to attack the cemetery, whilst the three others advanced against the " Schindel Vorstadt." In the meanwhile the main body of the advanced guard had come up, and was in the act of forming for action preparatory to making a concentric attack on the town.

About this time Colonel Mondl's Brigade, which was marching to Josephstadt, was halting only a mile and a quarter from Königinhof. On hearing firing so near to him, Colonel Mondl despatched three squadrons of Mensdorf Hussars to Königinhof. One of them (the 3rd, under Captain Macdonnel) advanced to the charge, and tried to check the advance of the Prussian Infantry from the "ziegelei" towards the town, but was repulsed with great loss. The 1st Battalion of the 1st Foot Guards now came up, and with this assistance Count Waldersee force his way into the faubourg. The Austrians made but a partial resistance, and lost many prisoners.

In the meantime four batteries of the Austrian Xth Corps came into action on the right bank of the Aupa, where they were joined by a battery of the 3rd Reserve Cavalry Division. This division had been recalled from its march to Horsitz, and had reached Daubrawitz. These guns fired on the faubourg of the town and on the Prussian columns that were following the advanced guard. To return their fire, the two batteries of the advanced guard unlimbered southward of the " Podharder Vorstadt," where they were joined somewhat later by the first

---

* Brickfield.

4 -pounder battery. The distance was however very great, and, as it was, the Infantry continued to advance rapidly, and soon entered the town itself.

In the interior of the town a most obstinate struggle was carried on on both sides, whilst at the same time the 12th Company of the Fusiliers was pressing forwards from the cemetery on the north, and the 1st Company of Rifles along the skirts on the east side of the town. Thus turned on both flanks, the position of the Austrians became one of great danger, as they had the defiles of the Elbe immediately behind them. The Prussian 12th Company was already drawing near the road to the upper bridge, and a detachment of the enemy attempting to retreat in this direction was driven back into the town. The 10th Company reached the bridge, and occupied the store-houses on the other side of the river. The Austrians could now only effect their retreat by the lower bridge. In a side street the 12th Company of the 1st Guards captured two officers, fifty men, and the colours of the 2nd Battalion of the "Coronini" Regiment; the latter were seized by Private Bochnia after receiving several wounds.

It was not part of the Prussian plan to cross the Elbe, therefore Count Waldersee rallied his troops on the market-place, and only sent some Hussars forward to watch the enemy's retreat on the other bank. Some Austrian columns again approached the town, but retired on finding the bridges occupied.

The 1st Division of Guards bivouacked in and to the north of Königinhof, with a line of outposts along the Elbe. General Von Alvensleben's Brigade, which was sent forward as relief, sent in about 300 prisoners, that had been for the most part concealed in the houses of the town.

The Prussian losses were 17 men killed, 2 officers and 50 men wounded, 1 man missing. The Austrians fell back on Schurz and Miletin. According to Hirtefeld's Calendar their losses were :—

|  | Killed. | Wounded. | Missing. | Total. |
|---|---|---|---|---|
| Regiment (Coronini) .. .. | 44 | 127 | 397 | 568 |
| Mensdorf Lancers .. .. | 4 | 1 | 24 | 29 |
| Total .. .. | 48 | 128 | 421 | 597 |

About 400 of these were taken prisoners, among others the Commander of the Austrian detachment.

The head-quarters of the Corps of Guards were moved to Rettendorf, at which place and at Komar the 2nd Guard Division, the Heavy Cavalry Brigade and the Reserve Artillery bivouacked.

## ACTION OF SCHWEINSCHÄDEL.

The outposts of the IVth Austrian Corps (General Count Festetics) held the line Langwasser-Trzebeschow in front of the Vth Prussian Corps. From the latter spot parties of skirmishers twice advanced against General Hoffmann's Brigade and short skirmishes ensued each time.

The Prussian troops were fatigued by the combats of the preceding days, and General Von Steinmetz gave the Vth Corps rest on the morning of the 29th. It was to march to Gradlitz to unite with the other corps of the IInd Army in the course of the afternoon.

The Chief of the Staff, Colonel Von Wittich, had reconnoitred the passages of the Aupa early in the morning, and personally convinced himself of the position of the Austrian outposts. From some papers that were found it was known that three corps had been in the neighbourhood on the 28th. In order, if possible, to reach Gradlitz without further combat, the Commanding General determined to turn the left flank of the enemy's outposts with the Vth Corps, General Hoffmann's Brigade and the Heavy Cavalry Brigade of the Guards, that had returned from Kosteletz, and to strike the Chwalkowitz-Gradlitz road by Zlitsch, Ratiboritz, and Wetrnik. To cover this march only a left-flank detachment, composed of the Infantry and Cavalry Brigades of Generals Wittick and Von Wnuck, was to advance on the right bank of the Aupa by way of Zagezd. It was to rejoin the main body of the corps at Miskoles.*

As soon as the foremost troops of the VIth Corps d'Armée reached Skalitz, and went into bivouac there, the new-formed advanced guard commenced its march at 2 o'clock, the left-flank detachment at half-past 2. The latter first encountered the enemy.

2 P.M.

On passing Zagezd, already General Wittich saw the Austrian outposts, which had been stationed in the Aupa valley towards Rzikow and Doubrawitz, falling back on Schweinschädel. Wishing to attract the enemy's attention, he brought the third 6-pounder battery into action southwards of the road, and fired on the retreating detachments. On the head of the column reaching Trzebeschow soon afterwards, it found the village unoccupied, but was met by the fire of a battery planted southwards of Schweinschädel.

The 52nd Regiment and the two batteries were ordered to continue their march in the deep valley leading to Miskoles, whilst the succeeding regiment, No. 47, covered this movement by holding Trzebeschow, after which it was to follow in the same direction.

---

* The detailed order of battle is given in Appendix XX.

Half way between Trzebeschow and Miskoles the Fusilier Battalion of the 52nd Regiment climbed up the steep bank of the valley, and covered the two batteries of the detachment that had come into action to the north of the church of Trzebeschow by dint of great exertion and under the enemy's fire. A skirmishing fire ensued between the battalion and some Austrian Infantry that was posted in the high corn at the top of the bank. As the nature of the ground obstructed the view, and the artillery fire was therefore of no effect, the batteries followed the musketeer battalions of the 52nd Regiment under cover of the Fusiliers, who drove the enemy back westwards in the direction of Miskoles.

In the meantime the 47th Regiment reached Trzebeschow, and was encountered by Austrian troops advancing from Schweinschädel. The 1st Company and two subdivisions of skirmishers of the 2nd Battalion were thrown forward to meet them, but General Wittich gave orders to break off this engagement, and to follow straight to Miskoles. Only Lieutenant Heidenreich and some volunteers of the 1st Battalion, who were trying to get up to the Austrian battery near Schweinschädel, still continued their fire, and soon forced the battery to withdraw.

Whilst General Wittich was thus proceeding on his somewhat perilous march, the first shots fired by his detachment had induced the advanced guard of the corps to prepare for action. General Kirchbach had marched by Zlitsch and Wetrnik, and had arrived at the ravine leading to Langwasser with the head of the advanced guard. On account of the defile the column could only march in sections, and the advanced. guard alone was upwards of a mile long. A patrol of Austrian Infantry had been made prisoners in Vorwerk Hermanitz, a detachment of Infantry seen between Augezdez and Langwasser. The 2nd Squadron of the Prussian Lancers was despatched towards Horicka to cover the right flank. As soon as General Kirchbach and the foremost patrols of the Lancers appeared north-westwards of Miskoles, they were fired on by Austrian artillery northwards of Schweinschädel; and the enemy's battery southwards of the village, which just then (about half-past 3 o'clock) opened fire on General Wittich's Brigade, was seen by the General. He immediately ordered General Tiedemann's Brigade to deploy at Miskoles, and resolved to march southwards to General Wittich's assistance as soon as he heard heavy firing in that direction.

Lieutenant Field Marshal Festetic's first line consisted of two brigades; Archduke Joseph's brigade extended from the Aupa to Schweinschädel, where the line to the left was taken up by Colonel Poeckh's Brigade, which reached as far as Sebuc. The latter occupied Schweinschädel with the 1st and 2nd Battalions of the 37th Regiment (Archduke Joseph), and the gully leading up to the heights west of the village with the 3rd Battalion of the same regiment, whilst the 51st Regiment (Archduke Charles Ferdinand) was posted on the heights themselves. The Brigade Battery and three battalions of the Reserve Artillery of the corps were in the neighbourhood of the latter regiment. The 8th Rifle Battalion and the 7th Regiment of Hussars were posted on the extreme left at Sebuc.

Further to the rear, General Brandenstein's Brigade and the two 8-pounder batteries of the Reserve Artillery of the corps were stationed in reserve at Dolan.

The four Austrian batteries on the hill, 1,200 paces south of Miskoles, strenuously attempted to prevent any débouché of the Prussians from the ravine; but in spite of their fire the 6th and 46th Regiments deployed, the former to the west, the latter on the slope to the north-east of Miskoles.

The Artillery first brought the 3rd 4-pounder battery into action southwards of the Miskoles-Chwalkowitz road; it held its ground here until the 4th 4-pounder battery had taken up a sheltered position on its left rear, and then fell back to the same spot.

By reason of the length of the column the formation of the advanced guard cost considerable time, but was effected with great order in spite of the enemy's heavy fire. As soon as the leading troops (Fusiliers and 2nd Battalion of the 6th Regiment) were formed, General Kirchbach sent them forward against the enemy's batteries. This first line of seven companies was then followed by the first batteries of the regiment as left-flank *échelon.*

The advance of the 6th Regiment and a simultaneous movement of the Fusiliers of the 52nd Regiment (General Wittich's Brigade) on the right flank of the Austrian batteries induced them to give up this position.

About 200 paces before they reached the batteries, the Prussian troops were halted, for about 20 minutes, on a strip of meadow land. The skirmishers drove in the enemy's riflemen that lay in front of the position. In the meantime the 46th Regiment had come up so near that it followed as right-flank *échelon* when the first line resumed its advance. The right flank of the line was covered by two squadrons of the Hussars; the two other squadrons watched the country towards the west and north-west. The Rifle Companies were posted in the "ziegelei," southwards of Miskoles.

Under cover of the Fusilier Battalion of the 52nd Regiment, which was thrown out on the left flank, General Wittich's Brigade continued its march to Miskoles, and formed on the south side of the village as reserve for General Tiedemann's Brigade.

General Wnuck's Cavalry Brigade also ascended the plateau between Trzebeschow and Miskoles, and deployed on the meadows by the side of the 6th Regiment.

Although the village of Schweinschädel lies in a hollow, still a large massive group of buildings, which takes up half its north side, gives it great defensive strength; walls 6 to 7 feet high, connect the different buildings, and surround the gardens; platforms were raised behind them for the Infantry, the buildings themselves loopholed, their doors and windows barricaded.

Assisted by the fire of General Wittich's two batteries (3rd 6-pounder and 3rd 12-pounder), and of General Wnuck's 1st Horse Artillery Battery, General Tiedemann's Brigade, now proceeded to attack the Austrian position. The two batteries of the advanced guard had expended all their ammunition. Although the enemy's artillery near Sebuc enfiladed the attacking columns, this did not check their advance. The skirmishers of the Fusilier Battalion of the 52nd Regiment, and the 11th and 12th Companies of the 6th Regiment stormed the massive buildings, into which Major Webern's half-battalion penetrated at the same time from the right. The latter half-battalion had previously gained possession of the northern part of the village. More than 300 Austrians surrendered in the buildings.

500 paces in front of Schwinschädel the right wing of the 6th Regiment, half-battalion Heugel, and 9th company, had encountered two columns of the Austrian 37th Regiment (Archduke Joseph), which came so suddenly out of the ravine north-westwards of the village, that the skirmishers met hand-to-hand. The half-battalion deployed and repulsed the attack with file-fire, and then following close on the flying enemy, seized the west skirts of the village, whilst the 9th company turned somewhat to the right to attack the wooded hill of the "Schäferei," against which the 46th Regiment was advancing at the same time in two lines of three half-battalions each. The enemy was dislodged from the wood; the "Schäferei" and the neighbouring "ziegelei" were taken, and a flag captured, by the 8th Company of the 46th Regiment. Captain Priebsch's half-battalion pressed on to a sand pit 300 paces south of the skirts of the wood.

The road to Jaromir was taken up by Archduke Joseph's Brigade, that was already on its way to occupy the town; the detachments that were driven out of Schweinschädel and the wood were, therefore, obliged to retreat to the north of the road. The Prussian skirmishers stepped out beyond the skirts of the village and the wood, and poured a rapid fire into the enemy's retreating columns, which caused them great loss.

Two half-battalions of the second line of the 46th Regiment had pressed on into the first line during the advance, the third one, commanded by Captain Gossnitz, marched on Sebuc. The village itself was taken, but an attack on the hills further to the south repulsed. Captain Von Gossnitz and the officers of both companies fell, Major Von Grolmann, General Staff Officer of the Division, and the Adjutant of the battalion, who came up at the moment, were wounded. Lieutenant Von Burghoff took command of the half-battalion, and kept possession of Sebuc. The two companies of rifles had in the meantime advanced from the "ziegelei" of Miskoles, and joined in the fire on the retreating enemy. As no further interruption of his march to Gradlitz was now to be feared, General Steinmetz most positively forbade any advance beyond the position already gained.

At this time the main body of the corps was forming between Miskoles and Chwalkowitz, the Cavalry Brigade of the Guards had come up by way of Augezdez and Langwasser, and stood by the side of General Wnuck's Brigade, its battery had an opportunity of firing on the enemy during his retreat from Sebuc.

General Von Steinmetz now resolved to resume his march to Gradlitz, and ordered General Tiedemann to reform his brigade north-eastwards of Schweinschädal.

Some Austrian Hussars appeared before the front, but retired immediately, as General Wnuck's Brigade advanced towards Schweinschädal, whereupon the latter returned to its former position on the meadows.

While the troops were occupied in collecting the dead and wounded, it seemed as if the enemy again meditated an attack. The Cavalry Brigade of the Guards trotted up to the "Schäferei," southwards of which its battery took post. The 3rd Company of Rifles, that also came up from Miskoles, established itself in the neighbouring sand pit, and kept up a skirmishing fire with some Austrian Rifles. The battery of the Guards first turned its fire on those detachments of the enemy that were visible in the foreground, and then on some columns on the Josephstadt road, 1,500 paces off, as well as on a battery at 1,800 paces distance, which was soon reinforced by a second battery. The Prussian fire was soon increased by the 3rd 4-pounder, the 3rd 6-pounder, and 3rd 12-pounder batteries, but as this cannonade did not agree with General Steinmetz's intentions, he ordered the engagement to be broken off.

7.30 P.M.   The main body of the corps resumed its march to Gradlitz at about half-past seven, it was covered by the 10th Division and the Cavalry Brigades. General Wittich's brigade and the 1st Lancer Regiment started first, as they were to form the outposts, they were followed by the 9th Division, and at about nine, by the 19th Brigade, as soon as the field of battle was completely cleared up. General Hoffmann brought up the rear, and was covered by the two Cavalry brigades that still watched the enemy from the plateau. General Wnuck's Brigade did not follow till midnight, and did not reach Gradlitz till 10 the next morning. In consequence of a report that the enemy's Cavalry was again advancing, the 4th Dragoons were sent to the rear to reconnoitre, and General Hoffmann halted the rear-guard at Wölsdorf until the return of the Dragoons, and then resumed his march.

The new line of outposts at Gradlitz extended from Schurz, on the Elbe, along the Ahn rivulet, nearly up to Wölsdorf. A few patrols of the enemy were seen in the foreground.

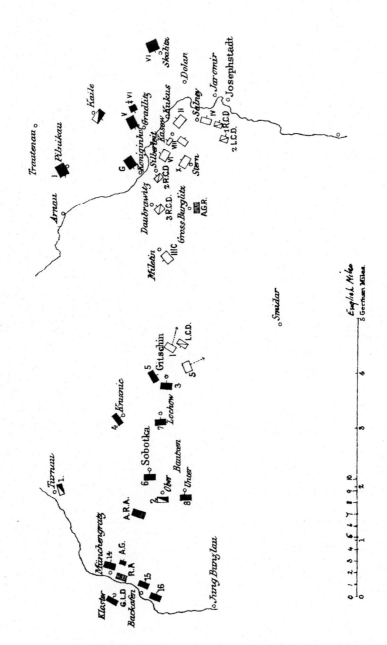

No. 7.

POSITION OF BOTH ARMIES ON THE EVENING OF THE 29TH. JUNE.

Weller & Graham, Ltd  Litho. London.

The losses of the Vth Corps in the action of Schweinschädel were—

| | Killed. | | Wounded. | | Missing. | | Total. | |
|---|---|---|---|---|---|---|---|---|
| | Officers. | Men. | Officers. | Men. | Officers. | Men. | Officers. | Men. |
| **10th Division.** | | | | | | | | |
| Staff .. .. .. | .. | .. | 1 | .. | .. | .. | 1 | .. |
| 46th Regiment .. .. | 4 | 32 | 1 | 123 | .. | 4 | 5 | 159 |
| 6th „ .. .. | 1 | 24 | 5 | 75 | .. | .. | 6 | 99 |
| 52nd „ .. .. | 1 | 7 | .. | 32 | .. | .. | 1 | 39 |
| 47th „ .. .. | 1 | 13 | .. | 48 | .. | 1 | 1 | 62 |
| 1st Lancer Regiment .. | 1 | 1 | .. | .. | .. | .. | 1 | 1 |
| 5th Field Artillery Regiment .. .. .. | .. | .. | .. | 5 | .. | .. | .. | 5 |
| **9th Regiment.** | | | | | | | | |
| 58th Regiment .. .. | .. | .. | .. | 2 | .. | .. | .. | 2 |
| 5th Rifle Battalion .. | .. | .. | .. | 2 | .. | .. | .. | 2 |
| **Cavalry Brigade, Von Wnuck.** | | | | | | | | |
| 4th Dragoon Regiment.. | .. | 1 | .. | 6 | .. | .. | .. | 7 |
| 8th „ „ .. | .. | .. | .. | 3 | .. | .. | .. | 3 |
| Total .. .. | 8 | 78 | 7 | 296 | .. | 5 | 15 | 379 |

According to orders of his Commander-in-Chief, Lieutenant Field-Marshal Count Festetics retired to the position on the right bank of the Elbe, near Salney, the details of which have been already described. His losses in the action were 37 officers and 1,447 men, of whom the 37th Regiment alone lost 1,026 men. Colonel Von Elbleinc, of the 67th Regiment, was wounded, and 3,400 men were taken prisoners without wounds.

The following sketch will show how the Prussian Armies were gradually drawing closer together, and what the positions of the different corps were on the evening of the 29th.

## THE 30TH OF JUNE.

On the morning of the 30th of June, His Majesty the King of Prussia went to the Army of Bohemia. Shortly before his departure from Berlin telegraphic news arrived that the IInd Army was in possession of the line of the Elbe. In consequence, during the King's journey, the following telegram was despatched to the headquarters of both armies, from Kohlfurt, at a quarter before one o'clock:—

" The IInd Army will hold its ground on the Upper Elbe; " its right wing will be prepared to effect a junction " with the left wing of the Ist Army, by way of " Königinhof, as the latter advances. The Ist Army " will press on towards Königgrätz without delay.

" Any forces of the enemy that may be on the right
" flank of this advance will be attacked by General Von
" Herwarth, and separated from the enemy's main
" force."

Even before he received these instructions, Prince Frederick
Charles had already resolved to push forward beyond Gitschin
on the Königinhof road, in order to draw near the IInd
Army. He gave orders that the Ist Army should start as soon
as the rations were cooked, and should reach the following
positions by eight o'clock P.M. :—

> The 6th Division Chotec, with outposts towards
> Miletin.
> The 7th Division Konetzchlum, with outposts towards
> Horzitz and Chomutitz.
> The 5th Division, Oulibitz.
> The 8th Division, Butowes and Milicowes.
> The IInd Corps, Gitschin and Podhrad.
> The Cavalry Corps, Dworetz and Robous.

The Army of the Elbe started in the morning, in two
columns, on the roads Fürstenbrück-Sobotka and Brizesno
Psinitz. The victory of Gitschin had removed all necessity
for halting at Sobotka, and the left flank column was, therefore,
able to turn off from the Gitschin road, which was crowded with
the trains of the Ist Army, and take the route to Liban. In the
course of the day, General Schoeler's advanced guard reached
Liban, the 14th Division, Sedlist, the 15th, Detenist, and the
16th, Rokitai. None of them had met with the enemy during
this march. The Division of Guard Landwehr arrived at Jung-
Bunzlau as ordered.

The IInd Army had reached the line of Arnau-Königinhof,
and the advance of the Ist Army must necessarily of
itself open the defiles of the Elbe. The Crown Prince, therefore, gave orders that all serious engagements were to be
avoided on the 30th of June, but that the different corps were
to take due precautions for their own security, to reconnoitre
the passages of the river, and to prepare for a further advance.
In the event of the latter, Burg and Schurz were appointed
as places for crossing for the Vth and VIth Corps, Königinhof
for the Guards and the heavy Cavalry Brigade of the corps,
Neustadt and neighbourheod for the 1st Corps and the Cavalry
Division.

The King did not receive the news of the brilliant and
successful action of Gitschin until he reached Reichenberg,
whither the wounded commander of the 5th Division, General
Von Tümpling, had been conveyed.

The Crown Prince only knew that Prince Frederick Charles
had passed Turnau, and ordered to 1st Corps to send Cavalry
detachments in this direction, to open communication with the
Ist Army.

In the meantime Prince Frederick Charles had also despatched Lieutenant-Colonel Von Barner, with the 1st Regiment of Guard Dragoons, for the same purpose. The latter found the advanced guard of the 1st Corps at Arnau, and direct communication was thus opened between both armies.

Even on this day, however, the troops of General Von Steinmetz were not destined to enjoy a day of perfect rest. As early as four in the morning the bivouacs of the corps were disturbed by the fire of an Austrian battery planted on the heights beyond the Elbe. The fire was answered by the Prussian 3rd 4-pounder and 3rd 6-pounder batteries, at distances of 4,400 and 3,600 paces. Their shells fell among the bivouacs of General Saffran's and Prince Würtemberg's Brigades, and even reached those of the Austrian VIIIth Corps.

The IInd Austrian Corps formed line of battle, and brought forward six batteries, some of which were posted behind earthworks, whilst the Prussian troops remained quietly in their bivouacs.

At nine o'clock the two batteries withdrew by order of General Steinmetz, whereupon the enemy's fire ceased also. In the course of the afternoon General Tiedemann's Brigade advanced to relieve the outposts, which induced the enemy to renew the cannonade for about an hour and a half, but with little or no effect.

General Von Steinmetz did not think it necessary to make any alteration whatever in the bivouacs of his corps, although one of the enemy's shells set fire to a building at his own headquarters. The losses of the corps amounted to six men killed, one officer and 19 men wounded. According to its own account, the Austrian IInd Corps lost four officers, 25 men, and two horses. Two of the enemy's limbers were seen to explode.

The other corps of the IInd Army made no material alteration in their bivouacs of the previous day. The 1st Division of Guards remained at Königinhof, the 2nd at Neu-Rettendorf; the Heavy Cavalry Brigade was moved forward to the latter village, the 1st Corps stopped at Pilnikau. The VIth Corps came to Brsitz, the Cavalry Division remained at Kaile.

On the part of the enemy, the Saxon Corps reached Smidar. The greater part of the 1st Austrian Corps, and of the 1st Light Cavalry Division, Sadowa. In consequence of this movement, the IIIrd Corps, with the Reserve Cavalry Division, which was attached to it for the day, fell back to Gross-Bürglitz.

The whole remainder of the Army, it is true, was now assembled on the heights of Dubenetz, in a position fronting mainly to the north and the east; but the army could neither remain in this position, for the Prussian Vth Army was within a day's march, and threatened both flank and rear, nor was it now any longer possible to attack one of the hostile armies without the other appearing in the rear of the action.

M

The losses which the Austrian Army had suffered in the previous engagements already amounted to 30,000 or 40,000 men.

The Feldzeugmeister, therefore, resolved to withdraw the army to the neighbourhood of Königgrätz during the night of the 30th of June to the 1st of July. He sent the following report to the Emperor from Dubenec :—

> "The retreat of the 1st and Saxon Corps d'Armée obliges
> "me to fall back in the direction of Königgrätz."

Thus the Prussian armies were now at liberty to unite immediately, if such a measure should be deemed expedient; but it was considered preferable to remain divided, as this caused no strategic change, and might produce considerable tactical advantage; should the enemy be found in a position too strong to be overcome by a mere frontal attack, one would only have concentrated all forces to separate them again for the necessary flank attack. The armies were but a short day's march apart, and neither ran any risk, if one were attacked, the other would be on the enemy's flank.

On this day the following Proclamation of their Sovereign was issued to the Prussian troops :—

### "Soldiers of my Army."

> "To-day I am coming to join you, my brave soldiers
> "in the field, and give you my royal greeting. Within
> "a space of a few days your bravery and devotion have
> "achieved results that may worthily rank by the side of
> "the great deeds of our forefathers. I regard all parts
> "of my faithful army with pride, and look forward to
> "the coming events of the war with joyful confidence.
> "Soldiers! Numerous enemies are in the field
> "against us. Let us, however, put our trust in God,
> "who is the Lord of all battles, and in the justness of
> "our cause. He will lead Prussia's oft victorious
> "standards to fresh victories through your bravery and
> "perseverance."

(Signed) "WILLIAM."

### The 1st of July.

Before the last mentioned telegram reached him, the Crown Prince too had arranged that the 1st Corps should advance on the 1st of July from Arnau to Ober-Prausnitz, and that the other corps should cross the Elbe on the 2nd, and unite with the 1st Army in the direction of Miletin.

On the 1st of July the VIth Corps was brought up to Gradlitz, where it was rejoined by General Hoffmann's Brigade.

On being informed of these movements, Prince Frederick Charles gave orders to the 1st Army to start at three o'clock in the afternoon, and to march as follows :—

The 5th Division to Miletin.
The 6th Division to Dobes.

The 7th Division to Horsitz, with an advanced guard at Gross-Jeritz.

The 8th Division to Gutwasser, its advanced guard to Milowitz.

The 3rd Division to Aujezd.

The 4th Division to Wostromer.

The Cavalry Division Alvensleben to Baschnitz.

The Cavalry Division Hann to Liskowitz.

The Army of the Elbe marked with the advanced guard to Hochwesely.

The 14th Division to Zeretitz.

The 15th Division to Cesow.

The 16th Division to Jicinowes.

The Division of Guard Landwehr remained at Jung-Bunzlau.

Prince Frederick Charles moved his head-quarters to Kamenitz, the Crown Prince stopped at Königinhof, and the King's head-quarters were moved to Castle Sichrow.

It was here that the approaching arrival of the French Ambassador Benedetti was first announced, and the immediate prospect of diplomatic negotiations was a still further reason for not relaxing in the hitherto restless course of military action.

The Austrians began to quit the position they had only just taken up at Dubenec, at one o'clock in the morning of the 1st of July ; their march was effected in four columns.

The IIIrd and Xth Corps, the 3rd Reserve, and the 2nd Light Cavalry Divisions, marched from Gross-Bürglitz and Liebthal to Lipa.

The 3rd Heavy Cavalry Division to a bivouac between Dohalitz and Dohalicka.

The VIth Corps and the 2nd Reserve Cavalry Division by way of Dubenetz, Horenowes to Wsestar.

The VIIIth and IVth Corps by Litic, Nenasow to Nedelist.

The 1st Reserve Cavalry Division, the IInd Corps, and the 2nd Light Cavalry Division by way of Dölzen to Trotina.

The troops did not reach their bivouacs between the Bistritz and the Elbe until the afternoon. The Ist Austrian Corps was already in bivouac at Wsestar, the 1st Division of the Saxons stood at Lubno, the 2nd at Nieder-Prim.

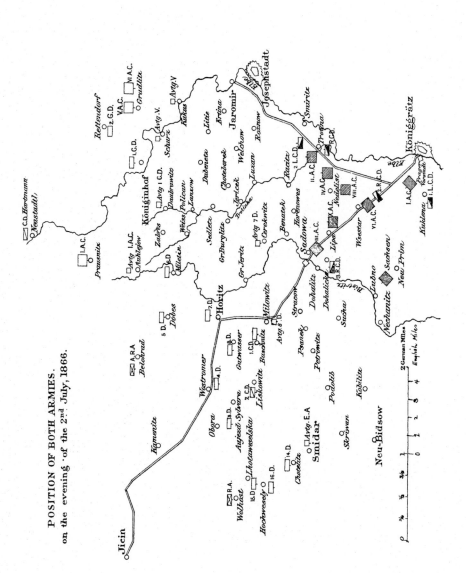

POSITION OF BOTH ARMIES.
on the evening of the 2nd July, 1866.

Weller & Graham, L.td Litho. London.

# BOOK THE SECOND.

## JULY 2ND.

ON the 2nd of July both armies remained essentially in their positions of the previous day. The Army of the Elbe alone moved the advanced guard to Smidar.

The 14th Division to Chotetitz,
The 15th Division to Lhota,
The 16th Division to Hochwesely, and
The Guard-Landwehr Division to Kopidlno.

The Austrian Army despatched its train to the left bank of the Elbe, that of the right wing by way of Sezenitz, that of the left by Jesnicau, near Pardubitz.

Thus the outposts of both armies faced each other on this day within a distance of $4\frac{1}{2}$ miles, without either army suspecting the near and concentrated presence of the other one.

On the Prussian side neither the advance of the Austrian man body to Dubenec, nor its nocturnal retreat from thence were known. The principal force of the enemy was rather supposed to be in position behind the Elbe with the fortresses of Josephstadt and Königgrätz on either flank.

In this case it would be necessary either to attack the Austrians in this position or to manœuvre them out of it.

The former eventually required an advance of the IInd Army against the enemy's right flank, while the Ist Army attacked in front; in the latter case the army would have to march to the right, across the enemy's front, to Pardubitz, where it would indeed threaten all its adversary's communications, but at the same time due precautions would have to be taken, lest an offensive movement of the enemy should disturb this flank march.

In the former case the IInd Army must remain on the left, in the latter be moved to the right bank of the Elbe.

Before any decision could be formed, it was most urgent to obtain more accurate knowledge of the enemy's position, and of the nature of the neighbouring country, most especially as to what impediments the Elbe in front and the Aupa in flank would oppose to the attack. Should the difficulties prove too great, the march to the right would alone remain feasible.

It was in consideration of these circumstances that the following orders for the 3rd of July were issued from the King's head-quarters at Gitschin :—

"General Von Herwarth will be pushed forward in "the direction of Chlumetz to watch the country towards

" Prague, and to secure the passage of the Elbe at
" Pardubitz.

" The other Corps of the Ist Army will move to the
" line Neu-Bidzow-Horzitz, a detachment from the left
" wing to Sadowa, to reconnoitre the line of the Elbe
" between Königgrätz and Josephstadt.

" Should the enemy be still in force in front of this
" line, he must be immediately attacked with, as far as
" possible, superior numbers.

" The Ist Corps d'Armée will march by Miletin to
" Bürglitz and Cerekwitz, will observe Josephstadt, and
" cover the flank march of the IInd Army, in case this
" movement should be ordered.

" The other Corps of the IInd Army will still remain
" on the left bank of the Elbe during the 3rd of July, and
" will reconnoitre towards the Aupa and the Metau.

" Reports on the nature of the country and the position
" of the enemy are to be sent here immediately. Should
" they show that a concentric attack of both armies on
" the main force of the enemy, which is supposed to be
" between Josephstadt and Königgrätz, would be
" attended with two great difficulties, or that the Austrian
" Army should already have left that position, then the
" general march will be continued in the direction of
" Pardubitz.

" The IInd Army will take into immediate considera-
" tion how the supplies of the army are to be ensured
" during this march.

" The commanders of both armies will send officers
" every evening to his Majesty's head-quarters for orders.

(Signed)      " VON MOLTKE."

" *Head-Quarters, Gitschin,*
     " *July 2nd, 1866.*"

Before, however, these orders were carried out, news arrived
which showed plainly the real position of the Austrian Army,
and rendered other measures necessary.

Colonel Von Zychlinsky, who occupied the castle of Cerekwitz with a detachment of the 27th Regiment, reported an
Austrian encampment near Lipa to Prince Frederick Charles.
It was stated that troops had marched thither from Bürglitz
from 8 A.M. till 3 P.M. of the 1st of July.

To verify these reports, scouting parties were thrown forward
in the direction of Königgrätz.

Major Von Unger (General Staff Officer of the Head-quarters
of the Ist Army) rode from Milowitz to Dub, and found the
heights near the latter village occupied; he was informed that
Colonel Prohaska's brigade was in a position there. Prisoners
stated that about four corps d'armée were at the Bistritz, namely,
the IIIrd Corps at Sadowa, the Xth at Langenhof, behind it the
Ist Corps, the Saxons at Problus, ten regiments of Cavalry, and
a numerous Artillery near Lipa.

Lieutenant Von Heister, of the 10th Hussars, had seen extensive bivouacs in front and rear of Benatek, and heard that the IIIrd Corps was at Sadowa.

Although sharply pursued by the enemy, these well-mounted officers got safely back, and this important information, the result of their own personal observation, reached the head-quarters of the Ist Army between 6 and 7 o'clock in the evening.

It has already been mentioned that only the positions of those four Austrian Corps that had been engaged were hitherto known on the Prussian side; of the movements of the other corps, one was as yet totally ignorant. The presence of such considerable masses at Sadowa seemed, therefore, to indicate, not a halt during the retreat, but an advance for the purpose of an attack. At all events the enemy was proved to be in the immediate neighbourhood, and Prince Frederick Charles ordered a concentration of his forces for the next morning. At 9 P.M. already he issued the following orders :—

"At daybreak to-morrow the Ist Army will be formed "on the Horzitz-Königgrätz road ready for action against "the position on the Bistritz, at Sadowa.

"1. General Horn's division will be in position at "Milowitz by 2 A.M.

"2. General Fransecky's division will march by Gross-"Jeritz to Cerekwitz, and will take post at the castle "there by 2 A.M.

"3. The divisons of Generals Manstein and Tümpling "will start at half-past 1 A.M., under command of General "Von Manstein, and will be posted as reserves south-"ward of Horzitz, Division Manstein eastward, Division "Tümpling westward, of the Königgrätz-Horzitz road.

"4. The IInd Corps d'Armée will move one division "to Psaneck, the other to Bristan. Both divisions will "be in position by 2 A.M.

"5. The Cavalry Corps will have saddled by daybreak, "and will await further orders in its bivouacs.

"6. The Reserve Artillery of the Army will move "forward as far as Horzitz; the Reserve Artillery of "the IIIrd Corps à cheval of the Horzitz-Miletin road, the "Reserve Artillery of the IInd Corps à cheval of the "Horzitz-Gitschin-Libonitz road.

"7. General Von Herwarth will march with all avail-"able troops to Nechanitz, where he will arrive as early "as possible.

"8. H.R.H. the Crown Prince has been requested to "take post with one or two corps in front of Josephstadt, "and to march with another corps to Gross-Bürglitz.

"9. As soon as possible the troops will open com-"munications, as well one with another, as also with the "troops of General Von Herwarth on the right, and "those of the IInd Army on the left flank.

"10. The trains will move at daybreak to the follow-
"ing stations, where they will park at the sides of the
"roads.

"Those of the 5th Division to Masowitz, eastward of
"this village;

"Those of the 6th Division by way of Belohrad to
"the right bank of the Jaworka.

"Those of the 7th Division by Domaslawitz to Smir-
"kowitz, westward of this village;

"Those of the 3rd Division near Wostromer, as far
"as Wojitz, on the Horzitz-Gitschin road;

"Those of the 4th Division at Aujezd-Sylvara, &c.,
"to Sobsitz, westward of the place;

"Those of the Cavalry Corps to Chomutitz;

"Those of the Reserve Artillery of the IIIrd Corps to
"Chotec, eastward of the village.

"Those of the Reserve Artillery of the IVth Corps
"beyond Wostromer, on the right bank of the Jaworka;

"11. From daybreak on I shall be near Milowitz.

"*The General of Cavalry.*

(Signed)     "FREDERICK CHARLES."

At a quarter before 10 o'clock P.M. the following letter was
written to the Crown Prince :—

"His Majesty the King has acquainted me with the
"orders which your Royal Highness has received for
"to-morrow (July 3rd), to make a reconnaissance to-
"wards the Aupa and Metau. A reconnaissance that
"was this morning already made from here, and the
"reports of the outposts having in the meantime proved
"that the enemy has concentrated a considerable force
"at Sadowa and Lipa, on the Horzitz-Königgrätz road,
"and has thrown forward an advanced guard as far as
"Dub, it is my intention to attack him to-morrow, July
"3rd, and to press him towards the Elbe, in accordance
"with the orders I have received.

"As, however, considerable bodies of the enemy's
"troops have crossed over to the right bank of the Elbe,
"at Josephstadt also, I can only look upon it as their inten-
"tion to operate against my left flank in case I push on
"towards Königgrätz. Such a diversion would compel
"me to divide my forces, and I should then not be able
"wholly to obtain the desired result, the destruction of
"the enemy's corps.

"I therefore request your Royal Highness to move
"the corps of Guards, or more, forward to-morrow,
"July 3rd, on the right bank of the Elbe, by way of
"Königinhof towards Josephstadt, and thereby to cover
"my left flank.

"I make this request more particularly, because I

" cannot reckon on General Bonin's corps arriving in time
" on account of the distance, and because, on the other
" hand, I presume that your Royal Highness will not
" meet any strong force of the enemy in the recon-
" naissance you propose to make to-morrow.

" I add that my left wing will stand at Gross-Jeritz
" and Cerekwitz.

(Signed)     " FREDERICK CHARLES,
" Prince of Prussia."

The following orders were despatched to General Von
Herwarth :—

" At daybreak to-morrow the Ist Army will be formed
" for action against the position of the Bistritz, at
" Sadowa, on the Horzitz-Königgrätz road.

" General Von Herwarth will move forward with all
" available troops to Nechanitz, where he will arrive as
" early as possible. At the commencement of the
" engagement I shall be near Milowitz.

" Report as soon as possible when and in what force
" you reach Nechanitz.

(Signed)     " FREDERICK CHARLES,
" Prince of Prussia."

General Von Herwarth received these orders at half-past 12
at night, and immediately issued the following disposition :—

" *Hochwesely, July 3rd,* 1866.

" The Austrians still hold the line of the Bistritz and
" the Horzitz-Dub-Königgrätz road. The Ist Army
" will attack on this road at daybreak. The Army of the
" Elbe will move forward in the general direction of
" Nechanitz, and will advance against the enemy's left
" flank. The divisions will start at 3 A.M., and will only
" take with them ammunition and medicine wagons, as
" well as empty carts with straw for the wounded. All
" other wagons will be left at the bivouac places of the
" divisions. General Schoeler's advanced guard will
" march by Skriwau, Kralic, and Kobilitz to Nechanitz ;
" General Canstein's division by Neu-Bidzow, Praseck to
" Nechanitz ; it will hold Neu-Bidzow until General
" Rosenberg's division comes up, and will guard the right
" flank. Patrols will be thrown out towards Chlumetz.

" General Graf Münster's division will start at half-
" past 3 A.M., will cross the Jaworka at Smidar, and march
" by Podolib on Lodin, whence it will, according to cir-
" cumstances, either turn off in the direction of Mzan, or
" push on over Sucha, or to Nechanitz.

" General Etzel's division will march past Smidar and
" follow the route of General Schoeler's advanced
" guard.

" The Reserve Artillery will start at half-past 3 A.M.,

"and will at first follow General Etzel's division. It will
"reconnoitre the roads early, and will, according to
"the result, follow, if possible, General Count Münster's
"division to Nechanitz, or else General Etzel's division.
"General Rosenberg's division will march at daybreak
"from Kopidlno to Neu-Bidzow.

　　"Head-quarters will march with the advanced guard.
　　　　　　(Signed)　　　"Von Herwarth,"

As soon as these arrangements had been made, the Chief
of the Staff, Lieutenant-General Von Voigts-Rhetz went to
Gitschin to report them, as well as the news that had been
received by the Ist Army. He arrived there at 11 o'clock P.M.

The King immediately resolved to attack the enemy on this
side of the Elbe with his whole force, whether the whole Austrian Army or only a large part of it should be found there.

One scarcely ventured to hope the first, but at all events a
successful action, for which, from the positions of the Prussian
Armies there was every chance, must materially facilitate an
attack of the Elbe position, in case it should afterwards be
necessary.

By order of His Majesty the following communication to the
IInd Army was immediately drawn up :—

　　"According to intelligence received by the Ist Army,
"the enemy has advanced beyond the line of the Bistritz,
"at Sadowa, with three corps d'armée, which may, how-
"ever, possibly be still further increased, and an engage-
"ment with the Ist Army may be expected there early
"to-morrow morning. Orders have been issued that the
"Ist Army is to take post to-morrow, July 3rd, at
"2 o'clock A.M., with two divisions at Horzitz, one at
"Milowitz, one at Cerekwitz, two at Psanek and Bristan,
"the Cavalry corps at Gutwasser.

　　"Your Royal Highness will at once make the neces-
"sary arrangements to advance with your whole force
"to the support of the Ist Army against the right flank
"of the expected advance of the enemy, and will attack
"as early as possible.

　　"The orders issued from here this afternoon, under
"different circumstances, are no longer valid.
　　　　　　(Signed)　　　"Von Moltke."

These orders were despatched at midnight. As the importance of the moment demanded, one copy of them was sent by
way of Kamenitz, a second one by the King's aide-de-camp,
Lieutenant-Colonel Count Finkenstein, direct to Königinhof.
As the route of this officer led close by the cantonments of the
Ist Corps d'Armée, he was at the same time the bearer of the
following communication to General Von Bonin :—

　　"In all probability an engagement will take place
"early to-morrow morning between the Ist Army and

" three corps of the enemy at Sadowa, on the Bistritz
" (on the road between Königgrät and Horzitz). Your
" Excellency will concentrate your corps at once, in order
" to be perfectly in readiness when the orders of His
" Royal Highness the Crown Prince arrive; or will, if
" necessary, act independently, as circumstances may
" demand.

(Signed)    " Von Moltke."

---

## The 3rd of July,

## BATTLE OF KÖNIGGRÄTZ.

### I.—Preparatory Dispositions and Movements up to 6 o'clock a.m.*

In order to be able to form an opinion on the battle of König-grätz, it is essential to bear in mind the positions of the different corps on the 2nd of July.

The accompanying sketch will enable the reader to see at a glance all that has been hitherto stated in this respect. There only remains to add that the head-quarters of—

His Majesty the King were at Gitschin ;
Prince Frederick Charles, at Kamenitz ;
The Crown Prince, at Königinhof ;
General Von Herwarth, at Hochwesely.

Feldzeugmeister Benedek had moved his headquarters to the " Prager Vorstadt " of Königgrätz.

The Prussian Armies had voluntarily kept a front of nearly 23 miles breadth. The troops nearest to the enemy were the advanced guards of the 7th and 8th Divisions; they were stationed at Milowitz, and as far forward as Gross-Jeritz and Cerekwitz.

The whole Austrian Army of the North was assembled behind the small river Bistritz, with the fortress of König-grätz and the Elbe in its rear; it extended over a space of about 5 miles.

A state of concentration like that in which the Army had been for the last five days renders the subsistence of the troops extremely difficult, and only admits of bivouacking, thereby weakening the strength of the troops, and opposing the greatest obstacles to all further movements. Under these circumstances the march of the army on the 1st of July, although only nine miles long, lasted 24 hours.

---

* *Vide* Appendix XXIIa– XIIg.

These are considerations which make a speedy decision urgent; they were probably not without weight when the Feldzeugmeister made up his mind to accept battle in case the Prussian armies advanced still further. Added to this, the Commanders of the Corps and the Chiefs of the Staff, who were summoned to the Austrian head-quarters on the 2nd of July, declared that the troops were in the best of spirits and wished for nothing more ardently than a speedy and grand decisive battle.

If Feldzeugmeister Benedek had intended—as Austrian accounts affirm—to commence his retreat towards Vienna, he now relinquished this idea, and the same evening issued the following dipositions for battle, which, however, did not reach several of the corps before between 4 and 5 A.M. of the 3rd of July.

"*Königgrätz, Prager Vorstadt,*
"*2nd of July,* 1866.

"Accounts, which have been received to-day, state " that the enemy is in great force in the neighbourhood " of Neu-Bidzow and in front of Horzitz; skirmishing " has already taken place between our outposts and " those of the enemy at Kobilitz and Sucha. Judging " from the enemy's position, it is possible that an attack " may be made to-morrow, and may be directed, in the " first place, against the Royal Saxon Corps d'Armée.

" In case of this taking place, I give the following " orders :—

" The Royal Saxon Corps will occupy the heights of " Popowitz; its left wing will be slightly refused and " covered by its own Cavalry. Nothing but outposts " will be pushed forward beyond this position. To the " left, and somewhat to the rear of them, the 1st Light " Cavalry Division will take up a position near Problus " and Prim, on suitable ground. The Xth Corps will " take post on the right of the Saxon Corps, and lastly, " the IIIrd Corps will occupy the heights of Lipa and " Chlum, on the right of the Xth Corps. The principal " duty of the VIIIth Corps will be to serve as support " to the Saxon Corps, behind which it will station itself. " Troops not herein-named have merely to hold them- " selves in readiness so long as the attack is confined to " our left wing; but should the enemy's attack assume " greater dimensions, and be directed against our centre " and right wing as well, then the whole army will be " formed in order of battle, and the following measures " will be taken :—

" The IVth Corps will move up on the right of the " IIIrd to the heights of Chlum and Nedelist, and the " IInd Corps on the extreme right flank, next to the " IVth. The IInd Light Cavalry Division will march to " the rear of Nedelist, and will remain there in readiness

" The VIth Corps will assemble on the heights of
" Wsestar, the Ist move to Rosnitz—both Corps formed
" in close order. The 1st and 3rd Reserve Cavalry
" Divisions will move to Sweti, the 2nd Reserve Cavalry
" Division to Briza.

" In the further event of a general attack, the Ist
" and IVth Corps, the five Cavalry Divisions, and the
" Artillery Reserve of the Army, which takes post behind
" the Ist and VIth Corps, will form the reserve of the
" army, and will be at my sole disposal.

" Early to-morrow the whole army must hold itself in
" readiness for a general action. The corps which is
" first attacked will immediately acquaint those corps of
" it that stand next according to these orders ; the latter
" will then send the intelligence further on.

" The VIIIth Corps will break up its camp imme-
" diately, and will send an officer on in advance to the
" head-quarters of the Saxon Corps d'Armée. In case
" the action should have commenced already, or be on
" the point of commencing, this officer will hasten back
" to meet the VIIIth Corps, and will lead it to the
" position which it is to take up behind the Saxon Corps.
" Should there be no prospect of an attack of the enemy,
" the VIIIth Corps will encamp on the appointed spot
" near Charbusitz.

" Should only the left wing of the army be engaged,
" I shall be with it, but in the event of a general action,
" my position will be on the heights of Chlum. Should
" the Army be forced to retreat, this will take place by
" way of Holic or the Hohenmauth road, without dis-
" turbing the fortress of Königgrätz.

" Immediately on receipt of these orders the IInd
" and IVth Corps will cause pontoon-bridges to be
" thrown over the Elbe, namely, the IInd Corps two
" bridges between Lochenitz and Predmeritz ; the IVth
" Corps two bridges also near Placka.

" Whatever materials may be wanted for this pur-
" pose will be given by the train of the 6th Battalion.
" Should it be necessary to make roads up to the bridges,
" this must also be done.

" The pioneers of the Ist Corps d'Armée will throw a
" bridge over the Adler at Swinar immediately. The
" execution of these orders is to be reported by Officers
" either verbally or in writing, and the spots selected
" for the bridges distinctly described.

" Dispositions for the event of a retreat will be issued
" to-morrow.

(Signed) " BENEDEK."

The last-mentioned dispositions for the retreat, in particular
which bridges were allotted to the different corps, and how

the march of such large bodies of troops to Holic was to be effected, seem not to have reached the corps d'armée. Some of the corps, at least, deny having received them.

A disposition with the VIth Corps, which General Ramming issued in his bivouac near Wsestar, at half-past 8 A.M. of the 3rd July, and which fell afterwards into the hands of the Prussians, states, as extracts from the above-mentioned general orders, where the places for crossing the river were, and also adds, that orders for the event of a retreat would follow.

We may here remark that Count Clam Gallas had been summoned to Vienna; he left on the morning of the 3rd of July, and Major-General Count Gondrecourt took command of his corps. Generals Henikstein and Krismanic were also removed from their posts, and the duties of Chief of the Staff entrusted to Major-General Von Baumgarten. In the place of Archduke Leopold, Major-General Weber had been in command of the VIIIth Corps since the 29th of June.

By way of adding to the strength of the battle-field, the Feldzeugmeister ordered the Director of Engineers, Colonel Baron Pidoll, to throw up some entrenchments in the position between Nedelist and Lipa. These instructions were given as early as the evening of the 1st of July. After a previous inspection of the ground, the 1st Battalion of Pioneers and half of the 12th Company of the 1st Regiment of Engineers constructed the following works in the course of the forenoon of the 2nd of July :—

Battery No. 1.—1,400 paces to the north of the church of Nedelist.
Battery No. 2.—1,500 paces north-west of the same church, on the slope of the Maslowed hill.
Battery No. 3.—1,000 paces to the east of the northern entrance of Chlum.
Battery No. 4.—Close to the west side of the same entrance.
Battery No. 5.—500 paces off the west entrance of the same village.

In the course of the afternoon and by the next morning other detachments, which were placed at Colonel Pidoll's disposal, completed still further:

An abattis in those patches of the Lipa wood that are nearest to Battery No. 4; it was made by half an Infantry pioneer detachment of Colonel Mondl's Brigade.

Battery No. 6, with powder magazine, forming a continuation of the west skirts of the same wood, constructed by the pioneer companies of the IIIrd Corps; this work was not completed before 10 A.M. of the 3rd of July.

The 6th Pioneer Battalion, which arrived at 6 P.M. of the 2nd of July, threw up two earthworks in front of battery No. 3. They had the form of a bastion. and were intended for the covering guard of the battery. Their total length was 390 paces; their breastworks were 8 feet high, with traverses; each work was to hold one company.

In addition to these, those detachments of the 1st Engineer Regiment which had been already at work on the 2nd of July, completed the following works :—

The 1st and 2nd Companies, two similar breastworks in front of Battery No. 1, 320 paces long.

The 3rd Company, an earthwork to flank Battery No. 4, and a small one at the north angle of Chlum, covering the entrance to the village.

The 4th Company, rifle pits flanking Battteries 4 and 5, and, jointly with the pioneer detachments of Colonel Mondl's Brigade, an abattis round the northern and part of the western skirts of the Lipa wood.

The question of strengthening the left flank of the Austrian line of battle was not yet settled when the Prussian attack commenced, on the morning of the 3rd of July. Colonel Von Pidol then despatched Major Von Ghyczy of the Staff of Engineers with the 6th Pioneer Battalion, to the left wing and, retained the Engineer detachments to add to the strength of the defences of Lipa and Chlum.

At this point two Engineer companies, and the three Pioneer detachments of the IIIrd Corps d'Armée placed the west front of Lipa, the two remaining Engineer companies the west side of Chlum, in a state of defence.

The 6th Pioneer Battalion did not reach Problus before 10½ A.M. With the assistance of the Saxon Pioneer detachments of the advanced guard and the " sappeurs " of the Infantry, one company placed the skirts of the village, a second one those of Nieder Prim, in a state of defence; the two other companies constructed an abattis along the west skirts of the wood between Problius and Charbusitz.

With the exception of those on the left flank and those which were on the ground occupied by the IIIrd Corps, these defences were only momentarily made use of during the retreat. The Austrian journal " Kamerad," of the year 1867, No. 4, makes the following remarks on this point :—

" Lastly, the IVth Corps d'Armée was not informed that " earthworks had been thrown up marking the front line of the " position. When they were first seen, early on the 3rd of July, " their position in the hollow of the ground only excited a " feeling of surprise, and led to the supposition that they were " merely intended, in the event of a retreat, to enable the " troops to make some slight stand on this slope, which was " overlooked from all sides."

Prince Frederick Charles's disposition were issued at 9 P.M. It was, therefore, late before the orders could reach the troops.

The most important divisions of the Army of the Elbe did not receive Von Herwarth's orders before half-past 2 A.M. of the 3rd; they were to start at three. The evening before, the 5th squadron of the King's Hussar Regiment (No. 7), came up with the enemy near Psanek; 1 officer and 6 men of the Austrian Regiment, King of Prussia Hussars (No. 10) were taken prisoners on this occasion; they stated that their supports consisted of Saxon troops. Due precautions were therefore necessary during the further advance of the army. Continued rain had rendered the country roads almost impassable, and darkness impeded the march, so that, in spite of the utmost exertions, the columns could proceed but slowly. Although the distance from Smidar to Nechanitz is only 9 miles, still General Schoeler's advanced guard could not debouch from the wood of Kobilitz before half-past 6 A.M.

The Ist Army was not either able to keep its appointed time. The formation of the 4th Division at Bristan was not completed before four o'clock, that of the Reserve Artillery of the IInd Corps d'Armée about 5 o'clock. By a still worse road the head of the 3rd Division reached the entrance of Petrowitz about the same time; the 5th Division, which did not receive its orders until half-past 1 A.M., did not take up its appointed position before 6 o'clock; similar circumstances attended the march of the other divisions.

Nevertheless, shortly after dawn of the dull, rainy day, the divisions occupied their positions as orders by Prince Frederick Charles, namely :—

General Fransecky's Division at Cerekwitz.
     „     Horn's Division at Milowitz.
     „     Herwarth's Division at Bristan.
     „     Werder's Division at Psanek.

The divisions of Generals Manstein and Tümpling were assembling in a reserve position near Horzitz. The Cavalry remained for the present in its bivouacs, according to orders.

Prince Frederick Charles's request to the Crown Prince, to co-operate with one or two corps in the expected action of the Ist Army, arrived at the head-quarters of the IInd Army, in Königinhof, about 2 A.M. But the Crown Prince was not able to accede immediately to the proposal in its full extent. From motives which have been already explained, the IInd Army had been instructed not to cross the Elbe as yet, and even as late as the 2nd of July orders had arrived from general head-quarters, to push a strong detachment on towards the Aupa. The reconnaissance of the preceding days, more particularly one which the Crown Prince made personally on the 2nd of July, had, however, proved that the enemy no longer held the line of the Aupa; that he had indeed quitted the neighbourhood of Josephstadt. The expedition towards the Aupa was, therefore, relinquished. Reports having, however, been received, stating that the enemy might possibly not hold Josephstadt, the VIth Corps d'Armée was instructed to advance on the right bank of the Aupa towards the fortress on the morning of the 3rd of July, in order to make sure on this point.

On the other hand, the Ist Corps d'Armée had already crossed the Elbe, and was therefore available to assist Prince Frederick Charles in the event of an action taking place, so that the bearer of the request returned with the following answer:

"*To H.R.H. Prince Frederick Charles.*

"By order of H.R.H. the Commander-in-Chief of the "IInd Army, I inform your R.H. that the VIth Corps will "undertake a reconnaissance of Josephstadt, on the left* "bank of the Elbe early this morning; this will, it is to "be hoped, draw off a portion of the enemy's forces from "the Ist Army. The Ist Corps d'Armée, followed by the "Reserve Cavalry, will advance, as His Majesty's orders "prescribe, by way of Miletin and Bürglitz, and will "eventually be prepared to assist your R.H. The Guards "and the Vth Corps are no longer at the disposal of the "IInd Army, because, according to the above-mentioned "orders, they are to remain in their present positions, and "are, moreover, absolutely necessary as supports of the "VIth Corps d'Armée, as the latter may possibly be very "much exposed.

(Signed)  "VON BLUMENTHAL,
"*Major-General.*"

"*Königinhof, 3rd of July,* 1866, 3 *a.m.*"

Corresponding orders were despatched to the Ist Corps d'Armée.

Shortly after leaving Königinhof, the officer bearing this answer met Lieutenant-Colonel Count Finkenstein with the orders for the advance of the whole IInd Army. Having been informed by the latter of this change in the position of affairs, he returned with him to Königinhof.

Although Count Finkenstein had to ride 22½ miles, from Gitschin to Königinhof, by night, and in a perfectly strange country, he was still able to deliver the letter which had been given to him for General Von Bonin to an officer of the outposts at Zabres as early as a quarter past 3 A.M. It reached the Chief of the Staff of the Ist Corps d'Armée by a quarter to 5 A.M. The letter which Count Finkenstein brought for the Crown Prince was in the hands of the Chief of the Staff of the IInd Army by 4 o'clock.

On the receipt of this despatch, His Royal Highness issued the following orders at 5 A.M. :—

"According to information received here, an attack "of the enemy on the Ist Army at Horzitz, Milowitz, and "Cerekwitz may be expected; the IInd Army will "advance to the support of the latter as follows :—

---

* General Von Blumenthal had just returned from Gitschin, and was not yet acquainted with the arrangement made by the Crown Prince that the VIth Corps was to advance on to the *right* bank of the Elbe.

" 1. The Ist Corps d'Armée will march in two columns
" by Zabres and Gross-Trotin to Gross-Burglitz.

" 2. The Cavalry Division will follow the Ist Corps to
" the same place.

" 3. The Corps of Guards will move from Königinhof
" on Jericek and Lhota.

" 4. The VIth Corps d'Armée to Welchow; on arriving
" there it will post a detachment to watch the fortress
" of Josephstadt.

" The demonstration originally ordered for to-day will
" not be made.

" 5. Two hours after the departure of the VIth Corps
" it will be followed by the Vth, which will advance as
" far as Choteborek.

" The troops will start as early as possible, and will
" leave trains and baggage behind, neither of which will
" be brought forward unless specially ordered by the
" Commander-in-Chief.

" In the name of the Commander-in-Chief, the Chief
" of the Staff.

(Signed)     " VON BLUMENTHAL,
" *Major-General.*"

" *Head-Quarters, Königinhof, July 3, 5 a.m.*"

The Commander-in-Chief of the Ist Army went from
Kamenitz to Milowitz at half-past 1 A.M. At a quater to 6 A.M.,
General Herwarth's report arrived at Milowitz, stating that he
would reach Nechanitz between 7 and 9 o'clock with 36
battalions.

The co-operation of all the Prussian troops which had
crossed the frontier of Bohemia for offensive operations, seemed
thus perfectly certain in the event of the enemy accepting a
general action. The Prussian outposts remained unchanged;
fog and dense rain had hidden the movements of the troops in
their rear, and the enemy's outposts had withdrawn in the
direction of Dub.

Under these circumstances, it seems both possible and
advisable without further delay to occupy the enemy's attention, and to engage his forces in front with the Ist Army, in
order that the double flank attack which had been concerted
might come into full play.

At 6 o'clock, therefore, Prince Frederick Charles ordered an
advance of his whole army, for the purpose of taking up such a
position in the neighbourhood of the Bistritz as would be
adapted to all contingencies. For the present it was not intended actually to attack, because the co-operation of the
IInd Army, the corps of which had to march between 9 and 12
miles, could not be reckoned upon before mid-day.

General Horn's division was ordered to advance on and
to the left of the high-road, as an advanced guard of those
troops which were approaching Sadowa in the centre; the IInd

Corps d'Armée was to keep on a line with the former on the right side of the high-road. The 5th and 6th Divisions were instructed to follow as reserve behind the 8th Division, at the side of the high-road, whilst the Reserve Artillery advanced on the road itself. The Cavalry Corps was set in motion at 5 o'clock from Gutwasser towards Petrowitz; it was to follow behind the right wing (IInd Corps d'Armée), and to keep up the communication with the Army of the Elbe.

General Fransecky's Division received instructions to advance from Cerekwitz as soon as the action commenced at Sadowa, and to join in it as circumstances might demand. The divisional Cavalry of the 5th and 6th Divisions was formed into a brigade under the command of Major-General Count Bismarck, and General Von der Goltz's Brigade of the Cavalry Corps was detached to IInd Corps d'Armée.

Thus, by 6 A.M. the columns of the Army of the Elbe and of the 1st Army were in full advance towards the Bistritz,

At this time (6 o'clock) the marching orders for the IInd Army had only reached the Corps of Guards and the Vth Corps d'Armée. The VIth Corps had received the first orders of the Commander-in-Chief to advance towards Josephstadt at half-past 12 P.M.; it was still in its bivouacs westward of Gradlitz, ready to start for the other bank of the Elbe, but the second orders, which modified the first, had not yet arrived. The letter from the Chief of the General Staff of the Army to the 1st Corps d'Armée was delivered at Prausnitz by a quarter past 5 A.M.; it authorized this corps to act immediately according to circumstances, and at a quarter to 6 the following orders were issued:

"The troops will hold themselves in immediate readi-
"ness to advance in the direction of Sadowa, and will
"prepare for action. Should the provision parks arrive
"before starting, they will make up their to-day's rations
"for man and horse.
"Further instructions will follow.
(Signed) "Von Bonin."

" Ober-Prausnitz, July 3, 1866."

This corps was therefore perfectly prepared.

---

II.—Advance against the Bistritz (6—8 o'clock a.m.).

The Austrian-Saxon Army had pushed strong detachments up to and beyond the Bistritz, as advanced guards and outposts.

To commence from the left flank, the Saxons had occupied Alt-Nechanitz ever since the 1st of July with the 8th Battalion and a peloton of Cavalry; outposts were posted still further forward. The 7th Battalion and one squadron were stationed in Nechanitz; the 11th and a peloton of Cavalry at Hradek;

two companies of the latter battalion were detached to Kuncitz; a Cavalry picquet was posted at Radikowitz.

The "Reiter" Division was stationed eastward of Nechanitz, in support of the outposts.

Further to the right, detachments of the Xth Austrian Corps and the 3rd Reserve Cavalry Division had thrown out outposts and patrols beyond the Bistritz, which watched the country on the right bank of the stream. The ground still further to the right was held by Colonel Prohaska's Brigade at Sadowa. Cistowes was occupied by a battalion of the 68th Regiment (Brigade Appiano), whilst the 4th Battalion of Rifles kept up the communication with the outposts of General Brandenstein's Brigade of the IVth Corps in the direction of the Maslowed wood. On the 2nd of July this brigade was employed in watching the line of country from the Bistritz eastwards past Benatek to Horenowes, but was obliged to extend its line still further, as far as Rasitz, when the VIIIth Corps d'Armée, whose outposts occupied that part of the field, was moved to the left flank of the army at half-past 4 A.M. of the 3rd of July. The 1st Battalion of the 32nd Regiment (Archduke Ferdinand d'Este), which was recalled from outpost duty, and the 2nd Battalion of the 21st Regiment (Baron Reischach, both belonging to the latter corps, still remained at Horenowes.

General Brandenstein stationed the 2nd Battalion of the 26th Regiment (Grand Duke Michael) and the 27th Rifle Battalion in the wood of Maslowed; the line of the latter stretched as far as Horenowes. The ring wing of the brigade, eastward of this village, consisted of the 1st Battalion of the 26th Infantry Regiment. Between the village and the wood two guns of the brigade battery, and a troop of the 7th Hussars (Prince of Prussia), were posted. The main body of the division, four battalions and six guns, bivouacked south-eastward of Maslowed.

The IInd Corps d'Armée took up the line still farther to the right, and reached as far the Elbe. In the course of the afternoon of the 2nd of July the bivouacs of this corps had been changed, the Infantry having been withdrawn behind the Trotina, its right wing resting on the village of Trotina, and the left extending in the direction of Sendrasitz. Colonel Thom's Brigade had posted the 1st Battalion of the 69th Regiment (Count Jellacic) on the wooded slope of the right bank of the Trotina; the 2nd Light Cavalry Division remained on the left bank of the stream, and covered the right of the Austrian position with its outposts. Two squadrons of the 6th Lancers (Emperor Francis Joseph) were detached to Smiritz.

According to the general orders, however, the Cavalry was also to fall back to the rear of Nedelist.

As has been already stated, the advanced guard of the Army of the Elbe, under Major-General Schoeler, debouched from the wood eastward of Kobilitz about half-past 6 A.M. Near Alt-Nechanitz a bivouac of the enemy was seen, whereupon the Fusilier Battalion of the 28th Regiment immediately advanced in front, the 2nd Battalion of the 33rd Regiment on the right, and the Fusilier Battalion of the 17th Regiment on the left, for a concentric attack on the village, whilst Captain Pilgrim's Battery opened fire from the south skirts of the wood. After a brief skirmish the 8th Saxon Battalion quitted the village and fell back to the small town of Nechanitz. In doing so it fired the bridge over the mill-stream, which flows past the north-eastern entrance of Alt-Nechanitz, as well as some neigbouring buildings. Captain Zenker's Battery, attached to the Saxon "Reiter" Division, which was destined as support for the outposts, came into action in a position near the churchyard of Nechanitz, and shelled the bridge so severely that it was not possible to quench the fire until the battery was dislodged by the Prussian battery of Captain Pilgrim.

The Fusilier Battalion of the 28th Regiment then advanced straight across the meadows against Nechanitz, which town was defended by the 8th Saxon Battalion, supported by the 7th. The bridge had been made impassable by removing the planks, but the Pioneer section of the battalion repaired it in face of the enemy's fire. The 2nd Battalion of the 33rd Regiment (Lieut.-Colonel Von Marschall) had advanced more to the right; the Fusilier Battalion of the 17th Regiment to the left, to find another passage over the Bistritz and its swampy meadows, which were very difficult to cross in consequence of the wet About 8 A.M. weather.

The advance of the Ist Army was executed in the following manner, commencing from the right wing :—

The Cavalry Corps reached Petrovitz at half-past 6 o'clock, and had established communications with the Army of the Elbe by this time; at 7 the corps continued its march by way of Psanek and Neresow. As soon as artillery fire was heard in the direction of Zawadilka, it trotted on to Sucha, and formed line there shortly after 8 o'clock, fronting the Bistritz; General Von Alvensleben's Division, with its right flank resting on Sucha; General Hann's Division on the left wing, as far forwards as the Sucha-Zawadilka road. The three batteries of the 1st Division took up a position further forward against the enemy's batteries beyond the Bistritz, but did not open fire on account of the distance.

General Werder's Division had moved forwards from Psanek on the Lhota-Zawadilka road, and was approaching the latter village at about 8 o'clock.

General Herwarth's Division, followed by the Reserve Artillery of the IInd Corps, marched across country over very heavy ground from Bristan towards the Mzan-Sadowa road, passing by the north side of Stracow. As soon as the 4th Lancer Regiment, which was with the advanced guard, debouched from Mzan, it was shelled by a battery posted at the wood beyond Sadowa. The 3rd Prussian 4-pounder battery (Captain Leo) took up a position against the latter southwards of Mzan, but had no sooner opened fire than, one after another, four hostile batteries on the other side of Dohalica, which had been hitherto concealed by the fog, poured in a crushing fire. The 4th 4-pounder, and at 8 o'clock the 3rd 6-pounder batteries (Prussian) took up positions by the side of the battery already engaged. The advanced guard of the division occupied Mzan; the main body and the reserve stationed themselves close behind the village in a sheltered position. The Reserve Artillery of the IInd Corps remained behind the division which had been joined by General Von der Goltz's Cavalry Brigade, near Psanek, as early as half-past 4. All villages on the Bistritz were found to be occupied by the enemy.

The advanced guard of General Horn's Division had been pushed forward from Milowitz to Klenitz at 4 o'clock, and the division advanced in line-of-battle order at 6, with the 6th Lancer Regiment in front. The enemy had quitted Dub, but still held Sadowa with Infantry.

The battalions of the advanced guard, formed in columns of companies, pressed on towards the brickfield (*ziegelei*) on the high-road in front of Sadowa, and the Infantry skirmishing commenced.

Even before 7 o'clock, as soon as the first Prussian columns became visible, an Austrian battery had opened fire from the other side of the Bistritz, between the woods of Sadowa and Maslowed. Cavalry was seen retiring behind the wood of Sadowa from the neighbourhood of Dohalitz and Dohalicka. Infantry was visible in the neighbourhood of the last-named wood.

To reinforce the battery of the advanced guard, General Von Hann ordered up the 3rd 6-pounder battery (Captain Anton). This latter battery fired the first shot at about half-past 7. The 3rd 4-pounder battery (Captain Von Schlotheim) took post on its left. At first these batteries were covered by the 12th Company, later in the day by the 1st Battalion of the 71st Regiment.

The 5th and 6th Divisions began to form line at Klenitz about 7 o'clock; the former to the west, the latter to the east of the high-road.

The Reserve Artillery of the army was on the march to the north-west of the Sadowa Brickfield, where it was to await further orders.

The main body of General Fransecky's Division had assembled at half-past 1 A.M. already, and the division was in its appointed position at Cerekwitz by 3 o'clock. From thence Lieutenant Count Hohenthal was immediately despatched to inform the nearest detachments of the IInd Army of the position of the division. In Daubrowitz this officer found outposts of the 1st Division of Guards, which had as yet received no order to advance.

Lieutenant Von Kleist, who had been despatched to the Commander-in-Chief of the 1st Army at 4 A.M., returned at 7 with the order that "the division was to join in the action of

" the 8th Division, which was advancing on Sadowa, according
" to circumstances." Accordingly General Fransecky determined to march on Benatek as soon as the first shot should be
fired by the 8th Division. This took place about half-past 7,
and at the same time Count Hohenthal was again sent to
Daubrowitz, with a request to the Guards to advance, in order
to cover the left flank of the division.

Shortly after half-past 7 the advanced guard of the 7th Division (Colonel Von Zychlinsky) formed for action ; the Fusilier
Battalion of the 27th Regiment to the west, the Fusilier Battalion of the 67th Regiment to the east of the road to Benatek,
the 1st squadron of the 10th Hussars covering the left flank.
The picquets of the Austrian 26th Regiment (Grand Duke
Michael), that were stationed northwards of Benatek, retired to
the village. As soon as the Prussian battalions arrived in front
of the village, they were fired on by the enemy's artillery from
the heights of Horenowes and Maslowed, and from the neighbourhood of the Skalka wood. At this spot the enemy's battery
was already engaged with the artillery of the 8th Division on
the Boskos-Berg. As soon, therefore, as the two 4-pounder
batteries of the 7th Division came into action southward of the
angle of the wood, at the road leading to Horenowes, and
opened fire on the right flank of the enemy's artillery at a
distance of 4,000 paces, the latter fell back towards Lipa, accompanied by some Infantry detachments. A few shells were
thrown into Benatek, which soon caught fire, upon which the
outposts and the two battalions of the Grand Duke Michael
Regiment quitted the village, which was then passed by the
Prussian advanced guard without further contest.

The 10th Company of the 27th Regiment occupied the
southern skirts of Benatek, the 9th Company the small copse to
the south-west. The 11th and 12th Companies were stationed
in the corn-fields immediately southward of the village. The
Fusilier Battalion of the 67th Regiment (Lieut.-Colonel Baron
Von Buttlar) was pushed forward towards the projecting angle
of the Maslowed wood, the skirts of which seemed to be occupied in force, and from whence a severe but ineffectual fire was
kept up. It was now necessary to wait until the remaining
detachments of the advanced guard came up.

During the advance of his army, Prince Frederick Charles
went to the right wing, to reconnoitre the country near the
Bistritz, and to make himself acquainted with the position of
affairs. Fog and rain prevented any extensive view, and it
was only from the numerous artillery, which was firing on the
heads of the Prussian columns, that the presence of considerable forces of the enemy could be surmised.

The Prince gave orders that the enemy's fire should be but
slowly returned until the weather cleared up, and that the divisions should on no account cross the Bistritz. On his return to
the heights of Dub he sent instructions to General Von Horn too,
merely to keep up the action of the advanced guard against

Sadowa, which village was prepared for Infantry defence, and to move the main body and the reserve somewhat more to the left towards Sowetitz, so as to establish communications with the 7th Division.

About 8 o'clock loud cheering from the rear announced the arrival of His Majesty the King. As soon as he appeared with his numerous suite on the heights of Dub an Austrian battery turned its fire in this direction, and shells fell on all sides.

After receiving the report of Prince Frederick Charles, His Majesty gave orders that the Ist Army should advance and take possession of the line of the Bistritz.

Even in case the enemy should assume the offensive, still the Ist Army and the Army of the Elbe would be strong enough to hold this line for a considerable length of time. The 5th and 6th Divisions were at hand as reserves, and even if the Prussian centre had been ultimately obliged to fall back, still the arrival of the IInd Army must have decided the day.

It was true that many hours might elapse before the Crown Prince came up with all his forces, but it was supposed that the arrival of the 1st Corps, which had been apprised so early, might soon be expected.

As we have heard, the IInd Army originally intended making a demonstration against Josephstadt with the VIth Corps, and General Von Mutius had arranged that General Von Prondzinski's Division (16 battalions, 4 squadrons, and 12 guns) should break up from Gradlitz at 6 o'clock, and cross the Elbe on a pontoon bridge near Kukus. General Von Zastrow's Division was to start with the 21st Brigade at 7, and the 22nd Brigade at 8 o'clock. The brigades were to cross the river respectively at Stangendorf and Schurz, where bridges had been thrown over by the Vth Corps.

Thus, General Prondzinski's Division was already on the march, when the Commanding General of the Corps (General Von Mutius) received the Crown Prince's orders to march on Welchow (half-past 6 A.M.). General Zastrow's Division, which was also on the point of leaving its bivouac, was instructed to start immediately, to cross the Elbe in two columns, as was previously ordered, to concentrate both brigades at Welchow, by way of Sibojed and of Litic, and then to bring forward its artillery and form for action.

On reaching Kloster-Schlotten the advanced guard of the 12th Division proceeded in the direction of Salney; it was followed by the main body, the strength of which was much diminished by the number of troops that were absent on other duties.

Cavalry detachments were thrown out in all directions, and met with Hussar and Lancer patrols of the enemy, which fell back towards Unter-Dolzen on a large body of Cavalry. Jaromir was found occupied, but the fortress Josephstadt opened fire on the Prussian skirmishers.

It was not before reaching Salney that General Von Proudzinski received the following pencilled note :—

"The 12th Division will march on Westetz, Ertina "as far as the Welchow-Jaromir road, and will cover the "left flank of the corps.

(Signed)    " VON MUTIUS."

" *Gradlitz, July* 3, 1866."

The troops that had been pushed forward towards Jaromir were therefore recalled, and the division was set in motion in the direction of Ertina.

Of the Corps of Guards it was the 2nd Division which was first called to arms in its bivouacs near Rettendorf. The instructions it received at 7 o'clock were to advance in close order until the head of the column reached Königinhof.

The 1st Division of Guards, in and near Königinhof, did not receive orders to march on Jericek until half-past 7 A.M.; it left at 8.

At the same time the Vth Corps started from Gradlitz.

The Ist Corps had thought necessary to wait for further orders from the Commander-in-Chief of the IInd Army before commencing its march. These orders arrived at a quarter to 8 A.M., or (according to the statement of the orderly officer who carried them) at a quarter past 7, at Ober-Prausnitz.

An hour later the Commander of the corps had issued his orders.

Consequently at 8 o'clock, when the Ist Army and the Army of the Elbe were already engaged on the Bistritz, no troops of the IInd Army were on the right bank of the Elbe, except the weak VIth Corps, the advanced guard of the Corps of Guards, and the Ist Corps. The two latter, however, had as yet no marching orders.

---

III.—THE AUSTRIAN ARMY TAKES UP ITS LINE OF BATTLE. THE PRUSSIAN IST ARMY AND THE ARMY OF THE ELBE ESTABLISH THEMSELVES ON THE BISTRITZ. THE IIND ARMY IS DRAWING NEAR THE BATTLE-FIELD. 8 TILL 11 A.M.

The first shots that were fired had called almost all corps of the Austrian Army to arms. The extent which the cannonade very soon assumed proved beyond all doubt that there was no longer any question of the partial attack, which Feldzeugmeister Benedek's dispositions had provided for, but rather that the general attack of the enemy was commencing, which was the second eventuality spoken of in these orders. Divers circumstances had, however, caused the army to take up a line of battle which essentially differed from the one originally intended.

On the extreme left the dispositions which reached the Saxon Corps d'Armée at midnight, instructed it to take up a position on the range of hills eastward of Popowitz and Tresowitz.

Now, when this tract of ground was closely inspected at

early dawn, it was found not to be suitable as a position for the whole Corps d'Armée, on account of a deficiency of communications within the position (wegen seiner beschränkten innern Wegsamkeit), but that the heights to the eastward, between Nieder-Prim and Problus, were well adapted to the purpose. No time was lost in requesting the Commander-in-Chief to permit a corresponding modification of the previous orders, which was immediately agreed to. Consequently the Crown Prince of Saxony made the following arrangements :—

A brigade of General Schimpff's division was despatched to the range of hills behind Lubno, Popowitz, and Tresowitz. It was intended to hold these hills merely as an advanced position, and the brigade was instructed to occupy the above-named villages and the neighbouring bridges, but to fall back on the main position at Problus, if attacked by superior forces of the enemy. Nechanitz was only to be occupied slightly by the outposts, in support of which the "Reiter" division was to take up suitable positions eastward of Nechanitz, and was to impede the débouché of the enemy.

The other brigade of General Schimpff's division was to occupy Neider-Prim and Problus; General Von Stieglitz's division and the Reserve Artillery were to take post between both villages. The original plan of occupying Nechanitz and the commanding heights in front of Hradek in force, especially with artillery, for which batteries had been already thrown up on the evening of the 2nd of July, was relinquished with reluctance, but the special orders of the Commander-in-Chief did not permit such an extension of the left wing of the line of battle.

The first shots were fired before the above-mentioned arrangements were completed.

At this time the VIIIth Austrian Corps—it had left two battalions at Horenowes, and was only about 19 battalions strong —was on the march from its bivouac near Nedelist, to the country between Ober-Prim and Charbusitz, where it was to take up a position as reserve for the Saxons; the 1st Light Cavalry Division was coming up for the same purpose.

The Xth Corps had bivouacked by Chlum, Lipa, and Langenhof, and had detached the 28th Rifle Battalion, before 6 o'clock, to garrison the sugar factory (zucker-fabrik) on the right bank of the Bistritz; two battalions of the 1st and 3rd Regiments (Emperor Francis and Archduke Charles) also arrived at the same spot. The remainder of General Knebel's brigade took up a position in support of these troops, partly at Unter Dohalitz, and partly in the wood of Sadowa. The *ci-devant* Brigade " Grivicic," now reduced to three combined battalions, under command of Lieutenant-Colonel Fabry, as well as the four batteries of the Reserve Artillery of the corps, and three squadrons of the 9th Lancer Regiment (Count Mensdorff) proceeded to Dohalicka. General Wimpffen's brigade was stationed more to the left, at Mokrowous, and Colonel Mondl's brigade remained for the present—at the request of Archduke Ernest—in the position of Chlum, until the IIIrd Corps d'Armée arrived, so that the Xth Corps occupied a somewhat advanced position in the general line of battle.

The IIIrd Corps was to join the right wing of the Xth Corps. As the troops of the former were getting under arms in their bivouacs, in front of the Xth Corps and westward of Cistowes, they received the following orders from Archduke Ernest:—

"According to orders of the Commander-in-Chief, "dated the 2nd instant, No. 961, the army will take up a "new position, and the IIIrd Corps will accordingly have "to form on the heights of Lipa and Chlum.

"As Brigade Prohaska is well acquainted with the "ground, it will remain advanced-guard brigade. The "main body of the brigade will stop in Sadowa, and be "joined by the Lancer Division.* The outposts must "avoid any disadvantageous engagement and unnecessary "loss.

"Brigade Kirchsberg will move up to the heights of "Lipa, and will take post behind this village, on the left "side of the road; Brigade Benedek will extend from "the right flank of the former brigade to Chlum. Ad- "joining the latter, Brigade Appiano will be stationed, "and will occupy the wood in front of the position; the "outposts of this brigade will open communication "with the IVth Corps and the advanced-guard brigade "of the IIIrd. The Reserve Artillery of the corps will "remain in Chlum. Ammunition park and ambulances "will encamp at Rosberitz. These measures will be "taken as soon as the men have breakfasted, unless "circumstances (gefechts-verhältnisse) should make it "necessary to occupy the new position immediately. "Brigade Prohaska will establish itself as well as possible "on the Bistritz, so as to be able to maintain a lasting "rear-guard action (nachaltiges Arrieregarden Gefecht), "but will not suffer serious resistance if the enemy should "attack with superior forces. The retreat of the brigade "will be effected *à cheval* of the high-road, and, if circum- "stances permit, between Lipa and Lengenhof; the "brigade will then take post behind Brigade Kirchsberg.

"The brigades are hereby further informed that the "Saxons are stationed on the left wing of the army "between Popowitz and Tresowitz. Adjoining them is "the Xth Corps d'Armée; the VIIIth Corps d'Armée stands "behind the Saxons, the 1st Light Cavalry Division "between Prim and Problus. To the right of the IIIrd

---

* The 1st and 2nd Squadrons of Mensdorff Lancers, No. 9, which was the Cavalry attached to the IIIrd Corps.—(Note by Translator),

" Corps will be the IVth Corps; the Reserves of the Army
" stand at Wsestar.

   (Signed)   " ARCHDUKE ERNEST,
         " *Lieutenant Field-Marshal.*"

" *Lipa, July 3rd,* 1866.
  " (*Despatched at a quarter past* 7 *a.m.*)."

The position indicated by these dispositions could only be
reached from the bivouacs of the corps by a retrograde movement. Colonel Prohaska's brigade was, therefore, reinforced by
the battery of Brigade Appiano, and ordered to hold Sadowa
and the line of the Bistritz as rear-guard until the corps had
taken up its position.

The 3rd Reserve Cavalry Division broke up from its bivouac
at Dohalitz and Dohalicka, and fell back to its appointed position
north-eastward of Sweti, where it arrived about half-past 8
o'clock.

Thus, the Austrian left wing and centre had on the whole
taken up the positions indicated by the Feldzeugmeister's dispositions, but the right wing deviated from his orders entirely.

It has been stated that the IVth Corps was to form line
between Chlum and Nedelist, and that the IInd Corps was to
occupy the ground between the latter village and the Elbe.
Instead of doing so, both corps formed on the line Cistowes-
Maslowed-Horenowes, therefore, 2,000 paces in advance of
the entrenchments that had been thrown up.

It is interesting to hear the reasons with which Austrian
military journals account for this fact.

As far as regards the IVth Corps, an article in the journal
*Kamerad,* of the year 1867, No. 64, remarks:—

  " The dimensions which the enemy's attack soon
" assumed gave reason to suppose that a general
" action would ensue. At the commencement of it the
" initiative of the enemy compelled us to act on the
" defensive. Above all things care had to be taken, so
" to form the line of battle, that the main body of the
" army might fight in a position where the ground was
" adapted to the defensive. In the neighbourhood of
" Nedelist, which lies in a hollow, there is no ground
" nearer than the village of Maslowed that affords those
" advantages which are requisite for a successful defence;
" but at this spot the formation of the country is highly
" favourable for a position facing the west as well as the
" east; indeed its advantages are so striking that one is
" convinced at the first glance that the possession of these
" heights must have considerable influence on the issue
" of the battle.

  " It was, therefore, resolved to post the right wing of
" the IVth Corps on the heights of Maslowed, under the
" impression that this would only be acting in accord-
" ance with the tenor of the Commander-in-Chief's orders.

" To be sure, these had fixed that the IVth Corps should
" take its stand on the heights between Chlum and
" Nedelist. On this line there are hollows, but no heights
" or well-defined positions, such as defensive tactics
" require. Such were only to be found further forwards.
'· Secondly, the ground which the IInd Corps d'Armée
" was to cover was not precisely defined in the general
" disposition for the battle; it was only stated 'that the
" 'IInd Corps was to form line on the extreme right
" ' wing, next to the IVth Corps d'Armée.'

"Now, if the right wing stood at Maslowed, the
" heights to the south of Horenowes and Racitz were
" the given position of the IInd Corps, heights which,
" similar to that of Maslowed, are seen even from a dis-
" tance to be peculiarly adapted to this purpose.

" In addition to this, the Trotina stream, with its
" swampy valley, forms an admirable *appui* for the right
" flank; it was only necessary to occupy the defile at
" the Trotina mill, where road and railway cross the
" stream, to make the flank perfectly secure.

"In case of an attack, not only from the direction
" of Neu-Bidzow and Horsitz, as was anticipated at
" head-quarters, but even still more so from the north-
" east, as was actually made by the Prussian IInd Army,
" the line Chlum-Maslowed-Racitz was a far more suit-
" able position for the right wing of the enemy than the
" line Chlum-Sendrasitz. . . . . ."*

The following are the movements that now took place :—

The IVth Corps d'Armée, from Nedelist, to take up a position
on the line Chlum-Maslowed.

The IInd Corps d'Armée to join to the right flank of the
former on the heights of Maslowed and Horenowes. General
Henriquez's brigade and the 6th Lancer Regiment (Emperor
Francis Joseph) were the only troops left in their position at
Trotina, to cover the right flank in case of need; the 1st Battalion of the 69th Regiment (Jellacic), which has already been
mentioned as posted in the small wood south-eastward of
Racitz, was afterwards reinforced by another battalion of the
same regiment.

The corps destined as reserve—the Ist and VIth—and the
Cavalry Divisions, took up their appointed positions; the VIth
Corps, as General Ramming's orders, which were found on
the field, show, on the heights between Rosberitz and Sweti,
in close order, Colonel Waldstätten brigade on the right,
Colonel Jonak's on the left, of the first line.

The Reserve Artillery of the army took up its ground to the

---

* The remainder of the article bears reference to the fact that the IVth Corps
d'Armée had not been informed of intrenchments having been thrown up. This has
been already mentioned at page 11.

north of the high road, on the heights between Wsestar and Sweti, at half-past 7 A.M.

Instead of the semi-circle originally intended, the Austrian line of battle now only formed a very gentle curve, the length of which, from Ober-Prim to Horenowes, was about 6¾ miles, and within which 4¾ corps d'armée were drawn up.  The left wing had a reserve of three weak brigades behind it, on the right wing only one brigade covered the ground between the right flank and the Elbe.  On the other hand, a main reserve of two corps of Infantry and five Cavalry divisions stood ready for action, full 2 miles behind the centre of the whole line of battle.

With the exception of General Rothkirch's brigade, all troops of the Austrian-Saxon Army of the North were assembled on the battle-field.

After deducting the losses in the preceeding actions and during the different marches, as well as the sick and the men absent on other duties, the actual fighting force of the Austrian Army on that day may be estimated at 206,000 combatants:—

|  | Men. |
|---|---|
| The Ist Corps d'Armée and the Light Cavalry Division (after their losses at Gitschin, &c.)  .. .. | 27,000 |
| The IInd Corps d'Armée (according to an official return)  .. .. .. .. .. .. | 28,520 |
| The IIIrd Corps d'Armée (still intact)  .. .. | 28,500 |
| The IVth Corps d'Armée (after its losses at Schweinschaedel and Koeniginhof), according to an official return)  .. .. .. .. .. .. | 26,980 |
| The VIth Corps d'Armée (after Nachod)  .. .. | 22,000 |
| The VIIIth Corps d'Armée (after Skalitz, and minus Brigade Rothkirch)..  .. .. .. .. | 15,500 |
| The Xth Corps d'Armée (after Trautenau and Soor) | 18,000 |
| The 1st Reserve Cavalry Division (after Nachod) .. | 3,600 |
| The 2nd  „  „  „  .. .. .. | 4,000 |
| The 3rd  „  „  „  .. .. .. | 4,000 |
| The 2nd Light Cavalry Division  .. .. .. | 3,000 |
| Reserve Artillery of the Army  .. .. .. | 3,000 |
| Saxons ..  ..  ..  ..  ..  ..  .. | 22,000 |
| Total ..  ..  .. | 206,100 |

On the Prussian side also, with the exception of the Guard-Landwehr Division, all the troops that had crossed the Bohemian frontier were brought together for the crisis; none were absent but the necessary detachments for securing the communications, for accompanying the convoys through the enemy's country, and for escorting the numerous prisoners.

The following was the strength of the different armies according to the official returns:—

*1st Army.*

|  | Men. | Men. |
|---|---|---|
| IInd Corps d'Armée.. .. .. .. | 28,353 | |
| The Divisions of the IIIrd Corps d'Armée.. | 24,202 | |
| The Divisions of the IVth Corps d'Armée .. | 26,525 | |
| Cavalry Corps .. .. .. .. | 8.467 | |
| | 87,547 | |

From which 161 medical men, 2,556 men of the Military Train must be deducted, leaving, combatants    84,830

N.B.—The Reserve Artillery of the Army is included in IIIrd and IVth Corps.

*Army of the Elbe.*

14th, 15th, and 16th Infantry Divisions, Reserve Cavalry and Reserve Artillery .. .. ..    39,088

*IInd Army.*

|  | | |
|---|---|---|
| Corps of Guards .. .. .. .. | 25,708 | |
| Ist Corps d'Armée .. .. .. .. | 26,098 | |
| Vth Corps d'Armée .. .. .. .. | 22,492 | |
| VIth Corps d'Armée.. .. .. .. | 19,404 | |
| Cavalry Division .. .. .. .. | 3,362 | |
| | | 97,066 |

Total .. ..    220,984

Of these only the 123,918 men of the Ist Army and of the Army of the Elbe were engaged at the commencement of the battle; the IInd Army did not come into action until the afternoon.

The 9,200 men of the Guard-Landwehr Division did not reach Nechanitz until the battle was over, for in spite of the utmost exertion and the eager desire of the men, the march from Kopidlno could not be completed sooner.

### ARMY OF THE ELBE.

After a skirmish of some duration the 8th Saxon Battalion left Nechanitz, and fell back towards Lubno with the 7th Battalion, under fire of Captain Wolff's battery. The Cavalry of General Schimpff's Division, and the Guard "Reiter" Regiment came forward to cover their retreat, and the battalions proceeded to join the other detachments of the 2nd Brigade, which were stationed behind the wood of Popowitz.

The Fusilier Battalion of the 28th Regiment took some gates off their hinges, and repaired the bridge with them, and then followed the enemy, and occupied the heights southwards of Lubno.

More to the left, the Fusilier Battalion of the 17th Regiment had advanced along the edge of the meadows as far as Komarow. To get at the enemy the battalion was obliged to wade or swim over the Bistritz, which is in some places 4 feet deep. After having been reinforced by the 8th Rifle Battalion (Major Zierold), the battalion then proceeded to attack Lubno.

The 3rd Saxon Brigade had already retired to the main position at Problus, but still held Lubno with the 9th Battalion.

Two battalions of the 2nd Brigade stood in Tresowitz and Popowitz, the remainder formed on the range of hills further eastward, by the side of and in the wood. In the neighbourhood of this wood Captain Leonhard's rifled battery, and at the side of Lubno, Captain Von der Pforte's howitzer battery, opened fire.

The Fusiliers of the 17th, and the 11th and 12th Companies of the 28th Regiment gained possession of Lubno, but not without a sharp fight, in which the former lost three officers and 80 men. The 2nd Saxon Brigade covered the retreat of the hostile battalion, and then retired in alternate lines, with Captain Von der Pforte's battery, to a reserve position north-westwards of Problus.

During their advance from Nechanitz, the 9th and 10th Companies of the 28th Regiment had an opportunity of firing a few vollies on the Saxon Cavalry. At a quarter past 10 they occupied the earthworks that had been thrown up on the hill of Lubno, and, as this position was important, the Fusilier Battalion of the 69th Regiment (Major Marschal Von Sulicki), and the 1st Battalion of the 40th Regiment (Lieutenant-Colonel Von Conrady) was sent forward by General Von Herwarth to secure it, as soon as they had passed the repaired bridge. In the low ground in front of the hill about 12 squadrons of Saxon Cavalry and a battery were seen on the march from Lubno towards Nieder-Prim, in close order. In spite of the soft nature of the ground, Captain Wolff's battery soon succeeded in gaining the height to the south of the intrenchments. The effect of its fire on the dense columns was evident, but no disorder could be perceived among the Saxon troops. In perfect order, and instantly filling up the gaps which the shells tore in their ranks, they marched to the reserve position eastward of Nieder-Prim.

Count Von der Goltz's Brigade of Hussars and the batteries of Captains Fuchsius and Pilgrim were brought forward at a trot, but were not able to get up in time. Captain Pilgrim's battery unlimbered on the hill; the Hussars remained in the dell to the south of Lubno.

On the right wing of the advanced guard, the 2nd Battalion of the 33rd Regiment had turned off southward, at Alt-Nechanitz, but could find no means of crossing the swollen ditches.

The bridges at Steiskal were destroyed, and the buildings of the stud-farm (Gestüte) at this place occupied by the enemy. The battalion did not therefore succeed in crossing until it had dislodged two companies of the 11th Saxon Battalion from

Kuncitz, and repaired the partially-destroyed bridge at this place. Both companies fell back fighting through the deer-park at Hradek, which the remainder of this battalion had quitted, to Neu-Prim. The Prussian battalion now advanced towards Hradek Castle, and General Von Schoeler despatched the 2nd Battalion of the 56th Regiment (Major Von Thielau) to its assistance.

The position of the advanced guard of the Army of the Elbe about 11 o'clock was as follows :—

On the right wing near Hradek :
Two battalions of the 33rd and 56th Regiments.

In the centre, on the heights extending from Hradek to-wards Lubno :
The 9th and 10th Companies of the 28th Regiment.
The 1st Battalion of the 40th Regiment.
The Fusilier Battalion of the 69th Regiment.
Two batteries (Captains Wolff and Pilgrim).

To the rear of the heights :
Ten squadrons of Hussars (Count Goltz).
A battery of Horse Artillery (Captain Fuchsius).

On the left wing, in and near Lubno :
The 11th and 12th Companies of the 28th Regiment.
The Fusilier Battalion of the 17th Regiment.
The 8th Battalion of Rifles.

The ground occupied by the advanced guard formed a natural *tête-du-pont*, under cover of which the Army of the Elbe was enabled to cross to the left bank of the Bistritz. About this time, therefore, the head of General Canstein's Division began to form eastward of Nechanitz.

## 1st Army.

The whole plan of the battle required the utmost resistance on the part of the centre of the Prussian forces (the 1st Army) to hold the ground which it had gained up to the present moment; but a farther advance, which could only be effected with considerable loss, and which might perhaps dislodge the enemy before the flank attacks of the other armies could take effect, was by no means necessary.

It was indispensable, however, to keep the Austrian Army occupied on all points of its front as long as the IInd Army was on the march. For this purpose the Bistritz must be crossed, and as the advanced guard of the 7th Division (General Von Fransecky) had already got a firm footing on the other bank, the advance gradually commenced from the left wing. The movement was successively followed by the 8th, 4th, and 3rd Divisions. The 5th and 6th Divisions and the Cavalry Corps were in the meantime held in continual readiness. In order to

o

keep up the communications between the 7th and 8th Divisions, and to cover the right flank of the latter during its advance on Benatek, the combined Brigade of Cavalry under Major-General Count Bismarck was sent in this direction, but was very soon employed in covering the left flank of the 8th Division.

The two Fusilier Battalions of General Fransecky's advanced guard (Colonel Von Zychlinsky) were now reinforced by the 1st and 2nd Battalions of the 27th Regiment, which General Von Gordon spread out to the right of and on the same line with them. With these four battalions the General then proceeded to attack the wood of Maslowed, which was apparently occupied in force, although Major Von Hymmen (10th Hussars) reported that four more battalions of the enemy had just entered the wood from the direction of Maslowed.

The Austrian Major-General Von Brandenstein had in fact moved forward the main body of his brigade from its bivouac south-eastward of Maslowed, to support both wings of his line of outposts. Two battalions of the 12th Regiment (Archduke William) took a northerly direction; the 3rd Battalion of the regiment, and that of the 26th Regiment (Grand Duke Michael), advanced southward of the village, where the battery of the brigade unlimbered.

The wood of Maslowed (otherwise called Swip or Wobora Wood) was not distinctly marked on the maps, so that its extent and depth were unknown. From east to west it is about 2,000, from north to south about 1,200 paces long. The ridge which it covers is very steep and difficult of access from the north, on which side it is intersected by numerous ravines; towards the Bistritz its fall is more gradual. The south-eastern slope of the hill, almost as far westward as the road leading from Cistowes to Benatek, is covered with oak scrub, in which there were at the time numerous piles of stack-wood. The triangular part of the wood westward of this road, and northward of the road which descends the hill from east to west, as well as that part of the wood farthest east which juts out like a bastion towards Horenowes, was of a similar kind. All the rest of the wood consisted of high timber, partly with and partly without undergrowth.

It was about half-past 8 when General Gordon's four battalions advanced against the wood. The main body of the 7th Division was ordered to deploy in the dell to the north of Benatek, and the reserve was to follow to the same spot. The 1st Squadron of the 10th Hussars was despatched to the right to open communications with the 8th Division. The three other squadrons of the regiment covered the left flank.

Lieut.-Colonel Weigelt, of the Artillery, brought up the 4th 12-pounder battery (Captain Von Notz) to the crest of the height, close to the eastern side of Benatek. The 1st 6-pounder battery (Captain Kühne) followed across the meadows, and opened fire to the left of the former battery, somewhat in its rear. Both batteries, however, were soon compelled to fall back behind the meadows by large bodies of skirmishers that pressed forwards from Horenowes, and fired on their left flank. The 12-pounder battery suffered some loss, and had one gun dismounted. Lieut.-Colonel Weigelt now led the 5th 4-pounder battery (Captain Von Nordeck) through the village, to support the attack of the Infantry; two guns of the battery unlimbered on the south, the other four on the east side of and close to the village. The two above-mentioned batteries, that had been obliged to withdraw, afterwards came to the same spot, and directed their fire principally against a massive building in front of Maslowed.

Benatek was already in flames, but the 1st 4-pounder battery (Captain Von Raussendorf) had passed through the village to the south of it, and was engaged with the enemy's batteries near Maslowed. With the exception of a few immaterial changes in their positions, the batteries remained on these spots as long as the engagement of General Fransecky's Division lasted. They lost on the whole 1 officer, 15 men, and 27 horses.

The enemy did not hold his ground at the skirts of the wood, but fell back, for the most part towards Cistowes. The battalions therefore followed into the interior of the wood,—namely, on the right wing the 1st Battalion of the 27th Regiment, through that part of the wood which projects westward; the 2nd and Fusilier Battalion of the same regiment on and at the side of the road leading to Cistowes; lastly, on the left wing, the Fusilier Battalion of the 67th Regiment to the northern part of the wood, which projects like a bastion.

In the meantime the IVth Austrian Corps was advancing in this direction to take up a position between Maslowed and Chlum, and had sent two Horse Artillery batteries, one 4-pounder, and the Rocket Battery of the Reserve Artillery of the corps, on ahead to cover this movement. The Rocket Battery was planted in Maslowed, the other batteries by the side of the village, so that 40 guns of the IVth Corps played upon the Prussian battalions during their advance. In vain the 18 Prussian guns attempted to draw the fire off from the Infantry; they were 3,500 paces off, and in the dull weather all they could do was to aim at the flashes of the enemy's guns.

As soon as the 27th Regiment entered the wood at the right wing, the enemy's guns, which were firing in this direction, gradually increased their fire until it attained an uncommon degree of vehemence. The connection between the different battalions was lost in climbing up the steep and wooded declivities, and the enemy's Riflemen and Infantry skirmishers gave way but slowly. However, the battalions succeeded in pressing forward to the other side of the wood, though not without losing officers and men.

In commencement of the action they had been encountered by detachments of the left wing of General Brandenstein's outposts—2nd Battalion of the 26th Regiment (Grand Duke Michael) and part of the 27th Rifle Battalion—and, as the engagement proceeded, probably also by part of the 4th Rifle Battalion, of the 2nd battalion of the 62nd Regiment (Archduke Henry), belonging to the IIIrd Corps, which advanced from Cistowes, and by the 1st Battalion of the 46th Regiment (Saxe-Meiningen). The left wing of the Prussian 27th Regiment then came in contact with the 3rd Battalions of the Austrian Regiments (Grand Duke Michael and Archduke Wilhelm, Nos. 26 and 12), which Major-General Von Brandenstein had pushed forward to the south of Maslowed.

The 1st Battalion of the 27th Regiment had only to pass through part of the wood, so that it was the first to reach the open country beyond, and then turned towards the Cistowes hill. The Commander of the battalion (Lieut.-Colonel Von Sommerfeld) fell, and Captain Schramm took his place. In the interior of the wood Lieut.-Colonel Von Zychlinsky himself directed the movements of the different detachments which were scattered over the ground in single columns of companies. The enemy was repeatedly driven back at the point of the bayonet, and all pressed forward, even if only to get out of the fearful shelling.

As soon as it was reported to the Colonel that the 1st Battalion was in possession of the corner of the wood towards Cistowes, he led the 2nd Battalion (Major Von Busse) to the same spot, where he found the 9th Company (Captain Von Buddenbrock) ensconced behind a bank of earth in front of Cistowes, and the 8th Company (Captain Von Kretschmann) at the south corner of the wood. Sharp skirmishing now commenced at the skirts of the wood, whilst those Austrian detachments that still held their ground in the interior of the wood kept up a continual fire there also. Colonel Von Zychlinski's horse was shot under him; Captains Von Kretschmann and Von Buddenbrock were wounded.

In the meantime the Fusilier Battalion of the 67th Regiment (Lieut.-Colonel Von Buttlar) had pressed forward on the left flank to the detached part of the north-eastern projection of the wood, where it was immediately engaged in a severe struggle with the 27th Austrian Rifle Battalion. The Infantry battalions which General Brandenstein sent forward came too late to save this part of the wood. An attempt they made to retake it was repulsed by the rapid file-fire of the Prussian Infantry, but the enemy still held the steep slope southwards of it. In consequence, the Fusilier Battalion (Lieut.-Colonel Von Schmeling) and the 1st Battalion (Major Schwager) of the 66th Regiment were sent forward from the main body of the division. Their concentric attack drove the enemy's Riflemen out of the oak-scrub, and repulsed repeated attacks of some Austrian reinforcements which had arrived. In this manner the Prussians gained possession of the greater part of the Maslowed wood, but were not able to occupy the whole line of outskirts on the opposite side of it, because of the great extent of the wood and the fierce struggle that was raging in parts of its interior.

These first successes of the 7th Division were, however, destined to be seriously endangered, and the struggle for the possession of the wood of Maslowed assumed momentarily increasing dimensions; for, even when the very first detachments of General Brandenstein's Brigade were being driven out of it, the main body of the IVth and the head of the IInd Austrian Corps were already approaching the scene of action, and then instantly joined in the combat.

The first part of the IVth Corps that arrived was General Fleischhacker's Brigade; it was despatched to the immediate assistance of General Brandenstein's left wing. The battery of the brigade took up a position near Maslowed; the Infantry formed in two lines and advanced on Cistowes, but detached the 13th Rifle Battalion into the wood on the right.

At this part of the field the left wing of the Prussian 27th Regiment had not yet reached the skirts of the wood, but was still fighting in the interior. The right wing, on the contrary (the 1st Battalion), was already pushing on towards Cistowes.

This village was occupied by two battalions of the Austrian 62nd Regiment (Archduke Henry), belonging to the IIIrd Corps, and by detachments of the 4th Rifle Battalion; but the 1st Battalion of the Prussian 27th Regiment nevertheless gained possession of the buildings which lie in front of the west side of the village, and the 2nd Battalion penetrated into the village itself from the north, and drove the enemy out. By degrees the Fusilier Battalion (Lieut.-Colonel Von Zedtwitz) also issued from the wood, and the 11th Company joined in the fight at Cistowes, the guidance of which had been taken by General Von Gordon and Colonel Von Zychlinski.

Now, however, as General Fleischhacker's six battalions drew near to the village, the Austrian detachments that had been driven out of it again advanced.

The shock of this overwhelming mass fell full upon the left flank, and, at the wood, even upon the rear of those Prussian companies that had pushed farthest forward. They were driven back in different directions. Lieutenants Von Schrœder and Von Hanstein, that were farthest ahead with their skirmishers, were cut off and taken prisoners. The 6th and 7th Companies were thrown back towards the south-west, and were obliged to retreat to the Sadowa wood; they were afterwards employed as support for the Artillery at the Skalka wood. The 5th Company fell back on the buildings that were occupied by the 1st Battalion. The 8th Company lost its officers, their substitutes, and the Sergeant-Major of the company. The Captain of the 1st Company (Count Finkenstein) had fallen, and parts of his company that were at this spot, and the 8th Company, were scattered, and retreated, partly to the wood of Maslowed, partly to that of Sadowa. Though perfectly isolated, the 1st Battalion, and those detachments that had joined it still kept up their fire against their far more numerous adversaries on the west side of the village.

General Fleischhacker now occupied the skirts of the village, and held a strong force in reserve behind it. The remainder of his brigade followed the Prussian detachments through the Maslowed wood, and there continued the fight.

The Commander of the IVth Corps, General Count Festetics, was severely wounded in these combats (his left foot was shattered by a shell), and General Mollinary took command of the corps in his place. General Count Thun, Commander of the IInd Corps, had also suffered a contusion of the head.

The horses of General Fransecky and his aide-de-camp were shot, as they were approaching the ravine at the north-eastern corner of the wood, by some Austrian Riflemen that were hidden by the corn. The General then passed the ravine on foot, and advanced to the foremost line of skirmishers to reconnoitre his adversary's position, when he suddenly found himself in the midst of the enemy's Riflemen. Some twenty Prussians that were cut off from their corps rallied around him, and by their assistance he succeeded in regaining his battalions.

Even before this took place the Quartermaster-General of the Ist Army, General Von Stülpnagel, had arrived with instructions from Prince Frederick Charles not to extend the line too far to the left.

It may have been about half-past 9 when the two last brigades of the Austrian IVth Corps (Poeckh and Archduke Joseph) appeared on the field, so that the 6 Prussian battalions were opposed to 28 Austrian battalions, behind which, and in their immediate neighbourhood, 14 more battalions of the Austrian IVth and two of the VIIIth Corps were stationed. 18 Prussian rifled guns were in fire against 96 guns of the enemy.

Nineteen more battalions of the Austrian IInd Corps now arrived on the field. We have already heard that this corps had moved to the left from the Trotina to keep in connection with the IVth Corps.

Colonel Thom's Brigade reinforced the battalion of the 69th Regiment (Count Jellacic), which was stationed southwards of Racitz, with a second battalion of the same regiment, and then marched towards the park (Fasanerie) of Horenowes. Prince Würtemburg's Brigade advanced to the left of the former, and General Saffran's Brigade in the direction of Maslowed.

Colonel Thom occupied Horenowes with a division of the 40th Regiment (Rossbach), and the park south of the village with the 2nd Rifle Battalion. The battery of the brigade, and the 5th 4-pounder battery of the Reserve Artillery of the corps which was attached to it, opened fire.

Prince Würtemburg's Brigade deployed in two lines between Maslowed and the park of Horenowes, and despatched the 20th Rifle Battalion to the assistance of the right wing of General Brandenstein's Brigade. When the Rifles arrived there they found the battalions of the latter brigade, that had been sent against the north-eastern part of the Maslowed wood, in full retreat, and the Brigade Würtemberg received orders to pre-

vent any further debouché of the Prussians from the wood.
A very severe skirmishing fire now ensued between the brigade
and the Prussian detachments on the opposite side, which had
also been reinforced by the main body of General Schwarzhoff's
Brigade. At the request of the IVth Corps, Prince Würtemberg
detached two battalions of the 47th Regiment (Hartung) to
occupy Maslowed. The 4th 4-pounder battery, two Horse
Artillery batteries, and the rocket battery of the Reserve Artillery of the corps, came into action in front of the brigade.

Under these circumstances the utmost exertions were necessary on the part of the Prussians to keep possession of the
wood of Maslowed, and by degrees all the battalions of the 7th
Division were brought forward in this direction.

The advance of Prince Würtemberg's Brigade had already
obliged General Schwarzhoff to send forward the last four battalions of the main body—the 26th Regiment (Colonel Von
Medem), and the 2nd Battalion of the 66th Regiment (Colonel
Von Blankensee).

The position of these four battalions during their advance
was one of very great difficulty.

On the right wing the Fusilier Battalion of the 26th Regiment (Major Löwenberger Von Schönholz) entered the wood
and reached the crest of the hill, but could not penetrate to the
detachments of the 27th Regiment that were engaged in front
of Cistowes.

The 1st Battalion of the same regiment crossed the summit
of the hill in the wood to the left of the Fusiliers, and had
almost gained the south-eastern skirts of the wood when it
was met by the fire of some masses of the enemy's troops
that were crowded together at this spot. Major Paucke, whose
horse had been shot, placed himself at the head of the 2nd and
4th Companies (Captains Von Westernhagen and Von Horn),
and led them on foot to the charge. The former officer, though
wounded, did not withdraw from the fight, which surged to and
fro for some time. The two companies even that were kept
back in reserve were so severely shelled, in particular by two
guns on their left flank, that they were withdrawn into the high
timber further to the rear, after suffering heavy losses.

At last the 2nd Battalion of the regiment (Major Von Gilsa)
succeeded in driving the Austrian detachments from the steep
northern slope, then wheeled to the left, and occupied the skirts
of the wood in front of Maslowed, where it however came into
the full force of the Austrian artillery fire, which struck down
whole ranks of the battalion. About 10 o'clock Austrian detachments appeared on its left flank. Though wounded several
times, and obliged to be supported by a bandsman, Major
Von Gilsa led three companies to meet them, and did not quit
the field until perfectly exhausted. He then took leave of his
men, thanking them for their conduct, and died a few days later.

On the left wing Major Wiedner advanced along the
northern skirts of the wood with three companies of the 2nd

Battalion of the 66th Regiment, in doing which he lost four officers. He reached the corner of the wood that juts out farthest towards Maslowed, to the left of the 2nd Battalion of the 26th Regiment, then advanced in line against the Austrian columns on the hill north-eastward of the wood, and poured several vollies into them, but was forced to fall back to the skirts of the wood by a heavy fire of shell and musketry from his right rear.

On the right wing Major-General Von Gordon had also been obliged to order up the two battalions of the Reserve—the 1st and 2nd Battalions of the 67th Regiment, the latter battalion only numbering three companies. He sent these troops, under Colonel Von Bothmer, to the assistance of the 27th Regiment, and requested the 8th Division, which was at that moment marching past the Skalka wood, to afford him still further aid. In consequence of this request, General Von Horn sent the 1st Battalion of the 72nd Regiment (Major Von Hänsel) and the 4th Rifle Battalion (Lieutenant-Colonel Von Colomb) to the Maslowed wood. Colonel Von Bothmer joined in the action somewhat after 9, the battalions of the 8th Division somewhat after 10 o'clock. By this time all 12 battalions of the 7th Division were already engaged. Inclusive of the two battalions of the 8th Division, 14 battalions and 24 guns were the whole force with which a struggle had to be maintained, which was becoming fiercer and fiercer every minute.

Colonel Von Bothmer advanced on and by the side of the Benatek-Cistowes road with the two battalions of the 67th Regiment, but was obliged to cover his left flank by throwing out skirmishers against the Austrians that were still in the interior of the wood, and with whom a brisk fire was kept up. On reaching the southern skirts of the wood he found parts of the 27th Regiment engaged with detachments of the brigades Fleischhacker, Brandenstein, and Appiano. The arrival of the Prussian reinforcements brought the action to a standstill at this spot.

At first starting, two of Colonel Bothmer's companies had taken the direction of Maslowed. The Brigade Würtemberg and the detachments of Brigade Brandenstein gained scarcely any ground by their attacks in this quarter, but a fierce struggle was still being carried on in the interior of the extensive wood and in the rear of those battalions that had pressed forward to its skirts.

The Prussian companies in this part were fighting singly, and without any connection with each other, and the powerful detachments of the enemy even succeeded in regaining the western skirts of the wood, and actually crossed the tract over which Colonel Bothmer had marched shortly before them. It so came to pass, that when the two battalions of the 8th Division reached the western skirts they found them occupied by the enemy in force, and had first to dislodge their opponents; a few hundred paces further on they fell in with skirmishing parties of the 27th and 67th Prussian Regiments in the interior of the wood.

In the eastern part of the Maslowed wood also General Brandenstein's battalions and the Rifle Battalion of General Fleischhacker's Brigade kept continually losing ground; General Mollinary, therefore, now sent forward Colonel Poeckh's Brigade, too. Archduke Joseph's Brigade was stationed as reserve behind it on the Maslowed–Chlum road, and the two 8-pounder batteries of the Reserve Artillery came into action by the side of Maslowed. In addition to this, the IInd Corps was requested, " to execute an offensive movement against the Prussian left "flank in order to disengage the troops fighting in the wood " as much as possible, to obtain possession of the latter, and " to force the enemy to retreat."

General Count Thun acceded to this request, and an attack of Colonel Poeckh's Brigade now commenced at half-past 10 o'clock, which was followed up by one of the IInd Corps further to the right. The 8th Rifle Battalion was at the head of the brigade, the first line of which consisted of the 51st Regiment (Achduke Charles), the second of the 37th Regiment (Archduke Joseph), the battery was brought into the line of artillery already engaged. The two battalions of the VIIIth Corps followed on the left flank of the brigade, and the 30th Rifle Battalion of Archduke Joseph's Brigade advanced on the right flank.

General Saffran's Brigade of the IInd Corps was the one detined to commence the attack, and Prince Würtemberg's Brigade was to advance again at the same time.

The 11th and 20th Rifle Battalions took the lead; they were followed by the 3rd Battalion of the 64th Regiment (Saxe-Weimar), and to the right of the latter by two battalions of the 47th Regiment (Hartung), and two companies of the 2nd Rifle Battalion.

To support this attack a column was formed out of the remaining battalions of both brigades; it consisted of three battalions of the 80th Regiment (Holstein), three of the 57th (Mecklenburg-Schwerin), and one of the 64th (Saxe-Weimar). The battery of the Brigade Saffran joined the artillery already in action.

Colonel Poeckh's attack was directed against the southeastern corner of the wood, where the Austrians still held the most ground; somewhat later General Saffran's Brigade and the reserve column advanced against the north-eastern part of the wood also.

The main forces of Colonel Poeckh's Brigade came in contact with the 1st and Fusilier Battalion of the 26th, the Fusilier Battalion of the 27th, and the 2nd Company of the 67th Regiment. These troops had only partially gained the skirts of the wood, and were still hotly engaged with detachments of the Brigades Fleischhacker and Brandenstein, but the charge of the first Austrian line was nevertheless repulsed, and almost all leaders of regiments and battalions put *hors de combat*. The charge of the second line, however, succeeded, and the Prussian battalions were driven back in various directions. Colonel Poeckh's left wing, on the other hand, met Colonel Bothmer's detachments, which had already repulsed several attacks of General Fleischhacker's battalions, and which had, whilst in pursuit of the enemy, pressed on beyond the strip of meadow land, and as far as the avenue of plum trees to the north of Cistowes. Colonel Bothmer was now met by a severe infantry fire in his front, whilst at the same time his line was enfiladed by one of the enemy's batteries, and strong hostile columns menaced his left flank. Lieutenant-Colonel Von Zedtwitz led the supports, that had been left at the meadow, against the latter and drove them back, but soon received so severe a fire from the wood in his rear that he was not able to maintain his position. The supports were driven back into the wood as far as the road leading from Maslowed along the crest of the hill; Colonel Von Bothmer, although almost entirely cut off, still remained with the 1st, 6th, and 7th Companies of the 67th Regiment in front of Cistowes, and kept up a very sharp fire against the villages. General Gon Gordon and Colonel Von Zychlinski still held their ground in the buildings westward of Cistowes and in the meadows leading down to the Bistritz with the 1st and parts of the other battalions of the 27th Regiment. The General and all the mounted officers had lost their horses, Colonel Zychlinski was wounded and the battalions 'were very much diminished, but they still kept up the combat with the strong garrison of the village.

Lieutenant-Colonel Weigelt's batteries played upon the IInd Austrian Corps during its advance; they were still in the same positions in front of Benatek, which have been already described.

General Saffran's first attack on the eastern part of the wood was repulsed; that of the reserve column, which had to cross the open country, totally failed. The Austrians suffered severely, especially the 80th Regiment (Holstein); a flank move-ment against the Prussian batteries was frustrated by the 10th Hussar Regiment. The progress which Colonel Poeckh's Brigade made in flank and rear of their position was, however, very soon felt by the defenders of the wood, and they were driven back into the north-eastern part of the wood.

11 A.M. It was now 11 o'clock; 40 Austrian battalions had been already engaged in this struggle; 11 were still in reserve.

128 Austrian guns had opened fire on the Prussian troops; 24 more were at hand, namely, the battery of Archduke Ernest's Brigade and the two 8-pounder batteries of the Reserve Artillery of the IInd Corps. General Brandenstein's Brigade was in the act of re-forming behind Colonel Poeckh's Brigade. The Austrians had gained possession of the greater part of the Maslowed wood, but still could not succeed in completely wrest-ing from General Fransecky's 14 battalions and 25 guns the

ground which had been conquered at so great a sacrifice and defended with so much devotion.

Certainly, so great a numerical superiority might prove very dangerous to the 7th Division—might even lead to its destruction, but even in the latter case, the issue of the battle would have been considerably influenced by the firmness with which this single division had held two corps d'armée of the enemy at bay, and had, by engaging their forces itself, drawn them away from their proper destination.

We must now interrupt the thread of our narrative and turn our attention to the events which were occurring at the other divisions of the Ist Army during the three hours which the struggle of the 7th Division had lasted.

Under cover of his advanced guard, which was posted at the brickfields. of Sadowa, and sheltered by the heights of Dub and the "Roskosberg," Lieutenant-General Von Horn led the main body and reserve of the 8th Division towards Sowetitz at 8 o'clock. The 6th Lancers halted near Dub. The fourth 4-pounder battery took up a position on the left wing, on a hillock to the north of Sowetitz, the third 6-pounder, third 4-pounder, and somewhat later the third 12-pounder batteries on the right wing of the Roskos Berg. The guns found excellent shelter here under the crest of the hill, and suffered no loss whatever. The battery of the Austrian Brigade Prohaska which was stationed on the north side of the high-road, and was fired on by the 3rd Division at the same time, lost both men and horses, and withdrew before 9 o'clock. Another battery, belonging to General Appiano's Brigade, instantly came up to take its place, but was soon compelled to retire by the accurate fire of the Prussian guns, which had now got their exact range, the more so, because its position was endangered by the advance of the 7th Division. A short pause now ensued in the artillery combat at this spot.

As soon as a patrol of Hussars brought the intelligence that General Fransecky was in possession of Benatek, and was gaining ground in the Maslowed wood, General Von Bose advanced through Sowetitz with three companies, and threw two small bridges for infantry (Laufbrücken) over the Bistritz, westward of the Skalka wood, and at the side of two other bridges that existed there already.

About this time, 9 o'clock, the 4th Division (Von Herwarth) had formed for action near Mzan, the 3rd (Von Werder) at Zawadilka; their batteries had been engaged for the last hour, and the smoke of the firing which rose beyond the burning village of Nechanitz indicated the progress of the Army of the Elbe. Under these circumstances Prince Frederick Charles gave orders, first to the 8th Division and then to the IInd Corps, to take possession of the passages over the Bistritz, but not to advance too far beyond the stream, nor up to the opposite heights. General Von Manstein, who commanded the two reserve divisions (5th and 6th) for the day, was then to advance as far as Sowetitz, General Schwarz, with the Reserve Artillery, as far as the Roskos Berg.

General Von Horn accordingly ordered the main body of his division and the Lancer Regiment to cross the Bistritz immediately, and then to turn towards the Königgrätz high-road as soon as they had established communications with the 7th Division. The Reserve and two batteries were instructed to follow, and lastly the advanced guard was to follow also under shelter of the Roskos Berg, whilst the third 4-pounder and the third 6-pounder batteries still kept up their position on this hill, covered by the 1st Battalion of the 71st Regiment.

Colonel Prokaska, whose brigade was stationed at Sadowa, had already reported to Archduke Ernest "that he was hard pressed "and could not withstand the enemy's overwhelming Artillery " fire any longer." The answer returned was that "the brigade " was not to expect any reinforcements, but could retreat, if " absolutely necessary, of which, however, it was previously to "apprize the neighbouring Xth Corps." The advance of the 8th Division threatening his flank and rear, Colonel Prohaska now fell back to the heights of Lipa, where the other brigades of the IIIrd Corps had been drawn up in the meantime; he took post behind the brigade of General Kirschberg, who stood in the foremost line southward of the high-road.

The four battalions of the main body of the 8th Division thus met with no resistance whatever at the Skalka wood; they crossed the Bistritz, and then wheeled to the right in the direction of the Sadowa wood, as they had been ordered to do. During their advance they were shelled from the heights of Lipa, but with slight effect. Skirmishing parties of the 31st Regiment made 60 Austrian prisoners in the bushes eastward of Sadowa.

The 15th Infantry Brigade now received orders to pass through the wood of Sadowa. This wood forms almost a regular square, and measures about 1,000 paces each way. In the immediate neighbourhood of the road it contains a good deal of high timber, oak, beech, and fir; but the other part of it consists principally of very dense undergrowth. Only trifling detachments of the enemy were found in it, which fell back at all points, but in pursuing them through the thickets the Prussian companies could not retain their close order, and when they reached the skirts of the wood on the opposite side suddenly found themselves in face of a powerful line of Austrian artillery, which the IIIrd and Xth Corps had planted on the brow of the heights sloping from Lipa towards Stresetitz, and which received the Prussian troops with a perfect hailstorm of shells.

Colonel Von Wedell posted the leading battalions (1st and 2nd) of the 31st Regiment in the skirts of the wood in front of Ober-Dohalitz and Lipa, but it was utterly impossible for the Prussian troops that were at the moment available, to advance against the Austrian Artillery. General Bose therefore gave orders to desist from any attempt of the kind, but to hold the skirts of the wood under all circumstances. Different detachments that were on the point of dashing on beyond the wood were held back, and the 3rd Company (Captain Giese), which had ensconced itself in the meadows, 800 paces further on, was recalled and sent to the south-east corner of Ober-Dohalitz, at which spot the 3rd and 4th Companies of the 71st Regiment also arrived; 1 officer and 64 men of the Austrians were taken prisoners here.

It was about this time that the detachments of the 7th Division were driven back from Cistowes, as has been already stated, and Colonel Von Bothmer tried to advance to their assistance from the high-road with the 6th and 7th Companies of the 71st Regiment, but the overwhelming fire of the Austrian artillery soon forced them to fall back again into the wood. An attempt to get at the enemy's guns by a flank movement met with no better success, and the only course adapted to the circumstances was to remain strictly on the defensive at this spot, a task that was far from agreeable on account of the shells which fell incessantly in the wood and the splinters they tore off from the trees.

We have already heard that the Reserve of the 8th Division despatched two battalions from the Shalka wood to the assistance of the 7th Division. The two remaining battalions of the 72nd Regiment were posted behind the wood of Sadowa in support of the 15th Brigade, and both battalions of the Advanced Guard sent to the same spot. Inclusively of the Fusilier battalions of the 31st and 71st Regiments, eight battalions of the divisions were assembled here at 10 o'clock. The 6th Regiment of Lancers had halted in a dell to the east of the Skalka wood. The 12-pounder battery remained in reserve, and the three rifled batteries took up a position on the ridge which rises towards Cistowes, but nevertheless all endeavours still failed to induce the enemy to turn his guns on the Prussian batteries, and thereby lessen the very severe fire which his numerous artillery kept up against the wood.

In the meantime the 4th Division (Von Herwarth) was also advancing, after having formed in line of battle near Mzan at 8 o'clock. The three rifled batteries of the division were already engaged with the superior artillery of the Austrian corps on the other side of the Bistritz.

The casualties caused by the enemy's fire were by no means trifling. One gun of the 6-pounder battery was for some time served by only two men; one limber was shattered, nevertheless the Prussian batteries punctually carried out the orders they had received and slowly and steadily returned the fire. In order to afford them some aid, General Von Schmidt sent instructions to the 3rd Division to hasten its march, and to send its artillery forward at a trot. The latter came into action on the right of the batteries already engaged as early as a quarter past 8 o'clock. The 12-pounders were soon obliged to be withdrawn, as the distance was too great for their fire to be of any effect, whilst they themselves suffered from the enemy's rifled guns, but General Von Lengsfeld brought the 2nd 4-pounder and 2nd 6-pounder batteries of the Reserve Artillery into action between Mzan and the brickfield of 'Sadowa, from which spot they were in some measure able to enfilade the enemy's position.

General Gablenz now felt himself obliged to request reinforcements for his artillery from the IIIrd Corps; they were, however, refused, because a serious action in the valley of the Bistritz was not in accordance with the general dispositions for the army.

In order to keep the Austrian skirmishers sufficiently far off from the Prussian batteries, the 2nd battalion (Major Von Tiedewitz) of the 49th Regiment was now sent forward against the "Zuckerfabrik;" the enemy's battalions that were posted there quitted the place, and left 25 prisoners behind them.

The Prussian battalion next turned its steps towards Unter-Dohalitz; it was followed by the advanced guard, whilst main body and reserve marched on Sadowa at a quarter to 10 A.M.

Nothing but trifling detachments of the enemy was met at this part of the field. Anyhow, the Xth Corps would not have been able to maintain its advanced position on the Bistritz after Colonel Prohaska's retreat from Sadowa. Under these circumstances General Gablenz resolved to withdraw the advanced brigades of his corps to the main position of the army, westward of Langenhof and Stresetitz, but the movement was only executed by degrees, according as the Prussian troops advanced, so that conflicts ensued in some places.

The Fusilier Battalion of the 49th Regiment (Major Von Rechenberg) waded through the Bistritz, made some prisoners in Unter-Dohalitz, and then marched to Ober-Dohalitz, where it took part in the capture of the village and the occupation of the wood.

Major Von Salpius led the 1st Battalion of the Regiment against Dohalicka, but found the village in the possession of the 3rd Division. He then advanced along a dip in the ground (Terrainfalte), and kept up the communication between both divisions.

The main body of the 4th Division was posted on the left bank of the Bistritz, 200 paces behind the Sadowa wood, with its left flank resting on the high-road; the reserves, with the artillery and the Lancer Regiment were at the village of Sadowa on the other bank of the stream. The mill buildings were occupied by the battalion. A reserve of 10½ battalions was thus at hand to maintain possession of the wood in case the enemy should assume the offensive at this spot.

The Austrian fire had forced the 3rd Division (General Von Werder) to form its line of battle near Zawadilka at 8 o'clock; this movement was completed by 9. The skirmishers of the Fusilier Battalion of the 42nd Regiment advanced against the

Austrian Infantry at the Bistritz by way of Kopanina; those of the Fusilier Battalion of the 54th Regiment on their right.

The 5th Brigade took up a position close by Zawadilka. The 6th Brigade occupied the skirts of the wood near Johanneshof. The 14th Infantry Regiment, the 5th Hussars, and the 12-pounder battery, stood farther to the rear, on the open part of the wood. The other batteries of the division continued their fire.

Two squadrons of Hussars were thrown forward on the right flank, and the 3rd Heavy Cavalry Brigade (General Von der Goltz), which was detached from the Cavalry Corps to the IInd Corps d'Armée, followed them as far as the corner of the wood which projects towards Johanneshof. The brigade fell back again upon General Hann Von Weyhern's Cavalry Division behind Sucha, after exchanging a few shots with a Saxon battery (Captain Heidenreich) which had come forward to reinforce the Artillery of the Xth Corps eastward of Tresowitz.

The Commandant of the Artillery of the Cavalry Corps, Lieut.-Colonel Von der Becke, wished to attempt to dislodge the enemy's batteries by enfilading their line. He advanced with Captain Roehl's Battery by Johanneshof towards Tresowitz, but suffered from the enemy's fire during his advance already. A gun-carriage was shattered, and it was soon evident that no result could be obtained in the low ground, especially not with smooth-bores. In turning round to retrace its steps the battery lost three men and five horses.

In the meantime the advance of the other Prussian divisions had induced the foremost Austrian batteries to retire, and General Werder now gave orders to cross the Bistritz and to seize on the foremost villages. When they were once gained, the opposite slopes must necessarily afford some shelter from the destructive fire of the enemy's artillery. About half-past 9, therefore, the division began to advance from the right wing. The 54th Regiment of the 6th Brigade took deploying intervals and marched on Mokrowous. On its left rear the 14th Regiment, with the Fusilier Battalion in second line, advanced against Dohalicka, whilst the 5th Brigade followed still further to the left by way of Kopanina. Preparatory to this attack, the 12-pounder battery now also came into action in front of Dohalicka. During its advance the division was shelled by the batteries near Langenhof, but with little effect. The enemy did not seriously defend the line of the Bistritz here either. The main body of General Wimpffen's Brigade was probably at this time already retreating, but the Fusilier Battalion of the Prussian 54th Regiment (Captain Von Pestel) was nevertheless fired on as it approached Mokrowous. It instantly rushed upon the outer boundary of the village, but found itself suddenly stopped by the Bistritz, which has very high banks at this spot. Without a moment's hesitation, and headed by its officers, the battalion sprang into the stream, waded through it, and took 9 officers and 60 men of their surprised opponents prisoners;

the latter belonged, for the most part, to the Austrian regiments Bamberg and Archduke Stephen.  The rest fled, leaving arms and knapsacks behind them.

The Prussian battalion was re-formed in the northern part of the village, and then advanced in the avenue of trees leading to Lagenhof; but the enemy's artillery concentrated so severe a fire on the battalion that it lost 60 men in a very short time, and was obliged, for the present, to desist from any further attempts to advance.

The supporting companies of the two other battalions of the 54th Regiment had also attacked Mokrowous as soon as the enemy had opened fire.  They captured some stragglers there, and were then rallied in a ravine and at the northern outlet of the village.  All attempts of the skirmishers and of the 3rd Company to advance still farther were frustrated by the severity of the Austrian artillery fire.

The remaining companies of the regiment, and the 14th Regiment, reached Dohalicka, just as the Austrian Infantry was leaving the place.  The village afforded them some shelter from the enemy's shells, and they placed the church and the school-house in a state of defence.

The 2nd Regiment (5th Brigade) took up a position in the brickfield (ziegelei) near the Bistritz; the 42nd Regiment by the side of the road between Dohalicka and Unter-Dohalitz. Two companies of the Rifle Battalion occupied Johanneshof.

There were very few practicable bridges over the Bistritz, so that it was not until later in the day that the 12-pounder battery could be brought forward southwards of Dohalicka, and the 5th 4-pounder battery to Unter-Dohalitz.  The other batteries of the division remained behind under cover of two companies of Rifles.  The Reserve Artillery of the IInd Corps re-filled the limbers of those batteries that had been engaged, and then followed to Unter-Dohalitz, where it crossed the Bistritz.

The 3rd Heavy Cavalry Brigade had been ordered by the Commander of the Cavalry Corps to rejoin the IInd Corps d'Armée.  When the brigade reached Zawadilka the 3rd Division was no longer there.  The brigade followed by way of Kopanina, and was afterwards stationed behind Dohalicka by the side of the Hussar Regiment.  The Commanding General of the IInd Corps d'Armée was, however, not informed of the arrival of the brigade.

At half-past 10 o'clock the Cavalry Corps was still in its first position near Sucha.

About this time the Commandant of the corps despatched an officer to the Commander-in-Chief, requesting permission for the Cavalry Corps to cross the Bistritz.  Soon afterwards Prince Albrecht received a request to support the Army of the Elbe. This was a mistake, for General Herwarth himself had made no such request; but it induced the Prince to detach General Alvensleben's Division to the Army of the Elbe—a proceeding which was, however, by no means in accordance with the intentions of the Commander-in-Chief.

Prince Frederick Charles now ordered General Hann Von Weyhern's Division to move to Sadowa.

It thus happened that the Cavalry Corps, which during the whole advance of the army had been held together at the cost of many a sacrifice, was now on the decisive day separated in two halves.

The divisions of the IIIrd Corps, that were united under General Manstein's command, had drawn nearer to Sowetitz, and received orders to halt between Ober-Cernutek and the Roskos-Berg.

The different detachments of the Artillery Reserve of the Army under General Schwartz moved into line between Dub and Sadowa.

If we contemplate the course of the action up to 11 o'clock we find that the Ist Army, advancing in échelons of divisions from the left wing, had wheeled one-eighth of a circle to the right, on ground originally held by the enemy, and now occupied the line wood of Maslowed—wood of Sadowa—Mokrowous.

The Army of the Elbe was in the act of forming to the rear of the line Hradek-Lubno, on the left bank of the Bistritz.

The Austrians had not attempted to make a permanent stand in this part of the field. Their main position on the heights further to the rear was not yet reached by their opponents. They had met the attack which was directed against their right wing by an offensive movement and with superior forces. In the centre and on the left wing of their line they made full use of those advantages of a superior artillery which are inherent to defensive operations. Planted in a series of most favourable positions, the Austrian artillery, whose excellence is an acknowledged fact, was enabled to shell the advance of its opponents from its very commencement, whereas the Prussian batteries came up singly, took up their positions under fire, and afterwards had to cross the Bistritz. By 11 o'clock there were but 12 Prussian batteries on the left bank, and only 7 of these had been able to come into action, making a total of 42 Prussian guns. On the other hand, the batteries of the Austrian IInd, IIIrd, IVth, and Xth Corps, as well as one Saxon battery, were available, and the fire of nearly 250 pieces of artillery opposed a mighty obstacle to any further advance of the Ist Army.

It was, however, by no means intended by the general plan of the battle that such an advance should take place. Enough had been done to keep the enemy fully occupied in his front. In a very short time the flank attack of the Army of the Elbe must now begin to take effect.

The Prussian centre was in no danger. The enemy had as yet attempted no offensive movement against it, besides which a corps of Infantry, a division of Cavalry, and a powerful reserve of Artillery were fully prepared to meet any such

P

attempt. The co-operation of the IInd Army also could therefore be awaited.

The left wing of the 1st Army, General Fransecky's Division, was certainly in very great danger; but then the more forces the enemy employed against it, the more decisive must be an attack proceeding from the north, between the Trotina and the Bistritz.

### ADVANCE OF THE IIND ARMY UP TO 11 O'CLOCK.

Meanwhile the time was come at which the co-operation of the IInd Army had been expected. Many a glance, therefore, was naturally cast in the direction from which it must approach, in anxious anticipation of its arrival.

The fierce thunder of the cannonade which came over from the battle-field to Daubrowitz had induced General Von Alvensleben not to wait for further orders, but to start at half-past 8 o'clock with the advanced guard of the Corps of Guards, and to march in the direction of Jericek, where, according to previous reports, he expected to strike on the right flank of the enemy.

A report of this proceeding was left behind for the main body of the corps, and Lieutenant Von Byern of the Guard Hussars despatched to General Von Fransecky with the assurance that the advanced guard would be at Jericek by half-past 11, but the troops stepped out so uncommonly well that this village was passed by 11.

As soon as the 1st Division of Guards had ascended the plateau of Daubrowitz by the sole existing steep road, it turned off to the left in the direction of Dubenetz, and continued its march up and down hill, straight across country, in order not to cross the line of march which the Commander-in-Chief of the IInd Army had appointed for the advance of the Ist Corps d'Armée. Soft and heavy as the rain had made the soil, the head of the column reached Choteborek as early as 11 o'clock; and, without interrupting his march, the Prince of Würtemberg pushed on even beyond his original destination.

The advanced guard of the 2nd Division of Guards had already passed Königinhof when it received orders from the Commander-in-Chief of the Corps that the 1st Division of Guards should be followed, first by the Reserve Artillery, then by the 2nd Division, and lastly by the Heavy Cavalry Brigade. Prince Hohenlohe therefore placed himself with the Artillery immediately behind the advanced guard of the 2nd Division. The head of the column reached the bridge at 10, so that the main body of the division could not cross till past 11 o'clock. On the heights of Daubrowitz the Reserve Artillery was ordered to place itself at the head of the main body of the 1st Division of Guards. The guns trotted past the columns, straight across country and through the high standing corn, but the long straw, mixed with the clayey soil, wound itself in thick wreaths round the wheels, and rendered such extreme exertion necessary that by the time they reached Jericek several horses had fallen dead before the guns from sheer fatigue.

After witnessing the passage of part of the Corps of Guards through Königinhof, the Crown Prince hastened on ahead past the marching columns, by way of Daubrowitz to Choteborek.

The VIth Corps had had to overcome similar difficulties during its advance. We know that it was already on the road when the direction of its march was turned to the battle-field of Königgrätz. On its left flank marched the 12th Division, which, as has already been mentioned, numbered only 7 battalions.

The 6th Regiment of Hussars (Colonel Von Trotha) was sent forward along the Ertina, and the patrols of the 3rd Squadron fell in with hostile Cavalry to the south of Josephstadt, in the neighbourhood of Jezbin and Semonitz. About 8 o'clock Captain Count Strachwitz advanced from St. Wenzel towards Holohlaw with the 1st Squadron. He let the two Austrian regiments, which were already retreating, pass close by him, and then harassed their rear-guard. At a rapid pace he followed them to Smiritz, continually skirmishing with them, crossed the bridge over the Elbe, and convinced himself that there were no columns of the enemy on the high-road to the fortress. A few prisoners were taken, among others an officer and a Sergeant-Major of the Austrian regiment Palffy Hussars. Count Strachwitz then fell back, and the regiment was formed at St. Wenzel and Habrina.

The main body of the 12th Division could only cross the swampy valley of the Ertina by the causeway leading to Jezbin, which the rain of the preceding days had made extremely bad. After crossing, the march was continued straight across country through the high corn.

General Von Prondzynski, who had to cover the left flank of the corps, occupied Ertina with the Rifle Battalion, and then marched towards the hill eastward of Roznow, from whence a good view of the surrounding country was obtained.

At this spot he formed his Infantry in two lines; his guns could only be brought up by help of the artillerymen. The enemy threw some shells from the outworks of Josephstadt, to which the 4-pounder battery answered by a few shots.

It was now half-past 9, and the march of the 11th Division was plainly visible in the low ground towards Welchow. A report on the state of affairs at the left wing were sent to the Commanding General of the Corps, and was answered by the following orders :—

"Keep the enemy in view. Do not lose the connec-
"tion with the 11th Division, which is marching towards
"the sound of the cannonade.
(Signed)    "VON MUTIUS."

General Von Prondzynski now resolved to proceed in the same direction. Colours were unfurled; the field chaplains of both confessions rode from battalion to battalion, and the march was resumed on a very broken road through Roznow and Nenasow towards Habrina.

The villages seemed to be deserted by their inhabitants; only a few old men were seen by the road-side, but long lines of flying peasantry, with their sick and children, and driving their cattle before them, met the troops from the direction of the battle-field.

The "Horicka-Berg," north-eastward of Racitz, was reached before 11 o'clock.

The advanced guard of the 11th Division was composed of the Fusilier Battalion of the 50th Regiment and the 4th Regiment of Hussars. It was followed by the 21st Brigade, with four batteries marching behind the leading battalion.

The roads in the direction of Stangendorf, more especially the steep ascents which lead from this village to the summit of the plateau on the other bank of the Elbe, were almost bottomless, and at the same time so narrow that the Infantry could only march in double file, the Artillery in column of single guns. It was to be foreseen that the passage of three bridges would cause some further delay.

General Von Hanenfeldt had given instructions that the close order of the columns should be carefully preserved, and that a report should be sent forward as each single battalion passed the defile, or when its distance from the preceding battalion exceeded 300 paces. In spite of these precautions, it was impossible for the troops to keep close up. When they descended the hills the guns had to put on the drag, and even if they themselves could regain their lost ground within the battery by increasing their pace, still the Infantry behind them must necessarily fall further and further to the rear. General Mutius therefore ordered the brigade to form line at a quarter before 9 o'clock, as soon as the leading battalion had ascended the side of the valley of the Elbe.

The heavy firing from the direction of the battle-field had been heard for the last half-hour. The troops pressed on as fast as possible, as the cannonade became more and more audible, for all felt the necessity of hastening their march, but in spite of all exertions, at a quarter before 10 o'clock two battalions of the brigade were still 3,000 paces to the rear. A report was received about this time from the 12th Division, that it had already occupied Roznow; and as in the meantime the 22nd Brigade, which had taken a better road by way of Schurz, was drawing near Welchow, so that the greater part of the 11th Division was assembled, General Mutius gave orders to advance. For this reason, when General Hanenfeldt resumed his march towards Litic, his brigade numbered only three battalions and four batteries.

About 10 o'clock the Commandant of the Division, General Von Zastrow, who had ridden on in advance, sent back orders for the division to form for action, and to bring the artillery to the front; consequently the 21st Brigade, which had been re-joined by the battalion of the advanced guard, formed in two lines between Neujahrsdorf and Welchow, with the 22nd Brigade on its right.

The former now advanced past Hustiran in a straight line over hills, meadows, and ditches, through copses and hedge-rows, until it reached the Trotina, somewhat above the influx of the Trotinka. The swampy valley of the former was a very serious obstacle. At the conflux of the two streams there was a bridge, but General Zastrow wished to shorten the delay that must necessarily ensue if the whole division defiled over this one crossing, and, having previously made himself acquainted with the nature of the country further on ahead, placed himself at the head of the brigade, and gave orders to attempt to cross higher up the stream also.

In order to prevent the necessity of moving his first line back again, General Von Hanenfeldt desired the two battalions of the 50th Regiment to cross the Trotina at the spot where they stood. The 1st Battalion got well over, although the water reached up to the men's chests, and the Commander of the 2nd cleared the stream on horseback; but the leading pelotons of the battalion got into so deep water that other places for crossing had to be found, where they got over by the help of some strong beams. The 2nd line crossed at the bridge.

The 22nd Brigade (General Von Hoffmann) followed, and took up its station on the right rear of the 21st.

As soon as the 11th Division had thus reached the heights to the north of Racitz, at about 11 o'clock, the first shells began to fall in its ranks.

About the same time, the foremost detachments of the Vth Corps d'Armée were approaching the village of Choteborek. The corps had started at 8 o'clock, and marched by way of Schurz, Sibojet, and Dubenetz. The head of the column was formed by the two Cavalry regiments of the corps under com-mand of General Von Wnuck. They were followed by the 9th and 10th Divisions, and then by the Artillery. The rear was brought up by the Fusilier Battalion of the 52nd Regiment. The Pioneer Battalion was left behind, partly at the bridges and partly to guard the train.

Detachments of the advanced guard of the 1st Corps d'Armée that were at Chroustow had for some time heard heavy firing from the direction of Sadowa, without having specially re-ported it to the Commandant of the corps at Ober-Praussnitz. It was not before 9 o'clock that the following orders were issued there:—

"A communication has been received from the Com-"mander-in-Chief of the IInd Army, stating . . . . (Here follow the dispositions of the IInd Army, as already given at p. 13.)

"Accordingly, the advanced guard, followed by the "Reserve Infantry and Reserve Cavalry, will march by

" way of Gross-Trotin, Weiss-Polikau to Gross-Bürglitz;
" the main body, followed by the Reserve Artillery, by
" Zabrez, Lanzow, Sedletz to Gross-Bürglitz. The main
" body will form its own advanced guard, and will start
' 'immediately by way of Swicin; it will leave a battalion
" by the side of the road near its bivouac, which will be
" placed at the disposal of the Reserve Artillery. The
" baggage of advanced guard, main body, and reserve
" will remain under cover of small detachments in their
" present bivouacs, by the side of the road, until further
" orders are received.

" I shall march with the advanced guard. The main
" body will appoint an officer with half a sub-division of
" Hussars to form my escort, which will await me in the
" neighbourhood of the bivouac.

" The General Commanding,
(Signed)    " Von Bonin."

" *Ober-Praussnitz, July* 3, 1866."

The advanced guard received these orders at 20 minutes
past 9, and started with its vanguard at half-past.

Before the corps started, the sound of the heavy cannonade
was heard at its head-quarters also, and the march hastened as
much as possible. An officer of the General Staff was sent on
ahead to inquire into the course of the action. In spite of all
haste, the advanced guard had not reached Gross-Bürglitz by
11 o'clock.

The Cavalry Division received the orders of the Commander-
in-Chief about a quarter past 8 o'clock, and started at 9. The road
was cleared of several baggage-wagons, but the reserve Artillery of the Ist Corps would not let the Division pass. The
latter now tried in vain to get ahead by way of Miletin, so that
nothing was left, in the heavy state of the roads, but quietly to
follow the parks of the Ist Corps.

If we sum up all that has been mentioned regarding the
advance of the IInd Army, we perceive that by 11 o'clock in
the forenoon the heads of the Guards and of the VIth Corps
had reached the Trotina, but were still more than 2½ miles off
from the sorely pressed left wing of the Ist Army.

The ends of the columns of the Guards, the Ist and Vth
Corps were still as far back as the Elbe.

IV.—COURSE OF THE BATTLE FROM 11 TO 3 O'CLOCK.  THE
IIND ARMY JOINS IN THE BATTLE.

Whilst still on the road to Choteborek, the Crown Prince had
become convinced that a battle must be raging along the whole
front of the Ist Army.

An extensive view opened out towards the valley of the
Bistritz, and, although the dull wet day rendered it impossible
to discern the exact positions of the troops, still the flashes of
the guns and the clouds of smoke hanging over the burning
villages indicated the line on which the battle was being
fought.

The view in front was limited by the ridge which extends
from Horenowes to the Trotina. On its highest points two trees
formed an object which was visible from very far off, and which
had long since attracted the attention of both armies. From a
distance of about 2½ miles, and in the dull atmosphere, these
heights resembled a mighty rampart which seemed to bar all
further progress.

By the first dispositions of the Crown Prince, the front of
the IInd Army, which had been originally about 22½ miles long,
was considerably contracted; it now occupied the line Bürglitz-
Jericek-Choteborek-Welchow, being a distance of only 9 miles.

It was evident that the mere advance of the different corps
must now lead the IInd Army on flank and rear of all those
forces which the enemy had already brought into action, but
that the crossing of the Elbe and the whole advance of the
IInd Army had been unperceived by the Austrians, and would
take them by surprise, was a thing which could never have been
anticipated. On the contrary, it seemed far more probable that
the enemy had stationed the troops destined to guard his flank
behind the heights of Horenowes, where they would have been
hidden from view, but where as yet only one single battery was
to be seen, close to the trees; but, even if this had not been
done, the Austrians could still throw forward their reserves in
this direction, whilst the Prussians were engaged in crossing the
2½ miles of intervening valley, where each single battalion
could be counted as it descended the opposite slope. The
heights of Horenowes fall steeply towards the north-east, and
are, moreover, covered by the swampy meadows of the Trotina.
They would have afforded the enemy so strong a defensive
position that an attack of them would have had but little
chance of success, unless undertaken by very considerable
forces.

Officers were therefore despatched to the different corps,
with orders to continue their march in case they should not
have done so of their own accord. At the same time, the group
of trees on the Horenowes hill was indicated as their mutual
point de vue.

The officers had hardly started, when General Mutius's report arrived, stating that he had reached Welchow, and that, on hearing the cannonade, he had continued his march in the direction from whence the sound proceeded. Besides this, General Wnuck's Cavalry Brigade appeared near Choteborek, and General Von Steinmetz reported that the heads of the Vth Corps were drawing near this place. Intelligence was next received from the Ist Corps that it was marching on Gross-Bürglitz, and the battalions of the Guards, which the Prince of Würtemberg had pushed forward with all possible speed, were descending into the valley, under the eyes of the Crown Prince. The latter thus knew that all available troops were in motion, and was convinced that the fate of the day would depend upon the issue of a struggle for the heights of Horenowes. One fact, however, nobody could foresee, namely, that by far the greater part of those troops which the enemy should have employed to guard against an attack from the north, and which therefore should have covered his right flank, were already engaged on the line Cistowes-Maslowed Horenowes, and that his main reserve was at that moment further from Horenowes than the heads of the IInd Prussian Army.

It must be left undecided, how far the full importance of this imminent danger was estimated at the Austrian head-quarters.

At all events the Feldzeugmeister must have been aware of the movement of the IVth Austrian Corps, which differed so materially from his own orders. As early as 8 A.M., Colonel Von Pidol, on riding to the entrenchments of the right wing, had found them unoccupied, and had seen the IVth Corps on its march towards Maslowed. He therefore rode to the heights of Chlum, expecting to find the Commander-in-Chief there, and, as the latter had not yet arrived, then hastened to Archduke Ernest, whom he found on the high-road in front of Lipa, and who received his report. Hereupon the Archduke himself went to the batteries 6 and 7 on the plateau, where at the same moment (10 o'clock) the Feldzeugmeister also arrived, and was informed by Colonel Pidol of the movement of the IVth Corps.

Two divisions of the Reserve Artillery, the 3rd and 4th, in the whole 64 8-pounders, under command of Colonel Von Gilles, were now, it is true, brought up to the plateau, and orders were sent to the IVth Corps to retire to its appointed position, but at the same time reinforcements were also wanted in the centre of the Austrian line, to assist the Xth Corps, as the 3rd Reserve Cavalry Division moved to the north-west of Langenhof.

The orders of the Austrian Commander-in-Chief were delivered to General Mollinary by 11 o'clock, but the latter deemed it his duty, first to inform the Feldzeugmeister of the progress of the action, because, as he said, " The state of affairs was such " that an offensive movement against the enemy's left flank " would have a fair chance of success."

The proposal to continue this offensive movement was rejected, and orders were despatched to General Von Mollinary, as well as now to Count Thun also, immediately to take up the positions as originally ordered.

We shall see that these instructions were even now neither immediately nor fully executed.

About 12 o'clock the Feldzeugmeister received a telegram from Josephstadt, stating that a Prussian corps d'armée, supposed to be the Vth, was marching towards the flank of the Austrian Army by way of Salney, along the Elbe. This was at a moment when 36 guns of the IInd Army were already in action against this flank.

On the Prussian side the advanced guard of the Ist Division of Guards, the head of which had debouched from Zizelowes at a quarter-past 11, had thrown the two battalions of the Guard Fusiliers into Wrchownitz and Zelkowitz, whilst the two battalions of the 2nd Foot Guards continued their onward march.

As far as one was able to judge in the dull state of the weather, it seemed as if the engagement of the 7th Division between Maslowed and Benatek was at this moment retrograding ; one saw the powerful line of the enemy's artillery on the height eastward of Horenowes, and a smaller line of batteries somewhat lower down, on the Wrchownitz-Maslowed road, firing in the direction of Benatek.

The two batteries of the advanced guard were now brought up ; the 4-pounder battery (Captain Eltester) took up a position between Zelkowitz and Wrchownitz, and opened fire about half-past 11. On its left, north-eastward of Wrchownitz, the 6-pounder battery (Captain Braun) unlimbered. The 6th Company of the 2nd Foot Guards and the 2nd Squadron of the Guard Hussars were detached to the left flank, the 3rd Squadron of the Hussars was thrown forward on the right flank to keep up the connection with the 10th Hussar Regiment of the 7th Division.

The Prince of Würtemberg now considered it of primary importance to gain possession of the heights of Horenowes. At 12 o'clock the Reserve Artillery was already southwards of Jericek ; the main body of the 1st Division of Guards (Gen. Von Hiller) was forming line on the left rear of the advanced guard, close to the Choteborek-Jericek road ; the heavy Cavalry Brigade of the Guards had also reached this spot, and was ordered up to the head of the column. The column of the 2nd Division of Guards had been broken through by the Reserve Artillery at the defile of Königinhof, and was divided in two parts, but General Von Plonski thought it advisable to relinquish for the moment all idea of re-forming his division, so as to be able to bring up at least his advanced guard to the aid of the 1st Division of Guards as speedily as possible ; he therefore marched from Choteborek, by way of Lhota and Luzan, straight towards the trees of Horenowes.

Until now the combined Cavalry brigade (Count Bismarck)

had covered the left flank of the 7th Division, and was stationed in the rear of the Artillery, but, as the division of Guards advanced, it crossed the dell between Zelkowitz and Benatek, and followed on the right flank of the Guards.

The 5th Squadron of the 2nd Dragoons tried to approach Horenowes, but was driven back by a volley delivered at point-blank range.

The VIth Corps had been informed that it was most desirable for it to come to the aid of the 7th Division as soon as possible, especially with its Artillery. At his own request, Major Broecker received orders from General Von Zastrow to advance with the artillery of the 11th Division, in company with the 4th Hussar Regiment, and to open fire on the enemy's artillery, which was just coming into line on the heights eastward of Horenowes. He passed the Trotinka by the bridge of Luzan, and posted four batteries on the other side of the stream, on the height beyond Racitz, at half-past 11 o'clock. It was soon, however, found that Austrian riflemen were still in this village, and, therefore, on the flank of the battery; Lieutenant-Colonel Von Buddenbrock was on the point of sending a detachment of dismounted Hussars against the village, when Prussian Infantry advanced to attack it.

It has already been mentioned, that the four battalions of General Hanenfeldt's brigade had arrived northwards of Racitz; General Hoffmann's brigade was stationed on their right rear.

We know further that, when the Austrian IInd Corps marched against the Prussian 7th Division, only the brigade of Major-General Henriquez, and two battalions of the 69th Regiment (Jellacic), belonging to Colonel Thun's brigade, were left at this part of the field. At 11 o'clock, the former brigade received orders to rejoin the IInd Corps, by way of Sendrasitz, preparatory to making the intended attack; it was on the point of starting thither, when the arrival of the Prussian VIth Corps fully occupied its attention at the Trotina, and prevented its departure.

Under these circumstances, General Henriquez took up the following position :—.

One battalion of the 14th Regiment (Hessen) was ordered to observe the country between Trotina and the Elbe, a second battalion of the same regiment occupied the bridges at Predmeritz and Lochenitz. The remainder of the brigade took up a position to the west of the high-road, with the 27th Regiment (Belgium) and the battery in the 1st, and the 3rd Battalion of the 14th Regiment in the second line. The artillery of the 2nd Light Cavalry Division was most probably employed here also.

Racitz and the wooded slope of the Trotina were occupied by two battalions of the 69th Regiment (Jellacic).

General Von Hanenfeldt received two orders simultaneously, one from General Von Mutius, to attack the wood on the Horicka-Berg with one battalion, and one from General Von Zastrow, directing him to take Racitz.

The Fusilier Battalion of the 10th Regiment was detached in the direction of the former; the 1st Battalion of the 50th Regiment, supported on its right flank by the 2nd Battalion of the same regiment advanced against Racitz, the Fusilier Battalion followed as reserve. Two companies covered the left flank of this movement, and advanced on the left bank of the Trotina.

The first assault of the 1st Battalion of the 50th Regiment carried Racitz, and drove the garrison, which consisted of Austrian Riflemen and Infantry, out of the village, which was in the hands of the former by 12 o'clock; one Austrian flag was captured.

The 7th Company of the 2nd Battalion took part in the engagement at Racitz, whilst Major Von Berken attempted to advance against the heights of Horenowes with the remaining three companies of the battalion, but was met by so severe a storm of shells that he lost two officers and 20 men within the first 150 paces.

The above-mentioned attack on the Horicka-Berg wood did not take place as was originally intended, because part of the Fusiliers of the 10th Regiment had joined in storming Racitz, and the remainder had taken a wrong direction during their advance, but the wood was carried soon afterwards by the 12th Division.

On the left wing of the VIth Corps General Von Prondzynski had in the meantime pursued his march with the 12th Division, and had reached the heights of Habrina and St. Wenzel shortly after 11 o'clock.

The three battalions of the 23rd Regiment and the artillery were at the head of the division, followed by the two battalions of the 22nd Regiment and the 1st and 4th Companies of Rifles, under Captain Von Minckwitz. The 6th Regiment of Hussars was thrown out towards Holohlaw and Rodow.

Detachments of the enemy were seen in the skirts of the wood on the Horicka-Berg, and, without waiting for his second line to come up, General Prondzynski ordered the 23rd Regiment to advance against the hill. The two batteries under Major Forst followed the regiment, after firing a few shots at the right flank of the enemy's line of Artillery on the heights of Horenowes. The weak detachments of the enemy gave way before this attack, and the Austrian Cavalry, which as yet kept on the left bank of the Trotina, now fell back behind the stream.

The second line of the division followed the first line, but had left the 1st Battalion of the 22nd Regiment (Major Herf), and the 2nd Squadron of the 6th Hussars behind to observe Josephstadt. The two Rifle Companies which had been left at Nesnasow now occupied Habrina and Rodow, in order to cover the retreat in case of a reverse.

The division, now numbering only five battalions, three squadrons, and two batteries, first advanced in the direction of Racitz, but was requested by General Von Zastrow to keep more to the left, so as not to get intermingled with the troops of the 11th Division. The necessary orders were given by General Prondzynski, but the half-battalion Von Tresckow (9th and 10th Companies) had already crossed the Trotina in immediate connection with the 11th Division; after much trouble, two other half-battalions waded through the stream somewhat lower down.

At 12 o'clock, therefore, the position of the IInd Army was as follows:—

The advanced guard of the Ist Division of Guards was advancing by Wrchownitz towards Horenowes;

The head of the 11th Division was in possession of Racitz;

The 12th Division was advancing from the Horicka-Berg;

Forty-eight pieces of artillery had already opened fire.

We know that the news of the approach of a Prussian corps, by way of Salney, had been telegraphed from Josephstadt, and that it had also been communicated to Lieutenant Field-Marshal Count Thun. At the same time, Major Von Sacken, of the General Staff, brought orders for the IInd Corps to cover the right flank of the Army.

Arrangements were made to carry out these orders, and the movement was executed under cover of 40 guns of the corps, which were planted eastward of Horenowes. The intended attack of Colonel Thom's brigade was, therefore, necessarily abandoned.

The brigades of the Prince of Würtemberg and General Saffran fell back by degrees to Maslowed (the village was held for the time by the 3rd Battalion of the 64th Regiment (Saxe Weimar), and then pursued their march towards Nedelist. In order to cover this movement, the five battalions of Colonel Thom's brigade were instructed to occupy the ridge between Maslowed and Nedelist, and were consequently withdrawn by degrees from Horenowes.

At midday the IVth Austrian Corps also received renewed orders to fall back to the position which it was to occupy according to the general dispositions for the battle.

General Mollinary now hastened personally to the Feldzeugmeister " to report the state of affairs," and " to recommend an " offensive advance of the IInd Corps on the right wing, ad- " joining the IVth Corps." He found the Commander-in-Chief still between Lipa and Chlum; of course, as matters now stood, his proposition could not be entertained, and he received orders —but not before a quarter-past 1—that his corps was to take up a position on the line Chlum-Nedelist.

General Von Brandenstein had been disabled by two severe gunshot wounds at about half-past 10 o'clock; his brigade was now rallied behind Maslowed, and then fell back to the heights eastward of Chlum. Archduke Joseph's brigade moved to the breastwork on its right flank, but still held Maslowed with the 2nd Battalion of the 68th Regiment (Baron Steininger). Colonel Poeckh's brigade had suffered severely in the fight in the wood, and the *débris* of its battalions were now rallied between the Batteries III and II. By reason of a misunderstanding General Fleischhacker's brigade still remained in Cistowes.

The retrograde movement of the Infantry of the IInd and IVth Corps naturally obliged the Artillery to give up the positions which it had taken up on the heights on both sides of Horenowes, but this was only done at the very last moment, when Major Petery had already taken Horenowes with the 1st Battalion of the 2nd Foot Guards and the 4th Company of Guard Rifles, and was advancing against the line of Austrian Artillery. First of all, the batteries westward of Horenowes, on the Wrchownitz road, retired; then by degrees those further eastward, until, last of all, the battery, which the Prussians had so long seen at the two lime-trees, disappeared also. In proportion as the Austrian artillery withdrew, so did the Prussian line of guns increase by degrees, in spite of the great difficulties which the nature of the ground everywhere opposed to their advance. The two advanced guard batteries of the 1st Division of Guards were already in action when, at half-past 12, Prince Hohenlohe brought forward the four rifled batteries of Lieutenant-Colonel Miesitscheck, which had crossed the Trotina at Jericek. Immediately afterwards the two other batteries of the 1st Division of Guards and the 4th Horse Artillery Battery, which had been detached to the left flank with the 3rd Regiment of Guard Lancers to open communications with the VIth Corps, took up a position on the left of Colonel Miesitscheck. This raised the number of Prussian guns to 90.

The batteries of the reserve now advanced within closer range and shelled the enemy's artillery and the Infantry columns, that were retreating from Horenowes over the south-eastern hills, with visible effect. A whole battalion was scattered by one of the first shells fired by Captain Werders' battery.

Whilst the Austrian right wing was still engaged in executing the above-mentioned extensive flank movement, the Prussian IInd Army advanced against it, it is true at first, with but trifling forces.

Still keeping possession of Wrohownitz and Zelkowitz, General Von Hiller sent Colonel Pape forward with three companies of the 2nd Battalion of the 2nd Foot Guards, and the 3rd Company of Rifles, in the direction of Benatek, where the 7th Division seemed to need immediate aid.

General Von Alvensleben then proceeded to attack Horenowes with only five companies, namely, the 1st Battalion Foot Guards and the 4th Company of Guard Rifles. The IInd Austrian Corps had already commenced its retreat, but some detachments were still in Horenowes; they were overcome, and for the most part taken prisoners. The village was in the hands of the Prussians before 1 o'clock; the advanced guard passed through and on both sides of it. and, after a slight skirmish, in which the park (Fasanerie) was taken, through the latter up to the heights. The combined Cavalry Brigade, under General Count Bismarck, had joined the advanced guard in this movement, and the 3rd Lancers and 1st and 5th Squadron of the 2nd Dragoons now trotted round the north side of Horenowes. An Austrian battalion was seen, which had suffered severely from the fire of the Prussian batteries, and Lieutenants Von der Planitz and Von Iagow with the Dragoons and some of the Lancers charged the supports of the battalion, round which the skirmishers had rallied, and took three officers and 70 men prisoners. In the meantime the battalion itself had disappeared behind the brow of the hill, and Count Bismarck gave orders to charge it. The Dragoons were soon re-formed, and Major Von Steinbrück charged with them and the 1st Squadron of the Lancers. He was received by the fire of the battalion, which stood in close order behind a ravine. The horses were tired by charging up hill in heavy ground, and could not break into the square. The 4th Squadron of the Guard Hussars, which advanced further to the left, was obliged to desist from attacking another body of Infantry, because the latter had found very good shelter in a clay-pit. The squadrons fell back on the three companies of the VIth Corps, which, as has already been mentioned, Major Von Berken was leading towards Horenowes, when Racitz was attacked by General Hanenfeldt's brigade.

In the meantime, Lieutenant-Colonel Heinichen, with the remaining three squadrons of the 2nd Dragoons, had advanced to the groups of trees on the heights of Horenowes, southeastward of Maslowed, in company with Major Von Petery's Infantry. On reaching the summit, a column of the Austrian IInd Corps was seen retreating on the road from Maslowed to Nedelist, the only compact body of troops that could be seen from that spot; the rear of the column was brought up by the 3rd Battalion of the 64th Regiment (Saxe Weimar), which, as has been already stated, had held Maslowed until the corps retreated; it was accompanied by six guns. General Von Hiller attracted Colonel Heinichen's attention to this Infantry, and the Prussian Cavalry advanced. The Dragoons ascended the Maslowed hill in a ravine, which leads up to its northeastern face, and charged immediately. The Austrian battalion had formed square, and the charge was met by its fire delivered at point-blank range, as well as by that of some other detachments of the enemy that were in the neighbourhood, besides which, the force of the charge was much broken by the steep bank on the roadside. Lieutenant-Colonel Heinichen fell at the head of the squadron, struck by four balls; besides their leader, the Dragoons lost one officer, 14 men, and 17 horses.

By order of the Commander of the corps, given at Horenowes, the whole 1st Division of Guards took the direction of the two lime-trees on the hill. Major Petery drove the last Austrian troops from the heights, and then the main body of the division assembled on the summit, detachments that were still behind having exerted themselves to the utmost to get up.

To the left of the Guards General Zastrow's division ascended the plateau northward of Sendrasitz, and took its place in this new line-of-battle. As soon as General Hanenfeldt's brigade had taken Racitz, namely, the 1st Battalion of the 50th Regiment advanced against the road which covers the steep right bank of the Trotina, and which was still occupied by the battalions of the 69th Regiment (Jellacic). Major Sperling debouched from the southern outlet of Racitz with three companies; the 3rd Company of the battalion advanced on the other side of the stream, and the 10th and 11th Companies of the 10th Regiment joined in the attack on the side of the meadows.

The enemy began firing at a very long range; the Prussian skirmishers established themselves as well as they could among the inequalities of the ground, and a skirmishing fire ensued, which had not lasted long, when the Austrian riflemen were seen making signs and waving handkerchiefs. As soon, however, as the Prussian skirmishers rose up from their shelter, the Austrians resumed their fire, whereupon the former rushed up the slope, and threw themselves on their adversaries from all sides. Major Von Neuman, who led the attack on the meadows, was wounded, but the battalion only lost 18 men, as the enemy gave way in great haste, leaving numerous prisoners behind.

The Fusilier Battalion of the 50th Regiment debouched from Racitz behind the 1st Battalion, and then turned to the right towards the plateau, on ascending which, the enemy was found to have retreated already. The battalion then pursued its march towards Sendrasitz without hindrance, and there met detachments of the 12th Division already. Nine companies of General Hanenfeldt's brigade established themselves in the village.

Of the companies which had been detached to the left bank of the Trotina, the 3rd Company of the 50th Regiment had taken the direction of Rodow, the 12th Company of the 10th Regiment re-crossed the stream under the enemy's fire, and proceeded to the eastern part of Sendrasitz. Lieutenant Salomon here advanced against a battery southward of the village, and got within Infantry range of it. In so doing, the company was severely fired on from the rear, it seems, by Prussian troops, and had besides to repulse a charge of Austrian Hussars, so that the battery had time to escape. One gun alone was left behind, and was captured by the company, with the assistance of skirmishers of the 50th and 23rd Regiment, notwithstanding all the exertions of the Austrian Riflemen and Hussars to save it.

When the 12th Division set off from the Horicka-Berg at half-past 12, to cross the Trotina below Racitz, it was met by a heavy fire from the batteries of General Henriquez's brigade, against which the two batteries of the Division took up a position.

General Von Prondzynski now gave orders to the 1st Battalion of the 23rd Regiment to cross the stream; Captain Von Elpons' half-battalion and Captain Von Minckwitz's half-battalion of rifles followed without orders. Lieutenant-Colonel Von Chamier first turned against the wood on his left, which was still occupied by the Austrians, but against which the 11th Division was advancing at the same time. He then proceeded to Sendrasitz, where he dislodged the enemy. Some of the latter retreated to Nedelist, but the greater part to Lochenitz.

General Prondzynski now led what little of his division remained on the left bank, by way of Rodow, against the mill and village of Trotina. At those two places, which the enemy defended but slightly, and abandoned with the loss of numerous prisoners, the half-battalions of Lieutenant-Colonel Von Fehrentheil (23rd Regiment), and Captain Müller (6th Rifle Battalion) crossed the Trotina; three Fusilier Companies of the 22nd Regiment, which were brought from St. Wenzel, crossed at the railway embankment. The regiment of Hussars was sent in pursuit of the detachments that were retreating from Sendrasitz to Lochenitz.

Thus, by 2 o'clock, the Corps of Guards had gained a firm footing on the heights of Horenowes, General Hiller's division had ascended the plateau of Maslowed, and occupied the south part of the village; the detachments that were sent towards Benatek were recalled, and those that were still in the rear brought up. On a line with the Guards the VIth Corps occupied Sendrasitz, and its left wing was advancing on Lochenitz, one of the bridges on which the Austrian Army relied, in case of a retreat.

As yet General Henriquez's brigade still covered the bridge by the position it had taken up at the high-road, but its connection with the other brigades of the IInd Corps was seriously endangered, now that the Prussians began to debouch from Sendrasitz, which important village had been but feebly defended. The last-named corps was still on its march, but at this moment in all probability only the leading brigade (General Saffran) had passed Nedelist, the ends of the long columns were still far behind this village.

The IVth Corps had set off later, and its last detachment was also still on the march to the entrenched position in front of the line Chlum-Nedelist; only the artillery, which has hastened on ahead, had as yet taken up its ground there. The whole flank movement of both corps was tolerably hidden from the sight of their opponents by the Maslowed-Nedelist ridge, but the shells of the Prussian batteries reached the Reserve Artillery of the army near Sweti, and forced it to change its position.

Lieutenant-Colonel Von Hofbauer brought forward the 64 guns of this reserve, which were still available, to the height behind the strip of meadow westward of Nedelist; their right flank rested on this village, on their left 40 guns of the IVth Austrian Corps stood in the entrenched position itself.

It was thus under the fire of above 100 pieces of artillery, and besides this taken in flank by some of the batteries of the IInd Corps, then retreating to Lochenitz, that the 1st Division of Guards had to advance against the position which the Infantry of the Austrian IVth Corps was still in the act of taking up.

At the time when the position was attacked, Chlum itself was occupied by the 2nd Battalion of the 46th Regiment (Saxe-Meiningen), belonging to General Appiano's brigade of the IIIrd Corps. The battalion was commanded by Lieutenant-Colonel Baron Schimmelpenning, the regiment by Colonel Slawetzki. The 3rd Battalion of the regiment (Major Jaczkowski) was posted behind the villlage at a ravine, the continuation of which leads to Nedelist. This Infantry had been here ever since 9 o'clock; on its left the Horse Artillery Battery, No. 7, of the 8th Artillery Regiment was stationed. All the available remains of General Appiano's brigade, namely, the 1st Battalion of the 46th Regiment (Saxe-Meiningen), commanded by Major Noak, ten companies of the 62nd Regiment (Archduke Henry), and the 4th Rifle Battalion, had been withdrawn behind the crest of the hill somewhat after 1 o'clock, and stood from 600 to 800 paces south-westward of Chlum.

The troops of the IVth Corps were stationed as follows:—

On the left wing the 8-pounder Battery, No. 10, in earthwork No. IV, westward of the north entrance of Clum; on its right the 8-pounder Battery, No. 9, and Horse Artillery Battery, No. 7, of the 4th Artillery Regiment were posted; the 3rd Battalion of the 67th Regiment (Schmerling) occupied the ground between the latter battery and earthwork No. III. In the earthwork itself, and in the adjoining breastwork to the right, the 4-pounder Battery, No. 4, and the Horse Artillery Battery, No. 8, were stationed, and from thence to earthwork No. II the remaining four battalions of Archduke Joseph's brigade were drawn up in two lines; on the right wing the remnants of 8th, 27th, and 30th Battalions of Rifles stood in and by the side of the earthworks.

The defence of the foremost line of the position was thus undertaken by Archduke Joseph's brigade. which was as yet unbroken, together with the Artillery and the Rifles.

The second line on the hill to the right of the southern part of Chlum consisted of the 4-pounder Battery, No. 1, three battalions, and one Rifle Company of General Brandenstein's brigade (the other battalions of the brigade were on the south face of the hill), then of the 4-pounder Battery, No. 5, and of the remnants of the 37th Regiment (Archduke Joseph), which were posted in the meadow-ground behind entrenchments Nos. III and II. The *débris* of the 51st Regiment (Archduke Charles

Q

Ferdinand) had pushed in between the two lines of General Brandenstein's brigade.

To the east of entrenchment No. II stood General Saffran's Brigade and then, extending as far as Nedelist, successively followed the Horse Artillery Batteries Nos. 4, 3, and 2 of the 6th, the Horse Artillery Battery No. 6 of the 12th, and lastly the 8-pounder Batteries Nos. 10, 9, 8, and 7 of the 6th Artillery Brigade, all belonging to the Army Reserve Artillery.

The Feldzeugmeister rode to Sweti about 1 o'clock, and returned to his former position on the heights between Chlum and Lipa at about half-past 1. It seems that even now he did not yet consider his right flank to be in any considerable danger; warning was certainly sent to the corps which stood in reserve that they might possibly have to change their front, but no orders were given to them to do so.

In order to prepare for and to assist the attack of the 1st Division of Guards, the Reserve Artillery of the Corps of Guards, and two batteries of the division pursued their march still further forward, whilst the two other batteries of the division stopped on the heights of Horenowes, and continued their fire against the enemy's line of artillery between Chlum and Nedelist. During its advance against Chlum General Von Hiller's Division was formed as follows:—

The four companies of the 1st Battalion of the 2nd Foot Guards were spread out in front, behind them followed the brigades of Colonels Von Pape and Von Obernitz; in the front line of the former the two battalions of the Guard Fusiliers, in that of the latter the 1st and 2nd Battalions of the 3rd Foot Guards; Colonel Von Kessel followed behind the left wing of Colonel Obernitz's Brigade; he had thrown the Fusilier companies of the 2nd Foot Guards and the two rifle companies, out in front of his brigade. By order of General Von Hiller, Colonel Von Pape stopped at the valley north-eastward of Maslowed and Major Von Petery at the strip of meadows between this village and Chlum; as Colonel Von Obernitz also halted for his battalions to take deploying intervals, Colonel Von Kessel's Fusilier Brigade came into the foremost line of the division.

In bringing forward the Reserve Artillery, Prince Hohenlohe first led the battery of Captain Von Mutius on beyond the avenue leading from Maslowed to Nedelist, to within 1,300 or 1,400 paces of the enemy's guns, and opened fire there about half-past 2 o'clock; the battery was soon reinforced by Captain Werder's battery on its left, and by the 2nd 6-pounder and 6th 4-pounder batteries on its right.

The 4th 12-pounder battery of the 1st Division of Guards took post on the right wing immediately to the south of Maslowed, and fired on Cistowes, which was still occupied by the enemy. The 1st 4-pounder battery came into action with the Reserve Artillery, and the 5th 4-pounder battery placed itself to the left of the latter; the 1st 6-pounder battery advanced on the left wing of the division, in the direction of Nedelist, and fired on the masses of the Austrian reserves that now became visible near Sweti. Count Pourtales' company of Guard Rifles covered the left flank. During the advance of the division the 4th Company of Guard Fusiliers had a slight skirmish with some Austrian detachments that were still in the ravine leading from Racitz up the Horenowes hill.

The main body advanced straight towards the church steeple of Chlum, leaving Maslowed about 1,000 paces on its right hand. In face of a very severe fire of shells, the men pressed forward so eagerly that the last detachments of Colonel Obernitz's Brigade very soon came up to the foremost line, and Colonel Von Knappe at last reached entrenchment No. III and the Austrian batteries planted eastward of Chlum with the right wing, the 1st Battalion of the 1st and the 2nd Company of the 3rd Foot Guards. The Horse Artillery battery, No. 7, of the IVth Austrian Corps had withdrawn already from want of ammunition; the 8-pounder battery, No. 9. left two guns in the hands of the Prussians. The left wing of the 2nd Battalion of the 3rd Foot Guards, the 6th and 7th Companies of Captains Von Arnim and Von Lobenthal, came upon entrenchment No. III itself. Here also the 4-pounder battery, No. 4, was on the point of withdrawing, but the Horse Artillery battery, No. 8, fired its last round of grape at 50 paces distance; the battery then managed to limber up its guns, but their teams were shot down by the rapid fire of the Prussian Infantry. On this spot and in the meadows behind the entrenchment this battery lost all, and battery No. 4 six, of its guns. Thus 14 guns were here captured by the 2nd Battalion of the 3rd Foot Guards, the skirmishing peloton of Lieutenant Chorus (2nd Foot Guards) and part of the 4th Company of the Guard Rifles (Captain Von Lettow).

The two battalions of Archduke Joseph's Brigade, which were stationed between Chlum and entrenchment No. III, did not hold out long. During this engagement the detachments of Colonel Von Kessel came up on the right, at their head the companies of the Fusilier Battalion of the 2nd Foot Guards (Major Von Erckert); behind these the 3rd Battalion of the Guard Fusiliers (Lieutenant-Colonel Count Waldersee), the Fusilier Battalion of the 1st Foot Guards (Lieutenant-Colonel Von Helldorf), and the 1st Company of the Guard Rifle Battalion. All these troops pressed forward between entrenchment No. III and Chlum, without noticing that the village was still occupied by the enemy. The Austrian 8-pounder battery, No. 10, that was stationed in entrenchment No. IV, being thus cut off from its corps, attempted to escape towards the north, but got into the fire of the 1st and 3rd Companies of the 1st, and the 3rd and 4th Companies of the 3rd Foot Guards, and instantly lost six guns. A seventh was overtaken by some officers of the divisional staff, and was captured by the Commander of the Guard Hussars (Colonel Von Krosigk), who was wounded in stopping the gun.

It was not until now that the enemy's fire in Chlum commenced, so that it seems as if his attention had been exclusively directed to the engagement which had been going on since the morning in the front of the army. The 1st Battalion of the 1st Foot Guards now wheeled to the right, and proceeded to attack the village; the 1st and 2nd Companies advanced against the east side of the southern and highest part, the 3rd Company surrounded the south end, and the 1st Company of Guard Rifles entered the northern corner of the village. The skirts were carried at all points at the very first onset; serious resistance on the part of the garrison (2nd Battalion of the 46th Regiment Saxe-Meiningen) was only encountered in the centre of the village, where Colonel Slawetzky fell, and the commandant of the battalion was seriously wounded. As soon as the 3rd Company of the Guards reached the further side of the village the Horse Artillery battery, No. 8, of the Austrian IIIrd Corps poured a perfect hailstorm of grape upon it, at a distance of 200 paces. In the meantime, however, the end of Colonel Von Kessel's columns, the Fusilier Battalion of the 1st Foot Guards, had reached the south end of Chlum and wheeled to the right against the battery. A destructive fire was poured upon the latter by the battalion and from the south corner of the village; the 10th, 11th, and 12th Companies of the 1st Foot Guards, under Lieutenant Von Griesheim, Captain Count Finkenstein, and Captain Count Rantzau, followed by the 3rd Company (Count Schlieffen), stormed the battery, which defended itself to the last with great bravery. The commander of the battery (Captain Von der Groeben) and one other officer fell, 52 men and 58 horses were killed or wounded, and 7 guns were captured; only one escaped.

Thus General Von Hiller was in possession of Chlum by a quarter before three o'clock.

The 1st and Fusilier Battalions of the 1st Foot Guards occupied the south end of the village and the hollow way to the right of it; the 3rd and 4th Companies of the 3rd Foot Guards were posted at the ravine to the left. Still further forward the 3rd Battalion of the Guard Fusiliers reached the hollow way leading from Chlum towards Sweti, from which it dislodged an Austrian battalion.

The 2nd Battalion of the 1st and the Fusilier Battalion of the 2nd Foot Guards advanced further eastward. General Brandenstein's Brigade was shaken by its previous combats, and opposed but slight resistance. Lieutenant-Colonel Gareis of the Austrian General Staff fell here severely wounded. The *débris* of Colonel Poeckh's Brigade, as well as the still fresh battalions of Archduke Joseph's Brigade at entrenchment No. II retreated likewise.

On the left wing of the division the 6th and 7th Companies of the 3rd Foot Guards and half of the Rifle Company halted between Chlum and Nedelist, and near the captured guns, but the 5th and 8th Companies advanced towards Sweti under

Major Von Barby; the troops on the right wing still pressed on, but were met by a severe fire of Artillery on their left flank, as soon as they reached the southern slope of the hill.

The Austrian Reserve Cavalry Division had come close up to the foot of the hill, and was within range of the Prussian Infantry on the summit. Each brigade of the division was formed in double column, the two Cuirassier regiments of Count Solm's Brigade on the left, General Schindlöcker's whole brigade on the right wing. As soon as both Horse Artillery batteries had opened fire, the latter brigade proceeded to charge the Prussian Infantry southward of Chlum, the different detachments of which had got much mingled together. The 9th Company of the 2nd Foot Guards (Captain Von Görne) followed, first by the 5th Company of the 1st Foot Guards (Lieutenant Baron Geyr), and then by the 10th and 11th Companies of the Guard Fusiliers (Captain Von Brederlow) were in the act of marching on the north end of Rosberitz, when the enemy's Cavalry appeared in the neighbourhood of the high-road. With full confidence in the force of their fire, these detachments faced towards the Cavalry, and deployed in line.

As far as could be distinguished, General Schindlöcher's Brigade was so formed that the Lancers and one regiment of Cuirassiers, were in the first line, and both in column, the other regiment of Cuirassiers followed close behind them.

The foremost detachments of the Prussian Infantry opened fire at little more than 200 paces distance, so that its results were most uncommonly successful; the remnants of the foremost Cuirassier squadrons swerved to the right, but got entangled with the Lancers, the following ones turned, and the brigade fell back to Langenhof, where Prince Solm's Brigade had moved to in the meantime. The loss was very considerable; the Commander of the 11th Cuirassiers, Colonel Kodziebrodzki, was severely wounded, the 1st squadron of his regiment almost totally destroyed; the total loss was estimated at more than 200 men.

On the Prussian right wing several Austrian attacks, proceeding from the direction of Langenhof and from the Lipa wood, with the intention of rescuing the captured guns, were repulsed by the 3rd, 10th, 11th, and 12th Companies of the 1st Foot Guards. Some detachments of the enemy, coming from the last-named wood, entered Chlum in the rear of the Prussian Division, the 11th Company therefore returned to the village and took an Austrian company prisoners at the church, after a short but sharp struggle.

In the meantime the Fusilier Battalion of the 2nd, the 2nd Battalion and the 9th Company of the 1st, and the 2nd Company of the 3rd Foot Guards, followed on the right by the 3rd Battalion of the Guard Fusiliers, pressed on towards and on both sides of Rosberitz. On the right wing of this advance a half battalion of the latter regiment, under Captain Von Brederlow, met a weak Austrian battalion—probably the 1st

Battalion of the 46th Regiment—which had already been thrown into disorder by the Lancers of General Schindlöcker's Brigade on their retreat, and the greater part of which now surrendered. A detachment rushed down to Rosberitz with the colours, but was dispersed by the 9th Company of the 1st Foot Guards; the colours were captured by Private Schellin. The 9th Company of the 2nd Foot Guards advanced towards the farm-house on the road to Langenhof. In the centre the 2nd Battalion of the 1st Foot Guards advanced by the Nedelist road and passed through and beyond the west skirts of the village, driving the enemy back over the high-road by its fire. A short time previously Major Von Erckert had got into a heavy fire of Infantry, whilst descending the hill eastward of Rosberitz with the 10th, 11th, and 12th Companies of the 2nd Foot Guards; on getting on a line with the village, he came upon a far superior force of Austrian Infantry and found a battery in the act of limbering up in front of the north-east corner of the village. The skirmishing fire of the 10th Company (Captain Captain Rantzau) forced the latter to abandon three guns, and the Austrian Infantry was driven back after a severe struggle.

Whilst Major Von Erckert was engaged in the pursuit of the latter, he came upon the left wing of the Austrian Reserve Artillery, which had been obliged to withdraw from its position when the Prussian Infantry advanced, and was now retreating towards Wsestar. The first battery reached was the Horse Artillery battery No. 4 of the 6th Regiment, which had already been obliged to abandon one gun by the loss of its whole team; it now turned its flank guns on its adverseries, and received the advancing skirmishers with a fire of grape, in spite of which however the 12th Company of the 2nd Foot Guards overcame the covering battalion and entered the battery. Major Von Erckert and his aide-de-camp dashed forward and stopped two guns which were on the point of driving off; Lieutenant Von Schrötter captured a third with part of the 8th Company of the 1st Foot Guards. Further towards Sweti the 5th and 8th Companies of the 3rd Foot Guards, under Major Von Barby, took three guns of the Horse Artillery battery No. 3 and two of Horse Artillery battery No. 2. By 3 o'clock Rosberitz was occupied, the enemy dislodged from the neighbourhood of the village, and an attack which the remnants of General Appiano's brigade attempted with ten companies of the 62nd Regiment (Archduke Henry) and the 4th Battalion of Rifles had been repulsed.

We must now turn to the combats which had covered both flanks of this advance.

The detachment which originally constituted the advanced guard of the 1st Division of Guards was now following *en échelon* behind the right wing of the main body. It consisted at present of the 1st and 2nd Battalions of the Guard Fusiliers, the 2nd Battalion of the 2nd Foot Guards, and the 3rd Company of Guard Rifles. About half-past 2 General Von Alvensleben had reached the meadow situated between the two roads leading from Maslowed to Chlum with these troops, when heavy columns of Austrian Infantry issued from the Lipa wood, as well as northward of the latter; they were accompanied by a battery, and several squadrons covered the flank of their march.

It was General Fleischhacker's Brigade of the IVth Austrian Corps which, as has been already mentioned, had remained by mistake in Cistowes, and was now proceeding towards Nedelist, whilst the 7th Hussar Regiment went round the north end of Chlum. The line of march of this considerable body of the enemy's troops brought them full upon the rear of the centre of the Ist Division of Guards, which was at that moment engaged in a most severe struggle eastward of Chlum.

Near to entrenchment No. III, the head of the Austrian Hussars first came upon two companies of Pioneers under Captain Von Adler, which were marching towards Chlum, then upon the batteries of the Reserve Artillery, which were on their road to the hill of Chlum, and lastly upon the 1st Battalion of the 2nd Foot Guards, which had been hitherto kept back in reserve. The 2nd 6-pounder and 6th 4-pounder batteries turned their guns quickly to the right, unlimbered, and opened fire. The leading sub-division of the Hussars was almost totally destroyed; the following ones suffered severely, and the regiment turned back. It then attempted to cut its way through Chlum, but got into the fire of the 1st Company of Guard Rifles, upon which some detachments of the regiment and two guns made a circuit round towards Maslowed.

Imagining the latter village to be still occupied by the Austrians, the remainder of the battery of General Fleischhacker's Brigade, accompanied by some Hussars and followed by a considerable body of Infantry, advanced towards the west entrance, three pelotons of Hussars and two guns towards the south entrance of the village. Rifle fire from Maslowed and grape fire from the 4th 12-pounder battery (Captain Von Schmeling), which was stationed here, compelled them to abandon the two guns. Their Cavalry escort, which likewise suffered great loss, dashed through Captain Schmeling's battery, was met by infantry fire from Maslowed, and then turned to the right towards the meadows leading to Sendrasitz. The confused mass then proceeded straight in the direction of the Crown Prince, who was at that moment riding towards the Maslowed hill with his suite, and was now forced to fall back to the nearest battalions of the 2nd Division of Guards, which were just then coming up. The 2nd Squadron of the Guard Hussars was already ascending the face of the hill, but faced to the right about and drove the fugitive Austrians—many of whom were taken prisoners—in the contrary direction, so that part of them fled towards Bürglitz, where they fell into the hands of other Prussian detachments. The remainder of the battery and the Infantry were met by the 5th, 6th, and 8th

Companies of the Guard Fusiliers, under Lieut.-Colonel Von der Knesebeck, whose fire dispersed them and drove them back towards Cistowes and Lipa with the loss of many prisoners; four guns of the battery were captured here.

General Fleischhacker's Brigade itself came upon the main body of General Alvensleben's Brigade. By his orders, Colonel Werder, who commanded the first line, charged the enemy's flank with the 1st Battalion of the Guard Fusiliers (Major Von Tietzen), and forced him back again into the wood. The three companies of the 2nd Battalion advanced on the right wing of the brigade, and captured the last two guns of the Austrian battery in Cistowes.

The remainder of the Advanced Guard had followed the Fusiliers and were still pursuing the enemy when they received orders to march to the assistance of the troops engaged at Chlum. General Von Hiller, who himself arrived at the spot at a quarter before 3, repeated the orders personally.

General Fleischhacker's Brigade was compelled to retreat westward to Chlum, and then sought to rejoin its corps in a southerly direction. Colonel Count Degenfeld led the *débris* of the 7th Hussar Regiment in a wide circuit round the flanks of the division of Guards.

As soon as Chlum was taken, and the Austrian line of artillery between this village and Nedelist had ceased firing, Colonel Prince Hohenlohe advanced with the Reserve Artillery on the left flank of the division; General Von Colomier had informed him that the 1st Division of Guards was engaged with considerable forces of the enemy, and was in great need of the assistance of artillery. The batteries were therefore set in motion towards the heights to the south of Chlum, without taking further notice of the Austrian Cavalry that was visible between Nedelist and Lochenitz. The above-mentioned encounter with the Austrian 7th Hussars, which had compelled the two batteries of the right *échelon* to unlimber whilst still in marching column, had, however, caused some delay.

The only Prussian Infantry between Rosberitz and Sweti consisted of the 5th, 7th, and 8th Companies of the 3rd Foot Guards, under Major Von Barby; the 6th Company (Von Arnim) was behind them, near to the guns which it had taken.

We have still to cast a glance at the simultaneous advance of the VIth Corps on the left wing of the IInd Army.

It will be remembered that during the taking of Racitz, Major Von Berken, of General Hanenfeldt's Brigade, had marched with the 2nd Battalion of the 50th Regiment towards the heights of Horenowes, under a heavy fire of artillery, and had soon afterwards covered the retreat of the Dragoons after their unsuccessful charge. As soon as the advance of the Guards had forced the enemy to quit the heights of Horenowes, and the 11th Division had occupied Sendrasitz, Major Von Berken pressed on westward of this village towards Nedelist, about on a line with the 1st Division of Guards. On reaching the road leading from Maslowed, the battalion was severely shelled, notwithstanding which the 8th Company (Captain John) proceeded to attack Nedelist, and entered the village in the first onset. It would seem as if the Austrians were completely taken by surprise here; crowds of them fled, and those remaining in the houses were taken prisoners.

In support of this undertaking, Major Von Berken had pushed forward the 5th Company (Captain Von Rechow) and the 6th Company (Captain Von Roux) past the west side of Nedelist. Whilst passing through the high corn, which made it difficult to see to any distance, the skirmishers (Lieutenant Von Both) was fired on by Infantry; they immediately returned the fire, and pressing further on, came upon the right wing of the Austrian Reserve Artillery, which Lieut.-Colonel Hoffbauer had placed here. The 8-pounder battery, No. 7, of the 6th Regiment, fired on the skirmishers with grape, in spite of which they rushed forward with cheers, drove off the Infantry supports, and captured all the guns of the battery, which lost 27 men and 41 horses on the spot. The commandant of the battery was shot through the head, two ammunition wagons had blown up before the attack, the remainder escaped; besides these, a 4-pounder gun that had been abandoned was taken here.

Further to the right the skirmishers of the 5th Company and part of the 7th Company, under Lieutenant Gehring, also came upon the enemy's line of Artillery—probably the 8-pounder Battery No. 8—which received them with a fire of grape. There, too, the skirmishers dashed on past two guns which had been previously abandoned, entered the battery in spite of the fire of its covering party, and captured two of its guns.

The 2nd Battalion of the 50th Regiment had thus taken 15 guns, and by gaining possession of Nedelist had obtained a *point d'appui* for the further advance of the corps; it was now, however, obliged to await the arrival of the other battalions of the regiment, which did not come up until 20 minutes later.

The *débouché* of these battalions from Sendrasitz had been for some time delayed by the cross-fire of Lieut.-Colonel Hoffbauer's batteries westward of Nedelist, and of those belonging to General Henriquez's Brigade, which were stationed to the south of Trotina; according to their own account they had to endure the fire of the 12th Prussian Division also. Whilst they were sheltering themselves behind the massive houses in the eastern part of the village and in the hollow ways to the north of it, they suffered from a disaster of a peculiar nature. A shell had fallen amongst a number of beehives, and the insects fell upon the troops, who could scarcely protect themselves from their fierce attack. About 3 o'clock the battalions drew near Nedelist, where the detached companies and the two battalions of the 10th Regiment, that had been behindhand during the march, arrived by degrees, and General Hanenfeldt's whole brigade was assembled.

General Hoffmann's Brigade and the Artillery of the 11th Division marched to the same spot as soon as the latter had refilled its caissons. The 8th Dragoons and 4th Hussars were formed in a brigade under command of Lieut.-Colonel Von Wichmann and followed over the heights of Maslowed, so that General Von Zastrow's Division was united again somewhat later.

The few companies of the 12th Division which General Von Prondzynski had kept in his own immediate neighbourhood had crossed the Trotina at the village and mill of the same name, and by the railway embankment. From the first-named spot, General Von Cranach had pushed forward the 6th Company of the 23rd Regiment (Captain Schmidt) along the high-road in pursuit of the enemy, who offered some resistance at the camp of huts near Lochenitz, but retreated into the village as soon as the 11th Company of the 22nd Regiment, which had crossed at the mill, turned his flank. An offensive movement which the enemy attempted to make from the village was checked by Colonel Von Ruville with the remaining companies of the Fusilier Battalion of the 22nd Regiment, which advanced between the high-road and the railway. Numerous prisoners were taken in the camp.

A struggle for the possession of Lochenitz now began, in which the 6th Company of the 23rd Regiment attempted to get round to the west of the village. The detachments which advanced against the village were met by a fire of musketry and grape; they returned it with a fire of skirmishers, and some of them even penetrated into the outskirts of the village and brought back some prisoners. Captain Count Henneberg was on the point of making a dash at the village when orders arrived from General Mutius that the few troops still available should be kept back as a reserve.

Thus, by 3 o'clock the right wing of the Austrian Army—the IInd and VIth Corps—was defeated and retreating on Wsestar, Sweti, Predmeritz, and Lochenitz.

Only five brigades of the Prussian Army had been as yet engaged; ten had not come in contact with the enemy. The former stood on the line Rosberitz-Nedelist-Lochenitz.

The 1st Division of Guards was furthest in advance; it had dislodged the IVth Corps from its entrenched position, and had —principally by its Infantry fire—forced its adversary's batteries to withdraw from their position. In its rapid and victorious course it had captured 55 guns and gained possession of the heights of Chlum. The head of the division stood on the high-road leading from Sadowa to Königgrätz, in the rear of the enemy's main position, but at the same time it was now in face of the mighty masses of the Austrian reserves, within a distance of only 2,000 paces. Two whole corps of Infantry, with a powerful Artillery, stood—as yet still motionless—in the low ground near Sweti, Wsestar, and Rosnitz; large bodies of cavalry menaced the flank of the division from the direction of Langenhof.

With the exception of the advanced guard of the 2nd Division of Guards, there were no Prussian troops within a mile and a quarter of these isolated detachments, from which any immediate assistance could be expected.

The head of the main body of the last-named division was at this time just ascending the ridge to the east of Maslowed, the 11th Division was still assembling behind Nedelist, the Vth Corps only approaching the heights of Horenowes, and the Ist Corps was still between Wrchownitz and Benatek. The 1st Division of Guards, must, therefore, be prepared to sustain a fresh and hard struggle with its own forces alone.

## 1st Army.

We left General Von Fransecky at 11 o'clock, as his adversary had penetrated into the wood with far superior forces, and had driven back the centre of his division, thereby totally separating both its wings.

In the south-eastern part of the wood the whole force of this mighty attack fell on the worn out Fusilier companies of the 27th and the 1st and Fusilier Battalion of the 26th Regiment. In vain these troops exerted their utmost energies to hold their ground. The Fusilier Battalion of the 27th Regiment had suffered severe losses in previous moments of the engagement, in the attacks which different detachments of the regiment had made on Cistowes, and on the enemy's artillery; Captain Count Finkenstein had fallen, Captain Von Westernhagen, and many of the officers were severely wounded.

The commandant of the Fusilier Battalion of the 26th Regiment, Major Von Schönholtz, was wounded, the leader of the 11th Company, Lieutenant Ewald, dead, and six officers *hors de combat.*

Parts of the 1st Battalion of the 26th Regiment, Major Paucke, under Captain Westernhagen and Von Horn, twice pressed forward from the summit of the hill to the skirts of the wood, but their attempts cost the battalion its commandant, Captain Von Westernhagen, five officers, and more than 200 men. The numerical superiority of the enemy was so great that the thinned ranks of the Prussians could no longer hold their ground; they were driven back partly to the northern projection of the wood, where the 2nd Company of the 67th Regiment, which now joined in the action, also repaired, and partly in the direction of Benatek.

The General Staff Officer of the Division, Major Von Krenski, rallied some of the detachments, and led them forward again, others occupied the village. The 12th Company of the 27th Regiment formed the nucleus of these troops, and Major Paucke soon arrived with such debris of his battalion as were still with him.

The 4th Battalion of Rifles and the 1st Battalion of the 72nd Regiment still held their ground in the western part of the wood, but here also they were partly forced out into the open country, as was also Major Von Zedtwitz, with the 8th Company of the 67th Regiment. In this struggle, which waved to and fro, Serjeant Müller and Private Bässler of the 2nd Company of the 72nd Regiment captured an Austrian flag, a second was also taken by Private Köhler of the Rifles, but was lost again through his being wounded.

Whilst the Prussian troops still made good their footing in this part of the wood, the Austrians gained more and more ground in other directions. The defenders of that part of the wood, which juts out towards Maslowed, were thus placed in an extremely difficult position; engaged in the interior of the wood, they were vehemently attacked from the direction of the village, and thereby menaced in front, flank, and rear at the same time.

At this spot the 2nd Battalion of the 26th and 66th Regiments, and the 3rd and 4th Companies of the 67th Regiment, were engaged. After Major Gilsa's mortal wound, Captain Fritsch made a successful attack on an Austrian battalion of rifles, with the 6th and 7th Companies of the 26th Regiment. Captains Von Pollern and Von Ploetz still held the road which leads into the wood from the south end of Maslowed with the 5th and 8th Companies of the same regiment, but the latter lost 2 officers, 8 non-commissioned officers, and above 80 men of his company. As, however, the enemy encompassed these detachments more and more, they were compelled to fall back to the northern part of the wood, disputing the ground step by step. Major Von Wiedner alone succeeded in maintaining his position at the front of the hill, where the road from Maslowed touches the corner of the wood, with three companies of the 2nd Battalion of the 66th Regiment. He was joined by Lieutenant Lademann with part of the 26th Regiment. Austrian rifles that had entered the wood at this spot were driven out again, and three different attacks of the enemy repulsed.

In the meantime the battalions of the IInd Austrian Corps had also began to advance against the northern projection of the wood. Here also an incessant struggle had been going on, but all exertions of the enemy were thwarted by the steadiness of the Prussian troops stationed here.

The companies had all become mingled together as the fight swayed backwards and forwards in the dense wood; no unity of guidance was possible on ground where hills and wood shut out all view of the surrounding country, and all that the commanders of the different detachments could do, was to lead their men by their own personal example. In all parts the officers rallied around them whatever men were in their neighbourhood, no matter to what regiment they belonged, and led them forward again and again. Troops that were driven out of the wood were sent back again into it, the debris of those detachments which were too far reduced in numbers were posted as reserves. It is true that numerous Austrian prisoners were still being continually brought back, but the numbers of wounded streaming to the rear, and of troops that had lost their leaders, was also increasing more and more. Behind them now appeared the enemy's skirmishers, and compact Austrian detachments soon issued out of the north-west corner of the wood, and advanced in the direction of Benatek.

Nevertheless, the defence of those parts of the wood which project towards Maslowed was still continued, and it was the aim of the Austrians to wrest this last position from the division. For this purpose strong bodies of troops advanced from the south, and those detachments of Prince Wurtemberg's and General Saffran's Brigades, which had been previously repulsed, as well as five perfectly fresh battalions of Colonel Thom's Brigade, which had just arrived from the heights of Horenowes, pressed forward from the east.

At this decisive spot, however, General Von Fransecky was personally present, and inspired all around him with the firm resolve to defend to the utmost the ground which had cost so much blood to conquer. He himself, General Von Schwarzhoff, Colonels Von Medem, and Von Blankensee were brilliant examples for the troops. Major Von der Burg of the General Staff had already announced the approach of the IInd Army, and the words "the Crown Prince is coming" flew through the thinned ranks of the defenders, and inspired the nearly exhausted strength of the hard pressed band with fresh life.

In reality, however this aid was still far off, and the situation became every minute more critical. Major Von der Burg was, therefore, requested to arrange that the first available detachments of the Guards should advance on Maslowed against the enemy's flank; riding through the line of the Austrian skirmishers this officer hastened to the heads of the Corps of Guards and the VIth Corps. The attempts of the enemy to debouch from the wood in the rear of the Prussian position had for the present to be resisted by the forces of the division alone.

In the course of the fight in the wood, a battalion of the 51st Regiment (Archduke Charles Ferdinand) had lost all idea of its whereabouts; issuing from the north-west corner of the wood it advanced towards the small copse on the Bistritz, in the direction of Horenowes, but was soon seen by Captain Von Humbert, who was stationed in a hollow way south-westward of Benatek with the 1st Squadron of the 10th Hussars. The squadron rapidly formed line and charged the enemy. At the first summons to surrender 16 officers and 665 men laid down their arms without resistance. One flag was captured; a second, that was at the rear of the battalion, escaped.

Some other detachments of the enemy coming out of the north-west corner of the wood, General Fransecky sent Captain Von Ploetz with the 5th and 8th Companies of the 26th Regiment against them. In company with part of the 4th Battalion of Rifles they also succeeded in surrounding those Austrian riflemen that first came out into the open, and in taking 3 officers and 200 men prisoners.

The arrival of fresh columns of the enemy, however, compelled Captain Von Ploetz to fall back eastward of Benatek; Captain Raussendorff's Battery southwards of the village was also obliged to withdraw. Detachments of the enemy were already pressing forward to attack Benatek, but as troops had been thrown into the village in due time, the former were unable to enter it, and were obliged to retreat again into the wood.

In the meantime the fight at that part of the wood where its north-eastern projection joins the main forest, raged with intense fury. Major Schwager and Lieutenant-Colonel Von Schmeling advanced here with the 1st and Fusilier Battalions of the 66th Regiment to cover the retreat of the troops that were retreating from the interior of the wood, as soon as the latter descended the hill. The enemy's pursuit was checked by repeated charges in which numbers of Austrians were taken prisoners.

The 3rd and 4th Companies of the 67th Regiment, under the command of Captain Ewald, also took part in these engagements. By order of General Fransecky, Lieutenant-Colonel Von Hochstetter took up a position with 2nd Company on the open ground more to the west, in order to prevent the enemy's débouché from the wood.

Lieutenant-Colonel Von Bothmer still held the ground in the extreme north-eastern corner of the wood. The 10th and 11th Companies of the 67th Regiment were twice driven back here, but each time Captain Liebeneiner succeeded in rallying his men and in regaining his former position.

At last it became necessary to withdraw Major Von Wiedner too from that part of the wood projecting towards Maslowed, in order to have some available reserve in the hour of need.

Between 1 and 2 o'clock, however, the enemy began perceptibly to relax in his attacks. We know this to have been caused by the mere approach of the Guards and the VIth Corps d'Armée, which induced, first the IInd, and then the IVth Austrian Corps also to turn their attention from the attempted destruction of the 7th Division to the preservation of their own army. The orders which were issued in consequence were not, however, immediately known by all the Austrian detachments, so that the fight in the wood of Maslowed lasted till half-past 2 o'clock.

During this whole time the right wing of General Fransecky's Division had held its ground outside of the wood in and near Cistowes. Here too the superior officers, General Von Gordon, Colonels Von Zychlinski and Von Bothmer, were in the foremost ranks of the combatants, leading them on by their own personal example.

Numerically weak as they were, the Prussian detachments maintained their positions in the western detached part of the village with the utmost steadiness. They were here in the centre of the violent artillery combat between the Austrian batteries on the heights of Lipa, and the Prussian Artillery at the wood of Maslowed; this prevented any further advance.

The struggle in which Colonel Bothmer was engaged at the avenue of trees further northward was sanguinary in the extreme; one after the other, Captain Von Hirschfeld and four officers were either killed or mortally wounded, and the Austrian columns, which pressed forward in considerable force from the northern outskirts of Cistowes, suffered very severely also by the fire of parts of the 1st, 6th, and 7th Companies of the 67th Regiment that were at this spot. Although wounded, Captain Müller and Lieutenant Vorberg hastened forward in pursuit; the former penetrated as far as the opposite side of the village, the latter took one of the massively built barns after a severe struggle, but fresh columns of the enemy compelled both of them to relinquish the advantages they had gained, and to fall back to their former positions. Inclusive of the Adjutant of the 2nd battalion, who fell here, the two divisions of the 1st, and the 6th and 7th Companies of the 67th Regiment lost 9 officers and 169 men at this spot, of whom 6 officers and 57 men were killed. In one of the enemy's attacks Corporal Görlitz and Private Hoebald of the 6th company captured an Austrian flag. Colonel Von Bothmer now withdrew these detachments, which were much diminished in numbers and perfectly isolated, but this did not take place until General Von Fransecky was already engaged in reforming his division.

It was not until now that the entrance of the Guard Fusiliers into Cistowes, which we have already related, released General Gordon's troops from their critical position.

On the left wing of the 2nd Division Major Von Wiedner had already returned to his position opposite Maslowed, and was on the point of advancing from thence against one of the massive buildings in front of the village, when detachments of the Guards appeared in the neighbourhood.

The artillery of the division was now brought forward to the heights of Maslowed, and opened fire on the last of the enemy's retiring columns, but it was above all things necessary to reform the infantry after its hard struggle. General Von Fransecky gave orders that this should be done on the meadows south-eastward of Benatek. Fighting with the last troops of the enemy, some detachments of his battalions, and the two battalions of the 8th Division, which had joined him, had regained the opposite side of the wood, where they were able to fire with effect on the retreating masses.

As General Fransecky's Division had to fight the hardest struggle of this day's battle, so were its losses also severer than those of any other division.

Exclusive of the artillery, they amounted to 84 officers and 2,036 men, of whom the 26th Regiment alone lost 26 officers and 709 men. The two battalions of the 8th Division, which had taken part in these combats lost 5 officers and 126 men killed and wounded. About 2,000 prisoners and 3 colours were the trophies which remained in the hands of the victors.

It is proved that 51 Austrian Battalions, and more than 100 pieces of artillery were here opposed to 14 Prussian battalions and 24 guns. It is not known for certain whether detachments of the IIIrd and 1st Austrian Corps did or did not also take part in this combat, but one of the captured flags is supposed to have belonged to the 38th Regiment (Haugwitz) of the latter Corps.

In just appreciation of the situation, Prince Frederick Charles had hitherto forbidden any further advance of the four divisions beyond the Bistritz; towards midday, however, he deemed it necessary to prepare for an offensive movement of the centre of his line of battle also, and brought forward his reserves for this purpose.

The 5th Division crossed the Bistritz at Unter-Dohalitz, and took ground to the right, the 6th Division at and by the side of the bridge at Sadowa, and was then massed behind the wood.

Thus, shortly after 12 o'clock, six divisions were in readiness to advance as soon as the flank armies (Flügel-Armeen) came up.

But the moment for this had not arrived yet, and the patience and endurance of the Ist Army had still to undergo a long trial.

Above all, the 7th Division would have been in dire need of assistance, but such could only be indirectly afforded by the IInd Army. It seemed neither advisable that still more forces should be absorbed in that destructive wood combat, nor admissible to withdraw the main reserves from the centre of the line of battle, where the enemy might possibly still attempt a general attack. As that combat could not be broken off, the division must necessarily be left for the present to its own resources. The possession of the Maslowed wood was, nevertheless, of the highest importance, as the means of ensuring the speediest possible connection with the IInd Army.

While General Von Fransecky was thus executing his difficult task in an unsurpassable manner, the battle—as far as regarded the other divisions—assumed essentially the character of a combat of artillery, to be sure of a most unequal one, in which the Prussian Infantry was for a long time condemned to the trial of passive endurance under a most severe fire of artillery.

The batteries which had been brought over the Bistritz, with both trouble and loss, found their range very much limited by patches of wood. Just those positions from which the Austrian Artillery did the most harm, were the most difficult to get at, so for instance, that of the powerful battery in front of Lipa, which poured an incessant shower of shrapnels and shells, not only on the Sadowa wood, but also on the reserves which stood behind it. It was in itself unfavourable to have to carry on a combat from low ground against artillery posted on the heights, and so hidden from view that the position of its guns could for the most part only be distinguished by the flashes of their fire, so that it was almost impossible for the Prussian artillerymen to test the accuracy of their own fire. Besides which the numbers on both sides were very disproportionate.

At the very commencement of the battle almost all the batteries of the IIIrd and Xth Corps, and of the 3rd Reserve Cavalry Division were brought into action on the heights which extended from Lipa to Tresowitz, and slope gently down towards the Bistritz, and when some of them had expended all their ammunition, towards the middle of the day, two more divisions of the Reserve Artillery of the Army, or 64 8-pounders, were brought into this position. We may, therefore, assume that 200 pieces of artillery came by degrees into action at this spot under the most favourable circumstances for defence that can possibly be imagined.

More than 80 Prussian guns still remained behind the Bistritz, because no use could be made of them further forward.

The Cavalry were in a similar position, sufficient ground had not yet been gained to afford room for its formation on the other side of the Bistritz, a circumstance which was not without influence later in the day when the fruits of the victory were reaped. In their reserved position both arms would certainly have been of eminent service if the enemy had assumed the offensive. The Austrians, however, attempted no attack in the centre of the line of battle, had they done so the advantages of a more effective artillery and infantry fire, as well as of the ground, would have passed over to their adversary's side.

Under such circumstances the Prussian Artillery could only imperfectly succeed in drawing the fire of the Austrian batteries off from the Infantry. As early as $\frac{1}{4}$ past 10, the 4th 4-pounder Battery (Captain Von Schlotheim) of the 8th Division took up a position between the woods of Sadowa and Maslowed, on the heights near the latter, where it was soon afterwards joined by the two other 4-pounder Batteries of the Division (Captains Kipping and Auton). The fire of these batteries was directed against the Austrian Artillery between Lipa and Chlum. The 12-pounder Battery was not brought into action. When the Infantry combat at the Maslowed wood drew near to the south border of the wood Captain Kipping's Battery was obliged for the moment to withdraw, but very soon resumed its former position.

The Artillery of the 4th Division could find no space for action, and was withdrawn over the Sadowa bridge when the enemy's shells began seriously to annoy the reserves behind the wood of Sadowa.

Captain Gallus's Battery of the 3rd Division had advanced beyond Unter-Dohalitz, and opened fire north-eastward of Dohalicka; the two other rifled batteries of this Division found no passage over the Bistritz and returned to Mzan. The 12-pounder battery joined the reserve.

R

All four batteries of the Reserve Artillery of the IInd Corps were now led through Unter-Dohalitz by Colonel Von Puttkamer, and went into action beyond Dohalicka. Captain Von der Dollen's Battery went on ahead as far as the position where Captain Gallus's Battery was already engaged.

Thus, by midday, only 18 Prussian guns were in action on the north, and 24 on the south side of the road, making on the whole 42 guns. As soon, however, as the troops of the IIIrd Corps now reached the Bistritz, Major Rüstow led the three rifled batteries of the 5th Division to the position beyond Unter-Dohalitz, between the wood and Dohalicka. Captain Hirschfeld's Battery of the 6th Division was brought up to the same spot, but the other batteries found no room, and remained in reserve.

The Commandant of the Reserve Artillery of the Army, General Schwarz, had ridden forward early in the day to reconnoitre the country on both sides of the Sadowa wood, and had personally convinced himself of the difficult position in which the batteries on the north side of the high-road were placed. In consequence of his report, Prince Frederick Charles dispatched two batteries from the Reserve (Captains Reinhardt and Von Schaper) to this spot. The General gave Colonel Roth the command of all the batteries planted on the western slope of the ridge which rises towards Cistowes. Of these Captain Schlotheim's battery had expended all, and Captain Kipping's nearly all its ammunition, and as the former was besides much damaged it was withdrawn. Its place was taken by the batteries of Captain Philipp and Meissner of the 4th, and lastly by Captain Eunicke's Battery of the 3rd Artillery Regiment, which raised the number of guns in this position to 42.

On the south side of the wood, Colonel Von Ramm brought forward the batteries of Captains Beneke and Burbach, of the 3rd Artillery Regiment; they found room in the intervals of the line in front of Unter-Dohalitz, and increased in to 60 guns.

Even counting two other batteries, which came into action later in the day, still the Artillery of the Ist Army at no time attained more than about half the strength of the Austrian artillery opposed to it.

The position of the batteries in front of Cistowes was very much cramped by the low meadows on their right flank, into which they could not descend without losing all view of the surrounding country. Even from the summit of the ridge it was very difficult to hit the enemy's battery westward of Lipa; nevertheless an uninterrupted fire was kept up against it and against the guns posted behind the entrenchments at Chlum, at times also against detachments of the enemy's artillery, which took the right wing of the line en écharpe from the direction of Maslowed, but which were soon driven off.

This artillery position, so near to the Maslowed wood, was

repeatedly in very great danger from the turn which the Infantry combat took there; it was, therefore, of primary importance that the line should be covered by other troops. Some detachments of the 27th Regiment, which were driven back from Cistowes towards the Sadowa wood, and were now trying to rejoin their regiment, had been already stopped here, and were posted in the Skalka wood. Later in the day General Schwartz found some men of the 4th Battalion of Rifles that had been forced out of the wood; these and a detachment of Pioneers were employed to guard the batteries at the edge of the wood, and at the same time he requested the squadrons of the 6th Lancers, that were in the neighbourhood, to act as the immediate support of the artillery. They most willingly undertook this difficult task, and stood in consequence for several hours under fire of the enemy's guns.

Having thus, in some degree at least, provided for the security of flank and rear, General Schwartz now turned his attention to the possibility of a retreat. Both he and General Lengsfeld personally interfered at the Sadowa bridge, which was at times completely stopped up by ammunition wagons and ambulances; a ford was also discovered near the Skalka wood. In this manner the artillery combat was kept up at this spot under difficult circumstances and with great perseverance, when all of a sudden, about 3 o'clock, the fire of the nearest batteries on the opposite side ceased. The cause of this has been already related. In consequence of the advance of the IInd Army, namely, the Austrian IVth Corps had marched to the right as early as 2 o'clock, but masked this movement for a whole hour by the fire of its artillery.

The artillery engagement south of the Sadowa wood did not proceed so favourably; a want of unity in the direction of the artillery was painfully evident on this part of the field. Two commandants of regiments were on the spot, but the eleven batteries there present belonged to five different artillery divisions, some of them to the divisional artillery and some to the reserve. This accounts for the want of unity of action at this spot; some batteries advanced perfectly isolated, whilst others retired behind the Bistritz at the same time.

The battery of Captain Gullus had expended all its ammunition, and received a false report that the Infantry was evacuating Unter-Dohalitz, in consequence of which the battery retreated to the line of artillery further to the rear; shortly before the battery left its position a gun was dismounted, but was brought back.

Captain Von der Dollen's battery, which was in the immediate neighbourhood of the former, and the Commander of which was mortally wounded, followed Captain Gallus. The Commandant of the regiment sent both batteries behind the Bistritz to repair their losses, because the bridges were so blocked up by the Infantry that the ammunition wagons could not cross the stream. Both batteries, however, returned to their former position as soon as they had made up their complement of ammunition.

Captain Moewes' battery was attached to the Cavalry Corps at the express desire of Prince Albrecht, and had retired from the left bank of the stream in consequence.

Captain Rautenberg's battery had fallen back to Dohalicka to complete its ammunition, and then went by way of Mokrowous to the 12-pounder battery of Captain Krüger, where it remained inactive. The latter had made repeated but unsuccessful attempts to get within closer range of the enemy's line.

Captain Bode's battery also retired to a reserve position.

Through the thick smoke of the firing Captain Gallus saw a battery not far off from his own position, which he took for a Prussian battery that had advanced still further than he had himself, more particularly so as its fire was not in any way felt; he therefore advanced with his own battery to a hillock in his right front, beyond his previous line of fire. One of the rifled batteries (Captain Munk), of the 5th Division, followed this movement. The commandant of the artillery of this division, Major Rüstow, an officer of much repute in the army, had fallen already. The two batteries soon got into so heavy and concentric a fire that they were obliged to fall back to a more sheltered position, and suffered considerable loss.

Major Von Held led Captain Bencke's battery of the Reserve Artillery along the skirts of the wood as far forward as the last houses of Ober-Dohalitz, but it could not hold its position there either.

The difficulty of keeping up the communication between the batteries and their ammunition wagons was universally felt as a very great inconvenience. It arose from the scarcity of available passages over the Bistritz. Only one of the serjeant-majors succeeded in bringing his wagons up to their battery, and in supplying it as well as some of the neighbouring 4-pounder batteries with ammunition. Determined not to give up their positions on any account whatever, the batteries of Captains Von der Goltz and Griess, of the 5th Division, fired their incendiary shells when they had expended all their other ammunition.

A favourable result could only have been obtained by the simultaneous advance of all the batteries; to effect this the support of both other arms would have been necessary. The Cavalry must have previously crossed the Bistritz, and the advance of masses of Infantry over the open plain against the advantageous positions of the enemy's numerous artillery would have caused the most disproportionate losses.

The task of patient and passive endurance weighed most heavily on the troops of the 8th Division, which had first entered the wood of Sadowa.

The fear of losing this important position by a sudden dash of the enemy made it necessary to occupy the wood, and especially its skirts, in force, and caused a greater quantity of reserves to be assembled behind the wood than would otherwise have been advisable. Only the great attachment of the men to their officers, and the example of the latter, made it possible to remain perfectly passive for more than five hours in so destructive a fire of artillery.

The skirts of the wood at the side of the high-road were held by detachments of the 71st, those further towards Ober-Dohalitz by some of the 31st Regiment. General Von Schmidt was in command at the former, General Von Bose at the latter spot. In and behind the village the 2nd and Fusilier Battalions of the 49th Regiment were stationed; the 1st Battalion of the regiment (Major Von Salpius) had been for some time exposed to the enemy's fire on the open plain somewhat further to the right, and had withdrawn to Mckrowous, when the Prussian batteries successively took up their positions in its rear, and commenced their fire.

It soon became necessary to reinforce the foremost line, and the last battalions of the 8th Division were sent into the wood. Some of the companies pressed on beyond it, but came almost immediately upon the enemy's Infantry and Cavalry.

At 12 o'clock already the severe losses from the enemy's artillery fire made it necessary to send forward part of General Herwarth's division also. First, the three battalions of the 61st and then the 1st Battalion of the 21st Regiment entered the wood. Parts of the latter battalion also attempted to advance beyond the skirts of the wood. In so doing the 2nd and 3rd Companies repulsed two charges of Cavalry, but were nevertheless compelled to fall back into the wood again. Their leader, Captain Von Bagensky, was killed. On the other hand, an attempt of some weak Austrian detachments to approach the wood along the high-road was instantly repulsed by companies of the 71st and 61st Regiments.

At 1 o'clock the 12th Company of the 61st Regiment (Capt. Kumme) established itself in an Austrian camp of huts in front of the wood, near the high-road, and some of the Fusiliers crept further on and began to annoy the battery of General Kirchsberg's brigade by their fire. A report being spread that an advance of the whole line was ordered, the 3rd and 11th Companies pressed forward near the road, two companies of the 71st Regiment followed further to the right. The two squadrons of the Austrian Lancer Regiment (Count Mensdorff), commanded to guard the battery, threw themselves upon the left wing of this unconnected line. The skirmishers at the high-road stopped lying in the roadside ditches; those in the camp of huts stood up in line, and both parties received the Lancers with so severe a fire that they retreated after losing four officers and half their men. The Austrian fire, which was now brought to bear upon the Prussian Infantry from all sides, compelled it to retire again into the wood. The same happened to the 2nd Company of the 61st Regiment, with which Lieutenant-Colonel Von Beckedorff attempted to ascend the slope on the right of the line. Captain Von Hirsch fell, and the remainder of the company fell back to Ober-Dohalitz, where they were formed into one strong battalion, with the *débris* of some other detachments. General Von Bose reserved the disposal of this battalion to himself. The camp remained occupied.

The different companies and battalions had got so mingled together that it was impossible to re-form them in the dense wood, behind it, however, Lieutenant Von Schrader assembled the Fusiliers of the 31st Regiment, whose leader, Captain Von Braun, was mortally wounded. Lieut.-Colonel Von Valentini, who was also wounded, rallied the men of the 71st Regiment. As this part of the field was very much overcrowded, the latter then went back as far as the Roskos Berg, in order to rally all the scattered men of the 15th Brigade. All men that had been separated from their different detachments under these difficult circumstances hastened to join him, in order that they might be led forward again, but His Majesty the King gave orders that they should rest for the present, there being troops enough in the wood without them.

The 5th Division had already moved the 1st and Fusilier Battalions of the 18th Regiment towards the right wing, and the 2nd Battalion of the 12th Regiment up to Ober-Dohalitz; the 2nd and 3rd Battalions of the 35th Regiment (6th Division) advanced to the skirts of the wood.

All the different attempts to advance beyond the wood, which we have hitherto described, arose from the eagerness of the troops, and a certain feeling of discomfort at the inactive state to which they found themselves condemned; it was therefore, difficult to prevent them, although they could not be successful, and must necessarily increase the losses, which were as it was very great. The ten companies of the 61st Regiment, for instance, lost 10 officers and 370 men; the 49th Regiment 5 officers and 327 men; the 71st Regiment, 9 officers and 291 men.

At the right wing of the 1st Army, General Von Werder forbade the 3rd Division to make any advance without orders, and took care that this prohibition was strictly adhered to. This division, which certainly had some shelter from the fire to which it was for five hours exposed, suffered, in comparison with the others, but little loss. The troops had prepared the villages and the line of the Bistritz for defence, and were equally prepared for offensive or defensive operations. Doubts had been expressed as to whether the artillery would be able to maintain its position alone in front of this line, but they were most decidedly refuted by Captain Gallus.

Supposing the heads of the IInd Army to be now sufficiently near, the 6th Division had been already instructed to advance beyond the Sadowa wood, but these orders were countermanded at head-quarters of the Army, where the opinion still prevailed that nothing but direct pressure on the flanks of the Austrian position would guarantee the success of an advance against the enemy's front, without causing too great a sacrifice.

The reader will be able to judge himself from the preceding narrative how heavy these losses would have been if the Prussian attack had been limited to the front of the Austrian position, even if it had been undertaken by the whole of the Prussian forces, and if the three armies had been concentrated for this purpose before the day of battle.

The first attempt of any consequence that the Austrians made to regain possession of the wood of Sadowa was undertaken by General Kirchsberg's Brigade between 1 and 2 o'clock.

At 1 o'clock, namely, Archduke Ernest had planned an offensive movement which he now purposed carrying out with his corps, beginning with the right wing; an officer of his Staff was despatched to request the permission of the Commander-in-Chief. This permission was refused, but the troops of General Kirchsberg's Brigade had commenced their advance before the answer arrived. The 49th Regiment (Baron Hess) advanced against Ober-Dohalitz, detachments of the 3rd Rifle Battalion, and two battalions of the 44th Regiment (Archduke Albrecht) against the corner of the wood at the high-road.

The attack was completely repulsed by troops of the 31st, 71st, 72nd, 61st, and 49th Regiments, all mingled together, which met the Austrian battalions in front, and threw out flank detachments from both wings. No Austrian soldier entered the wood after it was once taken by the Prussian troops. In this engagement the Commandant of the Austrian 49th Regiment, Colonel Von Binder, and very soon afterwards the Commandant of the Prussian 49th Regiment, Colonel Von Wietersheim, fell mortally wounded near the same spot.

The 4th Division had lost so many men in the wood that General Von Schmidt thought it necessary to extricate it from its position. Without further orders he drew the five battalions nearest at hand out of the wood towards the high-road. In consequence the 2nd and Fusilier Battalions of the 21st Regiment advanced as far as the corner of the wood, Colonel Von Sandradt formed the 1st and Fusilier Battalions of the 9th Regiment behind them, and the 1st Battalion of the 21st Regiment followed as reserve. As soon as the leading battalions came into the open country they suffered severely from the fire of the Austrian batteries, and General Schmidt ordered them to fall back behind the 9th Regiment—a command that was most unwillingly executed by both officers and men.

Soon afterwards Colonel Von Sandradt reported the advance of the IInd Army, the columns of which were just coming in sight on the slopes of the Chlum hill. General orders for the advance of the whole army very soon arrived, and the 4th Division marched forward. The details of this movement will be hereafter given.

### ARMY OF THE ELBE.

We left the Army of the Elbe at 11 o'clock when it was beginning to defile through Nechanitz under cover of its advanced guard. Before this could be effected, the Saxon Corps d'Armée had already taken up its position on the heights of Problus.

The 2nd Division, Lieut.-General Von Stieglitz, was stationed in a sheltered position, with its right wing behind Problus, the "Leib" Brigade on the right, the 1st Brigade on the left wing. The Cavalry Division kept up the communication with the Xth Austrian Corps.

The position of the 1st Division, Lieut.-General Schimpff, extended from Stresetitz to Nieder-Prim. The 2nd Brigade had withdrawn from Lubno, Popowitz, and Tresowitz, and had fallen back to a reserve position between Problus and Stresetitz on the right wing of the 2nd Division. The 3rd Brigade had posted the 3rd Rifle and the 9th and 10th Infantry Battalions in Problus, the 11th and 12th Infantry Battalions in Nieder-Prim. The 4th Rifle Battalion, belonging to the 2nd Division, was stationed at the latter village.

The reserve artillery was posted on the left rear of the 1st Division, in a dell near the wood which lies between Bor and Charbusitz.

After leaving Nechanitz and Lubno the "Reiter" Division took up a reserve position on the left rear of the 2nd Division at the west side of the same wood.

The rifled batteries Richter, Walther, and Leonhardi came into action on the brow of the hill, and opened fire on the two batteries of the Prussian advanced guard on the hill of Lubno.

The VIIIth Austrian Corps had also come up by this time. The Crown Prince of Saxony ordered it to take up a position in support of the Saxon Corps d'Armée, and reserved to himself to decide when and how it was to join in the action. The corps carried out these orders by taking its station in the wood south-eastward of Problus, between Problus and Charbusitz; General Schulz's Brigade on the right, Colonel Roth's* on the left wing; General Wöber's Brigade eastward of the wood in the second line. The 3rd Lancer Regiment (Archduke Charles) and the Reserve Artillery of the corps were on the right rear of the latter brigade.

Part of the Infantry of the corps seems to have been ordered forward to the wood of Stezirek and to Ober-Prim very early in the day, and the two 8-pounder batteries soon reinforced the line of artillery at Nieder-Prim, so that 34 guns were in action at this spot.

The Prussian Artillery on the heights of Lubno had also

---

* Colonel Roth and General Wöber commanded the two brigades, whose former Commanders, General Fragnern and Colonel Kreyssern, fell at Skalitz.

been reinforced by the two rifled batteries of the 15th Division, and now numbered 24 guns.

As the distance between the two lines was about 4,000 paces, the fire did but little harm on either side. It is true that shells, particularly those of the Saxon batteries, fell with great precision in the immediate neighbourhood of the Prussian position, but the angle of incidence in which they struck the soft ground materially lessened their effect. The Prussian batteries obtained no better results.

The position occupied by the Saxon Corps separated the Army of the Elbe from the 1st Army. The union of the two latter could be effected either by marching round or by attacking Problus. If the Army of the Elbe marched up the left bank of the Bistritz it would be well sheltered from the enemy's fire by the Popowitz range of hills, but it would have risked being jammed up against the stream if the enemy should energetically assume the offensive. Anyhow, it was not so desirable to reinforce the 1st Army in its front as it was to press as soon as possible on the flank of the enemy.

After due consideration of the circumstances, the Commander-in-Chief of the Elbe Army very rightly resolved upon a direct and immediate attack of Problus. As yet but a small part of the troops had been able to pass the narrow defile of Nechanitz, but the day was already half gone, the 1st Army had been engaged ever since the morning, and the main obstacle to its further progress (the formidable line of Austrian artillery) could be most effectively removed by advancing by way of Problus.

The course of the battle at the moment did not seem to require an immediate pressure on the Austrian line of retreat, nor were sufficient forces for this purpose as yet available on the left bank of the Bistritz.

General Herwarth had reconnoitred the enemy's position during the engagement of the advanced guard, and now gave orders to attack it on both wings, so as to avoid the full force of the Saxo-Austrian artillery in the open country in front. The Prussian batteries on the Lubno hill were to be reinforced, and the last detachments which crossed the Bistritz were to form behind them as reserves.

At half-past 11 the 15th Division (General Von Canstein), which was still in the act of crossing the Bistritz, received orders to advance by way of Hradeck towards Ober-Prim; Count Goltz's Brigade of Hussars was to follow. The 14th Division (Count Münster) was at the time still on the other side of Nechanitz, and was instructed to march along the west side of the heights of Popowitz, and through the wood towards Problus. General Kotze's Reserve Cavalry Brigade, and the 16th Division which was behind it, remained for the present at General Herwarth's disposal.

General Von Canstein personally led the 30th Brigade (General Von Glasenapp) in the prescribed direction, but gave orders that the 29th Brigade (General Von Stückradt) should follow as left *échelon* somewhat to the rear, and should advance in the direction of Neu-Prim, leaving Schloss-Hradeck on its right.

The Infantry of the advanced guard had also renewed the engagement, and was pressing forward on both wings so as to avoid the front of the enemy's strong artillery position.

The detachment which formed the left wing of the advanced guard position at Lubno advanced along the Bistritz, where it was pretty well sheltered by the range of hills on its right. The 11th and 12th Companies of the 28th Regiment reached Popowitz, and then turned to the right towards the north part of the wood, which they found unoccupied by the enemy. The Fusilier Battalion of the 17th Regiment, and the 8th Rifle Battalion, then followed in the same direction, and occupied the eastern skirts of the wood and the corner which projects towards Problus. These forces were not sufficient to attack the strongly garrisoned village, but the possession of this wooded hill gave an appui (stütze) for the advance of the 14th Division, which at this time was only just beginning to debouch from Nechanitz.

On the right wing of the advanced guard the 2nd Battalion of the 56th Regiment passed to the right of Neu-Prim, and advanced through the wood of Stezirek, where a skirmishing fire ensued with some detachments of the Austrian 15th and 8th Regiments (Nassau and Gerstner), which were met in a clearing in the wood. The 2nd Battalion of the 33rd Regiment advanced by Neu-Prim and the Schäferei in the direction of Nieder-Prim, and threw the 8th Company into the wood (fasaneri) between the latter village and Jehlitz. The three other companies halted in a severe fire of the enemy on the outside of the wood, and waited for the arrival of reinforcements.

From the centre of the advanced guard General Von Schoeler sent the 1st Battalion of the 40th Regiment by way of Jehlitz to the "fasanerie," which seemed, when seen from the heights, to extend so near to the position of the enemy's batteries that it was hoped it might be possible to dislodge them from thence. Lieut.-Colonel Von Conrady found the above-mentioned battalion of the 33rd Regiment (Lieut.-Colonel Von Marschall) engaged with the enemy in Nieder-Prim; he occupied the eastern part of the "fasanerie."

The advance of this comparatively small yet widely extended force was probably seen by the Crown Prince of Saxony, who deemed the moment to be opportune for making an attack in the direction of Hradeck.

For this purpose the "Leib" Brigade was ordered up from Problus, and in the meantime the attack was commenced by Captain Heringen-Göppingen's Howitzer Battery, which took up a position at the east end of Nieder-Prim, and opened a flank fire on the south skirts of the "fasanerie" (the companies there were still outside of it), and then placed itself on the right wing of the "Leib" Brigade as soon as the latter arrived. On reaching the meadows southwards of Nieder-Prim the " Leib " Brigade threw forward the 15th Battalion (formed in columns of companies, with a double line of skirmishers in front of them), and then advanced upon Neu-Prim and the fasanerie. Part of the garrison of Nieder-Prim, the 4th Battalion of Rifles, and half of the 12th Infantry Battalion, followed in the latter direction. The battery advanced within range of Infantry fire, and assisted the attack by a brisk fire of shrapnels.

The two Prussian battalions were obliged to give way before such superior numbers, and were driven back towards Jehlitz and Hradeck with a loss of 2 officers and 105 men. Deceived by the uniforms of their opponents, some of the Prussian skirmishers mistook them for Prussian Riflemen and ceased firing ; 32 men of the 40th Regiment were thus taken prisoners. Lieut.-Colonel Von Friesen, Commandant of the Saxon 16th Infantry Battalion, fell during this attack.

The " Leib" Brigade followed in hot pursuit, when all of a sudden the battalion of the 56th Regiment, which had driven the Austrians back through the wood of Stezirek, was seen issuing from the skirts of the wood opposite Ober-Prim.

This threatening movement against the flank of the Saxon Brigade brought it to a standstill ; the 13th Battalion faced towards the wood, and the others retreated in order to avoid the danger of having their line doubled up (aufrollen). The detachments belonging to the garrison of Nieder-Prim returned thither, the 14th and 16th Battalions retreated to a plantation of cherry-trees eastward of the village, and the 15th Battalion occupied the fasanerie.

It was now a quarter before 1 o'clock. The Saxon Crown Prince was by no means disposed to relinquish the offensive movement which had commenced so successfully. He ordered up the 2nd Infantry Brigade with the intention of employing it to cover the flank of the " Leib " Brigade when the latter again advanced. At half-past 1 the former brigade arrived on the left wing of the "Leib" Brigade, on the meadows southward of Nieder-Prim. An urgent request was despatched to the VIIIth Austrian Corps to guard the brigade from being again outflanked. The " Leib" Brigade sent the 14th Battalion to join the 15th in the " fasanerie," the 13th and 16th Battalions formed a second line behind them, and space was thus obtained for the 2nd Brigade, which pushed forward the 6th Battalion, and formed with the 8th and 5th Battalions in the first, the 7th Battalion and the 2nd Battalion of Rifles in the second line. The Battery Von der Pforte accompanied the advance, which took the direction of Neu-Prim and the wood of Hradeck beyond the former village. At the same time the Austrian Brigadiers Schulz and Wöber advanced from Ober-Prim along the north side of the Stezirek wood. The whole movement commenced shortly before 2 o'clock.

By this time, however, part of the Prussian 15th Division had arrived on the field, and was prepared to join in the action.

Ever since 1 o'clock General Canstein and the 30th Brigade had been waiting westward of a hill in the interior of the Stezirek wood for the arrival of the 29th Brigade. The latter had separated in different directions whilst passing through the wood westward of Schloss-Hradeck. At half-past 1 o'clock General Von Stückradt reached Neu-Prim and the neighbouring wood, but only with six companies of the 65th Regiment. The remainder of his brigade and the 12-pounder battery had got into the line of march of the 30th Brigade, and were still south-eastward of Hradeck. The Hussar Brigade was between this village and Schloss-Hradeck.

At first the Austrian Brigade Schulz succeeded in dislodging the 2nd Battalion of the 56th Regiment, which was skirmishing in front of Ober-Prim, from the skirts of the wood. The retreat of the battalion was covered by the 68th Regiment in the interior of the wood. On crossing an open space in the wood the Austrians came within sight of the 68th Regiment, and Colonel Von Gayl threw himself upon them with the leading battalion (the Fusiliers) of his regiment after brief firing.

The 74th Austrian Regiment (Nobili) was driven out of the wood, and the centre of the Austrian line, which extended from Ober-Prim to Neu-Prim, was broken through. This vigorous charge produced indescribable confusion in the ranks of the enemy. All Austrian troops in or in front of the wood, east-ward of the breach in this line, hastened to Ober-Prim or re-treated still further into the wood towards Stezirek. Those that were westward of that point fell back northwards, but were taken in flank by General Stückradt's detachment, and driven back by volleys delivered by the 68th Regiment at a range of 150 paces, the 1st and 2nd Battalions of this regiment having stepped out of the wood, and deployed right and left of the Fusilier Battalion.

The Nobili Regiment dispersed, leaving 600, and the Gerstner Regiment 230 prisoners behind them. The swarms of fugitives threw themselves upon the 2nd Saxon Brigade, where the 6th Battalion was just then attempting to cover its flank by effecting a change of front. They impeded this movement, and prevented the skirmishers from firing. Both the 6th and 8th Battalions were involved in the retreat, and suffered great loss, particularly in officers, among whom both leaders of the battalions and half the Captains of companies fell. The 5th Battalion, on the other hand, firmly withstood the shock of the flying mass, and the 2nd Rifle Battalion came forward from the second line and covered the menaced flank. Deployed in line, it let the fugitives pass through its ranks, then closed them again and received the 68th Regiment, which was advancing towards Brunnen, with its volleys.

The steady conduct of these two Saxon battalions checked the confusion, and enabled the 2nd Brigade to make good its retreat to Nieder-Prim. Captain Von der Pforte's Battery safely extricated itself from this perilous situation. Although exposed to Infantry fire, it succeeded in reaching Ober-Prim, where it immediately opened fire on the pursuing Prussian battalions.

Of course, after the retreat of the 2nd Brigade, the intended advance of the "Leib" Brigade was no longer feasible; both brigades were ordered to rally behind the hill of Problus.

The Austrian fugitives rushed on to Nieder-Prim, but the remainder of the two brigades came to a stand at Ober-Prim. An attempt which they made to attack the right flank of the 68th Regiment failed.

On this occasion also the Cavalry and Artillery afforded no direct assistance to the Prussian attack. The Prussian Artillery on the Lubno hill had, it is true, been considerably reinforced. At half-past 12 o'clock the two rifled batteries of the 14th Division arrived there, and half an hour later Colonel Von Bülow brought up the 2nd Division of the 7th Artillery Regiment. The 2nd 4-pounder battery of the 8th Artillery Regiment (Captain Von Zglinitzky) found room there also, so that after 1 o'clock Colonel Von Rozynski commanded 66 guns in this position, which prepared the advance of the Infantry on both wings by their fire. The distance was, however, too great for them to have any influence on the close combat in which friend and foe were intermingled in front of Nieder-Prim.

For this reason General Herwarth had already given orders for three rifled batteries to follow the 15th Division, but neither they nor Captain Theiler's 12-pounder battery had reached Neu-Prim yet.

The four battalions, which had advanced beyond the wood, availed themselves of the short lull which now ensued in the action to re-form their ranks. On their left hand, two battalions of the 40th Regiment (29th Brigade) were approaching, and the second line of the 30th Brigade, two battalions of the 28th Regiment, were coming up through the wood.

Although General Canstein momentarily had but seven battalions at his disposal, without either Cavalry or Artillery, still he was so fully convinced of the necessity of following up the advantages he had just gained, that he ordered the 30th Brigade to attack Ober-Prim immediately; whatever troops of the 29th Brigade had come up were to advance on Nieder-Prim.

General Von Glasenapp carried out these orders by marching with the 68th Regiment to the right against the western projecting corner of Ober-Prim; he was accompanied by some detachments of the 40th and 65th Regiments, which Colonel Zimmermann had rallied after the first attack of the Saxon brigade. The 1st and 2nd Battalions of the 28th Regiment drove the enemy before them through the wood, and advanced against the south side of the village; they were assisted by the Fusilier Battalions of the 56th and 65th Regiment.

The strong Austrian force in the village offered an obstinate resistance, but the Prussian battalions nevertheless forced their way in on the west side. Soon afterwards the detachments advancing from the wood reached the east side also.

An attempt to retake the village was repulsed, and the enemy retreated partly to Problus and partly to the wood south-eastward of this village.

The very great number of dead and wounded bore witness to the obstinacy with which the Austrians had defended Ober-Prim. General Schulz was killed, four officers and 120 men were taken prisoners, after making a gallant defence. The 68th Regiment also suffered severely; it purchased its victory with the loss of four officers and 140 men.

The left flank of the Saxon position at Problus was evidently much exposed by the loss of Ober-Prim and the retreat of the two brigades, which were still engaged between Ober- and Nieder-Prim immediately and seriously endangered. In order to extricate them from their perilous situation, the smooth-bore batteries of the Reserve (Captains Lengnich and Westmann), and the Horse Artillery Battery of Captain Hoch were despatched to the southern slope of the hill eastward of Nieder-Prim. The 1st Brigade, the last one which stood as reserve behind the latter village, was sent to occupy the abattis along the south skirts of the wood between Problus and Charbusitz. The *débris* of the Austrian troops, which had been driven out of Ober-Prim, rallied in the rear of the Saxon brigade. Colonel Wöber's brigade stationed itself westward of Charbusitz, the 24th Rifle Battalion at the south-east end of the wood. The 2nd Brigade of the "Reiter" Division and a Horse Artillery Battery had some time previously been already detached towards the left, to menace the Prussian right wing in company with the Austrian 1st Light Cavalry Division. Later in the day, this body of Cavalry did actually advance, by way of Techlowitz, towards Radikowitz, and appeared in the rear of the 15th Division, but found the latter village occupied by the 10th Company of the 68th Regiment (Captain Von Ketteler), and was fired on from the neighbourhood of the Hradeck church by the three batteries which were sent after General Canstein, upon which General Edelsheim fell back to Stösser, and merely observed the Prussian movements.

The batteries Von der Pforte and Heringen came into action by the side of the Artillery already in position eastward of Nieder-Prim. These 28 guns concentrated a rapid fire of shot, shell, and grape on Ober-Prim and the wood behind the village, and the two Saxon brigades retreated under its cover through Nieder-Prim to the hill behind Problus.

This fire could not be returned by the Prussian artillery. Captain Theiler's 12-pounder battery had, it is true, arrived, and was in position at the east entrance of Ober-Prim, but it was engaged with an Austrian battery only 1,000 paces off at the small wood northward of Stezirek. Ober-Prim was very soon in flames, and the Prussian battalions were forced to quit the village. They found some shelter in a neighbouring orchard and behind some piles of wood which were stacked there. The two battalions of the 40th Regiment drove the skirmishers of the Austrian 45th Regiment (Nassau) back towards Stezirek, and Colonel Von Gerstein led the Fusilier Battalion of the 69th and two companies of the 28th Regiment forward to Ober-Prim, but for the present further progress was impossible at this point.

In the meantime General Von Stückradt and his weak detachment had pressed forward for Brunnen towards Nieder-Prim, continually inflicting severe losses on the Saxon battalions, which were retreating to the latter village. He was followed by the advanced guard battalions of the 40th and 33rd Regiments, which had been re-formed, and by Colonel Zimmermann's detachment; the latter came from Ober-Prim, and was much harassed by the enemy's artillery fire.

By this time, however, the Prussian batteries had advanced from the Lubno hill. They took up one intermediate position, and then advanced to about 2,000 paces from Nieder-Prim. From this spot they fired with great effect on the Saxon battery northward of the village, and on the village itself, in which the castle brewery soon took fire. The 5th, 6th, and 12th Companies of the 65th Regiment, and Colonel Zimmermann's detachment now made a successful dash at the southern skirts of the village, the 6th Company (Lieutenant Merker) stormed the court-yard of the castle. The battalions of the 3rd Saxon Brigade (half of the 11th and the 12th Battalion of Infantry, with the 4th Rifle Battalion) disputed the ground step by step, but were forced back on Problus; 170 Austrians and Saxons were taken prisoners after a stout resistance. Two commanders of battalions (Lietenant-Colonel Metzradt and Major Hamann) fell here.

The 14th Division had been so delayed in defiling through Nechanitz that it was not able to complete its formation behind the Lubno hill before half-past 1 o'clock. The 27th Brigade (General Von Schwarzkoppen) was in the first, the 28th Brigade (General Von Hiller), and the 4th 12-pounder Battery in the second line. The 7th Rifle Battalion stopped in Lubno, and the 1st Battalion of the 16th Regiment was left to guard the artillery.

The leading brigade then formed for action, and advanced towards the wood between Popowitz and Problus, during which march the enemy's artillery caused but little loss, as it was engaged with the 15th Division. It has been previously stated that the wood was already occupied by Lieutenant-Colonel Koblinski's detachment.

By half-past two o'clock the division was ready to attack Problus, the last stronghold of the Saxon position.

From the height near the village the Crown Prince of Saxony had observed not only the continued advance of General Canstein's division against the Saxon line of retreat, but also the arrival of the Prussian IInd Army at Chlum, where the retreat of the Austrian right wing could be distinctly seen. As the neighbouring Xth Corps soon afterwards began also to fall back, it did not seem advisable to hold the present position any longer; about 3 o'clock, therefore, orders were issued for the retreat, which the troops that were still in Problus and the wood south-eastward of the village were to cover as rear-guard.

These orders were given just as the 14th and 15th Prussian divisions commenced a concentric attack on the heights of Problus.

General Schwarzkoppen's brigade was ordered to march against the village from the wood. General Hiller's brigade, which was 800 paces further to the rear, was in advance south-ward to the wood. To do this both brigades had to wheel to the right.

The position of the 27th Brigade previous to the attack was as follows:—

The Fusilier Battalion of the 56th Regiment, Lieutenant-Colonel Von Busse, was formed in columns of companies and stationed as advanced line in the south corner of the wood nearest to Problus. Behind it were the 1st Battalion of the same regiment (Major Von Hymmen), and the Fusilier Battalion of the 16th Regiment (Major Von Horn), the former on the right, the latter on the left wing; they constituted the main body of the brigade. The 2nd Battalion of the latter regiment (Major Von Grevenitz) was instructed to advance further to the left against the north entrance of the village. The detachments found already in the wood were to occupy it in the event of a retreat, but the Fusilier Battalion of the 17th Regiment (Lieutenant-Colonel Von Koblinski), the 12th Company of the 28th Regiment (Lieutenant Linz), and the 1st Company of the 8th Rifle Battalion (Captain Von Stülpnagel) joined the attacking troops.

The 28th Brigade was posted 300 paces behind the former. The three companies of the 1st Battalion of the 57th Regiment (Lieut.-Colonel Von Schöning) were spread out as advanced guard; the main body behind it consisted of the 1st Battalion of the same regiment (Lieutenant-Colonel Von Grolmann) on the right, and the 1st Battalion of the 17th Regiment (Major Von Rex) on the left; the 2nd Battalion of the 17th Regiment (Major Von Bieberstein) followed as reserve.

Before reaching the village from the wood the troops had to cover 1,600 paces of open country, over very heavy ground, and had, morever, to ascend the steep face of the opposite hill. As soon as General Schwarzkoppen's brigade stepped out of the wood it was met by the shells of the battery on the heights of Problus; at the same time its left flank was exposed to the fire of Captain Heidenreich's battery, eastward of Tresowitz.

The troops of the division had marched 13½ miles the pre-ceding night, over very heavy roads and through high standing corn; they had been for 12 hours under arms, and, like the rest of the army, had been without any provisions whatever. The troops were in no way flurried by the enemy's fire. Quietly stepping out to the sound of their bands, with the Commandants of the division and the brigades in front, the columns advanced in steady order, without regarding the gaps which the enemy's shells tore in their ranks.

Captain Schmelzer's 12-pounder battery took up a position on the south side of the road, and engaged the enemy's artillery; the rifled batteries of the division having arrived northeastward of Jehlitz opened fire here also with great effect. The fire of the Prussian skirmishers soon reached the front of the Saxon batteries, and the latter had to withdraw, before the battalions themselves ascended the hill. The foremost battalion of the attacking troops, the Fusiliers of the 56th Regiment, now turned to the right towards the south part of Problus, whilst the 1st Battalion kept to the direction of the church steeple of the village. Captain Schmelzer's battery went forward at a gallop to within Infantry range, and fired with shrapnels on the enclosure of the village, and on some detachments that showed themselves on the outside of it.

A bank of earth affording some shelter to the Fusiliers, they lay down behind it, and kept up a rapid fire on the skirts of the village until the other battalions came up, with which they then advanced in one dense swarm of skirmishers. In spite of the severe Infantry fire, they passed all the artificial defences erected outside of the village, and gained the enclosure. A new and obstinate struggle ensued in each farm-yard, each step in advance cost heavy sacrifices, and the enemy had to be driven from position to position until the further side of the village was reached.

It is meet that we should once more name the troops who so bravely defended Problus. They were the Saxon 9th and 10th Infantry and 3rd Rifle Battalions, with three companies of the 11th Infantry Battalion. They could only be overcome at the cost of grievous loss. The whole way from wood to village was marked by the bloody traces of the brave Westphalians. The Fusilier Battalion of the 56th Regiment lost 12 officers, among whom were four captains, and nearly 200 men; the 1st Battalion four officers and 86 men. The four battalions of General Schwarzkoppen's brigade lost altogether four officers and 67 men killed, and 17 officers, and 300 men wounded.

On the Saxon side General Von Carlowitz and Lieutenant-Colonel Von der Mosel were killed. Numerous dead and wounded covered the field, and 300 men, the most part of whom were wounded, were taken prisoners after a gallant resistance.

Problus was scarcely taken when a Saxon battery, north-eastward of the village, overwhelmed it with shells. The battalions of the brigade occupied the whole village under the personal superintendence of General Count Münster.

At the same time, and with equal bravery, the 28th Brigade advanced in like manner against the heights southward of the

s

village, with bands playing, and headed by General Hiller and Colonels Von Kottwitz and Von der Osten. The brigade soon got under cover of the brow of the hill, and therefore suffered less loss.

When the crest of the hill was nearly reached, two Saxon battalions, the 12th Infantry and 4th Rifle Battalions, which had fallen back from Rieder-Prim to a position to the rear of Problus, advanced in line to meet the attack. They were received with the file fire of the 1st Prussian line, and retreated to the wood south-eastward of Problus; Captain Schmelzer then planted his battery on the heights thus gained.

The Saxon Artillery between Problus and Nieder-Prim was the first that was obliged to give way before the Prussian skirmishers; when the latter village was taken, the smooth-bore guns on the eastern heights withdrew, and last of all the batteries of Captains Von der Pforte and Heringer; they took up fresh positions to the north of the Problus-Charbusitz wood, from which they covered the retreat of General Schimpff's division to Rosnitz and Briza, whilst General Stieglitz's division still held the wood and the copses south of it. Captain Heidenreich's battery remained in its position near Trosowitz, and prevented the Prussian 5th Lancer Regiment, which was despatched to open communications with the 1st Army from advancing beyond the Popowitz wood.

The seven rifled batteries of the Prussian Reserve Artillery had followed to between the Popowitz wood and the "fasanerie." The Reserve Cavalry was on the march to the fore-named wood. Five batteries of the Reserve Artillery of the VIIIth Corps were still at Nechanitz, through which town the 16th Division (General Von Etzel) was only just beginning to defile.

General Herwarth Von Bittenfeld was present at the storming of Problus. The following information regarding the progress of the battle was sent to him from the Chief of the General Staff of the Army:—

> "Crown Prince at Zizelowes; retreat of the Austrians "to Josephstadt cut off. It is of the utmost importance "that General Von Herwarth should advance on the "opposite wing, whilst the centre of the Austrians still "holds out.
> "Near Sadowa, quarter before 2.
> (Signed)  "Von Moltke."

These instructions had already been acted up to.

The evening before the battle the Army of the Elbe had been as far off the battle-field as the IInd Army. It had received its orders betimes, and had started early; but while the IInd Army had, from the commencement of its march, been able to advance in a broad line of front, the Army of the Elbe had been obliged to defile through one single point, Nechanitz.

Notwithstanding, if we take the Sadowa-Königgrätz high-road as the natural line of the Austrian retreat, by 3 o'clock this line was as much menaced in its left flank from Problus and Prim as in its right from Maslowed and Nedelist.

---

## V. Progress of the Battle from 3 to Quarter-past 4 p.m.

### IInd Army.

Feldzeugmeister Benedek does not seem even now to have fully appreciated the danger with which the right wing of his line of battle was menaced by the advance of the IInd Army. From his station between Lipa and Chlum he seems to have directed his whole attention to the course of the action in his front, when, about a quarter-past 3, the surprising news was brought to him that Chlum was occupied by the Prussians in his rear.

Hastening thither immediately, he was met by Infantry fire on approaching the village. One of his aides-de-camp, Major Count Grünne, was mortally wounded; General Henikstein's horse fell, and numerous casualties occurred in the Feldzeug-meister's personal escort. The accuracy of the news was therefore no longer questionable. The Feldzeugmeister now rode past Roberitz towards his reserves, but even here his Staff came within range of the Prussian Infantry in this village; Archduke William was wounded in the head.

The Feldzeugmeister still had powerful reserves at his command. The Reserve Artillery of the Army, the sole disposal of which he had reserved to himself, had, as we have seen, already been brought into action, but two intact corps d'armée and a reserve Cavalry of more than 70 squadrons were at hand and available at any moment.

It is true, on the Prussian side, two-thirds of the IInd Army had not been engaged yet, and the greater part of the Ist Army only waited for orders to assume the offensive. Still the situation demanded that the Austrians should now stake their last available troops, not indeed to bind victory to the Imperial standard (the insight we have since obtained into the position of affairs at this moment shows it to have been too late for this), but to protect the right wing of the army from destruction, and to enable the centre to make any retreat at all. However, even now the Feldzeugmeister still thought it feasible to send General Piret's brigade to Problus to the assistance of his left wing, and for the moment only despatched one brigade of the same corps to his right wing at Chlum.

The Prussian shells falling in the midst of its ranks were

sufficient inducement to the VIth Austrian Corps to take the necessary measures without waiting for further orders.

It is not known whether the corps engaged on the line of the Bistritz received any positive orders from the Feldzeugmeister to commence their retreat. As the circumstances were, the Commanding Officers were soon obliged to decide for themselves. Orders of this nature were, however, despatched to the corps on the left wing.

It was only by making considerable detours that the reports of the progress made by both Prussian wings on flank and rear of the Austrian position could be sent to the head-quarters of the army, at that time on the Roskos-Berg; they did not, therefore, reach the Commander-in-Chief until late in the day.

The first signs of the Crown Prince's approach had been the flashes of the guns at the two trees which, even from here, were visible on the heights of Horenowes; soon after, his columns were seen ascending the sides of the hill. It was not till later that some of the enemy's batteries in the front diminished their fire, and others turned their guns in a different direction. These batteries were all that could be seen of the Austrian main line of battle, the Infantry of the IIIrd and Xth Corps was hidden from view by the undulations of the ground up to the very last moment. At the very latest at 3 o'clock, the latter seems to have commenced its retreat, unobserved by the Prussians, concealed and protected by the devotion and energy of the Austrian Artillery. It was about 3 o'clock when the gradual decrease of the enemy's fire led to the supposition on the left flank of the Ist Army that the Austrians were beginning to retreat, and at half-past 3 His Majesty gave orders for the advance of the whole line.

We shall presently see that parts of the line had already begun to advance, but it had not as yet been possible to gain sufficient ground beyond the Bistritz for the Cavalry to deploy there. It was now necessary that the latter should cross as soon as possible, so as recover the start which the enemy had gained.

Before, however, the advance of the centre of the Prussian line could begin to take effect, the wings of the army had to sustain hard struggles.

We left the 1st Division of Guards at 3 o'clock in its advanced position at Chlum and Rosberitz, where it was exposed to the fire of numerous hostile batteries which came into action one after another on a wide circle between Wsestar and Langenhof. More than 100 Austrian guns poured a shower of grape on the two villages and the heights between them, whereas the Prussian Artillery had not been yet able to follow the advance of its Infantry.

Fresh forces now advanced from the Austrian reserves against this position, in addition to which the Prussian right flank was still menaced from the wood of Lipa, which was occupied by General Benedek's Brigade of the IIIrd Corps in great force; parts also of the IVth Corps had retreated there after their action with General Fransecky's Division. These troops kept up a brisk fire against the west side of Chlum; an offensive movement on their part might take place at any moment, the Prince of Würtemberg was, therefore, obliged to move the 2nd Division of Guards, which had hitherto been following as left *échelon,* more to the right; the main body of the division was, however, still as far back as Maslowed.

When General Von Hiller requested the assistance of the division, all General Von Plonski could momentarily do was to send Colonel Von Pritzelwitz with the advanced guard of the division to follow the Guard Fusiliers, which were then engaged with General Fleischhacker's Brigade. In their pursuit of the enemy the 2nd Battalion of the latter regiment had pressed on to Cistowes, as had already been mentioned; the skirmishers of the 2nd Company, the 1st and 4th Companies, and the 1st Company of the Guard Rifles, which latter had broken forth from Chlum, had advanced against the northern and lowest part of the Lipa wood, the 3rd Company and the supports of the 2nd Company of the Guard Fusiliers ascended the heights between Chlum and the wood. By reason of these movements two gaps were made in the line—in the right one of which the advanced guard of the 2nd Division of Guards pushed forward towards the northern skirts of the wood; the left one was filled up by Lieut.-Colonel Von Neumann with the 3rd Company of the Guard Rifles, and the 2nd and 1st Battalions of the 2nd Foot Guards, which advanced, partly northward of Chlum, and partly through the village against the eastern and highest part of the Lipa wood, which they proceeded to attack with six companies formed in one line.

During its march from the south of Maslowed to the eastern side of Chlum, the 1st Battalion of the 2nd Foot Guards had already disarmed one Austrian Battalion which burst forth from the wood, passed through Chlum, and then came upon the Reserve Artillery of the Guards, just then ascending the somewhat steep slope eastward of Chlum. The Artillery was compelled to turn back, and was therefore again delayed in its endeavours to come to the assistance of the Infantry.

All these different detachments on the left wing pressed eagerly forward, and by a quarter past 3 o'clock the Austrians in the wood of Lipa had succumbed to the concentric attack which was made on them from all sides. The skirts of the wood were carried in spite of a very severe fire; in the interior the enemy opposed an obstinate resistance, but suffered great losses, and was obliged to fall back to Lipa and Langenhof, leaving 1,600 prisoners behind them. The Commander of the Brigade, Colonel Von Benedek, was wounded, and went to the latter village.

The Prussian losses were compatively trifling, but Major Von Reuss fell at the head of his battalion; Lieutenant Vogeley, of the Guard Fusiliers, had been previously mortally wounded.

The wood was scarcely taken, when the Austrians advanced to the assault, and attempted to regain possession of the hill westward of Chlum. In close order, with skirmishers only a few paces ahead of them, the columns—apparently one brigade —crossed the high-road between Rosberitz and Lipa, and ascended the face of the hill with great bravery, utterly disregarding the fire which was poured upom them from Rosberitz and from the 9th Company of the 2nd Foot Guards westward of the village, as well as from Count Waldersee's Battalion of the Guard Fusiliers.

On the heights of Chlum, Colonels Von Pape and Von Werder could only meet this mighty attack with the 1st, 4th, and part of the 7th Companies of the 2nd Foot Guards, the 3rd Company and one division of the Guard Fusiliers and half a company of the 1st Foot Guards; the sole available reserves consisted of two divisions of the 2nd Foot Guards. The main force of the blow fell on the two first-named companies (Lieuts. Baron Von Lyncker and Von Froreich); they reserved the fire of their small force until the enemy was within the most effective range. When the Austrian masses were within 100 paces, they first delivered two volleys and then commenced a file-fire of most extraordinary effect. The enemy halted for a moment and then fell back behind the high-road, suffering enormous losses from the Prussian fire during his retreat.

The three companies, with which Lieut.-Colonel Von der Knesebeck advanced against Cistowes, were joined by some detachments of the 7th Division, which had for so long defended the wood of Maslowed. Cistowes was taken, the enemy losing 200 prisoners.

The IIIrd Austrian Corps had now no more intact troops with which it could reconquer the positions it had just lost. The brigade of General Appiano was beaten at Chlum, that of General Kirchsberg had been moved southward after the failure of its attack on the Sadowa wood; Colonel Prohaska's Brigade, which had been stationed as reserve at Langenhof, had already commenced its retreat; Colonel Benedek's troops were scattered in all directions by the combat in the Lipa wood, but the greater part of the artillery of the corps still held the positions it occupied at the commencement of the battle, and kept up a sharp fire on the 1st Army, in spite of the retreat of the Infantry.

Whilst the Guard Fusiliers were pursuing the flying enemy on the right and left of Colonel Von Pritzelwitz's detachment, the latter took the copses in his front with the advanced guard, and then marched against the north end of Lipa, the south end of which village was at the same time attacked by the 3rd Company of Guard Rifles.

The village was defended by the Austrian 3rd Field Rifle Battalion, around which divers scattered detachments had rallied. The Prussian Guard Skirmishers carried the enclosure of the village, though not without severe loss, but met with very determined resistance in the interior, the broad road through which was swept by several pieces of artillery. Captain Von Laue was mortally wounded; Major Von Besser lost his horse. In the meantime the 10th and 11th Companies of the 2nd Guard Grenadiers penetrated through the gardens into the farmhouses, although the leader of the former company, Lieut. Von Notz, was killed. In spite of a very severe fire, the remainder of the battalion, in company with the Fusilier Battalion of the 1st Guard Grenadiers, gained possession of the south part of the village. The conquest of the outlets in this part decided the fate of the combat. None but a few single detachments managed to escape from Lipa, and they only with very heavy loss.

During the attack on Lipa, Lieutenant Count Redern advanced along the north side of the village with the 1st Company of the Guard Fusiliers; pursuing the enemy, he saw a line of Austrian Artillery about 400 paces beyond the high-road. They were the remains of three batteries of the Austrian IIIrd Corps, which had kept up so long and so effective a fire on the Sadowa wood. The artillery of the Prussian IInd Corps had already been brought forward against this position, and the heads of the Prussian Infantry columns were advancing from the west. Under these circumstances, 14 of the Austrian guns had already withdrawn from their position; during their retreat they came within range of the Fusiliers of the 1st Guard Grenadiers, who advanced against them from Lipa and caused them some loss. The remainder of the guns, however, stopped in their position, and still kept up an uninterrupted fire against the front of the 1st Army. They were guarded by two companies of Infantry.

A skirmishing peloton of the Guard Fusiliers, and further to the left some detachments of the 2nd Guard Grenadiers opened fire on the covering Infantry, which retreated. This could not be accomplished by the guns, because almost the whole of their teams were struck down in a row behind the battery, and a great part of the artillerymen and drivers lay dead or wounded beside them. The Guard Fusiliers rushed forward closely followed by a company of Guard Skirmishers; within 50 paces of the battery one gun, which was only served by three artillerymen, fired its last shot, and the ten Austrian 8-pounders were taken. Their loss redounds to the honour of the Austrian Artillery.

A pause in the action now ensued at this part of the field, during which the troops were rallied.

Whilst the advanced guard of the 2nd and part of the 1st Division of Guards were thus fighting a separate and distinct action on the right flank, the main body of the latter division, which was engaged in the front, was left without aid, and the detachments which had entered Rosberitz were continually involved in a series of sanguinary combats.

Major Von Erckert held the extreme south end of the village with three companies of the 2nd Foot Guards; he had posted the 10th Company at the entrance from the high-road, the 11th

Company on the west, and the 12th on the east side of it. In the upper (northern) part of the village the 2nd Battalion of the 1st Foot Guards (Lieut.-Colonel Von Block) occupied the eastern, and the 3rd Battalion of the Guard-Fusiliers (Major Count Waldersee) the western part. The 9th Company of the 2nd Foot Guards (Captain Von Goerne) was pushed forward on the right towards a farm-house on the road leading to Langenhof. In addition to these troops, three other companies, which had been separated from their battalions in the rapid course of the action, had also entered Rosberitz, viz., the 4th and 9th of the 1st Foot Guards under Lieut.-Colonel Von-Helldorf, and the 2nd of the 3rd Foot Guards. The rest of the division was at Chlum where it occupied the brow of the plateau.

Captains Von Goerne and Von Oppel tried to gain possession of the solitary farm-house on the high-road westward of Rosberitz, but were obliged to relinquish the attempt, because the enemy's artillery completely swept the whole of the country. Their skirmishers, however, held their ground 200 paces in front of the enemy.

From the very beginning, several Austrian batteries had concentrated a cross fire on the south end of Rosberitz, and poured such a shower of shells, shrapnels, and rockets on its defenders that the road was covered with a mass of burning fragments. Austrian Riflemen esconced themselves in the foreground at a distance of little more than the breadth of the high-road from the village. Nevertheless the three Prussian companies still kept a strong line of skirmishers in the skirts of the village, who fired into the masses of the enemy.

Four separate attacks, each made by 2—3 battalions, and proceeding from the high-road, were directed against the west side of Rosberitz. They were beaten off by the concentric fire from the skirts of the village, and by that of the 3rd Battalion of the Guard Fusiliers.

The violence of the Austrian artillery fire against Rosberit were now redoubled. The foremost detachments outside were obliged to seek shelter behind the village and in the hollow way leading to Chlum, in doing which Captain Goerne was severely wounded.

By this time already the division received material aid from the artillery. Major Bychelberg had ordered the batteries of the division up to the heights of Chlum. By dint of the utmost exertions of men and horses, and after having been twice delayed on the road by the enemy, Prince Hohenlohe arrived there also at half-past 3 o'clock with the Reserve Artillery of the corps.

General Von Colomier planted the batteries along the ravine southward of Chlum. The 3rd and 4th Companies of the 3rd Foot Guards covered their left flank.

The 6th 4-pounder battery came up first and took up its position under an overwhelming fire of the enemy, but still managed to open fire in proper time on an Austrian Horse

Artillery battery, which drove up within close range with the intention of dislodging it, but, coming within range of the Prussian Infantry, was compelled to desist from the attempt. The remainder of the Reserve Artillery now came into line; Captain Eltester's battery took post on its left, and the artillery of the VIth Corps seconded its fire from Nedelist. Disregarding the fire of the enemy's batteries, fifteen of which were counted on a wide semicircle round Chlum, the Prussian Artillery concentrated its fire on the compact masses of the Austrian Reserves, which were visible at a distance of 1,000 to 1,800 paces, and first of all forced the 1st Reserve Cavalry Division to retreat towards Rossnitz. The densely crowded columns of the Austrian Infantry afforded a mark for the aim of the rifled cannon which could not be missed, and the losses at this spot increased to an enormous extent.

The losses of the Prussian Artillery were also very severe; it suffered especially from the flank fire of an Austrian battery posted between Sweti and Rosberitz, until the latter was silenced by Captain Werder's battery.

In the meantime the 6th 4-pounder battery had been very roughly handled, and reported that its ammunition had been expended. It therefore received permission to withdraw about half-an-hour later; but at the same moment Captain Heineccius' battery drove 200 paces further forward, in order to be better able to command the foot of the hill, in spite of the enemy's tremendous fire, and notwithstanding the Captain of the battery was wounded in so doing.

After their unsuccessful attempts to retake Rosberitz, the Austrians now changed their plan of attack. Three powerful columns, probably the brigades of Colonel Jonak and General Rosenzweig of the VIth Corps, made a concentric attack on the narrow end of Rosberitz. Strong detachments assaulted the south entrance and the eastern skirts: six battalions, formed in one dense mass, advanced along the west side of the village. The three companies of the 2nd Foot Guards were reduced to half their original strength, and had so completely exhausted their pouch ammunition that they only kept up the fire with the cartridges of the dead and wounded. The losses in this close and murderous fire were very heavy on either side. Major Erckert fell severely wounded by two musket-shots, and Captain Von Kropff assumed the command of the battalion. At length the overwhelming numbers of the enemy forced the Fusiliers to give up the skirts of the village, but they continued their resistance in the interior, and only fell back step by step.

The Austrians bore the utmost possible force of the Infantry fire with brave endurance and without giving way. The Prussian force was not strong enough to disengage itself by a bayonet charge.

A fierce struggle ensued for the colours of the battalion, the bearer of which, Serjeant Gursch, would not give way. Lieut.

Von Versen and Ensign Von Bülow rallied a few men and hastened to the assistance of the flag, in doing which the former was severely wounded. By an act of devoted self-denial, Lieut. Von Fallois and his men cut their way through, and brought back both flag and wounded officer.

The two companies which were posted as reserves at the other end of the village suffered almost as severely as those in the front line. Lieut.-Colonel Von Helldorf had fallen already; Prince Anton of Hohenzollern was severely wounded. In vain did these companies strive to check the stream of their opponents, who poured in on all sides. Lieut.-Colonel Count Waldersee led the half-battalion Von Brederlow into the village from the west, and detachments of almost all the battalions engaged in the action helf a brick-field on the north-east side of the village. The troops fought at a distance of but a few paces. The more the crowding in the narrow village street increased, and the companies from the rear pressed forward to the front, the more was all order deranged on both sides. After three-quarters of an hour's defence the village was no longer tenable, and was evacuated.

The losses had been heavy. Colonel Von Obernitz had been wounded on the heights eastward of Chlum, in the immediate neighbourhood of the enemy's skirmishers, before the struggle in Rosberitz commenced. General Von Hiller's aide-de-camp was killed; 70 men were left behind in Rosberitz as prisoners.

The 6th and 7th Companies of the 1st Foot Guards, which had been stationed eastward of the north end of Rosberitz, had some time before withdrawn to the heights eastward of Chlum by order of the Commander of their brigade; the companies now retreating from Rosberitz followed in the same direction. The officers succeeded in re-forming their scattered detachments outside of the north entrance of the village. At the ravine southward of Chlum Lieut.-Colonel Count Waldersee succeeded in checking the whole retreat by planting the flag of his battalion in the ground, and inspiring his men with the unanimous determination not to give way another step. He first rallied a nucleus of 6 officers and 200 men of his battalion, around whom men of all companies collected. A dense line of skirmishers was then posted in the hollow way, and the enemy's attack quietly and steadily awaited.

The latter advanced as far as the north end of Rosberitz, and was then brought to a stand-still by the measures which had been taken to cover the retreat of the troops from Rosberitz. A hollow way proceeding from Chlum, and running down the slope of the hill eastward, was occupied on the right by Prince Hohenlohe's batteries; in the centre, where the hollow way strikes the Chlum-Wsestar road, by the 3rd and 4th Companies of the 3rd Foot Guards, round which divers other troops had rallied. Further to the left Captain Eltester's 4-pounder battery was posted with its covering guard, the 7th Company of the

Guard Fusiliers. The 8th Company of the 1st Foot Guards, which had retreated from Rosberitz, halted and fronted by the side of the last-named company.

The enemy's columns, which had advanced through and by the side of Rosberitz, halted and commenced a standing fire. The horns of the Riflemen, however, soon sounded the advance again, and the music of the regimental bands was distinctly heard from the midst of the advancing columns.

As soon as the Austrian masses quitted the cover of the village they came within range of the Prussian Infantry and Artillery. The direct fire of Captain Werder's 6-pounder battery in front, and the flank fire of Captain Eltester's 4-pounders, proved especially destructive to them.

The Austrian columns now halted again and began to return the fire; only one rifle battalion turned half right, and dashed at the last-named battery. The attempt of the battalion failed, with enormous losses. The battery poured a fire of grape upon it until it came within 100 paces, the skirmishers lying in the hollow way enfiladed the movement with a most effective fire, and lastly the 3rd and 4th Companies of the 3rd, and the 8th Company of the 1st Foot Guards, accompanied by detachments of the Guard Fusiliers, broke forth and charged the battalion. The Rifles were completely routed and fled in great disorder. This defeat was the signal for the retreat of the other columns, which now fell back to the north end of Rosberitz, and established themselves there. After this no further advance was made by the Austrian right wing at this spot, but the left wing still made repeated attempts to press forward in the direction of the south end of Chlum.

The Reserve Artillery of the Guards had expended nearly all its ammunition in its position in front of Chlum. No supply could be obtained, and, as 50 horses had fallen, it was much to be feared that the batteries would lose all power of moving from this spot, especially so as Austrian skirmishers were already inflicting very painful losses on the Prussian left wing. Under these circumstances the Artillery was obliged to withdraw from its position about half-past 4 o'clock, and fall back to the next rise in the ground.

The Infantry, on the other hand, had managed to bring up an Infantry ammunition wagon, and a fresh supply of cartridges enabled it to meet the attacks of its adversaries with volleys and well sustained file-fire. Reinforcements also were now drawing near, sufficiently strong to frustrate any further attempt the enemy might make.

The losses of the 1st Division of Guards in this hard struggle had been very severe; they amounted to 38 officers and 1,022 men, the greatest share in which was borne by the 1st Regiment of Foot Guards, with 13 officers and 380 men, and the Fusilier Battalion of the 2nd Foot Guards, which lost 6 officers and 183 men.

The first fresh troops that arrived at this spot were the ad-

vanced guard of the Ist Corps d'Armée, which now moved up
into the widely extended line of the 1st Division of Guards at
Chlum, then the Heavy Cavalry Brigade of the Guards, and the
Guard-Hussar Regiment behind the left wing of the latter.
The detached squadrons of the Hussars had in the meantime
rejoined their regiment.

As soon as the advanced guard of the 1st Corps reached
Benatek it formed in line of battle, with the 41st Regiment in
the first, the 1st Regiment in the second line, and the Rifle Battalion in reserve, followed on its left rear by the Cavalry
Brigade. In this formation General Von Grossmann advanced
between Maslowed and the neighbouring wood in the direction
of Chlum. The two 4-pounder batteries turned off at Benatek,
and took the road leading past the west side of the wood to
Cistowes, in order to avoid the irregularities of the ground in
the other direction.

As the advanced guard passed Maslowed it was fired on by
scattered detachments of the enemy which had established themselves in some of the houses; and the left-flank battalion (the
2nd Battalion of the 41st Regiment) was sent into the village to
clear it. After doing so the battalion followed the brigade.

On reaching Wrchownitz the remainder of the corps took
the direction of the two lime-trees eastward of Horenowes,
according to the Crown Prince's first orders, but the reserve
Infantry followed the line of march of the advanced guard.

The Fusilier Battalion of the 1st Regiment passed along the
west side of the Lipa wood. The Rifle Battalion, which had
been brought forward to the head of the column, and was followed by the two battalions of the 41st Regiment, was instructed
to advance in the direction of the north end of Chlum. During
their march these troops crossed the line of fire of the enemy's
batteries, which were firing on the 1st Division of Guards, and
several shells fell amidst the battalions.

Passing partly through and partly on both sides of the village, the south end of Chlum was soon reached. About 30
hostile Riflemen were found still here, and the second line met
some Austrian stragglers.

Close to the south skirts of the village Major Von Sommerfeld
found Lieut.-General Hillier Von Gärtringen, Commander of the
1st Division of Guards. In the act of receiving the Major's
report, General Hillier was struck by a fragment of shell on the
breast, and sank from his horse without a word; he died whilst
he was being carried to the rear.

The face of the Chlum hill could not be swept by Infantry
fire from the skirts of the village. Major Von Sommerfeld
therefore threw forward the two first Rifle companies, that came
up, in skirmishing order as far as the brow of the hill, where
they stationed themselves between the two hollow ways, and
were soon reinforced on both wings by the 3rd and 4th Companies. Six companies of the 1st and Fusilier Battalions of the
41st Regiment, and a detachment of Pioneers, came up on

their right, between the hollow ways leading to Rosberitz and Langenhof.

The two Grenadier Battalions of the 1st and the 11th Company of the 41st Regiment were posted as supports, partly in rear of this line and partly in the south skirts of Chlum. The Cavalry Brigade of the advanced guard formed in the dell north-eastward of Chlum. Captain Körber's Horse Artillery Battery unlimbered near to the south entrance of the village; it was covered by the 4th squadron of the 1st Lancers. The 1st Horse Artillery Battery (Captain Preinitzer) had already opened fire from a position more to the left, but soon advanced still further, in order to engage two hostile batteries near Rosberitz; it was accompanied by a squadron of Dragoons.

The ten fresh companies that the 1st Corps had brought into action, and the detachments of the Guards which remained in their position, now swept the whole face of the hill towards Rosberitz with so effective a fire that, the Austrian columns westward of this village were also obliged to desist from all further attempts to advance; they commenced a standing fire in which they suffered severely.

Once again a mass of 2—3 battalions rushed up the hill, but was hurled back with heavy losses.

The batteries of the advanced guard now also arrived in the rear of General Grossmann's Infantry. The 5th, and soon afterwards the 1st 4-pounder battery, took up positions by the side of the south end of Chlum, on the road leading to Lipa.

The enemy's columns, which still held their ground in front of Rosberitz, were so shaken by the Prussian Artillery and Infantry fire that they gave up their position and retreated into the village. About the same time a strong column of Infantry, apparently two battalions, advanced at the high-road as far as the Chlum-Lagenhof road, but were met by the Fusilier Battalion of the 1st Regiment, and retreated to Rosberitz also.

The moment had now come for a renewed attack on Rosberitz, and Lieut.-General Von Crossmann gave Major-General Von Pape orders to carry it out.

As the greater part of the advanced guard of the 1st Army, and the nearest detachments of the Guards, were descending the hill of Chlum preparatory to attacking Rosberitz, they saw beyond the high-road a considerable body of Cavalry coming up at a rapid pace from the direction of Sadowa. This was the head of the Cavalry of the 1st Army in pursuit of the enemy, led by Major-General Count Groeben with the 12th Hussars.

Up to this moment the action of the VIth Prussian Corps had progressed as follows:—

Repeated attacks of the Austrian Haller Hussar Regiment attempted to disturb the formation of the 11th Division at Nedelist, but were repulsed by the volleys of the Infantry.

The village itself was occupied by the 1st Battalion of the 50th Regiment, the remainder of the 21st Brigade formed northward of it, and General Von Zastrow planted all available artillery on the slope of the hills facing the valley of the Elbe. There were at hand three Horse Artillery batteries of the Reserve Artillery under Major Arnold, that had exerted their utmost energies to hasten forward. The two 6-pounder batteries of the division soon came up on their right flank close to Nedelist. The two 4-pounder batteries were engaged in getting a fresh supply of ammunition. The 12-pounder battery had not been able to keep up with the rapid advance of the other batteries.

This Artillery directed its principal fire on bodies of Cavalry which were still to be seen in the neighbourhood of Lochenitz and Predmeritz, and which menaced the left flank of the division.

By way of covering this flank, the combined Cavalry Brigade under Lieut.-Colonel Von Wichmann, which had in the meantime arrived at the north side of Sendrasitz, received orders to advance against the Austrian Cavalry, and to avail itself of any possibile opportunity of attacking. The Hussar Regiment deployed; the Dragoons followed 300 paces behind its left wing in line of columns of divisions with deploying intervals. During their advance they were separated by a hollow way which gradually increased in depth, and were soon opened upon with grape by a battery which suddenly appeared at the highroad westward of Lochenitz.

In their eagerness to meet the enemy as soon as possible, the Hussars omitted to threw out éclaireurs in their front, and when they were already in a gallop they unexpectedly came upon a deep gully, which had been hidden from view in the high corn. Part of them pulled up in time, some got over to the other side, but the greater part fell into the ravine. The commander of the regiment tried to re-form the broken ranks behind this obstacle, and out of range of the enemy's grape, but those Hussars that were on the other side could only rejoin their regiment by riding round to the west end of the ravine. The Austrian Palffy Hussar Regiment took advantage of the situation and charged, and a *mêlée* ensued before the Dragoons could cross the ravine. Whilst the two Prussian regiments were engaged in re-forming the brigade, the Austrian Cavalry (the 2nd Light Cavalry Division) retreated to the bridges over the Elbe, under the fire of the Prussian batteries at Nedelist.

Previously to this, the main body of the Austrian IInd Corps had already retreated in the same direction. The advance of General Zastrow's Division had prevented General Count Thun from taking up the position in front of Nedelist as he was ordered to do. In addition to this, the progress of General Prondzynski's Division awakened lively apprehensions that this division might reach the Elbe bridges sooner than the IInd Corps. For this reason the latter had continued its retreat from Maslowed, without interruption, as far as Lochenitz and Predmeritz.

It now became the task of General Henriquez's Brigade to

impede the progress of its opponents as much as possible; this succeeded for a short time at Lochenitz.

We have previously seen in what manner General Prondzynski prepared to attack this village. Very soon horn signals were heard in all parts of the interior, and the enemy's battalions began to retreat eastward, but still held the skirts of the village by detachments of the 27th Regiment (Belgium). Major Von Lyncker occupied the watchman's hut on the railway with the 12th Company of the 22nd Regiment, and detached the 9th and 10th Companies of the battalion against the east entrance of the village on the side towards the Elbe. Both companies, led by Lieut. Sabel and Captain Von Gottberg, crossed the railway embankment in front of a severe fire, and then waded up to their breasts through the muddy waters of the Trotina, near to its influx in the Elbe.

An attempt of Captain Gottberg to wade through the Elbe also failed on account of the depth of water at the time. All that could be done here was to harass the enemy's retreat by file-firing at 400 paces distance. Major Lyncker posted a line of skirmishers in front of the Austrian detachments, which were spread out behind embankments in the immediate neighbourhood of the bridge, and then waded back again through the Trotina, in order to reach the bridges through the village. Assisted by the skirmishers of the 6th Company of the 23rd Regiment, the Fusiliers entered the village and advanced near to the bridges, which were only held by the 3rd Battalion of the 14th Regiment (Hesse). Captain Schmidt followed through the village street with the two other sub-divisions of his company, and captured part of a pontoon train which was just starting for Predmeritz. A cannon (overturned, but otherwise uninjured) and an ammunition wagon were left behind by the Austrians. Somewhat further on he opened fire on an Austrian Hussar regiment which was hastening from Predmeritz along the railway to the bridge at Lochenitz. The regiment succeeded in gaining the bridge, but suffered much loss. Other bodies of Cavalry, which were following the Hussars, turned back to Predmeritz in consequence.

Thus General Von Mutius had no longer any enemy either on his front or flank, but the increasing violence of the fire at Chlum was heard, and Prussian Infantry were seen retreating from Rosberitz to Chlum. The General resolved, therefore, to advance to the assistance of the Guards with all his available forces, and gave General von Zastrow orders to wheel the 11th Division half to the right, and to form it for an advance on Rosberitz, Wsestar, and Sweti, but not to begin this movement until the 12th Division should have covered his left flank by advancing beyond Lochenitz. At the same time the latter division received instructions to draw nearer to the 11th Division, and to continue to cover its left flank.

General Prondzynski now gave orders to discontinue the action in Lochenitz, and instructed Colonel Von Stein to withdraw the troops that were engaged there. By his orders Major Lyncker rallied the companies of his battalion, but left the 10th Company at the bridge over the Elbe, where it had the opportunity of repulsing the attack of an Austrian battalion. The bridge of Predmeritz was also occupied by a company. Soon afterwards the enemy's columns that had halted 6—800 paces eastward of the Elbe, continued their retreat, and General Prondzinski hastened to Nedelist with the 6th Hussars, and the 8th Company of the 23rd Regiment, the remainder of which soon followed in the same direction.

In the meantime General Von Zastrow had carried out the orders he had received. His brigades were formed in two lines southward of Nedelist; General Von Hoffmann's Brigade on the right wing, in front of Rosberitz, General Von Hanenfeld's on the left, in front of Wsestar and Sweti. The Fusilier Battalion of the 50th Regiment occupied Nedelist. The Artillery took up a position against the Austrian batteries that were engaged on the heights of Sweti and Wsestar. The communication with the 12th Division was kept up by the combined Cavalry brigade, which was soon joined by the 6th Hussars and the combined brigade of Count Bismarck.

General Von Zastrow had completed the formation of his division by about a quarter before 4 o'clock, and then started from Nedelist in the direction of Rosberitz and Sweti; his battalions were severely shelled during their advance. After being dislodged from its first position, the Artillery Reserve of the Austrian Army—still numbering 35 guns—had taken up a position on the range of hills extending north-westward of Sweti, where it was reinforced by some batteries of General Ramming's Corps. The Prussian Artillery tried in vain to draw the fire of these batteries off from the advancing Infantry, and the battalions, particularly those of General Hanenfeld's Brigade, suffered severely. Notwithstanding, they still continued to advance in perfect order, steadily and trustingly following their leaders (Von Zastrow and Von Hanenfeld), who rode at their head. It was not long before they came in sight of the high-road, on and at the side of which crowds of fugitives were hurrying back in full confusion. Officers and men now pressed forward, eager to participate in a victory of which there could now be no longer any doubt. Neither the fire of the enemy's artillery, nor the charges of his Cavalry, could check their advance. All attacks of the latter were frustrated by the cool fire of the Prussian Infantry, the skirmishers of which did not even think it necessary to form squares.

About a quarter-past 4 o'clock the 21st Brigade arrived before Sweti, where Archduke Joseph's Brigade of the IVth Corps had taken up a position to protect the batteries of the Reserve Artillery. The brigade and Artillery retreated on the approach of General Hanenfeld's troops, but still held the village.

The left wing of the Prussian first line—the 1st Battalion of the 10th Regiment—was now sent forward to take the village ; it advanced with impetuosity, and stormed the enclosure. Major Von Kalinowski occupied the south outlet with the 1st Company, whilst the 4th dislodged the enemy from some detached buildings eastward of the village. The Austrians retreated, hotly pursued by the fire of the Prussian Infantry ; at the same time the Austrian batteries concentrated the fire of their guns on the village.

General Von Hanenfeld now advanced with the other battalions of his brigade beyond Sweti, the right wing of General Hoffmann's Brigade drew near Rosberitz, which village was still occupied by the enemy.

This was about the time when, as we have already stated, the advanced guard of the 1st Corps and detachments of Guards were descending the hill of Chlum to retake Rosberitz.

The Prince of Wurtemberg had sent the main body of the 2nd Division of Guards in the direction of Lipa. Major-General Von Budritzki crossed the high-road at the village, and formed his troops westward of it, facing Langenhof, at a quarter past 4 o'clock. The 3rd 4-pounder battery of the advanced guard of the division took up a position in front of the main body.

General Clausewitz's Division of the 1st Corps was at this time advancing eastward of the Maslowed-Chlum road, in the direction of the latter village, accompanied by the Crown Prince. The Reserve Cavalry of the Corps was following the division ; the Reserve Infantry had just arrived between Benatek and Horenowes, but the Reserve Artillery and General Von Hartmann's Cavalry Division had not yet reached the scene of action.

The march of these troops had interposed between the Reserve Infantry of the 2nd Division of Guards and its main body. General Von Loen now followed the line of march of the 1st Corps d'Armée with the 4th Brigade of Guard Infantry.

The Vth Corps d'Armée was destined for the day as the general reserve of the Army ; it reached the height of Horen- · owes at 4 o'clock, and then continued its march southward.

We must now turn to the proceedings of the Army of the Elbe during the time from 3 till a quarter past 4 o'clock.

### ARMY OF THE ELBE.

The two divisions of the Army of the Elbe, which were for the moment available had wrested the heights of Problus from their adversaries, but the 1st Infantry Brigade of the Saxons still held the wood eastward of the village in force ; the Austrian Brigade of General Schulz was in the act of rallying behind the Brigade, and the Saxon Artillery had taken up a fresh position on the hill to the north of the wood.

The fire from the skirts of the wood was so severe, particularly against the 28th Infantry Brigade, which stood on the

T

heights without any shelter, that Major-General Von Hiller felt that no further progress could be made without gaining possession of the wood itself.

For this purpose the 1st Battalion of the 57th Regiment spread out in columns of companies and advanced in the foremost line, followed on its right by the Fusilier Battalion of the same, on its left by the 1st Battalion of the 17th Regiment. With these troops General Von Hiller attacked the skirts of the wood in front, whilst the 2nd Battalion of the 17th Regiment advanced against the enemy's flank. In face of a sharp fire from the Saxon skirmishers, and notwithstanding a most resolute defence, especially on the part of the 1st Saxon Rifle Battalion, the abattis was carried at the first onset, and the enemy, who retreated but very slowly, forced back into the interior of the wood. The latter being of considerable extent, it was feared that the troops might lose their touch, the Prussian Battalions were, therefore, soon halted, and the further pursuit entrusted to Captain Streccius with the 2nd Company and some skirmishing divisions of the 17th, and the 2nd Company of the 57th Regiment, with orders to press forward to the other side of the wood, where they were to establish themselves in the skirts, but not to advance beyond the wood. The Fusilier Battalion of the 17th Regiment followed in support of these detachments.

The skirts of the wood had been prepared for defence, and were obstinately disputed, so that they were not carried without much loss. The casualties in General Hiller's Brigade amounted to 10 officers and 190 men killed and wounded. The enemy's loss was in all probability not less; 2 officers and above 200 men were taken prisoners.

Whilst the last named companies were pressing on through the wood, and General Hiller was rallying his battalions on the side of it, the latter received orders from General Herwarth to advance no further, but to make sure his possession of the wood.

Almost simultaneously with the attack of the 28th Brigade, detachments of the 15th Division had penetrated into the south skirts of the wood. The 1st and Fusilier Battalions of the 28th Regiment were stationed at the east end of Ober-Prim, where they were much exposed to the fire of an Austrian battery posted in the direction of Charbusitz. Neither the burning village nor the neighbouring country afforded any shelter against this fire, and the leader of the 1st Battalion, Captain Von Quadt, resolved to extricate himself from this position by seizing on a fir copse eastward of Ober-Prim. Although the open country in front of the wood was completely swept by the enemy's shells, the 1st Battalion dashed forward and drove out the enemy, who retreated northward into the wood between Problus and Charbusitz. Captain Quadt threw forward the 2nd Company in pursuit as far as a wooded ravine in his front, and rallied his other companies, with which he then advanced to the right of the 2nd Company, and penetrated into the skirts of the above named large wood after a brief struggle.

The south-west skirts of the wood were attacked by three companies of the 2nd Battalion of the same regiment (the 4th Company was engaged with the enemy in front of Stezirek), and the 2nd and 3rd Battalions of the 40th Regiment.

These detachments met with no serious resistance. The Fusilier Companies of the 16th Regiment also advanced into the interior, where they drove back detachments of the Austrian 24th Rifle Battalion, and joined the companies of Captain Streccius. They then soon reached the north-eastern border of the wood, and occupied the farm buildings of Bor and the neighbouring copses, where they took a wounded Austrian Staff Officer and 20 men prisoners. Further advance was impossible at this spot, for two Saxon smooth-bore batteries fired with great effect on the skirts of the wood from a position north-eastward of Briza.

The 3rd 12-pounder Battery (Captain Theiler) followed this movement as far as the south-west corner of the wood, where it engaged the enemy's battery which was stationed to the north of Charbusitz, but could not hold its ground against the superior number of its adversary's guns, and soon withdrew behind the brow of the hill.

The Saxon Corps again formed line of battle on the heights between Rosnitz and the wood, but only for the purpose of covering the retreat of the troops from the wood and Problus. As soon as this was effected, and the last detachments—the 1st Saxon and the 24th Austrian Rifle Battalions—had arrived, the corps resumed its retreat.

Special orders for the retreat had not been received yet from the Austrian Head-Quarters; all that had been done in this respect was to designate Hohenmauth and some passages over the Elbe as the general line of retreat; the Saxon Corps, therefore, took the direction of the bridge at Placka, as the one furthest to the south, and the brigades started for this point immediately.

When the Crown Prince of Saxony arrived on the hill of Bor, he received the Feldzeugmeister's orders that the Saxon Corps should cross the Elbe at Opatowitz and Pardubitz.

Major-General Weber (Commander of the VIIIth Austrian Corps) was also on the same hill, and ordered the retreat of his corps. General Schulz's disorganized brigade was with the Saxons, those of Colonels Roth and Woeber were further southward at Charbusitz.

The Xth Austrian Corps had also begun its retreat, accompanied by the 3rd Reserve Cavalry Division. Here, as well as elsewhere, the Artillery still remained at its post with exemplary perseverance.

After having tried in vain to debouch from the wood of Popowitz, and to advance against the line of artillery at Stresetiz,

Major-General Von Kotze's Cavalry Brigade withdrew to a sheltered position in rear of Tresowitz.

The batteries at Stresetitz kept up a brisk fire against General Schwarzkoppen's Brigade, which stood near to the burning village of Problus, without shelter of any kind, and General Piret's Brigade, which the Feldzeugmeister sent up from the Austrian reserves, now proceeded to attack the Prussian Brigade. Parts of the Saxon Corps, viz., the 3rd Rifles, the 10th and parts of the 9th and 5th Infantry Battalions, discontinued their retreat, and joined General Piret's Brigade, following its advance as left flank *échelon*.

General Schwarzkoppen's Brigade was in the act of re-forming; its skirmishers occupied the enclosure of Problus, when the first line of General Piret's Brigade advanced, and forced the Prussian skirmishers, which were ensconced among the hedges outside Problus, back again to the skirts of the village. Here, however, the Austrian battalions were met by a very effective file-fire, whilst, at the same time, Prussian detachments broke forth from the north and south side of the village. The 12th Company of the 16th Regiment wheeled to the left, the 6th Company to the right, against both flanks of the enemy. The 1st Battalion of the 16th Regiment, which was employed as covering guard for the Artillery, also hastened to the scene, and arrived just as the Austrians reached the skirts of the village. The latter now suffered severely from a most destructive cross-fire, and fell back with the loss of numerous prisoners; during their retreat they were fired on by the Prussian troops in Bor.

The Saxon battalions only got to about 800 paces from Problus, and abandoned the attack, when General Piret's Brigade turned back.

This attack, which was made by considerable and fresh forces, took place about the same time as the attack on the wood south-eastward of Problus.

By 4 o'clock this wood was completely cleared of the enemy, and the 14th and 15th Divisions then assembled by order of General Herwarth at the following spots :—

General Schwarzkoppen's Brigade in Problus, where it was joined by the 7th Rifle Battalion from Lubno. Six companies of the advanced guard, which had taken part in the attack on Problus, remained at the north entrance of the village.

General Hiller's Brigade at the west skirts of the wood, which it had taken; the farm buildings at Bor were occupied by Captain Streccius's detachment; five companies of the 57th and 16th Regiment were posted at the north-east corner of the wood.

General Von Canstein assembled five battalions of his division on the right front of General Hiller's Brigade; two other companies were thrown forward as far as the north-east, and two into the south-east corner of the wood.

The 10th Company of the 68th Regiment, which had checked

General Edelsheim's Cavalry, had marched from Radikowitz into the wood of Stezirek.

At this time Captain Trautmann's Battery was engaged with the enemy's Artillery near Bor. the 12-pounder batteries of Captains Schmelzer and Theiler were with General Hiller's Brigade and the main body of General Canstein's Division; the other batteries were on the march, but none of them had yet reached the plateau. After the storming of Problus, the Reserve Artillery of the VIIth Corps and the Horse Artillery batteries had for a time taken up a position westward of the village, against the enemy's artillery near Stresetitz; the latter soon followed the general retreat of the Austrian Army.

At 4 o'clock the only part of the 16th Division eastward of the defile of Nechanitz was Colonel Von Senden's Brigade. The commander of the division, General Von Etzel, led it forward in the direction of Jehlitz without delay, and Captain Caspari's Battery, accompanied by the 3rd squadron of the 7th Lancers, hastened on ahead to Problus. General Von Alvensleben's Cavalry Division had pushed in between the Fusilier Brigade and Colonel Von Senden's Brigade, so that neither the former nor the Reserve Artillery of the VIIIth Corps had yet passed Nechanitz.

The last named Cavalry Division hastened on past Lubno in the direction of Stresetitz, but the difficulty of defiling through Nechanitz had been great, and the regiments of the division were separated from each other, even those of the leading brigade had not been able to keep together. Count Goltz's Hussar Brigade was still in the neighbourhood of Hradek.

It was an especially unfavourable circumstance that the nature of the lower Bistritz was such as to confine the whole army of the Elbe to one single place of crossing at Nechanitz, so that General Herwarth's forces could only come into action by degrees. His plan of attack had from the commencement been based on turning the enemy's left flank; two Prussian divisions had been engaged at this spot with two hostile corps, whose brave resistance, particularly that of the Saxon, had fully occupied the whole of the Prussian forces, so that General Von Canstein's right flank movement ended with the storming of the strong position of Problus, the joint deed of the 14th and 15th Divisions.

The fate of the day was undoubtedly decided by the taking of this position, and by the 1st Division of Guards holding its ground on the hill of Chlum, but great results might have been attained by General Von Herwarth's Army if he had had fresh reserves at hand to push straight on towards the Elbe. We know, however, that at the time when the pursuit of the enemy commenced, only the head of the 16th Division had as yet been able to pass Nechanitz, and was still nearly four miles and a half behind the 14th and 15th Divisions.

The Army of the Elbe was thus deprived of part of the fruits of this victory, which the men of the Rhineland and Westphalia had so materially assisted in gaining.

Having commenced their retreat betimes, and being covered by the Artillery, which had sacrificed itself for their safety, not only the Austrian left wing, but also the Xth Corps, and the 3rd Reserve Cavalry Division were able to effect their retreat without it being possible for these troops to throw any impediment in their way.

Although the 1st Army was the first to start in pursuit of the enemy, still it was not either able to reap the trophies which its long endurance of nine hours had prepared. Here also the difficulty, for the Cavalry, of defiling over the Bistritz was very manifest, and gave the enemy a considerable start on his retreat.

The struggle of the 1st Division of Guards in the rear of the enemy against three and four-fold numbers had forced the Austrian Army to give up the whole of its position, but had at the same time totally exhausted the strength of the division.

The VIth Corps was in the most favourable position for profiting by the victory; it was already in possession of two of the bridges by which the Austrian Army was to retreat, and was now approaching the immediate neighbourhood of the line of retreat of the Austrian centre.

## VI. The Pursuit.

It has already been stated that about 3 o'clock the foremost line of the 1st Army had perceived first a diminution of the enemy's fire, and then a retrograde movement of the Artillery in the Austrian centre. By degrees this was noticed along the whole line. This alteration in the state of affairs did not remain unnoticed on the Roskos Berg,* where at the same time reports arrived confirming the fact. Lieut.-General Von Schmidt and Von Manstein both requested Cavalry for the pursuit.

The available brigades of General Hann's Cavalry division, which were on the right bank of the Bistritz, now received orders to advance.

Prince Frederick Charles placed himself personally at the head of Count Groeben's brigade, which was instructed to cross the bridge of Sadowa. Prince Albrecht, senior, led Duke William of Meklenburg's brigade over the Bistritz at Sowetitz. His Majesty the King hastened on ahead of the latter to the foremost line of action.

All communication between the troops engaged beyond, and the rest of the army behind the Bistritz, had taken place during the day by way of these two defiles, so that they could not be passed by the Cavalry without difficulty and delay, still it had not hitherto been possible for it to deploy on the other bank of the stream.

Added to this, the masses of Infantry and long lines of Artillery, which were pressing on in pursuit of the enemy, blocked up the high-road and the whole country eastward and

---

* The station of the King of Prussia and his suite at this period of the action.

north-eastward of Sadowa. Through these the Cavalry had to wind its way.

For several hours these troops had been exposed to the hard trial of passive endurance; the long-wished for moment of the advance had now at last arrived. Before even the orders could reach all parts of the extensive line. the foremost detachments hastened forward, just as they were mingled together by the course of the action. Only those troops which had been held back in the second line advanced in compact order, and in their regular formation.

Colonel Von Sandrart, who was stationed north-eastward of the Sadowa wood, was the first to recognise the columns which appeared between Cistowes and Lipa as Prussian troops, and to report it. He immediately advanced with six companies of his regiment, and soon joined the Guard Fusiliers, who were pressing onward from Lipa, and with whom he then proceeded in the direction of Langenhof.

Major Von Wasielewsky galloped up with the three rifled batteries of the 4th Division, and unlimbered at the south-east skirts of the Sadowa wood against the Austrian Artillery that was covering the retreat, and upon which General Schwarz's batteries concentrated their fire, now that their former adversaries had withdrawn. Still further to the right Captain Müller's battery of the 3rd Division came into action, and the Horse Artillery batteries of Captains Von Gayl and Von Ekensteen hastened on ahead of the Cavalry Brigades, and soon arrived at this spot. We have already heard how the last of these Austrian guns were captured by the Infantry of the Guards a few moments later.

On leaving the wood, the 9th and 12th Companies of the 9th Regiment turned to the right towards Stresetitz, so as not to mask the fire of the artillery. The detachments which were posted in the skirts of the wood all advanced likewise. Captain Von Giese collected together stragglers of different detachments until his company, the 3rd of the 31st Regiment, almost attained the strength of a battalion, and pressed on towards Langenhof. Major-General Von Schmidt and four battalions of the 8th Division left the eastern corner of the wood, and proceeded in the same direction, in which also the main body of the 2nd Guard Division, just then arriving from the north, followed, as soon as it had crossed the highroad. On General Schmidt's right Colonel Von Rothmaler advanced with three battalions of the 35th Regiment, the 3rd Battalion, accompanied by Generals Von Manstein and Von Gersdorff, somewhat ahead of the others.

Major-General Von Bose broke forth from Ober-Dohalitz with the greater part of the 31st Regiment, and the combined battalion of Lieutenant-Colonel Von Beckedorff. Further to the right advanced the 2nd Battalion of the 12th Regiment, on a height with the 3rd Battalion of the 35th.

South of Sadowa the batteries of Captains Gallus and Munk were the first to follow the enemy in the direction of Langenhof and Stresetitz; they were followed on their left wing by the batteries of Captains Von der Goltz and Griess; on their right by Colonel Von Puttkamer, with the Reserve Artillery of the IInd Corps, and the 4th 12-pounder battery of the 3rd Division. The 2nd Battalion of Rifles spread out in columns of companies, and advanced towards Problus, to cover the artillery.

All these detachments pressed forward in somewhat loose order; they were followed in compact line-of-battle order by the bulk of the army, which had been hitherto kept back.

Immediately behind Colonel Sandrart's troops the 21st Regiment followed; behind Colonel Rothmaler the 60th Regiment, which advanced from Ober-Dohalitz towards Stresetitz, on its right hand the 12th Brigade. On a height with the latter General Schimmelmann's brigade advanced towards Problus; he was followed by the other brigades of the 3rd and 5th Division. The 5th Hussar Regiment and General Goltz's heavy Cavalry brigade crossed the Bistritz behind them.

The 61st and 49th Regiments were then collected together, and followed through the Sadowa wood towards Langenhof. As soon as the troops of General Fransecky's division were re-formed they advanced towards Chlum.

When the foremost detachments of Infantry drew near the line Langenhof-Stresetitz, at about 4 o'clock, they were overtaken by the heads of the Cavalry. The first to come up to Langenhof was Count Groeben's Brigade, which had taken the high-road, the best and most direct route. It had formed line of columns of divisions south eastward of the Sadowa wood, with the 12th Hussars on its left, and the 3rd Dragoons on its right wing.

The enemy's Infantry had disappeared, single detachments of it only were seen in the distance, but the Cavalry soon came within range of the Austrian batteries, which had taken up fresh positions further to the rear.

Count Groeben, who rode far on ahead of his brigade, saw some of the enemy's Infantry and Artillery retreating in loose order near Rosberitz, and at the same time perceived Prussian columns descending the Chlum Hill to attack the former village. He resolved to support this attack, and gave orders to Lieut.-Colonel Von Barnekow to charge, and to the Dragoons to follow the Hussars.

The 12th Hussars deployed, and moved somewhat to the left, then passed through an Austrian camp of huts and charged, hoping to reach the Austrian battalion, which was retreating in disorder, before it could fall back upon its supports.

The battalion defended itself both with volleys and with the bayonet. It was broken by the charge, but the Hussars were then fired on by Artillery and Infantry detachments, which still held their ground at the high-road. Count Groeben immediately threw himself upon the battery with part of the 4th Squadron; the Hussars cut the Artillerymen down, and captured four guns, the remainder of the battery fled, hotly pursued by the Hussars, Count Groeben was severely wounded here.

In the meantime the rest of the regiment came up with the

Infantry at the high-road, and broke into a square, which surrendered to them. The violent fire of an Austrian battalion in the neighbourhood caused several casualties among the 1st Squadron, and at the same moment a mass of hostile cuirassiers, the strength of which was not apparent, advanced from Rosnitz against the right flank of the Hussars.

This was Prince Holstein's Reserve Cavalry Division. Prince Holstein had already commenced his retreat, but no sooner perceived the danger in which the last detachments of the army were placed, than he instantly advanced to their support. With General Schindlöcker's brigade in line on his right wing, and Prince Solm's brigade as left *échelon* somewhat behind it, he reached the scene of combat in time to save the Infantry and Cavalry from still greater disaster. Part of the 2nd Regiment of Hussars (Grand Duke Nicolas) joined his brigade during this movement.

After their previous charges the Prussian Hussars were not in a position to meet such superior numbers of the enemy with a well-formed line. The left wing of the 3rd Dragoons, the 4th and 5th Squadrons, was the only support which had followed them. The other three squadrons of this regiment had not kept up with the Hussars during their advance through the masses of the Prussian Infantry and Artillery, but had proceeded in the original direction of the movement towards Stresetitz, with the commander of the regiment, Lieutenant-Colonel Von Willisen, at their head.

As soon as the leading Austrian brigade became visible, the 5th Squadron of the Dragoons, which was on the right of the 4th, wheeled to the right, and advanced to meet the enemy, whose first line consisted of the 9th Regiment of Cuirassiers (Count Stadion), and two squadrons of the 11th Cuirassiers (Emperor Francis Joseph). In spite of the far superior numbers of the enemy, Captain Von Görz broke through the Austrian line, and a fierce combat ensued, in which he himself was severely wounded. The Dragoons were obliged to fall back upon their 4th Squadron, with which Captain Groeben recklessly thew himself into the midst of the Cuirassiers. He was followed by the nearest divisions of the Prussian Hussars, whilst at the same time detachments of the 2nd Austrian Hussar Regiment (Grand Duke Nicolas) joined in the fight.

The *mêlée* lasted some time, and the weak Prussian force was eventually obliged to retreat between Langenhof and the high-road. This was, however, effected at a moderate pace, and with continual fighting with the Austrian Cuirassiers and Hussars, who followed close up. The long stream of pursuing Cavalry was now fired on by the Fusilier Battalion of the 1st Regiment, which just at this moment reached the high-road, and by the 2nd Company of the same regiment, which had advanced to the detached farm-houses on the high-road westward of Rosberitz. Part of the Austrian Cavalry turned back here already in consequence.

The Prussian squadrons derived still more effectual aid from the 4th Lancer Regiment, which now appeared on the field.

After crossing the Sadowa bridge this regiment had trotted forward in the dell northward of the high-road, on the right side of the latter. It was formed in column of divisions from the right. Colonel Von Kleist thus came straight upon the advancing mass of Prussian and Austrian Cavalry. The signal to form line to the front was sounded, and without waiting for the 1st Squadron to complete its formation, the foremost divisions charged into the crowd which was just then dashing past at scarcely 50 paces distance. Hard hand-to-hand fighting now ensued with that part of the pursuing Cavalry, upon which the shock of this charge fell, whilst the remainder continued its headlong career in the previous direction. Hereupon, two out of the three other Lancer squadrons, which were still in column, wheeled to the right and charged *en échelon*, so that the Austrians were forced back in the direction of Langenhof. In this movement the ranks of the Lancers were very naturally more or less broken, only one squadron of the regiment remained in compact order.

Behind this swarm of horsemen, the numbers of which had been much increased by the arrival of the Lancers, there now appeared a fresh line of Austrian Cuirassiers advancing in perfect order; it was the 4th Regiment (Emperor Ferdinand), the right wing of Prince Solm's brigade.

In the meantime, the head of the Prussian 3rd Hussar Regiment, belonging to Duke William of Meklenburg's brigade, arrived at the small brook which flows from Langenhof towards the high-road. The other regiments of the brigade had been much delayed in crossing the low and broken ground between Sadowa and Cistowes, and could only come up singly as they overcame this impediment to their progress.

Langenhof had already been taken by the 7th and 8th Companies of the 2nd Foot Guards (Lieutenants Von Rosenberg and Frankenberg). These companies had advanced on the village from the south corner of the Lipa wood, although fired on from the direction both of Lipa and of Rosberitz. Langenhof was occupied by Infantry, and flanked by two batteries; the latter were dislodged, one gun of each being captured, and the village stormed. The 7th Company then took the "schäferei,"* and the skirmishing division of Lieutenant Von Daum pushed on even still further. The 4th Company of the Guard Fusiliers very soon followed to the same spot. A large number of Austrians were taken prisoners here, among others Colonel Benedek, who had been carried here when he was wounded at Lipa.

The 2nd, 3rd, 10th, and 11th Companies of the 9th and the 5th Company of 21st Regiment (IInd Corps d'Armée), and the 6th and 7th Companies of the 12th Regiment (5th Division) had

---

* Schäferei: sheep-farm, a detached barn or sheep stable, about 250 paces southward of Langenhof.

also reached Langenhof by this time; some of them were inside some outside of the village.

The Austrian " Emperor Ferdinand " Cuirassiers kept to the left of the line of advance of General Schindlöcker's brigade, and rode straight on towards the "schäferei." Riding past it on both sides, the Cuirassiers then broke into a gallop and advanced towards the south end of Langenhof. They had already received Infantry fire from the schäferei, and from the enclosure of the village, and had swerved somewhat towards the south in consequence, when the 3rd Hussars arrived at the village. Lieutenant-Colonel Von Kalkreuth and Captain Von Thile crossed the brook close to the village with $1\frac{1}{2}$ squadron, and General Von Hann led them against the right wing of the Cuirassiers. The distance was so short that there was no time for the Hussars to form line, but their shock nevertheless sufficed to overthrow the Cuirassiers, who were already much shaken, and who now retreated towards Bor, a running fight continuing for some time between them and the Hussars.

During this pursuit a fresh line of Austrian Cuirassiers was seen advancing against the left flank of the Hussars; it seemed to consist of two squadrons, and proved to be the 6th Cuirassier Regiment (Grand Duke of Hesse). The "assemble" was sounded for the Hussars, and they rallied south-westward of Langenhof, where the remaining $2\frac{1}{2}$ squadrons of the regiment were drawn up. On the east of the "Schäferei" the 3rd and half of the 4th Squadron of the 4th Lancers advanced southward in columns of divisions.

The Cuirassiers trotted straight on towards Langenhof, and passed within a short distance of the head of the Lancers, who charged them in flank and rear without having had time to form line. The right wing of the Austrian line, which still advanced in close order, was thus completely surrounded by the Lancers at the moment when Duke William of Meklenburg charged them in front with the 3rd Hussars. The standing fight which now ensued ended with the flight of the Austrians in a south-westerly direction. In the meantime, Lieutenant-Colonel Von Kalkreuth had rallied his Hussars, and threw himself upon the head of the Cuirassiers, who now retreated first towards Rosberitz, and then in the direction of Rosnitz.

Part of the Hussars and Lancers followed in pursuit, another part turned to the south-west to meet some scattered detachments of Prince Windischgratz's brigade, as will be seen presently.

The Commander of the Cavalry Corps, Prince Albrecht, senior, was present during the action at Langenhof. The casualties among the Prussian Cavalry which took part in this engagement were considerable, particularly those of the two Dragoon squadrons, whose losses amounted to four officers, three cornets, and 96 men; the 12th Hussars lost four officers and 45 men, the 4th Lancers six officers and 30 men, and the 3rd Hussars 15 men.

The four Austrian Cuirassier regiments alone incurred a loss of 17 officers and above 300 men.

Towards the end of this action at Langenhof a similar encounter of Cavalry took place in the neighbourhood of Stresetitz.

It has already been mentioned that Lieutenant-Colonel Von Willisen advanced southwards past Langenhof with the 1st, 2nd, and 3rd Squadrons of the 3rd Dragoons. He reached Stresetitz under a severe shelling from the enemy's batteries, and halted there in an undulation of the ground, to await a favourable opportunity for charging.

On the point of attacking a retiring detachment of Austrian Rifles, he perceived a body of hostile Cavalry trotting up over the heights of Rosnitz, and resolved to advance to meet it.

Here also it was a body of Cuirassiers that appeared in the field, regiments of Major-General Count Coudenhove's 3rd Reserve Cavalry Division, which had turned back again on hearing of the approach of Prussian Cavalry, and were now advancing in a north-westerly direction towards Stresetitz.

From the very first moment of starting, Lieutenant-Colonel Von Willisen was fully aware that his three isolated squadrons could have but little chance of success against such far superior numbers, but he had perceived Prussian Infantry at Stresetitz, and his object naturally was to draw the enemy within range of its fire. The Dragoons therefore retreated towards Stresetitz, where Generals Manstein, Gersdorf, and Bose had, in the meantime, arrived with their detachments. Colonel Von Rothmaler and Major Von Papstein had advanced along the east side of Stresetitz with the 10th and 11th Companies of the 35th Regiment, which now deployed, four ranks deep, on a hillock near the village. Captain Munk's battery had been brought forward by Major Röckner, and took a position on their left, where it was covered by a battalion which Major Von Beckedorff had formed out of different detachments of the 49th Regiment.

Added to these, the 9th and 12th Companies of the 35th Regiment had reached the skirts of Stresetitz, and General Bose had advanced beyond the south enclosure of the village with parts of the 31st Regiment, which he had collected together; the lance-points of a regiment of Prussian Lancers were also visible in the undulations of the ground.

Lieutenant-Colonel Von Willisen thought the moment opportune for attacking his adversaries, in spite of their superior numbers.

The Austrian Cuirassiers had followed the Dragoons at a distance of about 800 paces. The leading brigade was that of Prince Windischgrätz, with the 8th Regiment of Cuirassiers (Prince Charles of Prussia) in the first line. The second line consisted of the 2nd Regiment of Cuirassiers (Count Wrangel), two squadrons of which followed en échelon behind each wing of the first line. Two squadrons of Lancers followed as reserve. The brigade of Major-General Von Mengen was still further to the rear.

The three Prussian Dragoon squadrons were retreating in line of columns of divisions with deploying intervals; they now fronted, formed line to the front, and trotted forward to meet the Cuirassiers; when within 150 paces of their opponents, they charged; the shock met the enemy's line obliquely.

The Austrian Cuirassiers had already received Infantry fire from the Langenhof "schäferei." They met the charge of the Dragoons with a firm, compact line, but did not increase their pace beyond a trot. The shock was very vehement, and the foremost lines of both parties broke through their opponent's line. The right wing of the Dragoons was overlapped by the Cuirassiers, and was forced back, but the 3rd Squadron of the former overlapped the right wing of the Austrians, and wheeling round it dashed at their rear. In doing so, however, they exposed their own rear to the 2nd Austrian line.

The Fusiliers of the 35th Regiment and Captain Munk's battery had kept up a sharp fire against the Cuirassiers during their advance, but could now no longer fire into the *mêlée*. However, they did so with such effect upon the supporting *échelons* of the Austrians that they recoiled.

In the meantime the two bodies of horsemen were enaged in a desperate and sanguinary hand-to-hand fight, which ranged over a confined space of ground, and from which the over-matched Dragoons were rescued by the arrival of Prince Hohen-lohe's Lancers.

This regiment, the 11th Lancers, belonged to Duke William of Meklenburg's brigade, and was following the 3rd Hussars, when the battalions of the Guards, which were advancing southward on the high-road, crossed its line of march, and pre-vented it from keeping up with the Hussars. Lieut.-Colonel Prince Hohenlohe, therefore, took the direction of Stresetitz, and was in the act of crossing a hollow way near this village when the Dragoons charged. As soon as the regiment, which was in columns of squadrons, had deployed, it dashed into the enemy's ranks. The three first squadrons came upon the left wing of the Cuirassiers; the 4th charged their right wing as soon as it got free of the defile; part of the latter had separated from their main line, and were engaged in a running fight with a small knot of Prussian Dragoons, whom they were forcing back in the direction of Langenhof.

The left wing squadron of the 8th, and the two squadrons of the 2nd Austrian Cuirassiers, which followed in second line, were the first to succumb to the charge of the Lancers. Whilst crossing the line of fire of General Bose's Infantry, they were caught by the 3rd and 4th Squadrons of the Lancers, and totally dispersed.

The remainder of the Cuirassiers were also forced to give way; they made a wide circuit round to the left, and dis-appeared in the direction of Rosnitz. A troop of about 100 horse-men only dashed past the south-east corner of Stresetitz, and then along a strip of meadow in the direction of Langenhof, where they incurred considerable loss from the fire of the Prussian Infantry in this village. Some Cuirassiers of the 2nd

Regiment passed Captain Munk's battery, and another party of
60 or 70 horsemen, friend and foe together, rushed through the
battery of Captain Gallus.

Two bodies of Austrian Cavalry had thus taken the direction
of Langenhof. One of them was pursuing some Prussian Dra-
groons, the other was itself pursued by part of the 2nd Squadron
of the Lancers; both were here again met by Prussian Cavalry.
Detachments of the 4th Prussian Lancers advanced against the
former, and drove them towards Stresetitz, where they again
came within the range of the Prussian Infantry and Artillery,
and were almost totally destroyed. The latter were met by
Duke William of Meklenburg with part of the 3rd Hussar
Regiment, who forced them back and pursued them southward.

These scattered Cuirassiers had come more or less in contact
with almost all the Prussian Infantry and Artillery, which was
advancing at this part of the field, and had naturally suffered
very considerable losses. The commander of the brigade,
Major-General Prince Windischgrätz, was left severely wounded
on the field; four officers of his Staff were also wounded,
22 officers and 248 men of the two Cuirassier regiments were
put *hors de combat*. But on the Prussian side also the losses
were by no means trifling; the three squadrons of the 3rd Dragoons, which were engaged at this spot, lost eight officers and
92 men, the 11th Lancers three officers and 39 men, the 3rd
Hussars and the squadron of the 4th Lancers suffered but
slightly, though four officers of the former regiment were
wounded. The Prussian Cavalry was rallied on the spot where
the action had taken place.

A few minutes after the commencement of the engagement
at Stresetitz, a third encounter took place between the Austrian
and Prussian Cavalry.

We left General Von Alvensleben's Cavalry division shortly
after its passage through Nechanitz, when the different brigades
and regiments were advancing singly, as they got clear of the
defile, from Lubno towards Stresetitz. The 1st Regiment of
Guard Dragoons was at the head of the division, the 1st Guard
Lancers were some distance behind it. The Austrian Cavalry
Brigade of Major-General Von Mengen had not been able to
support Prince Windischgrätz's brigade on account of the
Prussian Infantry and Artillery fire, and was retreating when
the Prussian Cavalry appeared near Problus. The Austrian
brigade fronted and advanced westward with the 11th Lancer
Regiment (Emperor Alexander) on its left, the 10th Cuirassier
Regiment (King of Bavaria) on its right wing, and the 12th
Cuirassier Regiment (Count Neipperg) following as reserve.

At this moment Lieutenant-Colonel Von Barner came up,
after a long and fatiguing trot, with the 1st Regiment of Guard
Dragoons in line of columns of divisions with deploying intervals,
and advanced round the north end of Problus to meet the
Austrian Cavalry. Almost simultaneously the 5th Regiment of

Prussian Hussars,* which had come from Under-Dohalitz, trotted past the west side of Stresetitz, and appeared behind the left wing of the Dragoons.

As soon as the Austrian Lancers were sighted, Lieut.-Colonel Barner gave the command for his regiment to deploy, which then dashed at full speed on its opponents, headed by Lieut.-General Von Alvensleben. The shock was very vehement, both lines meeting each other, so that their left wings overlapped their adversary's right. The Dragoons broke through the ranks of the Lancers, and, encircling their right wing, bore it back in hand-to-hand combat towards the south-west corner of Stresetitz, whilst, on the other hand, the Austrian left wing, which overlapped the right wing of the Dragoons, drove part of the latter back, and dashed on past the east side of Problus in pursuit of them. In the meantime, however, Captain Caspari's battery of the 16th Division had come up to Problus and resolutely advanced to the brow of the hill in face of the coming attack; it now stood unlimbered at this spot. Reserving his fire until the Austrian Lancers were in his immediate neighbourhood, Captain Caspari then received them with such a fire of grape that only a few Lancers, unable to turn their horses, dashed in between the guns of the battery, and then made a wide circuit to rejoin that part of their regiment, which was then being pursued towards Stresetitz. A second charge of a larger body of Lancers, which followed behind the left wing of the first Austrian line, was also repulsed by Captain Caspari's grape fire.

During the attack of the 1st Dragoons the 5th Hussar Regiment advanced to charge the 10th Austrian Cuirassiers (King of Bavaria), and came upon them before they had deployed. The 3rd Squadron of the Hussars, which had been held back in reserve, turned the right flank of the Austrians, and fell upon their rear. The Cuirassiers were broken, and were pursued for some distance by the Hussars. Some Austrian Lancers, probably those which were driven back in this direction by the Guard Dragoons, took part in this action.

The Austrian 12th Cuirassiers (Count Neipperg) took no perceptible part in the engagement, but a second line of hostile Cavalry was seen for a short time at a considerable distance. On the other hand, a fresh encounter ensued with those "Emperor Alexander Lancers" which had been driven back towards Stresetitz. Major-General Von Rheinbaben had by this time, namely, arrived with three squadrons of the 1st Guard Lancers between Problus and Stresetitz, and charged the Austrians in flank. The latter were at the same time fired on by General Bose's Infantry. Part of the Austrian Lancers turned back here already in consequence, but a confused mass of some 60 or 100 horsemen dashed past Stresetitz northward. This

---

* This regiment bears the name of "Blucher Hussars" in commemoration of its former Chief, Field-Marshal Blucher.

led them straight in the direction of His Majesty the King, who, after crossing the high-road between Lipa and the Sadowa wood at about 4 o'clock, and speaking words of greeting to the troops which were advancing at all points, had taken up his station some 400 paces north-westward of Stresetitz during the Cavalry engagement.

His Majesty's aide-de-camp, Lieutenant-Colonel Count Von Finckenstein, hastened forward with half a squadron of the King's personal escort, and was on the point of charging the Lancers, when the latter were met by the fire of the 1st and 2nd Battalions of the 35th Regiment, and of the 2nd Rifle Battalion, which happened to be in the neighbourhood.

Bnt few of the horsemen escaped the Prussian fire, and fled southward.

This engagement was also attended with very considerable losses on the part of the Austrians. According to such statements as are as yet known, the Emperor Alexander Lancers lost six officers and 160 men, the King of Bavaria Cuirassiers six officers and 123 men.

The Prussian Guard Dragoons lost three officers and 69 men, the 5th Hussars 11 men, the 1st Guard Lancers suffered no loss at all.

The retreat of the Austrian Cavalry, under circumstances such as we have just related, could not for the most part be effected otherwise than in disorder, more especially as the Prussian Artillery coming up to the front line of the engagement, brought the cross-fire of its batteries to bear on the retreating masses. Lieutenant-Colonel Von Scherbening brought the 24 guns of his Artillery division and the batteries of Captains Schäffer and Müller into action at the foot of the Chlum Hill, seven other batteries arrived one after the other, and opened fire between Stresetitz and Langenhof.

In face of such a fire no re-formation of those Austrian regiments, which had been the most engaged, was possible; they were obliged to fall back behind their own Infantry, the last detachments of which had gained a considerable start during the Cavalry combat.

The situation of these detachments also had, however, changed considerably for the worse in the meantime. Rosberitz and Wsestar had fallen into the hands of the Prussians, and the columns of the IInd Prussian Army had already crossed the high-road, so that the retiring Austrian Cavalry here again found itself met by Infantry and Artillery fire, which added to the confusion in its ranks. Part of it continued its flight in total disorder, over-riding the Infantry and overturning guns in its headlong haste, and thus raising the state of disorder which prevailed already among the retreating troops to a most alarming pitch.

Nevertheless, we must record the fact that the resolution of Prince Holstein and Count Coudenhowe, emanating as it did so entirely from themselves, and the meritorious bravery of their troops, very materially assisted the retreat of the Infantry and Artillery of the Austrian centre.

On the other hand, the want of Cavalry was principally felt on the right flank of the Austrian Army, which was so imminently menaced by the advance of the Prussian VIth Corps, and where the nature of the ground was peculiarly favourable for the action of large bodies of this arm.

On this wing not only had the 2nd Light Cavalry Division retired beyond the Elbe, as has been already stated, but the 2nd Reserve Cavalry Division also had been despatched to the left wing of the army at an earlier period of the day, in order to join General Edelsheim and the 2nd Saxon "Reiter" Brigade in protecting this flank against a threatening flank movement of the Army of the Elbe.

When we left the Prussian Ist Corps d'Armée at the commencement of the Cavalry engagement, it was advancing from the hill of Chlum on Rosberitz; at the same time the extreme right wing of General Hoffman's Brigade (VIth Corps) was approaching this village from the north-east; the main body of the brigade was advancing in the direction of the high-road between Rosberitz and Wsestar and towards the latter village. On its left General Hanenfeldt's brigade marched through and past Sweti towards Briza.

All these villages were still occupied by the enemy, and the intermediate country was covered with troops of all arms, whose retreat had led them in this direction.

Major-General Von Pape now led eleven companies of the advanced guard of the Ist Corps d'Armée, supported by four other companies in second line, to the attack of Rosberitz. The left wing of these troops, consisting of the 2nd Battalion of the 1st Regiment and the 3rd Company of the 1st Rifle Battalion, penetrated into the northern skirts of the village, the right wing, which extended as far as the high-road, wheeled to the left and attacked from the west. Detachments of the Guards namely, Count Waldersee's battalion, Fusiliers of the 1st and 2nd Foot Guards, and the nearest troops of the 2nd Battalion of the 1st, and of the 1st and 2nd Battalions of the 3rd Foot Guards, followed the attack, mostly on the left wing. Further to the left, Major Von Ostrowski (General Hoffmann's brigade) sent Captain Liebe with part of the 5th Company of the 51st Regiment against the east side of the village. At first the enemy held his ground with great obstinacy, in spite of which the Prussian troops entered the village on all sides, whereupon the greater part of its defenders laid down their arms. About 3,000 prisoners were taken at this spot. General Pape's skirmishers then advanced beyond the south skirts of the village, where they captured two guns; four more, which stood at the high-road, were taken by the 2nd and 10th Companies of the 41st Regiment, and part of the 3rd Company of the 1st Rifle Battalion. This took place simultaneously with the charge of the 12th Hussars, which we have related already.

U

The brief space of time which elapsed during the Cavalry combat was fully occupied in collecting together so large a number of prisoners and in searching the village, so that for the moment it fell to the lot of the Artillery to break up the retiring mass of the enemy still further.

The two 4-pounder batteries and the Horse Artillery battery of the advanced guard of the 1st Corps were already in position on the south slope of the Chlum hill. They were now joined by the 3rd Horse Artillery Battery, and by the 4th 4-pounder, the 3rd 6-pounder, and the 3rd 12-pounder Batteries of the 2nd Division. Thus 42 guns followed the retreat of the enemy with their fire from this spot. They were soon reinforced by the two 4-pounder batteries of General Fransecky's division.

Further to the left General Hoffmann's brigade in the meantime advanced uninterruptedly, and repulsed the attacks of some detachments of Cavalry without any difficulty; the 51st Regiment formed the first line of the brigade. The 8th and the skirmishing division of the 5th Company of the regiment, under the command of Captain Von Wunster, advanced against the north end of Wsestar; Major Von Ostrowski brought forward the 6th and 7th Companies against a strong column of the enemy, which issued from the east entrance of Rosberitz, even before the village was taken, for the purpose of gaining the high-road, at the side of which it deployed, and returned Major Ostrowski's fire. In the meantime Captain Von Wunster penetrated into the north end of Wsestar, in spite of the enemy's severe fire of grape and musketry. Three guns and two ammunition wagons fell into his hands at the skirts of the village; a Rifle detachment which defended them was taken prisoner. Captain Wunster then turned to the right and opened file fire at 250 paces on the flank of the Austrian line at the high-road, which was engaged with Major Ostrowski and the 9th and 12th Companies of the 51st Regiment. A body of Austrian Cavalry attempted in vain to charge the 8th Company; the fire of a single division of skirmishers sufficed to repulse it. Major Von Ostrowski now ceased firing, the band of the regiment struck up, and he proceeded to charge the enemy with the bayonet. The latter, much shaken already, could withstand no longer; his line began to waver. Many sought refuge in the neighbouring hollow ways, others rushed towards Captain Wunster's detachment, and 700 prisoners fell into the hands of the Prussians at this spot.

During this successful action of the 2nd Battalion of the 51st Regiment, the Fusilier and 1st Battalions of the Regiment also advanced on Wsestar, further to the left.

Advancing against the village with the 2nd and 3rd Companies, Major Von Haine came upon a battery of six guns, which kept up a strong and effective fire. After the skirmishers had returned this fire for a short time, Captain Von Lindeiner threw himself upon the battery with the two skirmishing divisions, and captured all of the guns. In addition to these troops, and at the same time when the 8th Company was entering the north end of Wsestar, there arrived before the east front of the village the 10th, 11th, 1st, and 4th Companies of the regiment, and the 1st Battalion of the 38th Regiment also advanced from the second line of the brigade.

The Prussian companies penetrated into several parts of the village at the first onset, although the enclosure was vigorously defended. The 10th and 11th Companies attacked the part northward of the church, where a battery of five guns stationed in the skirts of the village kept up a fire of grape; they captured the battery with its teams. All the Prussian detachments now hastened through Wsestar, which their astounded adversaries no longer defended, and spread out along the southern enclosure of the village. From here they poured a file fire upon the dense hostile masses of all arms, which were trying to escape through and round about Rosnitz to the high-road and to Briza. A skirmishing party of Major Haine's companies captured a gun here, just as it was on the point of driving off. As the companies were spreading out on the south side of Wsestar they were attacked by a regiment of Cuirassiers, probably one retreating from the Cavalry combat; they repulsed tha attack at a distance of 250 paces, and the Cuirassiers rode in wild confusion through the Infantry that was retreating behind them. On searching the village numerous prisoners were captured.

Whilst General Hoffmann's Brigade was thus engaged in taking Wsestar, General Hanenfeldt's Brigade, with the 2nd and Fusilier Battalions of the 10th Regiment at its head, pushed on further to the left, against Sweti, where it found itself in front of the Austrian Reserve Artillery, which had been dislodged from its position at Nedelist, and was now destined to suffer fresh losses.

During this advance, already, the 5th and 8th Companies had come upon the right wing of the Artillery, and had forced it to fall back with the loss of one gun. Two Cavalry attacks were repulsed, and the companies pressed on past the west side of Sweti, where they again reached a position of the enemy's Artillery, upon which the skirmishers and their supports rushed with such vehemence, that nine guns had no time to drive off, and were captured. Five others fell into the hands of the 10th and 11th Companies, which advanced further to the right.

Whilst the remnants of the Austrian Artillery, which had suffered severely, fled partly to Briza, and partly along the road to Königgrätz, the bulk of the above-named Prussian battalions pushed on further between Wsestar and Sweti. The 9th Company proceeded to the former village, where it participated in the capture of the garrison, of which it collected 12 officers and 500 men.

The 10th and 11th Companies made a vigorous dash and took possession of the "ziegelei," upon which Major Von Kalinowski also advanced with the 1st Battalion from Sweti, and the 12th Company further to the left.

By order of General Von Mutius, General Herkt had assembled all available Artillery of the Corps d'Armée behind the Infantry, in one large battery of 54 guns, on the heights of Wsestar and Sweti. This line of artillery consisted of the three rifled batteries of the 11th, the two 4-pounder batteries of the 12th Division, and the four 12-pounder batteries of the Reserve. From want of space between the two villages, the 2nd 6-pounder battery was obliged to take up a position westward of Wsestar; added to these, the 4th 6-pounder battery stlll continued its fire from the heights northward of Sweti.

The enemy's columns that were hurrying back to Briza and Königgrätz afforded an aim which the Prussian guns could not miss. In vain the Austrian Batteries, with the greatest self-devotion, took up even now fresh positions, and attempted to draw the Prussian fire upon themselves.

Thus, by 5 o'clock, General Zastrow's Division was in possession of the Königgrätz high-road from Rosberitz to the " ziegelei," and had even crossed it at some points. In their embrace of the Austrian Army, the two extreme wings of the Prussian Army at Wsestar and at the wood between Problus and Charbusitz had approached each other to within little more than a mile; the cross fire of their artillery swept the plain round Rosnitz and Briza, which was still covered by the enemy's masses.

The 42 guns of the Ist Corps d'Armée had come into action on the heights of Chlum, where the Crown Prince arrived with the main body of the Corps, the advanced guard of the corps was assembling to the south of Rosberitz. The 1st Division of Guards was being re-formed eastward of Wsestar. At the same time General Von Clausewitz was already descending the heights with the 2nd Division, and advancing in the direction of the north-east corner of the Charbusitz wood.

Further to the rear there were following in the direction of Rosberitz: Major-General Von Leon, with the Reserve of the 2nd Division of Guards, the Reserve Infantry of the Ist Corps d'Armée, and General Von Steinmetz with the Vth Corps, the latter preceded by General Wnuck's Cavalry Brigade.

The Cavalry combat at Langenhof and Stresetitz had only delayed the general advance of the army for a short time. The course of this action, however, and the obstinate *mêlées*, in which the regiments had been involved and mingled together, precluded all possibility of General Hann's Division following immediately in pursuit of the enemy as one compact body of Cavalry, and to have advanced otherwise than in perfect order would have been of no avail.

Even all endeavours of General Alvensleben's Division to take some share in the day's fight only resulted in the detachments coming one after another, and singly on the field. As soon as possible the General advanced with the two regiments of Guard Lancers of General Rheinbaben's Brigade, followed by the rapidly re-formed 1st Guard Dragoon Regiment, by Lieutenant-

Colonel Prince Hohenlohe with two and a half squadrons of his regiment, and by the 6th Lancers, but still did not succeed in overtaking the enemy's Infantry.

Further results could for the present only be obtained by the Artillery, the more so because the enemy had succeeded in forming a formidable line of Artillery near Rosnitz, even though this only lasted for a short time.

As soon, therefore, as the Austrian Cavalry had left the field, Prince Frederick Charles ordered the advance of a large force of Artillery, to silence these Austrian batteries at Rosnitz, which were covering the retreat of their army. The batteries of Captains Griess Von der Goltz, and Munck advanced on the left wing, they were followed, first by Lieutenant-Colonel Von Ramm with the two 6-pounder batteries of the Brandenburg Reserve Artillery, and the 4th 12-pounder Battery of the 6th Division, and then by the Horse Artillery Batteries of Captains Gayl and Ekensteen. On the right wing Colonel Puttkamer brought up two batteries of the 3rd Division, and Captain Von der Dollen's Battery of the Reserve, which was followed by Captain Hirschberg's Battery of the 6th Division. Lieutenant-Colonel Von Scherbening continued the fire of his 36 rifled guns from a position between Langenhof and Rosberitz, so that the enemy's artillery, being encircled on all sides, was obliged to give up its position at Rosnitz also.

Part of the foremost line of Prussian Infantry, Colonel Von Sandrart with the two battalions of the 9th Regiment, and the 5th Company of 21st Regiment, advanced on Rosnitz; Major-General Bose took the direction of a copse south-eastward of the village, the 1st and 2nd Battalions of the 35th, and the 2nd Battalion of the 12th Regiment followed also in the same direction.

Even now already, detachments of the 2nd Army unavoidably became mingled with those of the 1st Army, for, as long as the foremost troops were engaged with the enemy, those behind them followed in the same direction. If the advance were continued still further, every step must increase the confusion, by entangling the columns with those of the Army of the Elbe also.

Although the point of junction of the three Prussian Armies lay four miles and a half behind the front of the original Austrian position, still the enemy was already driven back beyond it, when the concentric advance of the armies brought them to the spot. A further advance from here could only be a movement towards the front (ein frontales Vorgehen), bringing the left wing within the sphere of action of the fortress of Königgrätz, whilst the Army of the Elbe on the right was not yet in a position to take an immediate and active part in the operations. On this wing General Von Etzel had led forward the only part of his division which was immediately at hand, Colonel Von Senden's weak brigade, by way of Jehlitz, and had reached Ober-Prim at 5 o'clock. He was here informed 5 P.M.

by His Majesty's Aide-de-Camp, Colonel Von Stiehle, of the general state of affairs, and that the heights in his front were occupied by the enemy's artillery, whereupon he ordered Captain Bastian's Battery to take up a position, and requested the Reserve Artillery of the VIIIth Corps, which was still further to the rear, to support the advance of his Infantry. The situation not being quite clear, General Von Herwarth had for the present held back the Fusilier Brigade of the 16th Division as soon as it had passed Nechanitz, as his sole available reserve. For the moment, therefore, the Army of the Elbe could not be expected to take any important active part in the operations.

Far more disastrous for the enemy was the continued advance of Lieutenant-General Von Zastrow's Division, whose two brigades were pressing irresistibly onwards against Rosnitz and Briza. The former village was resolutely defended, but was nevertheless taken by the troops which had been already engaged at Wsestar, in particular by the 8th and 11th Companies, and two sub-divisions of the 1st Battalion of the 51st Regiment, and the 9th Company of the 10th Regiment. Some of the Prussian detachments advanced along the east side of the village and intercepted the retreat of the Austrian garrison, of whom 13 officers and 6—700 men were taken prisoners; a battery planted on the slope eastward of the village was compelled to abandon two guns by the fire of the skirmishing division of the 5th Company of the 10th Regiment. In the meantime the 1st Battalion of the 51st Regiment, followed by the 1st Battalion of the 38th Regiment, had advanced against the south-east corner of Rosnitz, and the skirmishers of the half-battalion, Von Haine, captured a gun just as it was driving off. They were immediately afterwards attacked by several squadrons of Cuirassiers which they repulsed in company with the 9th Company of the 10th Regiment. The six other companies of the 51st Regiment advanced to the west of Rosnitz, as far as the height beyond the village, from whence they established communications with those detachments of the Army of the Elbe which occupied the north-east corner of the Bor wood.

Parts of General Hauenfeldt's Brigade had advanced towards Briza, of which the 2nd Battalion of the 10th Regiment now proceeded to attack the north-west, the 2nd Battalion of the 50th Regiment the west skirts of the village. The companies were formed in line of columns, with skirmishers in the intervals, and entered the village at the first onset, skirmishers of the 8th Company dashing at a battery which was still firing at the north-east entrance of the village and capturing two guns. The other guns fled along the east side of the village, and fell into the hands of other skirmishing parties which had already advanced thus far. Lieut. Ehrenkreuz, of the 50th Regiment, also captured two guns in the act of driving off at the west side of the village.

All detachments pressed forward to the south side of the

village, where they resumed their file-fire upon the dense crowds of all arms that were streaming to the rear.

The three Fusilier Companies of the 10th Regiment had advanced from the "ziegelei" and followed the attacking troops. The 10th and 11th Companies joined the right wing of the 2nd Battalion of the 50th Regiment, and increased its line of fire, in doing which they had an opportunity of capturing two guns and some wagons from a battery which was posted about 500 paces off Briza; the 12th Company took three guns on the east side of the village.

A few minutes later the 1st Battalion of the 10th Regiment arrived here also. General Von Hanenfeldt was now obliged to halt his brigade and to re-form his troops, whose ranks had got somewhat out of order by these continued village combats, and also to leave a clear range for the batteries, which were now by degrees coming up to Briza. Before, however, the necessary orders reached all detachments, the Fusilier Battalion of the 50th Regiment had already advanced beyond the line on which the other troops were engaged, and had taken possession of seven guns which the enemy had abandoned.

At midday the front line of the Prussian Army had still been above 16 miles long; now that Briza was taken, it was reduced to little more than two miles, the distance from this village to Bor.

The VIth Corps d'Armée had been almost incessantly on the march for the last twelve hours, during which it had been for the last eight hours engaged with the enemy. Rich fruits of victory had been reaped by its reckless and energetic advance. Nearly 5,000 prisoners and 52 guns had fallen into the hands of General Zastrow's Division merely within the last two hours, 36 of which had been taken by assault, for the most part by General Hanenfeldt's Brigade. It was now absolutely necessary that the troops should have some rest.

In the meantime all other detachments of the Ist and IInd Armies which were engaged in the pursuit of the enemy had also uninterruptedly continued their advance. The three batteries of General Clausewitz's Division, and the foremost batteries of the Ist Army unlimbered southward of Rosnitz and recommenced their fire. By this time, however, the Austrians had succeeded in assembling a considerable number of batteries and opposed a powerful line of artillery, which reached from Stösser, past Freihofen and Ziegelschlag, as far as Plotist, to the Prussian pursuit, which could now only be continued in the front.

The fire of these batteries was all the more effective, because the ground slopes gradually and regularly from the heights of Rosnitz and Charbusitz down to the valley of the Elbe; all troops descending the face of the hill were plainly visible and afforded admirable marks to the Austrian Artillery, which was itself posted among the gardens of the numerous farm buildings, and therefore scarcely to be seen.

For this reason the greater part of the Prussian Infantry took the direction of the wood between Problus and Charbusitz where the nearest detachments of the Army of the Elbe were stationed.

After meeting the Crown Prince near Chlum, Prince Frederick Charles rode on to the heights of Rosnitz.

At Chlum the Crown Prince ordered General Von Steinmetz to continue the pursuit with the Vth Corps d'Armée. These orders reached the corps during its advance, about 6 o'clock, when it was on a line with Rosberitz. Similar orders had been previously sent to General Von Hartmann, but had not been received by him ; he followed the movements of the Vth Corps of his own accord with the Light Brigade, the only available part of his division.

We left the 16th Division near Ober-Prim, where General Von Etzel covered his flanks by throwing ten companies into the two woods on his right and left.

Captain Bastian's Battery had opened fire in a position westward of Charbusitz, from whence the flashes of the enemy's guns in the low foreground were visible.

Columns of the enemy's Infantry were seen retreating eastward of Stösser ; considerable bodies of Cavalry between this village and the wood of Stezirek. Somewhat later the Reserve Artillery of the Prussian VIIIth Corps came up, and four rifled batteries came into action on the left of Captain Bastian's battery. As Captain Theiler's 12-pounder battery was also engaged at this spot, there was no room for placing the two Horse Artillery batteries of the reserve. These 36 Prussian guns had scarcely begun to play upon the enemy's artillery when they were suddenly enfiladed by shrapnel fire from a battery planted westward of Stösser, which the Cavalry now unmasked. This compelled Captain Bastian to fall back towards Ober-Prim. He was followed, first by the four batteries of the Reserve Artillery, and then by Captain Theiler's Battery. The retreat of the latter batteries was covered by Captain Zglinitzki's Battery, which remained in this position.

General Von Etzel had only $4\frac{3}{4}$ battalions and 3 squadrons at his disposal, and was therefore not able to continue his advance. He was forced to confine himself to taking the necessary precautions against any advance of the enemy. The 12th Company of the 29th Regiment occupied Stezirek ; the three other companies of the Fusilier Battalion, and the 1st Squadron of the 7th Lancers, were stationed in reserve behind the village. The 2nd Company of the regiment, and the 1st Battalion of the 69th Regiment, occupied the copse between the two large woods. The remainder of the troops at this spot either covered the left flank in the skirts of the Bor wood or were posted behind the copse as reserve.

Batteries of all the different corps now came into action against the enemy's line of artillery, and a fresh artillery combat ensued. As long as it lasted, all troops in the neighbourhood of the foremost line hastened towards the scene of action. The

Prussian batteries began to come into line at 6 o'clock, and took up positions wherever they could find room, from Briza to the north of Charbusitz, then to the west of Klacow and on the heights of Stezirek. In addition to the artillery of the Ist Army, the advance of which has been already mentioned, the following batteries now came into action :—The rifled batteries and the 4th 12-pounder battery of the VIth; five batteries of the Ist Corps; the two rifled batteries of the Reserve, and the 4th 12-pounder battery of the 2nd Division of Guards, and four batteries of the Army of the Elbe.

At half-past 6 the greater part of the Infantry of General Zastrow's Division again started in advance; five battalions of General Hanenfeldt's Brigade, and two battalions of the Brigade Hoffmann, reached Klacow, but found the village already occupied by troops of the Army of the Elbe.

By reason of the direction in which the two wings of the Army advanced, the Army of the Elbe and the IInd Army now crossed each other before the front of the Ist Army. Troops of the former, parts of the 29th and 28th Regiments, advanced as far as Charbusitz, Klacow, and even Ziegelschlag, where Captain Von Quadt captured two guns, whilst the 2nd Battalion of the 4th Regiment, belonging to the latter, entered the wood of Stezirek. The remainder of the 2nd Division took up a position in this wood and in that of Charbusitz.

Major-General Von Barnekow posted the reserve Infantry of the Ist Corps eastward of the latter wood, Major-General Von Loen the reserve of the 2nd Division of Guards on his right, and Major-General Von Pape the Infantry of the advanced guard of the Ist Corps at his rear. The 1st and 2nd Battalions of the 35th Regiment had arrived between Charbusitz and Stezirek; Major-General Von Bose at the south-east skirts of the wood of Bor.

Lieutenant-Colonel Wichmann's Cavalry Brigade, and the advanced guard Cavalry Brigade of the Ist Corps, were westward and north-westward of Klacow. Still larger bodies of Cavalry met at Briza. The 6th Hussars covered the batteries of the VIth Corps; General Von Alvensleben assembled the regiments of his Cavalry Division in this neighbourhood, and the Reserve Cavalry of the Ist Corps and the 6th Regiment of Lancers arrived here also, as well as the regiments of Duke William's Cavalry Brigade. Prince Hohenlohe had already advanced towards Plotist with the $2\frac{1}{2}$ squadrons of the 11th Lancers. General Von Hartmann had brought up the Light Brigade of his Cavalry Division to the neighbourhood of Briza by about 7 o'clock. The Cuirassier and Landwehr brigades were too much fatigued by their long march to proceed further than Rosberitz.

General Alvensleben's Division and the two brigades of the Ist Corps made several attempts to advance still further in the direction of Stösser, but were prevented by the shells and grape of the numerous Austrian artillery, which now covered the retreat of its own army, after having for so long retarded the advance of its adversaries.

The Heavy Cavalry Brigade of the Guards was at Rosnitz, where also the regiments of Count Groeben's Brigade were again united.

After the Cavalry combat at Langenhof His Majesty the King advanced with the foremost troops of the 1st Army, and was for some time exposed to the enemy's artillery fire at the south-east corner of Charbusitz wood.

At half-past 6 o'clock the enemy's Infantry had almost entirely diappeared, and the fire of his artillery began to diminish perceptibly. We have already heard upon what a very small space the Prussian troops were crowded and mingled together, the natural consequence of concentric attacks, the successful results of which are obtained on and not beyond the battle-field. This success had been attained. The Elbe formed a considerable barrier to any further immediate pursuit. As soon as the bridges over the river were once reached by the enemy—to whom moreover the fortress of Königgrätz, which commands so large a tract of the surrounding country, afforded a perfectly secure place of crossing—the pursuers were obliged to make a *détour* by way of Pardubitz.

The strength of the Prussian troops, the greater part of whom had started during the night, was in the highest degree exhausted. The day, which was to have afforded them the rest which they stood so much in need of, had become a day of battle. They had marched as far as 16 miles before the action commenced, many of them had been 19 hours on the march, and 10 hours engaged with the enemy. None of them had been able to cook their rations, the horses had not been fed, and very few of the men had provisions with them.

Added to this it required time to re-establish the formation of the different corps, divisions, and larger bodies of troops; a whole day's march was necessary to separate the different armies; this could only be effected the day after the battle.

Under these circumstances, as soon as officers of the different head-quarters were collected together, which was no easy task, the following orders were issued:—

" To-morrow will be in general a day of rest; only
" such marches will be made as are necessary for the
" comfort and the re-formation of the troops. Outposts
" will be thrown out towards Josephstadt by the IInd
" Army, towards Königgrätz by the 1st Army, and the
" troops of General of Infantry Von Herwarth will, as
" far as is possible, carry out the pursuit of the enemy,
" the greater part of whom had retreated in the direction
" of Pardubitz. The division of Guard Landwehr will
" be sent forward in the direction of Chlumetz.

(Signed)      " VON MOLTKE."
" *Near Königgrätz, the 3rd of July,* 1866,
"  $6\frac{1}{2}$  *p.m.*"

About 8 o'clock General Von Steinmetz had advanced as far as Klacow with the Vth Corps, which had been joined by General Von Hartmann with the light brigade of his Cavalry Division. Lieut.-General Von Kirchbach was on the point of pushing forward an advanced guard on Stösser, when the above-mentioned orders reached the corps from His Majesty's head-quarters, in consequence of which the plan of advancing still further was relinquished. The Corps had been on the march for 12 hours without break.

The positions of the other detachments of the armies were as follows:—

## Army of the Elbe.

The 15th Division, followed by the Fusilier Brigade of the 16th Division, had come close up behind Colonel Senden's Brigade. The two brigades of the 14th Division remained at Bor, and at the wood south-eastward of Problus. The advance guard of the Army of the Elbe was assembling at Ober-Prim. General Kotze's Cavalry Brigade had joined the 27th Brigade at Problus.

## 1st Army.

One brigade of the 3rd Division at Bor, the other at Problus. General Von der Goltz's Cavalry Brigade was with the latter.

The 5th Division had halted north-westward of the Bor farm. General Von Manstein was engaged in rallying the 12th and four battalions of the 11th Brigade further to the rear. Those troops of the 8th Division which Major-General Von Schmidt had led forward, and those which Lieut.-Colonel Von Valentini had assembled at the Bistritz, remained between Lipa and Langenhof. The 4th Division was behind the latter village. General Von Fransecky's Division was on the heights of Chlum.

## IInd Army.

The main body and advanced guard of the 2nd Division of Guards were assembled southward of Langenhof. The 1st Division of Guards was in front of them, westward of Wsestar. The Heavy Cavalry Brigade of the Guards (Major-General Prince Albrecht, junior) had advanced as far as the wood north-westward of Charbusitz. Lieut.-General Von Prondzynski had assembled his division at Sweti, in support of General Zastrow's advance, as early as 5 o'clock. Lochenitz and Predmeritz were occupied by two companies.

When the King left the Roskos-Berg he rode rapidly over the battle-field, where at first only dead and wounded were to be seen. The guns which had been abandoned by the enemy were either damaged or else Artillerymen and teams had been struck down and lay beside them. All this made the impression of an orderly retreat after a sanguinary combat.

On proceeding further the increasing quantity of knapsacks, czakos, and even uniform coats which the enemy had thrown away, as well as numerous side-arms and muskets lying about in all directions, bore evidence to a serious degree of disorder among the ranks of the Austrian Infantry. Still, the behaviour of the Cavalry and the well-sustained fire of the powerful line of Artillery at Placitz and Kuklena proved that part at least of the hostile army still retained its full power of resistance.

It is true that affairs behind this line of Artillery bore a very different aspect. At first the corps had for the most part taken the direction of the bridges northward of Königgrätz, but were prevented from reaching them by the advance of the Pussian extreme left wing. This caused the different bodies of troops to become promiscuously and confusedly mingled together. The flying Cavalry, shells bursting on all sides, still further increased the confusion, which reached its climax when the Commandant of Königgrätz closed the gates of the fortress.

Hundreds of wagons, either overturned or thrust off from the high-road, riderless horses and confused crowds of men trying to escape across the inundated environs of the fortress and the river, many of them up to their necks in water; this spectacle of wildest flight and utter rout, immediately before the gates of Königgrätz, was naturally hidden from the view of the pursuing enemy.

Thus, on the evening of the 3rd of July the feeling prevalent in the Prussian Army was that a victory had been gained, the strategical results of which would be of vast importance. It was known, although not to the full extent of the reality, that a very considerable quantity of war material had been captured, that numerous prisoners were taken, but the full extent to which the morale of the Austrian Army had been shaken could not be fully appreciated, either on that or even on the next day.

The IInd and IVth Austrian Corps, and the 2nd Light Cavalry Division, had crossed the Elbe at Lochenitz, Predmeritz, and Placka early in the day, but the bulk of the Army was still crowded together on the banks of the Elbe, in front and southward of Königgrätz. Only part of it succeeded in crossing the river at Placka, or at the bridges further southward.

Königgrätz had always been regarded at the Prussian headquarters as the natural and perfectly safe point of retreat for these masses, but the fortress did not open its gates until 11 o'clock at night, thereby forcing a great part of the Army to take the direction of Pardubitz.

The troops of the Saxon Corps maintained their order amongst this general dissolution. At the first it had retreated towards Placka, but received orders from Feldzeugmeister Benedek, at 5 o'clock, to cross the Elbe at Opatowitz and Pardubitz, in doing which it was divided into three parts by the mass of flying Austrians. Two battalions, 8 squadrons, and 2 batteries crossed at Placka ; 17 battalions and 2 batteries marched through Königgrätz ; head-quarters of the corps with 1 battalion, 8 squadrons and 6 batteries, together with the Austrian Cavalry Divisions of Generals Edelsheim and Zaitsek, reached Pardubitz after midnight.

During the night the Prussian Army bivouacked on the field as follows :—

*The Army of the Elbe.*—The 16th Division at Stezirek ; the 15th and the advanced guard at Ober-Prim ; the Reserve Artillery between Ober and Nieder-Prim ; the 14th Division at Problus.

*The 1st Army.*—The 3rd Division and General Goltz's Cavalry Brigade at Bor and Problus ; the 5th at Wsestar : the Divisions of Generals Fransecky and Horn at Lipa, Langenhof, and Stresenitz ; the 4th Division at the Sadowa wood ; the 6th at the Roskos-Berg. The Reserve Artillery marched back to Klenitz ; General Hann's Division of the Cavalry Corps remained at Rosnitz ; the Division of General Von Alvensleben went back to Nechanitz.

*The IInd Army.*—The Ist Corps on the west side, the Vth Corps southward of Rosnitz ; the 6th Corps at Briza and Sweti ; the Corps of Guards between Wsestar and Langenhof ; General Hartmann's Cavalry Division, with its Light Brigade at Briza, its main body at Rosberitz.

The outposts held the line Techlowitz, Stösser, Freihöfen, Plotist. The battalion of the 12th Division which had been left in front of Josephstadt, and one squadron, rejoined the VIth Corps during the night.

When His Majesty the King left his station at the corner of the wood eastward of Bor he visited different parts of the battlefield for the purpose of greeting the troops of his Army. With expressions of the utmost joy the latter welcomed their Sovereign, who had shared hunger and thirst, exertions and dangers of the day, with the humblest of his soldiers. The evening was far advanced when the King met the Crown Prince on the meadows north-eastward of Problus, after which he went back to Horsitz, where Prince Frederick Charles also established his head-quarters. The General Staff of the King returned to Gitschin, where the bureaus had remained during the battle, and went with them to Horsitz in the course of the morning of the 4th of July.

The Crown Prince went to Horenowes, General Von Herwarth to Problus.

Details of the losses of both Armies in the battle of Königgrätz are given in the Appendix.* Those of the Prussian Army amounted on the whole to 359 officers and 8,794 men, of which the Ist Army lost 206 officers and 5,054 men, the IInd Army 82 officers and 2,183 men, and the Army of the Elbe 71 officers and 1,557 men. The long-lasting defensive of the Ist Army

* *Vide* Appendix XXIII.

had thus cost nearly twice as great a sacrifice as the offensive of the two flank armies.

The total losses of the Austrian-Saxon Army consisted of 44,200 officers and men, of whom 19,800 were prisoners.

One hundred and sixty Austrian and one Saxon gun fell into the hands of the victors as trophies of the day. We have already mentioned in the course of this narrative in what an honourable manner most of them were lost. Five stands of colours were captured in the course of the action; the tassels of two other flags were brought in the next day. The amount of booty in the form of different kinds of war material was uncommonly large. Several thousand muskets, many hundreds of ammunition and baggage wagons and ambulances, as well as a pontoon train, were found next day on or in the neighbourhood of the battle-field.

## The 4th of July.

During the forenoon of the 4th of July, the Prussians were occupied in separating the corps and detachments of the different armies. Time and opportunity were afforded the troops for repairing damages and making all those arrangements which a battle of so unusually large a scale necessarily demands. The wounded and prisoners—the number of the latter exceeded all expectations—had to be provided for, and the battle-field cleared up; the parks and trains, which were a day's march to the rear, had to be brought up to the front, and the expended ammunition of the troops replaced.

The following General Orders were issued to the Army :—

" Soldiers of my Armies assembled in Bohemia.

" The timely union of all our forces in Bohemia has " been effected by a series of bloody and glorious en- " gagements. From all reports that have been sent to " me I have seen that this has been achieved by the " leadership of my Generals and the devotion and " bravery of all the troops. Immediately afterwards, " and notwithstanding the many exertions and privations " of the preceding days, the army under my command " attacked the enemy in his strong positions near König- " grätz, carried them after a severe struggle, and gained " a glorious victory. Many trophies, above a hundred " captured cannon, thousands of prisoners, bear fresh " witness to the bravery and devotion in which the troops " of all arms have vied with each other. The day of " Königgrätz has cost many a sacrifice, but it is a day of " honour for the whole army, which the Fatherland " regards with pride and admiration. I know that hence- " forward also you will fulfil my expectations, for Prussian " troops know at all times how to combine with bravery

" that discipline without which no great success can be
" obtained.

(Signed)   " WILHELM."
" *Haad-quarters, Horsitz, July 4th, 1866.*"

Early in the morning General Herwarth set his troops in
motion for the purpose of leading them out of the range of the
other armies.   General Schoeler's advanced guard reached
Lhota-unter-Libcan.*   General Canstein's Division Libisan, on
the Königgrätz-Bohdanetz high-road; the divisions of Generals
Etzel and Count Muenster, Urbanitz, and Libcan, on the
Chlumetz-Könnigrätz road.   Head-quarters of the Army of the
Elbe were moved to the latter place.   As soon as the Guard
Landwehr Division reported its arrival at Nechanitz it was sent
forward by the Commander-in-Chief of the 1st Army as far as
Kasalitz and Bela, on the road to Prelouc.

The latter division fell in with some hostile patrols in front
of Bela which retreated to Bukowka; nothing else was to be
seen of the enemy.   On the other hand, however, the leading
troops found ample proofs of hasty flight in the shape of
abandoned war material; ambulances, provision and ammunition
wagons were found in great numbers, as well as a pontoon
train and even several guns.

These traces were doubly visible before the gates of Königgrätz.   Lieutenant Von Wrangel of the Guard Hussars, who
was sent forward with 30 men to reconnoitre, found the high-
road as far as the faubourg of the town blocked up with
hundreds of wagons, besides several which were overturned
by the roadside; among the latter were about 20 guns.   An
advanced post of Austrian Infantry of about 12 men surrendered without resistance.   All signs proved the total dis-
organization of the troops which had retreated in this direction.
Under these circumstances this officer of his own accord undertook to approach the fortress, and to summon the commandant
to surrender.   At 3 in the afternoon the VIth Prussian Corps was
concentrated eastward of Briza, in order to give greater weight
to the negotiations which Major Von der Burg conducted by
order of the Crown Prince.   Austrian statements affirm that the
commandant of the fortress only seemingly entered into them
in order to gain time.   It was in the Prussian interest to grant
a truce at this spot, making it possible to march on Pardubitz
without either paying attention to the fortress or being disturbed by it.   This was done, but the negotiations produced no
other results.

Captain Mischke was sent from head-quarters of the IInd
Army with a flag of truce to Josephstadt also, but could not
reach his destination, being met and fired at by Austrian Infantry
near Holohlaw.   All his attempts to be recognized as flag of
truce were of no avail, and he was obliged to retire after his

---

* Lhota-unter-Libcan is a small village eastward of the Königgrätz-Chlumetz
road.   Lhota is an uncommonly frequent name of places in this part of Bohemia.

own and his trumpeter's horse had been wounded. In the course of the afternoon the 3rd Brigade of Guard Infantry and the Regiment of Guard Hussars were sent with two batteries, towards this fortress and marched as far as Racitz.

At 4 in the afternoon General Hartmann's Cavalry Division marched to Opatowitz and pushed forward advanced posts to Bohdanec and Pardubitz. They saw nothing of the enemy on this march but stragglers and abandoned war material.

In the ensuing night these detachments reported that they had been fired at from Pardubitz, that the bridge over the Elbe at this place was in flames, and that the planks had been removed from the railway bridge.

Prince Frederic Charles gave orders for concentrating the 1st Army further forward on the afternoon of the 4th. In consequence, the troops first cooked their rations in their present positions, and then moved to the district between Nechanitz Lhota-unter-Libcan, and Praskaska. Orders had been at the same time given for the Army of the Elbe to occupy the country northward of the Zdanitz-Opatowitz canal, but they were not carried out, on account of the movement which this army had already made in the course of the morning. This caused some confusion in quartering the men in some of the villages.

The Austrian army continued its retreat in several columns, as they had been formed by the different places at which the troops had crossed the Elbe on the evening of the battle.

The right flank column—the IInd Corps and the 2nd Light Cavalry Division—arrived at Hohenbrück with its main body during the night of the 3rd ; its rear guard—Brigade Henriquez —reached Swinarek. This column continued its march on the morning of the 4th, the main body to Kosteletz on the Adler, the rear guard to Tinist.

The IVth Corps remained at New Königgrätz, and between this place and Bohrohradek.

The centre column or main body of the army, which consisted of the Ist, IIIrd, and VIth Corps, the greater part of the Saxons and the Reserve Artillery of the army, and which was accompanied by the general head-quarters took the direction of Hohenmauth ; part of it remained at Holitz.

The left flank column—part of the Saxons, the VIIIth and Xth Corps, and the bulk of the Cavalry—had retreated on the right bank of the Elbe to Pardubitz, where its last detachments crossed the river between 6 and 7 A.M. of the 4th. The last troops evacuated the town during the night of the 4th, part of them marching by way of Dasitz to the Hohenmauth road, others, among whom were those Saxons who were with this column, taking the direction of Chrudim, Chrast, and Krouna to Zwittau.

The Austrian Commander-in-Chief now had to decide in which direction the retreat of his army was to be continued. He had the alternative of falling back on Vienna or on Olmütz.

In its present state the army could not pursue its march in

the former direction ; it would have been totally disorganized on this march of 135 miles. It was imperative first to rally the troops somewhere or other, in which case the start which they had gained upon the Prussian Army would be lost, and the latter would be again at their heels. On this route the Danube was the first line behind which any lasting stand could be made, and the whole country northwards of this river would fall into the hands of the enemy. In this case direct communication with the victorious Army of the South in Italy would certainly be secured, and this army alone, but not the filling up of the ranks with depôt troops, could counterbalance the superiority which was now unquestionably proved to be on the side of the enemy. At this period, however, Austria could scarcely be certain that the conduct of the war on the part of Italy would permit her to move the bulk of her army on the Mincio to the north of the Danube.

The entrenched camp at Olmütz was only half as far off, and afforded a safe place of refuge, which could be reached without danger of the army being totally dispersed, and where the latter could be rallied and could be restored to a fit state for again taking the field.

A force of about 100,000 men in this flank position would be a great obstacle to the enemy's march on Vienna, and would either protect a considerably tract of Austrian territory, or compel the enemy to divide his forces.

It must not, however, be overlooked that no flank position at all can be of any effect unless there is the possibility of undertaking offensive operations from it.

Whether or no the *morale* of the Austrian Army warranted the hope of being soon again able to assume the offensive, and whether Olmütz afforded the means of putting the troops in a state to do so, by giving them safety, rest, food, arms, and ammunition, were weighty questions, which had to be taken into consideration, and which must necessarily influence the decision of the Commander-in-Chief. According to all accounts, the place was in a very deficient state, and was so equipped as to be scarcely capable of defending itself, still less of repairing the losses of a beaten army.

Notwithstanding, Feldzeugmeister Benedek decided upon retreating to Olmütz.

He only devoted one corps d'armée and the bulk of his cavalry to the protection of Vienna. The aid of the railway was made use of for the transport of the former ; the latter was only to fall back towards the Danube in proportion as the enemy advanced.

This afforded the advantage of keeping continually acquainted with the enemy's movements in this direction, besides which, it may not have been possible to provide shelter and forage for so large a number of horses within the entrenched camp at Olmütz. At the same time, however, the latter lost a great part of its offensive power by being deprived of the cavalry.

x

In consequence of this determination, orders were issued in the course of the 4th of July, prescribing the following routes for the retreat of the different columns of the Austrian Army :—

| Date. | 1st Column.<br>Xth Corps d'Armée. | 2nd Column.<br>General Head-Quarters, Ist, IIIrd, and VIth Corps d'Armée, Reserve Artillery of the Army. | 3rd Column. | | 4th Column.<br>VIIIth Corps d'Armée, Saxon Corps. |
|---|---|---|---|---|---|
| | | | IInd Corps d'Armée. 2nd Light Cavalry Division. | IVth Corps d'Armée, Brigade Rothkirch (from Geiersberg). | |
| July.<br>4 | .. | Hohenmauth. | Tinist. | Neu-König-grätz. | .. |
| 5 | .. | Leitomischl. | Wamberg. | Borohradek. | .. |
| 6 | .. | Zwittau. | Wildenschwerdt. | | |
| 7 | Brüsau. | Mährisch-Trübau. | Landskron. Hohenstadt. | | Zwittau. Mährisch-Trübau. |
| 8 | Lettowitz. | Gewitsch. | | | |
| 9 | .. | Konitz. | Müglitz. | | Müglitz. |
| 10 | } Per railway | Olmütz. | Littau. | | Littau. |
| 11 | } to Vienna. | Olmütz. | Olmütz. | | Olmütz. |

AMMUNITION PARK OF THE ARMY.

| 4th of July | .. | Leitomischl. | 6th of July | .. | .. | Konitz. |
|---|---|---|---|---|---|---|
| 5th „ | .. | Mährisch-Trübau. | 7th „ | .. | .. | Olmütz. |

(Signed) BENEDEK.

With the exception of the Reserve Cavalry and the Xth Corps, the army was thus marching on only two roads, viz., three corps of Infantry and the Artillery by Hohenmauth; four corps of Infantry and a Light Cavalry division by Wildenschwerdt.

On the latter route the VIIIth Corps and the Saxons were a day's march behind the columns, and formed the rear guard of the army.

These orders were carried out with some trifling deviations.

The following general instructions were given to the 1st Light and the three Reserve Cavalry Divisions under Prince Holstein, as a guide for their movements :—

| 1st Reserve Division. | 2nd Reserve Division. | 3rd Reserve Division. | 1st Light Division. |
|---|---|---|---|
| Will remain at Policka on the 7th of July. The 8th of July, Brüsau, and will then continue its march by way of Zwitawka, Czernahora, Lipuwka, Brünn. | The 7th of July, Büstrau, and will continue its march by way of Oels, Nedweditz, Tischnowitz, Biliska, Rossitz. | The 7th of July, Ingrowitz, and will continue its march by way of Rossack, Straskau, Gross Bettosch, Namiescht. | The 7th of July, Saar; the 8th Radostin; the 9th Gross-Meseritsch, and will continue its march by way of Trebitsch, Jarmeritz, Mährisch-Budwitz. |

The further movements in the direction of Vienna will be regulated by the orders of His Serene Highness Lieutenant Field-Marshal Prince Holstein.

(Signed)      BENEDEK.

The Feldzeugmeister could not possibly deceive himself as to the state of his troops. It must have been of paramount importance to him not to be disturbed by the enemy, at least during the next few days.

On the afternoon of the 4th July, Lieutenant Field-Marshal Baron Von Gablenz, an officer who was well known from the Danish campaign, and highly esteemed for his distinguished bravery, arrived at the King's head-quarters at Horsitz.

He proposed a cessation of hostilities which were, as he said, now useless, as the fate of the campaign was already decided. The answer to these proposals was, that Prussia was perfectly ready to negotiate a definitive peace on a political basis, but that a standstill in the military operations was too much to expect of the Prussian Army.

A brief cessation of hostilities, if it did not hinder the movement of the troops, seemed indeed acceptable, as there was now no immediate hope of overtaking the Austrian Army. How the Prussian Army was to be supplied during its further progress was a question which required serious consideration. Supplies could not be brought up per railway, because the lines were barred by the Elbe fortresses; it was, therefore, hinted to General Gablenz, that Prussia might possibly be willing to agree to a three days' truce on the condition of Theresienstadt, Joseph-stadt, and Königgrätz being given up.

General Gablenz, who could not produce even a military, much less a political authority to enter into any negotiations, was obliged to content himself with this answer, and was escorted back Königgrätz late in the evening.

In order to continue the pursuit of the enemy, it was necessary that the left wing of the Prussian Army should march on Pardubitz, whilst the right wing wheeled round this place. The only means of lessening the detour with this movement involved was, by making the arc of the circle, which the right wing had to describe, as small as possible. This would, it is true, again increase the depth of the marching columns by diminishing the number of roads, the question was, therefore, where to find the proper medium.

During the afternoon reports came in from the different armies, stating what movements they had carried out in the course of the day, and at half-past 8 P.M. orders were issued that the IInd Army was to march on Pardubitz-Chrudim, the Ist on Bela-Prelouc, the Army of the Elbe on Chlumetz; the latter army was placed under the direct command of His Majesty the King. It now became necessary to guard the communications of the IInd Army with Silesia, by posting detachments of sufficient strength in front of Königgrätz and Josephstadt, not only on the right, but also on the left bank of the Elbe, as it would probably soon be possible to draw the supplies of the army

X 2

from the county of Glatz. The communications of the Ist Army and the Army of the Elbe by way of Turnau had also to be secured by occupying their line of march. The Division of Guard Landwehr was moved to the right towards Podiebrad, to cover the right flank of the army against any hostile forces that might be at Prague.

An advanced guard with an increased force of Cavalry was to follow the enemy in the direction of Leitomischl, in order to discover his line of retreat. The resistance met with by this advanced guard would determine, how far the troops of the two foremost armies could be allowed to take up their quarters in cantonments.

## The 5th of July.

Feldzeugmeister Benedek arrived at Zwittau on the 5th of July. The rear guard of his right flank column reached the line Wamberg-Borohradek, his centre column Leitomischl—its last troops Hohenmauth—his left flank column Krouna.

The main body of the army adhered to the above-mentioned line of march, but some detachments were still as far back as Wamberg-Borohradek, whereas crowds of stragglers and military train had hurried on far ahead of the columns.

The Prussian Cavalry Division of General Hartmann was the first to ford the Elbe near Pardubitz. A detachment had previously crossed the river at Dric, repaired the bridge at Nemcitz, and reached Pardubitz on the left bank. The horse-artillery batteries then marched by way of Nemcitz, as the river was too high to permit of their crossing by the fords.

The advanced troops which were thrown forward on the Holitz, Dasitz, and Chrudim roads captured numbers of stragglers, but otherwise only met some weak Cavalry detachments, which avoided any engagement. The only considerable body of the enemy, reported to have been seen, was at Holitz, but even this was found to have left, when a second detachment was pushed forward to reconnoitre the same evening.

General Hartmann instantly made arrangements for repairing the bridges at Pardubitz. A great quantity of stores fell into the hands of the Cavalry division at this place.

Major-General Von Wnuck then crossed likewise by a ford close to Pardubitz with the 1st Lancers and the 4th Dragoons. A Dragoon squadron, which was pushed on ahead of the brigade, met a squadron of hostile Hussars southward of Chrudim, but the latter evaded any encounter. The brigade bivouacked southward of Pardubitz.

The latter town was occupied by an advanced guard of the Vth Corps d'Armée, which had been formed under command of General Von Kirchbach out of all the Fusilier Battalions of the corps and two batteries. A pontoon train was now brought up, ann two bridges were immediately thrown over the river on either side of the former crossing.

The main-body of the Vth Corps reached Hradist, and bivouacked near this place. The Ist Corps marched to Ceperka, the Corps of Guards to Opatowitz, where it was rejoined in the course of the night by the 3rd Brigade of Guard Infantry, which had been relieved in its position in front of Josephstadt by the 12th Division. The Crown Prince established his head-quarters at Opatowitz.

As the IInd Army could only advance by one road, the different times of starting were distinctly fixed for each corps; all trains were united under one joint command at Stösser.

The 6th, 5th, and 7th Divisions of the Ist Army reached the Elbe at Prelouc, Melitz, and Lan; head-quarters of the army marched to the former place, and advanced guards were thrown forward on the left bank of the Elbe over the bridges which had not been destroyed at these spots.

In second line the Cavalry Corps marched to Breh, the 8th Division to Bohdanec. In third line the 3rd and 4th Divisions to Bela, the Reserve Artillery of the different corps to Bukowka, Wischnowitz, Praw, and Dobrenitz.

The Army of the Elbe also pushed its advanced guard up to and over the Elbe, to Kladrub and Recan, and General Canstein's division was detached to Wapno and Sobrc to keep up communication with the Ist Army. General Count Münster's division reached Zitzelitz, the Reserve Artillery Lucitz; head-quarters of the army and General Etzel's division moved to Chlumetz; General Rosenberg's division marched to Dlahopolsko.

The heads of the Prussian Army had thus reached the course of the Elbe from Pardubitz to Kladrub. The ends of the columns had moved up to the line Chlumetz-Opatowitz; the whole army was therefore crowded into a space of about 25 square miles. This circumstance and the continued advance of the army caused very great difficulty in provisioning the troops, and the greatest care was necessary for the security of the lines of communication to the rear.

For this reason the IInd Army left the VIth Corps d'Armée behind for the present, to protect its communications with Silesia, which were daily becoming longer and more vulnerable. At the same time the corps was to clear up the battle-field.

The 12th Division, now only mustering 6 battalions, 4 squadrons, 2 batteries, and 1 company of Pioneers, occupied the villages Ober-Dolzen, Ertina, and Unter-Dolzen in front of Josephstadt, the 11th Division moved up in front of Königgrätz.

Instructions were given to the latter division to test the firmness of the commandant of the fortress by firing on the place with rifled field guns, but not to expose itself to much loss. Four batteries therefore opened fire at a distance of 5,000 paces, and set some houses in the faubourg on fire. The guns of the fortress kept up a lively but ineffectual fire in return.

The country afforded no cover to get within nearer range of the fortress, and there seemed no chance of obtaining any material advantage; the batteries therefore ceased firing at half-past 7 P.M., and the division bivouacked at Freihöfen. Detachments were pushed forward to the left bank of the Elbe to watch the south-east front of the fortress.

The 1st Army had also left numerous detachments behind, to ensure uninterrupted communication with Turnau, the nearest station to which the railway could be made use of. Only one battalion remained at Horsitz. In addition to the above, the corps were much diminished by the different detachments which were necessary to escort and guard the numerous prisoners.

The field telegraph department, under Colonel Von Chauvin exerted itself to the utmost to perform all that was demanded of it, and succeeded in doing so in the highest degree. Nevertheless many lines which it laid down behind the front of the army were destroyed. All villages in whose neighbourhood this might occur again were threatened with severe reprisals, but the injury was very often done by the troops themselves, in ignorance of the value of the telegraph.

The empty triumph of entering the capital of Bohemia had been as yet disdained, but the moment was now come when it was worth while to devote part of the army to taking possession of so considerable a city as Prague, with its various resources. It was not known whether the enemy had forces at his command to defend the city.

The Army of the Elbe, therefore, received orders on the 5th to despatch General Von Rosenberg's. division in two marches from Podebrad to Prague; to provide against any contingencies, this movement was to be followed at a day's march by sufficient supports of about the strength of a division.

The passages over the Elbe at Elbe-Teinitz and Neu-Kolin were to be occupied, and the railway and its rolling-stock preserved from destruction.

We may here anticipate coming events, and state that General Rosenberg's division was reinforced by two rifled batteries of the 7th Artillery Regiment, and, marching by Sadska and Ober-Pocernitz, reached Prague on the 8th of July, where it found that all Imperial troops and authorities had evacuated the place. Thousands of the inhabitants were assembled at the roadside in expectation of the arrival of the Prussian troops; the Archbishop and the Head Burgomaster came to meet the division, and to consult with its leader. Most of the houses of the town had hoisted the white flag, and General Rosenberg was met at the gate by the remainder of the municipal authorities. The billeting and furnishing rations for the troops was arranged without difficulty by Lieutenant-Colonel Ranisch, the officer who was appointed Commandant of the city. Considerable war and railway material was seized, as well as several millions of cigars in the Sedletzer cigar manufactory. Besides this, the occupation of Prague was of high importance, as the line of railway from Turnau to Pardubitz, which passes the city, could now be rendered practicable.

On the 5th of July, General Von der Mülbe, who was released

from his office as Governor-General of Saxony, likewise received orders to march with General Bentheim's division from Dresden by way of Teplitz to Prague, and to reunite his corps at the latter place.

This division had previously pushed forward detachments to Hof and Teplitz, and from the latter place towards Theresienstadt, in consequence of which some trifling encounters of patrols had taken place. The division started on the 11th, and reached Prague on the 18th of July. The 3rd Landwehr Lancers were the only troops of the Reserve Corps that remained in Saxony at the disposal of General of Infantry Von Schack, who was appointed Governor-General of the kingdom.

## The 6th of July.

The Austrian head-quarters remained on this and until mid-day of next day in Zwittau. The end of the right flank column, at the head of which the IVth Corps had placed itself at Borohradeck, reached Wildenschwerdt; the last troops of the centre column Leitomischl; its main body, Zwittau; the left-flank column Policka; the 1st Light and the 3rd Reserve Cavalry Divisions spread out on a line reaching from Hlinsko (southward of Chrudim) to Policka.

The Cavalry of General Von Hartmann, who was placed under the orders of the Vth. the leading Prussian Corps, started at 4 A.M., and struck the Holitz-Hohenmauth road by way of Dasitz, Litetin, and Wysocka. Nothing was to be seen of the enemy but weak Cavalry patrols, which retreated hastily at all points. As soon as the men had cooked their rations, the division was ordered to advance again along the high-road as far as Neudorf, and to bivouack there. Detachments were pushed forward beyond Hohenmauth towards Leitomischl, and reported the former place to have been evacuated by the enemy, but that trains of the latter were still encamped near Leitomischl. A small detachment which was sent to Chotzen was prevented from advancing any further by a squadron of Haller Hussars.

The 5th Corps followed by way of Sezemitz to Holitz, and bivouacked at this place and at Chwajno; the advanced guard by the side of the high-road southward of Holitz, General Wnuck's brigade at Trauerndorf.

The 1st Corps reached Chrudim, and pushed its advanced guard forward to Slatinau, and its outposts to the line Worel-Skrowad.

The Guards were the last to debouch from Pardubitz; they marched by the Dasitz road, reached Zwiny with the head of the corps, and occupied Pardubitz and Sczenitz with one regiment each.

Head-quarters of the IInd Army moved to Pardubitz, at which the King's head-quarters likewise arrived in the evening from Horsitz. Duke Ernest of Saxe-Coburg-Gotha, who had reached the King's head-quarters on the 3rd of July, now joined those of the Crown Prince.

The Ist Army rested on this day, with the exception of the Cavalry Corps and an advanced Guard, which had been formed the day before. The latter was commanded by Duke William of Meklenburg, and consisted of the 60th Regiment of Infantry, the Fusilier Battalions of the 18th and 48th Regiments, the 4th Rifle Battalion, the 2nd Light Cavalry Brigade (2nd Guard Dragoons, 3rd Hussars and 11th Lancers), and three batteries, viz., the 1st Horse Artillery Battery of the 2nd, the 6th 4-pounder, and 2nd 6-pounder Batteries of the 3rd Artillery Regiments.

The Duke marched in the course of the afternoon to Choltitz, the Cavalry Corps to Zdechowitz, beyond the Elbe.

Count Münster's division of the Army of the Elbe was pushed forward to Neu-Kolin, so as to be in readiness to support General Rosenberg's division, but as news arrived this day already that Prague was evacuated, it did not seem necessary to move the division further westward. General Schoeler's advanced guard marched to Elbe-Teinitz, the other divisions were quartered between Chlumetz and the Elbe.

It was now already evident that the bulk of the Austrian Army was retreating to Olmütz, and His Majesty the King formed the important resolution of following in this direction with only the left flank army, and of leading the two other armies straight to Vienna, in order to bring the campaign to an end in the shortest possible space of time.

It was not intended to undertake the siege of Olmütz, nor was it possible to invest the place completely without causing a very dangerous division of forces. The task of the IInd Army could naturally be only to cover the Ist Army and the Army of the Elbe during their advance on the enemy's capital.

Credit was still given to the Austrian Army for having sufficient intrinsic worth (innern halt) to be able again to assume the offensive if afforded a short time to recover itself in the entrenched camp at Olmütz. In this case the army of the Crown Prince would be greatly outnumbered, and might be obliged to retreat.

If the Austrian Army directed its attack against the two other armies, they must interrupt their advance on Vienna in order to meet it. The issue of the battle of Custozza, however, made it of the utmost importance to reach the Danube before Austria was able to bring up any considerable forces from Italy.

If, on the other hand the line of retreat of the IInd Army led towards Silesia, then the latter would draw off the enemy's forces in this direction, and away from the decisive main operations.

The IInd Army, therefore, had to take up such a position in front of Olmütz as would enable it closely to observe the enemy; if the latter marched to Vienna to follow him, or, if he attacked with decidedly superior numbers, to evade his attack by falling back towards Silesia.

For the present Mährisch Trübau was given as direction for the march of the IInd Army. As soon as communications should be established with Glatz by way of Mittelwalde, the Königinhof route was to be abandoned, and the VIth Corps to leave its positions in front of the small Elbe fortresses and rejoin the army. Pardubitz was, however, to remain occupied until detachments of the Landwehr arrived to relieve its present garrison.

## THE 7TH OF JULY.

It was to be foreseen that the provision trains would not be able to keep up with the army, in case of a rapid advance on Vienna, and that the troops would only be able to provide themselves with food by making requisitions on the spot. The Imperial authorities had received orders everywhere to leave their posts, a measure which no doubt throws many an obstacle in the way of a hostile invasion, but at the same time greatly increases the sufferings of the country itself. The burden of the war must then be borne by the tract alone over which it passes, and which is therefore thus totally ruined. When, as was the case in Bohemia, and afterwards in Moravia, the nobility forsake their country seats, and the greater part of the inhabitants flee with their cattle and their goods into the forests, then the soldiers must unscrupulously take all that is left behind.

In order to render the maintenance of an army possible under such circumstances, and to facilitate the march of the troops by diminishing the length of the columns, it was necessary to change the state of close concentration, in which the army had been ever since the 3rd of July, to one of greater breadth of front.

Orders of the 7th of July assigned the Chrudim-Skuc-Policka and Chrudim-Kreuzberg-Neustadt roads to the Ist Army, the Deutsch-Brod-Iglau road to the Army of the Elbe. On reaching the Moravian frontier the columns were thus 40½ miles apart, but this was at a time when the hostile army was just reaching Olmütz, and could not yet be able to undertake any operations whatever. After crossing the frontier of Moravia the routes again converged towards Vienna.

The end of the right flank columns of the enemy reached Landskron on the 7th; the march over the mountain roads was attended with great difficulty. The heavy train of the IInd Corps d'Armée was sent by way of Reichenau and Alstadt to Müglitz. Brigade Rothkirch assembled in the neighbourhood of Böhmisch-Rothwasser. The centre column marched to Mährisch-Trübau and Zwittau; the left flank column likewise to the latter town, where the whole of the Saxon Corps was again united.

The ammunition park of the army, which had not reached

the army before the battle, but had only got as far as Leito-mischl, arrived at Olmütz on this day.

The last detachments of Prince Holstein's four Cavalry divisions remained on the line Hlinsko-Policka, the main bodies of the different divisions at Saar, Ingrowitz, Policka, and Bistrau.

The Xth Corps reached Brüsau and Lettowitz, and was conveyed to Vienna by rail on this and the following day.

On the Prussian side the IInd Army was the nearest to the enemy. The Vth Corps marched to Hohenmauth, the Guards to Chroustowitz, the Ist Corps by way of Statinan to the neighbourhood of Bela and Luze.

General Steinmetz ordered the Cavalry Division to advance as far as Cerekwitz and Böhmisch-Hermanitz, and then to take up quarters to the rear of this line.

An advanced detachment, which the division pushed forward to Leitomischl, brought back a few hundred Austrian stragglers; other patrols captured a convoy of about 80 head of cattle, an Imperial field-post and a military chest containing about 1,000 dollars. During his march General Hartmann learnt that the greater part of the enemy's forces had passed through Hohen-mauth as early as the 4th and 5th of July in a very disorgan-ized state, and that nothing but Cavalry had followed on the 6th, the last detachment of which had only left the town on the morning of the 7th. At half-past 1 P.M., therefore, the General gave orders for the formation of a special detachment still further forward at Nedosin, consisting of 700 horses and two Horse Artillery guns, under Lieutenaut - Colonel Von Barnekow. The 1st and 5th Cuirassiers and the 10th Hussars gave each 200, the 2nd Hussars 100 of their best horses, and Lieutenant-Colonel Von Barnekow was instructed to follow close upon the heels of the enemy, and to inflict as much damage as possible. This measure was reported to head-quarters of the Vth Corps, and the statement added that the division itself was prepared to make a forced march, and to follow Lieutenant-Colonel Von Barnekow next day.

The detachment of the latter started at half-past 6 P.M. from Nedosin, and arrived in front of Zwittau without meeting with any resistance at half-past 8, just as darkness was setting in. Bivouac fires of the enemy were visible in a wide circle round the town, but no ouposts were thrown out in front of them. The troops encamped here in the foremost line south-westward of the town were the Austrian VIIIth Corps, north-ward of the town the last detachments of the Saxons, two battalions, and four batteries, which had arrived in the course of the afternoon.

Lieutenant-Colonel Barnekow's two guns unlimbered, and disturbed the enemy's camp by throwing a few shells into it. As was discovered afterwards, this caused the greatest con-fusion among the Austrian military train which was parked there, and induced the Saxon detachment to fall back hastily through

Zwittau upon the main body of the corps, which was encamped at Mährisch Hermersdorf, south-eastward of the town. Westward of Zwittau the Prussian detachment came upon a wagon park, which was on the march escorted by Infantry. The combined squadron of the 5th Cuirassiers advanced against it, and a few shots were fired, upon which the escort, consisting of a company of the 4th Battalion of the 4th Regiment (Deutschmeister), which was on its way from Vienna to join the army, was taken prisoners. It did not seem advisable to advance any further, for some divisions of Hussars had been sent forward in the meantime, and had found the town to be occupied in force, one of the Saxon battalions having remained there as garrison.

Lieutenant-Colonel Von Barnekow now formed a line of outposts in front of Zwittau with four divisions of Hussars, but was obliged to give up his position, as Austrian Infantry of the VIIIth Corps came up under cover of the night, from the direction of Stangendorf, and disturbed the vedettes. The detachment retreated with its prisoners—4 officers and 112 men—to behind Mohren, where it bivouacked without fires in a pouring rain. The numerous wagons of the convoy were obliged to be left behind, but the detachment had succeeded in thoroughly alarming the enemy, both of whose corps remained under arms the whole of the wet night, thus adding considerably to the fatigue of the troops who were already well-nigh worn out as it was.

The main body of the Cavalry Division remained at Cerekwitz, the Light Brigade at Böhmisch-Hermanitz. The 4th Squadron of the 2nd Hussars was pushed forward to Sloupnitz.

General Wnuck's Cavalry Brigade of the Vth Corps occupied Chotzen, the advanced guard of the corps Hohenmauth. The main body was quartered on both sides of the high-road, northward of the town, the trains were at Holitz.

The Corps of Guard pushed its advance guard forward as far as Podecel, the remainder of the corps reached Chroustowitz, Hrochow-Teinitz, and Morawan. The trains were brought up to Pardubitz.

The Ist Corps came to Luze and neighbourhood, its advanced guard to Stremositz. Austrian Infantry having been reported as being at Richenburg, a detachment of three battalions and two squadrons was sent there, but found nothing of the enemy, and fell back again towards Luze. At 10 o'clock in the evening Lieutenant Field-Marshal Baron Gablenz again arrived at the latter place with a flag of truce, and proceeded to the Crown Prince's Head-Quarters, which had been transferred to Chroustowitz.

The advanced guard of the Ist Army marched to Bojanow, on the Hermanmestetz-Nassaberg road, without falling in with the enemy. The main-body of the army crossed the Elbe, and reached the Hermanmestetz-Caslau road with its foremost detachments. By the evening the Cavalry Corps was on the extreme right at Sbislaw and Podhoran, on its left in the front line, the 3rd, 5th, 6th, and 7th Divisions, extending from Turkowitz eastward to Morasitz and Rozhowitz; in second line behind the wings of the former, the 4th and 8th Divisions in Urbanitz and Jezboritz. The Reserve Artillery had moved up to Benesawitz, Jedonsow and Jenikowitz. Head-quarters were at Hermanmestetz.

The advanced guard of the Army of the Elbe marched to Czaslau, head-quarters and General Canstein's Division to Neuhof; General Etzel's Division to Schusitz, the Reserve Artillery Elbe-Teinitz. Count Münster's Division halted for the day at Neu-Kolin.

## THE 8TH OF JULY.

On the 8th of July the column which had hitherto been the centre one of the Austrian Army turned off from Mährisch-Trübau, southward to Gewitsch, and the former left flank column took the centre route and marched to Mährisch-Trübau. The Saxon Corps marched to the south of the latter town and proceeded to Türnau. The right flank column was joined by General Rothkirch's Brigade at Hohenstädt.

On the 7th of July, marching orders had been drawn up at head-quarters of the Prussian IInd Army, according to which the three corps were to take up the following positions by the 10th; the Ist Corps at Schirmdorf, the Vth at Böhmisch Trübau, and the Guards at Wildenschwerdt. This was a movement north-eastward, whereas the Austrian Army was leaning to the south-east.

Orders had been sent to the VIth Corps to leave only the 12th Division under General Von Prondzynski (6 battalions, 6 squadrons, and 3 batteries, to which were added 3 Landwehr Battalions, which were despatched to Pardubitz) to cover the communications of the army by masking the fortresses. The remainder of the corps was to march on the 9th to Holitz, the 10th to Chotzen, and the 11th to Rosocha, where it was to take up a position on the left flank of the IInd Army. The 63rd Regiment was likewise to be brought up from Glatz and Neisse, by way of Habelschwerdt as soon as possible.

In accordance with this disposition, General Von Steinmetz gave orders to General Von Hartmann to discontinue his advance on Zwittau, and to march by way of Leitomischl and Schirmdorf to Triebitz. The detachment which was stationed at Mohren was to rejoin the division at the latter place.

As this must naturally cause the division to lose sight of its adversary, whose traces it had just found, General Hartmann instructed Lieutenant-Colonel Von Barnekow to rejoin the division by way of Abstdorf, but added at the same time that he was not to hurry himself in so doing, but was rather to keep the enemy in sight, and to act at his own discretion.

The division marched to Schirmdorf, and despatched the 4th squadron of the 2nd Hussars on ahead from Sloupnitz by way of Böhmisch-Trübau to Landskron, hoping by this means to come up with the enemy on this new line of march. No traces were, however, to be found of the latter eastward of Leitomischl; even the small patrols which had hitherto watched the Prussian advance were now no more seen.

Lieutenant-Colonel Barnekow advanced in the course of the morning with the combined Hussar squadron to reconnoitre Zwittau, but found the ground in front of the town occupied by Infantry and Artillery in force, As soon, therefore, as General Hartmann's orders arrived, he started for Abstdorf, leaving only the Hussars at Nikel and Uberdörff. The detachment pushed forward its advanced guard about 200 paces ahead of its column, and was suddenly and unexpectedly charged by two divisions of Austrian Lancers, just as the main body in Abstdorf was drawing near the northern outlet of the village. The advanced guard was thrown back upon the main body, but the leading files withstood the stock, and repulsed the Lancers, who lost 2 officers wounded, 2 men killed, 3 wounded, and 1 prisoner. The Prussian loss amounted to 1 officer and 6 men wounded.

Lieutenant-Colonel Barnekow now deployed on the side of the village, and advanced against two squadrons of Austrian Lancers which appeared about 1,500 paces off, but which fell back towards Landskron without waiting for an attack.

The Austrian Lancers were part of the 6th Regiment belonging to the IInd Corps, which, as well as the 2nd Light Cavalry Division, was prevented starting from Landskron before midday, because the narrow valley of the Saczawa was crowded with the preceding columns of the IVth Corps. Some brigades of the IInd Corps, and the Light Cavalry Brigade, Westphalen, were still on this side of Landskron in the first part of the afternoon.

General Hartmann was on the point of dismissing the regiments of his division to their new quarters at Schirmdorf, when the news of Lieutenant-Colonel Barnekow's encounter arrived. He now gave orders to the Light Brigade to push on further beyond Trieblitz, and Major-General Von Witzleben sent two divisions of the 1st, two of the 2nd, and the 3rd Squadron of the 2nd Hussars on to Thomigsdorf. On riding through the west part of the village in the direction of Rudelsdorf, the advanced guard division reported hostile skirmishers and their supports to be on ahead among the undulations of the ground, which was covered by high standing corn. Lieutenant-Colonel Von Schauroth turned the head of the column off from the high-road to deploy his two squadrons, but was unexpectedly opened upon by artillery. Six shells bursting amongst his ranks in quick succession caused a loss of 16 men and 11 horses, and produced some confusion in the squadrons which were rallied behind a hillock somewhat to the rear. The Light Brigade then retreated to Sternteich.

In the meantime the 4th Squadron of the Hussars had passed Böhmisch-Thübau, and was in the neighbourhood of Rudelsdorf, to the west of which village it had come upon a bivouac of several battalions and squadrons. Hearing the firing at Thomigsdorf the squadron hastened to the spot, but found that the brigade had retreated already, and rejoined it at Sternteich. A patrol that had been previously sent to the north end of Rudelsdorf was taken prisoner by the Austrians. The enemy followed at some distance with about three squadrons.

By this time it was about 5 o'clock, and the horses suffered much from fatigue; no good view of the surrounding country could be obtained, but considerable forces of all arms of the enemy were known to be in front. Under these circumstances no advantage was to be derived from a further advance of the Cavalry, General Hartmann, therefore, assembled his division in a bivouac westward of Trieblitz, and threw forward outposts beyond the village.

General Wnuck's Cavalry Brigade reached Wildenschwerdt, and pushed a detachment forward towards Landskron. The enemy evacuated the town in the course of the afternoon, leaving the brigade Henriquez at Tattenitz, at the entrance of Saczawa valley, and reached Hohenstadt the same night.

The direction which the IInd Army had taken brought the Vth Corps d'Armée to Sloupnitz, its advanced guard to Privorat, the Ist Corps to Leitomischl, with an advanced guard at Scharhof, on the road to Schirmdorf. The Corps of Guards halted at Hohemmauth, so that it was now behind the two others. Head-quarters of the Army moved to Hohenmauth.

Although but short, the march in pouring rain had been extremely fatiguing, many detachments not reaching their quarters before 5 o'clock in the afternoon.

Duke William's advanced guard of the 1st Army marched to Hlinsko; patrols of the Ist Austrian Light Cavalry Division were met near Nassaberg, and some detachments which were pushed forward from Hlinsko came upon two squadrons of Lichtenstein Hussars at Kreuzberg, who retreated in the direction of Saar, after losing four prisoners.

The Cavalry Division of General Hann advanced to Chotebor, and also met patrols of the enemy. Having thus again felt Prince Holstein's Cavalry, sight was not lost of it during the remainder of the campaign.

The advanced guard was followed by General Manstein's Division to Kamenitz, General Hann by Alvensleben's Division as far as Kohl-Pribram.

The other divisions marched as follows: the 3rd to Bestwin, the 4th to Sec, the 5th to Nassaberg, the 7th to Zumberg, the 8th to Chrast. Head-quarters of the Army were moved to Chrast, the Reserve Artillery of the Corps to Bestwin, Lukawitz and Zajetsitz.

The advanced guard of the Army of the Elbe marched on the Iglau road to Habern, a detachment under the command of

Major-General Count Goltz, consisting of the 7th Hussar Regiment, two guns and 100 Infantry soldiers, the latter on carts, was despatched to Deutsch-Brod, to capture a large convoy of the enemy which was reported to have left for Iglau, and was said to consist of some thousands of wagons.

Head-Quarters of the Army and General Etzel's Division went to Goltsch-Jenikau, General Canstein's Division to Opatowitz, Count Münster to Caslau, and the Reserve Artillery to Chotusitz.

The Crown Prince and General Von Gablenz arrived from Chroustowitz in His Majesty's Head-Quarters at Pardubitz at the same time. The only credentials which the latter bore were "instructions" addressed to himself from the Minister, Count Mensdorff, who had in the meantime arrived at Zwittau.

These instructions authorized the General to conclude an immediate armistice, not only between the Prussian and Austrian-Saxon Armies in Bohemia, but one which should include all other allies of the Empire also, for whom Austria undertook to guarantee that they would respect it. This armistice was not to be for less than eight weeks, nor more than three months; 14 days' warning were to be necessary before re-commencing hostilities. As last as the truce lasted Josephstadt and Königgrätz were to be handed over, under the conditions that the garrisons should leave the places with full military honours, and that all war material and military stores contained there, as well as all buildings belonging to the fortification, should be returned in *statu quo* when peace was concluded.

The remainder of his instructions related to the proposed line of demarcation, and to questions of administration.

If one takes into consideration what the actual and evident position of affairs was at that time, not only in Bohemia, but also in South Germany, it is difficult to imagine how the Austrian Cabinet can ever have so far deluded itself as to believe that Prussia would entertain such propositions. Austria had ceded Venetia to France, and, even though this political move did not produce the results which had probably been anticipated at Vienna, still it afforded the possibility of transferring considerable reinforcements from the southern to the northern theatre of war. A truce which would give time for this to be done could never agree with the interests of Prussia.

Baron Gablenz was not admitted to an audience of the King, but expressing a wish for a written answer, received the following reply:—

*"Pardubitz, the 8th of July, 1866.*

"To the Imperial Lieutenant
    "Field-Marshal Baron Von Gablenz.

        "By your Excellency's permission I have obtained
    "an insight into your instructions for concluding a
    "suspension of hostilities, and have had the honour to
    "submit their contents to His Majesty the King.

" His Majesty expressed his willingness to grant an
" armistice for the purpose of conducting such negotia-
" tions as would tend to lead to a permanent peace
" between Prussia and Austria.

" No communications, however, have as yet been
" made which will form the political basis for this, besides
" which, the nature of our relations to Italy necessitates
" an understanding with this power, before we can form
" any definite resolution.

" Under any circumstances His Majesty would not
" be able now to accede to such conditions for a suspen-
" sion of hostilities as are contained in your Excellency's
" instructions.

" I beg your Excellency to accept the expression of
" highest esteem, with which I have the honour to be,

" Your Excellency's

" Most obedient,

(Signed)     " VON MOLTKE."

The same morning the outlines of the future operations were
drawn up.

Brünn was fixed as destination of the Ist Army, which it
was to reach by the Policka-Kunstadt and Kreuzberg-Rozinka
roads.

The Army of the Elbe was to advance on Iglau, from which
spot it could either be likewise be brought up to Brünn, or could
march straight on to Znaim.

The IInd Army received orders to advance to the line Littau-
Konitz, to disturb the re-organization of the hostile army at
Olmütz as much as possible, and to establish its own basis on
the county of Glatz.

### THE 9TH OF JULY.

The Austrian Army continued its retreat to Olmütz without
any interruption. The columns of the centre and the left wing
reached Konitz and Müglitz; the Saxon corps and the right
flank column deviated from the original orders and marched,
the former to Busau, the latter to Mährisch-Neustadt. Colonel
Thom's Brigade of the IInd Corps remained as rear-guard of the
latter at Aussee.

The head-quarters of the Prussian IInd Army were moved
to Leitomischl, and orders were issued that the 1st Corps should
march to the neighbourhood of Zwittau instead of to Schirmdorf, and should push forward advanced guards on the roads to
Brünn and Mährisch-Trübau. Permission was granted to the
Vth Corps to extend its line southward of Abtsdorf, but it was
at the same time advised to advance to Landskron to feel the
enemy; the Guards were moved still further to the left to
Brandeis.

At 2 A.M. two Landwehr Hussar squadrons of General Hartmann's Division were sent forward to reconnoitre in the direction of Landskron, and found the town evacuated by the enemy. The IInd Austrian Corps was said to have bivouacked there, but to have continued its march at 1 A.M. to Mährisch-Trübau.

Although the Commanding General of the Vth Corps had fixed the neighbourhood of Rudelsdorf, Sichelsdorf, &c., as the cantonments of the division for the day, still it seemed necessary under the existing circumstances to follow the enemy; Gen. Hartmann therefore started in the direction of Reichenau. When the advanced guard arrived there, it was ascertained for certain that only some small detachments could have turned off to Mährisch-Trübau, and that the greater part of the enemy's right flank column had retreated on and by the side of the railway to Hohenstadt. The patrols found Trübau evacuated, but all railway bridges, with the exception of one, were destroyed. A post of the enemy was stationed behind this one, and a bivouac of considerable hostile forces was to be seen in the neighbourhood of Hohenstadt. The division went into cantonments between Reichenau and Rudelsdorf. The 2nd Hussar Regiment was attached to the 9th Division for the day.

The advanced guard of the Vth Corps and General Wnuck's Brigade advanced to Landskron and Michelsdorff, the main body of the Corps to Mährisch-Trübau; the Corps of Guards came to Brandeis, Hradek, and Böhmisch-Hermanitz; the Ist Corps to Zwittau, where a considerable quantity of oats was found; the 12th Lancer Regiment opened communication with the 1st Army by way of Karlsbrunn and Policka. Intelligence was received that detachments of the enemy were at Brüsau, which was confirmed by a reconnaissance.

The Ist Army advanced in general as far as the Chotebor-Policka road; five divisions reached the line Studenetz-Oudaw-Krouma-Mladocow; the Reserve Artillery Libitz, Klodno, and Neuschloss behind them. The following troops were pushed forward beyond the above-mentioned line, viz., the advanced guard to Nemetzky, General Manstein's Division to Swratka and Krizanek and the Cavalry Corps to Slawetin and Kreuzberg. Prince Frederick Charles's head-quarters were established at Richenburg.

General Count Goltz's detachment of the Army of the Elbe arrived at Iglau at 9 A.M. already, but did not find the convoy there any more. The 2nd Squadron of the 7th Hussars made a very fatiguing forced march, and captured 20 wagons and 10 men. A small post, which was left as relay in Stöcken, was partly carried off by the Austrians.

Head-quarters and advanced guard of the Army of the Elbe reached Deutsch-Brod; General Etzel's Division, Radostin; General Canstein's, Swetla. Count Münster's Division marched to Habern, and the Reserve Artillery to Goltsch-Jenikau.

## The 10th of July.

With the exception of the Saxon Corps, which only reached Gross-Senitz, the left-flank column of the Austrian Army arrived at Olmütz, the centre column at Littau. The IInd Corps d'Armée and the 2nd Light Cavalry Division halted for the day at Aussee and Mährisch-Neustadt, and the IVth Corps continued its march towards Olmütz.

The head-quarters of the IInd Prussian Army were moved to Mährisch-Trübau. General Hartmann's Cavalry Division halted on this as well as on the following day, as it had great need of rest. Although its losses in action had been but trifling, still the regiments had suffered very considerably. They had marched 97 miles without break within the three last days. Besides those horses which had been left behind for lameness or sickness, the regiments still had upon an average 150 horses each that were unfit for service; one-third of the horses of the Landwehr were lame. This state of things had been partly caused by the exertions of marching, of picquet, patrol and orderly service, and partly by the impossibility of keeping the horses' shoes in permanent order. The latter suffered extremely from the varying nature of the ground, which was at times hard, at others clayey and wet.

The Vth Corps d'Armée went into cantonments in and round about Landskron. The advanced guard of the corps and General Wnuck's Brigade were broken up, and each division formed its own separate advanced guard out of the Fusilier Battalions of the division, two and three Squadrons of Dragoons, one and two Batteries and one company of Pioneers. These advanced guards· were pushed forward on the roads to Reichenau and Budigsdorf. The Corps of Guards halted further to the rear at Wildenschwerdt and Knappendorf; the Ist Corps marched to Mährisch-Trübau and Kunzendorf. One Brigade, with the 12th Lancers and a battery, remained in a bivouac near Greiffendorf, southward of Zwittau, as protection for the head-quarters of His Majesty the King, who moved to the latter town on this day.

General Field-Marshal Count Von Wrangel arrived at Mährisch-Trübau to-day for the purpose of sharing all the toil and exertion of the campaign with his regiment, the 3rd Cuirassiers.

Head-quarters of the VIth Corps and the 11th Division arrived at Chotzen.

Major-General Von Knobelsdorf was instructed to march with his detachment by way of Jägerndorf and Römerstadt to Hohenstadt. The distance from Jägerndorf to Hohenstadt was to be performed in two days.

General Hann's Cavalry Division, which was on the right

wing of the 1st Army, marched by Boran and Weprikow to Saar.

The head of the advanced guard (the 1st Squadron of the 9th Lancers) reached Strizanow, about 2 miles on this side of Saar, towards 9 o'clock in the morning, where it was fired on by patrols of Hesse Cassel and Radetzky Hussars. The leading files of the Lancers drove the latter back, but were themselves obliged to fall back on their supports when some 40 Hussars issued forth from one of the buildings. The Captain of the Lancer squadron threw himself upon the enemy with the advanced guard division, and a *mêlée* ensued in which the Hussars were driven back and hotly pursued. They lost ten men and as many horses. The Commander of the Lancer regiment had in the meantime arrived on the spot, and gave orders not to advance further than the south side of Saar, and to wait there until the two other squadrons of the regiment came up. The 2nd Squadron was absent on a foraging expedition. The leading peloton then passed through to the south side of the town, and was driven out again by a squadron of Hussars. The 1st Squadron of the Lancers, however, advanced, and forcing its way into the town completely dislodged the enemy. On reaching the south side of Saar the Lancers came upon two hostile squadrons, and immediately charged in column of threes, there being no room to deploy. A hard struggle ensued, which ended with the retreat of the Hussars.

In the meantime the 3rd and half of the 4th Squadron of the Lancers had come up, and Colonel Von Grüter sent the 3rd Squadron on in pursuit; two divisions of the 4th and the 1st Squadron followed as reserve. The remainder of the 4th Squadron had been sent by General Hann to reconnoitre the country on the right flank from the cross roads at Pelles. Keeping up a continual skirmish with the enemy, the 3rd Squadron arrived at the Wesseler brook beyond Wattin, and halted there from sheer exhaustion of the horses. Two divisions of the 4th Squadron came up afterwards and resumed the pursuit, but could not overtake the enemy, who had gained too great a start. Some hostile Cavalry was seen near Sasomin, and driven off by a few shots from two guns of the 2nd Horse Artillery Battery of the 2nd Artillery Regiment, which had come up from the advanced guard in the meantime.

Three Austrian officers and 30 men were brought in as prisoners, and 28 horses captured. The 1st and 3rd Squadrons of the 9th Lancers lost 1 man and 3 horses killed, 1 officer and 16 men wounded.

General Hann's Cavalry Division advanced as far as Hljny, General Alvensleben's Division to Jamny, the Duke of Meklenburg's advanced guard to Swolla and Rozinka on the Neustadtl-Tischnowitz road.

The other detachments of the Army reached the line Saar-Bistrau, where they were quartered in the villages. The 4th and 7th Divisions were in second line behind the former at

Skrdlowitz and Ingrowitz. The Reserve Artillery of the Corps marched to Strizanow, Wetzau, and Policka. Head-quarters of the Army were at Neustadtl.

The advanced guard of the Army of the Elbe reached Iglau, where Count Goltz's detachments had halted. Here also the enemy's Cavalry was felt. A division of the 3rd Squadron of the 11th Hussars, which was thrown forward on the left to reconnoitre, met a division of Lichtenstein Hussars, and made a Cornet and three men prisoners.

General Etzel's Division arrived at Stöcken, General Canstein's at Pollerskirchen, Count Münster at Deutsch-Brod, and the Reserve Artillery at Radostin.

The correctness of the opinion which had hitherto prevailed, that by far the greater part of the Austrian Army had retreated to Olmütz, and only a small part in the direction of Brünn, was fully confirmed by several papers that were seized at the Mährisch-Trübau post-office on this day. Among other documents they contained Marshal Benedek's orders to the Intendance of the Army, specifying the routes for the march of the Army as we have already given them under the head of the 4th of July (*vide* page 302).

## THE 11TH OF JULY.

With the exception of those troops that had taken the route to Vienna, the Austrian Army of the North was assembled at Olmütz in the course of the 11th of July. It had gained a start of 27 miles on the Prussian Ist Corps, and of 49½ miles on the Corps of Guards. By this uninterrupted retreat of eight days' duration, it was certainly enabled to avoid any conflict, but such a retreat must needs more and more ruin the fitness of the troops for action, both morally and physically, and the overcrowding of the Olmütz camp must be productive of difficulties of all kinds.

Added to this the advance of the Ist Army and the Army of the Elbe had been executed with so much energy that Prince Frederick Charles's advanced guard was already within one day's march of Brünn. When once there, a few days would suffice to interrupt the communication of Olmütz with Vienna at Lundenburg, and to menace the capital of the empire.

The peril of this situation was not overlooked on the part of the Austrians: on the contrary, it was resolved to move the greater part of the Army of the North to Vienna. On this day already, by command of His Majesty the Emperor, the Feldzeugmeister gave orders to the Commanding Generals of the different corps that the whole Army of the North, with the exception of one corps which was to remain in the Olmütz camp, was to proceed to Vienna immediately. The departure of the IIIrd Corps commenced the very same evening; the Saxon Corps was to be the next to follow in the same direction.

As yet the railway was still available for this purpose, because, for the moment, neither the IInd nor the Ist Army could possibly reach it; but it was by no means possible to convey the bulk of the Army of the North to the Danube in like manner, as, even with the utmost exertion, this transport would have required a month's time. The main body, therefore, had no alternative but to march on foot, and, if it took the direction of Vienna, it would expose its flank to the Prussian Army.

Notwithstanding this, the Feldzeugmeister's dispositions ordered part of the Army to take the road along the valley of the March by way of Göding and Malaczka to Pressburg. The Cavalry, which was to be the last to follow, and which had to protect rear and flank of the Army, was even instructed to march still further to the west, by Prossnitz, Eisgrub, and Walkersdorf to Vienna. As long as this march lasted, the VIth Corps, which remained at Olmütz, was to cover the line of railway between Olmütz and Prerau, the Ist Corps to guard the neighbourhood of the latter town. Colonel Mondl's Brigade was already stationed at Lundenburg for the same purpose.

The orders for the movements of the Prussian IInd Army, which had been given at His Majesty's head-quarters, were based on the supposition that a brief period of repose would enable the enemy to re-assume the offensive from Olmütz. All intelligence received since then proved, however, that the Austrian Army was in such a state that the security of the Prussian Army need only be a secondary consideration; the primary one now was to endanger the enemy's position.

For this reason, although no news of the diminution of the forces at Olmütz by the detachments which were being sent to Vienna, could yet have reached the Prussian head-quarters, His Majesty the King, nevertheless, immediately acceded to a proposition made by the IInd Army to take up a position on the line Prossnitz-Urschitz, instead of on that of Littau-Konitz.

If these positions were occupied sufficiently early, all further communication of the Army of the North with Vienna on the right bank of the March would be intercepted, and the enemy would be deprived of the use of the railway, if either Prerau were occupied or the line destroyed at this place.

It is true, this was in itself sufficient provocation to induce the enemy to attack the IInd Army with his far superior forces, and it was no longer possible to secure the communication with Glatz, so that the whole Army was now dependent on the line of Pardubitz for its supplies.

At this time the Intendance had to contend with difficulties which increased to an alarming degree. Railway transport was only practicable as far as Turnau; one of the lines leading further southward was barred by the fortress of Josephstadt; on the other one the tract between Prague and Pardubitz was not yet fit for traffic. The troops of the Ist Army and the Army of the Elbe could only subsist so long as their uninterrupted advance led them into fresh districts, where provisions were still to be found.

The IInd Army, which had a day of rest on this day, was specially instructed to break the line of railway between Olmütz and Vienna. Any arrival or departure of troops on this line was to be intercepted and reported.

The details of the march of the different corps to the right were settled at Mährisch-Trübau in the course of the evening of the 11th.

The frontier mountains of Bohemia and Moravia opposed considerable difficulties to this march, which was therefore so arranged that the four corps were to follow each other in succession, and by short stages on the road Mährisch-Trübau, Gewitsch, Stephanau, Ptin, and Plumenau. This prevented the Army from taking up its appointed positions before the 15th.

During this march, through a mountainous country with a scarcity of roads, it was necessary to reduce the number of wagons following the troops to a minimum, and to assign separate routes to the military train and the parks. The VIth Corps, which marched at the end of the column, was not affected by this measure, but the train and parks of all the other corps were turned on to the Brünn high-road, and were to arrive at Wischau, Plumenau, and Stephanau on the 15th.

As soon as this march was completed on the 15th, new lines of communication were assigned to the corps leading from their different positions to Brünn, Boskowitz, Brüsau, and Zwittau. At each of these points principal magazines were to be established, and filled either from the neighbouring country or by way of Pardubitz.

The Ist Army continued its march in the direction of Brünn on this day. During its march from Swolla to Tischnowitz the Duke of Meklenburg's advanced guard met some Cavalry detachments of the enemy which appeared in front and on both flanks. The 2nd Light Cavalry Brigade, which was at the head of the advanced guard, despatched one squadron to Zdiaretz and another to Daubrawnik to drive back the enemy's flank detachments, and if possible to cut off the retreat of his centre detachment, which was retiring on the middle Tischnowitz road.

The three roads meet near to the north entrance of the faubourg (Vorstadt), Vorkloster, which is separated by the Schwarzawa from the small town of Tischnowitz on the other side of the stream. The enemy escaped the danger which threatened his retreat, and it was not before reaching Vorkloster that the leading Prussian division (one of the 1st Squadron of the 2nd Guard Dragoons) met a division of the Austrian Wallmoden Lancers. The latter was thrown back on its supports, which were stationed on the market-place. The Dragoons then waited in a side street until the remainder of the squadron came up on the high-road. The Lancers advanced again, and both parties met on the bridge; the former were driven back and pursued until an Austrian division coming out of a side street brought the combat to a stand-still. In the meantime the Prussian advanced guard had waited in another side street, where it had repulsed a charge of Lancers by its carbine fire; dashing into the *mêlée*, it now decided the combat in favour of the Prussians.

The Lancers were reinforced on the market-place by about $1\frac{1}{2}$ divisions, in spite of which they were driven out of the town, making good their retreat under cover of the 3rd Austrian Cuirassier Regiment, 2 squadrons of Lancers, and a battery of Artillery.

The enemy, consisting of Brigade Soltyk of the 2nd Reserve Cavalry Division (apparently 10 squadrons), remained at Bitischka, behind the line of the Schwarzawa, until 6 in the afternoon. The Prussian Brigade halted at Tscheptin.

On the part of the Austrians the 1st and 4th Squadrons of Wallmoden Lancers had been engaged; they lost 2 officers, 53 men, and 30 horses killed, wounded, and prisoners. The loss of the Prussian Guard Dragoons amounted to 2 men killed, 1 officer and 10 men wounded, 7 men otherwise disabled, and 3 horses missing.

The Prussian advanced guard occupied Tischnowitz. The head-quarters of the 1st Army were moved to Pernstein, the 3rd and 4th Divisions to Pikaretz and Bobrau, the 5th and 6th to Daubrawnik and Olschy, the 7th and 8th to Hodonin and Kunstadt; the reserve Artillery of the different corps to Bobrau, Bystritz, and Oels.

The 1st Division of the Cavalry Corps reached Messiborz, the 2nd Straschkau.

When Prince Frederick Charles received the news of the action at Tischnowitz, he sent orders to the Cavalry Corps to surprise the Brigade Soltyk in its bivouac. If possible this was to be done the same evening, but if not then, Prince Albrecht was to advance as early as possible the next morning, either with the whole or with part of the corps, by way of Gross-Bitesch and Schwarzkirchen, towards the roads leading southward from Brünn, and to press forward as far as the condition of the horses permitted, in order to cover the march of the Army on Brünn. These orders did not arrive till $7\frac{1}{2}$ P.M.; the undertaking was therefore deferred until the next morning.

The following orders were despatched from His Majesty's head-quarters to the Commanders-in-Chief of the Armies:—

"According to intelligence which has been received, "Brünn will probably be but slightly occupied. The "Commander-in-Chief of the 1st Army will be able to "judge on the spot, how far any concentration of the "Army may be still necessary in order to gain possession "of Brünn, or whether circumstances may not permit of "the 1st Army making use of the Eibenschütz roads also,

" in order to facilitate and expedite the formation of the
" Ist Army and the Army of the Elbe on the line Znaym-
" Muschau behind the Thaya.

"The Ist Army will communicate the necessary in-
" formation to the Army of the Elbe, and according as
" this intelligence may be, the latter will either continue
" its march to Brünn by the Stannern-Trebitsch and the
" Gross-Meseritsch roads, or will advance with its whole
" force on Znaym.

(Signed)     " Von Moltke."

" Zwittau, the 11th of July, 1867."

This letter, and a communication stating that Brünn would
in all probability be already occupied by the Ist Army on the
12th, did not reach the Army of the Elbe until the afternoon of
the 13th, by which time the Army was already on its road to
Brünn.

Previous orders, however, sent from Hohenmauth on the
9th of July, had instructed the Army of the Elbe to form a
division with as much additional Cavalry as possible, as advanced guard of the Prussian Army during its march on Vienna.
In conformity with these orders, the advanced guard was reinforced by the Pomeranian Reiter Regiment and the 1st Horse
Artillery Battery of the 8th Artillery Regiment, thereby increased
to 7 battalions, 14 squadrons, and 24 guns, and despatched towards Znaym. Its foremost troops reached Markwatitz and
Horry, its main body Hungerleiden and Lang-Pirnitz on this
day. The detachment was directed to keep as much as possible
in communication with the other divisions of the Army of the
Elbe, and at the same time to send direct reports to the King's
head-quarters.

The 15th and 16th Divisions formed their own advanced
guards, the former marched to Pirnitz, the latter to Wollein.
The 14th Division and head-quarters of the army were moved
to Iglau, the Reserve Artillery to Polna.

## The 12th of July.

When the issue of the battle of Königgrätz had induced the
Emperor to cede Venetia, in order to be able to devote all his
forces to the maintenance of Austria's former position in Germany, the Government had at the same time taken the corresponding military measures. It was first of all intended to recall
as many troops as possible from the Army of the South, but at
Archduke Albert's request it was decided that the Field-
Marshal himself was to hasten to the Danube with the greater
part of his army.

The Archduke took the necessary steps immediately; the
Infantry Reserve Corps of the Army was broken up, and the
Vth and IXth Corps increased to four brigades each. The

former of these corps was then to march through Tirol, the
latter through Styria to the Danube, whereas one corps on the
Isonzo, and one division in Istria were all the troops which
were deemed necessary to check the advance of the Italian
Army.

On the 10th of July, the appointment of the Archduke as
Commander-in-Chief of all the Armies arrived at his head-
quarters in Vicenza, and at the same time a telegram desiring
him to start for Vienna immediately, attended by his Chief of
the Staff.

Early on the 12th, the Archduke gave up the command of
the Army of the South to Lieutenant Field-Marshal Maroicic,
and left for Vienna with his Chief of Staff, Lieutenant Field-
Marshal Baron John.

On the 13th, Feldzeugmeister Benedek gave orders for the
march of the remainder of the Army of the North from Olmütz.
It was to be effected in three *échelons*, by way of Kremsier and
Göding to Pressburg, from whence the troops were to proceed
to Vienna.

Better roads and a shorter distance were sufficient inducements to make the first half of this march on the right bank of
the March, but it is evident how much the advance of the
Prussian Army would endanger its execution.

The 6th Lancer Regiment and the Pontoon Train of the
army started on the same day, the 13th of July. As far as is as
yet known, the first *échelon*, consisting of the IInd and IVth
Corps, with 16 squadrons of Saxon Cavalry, were to set off on
the 14th, the VIIth and Ist Corps and the 2nd Light Cavalry
Division on the 15th; the VIth Corps was to follow on the 16th.
This corps was eventually to be joined by part of the Saxon
corps, the transport of which was soon interrupted by events
which will be related hereafter.

The IInd Prussian Army commenced its movement southward on the 12th of July. Head-quarters of the army remained
in Mährisch-Trübau. The Ist Corps reached Gross-Gewitsch
with its main body, Jaromierzitz with its advanced guard, and
Ungendorf with a right flank detachment. General Pape's
brigade at Greifendorf marched by way of Brüsau, at which
place it stopped until the King, who moved his head-quarters
to Czernahora to-day, had passed. The brigade reached
Opatowitz in the evening.

The Cavalry Division went into quarters in Türnau and the
environs of the town; the 2nd Hussars were thrown forward
towards Brannöhlhütten to cover the left flank.

The 9th Division of the Vth Corps reached Mährisch-Trübau,
the 10th Division, and the Reserve Artillery Altstadt, where
they were billetted in the neighbouring villages. Outposts were
stationed at Pohres and Pirkelsdorf.

The corps of Guards came to Sternteich and Kötzelsdorf, the
VIth Corps to Landskron. The latter received orders from the
Commander-in-Chief to reinforce General Knobelsdorff's detach-

ment by the 63rd Regiment (to be brought up from Glatz and
Neisse), and to leave it at Grulich, so as to check any communication which might be attempted between Olmütz and the
fortresses on the Upper Elbe. The railway to Pardubitz was
to be guarded by stationing a detachment at Wildenschwerdt;
on the other hand, the line from Olmütz was to be broken at
Hohenstadt, and a line of communication to be opened from
Wildenschwerdt to Glatz.

The advanced guard of the Ist Army entered Brünn.

It had been ascertained the day before already that the town
was no longer occupied by the enemy. Prince Frederick Charles
followed at the head of the 6th Division at half-past 7 in the
evening. Whatever demands had to be made of the town were
fully satisfied by the citizens; indeed at the moment of the
entrance of the army and during the whole time of occupation,
the Burghomaster, Dr. Giskra, knew so well how to combine his
duty as Austrian subject and representative of the town, with
the fulfilment of the unavoidable requirements of a hostile army,
that his services were deservedly appreciated by both sides.

The Cavalry corps started at daybreak, and advanced by
Gross-Bitesch and Schwarzkirchen to Rossitz, where it heard
that General Zajtsek's Cavalry division had left the place for
Eibenschütz a few hours previously. Prince Albert set off again
as soon as the horses had been fed, but did not overtake his
adversary, who had passed Eibenschütz in the forenoon already.
The 1st Prussian Cavalry Division advanced as far as Gross-
Raigern, the 2nd remained in Kanitz and Eibenschütz. This
march of full 38 miles, over rocky ground and in very hot
weather, had been very fatiguing. Towards evening several
Austrian squadrons approached the outposts of the 2nd Cavalry
Division, but did not attempt an attack.

The 3rd, 5th, and 7th Divisions of the Ist Army marched up
to the line Gross-Bitesch, Gurein, Blansko; the 4th reached
Bitischka-Ossawa, the 8th Czernahora and Daubrawitz behind
both wings of the former; the Reserve Artillery of the different
corps came to Wlkau, Tischnowitz, and Porstendorf. The
evening before Count Goltz's brigade had sent back a report to
head-quarters of the Army of the Elbe that the enemy's line of
outposts had been reinforced by Infantry. The advanced guard
therefore started from Hungerleiden and Lang-Pirnitz at 3 A.M., but
the enemy withdrew his outposts, and formed line near Martinkau
with a few squadrons and eight guns. On debouching from the
wood southward of Horka the Prussian advanced guard was
fired on by a battery on the hill of Jakobau. The Ist 4-pounder
battery of the 7th Artillery Regiment opened fire in return, but
the enemy withdrew before the ten squadrons of Hussars could
deploy in front of the wood. The latter advanced still further
until they were met by musketry and carbine fire from the
village of Littahorn, on which they marched round about the
village, whilst the above-named battery and the 3rd Horse
Artillery Battery of the 8th Regiment continued their fire; they

only succeeded in capturing a few prisoners. Count Goltz's brigade advanced to Gröschelmauth, the main body of the advanced guard to Mährisch-Budwitz.

The 14th Division reached the neighbourhood of Startsch and Okrzischko, the 15th Wladislau and Trebitsch, the 16th Eisenberg and Gross-Meseritsch, the Reserve Artillery Ratzerowitz and Czechtin.

## THE 13TH OF JULY.

The head-quarters of the IInd Army were moved to Opatowitz, the army itself continued its march as follows :—

The Ist Corps to Stephanau, advanced guard to Wachtel, a detachment of 3 battalions, 2 squadrons, and 1 batttery under Major-General Von Buddenbrock was pushed forward towards Hrochow :—

The Vth Corps to Jaromiersitz, Gewitsch, and Konitz :

The Corps of Guards to Mährisch-Trübau and Türnau ;

The VIth Corps halted at Landskron.

The Cavalry Division marched to the neighbourhood of Konitz, and was billeted in the villages there. The 2nd Regiment of Hussars was pushed forward on the road to Olmütz, the 10th Lancers on that to Prossnitz.

A patrol of Hussars which advanced past Drahanowitz as far as the outworks of Olmütz at 10 o'clock in the evening, saw nothing of the enemy in this direction, and reported that the latter was said to be behind and at the side of the entrenched camp.

His Majesty the King entered Brünn at 2 in the afternoon, the 5th and 7th Divisions marched there also, and the 6th Division halted for the day in the town. The Cavalry corps remained in the position it had reached the day before. In case the latter should need support, the advanced guard of the army was pushed forward as far as Medritz, close to the river Obrawa.

As Brünn had been occupied without opposition, the IInd Corps d'Armée could now make use of the Eibenschütz road. General Rheinbaben's Cavalry Brigade was attached to the corps to do advanced guard duty; the 3rd Division reached Eibenschütz, the 4th Rossitz, the Reserve Artillery of the IInd Corps Nesslowitz, that of the IIIrd and IVth Corps Komein and Ugartsdorf, the 8th Division halted to-day.

At the request of the Ist Army the King granted it two days' rest, of which it stood in great need, not only on account of the long and continued marches it had made, but also because the supplies obtained by means of requisitions were but scanty.

Arrangements were made for bringing up the bridge trains from Turnau, and the orders of the 11th, instructing the Army of the Elbe to march on Znaym were repeated.

This order arrived in the course of the afternoon, but intelligence which he had received, and the retreat of the Austrian Cavalry (General Edelsheim's division) in front of him to Znaym had already convinced General Herwarth that it could not be the enemy's intention to hold Brünn. The 16th Division had met the IInd Corps at Gross-Meseritsch on the 12th of July already. It was therefore settled that the Divisions of the Army of the Elbe should advance on the 13th, move to the south-east instead of continuing their march on Brünn, and reach the line Jarmeritz-Namiest on this day. Head-quarters of the army remained in Trebitsch; the 14th Division came to Ratkowitz and Missliborzitz, the 15th to Slawietitz and Dalleschitz, the 16th to Hartikowitz and Namiest, the Reserve Artillery to Trebitsch.

The advanced guard of the Army of the Elbe continued its march towards Znaym. The Commanding General of the army had ordered that it was to reach Wolframitz-Kirchen with its main body on this day. Intelligence was brought in, stating Znaym to be occupied in force and entrenched. Count Goltz was in consequence sent forward from Mramotitz with the two Hussar Regiments and the 2nd Battalion of the 33rd Regiment to reconnoitre. He met several squadrons of Austrian Dragoons, and some skirmishing ensued between them and the 3rd Squadron of the 7th Hussars. The enemy, however, soon fell back on Znaym, then passed this town and retreated behind the Thaya, burning down the bridge over the river. The Prussian Cavalry was obliged to ford the river, which gave the enemy so much start, that he evaded all further pursuit. A few prisoners were made and some horses captured. General Von Schoeler entered Znaym with the main body of his advanced guard, and threw a temporary bridge over the river by the side of the former one.

Thus, ten days after the battle on the Bistritz, the army had reached the Thaya, having completed a march of nearly 112 miles in this time.

## The 14th of July.

The Austrian Army could not be attacked in its entrenched camp at Olmütz, but at the same time it was not to be expected that it would issue forth from it and assume the offensive. The campaign could therefore only be decided by the further advance of the Prussian Ist Army and the Army of the Elbe. On the 14 of July, at Brünn, the King gave orders for this to be done.

The Austrian Cavalry in front was not able to check this march, and if the troops, that might perhaps be assembled at Vienna already, were to advance to its support, then the second battle, which was necessary to end the war, would be fought under more favourable military and political auspices now than if the Prussian Army were to seek it later. The great thing now was to cross the intervening space between the Thaya and the Danube as quickly as possible, and to prepare the means of crossing the latter stream.

In order to carry out these intentions, the following instructions were given :—

> "*Head-Quarters, Brünn, July* 14*th*, 1866.

"As soon as the two days' rest which His Majesty the King "has granted to the troops of the 1st Army have expired, this "army will commence its march beyond the Thaya and on "Vienna, for which purpose the following routes :—

"*a.* Eibenchutz, Laa, Ernstbrunn ;
"*b.* Dürnholz, Ladendorf ;
"*c.* Muschau, Nikolsburg, Gaunersdorf ;

"will be at its disposal.

"In addition to this, a detachment, the strength of which "will be fixed by the Commander-in-Chief of the 1st Army, will "be sent towards Lundenburg. The advanced guard of this "detachment will be pushed far on a-head, and will destroy the "railway leading to Prerau as soon as possible; on the other "hand, as the railway Brünn-Lundenburg-Gaunersdorf may be "useful to us, it is to be occupied as the detachment advances, "and any injury to it will be prevented.

"Yesterday's orders directed the Army of the Elbe to pro-"ceed to Znaym; it will now march from there by the two "routes—

"*a.* Jetzelsdorf, Ober Hollabrunn ;
"*b.* Jaslowitz, Enzersdorf im Thale ;

"and will send a detachment to Meissau, so as to be able later "to make demonstrations from there against the Upper Danube, "between Tulln and Krems.

"In order that the 1st Army and the Army of the Elbe may, "if necessary, be able to afford each other mutual assistance "during these operations, they are both hereby instructed to "cross the Thaya at Muschau and Znaym on the 17th instant "with their main bodies.

"The 1st Army will move both of its pontoon trains per "road by way of Pardubitz and along the Brünn railway to "Brünn.

"The IInd Army will also immediately send the whole of "its pontoon trains to Brünn. The Commander-in-Chief of "both armies will, as soon as possible, send the routes of the "pontoon trains here, so that their further transport per rail "may be arranged.

"The Guard Landwehr Division will set out for Pardubitz "on the 16th, leaving for the present a detachment in Prague.

"It may be remarked now already that it is intended, as "soon as General Bentheim's division arrives at Prague, to "move it forward per rail from this town to the main army, in "company with the detachment of General Rosenberg's division "which is now stationed there. The latter division itself will

" also be eventually conveyed per rail from Pardubitz to the
" main army. When this takes place, one brigade of Infantry,
" one regiment of Cavalry, and one battery of General Ben-
" theim's brigade will be left in Prague. The special orders
" for this transport will not be issued until the Prague-Brünn
" line of railway is opened.

" Head-quarters of His Majesty the King will remain at
" Brünn until further orders, which town will be garrisoned
" by a detachment of the Ist Army.

" All three armies will establish letter-carrier stations be-
" tween their head-quarters and Brünn. By means of these
" letter-carriers the latest occurrences and measures proposed
" for the following day will be reported here. The Ist Army
" must pay particular attention to its line of communication
" with Brünn.

(Signed)     " Von Moltke."

Instructions were telegraphed to Colonel Von Mertens at
Dresden to hold in readiness 50 heavy guns, which had been
conveyed there, so that they might be sent on per rail without
any delay as soon as ordered.

The Austrians had recognized the necessity of assembling
a fresh army in the neighbourhood of Vienna, and the transport
of troops from Italy thither began on the 14th of July. Those
from Olmütz were likewise continued. The IVth Corps was to
reach Kojetein from the latter place on this day, the IInd
Tobitschau, both marching on the right bank of the March.
Twelve squadrons of Saxon Cavalry were attached to the former,
the 3rd Saxon "Reiter" Regiment to the latter, and both were
instructed to cover the right flank of this march by a brigade.
The heavy trains were sent on the left bank by way of Prerau
to Moschtienitz.

One single brigade detached in the right flank might protect
a corps at one stage, but could not cover the march of an army
for any length of time, as soon as more than the mere heads of
its adversary's columns approached on its flank.

To reach Göding on the right bank of the March was a
thing which the Austrian Army could only expect with any
degree of certainty, if a strong force first freed it from the
neighbourhood of the IInd Prussian Army, by assuming the
offensive and driving the latter back westward.

It is true, on the 14th, the Prussian VIth Corps only reached
Mährisch-Trübau, the corps of Guards Opatowitz and Jaromierzitz, but the Vth Corps was already drawing near to Laschkau
and Neustift, the Ist Corps to Prossnitz.

The Cavalry Division had been sent on in advance to Kosteletz, and saw from the heights of Hluchow very long clouds of
dust, apparently denoting the march of considerable forces.
It could not be distinguished, whether they were on the right or
the left bank of the March. Patrols that advanced towards
Prossnitz met a hostile Cavalry regiment, but nothing more was

to be seen of the enemy when General Von Hartmann arrived there at half-past 11 A.M. Scouting parties were then thrown forward in different directions, and the division halted at Kosteletz.

This was reported to the VIth Corps at 9¾ A.M., and General Von Steinmetz gave orders that the Cavalry Division should advance as far as Prossnitz, and send as strong a detachment as possible in the course of the day to Prerau, to obtain information whether troops were marching on Tobitschau or Prerau, or behind these places, and in what force; besides which the detachment was to seize on the telegraph and railway stations, and was to inflict as much injury on the enemy as possible.

Soon after these orders were despatched, the following communication arrived at head-quarters of the Vth Corps from Prossnitz:—

"12¼ P.M.

"I have received reports from Ollschann and from far "southward of Prossnitz. There is nothing more to be "seen of the enemy anywhere. An Austrian regiment "of Hussars, and one of Saxon 'Reiter,' have been in "Prossnitz this morning. The Austrians are said to "be in Tobitschau at this moment. I shall keep my "advanced guard beyond Kosteletz, throw forward "outposts towards Prossnitz and Ollschann, and shall "quarter the main body, as far as possible, in and in the "neighbourhood of Kosteletz.

(Signed) "VON HARTMANN."

"P.S. I am on the point of pushing a reconnaissance "on towards Tobitschau."

In the course of the afternoon the General again reported from Kosteletz:—

1. That the 2nd Hussars had this morning observed from Drahanowitz columns, consisting of all arms, marching on the road from Littau to Olmütz, and that prisoners had stated the troops to be on the point of starting from Olmütz to Vienna by way of Prerau. From the heights of Rittberg an officer of the Hussars had seen considerable columns marching on one of the roads leading southward from Olmütz.

2. The aide-de-camp of the division, Lieutenant Von Rosenberg, reported from Whrahowitz that Ollschann and Dubau were not occupied by the enemy, but that Infantry was in Wrbatek, and that a squadron and a half of Cavalry were moving towards Hrdiborsitz. A patrol of the 3rd Saxon "Reiter" Regiment had been taken prisoner, and stated that the Army was marching to Vienna, and that its marching discipline was very slack. Lieutenant Von Rosenberg was continuing his observations.

3. The General Staff Officer of the division, Captain Von Versen, reported that he had met no enemy in Kralitz, but that, according to the statements of several inhabitants, it might be taken for granted that one regiment of Saxon Cavalry, two regiments of Austrian Infantry, and one Austrian Rifle Battalion, had passed Kralitz early this morning in the direction of Kojetein. The retreating troops were said to be marching to Kremsier. The reconnaissances towards Tobitschau were being continued.

To these reports General Von Hartmann added:—

" The result of all observation is that the enemy is " retreating southward. I request permission either to ' throw myself by way of Dub on his line of retreat near " Krzmann or Kokor, or else by way of Tobitschau on " Prerau. For this purpose I beg for the assistance of " Infantry and of a Light Cavalry regiment in the place " of the 2nd Regiment of Hussars, which is detached to " Drahanowitz."

After waiting some time for the orders granting the desired permission, General Von Hartmann went himself to Neustift to urge General Von Steinmetz to agree to the undertaking.

All these reports were sent to the Commander-in-Chief, whose head quarters were moved to Konitz, accompanied by the following letter from General Von Steinmetz:—

" The Vth Corps is unfortunately not near enough for " me to be able to assist General Von Hartmann with " Infantry; it would be good if the Ist Corps were in- " structed to do so. I am perfectly of the same opinion, " that the Austrians are retreating from Olmütz to " Vienna. The state in which the troops are retreating " is such that I consider it highly desirable to pursue " them rapidly, and to attack them wherever they may " be found, from which I anticipate good results. I have " authorized General Hartmann to push on towards " Prerau.

(Signed) " VON STEINMETZ."
" Head-Quarters, Neustift, July 14th, 1866."

The main body of the Ist Corps had reached Plumenau already, the advanced guard Leschau and the Reserve Ptin. General Buddenbrock's detachment was pushed forward to Prossnitz, where it arrived at 4 in the afternoon, and where it was only about 4½ miles from Kralitz and Biskupitz.

Heavy clouds of dust were visible beyond Wrahowitz, in consequence of which the 1st Regiment of Hussars (attached to the 2nd Division) was ordered to send a squadron on in advance in that direction, and then to follow with the remainder of the regiment. One squadron had been previously detached to Kosteletz.

The 2nd Squadron (Captain Von Winterfeld) went on ahead of the regiment, and was met by Lieutenant Von Rosenberg with the intelligence that the 1½ squadrons of Saxon "Reiter," which he had already reported were approaching, and had chased him. Captain Von Versen also joined the squadron. Wrahowitz was scarcely passed, at half-past 4, before the skirmishing division of the Hussars come upon the enemy's skirmishers, and two squadrons were seen in the direction of Kralitz. When first seen they were retreating, but they now fronted again. The Hussar squadron deployed eastward of Wrahowitz with the 4th Division on its right flank, and then advanced to the attack. The enemy stood still, and received the charge with a volley in the neighbourhood of the Kralitz cemetery; his line was however broken, and he was forced back in a running fight towards Kralitz. Foreseeing the chance of hemming the enemy in between two walls, and thereby placing him in a very unfavourable position, Captain Winterfeld now rallied about two divisions, and threw himself in flank and rear of his adversary. Another obstinate hand-to-hand fight ensued, in the course of which the Saxons succeeded in shaking themselves free of their assailants, and rallied to the rear of the village. The disorder which the action had produced in the ranks of the Hussars rendered it necessary to halt them also, but Captain Winterfeld succeeded in again overthrowing the enemy with the first Hussars (about 40), that were re-formed. The Saxons were driven back towards Biskupitz, where Artillery and Infantry fire, and a fresh hostile squadron which appeared in the distance, as well as the fatigue of the horses, checked further pursuit.

The 1½ squadrons of the regiment which were following Captain Winterfeld joined him in front of Biskupitz, and Lieut.-Colonel Von Barnekow hastened hither from Prossnitz with the 4th Squadron of the 10th Lancers.

The enemy's artillery fire caused some losses here. The Hussars had 2 men killed, 2 officers and 18 men wounded, and 25 disabled horses. The greater part of this loss was suffered by the 2nd Squadron. The Saxon 3rd "Reiter" Regiment left 1 officer, 18 men, and 13 horses on the field.

At half-past 8 P.M. Captain Von Versen reported the results of this action from Kralitz. He stated also that two battalions and some artillery had advanced from Tobitschau, and that the inhabitants affirmed that considerable forces of the enemy still stood behind Tobitschau.

In the course of the afternoon the Crown Prince had ridden to Neustift, accompanied only by one of his personal aides-de-camp, with the intention of personally presenting General Von Steinmetz with the Order of the Black Eagle, conferred upon him by His Majesty the King. He received the above-mentioned letter of the General with the accompanying reports on the road.

z

The Prince gave the following orders in consequence :—

" The 1st Corps will send a brigade of Infantry, with
"a battery, to Tobitschau this evening (July 14th), and
"will occupy the passages over the rivers between
" Tobitschau and Traubeck, in order to support an
" undertaking of the combined Cavalry Division on
" Prerau, which will be carried out early on the 15th, or
"if necessary, to cover the retreat of the Cavalry.
(Signed)        " FREDERICK WILLIAM."
" *Neustift, July 14th*, 1866.
" *To the Commanding General of the 1st Corps d'Armée.*"

General Von Hartmann, who was still at Neustift, received
corresponding instructions, and took the letter to General Von
Bonin himself. By this time, however, it was half-past 10 P.M.;
and it was arranged between the Ist Corps and the General
Staff Officer of the Cavalry Division, that the expedition should
be carried out by both parties early the next morning.

In consequence of the former orders of General Steinmetz,
however, General Von Borstell had set off for Prossnitz with
the main body of the Cavalry Division at 4 P.M., and had sent
Colonel Von Barby with the 1st Cuirassiers on in advance in
the direction of Tobitschau. Avoiding the different villages on
his road, Colonel Barby reached the neighbourhood of Kralitz as
darkness was setting in, and Captain Von Versen made him
acquainted with the position of affairs. Thinking he saw a
hostile squadron about 1,000 paces westward of Biskupitz, the
Colonel ordered the 2nd Squadron to charge it, and rode forward
himself to reconnoitre, whilst the squadron was forming line.
When about 200 paces from the enemy, he perceived that
Infantry, apparently about a battalion, had formed square here
in the open country.

The 1st Squadron charged with great boldness. Although
the squadron received first two volleys, one at 100 and another
at 40 paces distance, and then file-fire, its losses were not considerable.

In the meantime the 2nd Squadron charged likewise against
the left flank of the square. The left wing of the squadron was
somewhat impeded by the 1st Squadron, but the right wing
partly penetrated into the square. About the same time two
divisions of the 4th Squadron came up on the rear of the square,
and charged it from this side.

The enemy—according to Austrian accounts two companies
of the 64th Regiment (Saxe-Weimar)—was divided into two
parts by these charges, but each one of them still held together. One part was forced somewhat northward, and was
again attacked by the 3rd Squadron of the Cuirassiers. Here
also a combat between the bayonet and the sabre ensued.

By this time darkness had completely set in; the horses
shied at the fire, and could not be forced up to the squares any
more; fresh detachments of the enemy came out of Biskupitz,

and Infantry as well as Artillery opened fire on the Cuirassiers. Under these circumstances the regiment was rallied, and retreated to Prossnitz. Its loss amounted to two officers and five men killed, three officers and nine men wounded; one officer, whose horse was killed, was taken prisoner. The enemy states his loss to have been three men.

This Infantry, as well as the Cavalry which Captain Winterfeld had met, belonged to the troops which covered the flank of the IInd Austrian Corps, and which left the entrenched camp at 9 A.M., marching, by way of Neustift and Dub, over the same ground in the afternoon which the flank guard of the IVth Austrian Corps passed in the course of the forenoon. The latter arrived safely at Kojetein, the former reached Tobitschau.

The march of the 1st Austrian *échelon* was thus only reached by the heads of the Cavalry of the Prussian Army.

Among the various reports and accounts, that were brought to the Crown Prince's head-quarters at Konitz, were some which stated, on the assertions of the country people, that the Austrians had been evacuating Olmütz for several days already. This gave rise to the opinion that the troops which had been seen retreating to-day had been the last and not the first *échelon*. Was this the case, it would be unnecessary to take up the position Prossnitz-Urtschitz, as the latest orders prescribed. If the bulk of the Austrian Army had made good its retreat to Kremsier, then it was thought that no further results would be obtained by pursuing it, and it was considered advisable to observe Olmütz henceforth with part of the Army only, and to rejoin the Ist Army, then marching straight to Vienna, with the remainder.

On the evening of July 14th already the following orders were given :—

"*Konitz, July* 14*th.*

" Intelligence having been received of the departure " of part of the enemy's forces from Olmütz, the orders " regarding the occupation of the position at Prossnitz " and the formation of a 2nd Cavalry Division are hereby " annulled, and the following instructions given instead: " The Ist Corps d'Armée will cross the Olmütz-Brünn " road ; part of the corps will bivouac between Zeschow " and Weischowitz; the remainder will take up canton- " ments behind the former in Urtschitz, Ottaslawitz, and " neighbourhood ; the corps will push forward an ad- " vanced guard in the direction of Kralitz, and will pro- " tect its right flank towards Tobitschau.

" The Vth Corps will occupy Prossnitz with an ad- " vanced guard, behind which it will be quartered as far " as Plumenau.

" The Cavalry Division will remain under the com- " mand of General Von Steinmetz.

" Both corps will push forward detachments to Olmütz " early to-morrow morning, to procure reliable informa-

" tion as to whether the enemy has really retreated, and
" in what force he has done so.

" On the 15th the Corps of Guards will not march to
" Konitz, but to Boskowitz, and will be billetted there.
" It will bring up its train and parks there, and will have
" a new line of march assigned to it.

" The VIth Corps will not march to Gewitsch to-
" morrow, but to Lettowitz on the Krönau road. It will
" receive the orders for resuming its march at Boskowitz
" from the Corps of Guards.

(Signed)    " FREDERICK WILLIAM."

THE 15TH OF JULY.

In the course of the night of the 14th reports were forwarded to His Majesty's Head-quarters at Brünn, that seemingly
large bodies of troops had for some days past been leaving
Olmütz in a southerly direction.

This rendered it imperative to meet that part of the enemy
which had marched past the IInd Army at Prossnitz, with the
Ist Army at Lundenburg, so as to bar his route to Vienna as well
as to Pressburg.

For the present, therefore, the direct march to the Danube,
as was ordered yesterday, must be abandoned, and the advance
of the Army must take a more easterly direction.

If the whole Army of the North, or at least a considerable
part of it, was moving along the Bank of the March to Vienna,
then there was every prospect of another battle.

In order that part of the IInd Army at least should, if possible, take part in the decisive action, the Crown Prince, whose
change of orders to the Guards and the VIth Corps were not
yet known, was directed to despatch the two corps nearest at
hand (the Ist and Vth) to Kremsier and Napagedl, so as to
follow up the enemy, and to enter into communication with the
Ist Army.

The latter was ordered to set off for Lundenburg; the Army
of the Elbe to advance by way of Laa towards Wülfersdorf, so
as to cover the right flank of the army on its march to Vienna.

According to the dispositions of Feldzeugmeister Benedek,
it was, however, in reality only the 2nd *échelon* of the Army of
the North (the Ist and VIIIth Corps, the 2nd Light Cavalry
Division, and the head-quarters of the Army) which commenced
its southward march from Olmütz to-day. The VIIIth Corps
was even to-day still to march by way of Tobitschau to Kojetein,
the Ist was to make use of the Prerau road.

General Rothkirch's Brigade and three batteries of the
Reserve Artillery of the VIIIth Corps were to cover the right
flank of this march.

On the 14th the head of the IInd Prussian Army (the Ist
Corps) had come within 9 miles of the former line of the enemy's
march. This led to the actions of Tobitschau and Rokeinitz on
the 15th of July.

## ACTIONS OF TOBITSCHAU AND ROKEINITZ.

The Ist Corps d'Armée ordered the 3rd Infantry Brigade to support the Cavalry Division during its advance on Prerau. General Von Malotki started from his bivouac near Stichowitz at 4 A.M., and marched by way of Prossnitz, Wrahowitz, and Kralitz towards Hrubschitz. General Hartmann's Cavalry Division had not arrived yet, and did not come up before the brigade reached Kralitz, where the 4th Squadron of the 10th Lancers joined. This squadron then went forward as advanced guard, and very soon discovered that hostile Infantry and Cavalry were at Tobitschau. Soon after passing Hrubschitz, General Malotki perceived a considerable column marching along the high-road from Olmütz towards Tobitschau, and just then passing Dub. This column was General Rothkirch's Brigade of the VIIIth Austrian Corps, the only brigade which had not yet been engaged. Two companies were somewhat carelessly following the course of the Blatta.

Although it was not possible to see how strong the enemy was, still General Malotki determined to attack immediately. The main object was to reach Tobitschau before the enemy, thereby wholly intercepting his retreat on the right bank of the March, and seriously endangering it on the left bank.

General Von Bonin, who was on the spot, perceived how desirable it would be to have more forces at hand then one brigade of Infantry for so important a purpose. He therefore gave orders that the remainder of the corps was not to form line between Urtschitz and Weischowitz, but was to concentrate near Hrubschitz-Ottonowitz.

On advancing further towards Tobitschau, Klopotowitz and the Wiklitzer Hof (farmhouses) were found to be still unoccu- 9 A.M. pied, but the bridge eastward of the latter was barricaded. Hostile skirmishers opened fire from behind an embankment on the other side of the stream as soon as the 10th Company of the advanced guard battalion (Fusiliers of the 44th Regiment) approached the bridge. The Prussian skirmishers found shelter on the right bank and returned the fire ; at the same time they proceeded to remove the barricade.

Meanwhile the 11th Company forded the Blatta westward of the farmhouse, stormed the embankment immediately in front of this spot, and so outflanked the enemy's skirmishers that the latter were obliged to withdraw from the whole line of the embankment. Both companies then spread out on the opposite bank of the stream, but could not for the present gain any ground, because some ditches and a dense wood northward of their position were held by the enemy in force. All they could do was to repulse several detachments which attempted to advance from the wood by their volleys.

At the first commencement of the action 16 Austrian guns unlimbered 500 paces north-eastward of the wood, and opened fire on the advancing Prussian columns. They were answered by the 1st 4-pounder battery, Captain Magnus, from a position south-eastward of Klopotowitz. The two Horse Artillery batteries of the Cavalry Division, the head of which was just then debouching from Hrubschitz, were now sent forward to reinforce Captain Magnus, and took up a position on his left, whereupon he moved his own battery to a more favourable position nearer the Wiklitzer-Hof. The Prussian guns, could not, however, silence the Austrian artillery, which had been reinforced by a third battery, and now turned its fire on the Prussian 4th Regiment at the farm buildings. The 5th Company, Captain Anders, was therefore ordered to advance as near as possible to the enemy's guns and to drive them off by skirmishing fire.

In the meantime the 44th Regiment had followed its two Fusilier companies over the Blatta, and formed for the attack of the wood with five companies in the first and seven in the second line. A rapid assault carried the skirts—an advantage which was followed up by driving the enemy totally out of the wood. The 5th Company of the 4th crossed the Blatta, advanced near to the Austrian guns in spite of their grape-fire, and compelled them to make a slight change in their position. Being then obliged to turn off to the right to get out of the line of fire of the Prussian artillery, this company also entered the same wood.

The foggy weather kept down the smoke of the firing, and obstructed all view of the surrounding country from the wood, a circumstance of which the Austrians availed themselves and attempted to retake the wood. They were, however, discovered in time, before they reached the east skirts, and were driven back with great loss. A brief pause now ensued in the Infantry fire.

About this time the 4th Regiment likewise crossed the Blatta, and sent Lieut.-Colonel Von Pannwitz, with the 10th and 11th Companies against Tobitschau.

When the atmosphere cleared up in the neighbourhood of the wood, the enemy's Infantry was seen in a new position beyond and almost parallel with the high-road. Dense swarms of skirmishers lined the ditches, columns were stationed behind them, and one battalion was posted at the chapel. The Austrian artillery had gone somewhat further back, on the west side of the high-road, and now stood in a flank position with its left wing at the bend in the road northwards of the chapel.

10.30 A.M.    The Prussian Infantry immediately proceeded to attack this position: Colonel Von La Chevallerie led the 44th Regiment out of the skirts and charged in front, whilst the 1st Battalion, which had marched round the south side of the wood, fell on the enemy's left flank; the latter—a brigade—met the attack with a very severe fire, but was nevertheless dislodged with heavy losses, and retreated partly to Wirowau and partly beyond the mill-stream in the direction of the Opleta wood.

The Austrian batteries, on the other hand, did not quit their position, but kept up a brisk fire, even though the 1st Prussian

4-pounder battery opened fire from a position eastward of the high-road, on a line with the north side of the wood. In the meantime the 5th Company of the 4th Regiment, which had driven off the Artillery once before and had advanced against the Austrian battalion at the chapel during the attack of the Infantry, and the 12th Company of the 44th Regiment had crept so close up to the Austrian Artillery that their fire reached the artillerymen at their guns, and forced the batteries to withdraw. Twenty guns of the latter took up a fresh position on a hill westward of Wirowan, the remainder recrossed the March by the bridge eastward of this village.

The Cavalry Division had detached three squadrons of the 10th Lancers to watch the passages over the Blatta above Biskupitz, and to observe the country towards Olmütz; the 4th squadron of the regiment was attached to the Infantry Brigade and had marched along the right bank of the Blatta towards Annadorf. The 2nd Hussars had not yet rejoined the division, so that General Hartmann had only 16 squadrons at his disposal with which he proceeded to Klopotowitz, passing by the left flank of his two batteries which had been sent forward at the commencement of the action.

The Brigade of Cuirassiers, at the head of the division, despatched the 5th Squadron on in advance to find a place for crossing the stream. The aide-de-camp of the division, Lieut. Von Rosenberg, had in the meantime discovered a bridge somewhat higher up between Biskupitz and Klopotowitz, and riding further on noticed that the large Austrian battery westward of Wirowan was without any guard. As soon as he reported this circumstance, Lieut.-Colonel Von Bredow led the three squadrons of the 5th Cuirassiers that were still with him over the very shaky bridge.

Guessing his motive, General Hartmann planted the two Horse Artillery batteries on the bank of the Blatta southward of Klopotowitz, from where they could engage the enemy, draw his attention off from the Cuirassiers, and assist their attack.

As soon as the latter had crossed the bridge, they advanced to the charge, which was led by the 2nd Squadron, Captain Von Schach; the 4th, Captain Von Massenbach, followed as left échelon; the 1st, Captain Von Schönaich, as reserve, on the right flank. The undulating ground afforded some shelter until the squadrons were close up to the guns, and the discharges of grape which they received at the last moment did not prevent their entering the batteries. The guns on the left wing had time to limber up, but were overtaken, and only two escaped.

A squadron of the enemy advanced from Nenakowitz, but was driven back again into the village by Lieut.-Colonel Von Bredow, with the 1st Squadron, and lost some prisoners.

By this successful charge 18 guns, 15 limbers, 7 artillery ammunition wagons, 2 officers, and 168 men fell into the hands of the Cuirassiers who themselves only lost 10 men.

11 A.M. The whole of the Cuirassier Brigade now assembled on the left bank of the Blatta, where it was joined by 3 squadrons of the 1st Landwehr Lancer Regiment and a Horse Artillery battery; all of these troops were under command of Major-General Von Borstell, and were to act as supports for General Von Malotki's Infantry brigade.

As soon as the Infantry Brigade was re-formed after the action at the high-road, General Malotki proceeded to attack Wirowan with the 2nd Battalion of the 44th and the 5th Company of the 4th Regiment, followed by the 1st Battalion of the latter regiment and the 4-pounder battery. The village was surrounded on three sides, and the enemy not only driven out of this, but also out of the adjoining villages, Rakodau and Nenakowitz, in great disorder and with the loss of many prisoners. The 4-pounder battery unlimbered south-eastward of Wirowan and opened fire on the Infantry, which retreated over the March to Zittow and on some guns at the Opleta wood. The 1st Battalion of the 44th Regiment stationed itself on the right of the battery at the foot of the hill.

General Von Hartmann now went to Tobistchau with the 4th Squadron of the 10th Lancers and the Horse Artillery battery of the 6th Artillery Regiment; the Landwehr Hussar Regiment and three squadrons of the 2nd Hussars, which had in the meantime rejoined the brigade, had been already ordered to proceed thither. Thus eight squadrons and six guns were available for carrying out the reconnaisance on Prerau as soon as the defiles were opened. In place of the 4th squadron of the 10th Lancers the 4th squadron of the Landwehr Lancer Regiment remained at Tobitschau, to cover the right flank towards Annadorf.

12 o'clock. General Malotki had himself sent Colonel Von Wedell with the remaining five companies of the 4th Regiment to the right wing to assist in the attack on Tobitschau, but the town had already been taken by Lieut.-Colonel Von Pannwitz, after a determined resistance on the part of the garrison, consisting— according to the statements of the prisoners—of three companies of the 71st Regiment (Toscana).

Seven companies were now at this spot, and they pressed the enemy, who at first made an obstinate resistance, back towards Traubeck.

The appearance of the Lancer squadron converted the enemy's retreat into a complete flight, which cost him numerous prisoners; a division of Lancers dispersed a small square, which still defended itself, and took 1 officer and 30 men prisoners.

Colonel Von Wedell then occupied the bridges over the March with the 10th and 11th, Traubeck with the 6th, 7th, and 8th, and the entrance of this village from Prerau with the 12th Company. The necessary preparations were made for sending the 9th Company forward on country carts, to accompany the Cavalry on its expedition to Prerau.

By some mistake the Lancer Brigade, which was to make this expedition, had taken the direction of Wirowan and had to be recalled as quickly as the fatigue of the horses permitted, and then had to start for Traubeck.

As soon as Wirowan and the adjoining villages were taken, fresh hostile batteries appeared near Dub. A still further advance was not within General Malotki's instructions, he therefore confined himself to holding his present position with his small detachments, and to securing the defile of Tobitschau, thus covering General Von Hartmann's reconnaissance on Prerau. Wirowan and Rakodau were occupied by the 2nd Battalion of the 44th, the bridge over the mill-stream eastward of these villages by the 5th Company of the 4th Regiment; the three other battalions were posted southward of Wirowan as reserve. General Borstell's Cavalry Brigade was hidden in the low ground westward of the high-road.

It was half-past 1 o'clock before the batteries at Dub 1.30 P.M. opened fire.

Dense clouds of dust on the Olmütz road now announced the approach of fresh forces. The 1st 4-pounder battery un-limbered on the hill between Wirowan and the high-road, and at the same time the 4th 4-pounder battery of the Advanced Guard, Captain Böhnke, arrived from Hrubschitz under cover of two squadrons of the 8th Lancers. It had been ordered up by General Von Bonin, and now unlimbered on the left of the 1st battery.

The Advanced Guard of the Corps itself did not reach Bis-kupitz until 2 P.M. and then planted its batteries—the 3rd 6-pounder and the 4th Horse Artillery—on the slope westward of the village where they opened fire at a long range. The Fusilier Battalion of the 3rd Regiment was pushed forward to the ford eastward of the village.

Under cover of his batteries the enemy now formed a body of Infantry of about the strength of a brigade with several squadrons of Lancers; the former then throw out dense swarms of skirmishers and advanced against Nenakowitz and Rakodau. It seems that the main body of the VIIIth Austrian Corps had sent forward reinforcements for the Brigade Rothkirch in order to cover its retreat from Dub to the left bank of the March, which had already commenced.

The attack of the enemy's skirmishers was unsuccessful, and the right flank of the brigade was very soon threatened by detachments of the advanced guard of the 1st Prussian Corps. The Fusilier Battalion of the 3rd Regiment and the 1st Regiment of Dragoons had crossed the Blatta eastward of Biskupitz and were joined by the 1st Cuirassiers during their advance.

The enemy eluded this attack by so hastily retreating to his artillery position that he could not be overtaken, but a sub-division of the 3rd Regiment made a few prisoners in Dub belonging to the 71st and 32nd Regiments, Toscana and Este.

Thus ended, at half-past 2 P.M., the share of the 1st Corps 2.30 P.M.

d'Armée in this day's action. General Von Malotki held his positions in Wirowan, Tobitschau, and Traubeck, and the remaining detachments of the corps assembled in a bivouac between Hrupschitz and Klopotowitz, where they were joined in the course of the afternoon by the 4th Infantry Brigade with the 1st Hussar Regiment and the 5th 4-pounder battery from Prossnitz. The Hussars and the battery had made a reconnaissance this morning between Czechuwek and Seilerndorf, in the course of which they had an encounter with a detachment of the enemy advancing from Stichowitz.

The losses of the Infantry in these different engagements amounted to 4 officers and 127 men, of whom all the officers and 79 men fell to the share of the 44th Regiment.

## ACTION AT ROKEINITZ.

The Brigade of Hussars did not reach Traubeck until 2 P.M. where the horses were hastily fed and re-saddled; they had been watered on the road already, the banks of the March descending so gradually to the water that whole squadrons could ride in at once. General Hartmann then immediately proceeded to carry out the reconnaissance, which had been entrusted to him, without being deterred, either by the length of the Tobitschau-Traubeck defile, or the sound of the cannonade in his rear at Dub.

The General Staff Officer, Captain Von Versen, who was on in advance of the division, found a ford through the Beczwa, eastward of Wrbowetz; riding on along the Olmütz railway, he came upon a numerous suite, which he took to be that of Feldzeugmeister Benedek himself.

About 3 o'clock the Cavalry crossed the ford. Several detachments of the enemy were marching between Rokeinitz and Dlaluwitz, and a considerable train of wagons was seen on the Olmütz road, in the direction of Prerau. These were parts of the Ist Austrian Corps on its march to Prerau, the Generals and Staff Officers of which were not with their troops at the moment, having been called to General Count Gondrecourt. The unexpected appearance of the Prussian Cavalry visibly produced no slight commotion.

The 9th Company of the 4th Regiment had followed on carts and was left by Major-General Von Hartmann at the ford. The Horse Artillery battery, Captain Le Bauld de Nans, was sent 1,200 paces north-eastward, covered by the 4th squadron of the 1st Hussars. The Landwehr Hussar Regiment formed line to the right of the battery, the 4th squadron of the 10th Lancers was on the right wing of the Hussars and the 2nd and 3rd squadrons of the 2nd Hussars were in second line.

The first line advanced to the attack soon after the battery had opened fire. The Lancer Squadron came upon a body of Infantry standing 300 paces westward of Dlaluwitz, a great part of which was either pierced by the lances or ridden over, the remainder fled into the village. The squadron lost 3 men and 12 horses killed and 2 men and 8 horses wounded, and withdrew out of range of the village with a considerable number of prisoners.

The charge of the 1st and 2nd squadrons of the Landwehr Hussars under Colonel Von Glasenapp came upon a larger square of Infantry which stood further to the rear, midway between both villages. The order in its ranks had been much shaken already by the shells of the Horse Artillery battery. After firing a precipitate and therefore ineffectual volley, the enemy retreated hastily to Przedmost, but was overtaken by the Landwehr Hussars. The Infantry tried to form square, but the greater part was cut down, and above 300 prisoners captured.

The 3rd Squadron of the same regiment likewise dispersed a detachment of Infantry 500 paces from Rokeinitz, by the side of the road leading from the east end of the village to the west skirts of Dlaluwitz, and then dashed on after the train of wagons on the Olmütz road. The greatest confusion prevailed at this spot. Many drivers cut the traces and endeavoured to escape, others upset their wagons in trying to turn, and the whole train was in the utmost disorder.

The charge of the 4th Squadron was attended with equal success. Trotting past the right wing of the 1st and 3rd Squadrons it attacked and scattered a detachment of Infantry some hundred paces from the north entrance of Dlaluwitz.

The Horse Artillery battery advanced about 700 paces further, and opened fire on two battalions which appeared at the east outlet of Rokeinitz.

These successes now induced the second line to join in the engagement. It proceeded to attack the two last-mentioned battalions. The 3rd Squadron of the 2nd Hussars came upon a ravine, and was fired on in front and from the skirts of the village, so that it was obliged to turn back; it immediately returned to the attack, but with no better success. The 2nd Squadron broke into a square and took an officer and some men of the 33rd Regiment (Gyulai) prisoners, but got into a flank fire at close range, and was also obliged to retreat without obtaining any further result. The squadron which was attached to the battery as covering guard now alone remained intact.

Strong columns of Austrian Infantry and Cavalry now deployed northward of Rokeinitz and several batteries unlimbered on the heights north-eastward of this village. The Hussars that were occupied with the train on the high-road were very soon engaged with Austrian Cuirassiers.

For these reasons General Hartmann sounded the recall. The 2nd and 3rd Squadrons of the 2nd Hussars, the 4th Squadron of the Landwehr Regiment and the Lancer Squadron were very soon re-formed at Wrbowetz, and the Horse Artillery battery fell back to the same spot. This could not be so soon effected by the three other Landwehr squadrons, the struggle they had been engaged in had caused more disorder in their ranks. Colonel Glasenapp re-formed them on their way back, and was still occupied in so doing, when he perceived three squadrons of the Austrian "Haller" Hussars on his flank, trotting up past Dlaluwitz from the direction of Prerau ; almost at the same moment two other squadrons were seen coming from Przedmost.

Thinking to impose upon the enemy the Colonel changed the pace of the Hussars from a trot to a walk, and moved somewhat nearer to Rokeinitz. The enemy showed no inclination to charge and fell into a walk likewise, but threw out skirmishers which followed so close up to the Landwehr Hussars—at times within 10 paces—that Colonel Glazenapp determined to charge himself, under the supposition that the remainder of the Prussian Cavalry must be in the neighbourhood and would join in the action.

There were but seven divisions of nine rank and file each, or about 130 Landwehr Hussars on the spot, the remainder of the 1st, 2nd, and 3rd Squadrons were either engaged in escorting prisoners or had not yet rejoined the regiment. A few words of instruction sufficed to prepare the Hussars, who fronted towards the enemy, and then immediately charged with as much vehemence as the strength of their horses permitted. The enemy was completely taken by surprise, halted, and received the shock in compact order, but standing still. A prolonged and obstinate hand-to-hand fight ensued. The Landwehr Hussars being considerably overmatched were ultimately obliged to give way. Colonel Glasenapp fell covered with nine wounds, and was taken prisoner.

The Austrian Hussars followed slowly and cautiously. The attack of so small a detachment led them to suspect the neighbourhood of considerable supports. This was in reality the case, but the action had not been seen at Wrbowetz, being hidden from view by a gentle rise in the ground. As soon, however, as the Landwehr Hussars were seen retreating in a running fight with the enemy, General Hartmann advanced with three squadrons to their support, upon which further pursuit ceased on the part of the enemy. The Prussians remained a full hour on the battle-field to remove the wounded, the prisoners, and the captured horses, without being disturbed by the enemy ; only a patrol of four Landwehr Hussars, who rode back to seek their Colonel on the field, were surrounded and taken prisoners by the enemy.

The unexpected appearance and the attack of the Prussian Cavalry had caused the greatest confusion amongst the marching columns of the 1st Austrian Corps. Although many of the prisoners found opportunities for escaping in the high corn, still 5 officers and 250 men were brought back.

General Von Hartmann did not leave the field until 5 o'clock, and then returned by the way he came, and bivouacked westward of Tobitschau. General Malotki's Brigade remained in its position until darkness set in, and then rejoined its corps between Klopotowitz and Hrupschitz, but kept Biskupitz and Tobitschau occupied.

The losses of the Cavalry in the action of Tobitschau and Rokeinitz were—

| | Killed. | | | | Wounded and Missing. | | | |
|---|---|---|---|---|---|---|---|---|
| | Officers. | Non-Commissioned Officers. | Privates. | Horses. | Officers. | Non-commissioned Officers. | Privates. | Horses. |
| 1st Regiment of Cuirassiers .. | .. | .. | .. | 9 | .. | 2 | 7 | 2 |
| 5th ,, ,, .. | .. | .. | .. | 12 | .. | .. | 10 | 3 |
| 4th Squadron of 10th Lancers .. | .. | .. | 3 | 12 | .. | 1 | 2 | 8 |
| 2nd and 3rd Squadrons of 2nd Hussars .. .. .. | 1 | 3 | 8 | 2 | 3 | 13 | 3 | |
| 2nd Landwehr Hussars .. .. | .. | .. | 3 | 7 | 5 | 10 | 42 | 39 |
| Total .. .. | .. | 1 | 9 | 48 | 7 | 16 | 74 | 65 |
| The Artillery lost.. .. | .. | .. | .. | .. | 1 | .. | 6 | 10 |

The total losses of the Prussian troops in both actions of the 15th of July thus amounted to 12 officers and 235 men. Their adversaries lost, according to Austrian accounts, 40 officers and 1,965 men.

Hirtenfeld's calendar states the casualties of the Austrian troops, exclusive of officers, as follows:—

| | Killed. | Wounded. | Missing. | Total. |
|---|---|---|---|---|
| 21st Infantry Regiment .. .. | .. | .. | 30 | 30 |
| 25th ,, ,, .. .. | 5 | 12 | 31 | 48 |
| 32nd ,, ,, .. .. | .. | .. | 148 | 148 |
| 71st ,, ,, .. .. | 97 | 407 | 539 | 1,043 |
| 77th ,, ,, .. .. | .. | .. | 68 | 68 |
| 33rd ,, ,, .. .. | 5 | 14 | 167 | 186 |
| 38th ,, ,, .. .. | .. | 10 | 46 | 56 |
| 5th Battalion of Rifles .. .. | .. | .. | 2 | 2 |
| 32nd ,, ,, .. .. | .. | .. | 6 | 6 |
| 4th Regiment of Hussars .. .. | .. | .. | 13 | 13 |
| 14th ,, ,, .. .. | .. | .. | 4 | 4 |
| 11th Regiment of Artillery .. .. | .. | .. | 11 | 11 |
| 9th ,, ,, .. .. | .. | .. | .. | 332 |
| Covering Guard of Artillery .. .. | .. | .. | 3 | 3 |
| Pioneer Detachment .. .. .. | 2 | 2 | 2 | 6 |
| Total .. .. .. | 109 | 445 | 1,070 | 1,956 |

During the action at Tobitschau the Vth Prussian Corps marched according to the orders it had received, occupied Prossnitz, and pushed an advanced guard forward towards Ollschau. The Guards and the VIth Corps reached Boskowitz and Lettowitz; the Crown Prince's head-quarters remained at Konitz. The latter now resolved to leave only the Ist Corps in front of Olmütz to check any attempts of the enemy to intercept the communications of the army, and that the Guards and the VIth Corps should continue their march by way of Blansko and Czernahora, so as to arrive at Brünn on the 17th. The Vth Corps and the Cavalry Division were to follow on the flank of the enemy's march, and were to throw detachments over the March, or even altogether to cross the river, if an opportunity occurred of disturbing the enemy's retreat.

The necessary arrangements were made to carry out these intentions the next day, and a report sent to the King's head-quarters. The Quartermaster of the IInd Army, Major-General Von Stosch, himself repaired to Brünn, to explain the Crown Prince's motives, and to request further instructions.

The Ist Army resumed its march towards Vienna on this day.

The advanced guard, Duke William of Meklenburg, advanced by way of Pohrlitz to Muschau, in order to secure this important passage over the Thaja. The bridge was found to have been destroyed, but the 2nd Squadron of the 11th Lancers forded the river, and about ten men of the 60th Regiment swam across, upon which some Austrian patrols of "Mexico" Lancers that were on the opposite side retreated, so that the Prussian Lancers only succeeded in capturing four of them at Nikolsburg. The remainder of the 11th Lancers and two battalions of Infantry crossed the Thaja in the course of the afternoon; the latter by means of a small bridge which was thrown over. The 6th Division followed the advanced guard as far as Pohrlitz; on its left the 7th Division advanced to Gross-Niemschitz, the 8th to Koblank.

On the right wing the Cavalry corps was instructed to advance with its whole force towards Dürnholz and Grusbach, and to drive back any detachments of the enemy that might still be northward of the Thaja and the Jaispitz. When this was done, General Rheinbaben's Brigade was to join the advanced guard of the IInd Corps d'Armée, which was pushed forward to Laa, the latter corps itself was to reach Mislitz. The 5th Division was to remain for the present at Brünn.

The troops were already on the march in the above-mentioned directions, when Prince Frederick Charles received orders from His Majesty's head-quarters, dated 8 A.M. of the same day, to advance towards Lundenburg. These orders were given in consequence of the report received from the IInd Army.

No immediate alterations could be made in the arrangements which had been made for to-day, but orders were despatched to the 7th Division to establish communications with the 8th Division, and to push its head on to Auspitz to-day for this purpose. The 5th Division was ordered to leave Brünn for Mönitz and Tellnitz.

The 8th Division had been instructed to take possession of

Göding next day, and as far as possible to prevent any demolition of the railway, so that the army might be able to make use of it later. The intelligence, however, which now arrived, that the enemy had been transporting his troops on this line for several days, rendered it important to check this traffic as soon as possible, by breaking up the rails in such a manner that the line might afterwards be easily repaired.

For this purpose General Von Horn sent a detachment of 150 of the best horses of the 6th Lancers, with a pioneer section from Koblank to the railway northward of Göding. This detachment was watched by the enemy's patrols, but arrived at its destination by 6 o'clock the same evening. Before it reached the line two trains were seen to pass from the direction of Olmütz. Several rails were now taken up and the telegraph wires cut. During this occupation a third train, containing Saxon troops, came up, but must have received timely warning, for it halted and turned back. Austrian Infantry and Cavalry now approached, and the detachment retired to Koblank. It had started from beyond Brünn at 3 A.M., and reached its bivouac at Koblank at 12 P.M., having made 56 miles on this day.

In consequence of the presence of Prussian troops near Göding, telegraphic orders were despatched from Vienna for Colonel Mondl's Brigade of the Xth Corps, which was stationed at Lundenburg, to retreat per rail to Marchegg the same night.

Not having received any further orders by the forenoon of the 15th, the Army of the Elbe continued its march to Znaym, and occupied this town with the 14th Division.

The advanced guard marched to Haugsdorf and Jetzelsdorf, and had a slight encounter at the latter village. On debouching from the village the leading squadron of the 11th Hussars was shelled from the heights southward of the Pulkau brook. Captain Pilgrim's 4-pounder Battery returned the fire, and after a few shots the enemy's battery withdrew under cover of some squadrons of "Savoyen" Dragoons and "King of Prussia" Hussars. The 11th Hussars pursued them, but only brought back four prisoners and three horses, as the enemy did not make any stand.

On the Austrian side the IVth and IInd Corps reached, the former Zdaunek, and the latter Kremsier, to-day, without being disturbed, but two Prussian brigades had sufficed to render the retreat of the second *échelon* impossible on the right bank of the March, a Cavalry detachment had materially disturbed it on the left bank. The VIIIth Corps had retreated beyond the river, which it probably crossed at Dub, and was now at Prerau with the Ist Corps. Feldzeugmeister Benedek spent the night at the same place.

The same evening the news arrived that the Ist Prussian Army had reached Göding also.

Under these circumstances all idea of reaching the Danube through the valley of the March was necessarily abandoned as totally impossible. All that could now be done was, to try how far this object might be attained by making a detour through the mountains, and down the valley of the Waag.

Feldzeugmeister Benedek issued the following orders in consequence.

The IVth Corps which was at Zdaunek was directed to cover the march of the army, and to retreat by way of Kunowitz, near Ungarish-Hradisch, and Welka to Miawa, where it was to arrive on the 18th, on which day the IInd Corps was to reach Waag-Neustadtl from Kremsier, by way of Ungarisch-Hradisch and Strany.

The Ist Corps was to march from Prerau by way of Freystadtl, Slawitschin, and over the Wlar pass, the VIIIth by Holleschan, Zadmerzitz, Boikowitz, and over the Hrosenkau pass to the river Waag.

The VIth Corps, which was still at Olmütz, was to make a still greater detour, and take the route Leipnik, Wallachisch-Meseritsch, Wsetin, and Klobank. A second *échelon*, consisting of six battalions and three batteries of the 2nd Saxon Division, whose transport, per rail, had been interrupted, and of some thousand men of the VIIIth Austrian Corps, was to leave Olmütz on the 16th, and follow the route of the VIth Corps.

The orders for the continuation of this movement as far as Pressburg were not issued from head-quarters at Slawitschin until the 17th.

### THE 16TH OF JULY.

Head-quarters of the Prussian IInd Army were moved to Prödlitz, the Guards and the VIth Corps continued their march in the direction of the day before ; the former reached Czerna-Lora, the latter the neighbourhood of Raitz and Petrowitz.

The corps that were still in front of Olmütz received orders this morning for the Vth to march to Prerau, and for the Ist to support this movement with a strong division ; the Cavalry Division was instructed to cover its right flank.

In consideration of the position of both corps, and at the proposal of General Von Steinmetz, the Generals commanding the two corps mutually agreed that the Ist Corps should advance to Prerau, and be supported by a division of the Vth. In conformity with this arrangement, the dispositions of the Ist Corps were so planned that General Von Clausewitz should advance with the 2nd Division on the Tobitschau road to Prerau, and break up the railway there ; Colonel Von Bredow's combined Cavalry Brigade was to follow the 2nd Division to Traubeck, and then to keep along the right bank of the Beczwa. In order to secure the passage of the defiles the advanced guard brigade was to take post at Traubeck, the reserve at Wiklitzer-Hof and Tobitschau.

The 9th Division of the Vth Corps set off early and reached Kralitz in the course of the forenoon, where it found the Ist

Corps still in its bivouac, intending not to commence the expedition until the men had cooked their rations. For this reason the 9th Division returned to its quarters at noon, and the 10th Division, with General Von Wnuck's Cavalry Brigade, were assembled at Dub in the afternoon, from whence the latter made a reconnaissance towards Kokor, whilst the Ist Corps marched to Prerau.

When the head of the latter corps reached this town, at half-past 5 P.M., it was found to have been evacuated by the enemy, whose last detachment had left by the road to Moschteinitz as early as 9 A.M. Upon this being reported, the 10th Division, and those detachments of the Ist Corps that were further to the rear, were recalled to their bivouacs.

The 2nd Division not only broke up about 1,000 paces of the railway northward of the Beczwa, but also blew up an iron bridge across the river, thereby intercepting the communications with Silesia, which was not the intention of the Commander-in-Chief of the IInd Army. The division did not return to its bivouac before 3 o'clock the next morning, after seizing considerable stores of provisions and oats, which were found at Prerau.

General Hartmann's Division did not return to its bivouac, near Klopotowitz until between 12 and 2 in the night, without having come in contact with the enemy.

The Ist Army continued its advance southward according to its instructions.

The 8th Division reached Göding at 4 P.M., and found the place occupied by a small detachment which had been left to guard the stores there, and which now fell back to Holitsch. The light bridge train of the corps repaired the bridge over the March, and the 2nd squadron of the 6th Lancers then crossed the river with the 4th Company of the 31st Regiment, and advanced to Holitsch where they were received by Infantry fire. The company entered the town, and the squadron rode round the north side of it, where it met and charged some detachments of Lancers and Cuirassiers.

An officer and 17 men of the 79th Regiment (Frank) were taken prisoners in Holitsch. As this regiment belonged to the VIth Austrian Corps, they were most probably part of its fourth battalion. Darkness prevented any further advance.

The 7th Division marched on the left, the advanced guard on the right bank of the Thaja to Lundenburg. The Infantry of the latter crossed the river by a small bridge which was thrown over the day before, the Cavalry by a ford. A more solid bridge had to be constructed for the Artillery and the train which was not completed until 10 o'clock. As news in the meantime had arrived that Lundenburg was occupied by the 7th Division, the advanced guard remained at Eisgrub, and only pushed forward a squadron of Lancers to Lundenburg.

The 5th Division advanced to Czeitsch behind the 7th.

The Cavalry Corps marched to Felsberg and Drasenhofen,

2 A

and watched the high-road to Vienna.  Under its cover the 6th Division advanced to Nikolsburg, and the IInd Corps marched from Mislitz to Gutenfeld and Unter-Danowitz.

Head-quarters of Prince Frederick Charles moved to Pawlowitz.

The Commander-in-Chief of the Army of the Elbe had already given his instructions for marching to Ober-Hollabrunn and Enzersdorf-im-Thal on the 16th, but the despatch from the King's head-quarters ordering the army to march by Laa to Wülfersdorf, arrived on the night of the 15th, and made some alterations necessary.  In consequence, the divisions of the army marched to Wülzeshofen, Erdberg, Höflein, and Neudorf, villages near Laa; the advanced guard was pushed forward southward to Eichenbrunn, where it surprised two squadrons of Austrian Cuirassiers in their bivouac.  In order to mislead the enemy as to the direction in which the Army of the Elbe was marching, two squadrons of the 7th Hussars remained on the Znaim-Ober-Hollabrunn road.  At the latter place they again came upon the same detachment of " Savoyen " Dragoons and " King of Prussia " Hussars that had been met at Jetzelsdorf; nothing occurred, however, beyond a few shots fired by the Austrian battery.

The IVth Corps of the Austrian Army of the north, and the bulk of the Saxon Cavalry, marched during the night of the 15th to Ungarisch-Hradisch, and proceeded from thence to Ostra.  The IInd Army and a Saxon " Reiter " Regiment reached Ungarisch-Hradisch by the Kwassitz-Tlumatschau-Napagedl road ; a few battalions kept up the communication with the IVth Corps, by way of Allenkowitz and Neudorf, and covered the flank of the march.

The stores at Ungarisch-Hradisch were either distributed among the troops or brought to a place of security.  Whatever locomotive engines could not be removed were rendered unfit for use.

The Feldzeugmeister marched with the Ist and VIIIth Corps to the neighbourhood of Freistadtl and Holleschau on this day ; the VIth Corps started from Leipnik ; at which place the Saxon Division of General Von Stieglitz arrived from Olmütz.  The latter, however, left again after a few hours' rest, and marched the same night as far as Weisskirchen.

### The 17th of July.

Having once recognized the necessity of making this detour over the Lesser Carpathian Mountains, in order to unite his army with the Army of the South, then assembling at Vienna, Feldzeugmeister Benedek made energetic efforts to regain the time which was thus unavoidably lost, by making long marches, which were most creditable to the perseverence and endurance of his troops.

In spite of the difficulty of crossing so mountainous a

country, the ends of his long columns reached the following line by the 17th of July:—Welka, IVth Corps; Strany, IInd Corps; Zadmersitz, Ist and VIIIth Corps; Meseritsch, VIth Corps; head-quarters were established in Slawitschin.

The direction which the Austrian Army had thus taken was naturally not known at the Prussian head-quarters. It was indeed evident that only part of the Army of the North could be between Kremsier and Skalitz, but even in this case sufficient troops must have been left to occupy the country between Lundenburg and Göding for the present, so as to bar the roads to Pressburg and Vienna. It was therefore necessary that one corps at least of the IInd Prussian Army should be brought up along the March, in order to drive whatever detachments of the enemy might still be in the valley of the river into the mountains.

To follow the enemy eastward with any considerable force, in case he made this detour, would have interrupted the communications with the Ist Army. It was deemed preferable to take the most direct route to the Danube, to cross this river either at Vienna or further westward, and thus to separate both hostile armies.

Olmütz could be sufficiently observed by leaving the Ist Corps in a position on the left bank of the March, between Tobitschau and Prerau, from whence detachments and small parties of Cavalry could watch the neighbourhood of the fortress. This position, however, was not occupied until the next day, because the corps thought it necessary to take up the cantonments which were ordered on the 13th, viz., Urtschitz, Ottonowitz and Weischowitz on the road to Brünn, to which it marched from Tobitschau on the afternoon of the 17th.

The Vth Corps and Gen. Hartmann's Cavalry Division were ordered to advance along the March, and it was left to General Steinmetz to act according to his own discretion in case he met the enemy. This march was, however, likewise deferred until the following day, because it was necessary to give the troops a day's rest, which they had not enjoyed since the 11th.

The Guards and the VIth Corps continued their march behind the Ist Army and reached Brünn, the heads of both corps advancing as far as Turas and Mederitz.

The 8th Division of the Ist Army advanced to Holitsch, the 5th Division and the Reserve Artillery of the IVth Corps to Göding; the 7th Division still occupied Lundenburg, and the Reserve Artillery of the IIIrd Corps marched in the direction of Kostel and Rampersdorf.

The remainder of the army moved on towards the Danube.

The Cavalry Corps marched in *échelons* down the right bank of the March as far as Hohenau and Bernhardsthal.

The Duke of Mecklenburg's advanced guard was sent forward on the high-road to Vienna, but finding Wilfersdorf already occupied by the Army of the Elbe, it turned off to the left to Prinzendorf and Hauskirchen, where it went into cantonments.

The 6th Division followed on the same road to Poisdorf and Wetzelsdorf, the 4th Division to Nikolsburg. General Rheinbaben's Cavalry brigade, which was attached to the IInd Corps, advanced on the right wing of the army to Neudorf and Kirchstädten ; it was followed by the 3rd Division.

The Army of the Elbe executed the orders of the 15th by moving likewise towards the Nikolsburg-Vienna road, and occupied Wilfersdorf and Mistelbach with its advanced guard. The Ist Army had already reached the villages further to the rear. For this reason the 16th Division went into cantonments on the west side of the road at Erdberg, the 15th at Ameis and Föllin, the 14th round about Enzersdorf and Staatz.

One battalion, two squadrons, and two guns were pushed forward towards Gaunersdorf, and met a few squadrons of Cuirassiers beyond Schrick. The latter were driven off by the fire of the two guns and left eight men killed on the field.

The same evening an Austrian Cavalry detachment surprised a picquet of the Prussian 11th Hussars, and wounded two men.

## The 18th of July.

His Majesty's head-quarters were moved to Nikolsburg on this day.

Prince Frederick Charles did not issue any orders to the Ist Army on the 17th for the continuation of its march on Vienna, because a telegram had been received from the King's head-quarters stating that fresh orders might soon be expected. The latter arrived at 6 A.M. of the 18th. They were dated Brünn the 17th, and the following were their principal contents :—

" His Majesty intends the general advance of the " army towards the Danube to be continued, but it " remains to be decided whether this will take place in " the direction of Vienna or of Pressburg.

" The Army of the Elbe will follow the Brünn-Vienna " high-road, and will watch the road from Dürnkruth " and Laa to Vienna.

" The Ist Army will advance on both banks of the " March, and will secure, and if necessary repair, the " bridges over this river. The army will prevent the " retreat of the enemy from Olmütz to Vienna and " Pressburg.

" As soon as the IInd Army can be dispensed with in " front of Olmütz, it will assemble on the line Nikolsburg-" Lundenburg, and will closely follow the advance of the " Ist Army and the Army of the Elbe.

" The Ist Army and the Army of the Elbe will keep " on the same height with each other during their " advance. In order to arrive at the Danube with con-" centrated forces, only short marches will be made " until the IInd Army can come up. As it is possible " that the enemy may assume the offensive from Vienna,

" or perhaps from Pressburg also, the situation of affairs
" makes it requisite for the armies to keep closer together,
" and to increase the strength of their advanced guards,
" especially that of the Army of the Elbe. The latter
" army will concentrate to-morrow, the 18th, round about
" Wilfersdorf, and will await further orders for its ad-
" vance. The Ist Army will take into consideration that
" a division may possibly be ordered to make a rapid
" march from Malaczka to Pressburg, to seize on the
" town and the passages over the Danube, and if possible
" to secure Hainburg and Kitsee also. This will, how-
" ever, not be done without further orders.

(Signed)    " VON MOLTKE."

When the corresponding orders, which were issued to the
different armies were carried out, the situation of the Ist Army
westward of the March was as follows:—The advanced guard
at Spanberg, on its left the Cavalry Corps at Götzendorf, Dürnkruth, and Jedenspeigen; the 7th Division at Drösing, the 6th
Division in Zistersdorf; the IInd Corps further to the rear at
Feldsberg and Herrenbaum-Garten; the Cavalry brigade of
General Von Rheinbaben rejoined the Cavalry Corps on
this day.

Eastward of the March the 8th Division was pushed forward
to St. Johann, where it opened communication with the 7th
Division. The 5th Division was moved up to Holitsch to watch
the Olmütz and Tyrnau roads; head-quarters of the Army
were moved to Hohenau.

The concentration of the Army of the Elbe took place on
the line Asparn, 14th Division; Mistelbach, advanced guard;
Wilfersdorf, 16th Division; the 15th Division behind the latter
at Wetzelsdorf. The detachment at Gaunersdorf remained
there without encountering the enemy any more. The detachment on the Znaym-Stockerau road advanced to Göllersdorf,
and only met with small parties of Cavalry, which retired to
Stockerau with the loss of a few prisoners.

The Guards and the VIth Corps continued their march
beyond Brünn on both sides of the Schwarzawa; the former
as far as Lauschitz and Gross-Raigern, the latter to Mödlau and
Rohrbach. General Von Steinmetz reached the river Hanna at
Mierowitz and Kojetein, and pushed his advanced guard over
the stream; General Hartmann's Cavalry Division advanced to
Kremsier and Hullein. From there the 10th Lancers and 2nd
Hussars marched to Tlumatschau and Kwassitz without meeting
the enemy anywhere.

Information which General Von Hartmann obtained from
some Austrian stragglers proved to a certainty that the Ist and
VIIIth Austrian Corps had retreated by way of Holleschau and
Wisowitz, the IInd and IVth by Kremsier and Hradisch, over
very bad roads, into the mountains, and that much disorder
prevailed upon this march—at least among the Infantry.

In reality the IVth Corps reached Miawa already on this day, the IInd Waag-Neustadt. The rear guard of the latter (Colonel Thom's brigade) remained in Szrnye; the Ist and VIIIth Corps were drawing near the valley of the Waag, the former having arrived between Stitna and Nemsowa, the latter at Boïkowitz; whereas the VIth Corps reached Klobank, and General Von Stieglitz, Wsetin. The Feldzeugmeister transferred his head-quarters to Trentschin.

Orders from the Commander-in-Chief reached General Count Thun at Waag-Neustadl, directing him to march to Trebéthe on the 19th, to halt there for a day, and then to proceed by way of Malzenice, Cziffer, and Wartberg to Pressburg, where he was to arrive on the 24th. Simultaneously with these orders, however, Major Fejervary, aide-de-camp of the Emperor, arrived from Vienna, and urged the pressing necessity of supporting Colonel Mondl's brigade, which had retreated from Marchegg by way of Blumenau to Pressburg, as well as of protecting Pressburg, which was seriously endangered by the advance of considerable hostile forces from Göding.

In spite of the fatigue of his troops Count Thun immediately determined so to hasten his march as to reach Pressburg on the 22nd already.

Major Fejervary proceeded to head-quarters of the army, and at his request fresh orders were despatched to the IInd Corps, according to which it was to reach Pressburg in four days. As far as possible part of the troops were to be conveyed there in carts. The instructions for the corps were " to secure Pressburg " and the adjoining part of the Lesser Carpathian Mountains." These orders reached the IInd Corps the next day after it had already started.

The Ist Prussian Corps took up the necessary positions for investing Olmütz. A detachment under Colonel Von Bredow, consisting of three battalions and the Reserve Cavalry, occupied Prossnitz, and watched the different roads which meet at this town. Major-General Von Barnekow occupied Rakodau, Wirowan, and Dub with the 2nd Brigade of Infantry, two squadrons of Dragoons, and one battery, and placed outposts northward of these villages between the Blatta and the March.

The country on the left bank of the latter river was watched by the 2nd Division of Infantry, which was reinforced by the 12th lancers and a battery. A combined brigade of the division was stationed at Prerau, the other brigade at Traubeck; the line of outposts of the division observed the country between the Olleschnitza brook and the Beczwa at Legsek. The former advanced guard brigade of the corps was posted at Tobitschau and neighbourhood, the Reserve Artillery at Lobeditz, Annadorf, &c. Head-quarters of the corps were at Tobitschau.

## THE 19TH OF JULY.

The heads of the Prussian Army were now within two days' march of Vienna, but a considerable part of the troops were still as far behind as Brünn and Kojetein.

At 11 P.M. of the 18th a communication was sent from the King's head-quarters, stating that the Army of the Elbe would have a day's rest in its present position at Asparn and Wilfersdorf after its fatiguing marches, and that the IInd Army could not reach the line Muschau-Pawlowitz with two of its corps until the 20th; that it was therefore advisable that no general advance of the Ist Army beyond the line Malaczka-Gaunersdorf should take place on the 19th.

When Prince Frederick Charles received this letter, at 4 A.M., he had already given his instructions for the advance of his army; they were now so far modified that the army reached the following positions:—

On the right bank of the March the advanced guard and the Cavalry Corps occupied the line of the Weiden brook from Schönkirchen to Zwirndorf; behind these troops were the 6th Division, at Prottes, Ollersdorf; and the 7th Division at Dürnkruth. The IInd Corps marched to Zistersdorf and Drösing.

On the left bank the 8th Division advanced to Gross-Schützen, the 5th Division to Kuti.

Railway and telegraphs were destroyed at Unter Gänserndorf, but the bridges at Dürnkruth and Anger were repaired. Nothing was seen of the enemy but patrols.

The Army of the Elbe remained in its position of the 18th, in which, if attacked by the enemy, it was to hold the line of the Zaya. The 14th Division pushed an advanced guard forward to Ladendorf, the right flank detachment advanced to Sierndorf.

The VIth Corps of the IInd Army reached the neighbourhood of Muschau, the 1st Division of Guards, Auspitz; the 2nd had a day's rest in Gross-Raigern, in order to make arrangements for regulating its supplies.

The Crown Prince moved his head-quarters to Gross-Seelowitz.

General Von Steinmetz advanced to Napagedl with General Von Hartmann's Cavalry Division, and sent forward detachments from here as far as Zlin and Hradschowitz. The 9th Division reached Kwassitz, the 10th Tlumatschau, their advanced guards the line Bielow-Ottrokowitz. Thirteen locomotive engines and 125 railway carriages were seized at the station of Altstadt.

The IInd Corps of the Austrian Army continued its march on the road to Pressburg as far as Trebéthe and Kosztolan; the IVth left General Fleischhacker's brigade and the 2nd Saxon "Reiter" Regiment at Miawa, the Brigade Kaminiecki and the 1st Saxon "Reiter" Regiment were sent to Jablonitz, the main body of the corps took up a position at Verbocz, on the Göding Tyrnau road.

The Ist Corps descended the valley of the Waag as far as

Trentschin, the VIIIth as far as Kosztolna; the VIth Corps reached Nemsowa, the Saxon Division Stieglitz Klobank.

It was not known for certain at Prussian head-quarters how great a part of the Austrian Army of the North had been sent per rail from Olmütz to Vienna previous to the arrival of the IInd Prussian Army in front of the fortress, or how much had afterwards marched along the Waag to Pressburg. It was moreover doubtful whether it had yet been possible to form a Reserve Army out of the Austrian 4th and 5th Battalions, and to assemble it behind the Danube, and above all how much of the Army of the South had been conveyed to Vienna by the railway transports, which had commenced six days ago. Nothing was heard of any activity on the part of the Italian Army, by which they might have been prevented. Austrian accounts, unauthenticated it is true, stated the number of available forces there to be very considerable. The great extent of the fortifications in front of the Danube seemed calculated for a large body of troops, and it was, to say the least, not impossible but that the Austrians might, by making use of their very last resources, have already assembled an army which could issue forth from the lines of Florisdorf and offer battle on the Marchfeld to save the capital.

On the part of the Prussian Army great vigilance and close concentration of the troops were necessary. Their numbers sufficed for all purposes.

Circumstances might occur in which the King's orders must reach the Commanders-in-Chief too late to ensure the necessary co-operation of their armies; it was therefore deemed necessary to make them fully acquainted with His Majesty's intentions.

A rescript from head-quarters, dated the 19th of July, states on this point:—

"It is the intention of His Majesty the King to con-"centrate the army in a position behind the Russbach, "with the Army of the Elbe at Wolkersdorf, the Ist Army "behind Deutsch-Wagram, and the IInd as Reserve at "Schönkirchen.

"The objects of this position are to enable the army "in the first place to meet any attack which the enemy "might make with about 150,000 men from Florisdorf, and "secondly, either to reconnoitre and attack the Floris-"dorf entrenchments, or else to leave a corps of observa-"tion in front of them, and to march as quickly as possible "to Pressburg.

"For this purpose those detachments which are already "available, viz., the Army of the Elbe, the IInd Corps, "the 6th Division, the Cavalry Corps, and the advanced "guard of the Ist Army will advance to-morrow, the "20th, no further than the 'Weidenbach,' between "Gaunersdorf and Weikendorf, so as to give time to "those detachments of the army which are following to "come up. Both armies will push outposts and recon-

" naissances on to the ' Russbach,' in the direction of
" Wolkersdorf and Deutsch-Wagram.

" Simultaneously with this movement an attempt will
" be made to gain possession of Pressburg by surprise,
" and to secure the passage of the Danube at this spot.
" It is left to the Commander-in-Chief of the Ist Army
" to give the necessary orders to the troops which are
" available for this purpose on the left bank of the
" March, at Malaczka. The Commander-in-Chief of the
" Ist Army will likewise take measures for bringing up
" the 5th Division from Holitsch as soon as circumstances
" will permit.

" The IInd Army will arrange the continuation of the
" march of the Guards and the VIth Corps in the direction
" of Lundenburg and Nikolsburg. It is taken for granted
" that these corps will reach the line Drösing-Wilfersdorf,
" and be ready to support the Ist Army and the Army of
" the Elbe by the 21st. The Commander-in-Chief of the
" IInd Army will be able to judge how soon the Vth Corps
" can be brought up, and will then give the necessary
" orders, as it is in any case desirable to commence
" operations at the Danube, if possible, with the entire
" force of the army.

" Arrangements have been made for eventually bring-
" ing up the Ist Reserve Corps from Prague and Pardu-
" bitz per rail.

(Signed)    " VON MOLTKE."

The necessary preparations were made at His Majesty's head-
quarters for attacking the Florisdorf lines, as well as for crossing
the Danube.

Fifty mobilized rifled 12-pounder guns were in readiness at
Dresden to be despatched per rail to Lundenburg at a moment's
notice. The Inspector-General of Artillery was instructed to
assemble a park of horses and wagons at Lundenburg for con-
veying them on further.

The three pontoon trains of the IInd Army had already arrived.
at Kostel near Lundenburg; the two pontoon trains of the Ist
Army were on the road to Bernhardtsthal and Drösing. A company of Pioneers that was left at Dresden was brought up per rail.

General Von Bentheim's Division of the 1st Reserve Corps
reached Prague on the 18th, where it relieved the detachment
which General Von Rosenberg had left there, and which now
rejoined its division at Pardubitz.

By dint of very great exertions, made under the superintendence of Councillor Vogt, the line of railway Turnau-Kralup-
Prague-Pardubitz-Lundenburg was rendered fit for traffic as far
as the broken bridge at the latter place. This was a very great
help, but the scarcity of railway officials, and the want of railway signals and telegraphs, prevented more than two trains
a-day being despatched from Prague, and four from Pardubitz.
The exigencies of the provisional department were so pressing

that only five trains could be given to General Rosenberg's Division, and the troops that could not be conveyed per rail had to march on foot, at least as far as Pardubitz.

Major-General Count Stolberg's Detachment in Upper Silesia was now no longer wanted for the purpose for which it was originally put together, and became available for the main operations of the Army. The Commander-in-Chief of the IInd Army therefore sent orders to Count Stolberg to establish himself at Teschen, and to form a basis there for an expedition which it was intended afterwards to make to Hungary. At the same time the repair of the railway from Oderberg to Prerau was to be hastened and secured.

### THE 20TH OF JULY.

On this day the IInd Corps of Feldzeugmeister Benedek's Army reached Tyrnau. Orders had been sent on in advance to this place to hold 1,000 country carts in readiness, in which the leading brigade (General Henriquez, at the time commanded by Colonel Von Schütte) was immediately conveyed to Pressburg. It arrived there at 8 P.M., and was stationed in the "Mühlenthal"* as support of Colonel Mondl's Brigade. The two Horse Artillery batteries of the Reserve Artillery of the corps, accompanied by two squadrons of the 3rd Saxon "Reiter" Regiment, made a forced march and followed the same day.

The IVth Corps left the Brigades Fleischhacker and Kaminiecki in their flank positions at Kraina and Jablonitz, and marched with the main body to Binowitz near Nadas, where it covered the Göding-Tyrnau road.

The other corps had made such considerable detours that they were unable to take any active part in the operations of the next few days. With the exception of the Saxon Division Von Stieglitz, which crossed the Wlar pass to Srnye and then joined the VIth Corps, all these corps had a day's rest on the 20th in the stations they had reached on the 19th.

Thus the only troops of the Army of the North, that were available at the Danube, were the IIIrd and Xth Corps, 8 battalions and 28 guns of the Saxon Corps, and the 4 Cavalry divisions of Prince Holstein, on the whole perhaps 55,000 to 60,000 combatants.

In the meantime the orders for bringing up as many troops of the Army of the South as could be spared in Italy were being carried out.

According to the instructions given by Archduke Albrecht when he left the southern threatre of war, the Austrian Army in Italy had retired behind the Piave on the 14th of July. On the same day the railway transport of the greater part of the Vth Corps commenced on the western line (Innsbruck-Salzburg), and on the 15th that of the IXth Corps and Brigade Biehnert of the Vth Corps on the eastern line (Austrian Railway of the South).

---

* The valley of a small stream which flows into the Danube westward of Pressburg, after turning several mills.

The Vth Corps reached Innsbruck between the 14th and 17th of July, St. Pölten between the 17th and 19th, and was very soon moved on to Vienna from the latter place.

On the night of the 15th Brigade Kirchsberg of the IXth Corps embarked on the railway at Conegliano, on the 16th Brigade Kluedgen at Pardenone, Brigade Welsersheimb at Casarsa, and Brigade Weckbecker at Cordroipo. The head of the corps reached Vienna on the 17th, the last detachments on the 20th.

The first Regiment of Hussars (Emperor Francis Joseph) was conveyed with the IXth, the 12th Regiment of Lancers (Sicily) with the Vth Corps. The 3rd and 13th Regiments of Hussars (Prince Charles of Bavaria and Prince Liechtenstein), and the 13th Regiment of Lancers (Count Trani), marched to Villach, where they arrived on the 22nd. They were conveyed from there to Lower Austria per rail, but were not assembled at Vöslau before the 26th.

The reinforcements which had reached the Danube from Italy by the 20th thus amounted to about 50,000 men.

According to the orders received from the King's head-quarters, Prince Frederick Charles only ordered the troops of his Army westward of the March to close up to the foremost detachments at the Weiden brook on the 20th, and directed the 8th and 5th Divisions to advance, the former to Malaczka and the latter to Gross-Schützen.

The orders which arrived from Nikolsburg on the morning of the 20th caused the 8th Division to be pushed forward the same day to Stampfen, where it opened communications with the main body of the Army by way of Auger.

The Cavalry Corps stood on the right bank of the Weiden brook as far as Weikendorf; the line of the stream from this spot to Schönkirchen was occupied by the advanced guard. The 6th Division was stationed at Ollersdorf, the 7th at Matzen. The IInd Corps had moved up to Spannberg-Dürnkruth. Prince Frederick Charles established his head-quarters at Ebenthal, in the centre of his closely concentrated Army.

An encounter took place at the outposts between the 3rd Hussars and some Austrian Hussars near Deutsch Wagram.

The Army of the Elbe moved to the line Wolfpassing (14th Division), Gaunersdorf (16th Division), Hohen-Ruppersdorf (15th Division); the advanced guard occupied the valley of the Russ brook at Wolkersdorf. A line of outposts was pushed forward to the heights northward of Eibesbrunn, in consequence of which a skirmish took place near Ebersdorf. Reports having namely been sent in, that a detachment of the enemy, consisting of Infantry and Cavalry, was foraging in this village, the 1st Squadron of the 7th Hussars and the 3rd Company of the 33rd Regiment were sent forward to prevent it. The enemy was driven off, and 3 Infantry soldiers and 12 men and horses of the Lichtenstein Hussar Regiment were brought back as prisoners; one Prussian Hussar was carried off by the enemy.

The right flank detachment took possession of Stockerau on this day, and advanced beyond it as far as Spillern, which place was occupied by Austrian Infantry. The two squadrons then fell back to Sierndorf, after having made a requisition of provisions in Stockerau. The enemy attempted a surprise in the course of the evening, but was repulsed by the outposts.

The VIth Corps advanced to the neighbourhood of Drasenhofen and Poisbrunn, the 1st Division of Guards to Lundenburg, the 2nd to Kostel. The Guards took up the positions appointed for them by the King's head-quarters on the following day; they were at the same time ordered to collect 140 2-horse and 125 4-horse carts for the wagon park at Auspitz.

The Crown Prince established his head-quarters at Eisgrub.

General Von Steinmetz reached Ostra with the Cavalry Division, from whence detachments advanced to Hluk, Velka, and Strassnitz.

The 9th Division marched on the right bank of the March to Altstadt and neighbourhood, the 10th Division on the left bank to Ungarisch-Hradisch. The bridges at Ostra, Wessely, and Strassnitz were repaired, and a considerable quantity of railway materials again seized at Pissek and Hullein.

The Ist Corps had a day's rest on the 19th, and the situation of affairs in front of Olmütz remained unaltered on the 20th also. The two detachments of Colonel Von Bredow and Major-General Von Barnekow were placed under the command of Lieut.-General Von Grossmann, and a detachment was stationed at Kralitz to keep up the communication between them. A special reserve for the corps, consisting of three battalions and one battery, was formed at Tobitschau. Kojetein was occupied by a detachment of all arms, in order to guard the Wischau road. Hospitals were obliged to be established at Prossnitz and Prerau on account of the cholera, the first cases of which had appeared on the 9th in the Ist Corps.

## THE 21ST OF JULY.

The Ist Army and the Army of the Elbe were instructed to remain in their present positions on the " Weidenbach," and to await the arrival of the IInd Army, which was drawing near; but they were at the same time informed that they were to accept battle on this line if the enemy should attack, in which case Prince Frederick Charles would have the command of the Army of the Elbe until His Majesty arrived upon the field.

The Ist Army therefore made no alterations in its positions, with the exception of those movements which were necessary for carrying out the expedition to Pressburg.

The 5th Division was recalled from Gross Schützen and Gayring, and marched by way of Dürnkruth to Stillfried and Ollersdorf. The 7th Division crossed the March at Anger, and advanced to Stampfen. The Field Artillery Division of the 4th Artillery Regiment followed as far as Zohor. At General

Fransecky's request the 2nd Division (General Hann) of the Cavalry Corps was sent to Marchegg in the afternoon, and placed at his disposal.

Some slight encounters again ensued at the outposts on the " Weidenbach," and the enemy evacuated Deutsch-Wagram in the course of the afternoon.

General Von Horn was appointed to the command of a 2nd Reserve Division which had been formed at Leipzig. Until his successor (General Von Schoeler) arrived, General Von Bose took the command of the 8th Division, and was placed *ad interim* under the orders of Lieut.-General Von Fransecky. General Von Schoeler was replaced by Major-General Count Goltz in the command of the advanced guard of the Army of the Elbe.

Intelligence had been obtained from the inhabitants of the country, stating that a hostile force of 30,000 men was stationed southward of Bisternitz and Marienthal, but a reconnaissance of the country near Blumenau and Kaltenbrunn, made by General Fransecky in company with General Bose and the Quarter-master of the Ist Army (General Stülpnagel), proved this information to be false. As had been the case during the day, only slight forces of the enemy were found there. A body of Infantry (about a battalion), a few squadrons, and some guns were to be seen in a position between both villages.

Captain Count Haeseler, of the General Staff, rode back to Ebenthal at 8 P.M. with this report, and with a letter from General Stülpnagel, expressing the wish of the Generals to reconnoitre Pressburg the next morning.

The VIth Corps reached Wilfersdorf, the Corps of Guards the neighbourhood of Drösing. General Steinmetz crossed the March at Ungarisch-Hradisch with the 9th Division, and led the Vth Corps to the neighbourhood of Strassnitz and Wessely. The Cavalry Division reached Skalitz, and pushed an advanced guard forward to Holitsch. The 4th Dragoon Regiment of the 9th Division advanced on the left flank by way of Velka to Verborcz. Patrols that reconnoitred the road to Jablonitz as far as Szenicz, met with some slight detachments of the Saxon Cavalry that was attached to the IVth Austrian Corps.

The same evening General Steinmetz received orders from the Commander-in-Chief to draw nearer to the Army, so as to take up a position at Hohenau on the left flank of the Corps of Guards by the 24th. It was left to his discretion to effect this either on the left or on the right bank of the March, but he was advised to leave General Hartmann's Cavalry Division on the left bank. Göding was to be occupied by a detachment of the ·Vth Corps, which was to watch the road to Tyrnau.

Nothing but some trifling skirmishing of the outposts took place in front of Olmütz. On the evening of this day a telegram from the Commander-in-Chief of the IInd Army reached General Von Bonin, ordering him to despatch a brigade of Infantry, a regiment of Cavalry, and two batteries by way of Wischau. Austerlitz, and Theresiendorf to Holitsch.

The IInd Austrian Corps continued its strenuous exertions to send more troops up to Pressburg. On the 21st the 2nd and 20th Battalions of Rifles were sent from Tyrnau by a tramway to Gross-Schenkwitz, in order to occupy St. Georgen, Bösing, and Modern, and to watch the roads leading from here over the Carpathian Mountains in company with the 9th Regiment of Lancers (Xth Corps), which had been sent by the Commanding Officer in Pressburg to Ratzensdorf, Bösing, and Cziffer. In the course of the same day the 47th Regiment (Hartung) was likewise sent per tramway to Pressburg, but did not arrive there until early on the 22nd. The main body of the corps marched to Wartberg, and bivouacked there. In the course of the afternoon and evening the Staff of the Duke of Wurtemberg's Brigade and the 57th Regiment (Meklenburg), with the 4-pounder Battery No. 4, were conveyed per rail to Pressburg. During the night and early in the morning of the 22nd the two Infantry regiments of Colonel Thom's Brigade were sent there in like manner. Two squadrons of the 3rd Saxon "Reiter" Regiment started at 2 A.M. of the 22nd from Wartberg, and arrived at Pressburg at half-past 6. Colonel Mondl's troops remained in their positions at Blumenau and Kaltenbrunn, on the road from Pressburg to Stampfen.

The other corps of the Army of the North continued their march on the 21st. The 1st and VIIIth Corps reached Neustadtl and neighbourhood, the VIth and the Saxon Division Trentschin.

For some days already negotiations had been pending at Nikolsburg—a castle of the Austrian Prime Minister Count Mensdorf, where His Majesty's head-quarters were for the moment established—the object of which was a cessation of hostilities for five days, and in which a difference was made between "*trève d'hostilités*" and "*armistice*." The primary object of these negotiations was to gain time for diplomatic action. The rapid course of the campaign had hitherto prevented any negotiations, the changes in the situation of affairs eventually altering the basis upon which they had been originally commenced. Now, however, that the Prussian Army appeared upon the Marchfeld a fresh catastrophe was near at hand.

By dint of great exertions, and after much travelling to and fro, the French Ambassador at the Court of Berlin succeeded in finding a basis upon which definite peace proposals could be made.

Hostilities were to cease at noon of the 22nd, and were not to be resumed until noon of the 27th.

Information of this was sent to the Commanders-in-Chief of the armies, and it was at the same time stated that no operations were to be commenced on the 22nd which might lead to a conflict with the enemy. General Staff officers were summoned to Wolkersdorf to the Quartermaster-General of the Army, Major-General Von Podbielsky, at 9 A.M. of the 22nd, to receive further orders.

## The 22nd of July.

At 10 o'clock in the morning Major-General Von Podbielsky and Lieutenant Field-Marshal Baron John met at Eibesbrunn to make whatever arrangements were necessary during the cessation of hostilities and to settle a line of demarcation.

The latter was to begin at Krems, was then to follow the course of the Danube to Stockerau, to run from here up the "Göllersbach" as far as the castle of Schönborn southward of the village of Göllersdorf. The line was then to be drawn eastward to Wetzleinsdorf, from whence it was to follow the course of the "Russbach" to Leopoldsdorf. Running then further eastward past Lassee and the railway bridge over the March, it was to continue by way of Bisternitz and Stampfen to Lozorn, and then along the eastern skirts of the Lozorn firwood to Szenicz.

The articles of this agreement were signed at noon, therefore at the very moment when it was to come into force already.

In accordance with orders given by Prince Frederick Charles at 3 P.M. of the 21st already, the advanced guard of the Ist Army moved up to the "Russbach" between Wagram and Markgraf-Neusiedel. In so doing its foremost detachments of the 11th Lancers and 2nd Guard Dragoons came in contact with the enemy's patrols at Deutsch-Wagram and Gross-Enzersdorf.

The 1st Division of the Cavalry Corps advanced to Siebenbrunn and Schönfeldt. The 5th and 6th Divisions followed to Schönkirchen and Bockfliess.

A greater extent of country was thus gained for the cantonments during the armistice, those of the Ist Army comprising the district southward of the Zaya and Laksar rivulets as far westward as the Brünn-Vienna high-road. The Army of the Elbe only had to recall its right flank detachment within the line of demarcation, and cantoned westward of the high-road. The cantonment of the IInd Army lay northward of the two above-mentioned brooks, with the exception of Nikolsburg and a tract northward of this town, which was kept free for the Ist Reserve Corps, the foremost detachments of which reached Brünn on this day.

General Steinmetz advanced with the Vth Corps to the neighbourhood of Skalitz and Holitsch. The Dragoon Regiment covered the left flank at Radosocz.

General Hartmann's Cavalry Division reached Egbell, his advanced guard Schossberg, and pushed forward a squadron on each of the two roads leading to St. Johann and Jablonicz as far as Kuti and Szenicz.

Intelligence of the cessation of hostilities had not arrived yet at the latter place, and the 3rd Squadron of the 10th Lancers was surprised at 2 P.M. by two squadrons of Saxon "Reiter" which belonged to the troops at Jablonicz. The Lancers lost some men and horses in the *mêlée*. The loss of the enemy amounted to more than twenty men,

In accordance with the orders received in the night of the 21st, the 1st Corps despatched Lieut.-General Von Clausewitz with the 3rd Brigade of Infantry, the 12th Lancers, and two batteries to Wischau on the 22nd. The alterations that became necessary in consequence in the positions of the troops before Olmütz were made in the course of the day.

At half-past 6 P.M. the news arrived that hostilities had ceased for the time and was communicated to the Commandant of Olmütz, who refused to respect the armistice, on the ground that he had as yet received no official instructions.

The lateness of the hour at which the intelligence of the armistice reached the different troops on the forenoon of the 22nd had more serious consequences on the left bank of the March, where the action of Blumenau had commenced before the news arrived.

## ACTION OF BLUMENAU.

During the night of the 21st General Von Fransecky's troops occupied the following positions :—

The 8th Division southward of Bisternitz, with an advanced guard pushed forward on the Blumenau road.

The 7th Division at Masst and Stampffen.

The Field Division of the Reserve Artillery at Zohor.

General Von Hann's Cavalry Division at Marchegg.

Appendix XXVI. This whole force amounted to 18¼ battalions, 2 companies of pioneers, 24 squadrons, and 78 guns.

Captain Count Haseler returned to Stampffen at half-past 3 A.M. of the 22nd. He had left Ebenthal before the news of the cessation of hostilities had arrived there, and he brought the Prince's permission to make the proposed reconnoissance toward Pressburg.

The Austrian Brigade Mondl, reinforced by Cavalry and Artillery, had been in its position at Blumenau ever since the 18th. According to orders received from the Commander-in-Chief this position was to be defended to the utmost.

The outposts, one battalion of the 10th Regiment (Mazzuchelli), stood 2,000 paces in front of Franzhof and along the line of railway as far as a range of bare hills northward of Kaltenbrunn. The 12th Rifle Battalion and the 1st and 3rd Battalions of the 24th Regiment (Parma) were stationed as support behind the right wing, the 2nd Battalion of the latter regiment stood behind Blumenau. The two other battalions of the "Mazzuchelli" Regiment were behind the left wing, in front of Kaltenbrunn.

Northward of both villages was a ridge of hills sloping gently to the north and commanding the plain in front of them. These hills afforded an admirable artillery position and were occupied by the battery of the brigade and two 8-pounder batteries of the Reserve Artillery of the Army.

A combined Brigade of Cavalry, under Colonel Von Waldegg, consisting of four squadrons of the 2nd, four of the 6th, and one of the 9th Lancer Regiments, but mustering little more than 500 to 600 men, was posted behind the heights.

The Reserve—the brigade of Colonel Von Schütte (formerly commanded by General Von Henriquez) belonging to the IInd Corps—had been stationed since the 20th in the " Mühlthal," at the Kunstmühle.* It had detached the 9th Rifle Battalion and the 1st Battalion of the 27th Regiment (King of Belgium) to the " Eisenbrünnel," the 2nd Battalion of the same Regiment to the " Gämsenberg," to cover the right flank, and had also occupied the Castle hill of Pressburg.

The 40th Regiment (Rossbach), of Colonel Thom's Brigade had been brought up per rail in the course of the night and was now assembling in the " Fürsten-Allee " of Pressburg. The 69th Regiment (Jellacic) was still on the road, and the 2nd Rifle Battalion had remained in St. Georgen.

Prince Würtemberg's Brigade had disembarked from the rail at Ratzersdorff and had been in readiness there ever since the morning.

General Saffran's Brigade, with two squadrons of the 3rd Saxon " Reiter " Regiment and four batteries, had been on the march from Wartberg to Pressburg since 2 in the morning.

The troops momentarily available thus amounted to 24 battalions, 11 squadrons, and 24 guns.

The state of fatigue, in which these troops must have been, may be well imagined, if one considers what exertions had been demanded of them during the whole of the retreat from Olmütz most especially on the 21st and the following night.

The reconnaissance which General Von Fransecky had made on the preceding day had convinced him, that to attack the enemy in front, in face of his strong artillery position, must cause heavy losses ; he therefore determined only to keep his adversary occupied at this spot until his flank was effectually turned. For the latter purpose General Von Bose was to march from Bisternitz and Mariental to the " Prohaska " and " Jäger " mills in the rear of the position at Blumenau.

The corresponding orders were as follows :—General Von Bose was to start immediately with 6 battalions in the direction which he had himself proposed the day before. Two hours later the enemy's attention was to be occupied in front of his position by the 72nd Regiment and the artillery, the latter being stationed southward of Bisternitz ; the 7th Division was to follow in the same direction ; the Cavalry Division was to be brought up from Marchegg, the Reserve Artillery from Zohor. General Bose was to establish a succession of letter-carrier stations during his advance ; his reports of the progress made by the flank detachment and the situation of affairs after gaining possession of the Blumenau-Kaltenbrunn position would

---

* One of the mills on the Mühlthal.

2 B

determine when and how the expedition to Pressburg would be carried out, in which case special orders would be then given by General Von Fransecky. The whole engagement was thus from its very commencement divided into two separate actions.

These orders reached Gen. Von Bose at a quarter past 4 A.M. His troops had had their morning's meal already, but the departure of the brigade was delayed until half-past 6, because the outposts which belonged to the 31st Regiment had first to be relieved by the 72nd Regiment, and then to return to Marienthal.

By this time the action had already commenced in the front, the advanced guard of the 7th Division having moved into a sheltered position southwards of Bisternitz and westward of the 6.30 A.M. high-road at half-past 6.

Colonel Mondl had thrown forward two squadrons of the 6th Lancer Regiment, under Lieut.-Colonel Dorner, to reconnoitre the country beyond the railway embankment, which they passed at two different openings. One of these squadrons advanced against a squadron of the Prussian 10th Hussars which had been sent forward to drive in the Austrian patrols and which now retreated because its flank was menaced by the second Austrian squadron. The enemy followed in pursuit, the Commander of the Prussian squadron, having first made his men acquainted with his intention, sounded the signal, upon which the squadron fronted and charged its pursuers. After a brief hand-to-hand combat the Lancers fled, pursued by the Hussars.

An Austrian battery now opened fire and the second squadron stood at the railway crossing, so that the pursuit was soon checked, but on General Von Fransecky sending forward the 2nd and 4th Squadrons of the 10th Hussars, both Lancer squadrons withdrew behind the railway embankment. In this encounter 3 Prussian officers and 7 men were wounded, 1 Hussar and 6 horses were missing. The Lancers lost 10 men and left 5 men and 7 horses in the hands of the Hussars.

The latter advanced to within 1,000 paces of the embankment and stationed themselves behind a rise in the ground, where they were sheltered from the fire of the 24 guns which Colonel Mondl had placed on both sides of the Neudorf road on the bare heights in front of the two villages.

As it was not as yet intended to press the engagement at this spot, the Artillery did not cross the plain, but opened fire with 36 rifled guns at 4,000 paces distance, on a rise in the ground southward of Bisternitz. The flanks of this position were protected by pushing forward the Fusiliers and half the 1st Battalion of the 72nd Regiment to the wooded heights on the left and the 2nd Battalion of the same Regiment to the projecting corner of the "Theben Kogl" on the right.

The 6th Prussian Lancer Regiment was sent forward to join the 10th Hussars, in order to prevent the enemy's Cavalry from again advancing.

As the 15th Brigade had started so late, it was feared that a long time would elapse before the flank movement could take effect. General Von Fransecky therefore now resolved to press direct upon the wings of the enemy's position.

In consequence of a previous report that a strong detachment of the enemy was advancing over the heights between Kaltenbrunn and Neudorf, the Fusilier Battalion of the 66th Regiment and the 4th 12-pounder battery had already been sent to reinforce the 2nd Battalion of the 72nd Regiment. These troops were now instructed to advance along the front of the hills and over the wooded heights in the direction of Kaltenbrunn, whilst General Von Gordon advanced on the left with the advanced guard—the 67th Regiment, the Fusilier Battalion of the 27th Regiment, and the 4th Company of Pioneers—against the enemy's detachments at Franzhof. He followed the above-mentioned one and a-half battalion of the 72nd Regiment, which had previously advanced in this direction.

The reserves therefore now consisted of four battalions of the main body of the 7th Division and a 12-pounder battery; the Reserve Artillery accompanied by the 1st Battalion of the 27th Regiment was drawing near; General Von Hann's Cavalry Division had already arrived westward of Bisternitz.

Colonel Mondl, seeing his flanks thus menaced, reinforced the troops on both wings by the 10th Regiment (Mazzuchelli), and moved the 2nd Battalion of the 24th Regiment (Parma) from Blumenau on to the heights of the Rosalien chapel; at the same time he sent a request to Count Thun, who had arrived at Pressburg, to assist him with the IInd Corps.

At this time General Von Fransecky received a letter from the Chief of the Staff, Lieut.-General Von Voigts-Rhetz, dated Ebenthal, the 22nd of July, 4 A.M., announcing the approaching cessation of hostilities, the news of which had reached Ebenthal half an hour before, and instructing him to act accordingly.

All operations were to cease precisely at midday, and officers, accompanied by trumpeters, were to inform the enemy in front of the commencement of the armistice.

No line of demarcation being as yet settled, it was stated that, in case Pressburg should be already occupied, the troops were to be quartered there, but otherwise further to the rear.

General Von Fransecky was sharply engaged. The detachments which were pushed forward on both flanks in different directions could not be momentarily recalled, nor could this be done without danger for the centre of the line.

Great results might be expected from the measures that had been taken. Being perfectly justified in making full use of his freedom of action until midday, the General saw no reason for breaking off the action which he had commenced until this hour.

He first of all reinforced his line of artillery by bringing up the four batteries of the Reserve Artillery, which arrived about half-past 8 on the right of the batteries already engaged. When this fire had continued for an hour at a long range which prevented its having much effect on either side, Lieut.-Colonel Von Scherbening led the five batteries of the right wing that were on the west side of the high-road closer up to the enemy. The five batteries of the left wing were stationed behind a steep and impassable ravine, and remained in their present position. As covering guard for the artillery, the Fusilier Battalion of the 26th Regiment was brought forward from the main body of the 7th Division and stationed behind the right wing of the batteries, where it was afterwards joined by the 1st Battalion of the 27th Regiment. Both battalions found good cover in the undulations of the ground. The Cavalry Division deployed on the right wing; Count Bismarck's Brigade, with extended skirmishers, in the first, General Hann's Heavy Brigade in the second line, and extending somewhat beyond the right wing of the first line.

In the meantime part of the reinforcements which Colonel Mondl had requested—Colonel Von Schütte's Brigade—arrived from the "Kunstmühle." The brigade had already detached some troops to Franzhof. The 1st and 3rd Battalions of the 14th Regiment (Hesse) were now sent to Kaltenbrunn and posted on the heights westward of the village, where they formed the extreme left of the position, and watched the country as far as the Danube. The Horse Artillery Battery No. 7 came into action northward of the village, and the two Saxon "Reiter" squadrons joined Colonel Waldegg's Brigade. The remainder of the 14th Regiment occupied the railway viaduct near the "Kunstmühle," only one battalion of the 27th Regiment remaining at the mill itself.

The 40th Regiment (Rossbach) of Colonel Thom's Brigade had just arrived at Pressburg and received orders to advance with all haste. Six guns of the Horse Artillery Battery No. 8, which were hitherto stationed at the Kunstmühle, advanced with the regiment, the two other guns of the battery were withdrawn to Pressburg to occupy the "Calvarienberg." The 69th Regiment (Jellacic) was coming up to Pressburg by degrees, and was ordered to move to the front without delay.

The 20th Rifle Battalion and the 57th Regiment (Mecklenburg), belonging to Prince Würtemberg's Brigade at Ratzersdorf, advanced towards Marienthal.

The remainder of the IInd Corps was assembling at the brickfields eastward of Pressburg after a march of six hours.

9 A.M.    By 9 o'clock the Prussian right wing detachment had reached the railway embankment without suffering much from the enemy's fire while passing the open plain. A patrol of Hussars having reported that the enemy was sending troops toward the March induced the 2nd Battalion of the 72nd Regiment to advance more to the right, and the Fusilier Battalion of the 66th Regiment took up a position behind the railway embankment with the intention of covering the right flank, thus

deviating still more from the direction originally pointed out. Orders were however soon sent for both battalions to march on Kaltenbrunn, upon which the former battalion immediately advanced in columns of companies across the wooded heights whilst the latter ascended the side of the valley and joined it. The enemy's skirmishers in the wood retreated at all points without offering much resistance, but the dense thicket and the steepness of the hills prevented the battalions from making any rapid progress. The Fusiliers suffered some loss from the enemy's left wing battery; that of the 72nd Regiment was very trifling.

The 12-pounder battery was not able to follow the battalions and remained at the railway embankment.

The six companies of the 72nd Regiment which were advancing from the left wing, pressed forward under cover of the wooded heights at the side of the road to within 800 paces of Franzhof. The country was very impracticable and they gained but little ground. About half-past 9 they commenced a standing 9.30 A.M. fight in front with the skirmishers of the Austrian 12th Rifle Battalion and of the "Mazzuchelli" and "Parma" Regiments; at the same time the 12th and soon afterwards the 9th Prussian Companies moved more eastward to guard the left flank.

The advanced guard followed these six companies. The two Fusilier battalions could make but slow progress, the broken nature of the ground causing much loss of time. After advancing to about half way between the artillery position and Franzhof they halted, because two companies of the 72nd Regiment were on before them. The 2nd Battalion of the 67th Regiment soon arrived behind the left wing of the six companies, but the 1st Battalion had got too much to the left in the thick wood.

Meanwhile the 15th Brigade had set off on its expedition against the enemy's right flank in two columns. The first, or left, column was led by General Von Bose himself, and consisted of the 31st Regiment, a division of Lancers, and half a company of Pioneers. It started half an hour before the second or right column, which set out from Leopoldshof, and consisted of the 71st Regiment; it was led by Colonel Von Avemann.

A gamekeeper and some country people who were perfectly acquainted with the country accompanied each column, which they were to lead, so as to unite on the Gämsenberg at 10 o'clock.

The troops marched without knapsacks and in foraging caps, but this march over the heights and ravines of these wooded mountains was excessively fatiguing; the heads of the column were often obliged to halt for the files to close up. At the spot settled by the guides both columns met, but from this spot the guide of the left column made a detour which caused fresh delay. The march was not in any way disturbed by the enemy,

The 12th Company of the 31st Regiment had been on outpost duty during the night and was instructed to wait until the main body of the brigade had passed and then to assemble and follow. It started half an hour later alone, and probably took a road too far to the east, for about half-past 9 it come upon au Austrian picquet of the 57th Regiment (Mecklenburg), 1 officer and 26 men, who surrendered without a shot. The commander of the company had ridden on ahead after the Brigade in order to ask for instructions, and on his return saw a detachment of the Austrian 20th Rifle Battalion. In company with two Lancers who were posted in the neighbourhood as letter-carriers, he rode after the riflemen, 15 of whom surrendered at his mere summons, the rest fired a few straggling and ineffectual shots and disappeared in the thicket. The enemy now appeared in greater force and the company was obliged to retire; part of it rejoined its regiment, part was separated from it but still brought all the prisoners safely to Marienthal. The company only lost 1 non-commissioned officer and 2 men missing.

10 A.M. It was now 10 o'clock. General Von Fransecky had as yet heard nothing of the 15th Brigade, the heads of which were at this time reaching the valley of the "Mühlbach." The above-mentioned slight encounter had driven the letter-carriers away from their stations. Having but two hours left for action, the General now determined to attack the enemy immediately.

On the right wing the enemy's skirmishers in the wood were driven back over the heights of Kaltenbrunn, and the position of the Austrian Artillery was threatened from there.

In the centre of the line the six batteries of the right wing advanced *en échelon* to 2,000 and 2,500 paces of the enemy's position, and brought the whole force of their fire to bear upon the artillery at Kaltenbrunn, without paying any regard to a rocket battery which fired with but slight effect from the "Theben Kogel."

Colonel Mondl's batteries were already beginning to feel the want of ammunition, the two 8-pounder batteries of the Reserve Artillery had so completely expended theirs that they had to be sent back to Pressburg. However, the six guns of the Horse Artillery Battery No. 8, which had hastened on in advance of Colonel Thom's Brigade, came up just in time to take their place.

On the Prussian left wing the 10th Company of the 72nd Regiment gained possession of the Franzhof, which was but slightly defended by a detachment of the "Mazzuchelli" Regiment. A ditch in front of the farm afforded a good opportunity of firing at a railway cutting, which was occupied by the enemy in force. The battalions of the advanced guard came up to this spot, from whence they completely commanded the country up to the railway and the cemetery of Blumenau. The 1st Battalion of the 67th Regiment advanced more eastward, and drove back an Austrian detachment, but soon came upon far superior forces in a favourable position—most likely the 57th Regiment

(Mecklenburg), which had advanced thus far from Ratzersdorf. The action at this spot was confined to a standing fire of skirmishers.

Shortly after 10 o'clock the leading battalion of the 15th Brigade, Fusilier Battalion of the 71st Regiment, met the advanced posts of the 2nd Battalion of the 27th Austrian Regiment, at the foot of the Gämsenberg. As soon as the other battalions of the Prussian regiment had come into line the order was given to advance. The battalion was met by a well-delivered fire on the part of the enemy. Colonel Von Avemann then sounded the charge, and with bands playing and colours flying the 2nd Battalion rushed up the side of the hill and threw itself upon the enemy's left flank. The summit was soon gained, and the enemy driven back with great loss. With joyous cheers the men of Thuringia hailed the sight of Pressburg and of the valley of the Danube at their feet.

The regiment, which had lost two officers and 50 men, now waited for the 31st Regiment to come up; the 5th Company followed the enemy through the thicket and down the face of the hill towards the railway station of Pressburg.

Lieutenant Field-Marshal Count Thun did all in his power to check the advance of his adversary. The 69th Regiment (Jellacic), which had just arrived, sent its 1st Battalion from the railway station to the heights northwards, to cover the retreat of the 27th Regiment. The two other battalions occupied the "Calvarienberg," and the last battalion of the 40th Regiment (Rossbach), with which Colonel Thun had just reached the "Jager" mill, was detached to the Gämsenberg. Finally the 47th Regiment (Hartung), which had stopped at Ratzersdorf, was instructed to advance against the rear of the 15th Brigade.

At this moment Count Thun was informed by the Commander-in-Chief of the cessation of hostilities, which was to commence at 12 o'clock. He communicated the intelligence to the commanding officers, and instructed them to send flags of truce to their adversaries with the information of it as soon as the hour arrived.

General Bose reached the Gämsenberg with the 31st Regiment soon after the position had been carried. He here received information from General Fransecky of the impending armistice, and sent back word that he was already in the rear of the Blumenau position, and should proceed along the road to attack it without delay. This report did not, however, reach General Von Fransecky, as the line of letter-carriers was already intercepted, and the latter general thus remained in ignorance of the progress of the 15th Brigade.

General Von Bose was now obliged to cover the rear of his intended march on Blumenau, by detaching troops in the direction of Pressburg, and the Fusilier Battalion of the 71st Regiment was appointed to this duty. The other battalions wheeled to the right and advanced on Blumenau, with the exception of the 2nd and Fusilier Battalions of the 31st Regiment, which missed the direction in the dense and high thicket, and followed the Fusiliers of the 71st Regiment towards Pressburg.

The 64th Austrian Regiment (Saxe Weimar) and two 8-pounder batteries of General Saffran's Brigade had just arrived at Pressburg, and Count Thun sent them immediately through the vineyards to the heights northward of the railway station, and on the right of the battalions of the Regiments "Jellacic" and "Belgium." They ensconced themselves behind some heaps of stones, and received the Prussian Fusiliers with a brisk but ineffectual fire as they descended the hill from the "Strohhütte." The latter occupied the skirts of the wood 200 paces southwards of the hut, and waited for the two battalions of the 31st Regiment to come up.

The fire which now ensued at this spot was of but little effect on either side, from the sheltered position of the skirmishers, but it nevertheless had the desired result of covering General Bose's march against any undertaking from the direction of Pressburg, by occupying twofold forces of the enemy. The latter had seven battalions northward of the station and on the "Calvarienberg."

The broken state of the ground opposed uncommon difficulties to General Bose's advance on Blumenau. Ravines and steep hills, tracts of large stones and dense thickets had to be passed. Continual signals were the only means of keeping the different columns together.

On the right wing the Fusilier Battalion ot the 71st and the 1st Battalion of the 31st Regiment met the 9th Austrian Rifle Battalion, at the Eisenbrünnel, and the latter fell back fighting upon the 1st Battalion of the 27th Regiment (Belgium), which was posted at Mill No. 9. The 3rd Battalions of the latter and of the 40th Regiment (Rossbach) were despatched to the same spot; Colonel Thom remained with the 2nd Battalion of the latter regiment at the "Kunstmühle" in reserve.

A sharp skirmishing action now ensued along the whole front of the three Prussian battalions. The conviction felt by each soldier in their ranks, that it now needed but brief exertion to achieve signal success, made them forgetful of their fatigue, and the enemy was driven back at all points in spite of his superior numbers. On the left wing parts of the Austrian regiments "Belgium and Rossbach" were seen flying in complete disorder and great haste across the high-road and into the woods on the heights beyond.

It was, however, now noon, and the time for action had passed; one hour still was wanting to reap the fruits of so much exertion.

Had Colonel Mondl's Brigade not known for certain that hostilities would cease at 12 o'clock, it would scarcely have ventured to wait until affairs assumed so menacing an aspect, its adversaries being in the immediate neighbourhood of both its flanks, and the sole line still open for its retreat leading through the narrow wooded valley to Carlsdorf.

Whilst the Austrian Artillery, both flanks of which were in danger, drove off in *échelons*, Austrian flags of truce proclaimed the commencement of the armistice in all directions. On the Prussian side the signals to halt and to cease firing were immediately sounded, but were not everywhere heard.

At some parts of the field, in particular at the "Kunstmühle" on the high-road, the firing was kept up on both sides for more than half-an-hour. It was with great difficulty that the fierce struggle was everywhere put an end to.

The line of demarcation which the commissioners from both head-quarters settled at Eibesbrunn, at the same time, a quarter before 12 o'clock, that the trumpets were sounding peace signals in front of Pressburg, was based upon the positions of both armies as they were known at that moment, but by no means suited the totally changed positions of the 7th and 8th Divisions.

General Von Fransecky was discussing this question with the officers of the Austrian General Staff, when General Bose's report arrived that he had advanced as far as the Prohaska mill, and had come to an arrangement with the Chief of the Staff of the Austrian IInd Corps at the Jäger mill on the high-road, that this mill should remain neutral, and that the Austrian troops near Blumenau should fall back behind it.

General Von Stülpnagel, Quartermaster of the Ist Army, rode to Pressburg to the Commanding General of the Austrian Corps to press the well-founded claim of the Prussian Division, and demanded that General Bose's brigade should remain on the line of the "Mühlthal" until noon of next day, thus proving its success and the position it had gained. Count Thun showed a telegram from Archduke Albrecht, pointing out the line Marchegg-Bisternitz-Stampfen as line of demarcation, but nevertheless acknowledged the justness of General Stülpnagel's claim, and himself sent the necessary intelligence to General Von Bose.

The 15th Brigade was then formed between the Kunst and the Prohaska mills, where it bivouacked.

On proceeding from the Strohhütte to this spot, the Fusilier Battalion of the 71st Regiment had to pass through the ranks of Austrian Corps, and the Austrian brigades of Colonels Mondl, and Waldegg marched close by the 15th Prussian brigade when they retreated to Pressburg.

Colonel Von Fransecky retired behind the line of demarcation the same afternoon, but General Von Bose did not follow with his brigade until 2 P.M. of the following day.

The action had lasted for five hours, but the losses were, comparatively speaking, trifling; those of the Prussian troops amounted to—

| 7TH DIVISION. | Killed. | | Wounded. | | Missing. | | Total. | |
|---|---|---|---|---|---|---|---|---|
| | Officers. | Men. | Officers. | Men. | Officers. | Men. | Officers. | Men. |
| Fusilier Battalion, 26th Regiment .. | .. | .. | .. | 2 | .. | .. | .. | 2 |
| Fusilier Battalion, 66th ,, .. | .. | 1 | 1 | 5 | .. | .. | 1 | 6 |
| 1st and Fusilier Battalion, 27th Regt. | .. | 1 | .. | 4 | .. | .. | .. | 5 |
| 1st and Fusilier Battalion, 67th ,, | .. | .. | .. | 16 | .. | .. | .. | 16 |
| 10th Regiment of Hussars .. .. | .. | .. | 3 | 8 | .. | 1 | 3 | 9 |
| Artillery .. .. .. .. .. | .. | 1 | .. | 7 | .. | .. | .. | 8 |
| Total of 7th Division .. .. | .. | 3 | 4 | 42 | .. | 1 | 4 | 46 |
| Reserve Artillery .. .. | .. | .. | .. | 35 | .. | .. | .. | 35 |
| 8TH DIVISION. | | | | | | | | |
| 31st Regiment .. .. .. .. | .. | 1 | .. | 8 | .. | 7 | .. | 16 |
| 71st ,, .. .. .. .. | 2 | 16 | 2 | 44 | .. | .. | 4 | 60 |
| 72nd ,, .. .. .. .. | .. | 4 | .. | 28 | .. | 3 | .. | 35 |
| 6th ,, of Lancers .. .. | .. | 1 | .. | 4 | .. | .. | .. | 5 |
| Artillery .. .. .. .. | .. | .. | .. | 2 | .. | .. | .. | 2 |
| Total of 8th Division .. .. | 2 | 22 | 2 | 86 | .. | 10 | 4 | 118 |
| Total of both Divisions.. .. | 2 | 25 | 6 | 163 | .. | 11 | 8 | 199 |

According to Hirtefeldt's calendar and Count Thun's own report the Austrian losses were as follows:—

| IIND CORPS D'ARMEE. | Killed. | Wounded. | Missing. | Total. |
|---|---|---|---|---|
| 14th Regiment (Hesse) .. .. .. | .. | .. | 1 | 1 |
| 27th ,, (Belgium) .. .. .. | 29 | 103 | 65 | 177 |
| 40th ,, (Rossbach) .. .. .. | .. | 4 | 5 | 9 |
| 69th ,, (Jellacic) .. .. .. | 2 | 5 | 3 | 10 |
| 57th ,, (Mecklenburg) .. .. | .. | .. | 24 | 24 |
| 64th ,, (Weimar) .. .. .. | 4 | 15 | 3 | 22 |
| 9th Rifle Battalion .. .. .. | 2 | 12 | 15 | 29 |
| 20th ,, ,, .. .. .. | .. | .. | 23 | 23 |
| 2nd Artillery Regiment .. .. | 1 | 9 | 6 | 16 |
| 6th Regiment of Lancers .. .. | 1 | 9 | .. | 10 |
| Total of IInd Corps .. .. .. | 39 | 157 | 145 | 321 |
| COLONEL MONDL'S BRIGADE. | | | | |
| 10th Regiment (Mazzuchelli) .. .. | 6 | 38 | 28 | 72 |
| 24th ,, (Parma) .. .. | .. | 9 | 10 | 19 |
| 12th Rifle Battalion .. .. .. | 7 | 21 | .. | 28 |
| 3rd Artillery Regiment .. .. .. | 5 | 11 | .. | 16 |
| 2nd Battery of Reserve Artillery .. | 4 | 9 | 1 | 14 |
| Total .. .. .. .. .. | 22 | 88 | 39 | 149 |
| Total of IInd Corps and Brigade Mondl.. | 61 | 245 | 184 | 470 |

Among these are included 19 officers, but the five prisoners who were taken by the 10th Prussian Hussars are not mentioned among the missing.

---

## THE ARMISTICE FROM THE 22ND TO THE 27TH OF JULY.

The troops of Ist Army and the Army of the Elbe took up quarters within the appointed districts, but were obliged to overstep these bounds to procure the necessary supplies.

The preparations for attacking Florisdorf, as well as for crossing the Danube, were continued without interruption, although the diplomatic negotiations had already taken such a turn that it was not deemed necessary to bring the troops of General Rosenberg's division up further. They were arriving by degrees at Brünn, and were quartered in the neighbourhood of the town. General Bentheim's division remained near Pardubitz and in Prague.

On the 23rd the Ist Corps received telegraphic orders to leave only one division and two regiments of Cavalry in front of Olmütz, and to proceed with the remainder of the corps along the valley of the March, so as to reach Holitsch on the 27th. Lieut.-General Von Clausewitz's division was to be brought up to the latter place also; it left its present position on the 22nd by way of Austerlitz.

A reconnaissance which was made in the direction of Littau met troops of General Knobelsdorff's detachment in Schmirzitz on the evening of the 22nd.

The latter General had occupied Austrian Silesia since the 5th of July, had started from Troppau on the 14th, and marched over Römerstadt and Hohenstadt to Schönberg and Müglitz, from whence Colonel Von Malachowsky was detached to Schmirzitz.

General Von Knobelsdorff had already established communications with the 63rd Regiment when he reached Schönberg on the 17th. This regiment was marching by way of Hohenstadt and Wildenschwerdt on Zwittau. The General then continued his march through Gewitsch to Brünn, and reached the neighbourhood of the latter town on the 30th.

The Vth Corps went into its appointed cantonments southward of Feldsberg on the 25th. General Von Hartmann's Cavalry division halted near Holitsch.

As the state of politics very soon made a still closer concentration of the Army unnecessary, the advance of the 2nd Division of Infantry was checked, and it remained in the neighbourhood of Strassnitz and Theresiendorf.

General Count Stolberg's operations were interrupted in the beginning of July, because the Infantry of his detachment was wanted to form the fourth battalions of the Silesian regiments, to the depôts of which it was recalled for this purpose. This force being thus reduced to one company of Rifles and two regiments of Cavalry, Count Stolberg was compelled to refrain from any expedition on a large scale, in particular from any beyond Myslowitz, this being the direction in which he knew the bulk of the enemy's forces to be. He thought the best plan to effect his object of guarding Upper Silesia would be to menace the rich manufacturing districts of Bielitz and Biela, thereby inducing the enemy to leave the neighbourhood of Myslowitz, and to march to meet him. To do this he moved his detachments from Nicolai to Pless, from which spot he daily despatched strong patrols to Kenty and other places of this district, in consequence of which a slight skirmish took place at Kenty.

These expeditions alarmed the enemy, and an Austrian detachment of all arms attacked the passage over the Vistula between Dzieditz and Goczalkowitz on the 16th, but was repulsed by Captain Von Kusserow's company of Rifles, which was stationed at this spot. As soon as the five fourth battalions had rejoined the detachment, Count Stolberg commenced his march to Teschen, according to the orders he had received from the Commander-in-Chief of the IInd Army.

During the time between the 23rd and 27th of July, the Ist, IVth, VIth, and VIIIth Austrian Corps, the Saxon troops that were still with these corps, and the 2nd Light Cavalry Division, retreated through Pressburg to the right bank of the Danube. The IInd Corps followed on the 27th, and then broke up the bridge of boats there. Pressburg was not re-occupied until some time afterwards.

When two hostile armies, whose active operations, though momentarily suspended, may be resumed within a few hours, are separated from each other only by the breadth of a small brook or a cross-road, it is not to be wondered at if the limits prescribed by the convention are here and there overstepped. The military authorities, however, on both sides made every exertion to prevent any such trifling transgressions on the part of their inferiors. By way of adhering precisely to the line of demarcation, the Prussians evacuated Leopoldsdorf as lying southward of the "Russbach" and the road to Lassee, but still held the latter village, which was northward of this line.

The Commandants of Olmütz, Josephstadt, and Königgrätz refused to acknowledge the armistice, alleging that no official communication had reached them respecting it.

As it was necessary to fix some spot where the line which neither army might cross ended, the terms of the convention stated that this line was to follow the course of the Danube below Krems. The movements of either army were free behind this line, but no positive conditions prohibited detachments from crossing the river "above" this point. Austrian troops of all arms appearing at Pulkau and Schrattenthal, westward of the Znaym-Stockerau road, led to some trifling skirmishing, in which prisoners were taken on both sides, which compelled the Prussians to send a brigade to this district, in order to prevent the chance of Znaym—where Prussian reconvalescent patients were quartered—from being seized on in case the armistice ceased.

On the 26th the necessary orders were drawn up at Nikolsburg for concentrating the Army of the Elbe and the Ist Army on the line Wolkersdorf-Stampfen, and for assembling the IInd Army at Gaunersdorf in the course of the afternoon of the 27th.

The following summary will show with what forces the Prussian Army would have been able to resume its operations :—

### A. *The Ist Army.*

|  | Combatants. |
|---|---|
| The 5th, 6th, 7th, and 8th Divisions, the IInd Corps d'Armée, the Cavalry Corps, the Reserve Artillery of the Army ; according to the last official report.. | 76,000 |

### B. *The IInd Army.*

|  | Combatants. |
|---|---|
| The Corps of Guards, the Vth Corps d'Armée, the 11th Division, and the Reserve Artillery of the VIth Corps, the 2nd Division of the Ist Corps, and the Cavalry Division .. .. .. .. | 72,000 |

(N.B.—The 12th Division was not yet available for this purpose, because the corps of observation which was being formed at Königinhof under the command of Lieutenant-General Von Lehwald, was not ready to relieve it.)

### C. *The Army of the Elbe.*

| | |
|---|---|
| The 14th, 15th, 16th Divisions, the Reserve Artillery of the VIIth and VIIIth Corps d'Armée .. .. | 36,000 |
| The 1st Division of Guard Landwehr .. .. | 10,000 |
| There were thus available in the first line .. .. | 194,000 |

In second line behind these three armies there were :—

| | Combatants. |
|---|---|
| 1st. General Bentheim's Division of Landwehr at Prague .. .. .. .. .. .. | 10,500 |
| 2nd. The 12th Division and General Von Knobelsdorff's Detachment at Brünn .. .. .. | 10,500 |
| 3rd. The 1st Division in front of Olmütz .. .. | 10,000 |
| 4th. Fifteen fourth-battalions that were on the march to join the IInd Army .. .. .. .. | 12,000 |
| 5th. Two fourth-battalions on the march to join the Army of the Elbe .. .. .. .. .. | 1,600 |
| 6th. Count Stolberg's detachment .. .. .. | 5,000 |
| Total in second line .. .. | 49,600 |

In addition to these forces, a Decree of the 14th of July had ordered the formation of a partizan corps, in which it was intended to employ such of the numerous prisoners who voluntarily offered to join it, for the purpose of invading Hungary. The formation of this corps was not completed until the end of July, when it consisted of 2,000 men. Part of it was quartered in Neisse, and part of it bivouacked along the frontier. In opposition to the orders of the Prussian Government, this corps left its bivouacs on the 1st of August, under the pretence of making a march for the purpose of exercising the troops, and crossed the frontier in the direction of the Jablunka mountains. The Prussian authorities immediately despatched officers to overtake the expedition, with orders summoning its leader to return, and at the same time pointing out the actual position of affairs, in consequence of which the detachment returned behind the line of demarcation on the 6th of August.

On the 26th of July the plenipotentiaries of both powers signed preliminary articles of peace at Nikolsburg, and operations ceased on the eastern theatre of war.

---

If we cast a retrospective glance upon the principal occurrences of the campaign, we see that when the war broke out the Prussian forces formed three separate armies, which had taken up positions for the defence of the Marches and Silesia, whereas the bulk of the Austrian troops was assembled in one army in Moravia. The forces were equal on both sides.

As soon as war was determined upon at Berlin, orders were issued for the junction of the armies by the shortest possible routes forwards, therefore within the enemy's country.

The point selected for this purpose was equally distant from Görlitz, Glatz, and the Bohemian-Moravian frontier, as well as from Torgau, Brünn, and Olmütz. For this reason, first of all, the Army of the Elbe entered Saxony (16th of June), but at the same time (17th of June) Feldzeugmeister Benedek commenced his march from Moravia to Bohemia, where the advantages of the inner line of operations could alone be made full use of.

Such large masses must necessarily march in deep columns. Whilst advancing to effect their junction, the Prussian armies could not, therefore, find the passage barred by the whole of the Austrian Army, but might well meet, not only the Ist and the Saxon Corps, but also the heads of the enemy's main army. The only safeguard against this danger lay in the initiative and in rapid execution of the necessary marches.

Prince Frederick Charles had to wait for the junction of the Army of the Elbe from the direction of Dresden. On the 26th the heads of his army occupied the defiles of the Iser at Turnau and Podol. He was only half as far from Gitschin as the IInd Army on the line Liebau-Reinerz, and therefore facilitated the advance of the latter. The difficult task of the Crown Prince was, however, to concentrate the IInd Army by mountainous roads, and on the other side of the frontier, and this at a time when the enemy's foremost troops were already appearing at the issues of the defiles.

The centre of the IInd Army crossed the frontier on the 26th, the two wings on the 27th.

On the right wing Lieutenant Field-Marshal Von Gablenz succeeded in checking the advance of the Ist Prussian Corps at Trautenau, but having exposed his flank to the attack of the Corps of Guards, is routed at Soor the next day.

Lieutenant Field-Marshal Von Ramming throws himself upon the Prussian left wing, and is defeated. The Prussian Vth Corps, although only intended to march up to the defile on this day, debouches with its whole force beyond it. The VIIIth Austrian Corps reaches Dolan too late to afford any assistance to the VIth Corps at Nachod, but relieves it next day at Skalitz, and the IVth Corps is brought up to Dolan. Thus three Austrian Corps—minus two brigades, which were otherwise employed—might certainly have been opposed to the Vth Prussian Corps at Skalitz, but one of them was much shaken by the action of the preceding day, and the second one would only have been able to reach the position in the course of the afternoon, at the time when the third was already leaving it. Besides this, General Steinmetz's measures were so taken that he could not have been thrown back into the defile of Nachod, but at the very utmost only upon the main body of the IInd Army. On the 29th he defeats the IVth Austrian Corps also at Schweinschädel. A sanguinary combat of three days' duration, in which 22 Prussian battalions were successively opposed to 72 of the enemy, thus opens his way to join the army. The only support afforded in these engagements was that of the 22nd Brigade of the VIth Corps in the action of the second day.

The main body of the Ist Army turned off from the road to Gitschin, in order to dislodge the enemy from his position on the Iser at Münchengrätz; but on the 24th already the divisions of General Tümpling and Werder—together only 25 battalions—wrested Gitschin, the primary object of the campaign, from the enemy, who had 45 battalions on the field.

Shortly before this occurred, Feldzeugmeister Benedek had become convinced that the progress of the IInd Prussian Army rendered offensive operations against the Ist Army impossible. Two of his corps were now (30th of July) concentrated in front of the former on the plateau of Dubenetz. The three other corps were also ordered to the same spot, but were followed by the whole of the Prussian Ist Army, and forced to take a more southerly direction. In the course of the preceding three days the Austrian Army had been engaged in eight different actions, in which it had lost far above 30,000 men, and nearly 1,000 officers. It could no longer move to attack one of the hostile armies, which were now already in immediate communication with each other, without having to sustain the attack of the other on its flank. The reunion of the Army with the 1st and the Saxon Corps could only be effected by retreating in the direction of Königgrätz, and even the iron will of the Austrian leader was forced to yield to this necessity.

On the 1st and 2nd of July the Austrian Army assembled on the Bistritz, and the resolution which His Majesty the King of Prussia immediately took led to the decisive battle of the 3rd, for which both combatants succeeded in assembling the whole of their available forces.

Even though the Austrian Army lost 40,000 men on this day, it nevertheless still numbered 180,000 men, and only needed time to recover itself, in order to be able to offer fresh resistance. Safety and rest might both be expected in the entrenched camp of Olmütz. By retreating thither the Austrian main forces might well hope to lead their adversaries after them, and away from the Capital.

However, only one of the Prussian armies follows in this direction, an army much inferior in numbers to the enemy, but buoyed up by victory. More than 100,000 Prussians, on the other hand, marched straight on Vienna.

Even in spite of the cession of Venetia, it had not been possible to assemble sufficient forces for the immediate protection of the capital. Lightly as Austria may have estimated the enterprising spirit of the Italian head-quarters after the battle of Custozza, still not more than two of the three corps d'armée in Italy could have been brought up to the Danube, and they not until the 20th of July. Including the Xth Corps and the Cavalry, then on their march from Bohemia to Vienna, there can have been scarcely more than 60,000 to 70,000 combatants available there.

No time, therefore, could be granted to the Army of the North to recover from the effects of its defeat, and on the very first day of its arrival at Olmütz the transport of the IIIrd Corps commenced.

Although the railway was of great assistance on this transport, still the greater part of the troops had to start for Vienna on foot.

Having but few roads at its disposal, and because of the mountainous nature of the country, the Prussian IInd Army could not arrive in time to prevent this movement, which the first Austrian *échelon* carried out on the 14th of July on both banks of the March. On the 15th the second *échelon* was driven back from the right to the left bank of the river in the action of Tobitschau, and its march on the left bank even is disturbed by the combat of Rokeinitz. The Prussian Cavalry alone was not, however, able to bar all roads, and the Feldzeugmeister advanced along the valley of the March to Kremsier and Hradisch.

Forty-five miles behind Olmütz, however, Göding was already in the hands of his adversary.

Marching with a broader front, and, therefore, with greater rapidity, Prince Frederick Charles reached Brünn on the 12th, and dislodged Colonel Mondl's Brigade from Lundenburg on the 16th.

From this moment railway and roads along the valley of the March were intercepted, and the Austrian corps compelled to make a detour over the mountains and along the valley of the Waag. Were they to find Pressburg already occupied by their adversaries, then Komorn would be the nearest possible spot for crossing the Danube.

Exerting themselves to their utmost the Austrian columns descended the mountains into the valley of the Waag on the 18th already. Their nearest corps, the IInd, was still at Neustadtl, 54 miles from Pressburg, on this day, on which the 8th Prussian Division reached St. Johann, only 27 miles from this important place.

On the 21st even there were but two Austrian Brigades at hand to defend the town, but during the night, and in the course of the next day, the energy of Lieutenant Field-Marshal Count Thun succeeded in bringing up his whole corps, to do which he availed himself of the tramway and of peasants' carts. Nevertheless, the turn which the action of Blumenau took leaves no doubt but what the Prussians would have gained possession of Pressburg if the commencement of the armistice had not put a stop to the engagement.

The Prussian forces which started from Dresden, Gorlitz, and Frankenstein on the 22nd of June were in front of Vienna and Pressburg on the 22nd of July, having made 225 miles in the direction of the main operations within these thirty days.

For the most part in the eight days, which comprised the principal actions of the campaign, they had captured 200 pieces of artillery, 11 flags and standards, and 39,800 prisoners. After deducting all losses, and without including those detachments which were left in front of the enemy's fortresses, or were employed in guarding the lines of communication in rear of the army, 184,000 out of 254,000 men, or three-quarters of the original force, arrived at the Danube.

Within a very short time this number could be increased to 200,000 by bringing up the troops that were already on the march. Siege artillery and materials for bridge-building were at hand in sufficient quantities; the spirits of the troops were raised by their preceding victories, and the scene of operations was on the point of being transferred to the opposite bank of the Danube, when French mediation succeeded in finding a basis for peace negotiations.

The marching orders which had been already drawn up for a renewed concentration of the army were not despatched to the different headquarters, and the following military convention was signed on the 26th of July, simultaneously with the preliminary articles of peace :—

" The undersigned, the Royal Prussian General of Infantry, " Baron Von Moltke, and the Imperial Feldzeugmeister, Count " Degenfeldt, having been empowered by His Majesty the King " of Prussia and His Majesty the Emperor of Austria, and having " mutually proved their credentials, conclude a truce under the " following conditions.

" The preliminary articles of peace having been signed to-day, " hostilities will now cease between the Royal Prussian troops on " the one side, and the Imperial Austrian and Royal Saxon " troops on the other side, and a four-weeks' truce will commence " on the 2nd of August. While it lasts, the following conditions " will be observed :—

" § 1. During the truce the Royal Prussian troops will occupy " a district, bounded on the west by the line Eger, Pilsen, Tabor, " Neuhaus, Zlabings, Znaym, inclusive of the forenamed places. " The Thaya will form the boundary down to the influx of this " river into the March, on the east, the latter river as far as " Napagedl, and from thence a straight line to Oderberg.

" § 2. An extent of nine miles round the fortress of Olmütz, " and of 4½ miles round the fortresses of Josephstadt, Königgratz, " and Theresienstadt will be exempted from the Prussian occupa- " tion, and these fortresses can draw their supplies from these rayons. " The fortress Olmütz will have a line of communication over " Weisskirchen to Meseritsch, leading through the Prussian rayon, " on which line Prussian troops will not be quartered.

" § 3. To enable the Prussian troops to reach the districts " settled in § 1 from their present positions, the routes Meissau, " Scheiteldorf, Wittingau to Tabor, and Malaczka, Skalitz to " Napagedl, will be given up to them, and they will be permitted " to take up quarters within nine miles on either side of these " routes.

" § 4. The Prussian troops will make free use of all land and " water communications, and railways within the district settled " in § 1, as long as the truce lasts, and will be in no way hindered " from so doing by the fortresses named in § 2.

" Exempted herefrom is the tract of the Prerau-Trübau rail- " way, which passes through the wood of Olmütz.

" § 5. The Imperial Austrian troops will not cross the line of " demarcation fixed on the 22nd of this month, until the end of " the Prussian column has passed the Thaya.

" A notification will be sent to the Imperial Government as " soon as this has taken place.

" § 6. The sick and the surgeons, and the officials tending " them, who remain behind in the districts evacuated by the Royal " Prussian troops, will remain in possession of whatever buildings " they now occupy. In addition to this, the assistance of the " authorities, supplies, and means of transport, will be afforded " them on the part of the Austrians. Neither during nor after " the truce will any obstacle be opposed to their return to their " homes, which the Prussian authorities will hasten as much as " possible.

" § 7. The Royal Prussian troops will draw their supplies

" from the districts in which they are quartered. No contribution
" of money will be raised on the part of the Prussians.

" § 8. No property, magazines and stores belonging to the
" Imperial Austrian Government, which are not in possession of
" the Prussian troops before the commencement of the truce, will
" be seized by them.

" § 9. The Imperial Government will provide for the
" immediate return of the civil authorities to their posts, in order
" that they may render assistance in provisioning the Prussian
" Army.

" In the time intervening between the 27th of July, and the
" 2nd of August, the Austrian-Saxon troops will keep two and a
" quarter miles off the line of demarcation fixed on the 22nd
" instant, in so far as the line runs on the left bank of the Danube,
" and no Prussian troops will cross the aforesaid line.

(Signed)·   " COUNT DEGENFELD,
" <i>Imperial Feldzeugmeister</i>,
" BARON VON MOLTKE,
" <i>General of Infantry</i>."

" <i>Nikolsburg, the 26th of July</i>, 1866."

When this convention was announced to the troops they
were warned, with reference to the concluding sentence, that
misunderstandings might possibly produce casual conflicts, and
that, therefore, the troops were to maintain their perfect
readiness for action until further orders.

# BOOK THE THIRD.

## THE CAMPAIGN IN WESTERN GERMANY.

WE still have to narrate the course of those events which took place in the west of Germany during and, for the most part, after the main operations which decided the fate of the war in the east.

As is known, a decree had been passed in Frankfort to mobilize four Federal Corps, the VIIth, VIIIth, IXth, and Xth, for the purpose of Federal execution against Prussia. Only the two former of these Corps, however, actually took the field, and formed the German Federal Army, with which war was waged against the German Federal State, Prussia.

The VIIth Corps consisted of the Bavarian Army, the VIIIth of the contingents of Würtemberg, Baden and Hesse Darmstadt, which were also joined by an Austrian Brigade formed out of the garrisons of the Federal fortresses, and by the contingent of Nassau, otherwise belonging to the IXth Federal Corps.

It was intended that the troops of Hesse Cassel should also form part of the VIIIth Corps, but having left Cassel without any war equipment, they were not ready to take the field, and were, therefore, employed to reinforce the garrison of Mayence; two squadrons only joined the VIIIth Corps.

The contingents of the Xth Federal Corps and the Reserve Division were divided. Those of Saxe-Weimar, Saxe-Meiningen, Schaumburg-Lippe, and Reuss were sent to relieve the Prussian and Austrian troops in the Federal fortresses; Brunswick remained for the present neutral, all of the remainder espoused the cause of Prussia.

The strength and formation of the Federal Army are given in Appendix No. II.

The supreme command of this army was entrusted to Prince Charles of Bavaria, who was at the same time Commanding General of the Bavarian troops. Although above 70 years old, this Prince possessed great mental activity. His high birth and experience of war, as well as the antecedents of his military life, all combined to render him peculiarly fit for the difficult task of uniting so many different elements.

His chief of the Staff was General Von der Tann, a general who in the campaign of 1848–50 in Schleswig-Holstein had won for himself the reputation of a brave and enterprising officer. His military career had been rapid and brilliant.

Prince Alexander of Hesse was appointed Commanding General of the VIIIth Corps. Originally in the Russian service, he afterwards entered that of Austria, in which he obtained much credit in the campaign of 1859, and rapidly advanced to the rank of Lieutenant Field-Marshal and Commander of a Division. His Chief of the Staff was the Würtemberg General Von Baur.

It was intended that the whole of the Federal Army should muster above 90,000 combatants, but it did not attain this number. When war broke out the mobilization of some of the different contingents was not completed.

Most of the south and central German States had, it is true, begun their preparations in the spring, when war first became imminent, but were not ready when hostilities commenced. They either failed to appreciate the serious position of affairs, or else had in time of peace neglected those measures, without which a State cannot be prepared for war.

In Bavaria purchases of horses had been decreed in the beginning of April, and men on furlough were called in to fill the numerous vacancies in the ranks. At the same time, the customary contingent of recruits was enrolled to make up for the one-sixth of the older men who had been dismissed in March. When the question of disarming was started, and affairs seemed to obtain a more peaceful tendency, the purchase of horses was discontinued, but was recommenced in the beginning of May. On the 10th of May the order was issued for the mobilization of the whole army, and the day following all men on furlough were called in.

The cadres which were kept up in time of peace were very weak, and incomplete. Numerous vacancies were always customary among the commissioned and non-commissioned officers of the Infantry; in the beginning of April the companies had but 25 men each on duty, exclusive of recruits, whereas the war complement required 127 rank and file. The other arms were similarly situated.

Raising the existing cadres to their war strength was, however, not all that was necessary to be done; there were also very considerable perfectly new formations to be made. Two fresh battalions in each Infantry, a reserve squadron in each Cavalry regiment had to be formed, as well as a corresponding number of new batteries, sanitary companies, and squadrons of military train. Besides these, all the different depôt detachments, field hospitals, commissariat departments, and provision parks had to be put together.

Very great exertions, therefore, were necessary before the army could take the field. The peace vacancies could only be filled up, and the necessary new formations effected at the cost of the existing cadres, and the government was obliged to call in men who had been from four to six years out of all connection with military life, before the ranks could be filled.

The procuring the horses for the army was a matter of peculiar difficulty. To take them by compulsion not being legally permitted, and the country itself not being able to furnish a sufficient quantity, they were obliged to be purchased in other countries. Under these circumstances the intended formations were not nearly completed when the war broke out. The battalions were incomplete; the field hospitals and parks were almost totally wanting.

The local distribution of these troops in the middle of June has been already mentioned in a previous chapter.

Würtemberg and Baden were still more behindhand than Bavaria in their preparations.

In the former State orders for mobilizing the troops had, it is true, been also issued as early as the 5th of May, but they were but very gradually carried out.

In the middle of May a compulsory levy of horses was decreed, and a number of men called in; but the men on furlough were not regularly called in before the beginning of June, and did not join their standards until the middle of the month.

In order in some degree to keep pace with the armaments of the other South German States, the government of Baden requested a grant from the chambers in the beginning of May, for the purpose of buying horses and calling in men; but as neither government nor chambers were particularly eager about the matter, the loan was not effected before the beginning of June. By reason of the resolution taken by the Federal Diet still further grants were voted in the middle of the month, and the chambers gave their necessary permission for the mobilization of the troops. The men on furlough were then called in on the 17th of June.

Hesse Darmstadt and Nassau were the only States in which greater activity was shown in preparing for war. In both the levy of horses and enrolling of men commenced as early as the middle of May, and the troops were ready for marching by the middle of June.

Nevertheless, the actual outbreak of hostilities took all South German States by surprise before they were prepared to take the field.

During the first period of the operations which we are now going to describe, the forces opposed to each other amounted in round numbers to—

|  | Men. | Guns. |
|---|---|---|
| Prussian Army of the Main.. .. .. | 45,000 | 97 |
| Bavarian Corps .. .. .. .. | 40,000 | 136 |
| VIIIth Corps .. .. .. .. .. | 46,000 | 134 |

Each of the two separate halves of the West German Armies was thus about equal to the united Prussian Forces; to which their Cavalry and Artillery was numerically far superior.

No mutual plan of operation had been settled. Towards the end of May delegates of the South German States met in Munich for military conferences, but the only agreement they arrived at was that the different contingents should be assembled ready for marching by the 15th of June, either in stationary camps, or in the neighbourhood of the main lines of railway. This was by no means possible for all of them to effect, from reasons which we have already explained. The conferences which were held at Olmütz, as mentioned in our introductory chapter, only fixed the general outline of the co-operation of the VIIth and VIIIth Federal Corps, besides which they took place so late that the decisions arrived at could not be carried out. The commencement and course of the war were, however, unexpectedly rapid, and rendered speedy action imperative.

In the first place, the position of the Prussian Division Beyer, near Wetzlar, caused apprehension that an expedition against Frankfort or Mayence might be intended. The Federal Diet, **16th to 25th June.** therefore, desired the governments to send all available troops that were ready for action as speedily as possible to Frankfort, and requested the Prince of Hesse to undertake the defence of the town.

In consequence the greater part of the division of Hesse Darmstadt was moved to Frankfort, and the brigade of Nassau concentrated near Höchst, besides which a brigade of Würtemberg troops, 5,000 men strong, but very insufficiently equipped, arrived there on the 17th.

The same day, however, the news of General Beyer's advance on Cassel arrived. The dreaded danger seemed to be happily averted, and the increased activity which was momentarily aroused, again quietly subsided.

The Prince of Hesse devoted the next few days to forming his head-quarter staff, to inspecting the troops, and issuing grandiloquent proclamations.

On the 21st, the Austrian Brigade Hahn reached Darmstadt from Linz. It had only been sent to the latter town a week before from Frankfort and the Federal fortresses. A brigade from Baden arrived at Frankfort on the 25th.

A Council of War, at which the ministers were present, was held at Munich on the 17th, and operations in a north-easterly direction were taken into consideration. It was therefore decided that the first concentration of the army should take place around about Bamberg.

The transport of the troops from the south of the kingdom to the Main was therefore forthwith commenced, and the Bavarian Army was assembled at the following points by the 21st:—

Division Feder, at Forchheim.
    „    Hartmann, at Schweinfurth.
    „    Zoller, at Bamberg.
    „    Stephan, at Lichtenfels.
The Reserve Cavalry, in Upper Franconia, between Bayreuth and Hof.
The Reserve Artillery, at Erlangen.

In the meantime, Prussian operations against Hanover had commenced. In describing them we have already briefly mentioned the movements of the Bavarian Army, which bore reference to them, but have still to add the following remarks :—

On the 18th of June a Hanoverian emissary passed through Schweinfurth on his way to Frankfort, and inquired of General Von Hartmann whether the troops, then at Göttingen, would be received in Bavaria in case they marched thither.

The answer was in the affirmative, and when the officer returned next day, a request was sent by him to the Hanoverians to communicate their intended route as soon as possible.

On the evening of the 21st the Prince of Hesse reported that the Hanoverians intended to march on Fulda, and the Bavarian Army was in consequence moved in this direction on the 22nd and 23rd. The army, however, progressed but slowly, as much was still wanting in its equipment for the march. The news soon arrived that the occupation of Cassel by the Prussians, had induced the Hanoverians to turn off in the direction of Mühlhausen, and that considerable forces of the enemy were assembling at Eisenach; the Bavarians, therefore, took a more northerly direction on the 25th, so as to be able to march either through the valley of the Fulda or the Thüringer-Wald, as circumstances might demand.

On the 26th of June the Division Hartmann, which formed 26th June. the advanced guard, in company with the 1st Light Cavalry Brigade, moved one Brigade of Infantry to Neustadt, the other one to Unsleben, Mellrichstadt, Fladungen, and Tann. The Light Cavalry Brigade was pushed on towards Meiningen.

The Division Zoller stood at Münnerstadt, Division Feder at Lauringen, Division Stephan at Königshofen.

The reserves were still in the act of assembling at Schweinfurth, at which place Prince Charles had established his head-quarters.

It was high time that some decision should be agreed upon with respect to mutual operations. Prince Charles of Bavaria and Prince Alexander of Hesse, therefore, arranged, in a conference held at Schweinfurth on the 26th of June, that both corps should unite at Hersfeld, and the following routes were fixed for this purpose :—

|  |  |  | VIIIth Corps. | VIIth Corps. |
|---|---|---|---|---|
| 30th of June | .. | .. | Friedberg. | Brückenau. |
| 1st of July | .. | .. | Hungen. | Löschenroda. |
| 2nd „ | .. | .. | Grünberg. | Fulda. |
| 3rd „ | .. | .. | Ruppertenrod. | Fulda. |
| 4th „ | .. | .. | Alsfeld. | Hünfeld. |
| 5th „ | .. | .. | Alsfeld. | Hünfeld. |
| 6th „ | .. | .. | Grabenau. | Neukirchen. |
| 7th „ | .. | .. | Niederaula. | Hersfeld. |

The united Federal Army most certainly guarded all Federal territories if stationed at Hersfeld, and did so all the more effectually the further it advanced in this direction; but the question to be considered was whether the enemy would allow it to reach this point, from which he was only half as far off as the Federal Army.

It was without doubt the state of unreadiness in which the different contingents still were, which compelled the armies to defer their advance until the 30th of June. The roads selected for this purpose only converge after passing Alsfeld and Hünfeld. These points were to be reached on the 5th of July, and even then the corps were still two days' march separate. They could scarcely expect, with any degree of probability, to find one or the other of these points unoccupied by the enemy after a space of 11 days.

If the Prince of Hesse had taken the high-road to Gelnhausen instead of the road by Grünberg, both corps might have been at Brückenau and Schlüchtern, one day's march from each other, on the 2nd of July, and could then have effected their junction, either forwards at Fulda, or further to the rear at Gemünden.

In judging these first and so momentous measures, we must not forget that all strategical arrangements made between allied armies are necessarily but compromises, based upon the separate interests of the different States. Those of the minor States required protection against an invasion from the Prussian Rhenish provinces, and the safety of Frankfort and Mayence. To guard the Hessian territories by his advance was naturally a welcome task to the commander of the VIIIth Corps. Better shelter and provisions for the troops were to be found westward of the "Vogelsgebirge," and an advance in this direction afforded the advantage of a line of railway for the numerous and necessary supplies which still had to be brought up from the rear. General Von Baur, Prince Alexander's Chief of the Staff, pronounced himself very decidedly in favour of an advance on Cassel. The Bavarians, on the contrary, naturally preferred to keep on a line between the enemy and their own native country. They recommended a line of operations on Eisenach which would cover the roads leading from thence to Würzburg and Bamberg. It was thought that the operations might be continued from Eisenach as well against Cassel as against Hanover, or even in the direction of Leipzig. By way of reconciling these adverse opinions, the Austrian General Count Huyn, whose wish was principally that an advance in any direction should be made, proposed the intermediate point Hersfeld as place of junction, a proposition which was ultimately agreed to.

It was then also arranged that the plan of route which had been settled should not be deviated from unless from the most pressing reasons. The preceding movements of the VIIth Corps had, however, already caused it totally to swerve from the prescribed direction. As we know, this had been caused by the idea of being nearer at hand, in case it should be necessary to afford assistance to the Hanoverians. At the same time the position of the latter was not thought to be one of such imminent danger, and the opinion prevailed that 19,000 men were strong enough to force their way through the enemy. When nothing was heard that showed any intention of so doing, but on the contrary rumours spoke of negatiations being carried on with Prussia, then all confidence was lost in the resolution of their allies, and the Bavarian troops remained quietly in their above-mentioned quarters on the 27th and 28th of June, just during those days in which the fate of Hanover was decided. In like manner the VIIIth Corps threw difficulties in the way of uniting both corps at Hersfeld by detaching several portions of troops in its left flank. On the 28th the latter corps was reinforced by a Würtemberg brigade, but reports arising that Prussian detachments had entered the northern part of Nassau and the " Rheingau,"* the Austrian-Nassau division was pushed forward towards Friedberg and Wiesbaden, and the garrison of Mayence was increased.

27th and 28th June.

It was a fact that small detachments, formed out of garrison troops, had been sent from Coblentz and Cologne in the direc-tion above-named for the purpose of alarming the enemy and attracting his attention in that direction. On the 28th and the following days they occupied Ems, Montabaur, &c., in the former, and Bingen, Rüdesheim, Geisenheim, and some other places in the latter direction.

On the 28th Prince Charles was informed for certain by an emissary coming direct from the King of Hanover, and also by telegraphic despatches from Munich and Vienna, that the Hanoverians were still at Langensalza and hoped to be able to hold their ground there until the arrival of reinforcements. In consequence of this information it was now determined to continue the march of the VIIth Corps over the Thüringer Wald, in the direction of Gotha. Two divisions were to ad-vance over Hildburghausen and Suhl, two over Meiningen and Schmalkaden. The Reserve Cavalry was to keep up the com-munication with the VIIIth Corps by marching on Vacha. These movements commenced on the 29th, and on the 30th the Bavarian Army was at Wasungen, Meiningen, Schleusingen, and Hildburghausen, instead of at Brückenau. The advanced guards were thrown forward on both roads as far as Schmal-kalden and Suhl, reserve artillery and parks were still as far back as Neustadt.

30th June.

With the exception of the 1st Light Brigade, the Reserve Cavalry was detached to the neighbourhood of Kissingen.

The head-quarters of the Prince Field-Marshal were moved to Meiningen.

Although this advance towards Gotha was communicated to Prince Alexander the day before, still no alteration whatever was made in the route of the VIIIth Corps; on the contrary, in the letter on the 29th, it was said :—

---

* The valley of the Rhine between Mayence and Bingen.

" I have received your Highness's communication
" stating that you will commence your march on Hers-
" feld to-morrow, the 30th."

In consequence, the VIIIth Corps started on this day, according to the route which had been agreed upon.

On arriving at Meiningen Prince Charles, however, already
received the intelligence of the capitulation of the Hanoverians. His march on Gotha had no longer any object, and
he now returned to the original idea of effecting a junction
with the VIIIth Corps. The latter was on this day round about
Friedberg, 80 miles from Meiningen as the crow flies, and an
immediate junction of the two corps could now only be effected
by means of flank marches in the neighbourhood of the enemy
and across heavy mountain roads.

In a letter written to the Prince of Hesse on the evening of
the 30th the Field-Marshal announces his intention of concentrating his forces at Meiningen, fronting towards Eisenach. In
case the enemy should not prevent it, he hoped to draw near
the VIIIth Corps by means of the cross roads Hilders-Fulda and
Geisa-Hünfeld. This of course necessitated the continued
advance of the latter corps past the north side of the Vogel
mountains. In case the Bavarian Army should be forced to
retreat, this would be effected by way of Mellrichstadt and
Neustadt, and the Field-Marshal then expected the " co-
" operation of the VIIIth Corps between Neustadt and Schwein-
"furfth," for which purpose it would necessarily be obliged to
fall back *southward* of the Vogel mountains. The end of this
letter is as follows :—

" I therefore return to the plan of operations which
" we concerted at Schweinfurth, and earnestly request
" your Highness to waive all secondary considerations
" and to join me with all your available forces, partly by
" the line Hanau-Fulda-Hunfeld ; partly, and in par-
" ticular, by the line Frankfort-Gemünden per railway,
" and from there over Hammelburg to Kissingen."

The Prince of Hesse received this letter at Friedberg on the
1st July. evening of the 1st of July.

The Hessian Division was already at Laubach and Münster ;
the Würtemberg Division, as yet only two brigades, was at
Borstadt ; a right flank detachment in Ober-Schmitten in the
Nidda valley ; the Brigade of Baden on the left, in Gross-Linden.
The latter was to clear up the neighbourhood of Wetzlar and
Giessen, where hostile troops had been seen, for which purpose
it had been reinforced by the Reserve Cavalry.

The Austrian-Nassau Division was left at the Maine in order
to protect Mayence and Frankfort against any expedition that
the enemy might undertake from Coblentz. If it had not been
for this object, the division might well have been sent per rail
to Gemünden, but it was neither in the immediate interest of

the Corps to diminish its forces by so doing, nor indeed to march in the direction of Neustadt-Schweinfurth, which would leave the whole territories of the minor States without any protection. It is not in the nature of coalitions to perceive that the great objects of war are not to be obtained without such partial sacrifices. The Prince of Hesse, nevertheless, agreed to march to Fulda.

Although it would even now have been advisable to effect the junction of both corps further to the rear, still this measure was repugnant to the chivalrous feelings of both commanders. In a political view it would have made an unfavourable impression if the campaign had commenced with so retrograde a movement, and it would also have had a depressing influence on the spirit of the troops if the army were to retreat even before the Prussians were seen.

It was very probably in opposition to the better military judgment of their leaders that both corps thus marched separately towards the Fulda road, where they might almost for certain expect to meet the united forces of their adversary.

The VIIth Corps brought up its detached troops to Meiningen, and the flank march commenced by General Zoller's division leaving the valley of the Werra and crossing the mountains by way of Ober-Katz and Kalten-Nordheim to the valley of the Felde.

General Hartmann's Division was left at Wasungen and Wernshausen to cover this movement against any hostile advance from Eisenach. A patrol which was thrown forward in the Werra valley met Prussian troops on the evening of the 2nd. Colonel Aldosser advanced towards Barchfeld late the same evening to reconnoitre with one and a half companies and a squadron. A Prussian picquet was discovered at Immelborn, but was on the alert and repulsed the attack of the Bavarians with file-fire. The latter lost 2 men killed, 5 officers, and 17 men wounded, among whom was Colonel Aldosser himself. It was thus proved that the Prussians were advancing from Eisenach.

Prince Alexander continued his march in an easterly direction in order to reach the line Hanau-Fulda-Hünfeld.

The Hessian Division arrived at Herbstein on the 3rd of 3rd July. July; one of the Würtemberg Brigades at Ruppertenrod, the other at Schotten. Lauterbach and Alsfeld were occupied.

The Austrian-Nassau Division did not get further than Friedberg, so that it could not become available within the next few days. This was of all the more importance as the forces of the Corps were already much diminished by the absence of the troops of Baden and of the Reserve Cavalry, both of which left at the Lahn, both to cover the base of operations on the Maine and to protect flank and rear of the army during its advance in the valley of the Fulda.

The great apprehension which was felt for the line of communication in rear of the army arose partly from exaggerated reports with regard to the strength of the hostile detachments which had entered Nassau and partly from the dread lest the Prussians should advance per railway from Cassel direct on Frankfort. The instructions given to the Commander of the Baden troops expressly state that he was to advance towards Wetzlar, but was to avoid any serious engagement. and was to select a suitable central position in the neighbourhood of the Lahn, in which he could assemble his troops if attacked by superior forces. In addition to this, stress is laid on the security of the Marburg road, and permission is granted to destroy the line of railway leading there.

Prince William of Baden, who joined with the remainder of his division on the 2nd of July, occupied Gissen with one brigade, whilst the other one and the Reserve Cavalry cantoned further to the rear near Butzbach.

On the 3rd of July the Bavarian division Zoller marched on Dermbach. The advanced guard found the place occupied by the enemy, suffered some loss by his fire and then fell back again to Neidhartshausen. The main body halted at Diedorf. Tann was occupied by a battalion.

The divisions Stephan and Feder followed as far as Kalten-Nordheim, Ober-Katz. and Kalten-Sundheim; the Reserve Artillery immediately behind them. Division Hartmann advanced towards Rossdorf. The advanced troops of the division occupied Helmers, Rosa, and Wiesenthal, a detachment of the enemy retreating from the latter place without offering opposition as the Bavarians approached; on the other hand, they were met with artillery fire on drawing near Urnshausen.

Head-quarters moved to Kalten Nordheim.

The corps had thus succeeded in *écheloning* three divisions on the Mellrichstadt-Berka road and in drawing somewhat nearer to the VIIIth Corps, whose approach was expected from the direction of Fulda. The junction with the 4th division of General Von Hartmann, which was coming up on the right, was, however, not yet effected, as the enemy held possession ot the cross roads at Dermbach. If the avowed intention of meeting the allied corps at Hünfeld was still to be carried out, it was necessary to open the road to Geisa by an engagement.

We left the Prussian troops under command of General Von Falckenstein in their quarters round about Eisenach, Langen-salza, and Gotha.

The breaking up of the Hanoverian army had cleared North Germany of the enemy, the communication between the east and west of the monarchy was secured, and a basis established for operations against South Germany.

In directions which had been previously given to General Von Falckenstein by the Chief of the General Staff it was expressly mentioned, that like as the centre of opposition for the whole war might be sought in the Austrian Army, so Bavaria formed the nucleus of the South German coalition. It was to be feared that offensive operations from Cassel direct on Frankfort would induce the VIIIth Corps to take refuge in

Mayence, in which case no enemy would be found in the field. It was therefore more advisable to take the route Fulda-Schweinfurth. One might be sure of meeting the Bavarian Army if one sought it in its own country, and might well hope to prevent the junction of the VIIth and VIIIth Corps by advancing in this direction.

These operations were forthwith commenced on the 1st of July.

General Beyer's Division advanced on the right wing by way of Berka and Vacha, General Goeben's Division on its left on the road to Marksuhl and Wilhelmsthal. General Manteuffel's corps followed the latter division.

The tactical formation of the troops, which had been disturbed during the pursuit of the Hanoverians, was restored during the two first days' march. The 19th Regiment of Infantry was transferred from General Beyer's Division to that of General Goeben, and the latter was further increased by a horse artillery battery, and a light field bridge train formed out of Hanoverian materials. The two Coburg-Gotha battalions and a horse-artillery battery were added to General Manteuffel's Corps and two 12-pounder batteries to General Beyer's Division.

The two battalions of the Guards and all garrison and depôt troops which had been employed in surrounding the Hanoverian Army returned to their former garrisons.

In all other respects the formation of General Falckenstein's troops remained the same as is shown in Appendix No. II, but the whole of the forces assembled under his command now received the name "Army of the Maine."

On the 3rd of July General Von Beyer's Division was at Rasdorf, Geisa, and Buttlar on the Vacha-Fulda road, General Goeben's Division in Oechsen and Lengsfeld, on the road to Mellrichstadt, on which we have just left the Bavarian Army in the act of crossing over from the valley of the Werra. Its further advance along the valley of the Felde was now checked by General Von Goeben in Dermbach, which place, together with Urnshausen, he had occupied to cover his left flank. General Von Manteuffel had followed beyond Marksuhl.

Nothing could in reality have been more welcome to the Army of the Maine than to be able to meet with its whole force one of the enemy's corps alone, the more so if it was that one the importance of which held the component parts of the whole army together.

It was, however, thought that the enemy immediately in front of the Prussians was but a detachment of perhaps a division thrown forward to cover the march of the main body to Fulda.

General Von Falckenstein was determined at all events to prevent a junction of his adversaries at the latter spot, and resolved to attack the enemy immediately in front of him, but not to interrupt the advance of his main force in the direction of Fulda.

General Von Goeben was therefore directed to throw back any columns of the enemy that might advance against him, but not to pursue them far, and to march towards Fulda the same day, in which direction Generals Von Beyer and Von Manteuffel were to continue their march.

## ACTIONS NEAR DERMBACH ON THE 4TH OF JULY.*

Under this head are generally comprised two separate actions, which were simultaneously fought on the 4th of July by the troops of General Goeben's Division, but between which there was no immediate connection, viz., General Von Kummer's Brigade against the Bavarian Division Zoller, at Zella, and General Von Wrangel's Brigade against General Hartmann's Division, at Wiesenthal.

### 1. ACTION AT ZELLA.

At 8 o'clock A.M., General Goeben gave orders to General Kummer to advance from Dermbach to attack Zella with four battalions of his brigade, two squadrons of the 8th Hussars, and the 3rd 6-pounder battery. At the same time General Wrangel's Brigade was ordered up from Oechsen by way of Ober-Alba, and then sent towards Wiesenthal with the three remaining squadrons of the Hussars and the 3rd 4-pounder battery. Two battalions of General Kummer's Brigade and the 4th 4-pounder battery remained in reserve at Dermbach until General Wrangel's Brigade arrived there.

The former, thus reduced to four battalions, started immediately. The Fusilier Battalion of the 53rd Regiment was sent on Neidhartshausen, the 1st Battalion of this regiment across the mountainous country eastward, and the 2nd Battalion by a road westward of the high-road, in order to attack both flanks of the Zella position, which was difficult to force from the north. The Fusilier Battalion of the 13th Regiment, the Cavalry and the Artillery followed along the high-road.

The nature of the ground made the position Zella-Neidhartshausen one of great strength for defensive purposes. Deep marshy meadows cover the front. Zella itself lies on a height with steep slopes, commanding the neighbouring country, and an old convent surrounded by walls afforded an admirable redoubt in the interior of the village. The Bavarians occupied the position with three and a-half battalions, a small detachment of cavalry and two 12-pounder guns of General Zoller's Division. In the place itself four companies of the 14th and one of the 6th Regiment were stationed, the two guns were planted in a favourable position immediately at the side of the village, close behind which the cavalry was hidden. The 1st

* *Vide* Appendix XXVIII.

Rifle Battalion and a company of the 6th Regiment occupied Neidhartshausen, a battalion of the 14th Regiment was on the right bank of the Fulda.

When the Prussian troops approached this position at about 9 A.M. they were shelled by the two Bavarian guns. General Kummer brought forward his 6-pounder battery, and opened a very effectual fire, after which the Infantry proceeded to attack the position. It was carried at the first onset, the 2nd Battalion of the 53rd Regiment entering Zella from the west and the 9th Company of the 13th Regiment from the north at the same moment. Neidhartshausen was taken by the Fusilier Battalion and the woods eastward of the road by the 1st Battalion of the 53rd Regiment. It was, however, not without a long and hard struggle that full possession of the whole position was gained.

The company of the 6th Bavarian Regiment in particular held its ground in Zella with great obstinacy, and was almost totally destroyed. Only 1 officer and 19 men succeeded in cutting their way through.

The beaten troops fell back upon their main body at Diedorf after suffering severely from the fire of the Prussian Infantry and Artillery. The Prussian battalions were then re-formed.

Captain Eynatten's battery unlimbered close to Zella and shelled the retreating enemy. General Kummer did not consider it advisable to pursue any further, as considerable forces of the enemy near Diedorf could be seen from a height near Zella, which commanded an extensive view of the surrounding country.

At Diedorf, the whole of General Zoller's division was now assembled, and its two batteries opened a brisk fire against the position now occupied by the Prussians.

General Goeben had sent forward the 4th 4-pounder battery (hitherto held back in reserve), the Fusilier Battalion of the 55th Regiment, belonging to General Wrangel's Brigade, and the 4th Cuirassier Regiment, with the Horse Artillery from the reserves of the division to reinforce General Kummer's brigade. The 4-pounder battery unlimbered at the high-road immediately eastward of Zella, and the Cuirassiers drew up in a sheltered position on its flank. The Horse Artillery battery could not be brought into action as there was no room to place it. The two rifled Prussian batteries now engaged the enemy's artillery.

General Zoller's Division made an energetic attack with its whole force to reconquer the position, but was beaten back by the fire of the Prussian guns and by that of the foremost Infantry detachments.

The action was kept up for some time by the batteries on both sides, but their fire ceased about 3 P.M.

According to official accounts the following are the losses of both parties :—

2 D

| | Prussians. | | Bavarians. | |
| --- | --- | --- | --- | --- |
| | Officers. | Men. | Officers. | Men. |
| Killed .. .. .. .. | 1 | 10 | 2 | 8 |
| Wounded .. .. .. | 3 | 58 | 3 | 46 |
| Missing and prisoners.. .. | .. | 2 | 2 | 103 |
| Total .. .. | 4 | 70 | 7 | 157 |

The number of dead and wounded left by the Bavarians on the field are included among the missing.

## 2. ACTION OF WEISENTHAL.

General Von Wrangel's Brigade reached Dermbach about 9 o'clock, just as the first cannon shots were fired at Zella.

General Von Goeben had already sent the two battalions of General Von Kummer's Brigade which had been kept back in reserve to the bridge over the Felde, near Lindenau, in order to secure this defile. Colonel Von Gellhorn found the enemy there, pressed on to Lindenau, and occupied the neighbouring woods. His battalions were therefore attached to General Von Wrangel's Brigade and a fresh reserve, formed in their stead out of the 1st and Fusilier Battalions of the 15th, and the Fusilier Battalion of the 55th Regiment, was left at Dermbach. It has been already mentioned that the latter battalion was afterwards sent forward to Zella.

General Von Wrangel threw forward a squadron of Hussars to reconnoitre the country in his front: the 2nd Battalion of the 15th Regiment followed.

The Bavarians occupied Wiesenthal and the country in front of the village with the 6th Rifle Battalion and a battalion of the 4th Infantry Regiment. Their foremost troops fired on the heads of the Prussian Columns, but the latter continued their advance without any interruption, altough a pouring rain prevented any view of the surrounding country. The Bavarians did not hold their ground, the outposts fell back upon their supports, and the latter then retired to Wiesenthal, but were driven out of the barricaded village also, upon which they fell back to a wooded hill in front of Rossdorf, called the Nebelberg. They were here supported by General Cella, who had brought up the main body of his brigade—three battalions, four 12-pounder guns, and two squadrons—from Rossdorf, with which he took up a position on the slope of the hill.

This position was now attacked by the Prussian Infantry, the 2nd Battalion of the 13th Regiment advancing on the right, the 2nd Battalion of the 15th Regiment on the left, the former crossing the valley at the south, the latter at the north entrance of Wiesenthal. Both battalions were formed in columus of companies. The 2nd Battalion of the 55th Regiment which had come up in the meantime, kept up the communication between them. All three battalions were placed under the command of General Gellhorn, who was instructed not to push his advance on too far, as General Von Goeben's movements in this direction were only intended to cover the left flank of General Kummer's Brigade.

General Von Wrangel brought up his 4-pounder battery, and planted it on the heights close to and north-westward of Wiesenthal, where they fired with great effect on the enemy's position. The 1st Battalions of the 13th and 55th Regiments and the 12-pounder battery remained in a sheltered position westward of the village as special reserve.

The highest point of the Nebelberg is about 400 feet above the neighbouring valleys. Its summit is very steep, and is covered with high wood. The Bavarians were soon driven back from the western face of the hill by the admirable fire of Captain Cöster's battery and by the impetuosity with which the Prussian company columns pressed forward without being checked either by the steepness of the hill, the deep ground, or the considerable loss which they suffered.

Three of the Bavarian battalions opposed to them hastily took refuge in the wood which covers the summit of the hill; a fourth went round the north side of the hill in some disorder; the 12-pounder guns took up a position further to the rear, and the Cavalry disappeared from the field altogether. The Prussian skirmishers followed close on the heels of the retreating enemy, and established themselves in the skirts of the wood.

General Cella's Brigade reached Rossdorf about midday and was re-formed in the same position near the west entrance of the village which it had occupied when the action commenced. General Faust soon after arrived there with four battalions and the remaining four 12-pounder guns.

These reinforcements now induced General Hartmann to assume the offensive in order to regain possession of the Nebelberg. Leaving General Faust and his troops in a reserve position near Rossdorf, he personally led the five battalions of General Cella's Brigade against the hill, in particular against its northern face. The eight 12-pounder guns prepared and supported his attack by a very severe fire.

General Von Wrangel now also brought a second battery into action, and succeeded in repulsing the attack, although the foremost troops of the enemy came close up to the skirts of the wood.

Deceived by the echoes among the mountains the Prussians thought they heard artillery and musketry fire north-eastward of the Nebelberg and imagined that General Manteuffel had advanced from Lengsfeld and was engaged. In order to co-operate with him, General Wrangel now thought it necessary to occupy the whole of the Nebelberg and of the wood which crowns its summit. A renewed attack of the Bavarians was repulsed at this spot, although supported by General Faust with

2 D 2

his four battalions and half a 6-pounder battery posted southward of Rossdorf. The General himself lost his life at the
head of his troops.

General Wrangel now resolved to attack Rossdorf and was
engaged in forming his troops for this purpose, when orders
were received from General Goeben directing him to break off
the engagement.

In consequence, one battalion, a battery, and a squadron
were first sent to a reserve position eastward of Wiesenthal
under cover of which the troops which had been engaged were
successively withdrawn and the dead and wounded removed
from the field.

Several attempts of single Bavarian battalions to follow in
pursuit of the Prussians and to occupy the ground evacuated
by them were thwarted.

Captain Cöster's battery distinguished itself here also by its
well-aimed fire, and obliged a considerable detachment of the
enemy, which attempted to advance northward of the Nebelberg
on Wiesenthal, to retreat hastily out of its range by a few well
directed shells.

The action was completely over by half-past three o'clock.
The losses amounted on both sides to—

|  |  |  |  | Prussians. | | Bavarians. | |
|---|---|---|---|---|---|---|---|
|  |  |  |  | Officers. | Men. | Officers. | Men. |
| Killed .. | .. | .. | .. | 5 | 32 | 7 | 147 |
| Wounded | .. | .. | .. | 5 | 208 | 14 | 251 |
| Missing .. | .. | .. | .. | .. | 20 | .. | 190 |
| | Total | .. | .. | 10 | 260 | 21 | 588 |

In this case also the greater part of the missing Bavarians
may be accounted for by the dead and wounded left on the
field.

In accordance with the orders he had received General Von
Goeben sent orders to both brigades of Generals Wrangel
and Kummer to break off the engagements and to return to
Dermbach.

There were no supports at hand which could have secured
any decisive advantage from the success obtained by General
Goeben's Division.

General Von Wrangel marched the same afternoon as far as
Geisa, which place General Von Beyer held until his arrival;
General Von Kummer remained at Dermbach to provide for
the transport of the wounded.

The Bavarians had no intention of avoiding a battle if offered
by the enemy, but they hesitated even at availing themselves of any advantageous situation before they were united
with the VIIIth Corps. It is true, they could not assume

the offensive unless victorious at Zella and Wiesenthal, or unless they had at least held their ground there. The mountainous country afforded the enemy also very strong positions, and it had been just proved that it was doubly difficult to take them if defended by Prussian troops armed with the needle-gun. The Bavarian Artillery was superior in the number of its guns, but the country did not permit it to develop its strength, and in case of a reverse there was great danger of the corps being thrown back upon the intricate defile Diedorf-Kalten-Nordheim.

It was therefore decided to fall back behind the defile, and to await any further attack of the enemy in a suitable position. Both Bavarian divisions received orders to retreat almost exactly at the same time when the Prussian brigades broke off the engagement. Small detachments held the ground eastward of Wiesenthal and southward of Dermbach until nightfall.

A detachment of two battalions, half a squadron, and half a battery was sent to Hilders, in the Ulster Valley, to cover the left flank, because hostile troops were reported to be advancing from Geisa.

During the actions of General Goeben's division the other Prussians had continued their march on Fulda, according to the general disposition.

General Manteuffel sent a strong detachment to Lengsfeld early in the morning, to open communications with the Division Goeben, and to assist it if necessary. The remainder of his troops went into cantonments round about Vacha.

General Beyer's division had scarcely commenced its march to Hünfeld when the outposts reported hostile Cavalry to be at the New Inn, in front of Kirchhasel, and that at least a regiment had been seen near Hünfeld.

This was the advanced guard of the Bavarian Reserve Cavalry, which, as we have already heard, was sent quite alone from Schweinfurth towards Vacha, to open communications with the VIIIth Corps.

Prince Taxis had reached Neustadt on the 1st of July, Bischofsheim on the 2nd, and Fulda on the 3rd. As the information that he received regarding the enemy was very vague, he determined to advance still further, according to his instructions, but being totally without Infantry, addressed a request to the VIIIth Corps, then only 13½ miles from Fulda, to assist him in this respect. The Prince of Hesse had granted his troops a day's rest on the 14th, and refused the request, so that Prince Taxis started from Fulda at 4 A.M. without the desired reinforcements, having sent the 1st and 2nd Regiments of Cuirassiers and four 12-pounder guns on a-head as advanced guard in the course of the night.

The latter met the head of General Beyer's division about 7 o'clock as it debouched from the high wooded district called the Queckmoor, in the neighbourhood of the New Inn. A few rounds of grape fired without any effect were immediately answered by two 4-pounder guns, which opened upon the Bavarian Artillery and the columns of the Cuirassiers at the road-side with so much effect that the Bavarians retreated in haste to Hünfeld after a few shots, and left a 12-pounder gun behind them. The Prussian Artillery followed rapidly, and again threw some shells among their ranks in the neighbourhood of the latter town.

The total losses of the Bavarian Cavalry did not exceed 28 men, and the presence of Prussian troops at this spot cannot have caused them much surprise. Nevertheless the advanced guard immediately retreated, as it seems, in a somewhat disorderly manner.

This conduct was not without influence on the main body of the Cavalry which was advancing behind the advanced guard, but which now hastily retreated to Fulda. Being totally without Infantry, the Cavalry felt itself to be in great danger in this mountainous and wooded district; many alarming rumours arose, and although a start of thirteen miles had been gained, so that nothing but hostile Cavalry could possibly have followed, still a retreat in the direction of Bischofsheim was ordered, and commenced the same afternoon. The imagination of the men being once excited, every trifle gave fresh cause for alarm. When passing the extensive forest between Hettenhausen and Gersfeld towards evening, some carbines were incautiously discharged in the midst of the column, and a report was spread that the road was already occupied by the Prussians, and the retreat of the Cavalry cut off. This was sufficient to induce the latter to take the road to Brückenau, and in the general confusion and the dark night the retreat then degenerated into actual flight.

Only the 3rd Regiment of Cuirassiers and a Horse Artillery battery kept together, and formed a rear guard under the personal command of Prince Taxis, which occupied the pass of Döllbach towards morning. Other regiments rode as far back as Brückenau and even Hammelburg, and were not rallied until several days afterwards near the former town. Single bodies of scattered horsemen are said to have spread terror and dismay as far back as the Maine.

General Beyer's division continued its march as far as Hünfeld, and took up cantonments there, throwing forward an advanced guard to Rückers.

5th July. The Prussians were not aware of the fact that the divisions of Generals Zoller and Hartmann had also retreated as soon as the actions at Zella and Wiesenthal were broken off.

The Bavarian outposts were visible on the neighbouring heights until darkness set in. The enemy had shown considerable numbers at both points, and it was to be expected that he would soon advance with his whole force against the flank and the communications of the army. Under these circumstances it did not seem advisable to continue the march to Fulda without some precautions; General Von Falckenstein, therefore, concentrated his army more closely early on the 5th.

General Manteuffel's Corps was brought up to Lengsfeld, General Goeben's division assembled between Dermbach and Oechsen, and General Beyer's division recalled to Geisa. The latter, however, still occupied Hünfeld with its advanced guard.

More extensive reconnaissances made at daybreak soon proved the enemy to have retreated, and orders were immediately given to resume the march on Fulda.

General Beyer returned to Hünfeld; General Goeben advanced to Geisa; General Manteuffel remained between Oechsen and Lengsfeld.

The Bavarian Army kept in its position at Kalten-Nordheim during the whole of the 5th of July, to give the military train time to retire.

When the determination to assume the offensive was once given up, it became necessary to renounce all idea of joining the VIIIth Corps in the neighbourhood of Fulda, although the latter had approached within seven miles of this town already. On this day, namely, the Hessian division reached Gross-Lueder, the Würtemberg division assembled round about Lauterbach, and the Austrian-Nassau division followed as far as Schotten. It is true, but little progress had been made in the direction of Fulda, but if the corps was to be concentrated, its head could only make short stages.

On the morning of this day Prince Charles issued the following orders to the VIIIth Corps :—

> " The Prussian columns advancing on all sides beyond
> " the Werra renders it impossible to effect a junction of
> " the VIIth and VIIIth Corps northward of the ' Rhön.
> " I purpose, therefore, to retreat to the line Neustadt-
> " Bischofsheim, and request the VIIIth Corps to keep on
> " the same height with me, and to open communications
> " as soon as possible by way of Brückenau and Kis-
> " singen.
>
> " It is impossible to make any further arrangements
> " at present. On the 7th I shall be in the neighbourhood
> " of Neustadt.
> <div align="center">(Signed)   " CHARLES, Prince of Bavaria.<br>" <i>Fieldmarshal.</i>"</div>

This time again the place of junction was so chosen that the VIIIth Corps had by far the most difficult task to perform. The Bavarian Army might possibly reach Neustadt from Kalten-Nordheim in two days. It had at least one good road for its march, and was separated from the enemy by the Rhön mountains.

The VIIIth Corps, on the other hand, was itself not yet concentrated, had double the distance to march, and to traverse these mountains by cross-roads and in the presence of the enemy.

Head-quarters of the Prince of Hesse were in the castle of Eisenbach, near Lauterbach, when these altered dispositions of the Commander-in-Chief arrived in the course of the afternoon. At the same time an aide-de-camp, who had been despatched to Prince Charles on the 3rd, sent a telegram announcing the result of the actions on the 4th, and the advance of the Prussians in the valleys of the Felde and Ulster. The retreat of the Bavarian Cavalry Corps and the Prussian advance beyond Hünfeld now also became known.

Under these circumstances the Prince determined to concentrate his corps at Sclüchtern.

6th July.   The troops were set in motion with this object on the 6th of July.

The Würtemberg division marched to Grebenhain and Freiensteinau, and very judiciously the same day despatched a detachment on carts to Flieden, in the valley of the Fliede, on the Fulda-Hanau road.

The Hessian Division cantoned at Herbstein and Altenschlirf. The Austrian-Nassau Division advanced to Wennings and Seemen.

Thus, three divisions were in some degree concentrated, and the last Würtemberg Brigade, which had at last become available, and had reached Gelnhausen, was brought up to Sallmünster, and was, therefore, in close connection with the corps.

The Bavarian Army commenced its retreat on the 6th, but having only one road at its disposal did not get beyond Ostheim and Fladungen that evening.

On the part of the Prussians the Divisions Beyer and Goeben reached the neighbourhood of Fulda, General Von Manteuffel Hünfeld.

General Goeben's division was reinforced by the Lippe-Detmold Fusilier Battalion, which joined the army on this day.

In the course of the day the Prince of Hesse received the news of the catastrophe of Königgrätz. Position and task of the VIIIth Corps now appeared in a somewhat different light.

The severe defeat sustained by the Austrian Army completely paralysed the joint offensive operations of all forces allied against Prussia. No result obtained on the Western theatre of war could make up for the loss in the East. The main point of the campaign was decided, and peace might soon be expected. Until then each of the allied States must wish to guard its own territories against hostile invasion, and it was very natural that the leaders of the contingents of Hesse, Nassau, Bade, and Würtemberg could not easily make up their minds to abandon all these States to the incursions of their opponents by marching to the right to Bavaria, and giving up the communication with their own countries. This diversity of interest (partikularen rücksichten), which does not prevail in a united state (einheits staat) no doubt made the guidance of the operations by the Bavarian Commander-in-Chief a very difficult matter, and in the same degree prevented the Prince of Hesse from freely disposing of his corps, which was composed of five different contingents.

✗ Now that Fulda could be no longer reached, Schlüchtern was very judiciously selected by Prince Alexander as the place for concentrating his corps; it was the last point where the joint interests might be jointly guarded by defensive operations. After deducting the Baden Division and the Cavalry, the VIIIth Corps mustered about 30,000 men, with 42 guns. At the entrance of the Kinzig valley were strong positions, in which the corps might offer very considerable resistance to the advance of the Prussians, and might possibly await the approach of the Bavarians, slow as it was. At the same time the retreat of the corps to Frankfurt would have been perfectly secure. At all events it would even now have been still perfectly feasible to effect the junction of the South German forces on the Lower Saale—for instance, on the line Hammelburg-Gemünden.

The Prince of Hesse thought that under the existing circumstances the most pressing necessity was to regain the line of the Maine between Hanau and Mayence, and set off thither immediately. In announcing his intention to the Field-Marshal he expressed the hope that the junction of the two armies might now be attempted between Hanau and Aschaffenburg, instead of in Franconia.

On the 7th of July the Bavarian Army marched to Mellrich- 7th July. stadt-Neustadt. If any measures were intended to be taken to secure the approach of the VIIIth Corps, the Cavalry Corps, which had been assembled at Brückenau in the meantime ought to have been again sent forward towards Fulda, instead of which, however, it retreated to Hammelburg.

We have heard that the Prince of Hesse had already given up all idea of marching in this direction. The VIIIth Corps retreated on this day by parallel roads over Ortenberg and Birstein without even having seen the enemy. On the former road the Austrian-Nassau Division reached Allenstadt and Lindheim, the Hessian Division Gedern and Lisberg; on the latter two Würtemburg brigades marched to the neighbourhood of Birstein; the third brigade returned to Gelnhausen. The Prince's head-quarters were established at Ortenberg.

This rendered the junction of the two corps for the present impossible, and exposed the flank of the Bavarian Army during its retreat.

The very same day the Commander-in-Chief desired the VIIIth Corps to retrace its steps, and ordered it to advance as far as possible towards Schlüchtern, but at the same time to detach a brigade to Gemünden.

From other quarters perfectly different requests were addressed to the Prince.

At Frankfort the opinion prevailed that the change which had taken place in the political situation rendered the defence of Mayence and Frankfort of primary importance, that the so doing would protect the whole of South-West Germany, and be preferable to marching eastward. The Prince was requested to take measures to this effect, but at the same time, with diplomatic shrewdness, the writer disclaimed any intention of influencing his military operations, and least of all, of preventing an engagement with the enemy.

We left the Baden Division and the Reserve Cavalry on the 3rd in the neighbourhood of Giessen.

Prince William's instructions were to ensure the safety of Frankfort and the line of the Maine, and to cover the left flank of the VIIIth Corps.

These two objects could not be combined if the latter advanced as far as Fulda.

The Cavalry had reconnoitred the country in a north-easterly direction, advanced from Giessen over Heskern and Homberg to Alsfeld, and returned by way of Grünberg and Hungen to Friedberg, confirming the advance of the enemy in the valley of the Fulda, and reporting that no hostile troops were stationed between Friedberg and Cassel. No danger threatened from this direction, but in Mayence and Frankfort there was still great fear of Prussian expeditions in the valley of the Rhine. Instead of scattering his troops along the Lahn, Prince William of Baden therefore retreated on the 5th to Butz-bach, and on the 6th to Vilbel, behind the Nidda.

The Prince of Hesse disapproved of this movement, although it was made for the same purpose which had induced the VIIIth Corps to retreat—anxiety for the safety of Frankfort and the line of the Maine. The division was ordered to return to Friedberg.

The march of the VIIIth Corps to Frankfort removed it out of all connection with the military events of the next few days; we therefore lose sight of it for the present.

The Prussian Army halted on this day in its cantonments round about Fulda.

The bad weather of the last few days succeeding to a period of great heat, and the total want of straw in the bivouacs, had injuriously affected the condition of the Bavarian troops. It was thought necessary, for the sake of their health and fitness for action, to avoid any great exertions. The army was therefore to proceed to Poppenhausen in short stages; the marches on the 6th and 7th had also been but short. It was intended to hold the defiles of the Saale but slightly, and to offer battle to the enemy in a favourable position near Poppenhausen. From some unknown reasons the impression prevailed that the Prussians would not appear on the Saale before the 11th, and that there would be time for preparation up to the 10th.

On the 8th the main body of the army reached Neustadt; the advanced guard Münnerstadt. The flank detachment, which was retreating from Hilders to Bischofsheim was left at the latter place to watch the advance of the enemy; the 1st Light Cavalry Brigade and some Infantry were pushed forward to Poppenroth, and the Reserve Cavalry, which was at Hammelburg, threw out detachments towards Brückenau.

On the Prussian side, General Goeben's division marched on the Brückenau road as far as Döllbach, General Von Beyer on the Frankfort road to Schlüchtern, General Von Manteuffel followed as far as Fulda.

General Beyer had not come up even with the rear-guard of 9th July. the VIIIth Corps.

It was by no means General Falckenstein's intention to follow the Prince of Hesse; on the contrary, he determined to pursue the Bavarians with his whole force. By pushing forward General Beyer's division on the Frankfort road he gained the twofold object of hiding this intention and of giving the division a separate road for its advance. It marched direct from Schlüchtern to the baths of Brückenau, General Manteuffel's corps to the town of the same name, General Goeben's division advanced beyond this town as far as Geroda.

According to positive intelligence which had been received, the enemy was supposed to be assembled in force at Hammelburg and Kissingen. Prussian patrols thrown out on the roads leading to both places repeatedly met hostile Cavalry and the leading files of General Goeben's division, exchanged some shots with the enemy's foremost detachments at Platz and Waldfenster. As soon as more troops came up the latter fell back on Kissingen.

The Bavarians occupied Kissingen and Hammelburg, each with one brigade of General Zoller's division. The Division Feder and the Reserve Artillery reached Münnerstadt; General Hartmann's division stood southward of this town; head-quarters of the army and General Stephan's division remained in Neustadt.

The Bavarians thus stood from Neustadt to Hammelburg on a line 22½ miles long, whereas the Prussian Army now appeared in a state of close concentration nine miles in front of them, two days before it was expected.

General Beyer's march probably gave rise to the opinion that part of the Prussian forces had followed the VIIIth Corps. It was thought that the enemy would not venture to cross the Rhön mountains between the two corps, and would only make a slight attack on the Saale, as had been the case at Dermbach. The Bavarians intended meeting any such attack at this river.

On the evening of the 9th General Von Zoller received orders to hold Kissingen if he should be attacked, in which case he would be reinforced by troops from General Feder's division in the course of the 10th. General Hartmann's division and four 12-pounder batteries of the Reserve Artillery were despatched to Poppenhausen in order to be prepared to meet any attempt on the part of the enemy to cross the river at Euerdorf.

## THE ACTIONS ON THE FRANCONIAN SAALE
## ON THE 10TH OF JULY.

10th July.   In accordance with General Falckenstein's dispositions, General Beyer marched towards Hammelburg on the 10th July, General Goeben to Kissingen. General Manteuffel's corps was at first sent towards Waldaschach, but was afterwards directed to follow General Goeben's division.

Thus, during the day engagements took place on the Saale at five different spots, viz., at Hammelburg, Kissingen, Friedrichshall, Hausen, and Waldaschach. They resulted in the passage of the river being forced at all points.

The action at Hammelburg was a perfectly isolated one, whereas all the other engagements were more or less in connection with each other.

### 1. ACTION AT HAMMELBURG.*

About 10 o'clock A.M. the heads of General Beyer's advanced guard came upon some Cavalry patrols of the enemy near Neu-Wirthshaus. After marching some distance further it was reported to the Commander of the advanced guard, General Von Schachtmeyer, on the heights north of Unter-Erthal, that a large column of hostile Infantry and Cavalry was visible southward of this village, and that the enemy had not thrown out any guards.

The 4-pounder battery of the advanced guard was forthwith brought up to the face of the hill westward of Unter-Erthal, and opened fire on the enemy with such effect that he very soon retreated to Hammelburg. Two Bavarian rifled guns took up a position on the other side of the Thulba and returned the fire, but soon withdrew.

These advanced troops, consisting of the 1st Rifle Battalion, two squadrons of Lancers, and the two above-mentioned guns, did not rally until they had crossed the bridge over the Saale at Fuchsstadt, and took no further part in the action.

General Schachtmeyer followed the retreating enemy with the advanced guard. He left the 1st Battalion of the 39th Regiment in Unter-Erthal, with orders to hold this village until the main body arrived.

The bridge over the Thulba, below the village, was barricaded, and some hostile skirmishers were seen on the other side of it. The 7th Company climbed over the barricade, and commenced a skirmishing fire. The obstacle was soon removed; the other companies then passed the bridge, and the 3rd Battalion followed as reserve.

As soon as the heights to the north of Hammelburg, between

---

* *Vide* Appendix XXIX.

the Thulba and the Rechbach, had been cleared of the enemy's Riflemen, the advanced guard battery (Captain Schmidt) took up a position westward of the high-road, about 1,600 paces from the north entrance of Hammelburg, and opened so well-directed a fire on a regiment of Cavalry, and a detachment of Infantry in the low ground immediately to the north of Hammelburg, but they very soon retreated through the town.

Another Cavalry regiment which was stationed somewhat lower down the valley of the Saale near Dibbach, was also driven off by two guns which were brought forward by General Schachtmeyer's right flank. The advanced guard squadron tried to follow the retreating enemy, but could not get over the Thulba.

In the meantime a Bavarian rifled battery, planted in two very favourable positions on the face of the heights south-eastward of Saaleck, opened fire on the Prussian Artillery. Battery Schmidt returned the fire, which was kept up for some time with much vigour, but without any result whatever, on account of the distance—3,000 paces.

Although the enemy had as yet shown few troops, still the nature of the country allowed of considerable forces being close at hand, in positions where they would be completely hidden from view. Precaution seemed necessary, and General Von Falckenstein directed General Von Beyer to keep up a standing skirmishing fire in front, and in the meantime to bring up his main body and reserve to a position where they could form line unseen by the enemy. At the same time he acquainted General Von Goeben of all that had passed since the commencement of the action, and directed him to operate against the right flank of the enemy at Hammelburg in case he himself should not be engaged. We shall see presently that General Goeben was by this time hotly engaged at Kissingen, and could not therefore follow these instructions.

The enemy kept up a brisk musketry fire from the skirts of Hammelburg, and from the heights of the Heroldsberg and Offenthaler Berg. Four companies of the 2nd, and the 9th and 10th Companies of the Fusilier Battalion of the Prussian 39th Regiment, that had found some slight shelter in the vineyards and road-side ditches, returned the fire at a range of 400 and 600 paces. Later in the day they were joined at their extreme left by troops of the main body of the division. The 10th and 11th Companies were stationed as supports eastward; the 1st Battalion, which had come up in the meantime, westward of the high-road. General Schachtmeyer, whose horse had been already killed under him, was here wounded in the right hand, and struck by several spent balls.

The action on the Prussian left wing was thus solely maintained by skirmishers, whilst the number of batteries that were engaged on the right wing kept continually increasing without attaining any material result. A 12-pounder battery came into

action by the side of Captain Schmidt's Battery, and another
12-pounder battery opened fire upon Hammelburg from a position eastward of the high-road. The Bavarians also reinforced
their rifled battery by half a 12-pounder battery, which took up
a position eastward of Kloster-Saaleck.

Part of the Bavarian guns was engaged with the Prussian
Artillery; others fired over the heads of the latter upon the
main body, which was then forming line in the narrow valley,
and upon the reserve of the division as it passed the bridge over
the Thulba, but in both cases without much effect.

Towards the end of the action the two 12-pounder batteries
of the reserve unlimbered on the extreme left of the Prussian
Artillery.

As soon as the main body was formed, and the reserve had
crossed the Thulba, General Von Falckenstein deemed it advisable to proceed to the attack of the enemy.

In order to avoid unnecessary loss, General Von Glümer was
sent over the Rechbach to attack the Offenthaler Berg, and to
turn the enemy's right wing. The hill was only occupied by
one battalion, which retreated before the attack of such overwhelming forces. The advanced guard took advantage of the
moment, and proceeded to storm the skirts of Hammelburg,
upon which Captain Hoffbauer's Battery was playing. They
were carried at the first charge. The enemy then evacuated
the burning town, and his whole force retreated in different
directions.

The Bavarians only defended Hammelburg with comparatively trifling forces, consisting of one brigade (the 6th) and
11 guns.

It has been already mentioned that the 1st Rifle Battalion
retreated at the very commencement of the action, in which it
took no further part.

The other detachments had been much scattered; one battalion in and near Hammelburg, a third on the Herolds and
Offenthaler hills, a fourth as support behind them, the fifth still
further eastward in the direction of Westheim. The nature of
the country prevented the reserve Cavalry from joining in the
action.

It was 3 o'clock by the time Hammelburg was completely
occupied by General Beyer's troops. A short time previously
General Von Falckenstein had received intelligence of General
Goeben's engagement. He gave orders to General Beyer to
remain at Hammelburg with his division well concentrated, and
rode for his own person to Kissengen, where he arrived near
evening.

General Beyer threw out scouting parties to watch the enemy's
retreat, and his division took up close cantonments and bivouacs
in and in the immediate neighbourhood of Hammelburg. The
town was burning, and the fire could not be quenched before
evening by the Prussian troops, almost all the inhabitants
having fled.

The casualties in the action amounted to :—

|  | Prussians. | | Bavarians. | |
| --- | --- | --- | --- | --- |
|  | Officers. | Men. | Officers. | Men. |
| Killed .. .. .. .. | .. | 10 | .. | 7 |
| Wounded .. .. .. | 6 | 66 | 2 | 40 |
| Missing and prisoners.. .. | .. | .. | .. | 15 |
| Total .. .. | 6 | 76 | 2 | 62 |

## 2. ACTIONS AT KISSINGEN.

### (a.) *Taking of Kissingen.*

When General Von Goeben arrived at Schlimphof, on his march from Waldfenster to Kissingen, he received the intelligence that the enemy held the latter town in force, upon which he immediately despatched the leading brigade (General Kummer) by way of Albertshausen to Garitz. The main body, General Wrangel's Brigade, and the reserve under General Von Tresckow, followed immediately in the same direction. At the same time General Goeben detached the 2nd and Fusilier Battalions of the 15th Regiment, belonging to the main body, under command of Colonel Von der Goltz in his left flank over Poppenroth and Claushof, on Kissingen. As we shall presently see, this flank detachment engaged the enemy at Friedrichshall.

About 10 A.M. the head of the advanced guard brigade reached Garitz, and found the place only slightly occupied by the enemy, who hastily fell back on Kissingen without offering any resistance. Two Bavarian batteries, north-eastward of Kissingen, opened fire. General Kummer planted his artillery on the heights to the north of Garitz, between the " Clauswald " and the " Marbachsgraben," and his Infantry formed for action under cover of its fire, with the 53rd Regiment in first and the 2nd and Fusilier Battalions of the 13th Regiment in second line. The 1st Battalion of the latter regiment had turned off from Albertshausen to Aura, to cover the right flank of the division, and to open communications with General Beyer. The battalion in consequence took no part in the action. General Kummer's Brigade now wheeled a quarter left towards Kissingen, and advanced against the west skirts of the faubourg on the right bank of the Saale, which were carried by the Fusilier Battalion of the 53rd Regiment at the first onset. The two other battalions of the regiment followed, and the enemy retreated, fighting and hard pressed to the left bank of the river.

Three bridges cross the Saale at Kissingen, of which the centre one, a massive stone bridge over which the high-road enters the town, was strongly barricaded and defended by two pieces of artillery. The wooden bridge higher up the river was almost totally destroyed, and the planks had been removed from a small iron bridge for foot passengers which leads to the gardens of the bathing establishment lower down the river. As the Saale could not be forded, there was for the moment no possibility of pursuing the enemy further at this spot, and a standing fight ensued between the skirmishers on both banks of the river.

In the meantime the main body had arrived at Garitz, and was sent by General Goeben to the right wing of General Kummer's Brigade, with orders to take possession of the Altenburg, and if possible to turn the enemy's left flank from this spot.

Skirmishing detachments of the 53rd Regiment had already ensconced themselves on this hill, and covered by their fire and by the leading battalion of General Wrangel's Brigade, the 1st Battalion of the 15th Regiment, Captain Coester's 4-pounder battery took up an advantageous position on the north-west face of the hill and opened fire. The 2nd Company of the latter regiment had in the meantime cleared the whole hill of the enemy's skirmishers, and now advanced to a bridge which crossed the river somewhat above the Lindenmühle, but which had also been destroyed. In spite of the enemy's severe Infantry fire the bridge was so far repaired that it could be passed in single file. Captain Von dem Bussche then led the way over at the head of his company. The other companies followed, and were then formed into two half battalions at the Schweinfurth high-road, and in the thickets on the north face of the "Bodenlaube," after which they threw out a heavy line of skirmishers, and proceeded to attack the south entrance of Kissingen under cover of their fire. A division of the battalion remained on the Bodenlaube, and repulsed a detachment of Bavarian Infantry which attempted to approach the hill from the direction of Reiterswiesen.

The bridge having been in the meantime still further repaired, first the 1st and 2nd Companies of the Lippe Fusilier Battalion, and then the 1st Battalion of the 55th Regiment, followed the 1st Battalion of the 15th Regiment across the river, and joined in the attack on the town, the skirts of which were soon carried. An obstinate fight ensued in the streets of the town, the Prussians only gaining ground step by step.

The remaining two and a half battalions of General Wrangel's Brigade remained for the present on the other bank of the river, on the right flank of General Kummer's Brigade, and in front of the high-road bridge.

In the meantime the concentric fire of the three Prussian batteries had compelled the Bavarian Artillery to withdraw to a position further backward.

The advance of the Prussian right wing in the south part of the town soon made itself felt in the centre of the line, and the 3rd Company of the "Lippe" Fusiliers, with some men of different other regiments, now succeeded in crossing the river over the remains of the small iron bridge, and in entering the garden at the baths. The Fusilier Battalion of the 53rd Regiment climbed over the barricade on the centre bridge, and the remaining troops of both brigades rapidly followed over the river. The steady progress which was made in front and flank of this position ultimately drove the Bavarians out of the whole town, in spite of their determined defence of the place. The fighting was especially severe at the churchyard, which lies on a hill at the east entrance of the town.

After suffering a considerable loss of killed and wounded, and in particular of prisoners, of whom several hundreds fell into the hands of the Prussians during the street fight, the Bavarians now retreated to the heights of Winkels. The three Prussian batteries that were still in position on the right bank kept up a heavy fire on the retreating troops. The Bavarian Artillery fired exclusively on the town, which was now in the hands of its adversaries.

### (b.) Advance against Nüdlingen.

General Goeben had brought up the 19th Regiment from the Reserve, and sent it forward through Kissingen to General Von Kummer. After the action the 53rd Regiment and the Fusilier Battalion of the 13th Regiment were rallied in and eastward of the town, and the 2nd Battalion of the latter regiment occupied a position at the south entrance, fronting southward. While this was being done General Kummer advanced with the 19th Regiment against the heights of Winkels, assisted by a simultaneous advance of General Wrangel's Brigade across the hill "Winterleite" towards Nüdlingen. The movement was crowned with complete success. The enemy was dislodged from his strong position, and driven back from height to height into the village of Nüdlingen.

Whilst General Wrangel's Brigade was advancing against the heights of Winkels the skirmishers of the 55th Regiment, led by Lieutenant Von Papen, fired upon a battery of the enemy, and about twenty men then dashed forward to capture the guns. The battery ceased firing and drove off, but at the same time a Bavarian squadron that had been previously hidden in an undulation of the ground charged the party, of whom the officer and about six men were carried off as prisoners after a very obstinate resistance, in which the officer was severely wounded.

During the pursuit of the enemy towards Nüdlingen the 1st and 4th Companies of the 15th Regiment, the foremost troops on the right wing, came upon a Bavarian smooth-bore 12-pounder which was in the act of withdrawing from a position southward of the village. The fire of the Infantry killed several horses, and the gun again unlimbered, but was captured before it could discharge a single shot. A column of Bavarian

2 E

Infantry advanced in compact order, *tambour battant*, and attempted to save the gun, but was driven back by the Prussian file-fire.

About 4 P.M. the enemy was compelled to evacuate Nüdlingen also, with which the action ended. The 4th Cuirassiers and Captain Metting's Horse Artillery Battery had been brought up from the reserve, and were drawn up in line on the extreme left on the open ground to the north-west of the "Sinnberg," but did not come into action.

General Goeben now placed the 19th Regiment under the orders of General Wrangel, and gave orders to throw out a line of outposts in front of Nüdlingen.

General Von Zoller, the Commander of the Bavarian troops engaged, had at the commencement of the action, in and near Kissingen, only the 5th Brigade (Ribeaupierre), but little Cavalry, two rifled and one 12-pounder battery, at his disposal. In the course of the day he was reinforced by six battalions of General Feder's Division and two batteries which came from the direction of Münerstadt.

Lieut.-General Von Zoller was struck down by a shell during the retreat to Nüdlingen.

### (c.) *Evening Combat near Winkels.*

The troops had just begun to establish themselves in their bivouacs, and the 2nd Battalion of the 55th Regiment was on the point of relieving the 19th Regiment at the outposts, when, about half-past 6 P.M., a report was received by General Wrangel that a heavy force of the enemy was advancing from Nüdlingen. It was the 1st Bavarian Division (General Stephan), just then arriving from Neustadt, which now assumed the offensive, with the intention of regaining the lost ground and of retaking Kissingen.

General Wrangel immediately sent forward the Fusilier Battalion of the 55th Regiment, a 12-pounder battery, and a squadron of the 8th Hussars, to the assistance of the 19th Regiment, and himself hastened on to the outposts in advance of them.

General Stephan's Division had very cleverly availed itself of the nature of the ground, and had already succeeded in forming for action. The left wing of the Prussian line of outposts being somewhat exposed, was unexpectedly charged in its flank and driven in.

Before the Prussians had time to take any measures to meet this unexpected attack, their numerically far superior adversaries succeeded in gaining the foremost heights of the Sinnberg. Two Bavarian batteries very soon came into action, and played with great effect upon the dense columns of the 19th Regiment beneath them, whilst the main body of the division continued to advance.

Under these disadvantageous circumstances the foremost Prussian detachments fell back, suffering considerable loss from the enemy's severe fire, which was delivered within a very close range. The 12-pounder battery attempted to check the rapid advance of the enemy's columns, but got within range of Infantry fire, and was compelled to withdraw. In the meantime, however, the Fusiliers of the 55th Regiment had reached the spot where the high-road makes a sudden turn, and crosses the heights between the "Sinnberg" and the "Schlegelsberg." They immediately took possession of a ravine southward of and parallel to the high-road, from whence they then advanced to attack the enemy.

Their rapid fire, delivered at point-blank range, checked the advancing Bavarian columns, and gave the 12-pounder battery time to withdraw.

General Wrangel posted the troops that were still at his disposal—viz., the 1st Battalion of the 55th Regiment, and the Lippe Fusilier Battalion—on the heights eastward of Winkels. Captain Coester's 4-pounder battery unlimbered on their right, and Captain Eynatten's 12-pounder battery on their left wing. Under cover of this position he then proceeded to rally the retreating troops.

At the very beginning of the action the 6th and 7th Companies of the 55th Regiment had been despatched to the woods southward of the high-road. Part of the 19th Regiment had joined them there, but their right flank being turned they were by degrees pressed back, so that the Fusiliers of the former regiment, who had hitherto held their advanced position in spite of heavy losses, were now fired on in front, right flank and rear.

The Commander of the Brigade, whose horse had been killed and fallen on him, was momentarily disabled, and Colonel Stoltz of the 55th Regiment assumed the command. He gave orders that the companies of the Fusiliers should successively withdraw from their far advanced and isolated position. The movement was effected with great steadiness and without much loss. Indeed, by taking advantage of whatever shelter the ground afforded, and with the assistance of the fire of the two batteries the Prussians now succeeded in checking the advance of the Bavarian columns.

The brigade was now assembled and re-formed. General Wrangel, who had recovered from the stunning effects of his fall, resumed the command of the brigade, and determined to assume the offensive himself.

The 2nd Battalion of the 55th Regiment and two companies of the "Lippe" Fusiliers were pushed forward to the wooded heights southward of the high-road; the other two companies of the Fusiliers, and a battalion of the 19th Regiment, into the woods on the north of the road. As soon as these flank detachments had taken up their positions the General gave the signal to advance along the whole line.

With drums beating, all troops set off simultaneously. The enemy's fire was vehement and the losses considerable, but the

Schlegelsberg and Sinnberg were, nevertheless, both stormed, and the lost position again occupied. Major Robdewald, Commander of the Lippe Battalion, fell in this charge. After a stout resistance the enemy was forced to retire towards Nüdlingen.

Darkness and the great fatigue of the troops, who had been on the march incessantly since a very early hour of the morning, in great heat and over very mountainous ground, put an end to any further pursuit.

General Wrangel himself now posted his outposts on the reconquered heights in front of Nüdlingen. In the course of the night they were relieved by a battalion of the 36th Regiment, which was sent forward from Kissingen for this purpose. The main body of General Goeben's Division stood in and close by Kissingen.

### 3. ACTIONS AT FRIEDRICHSHALL AND HAUSEN.

It has been already mentioned that Colonel Von der Goltz received orders at Schlimphof to march on Kissingen by way of Claushof with two battalions of the 15th Regiment. On passing out of the wood opposite Friedrichshall, at about a quarter past 10 o'clock, the head of this column was fired on by the enemy. The latter occupied two saltworks, from whence he kept the whole open country, from the right bank of the river to the skirts of the wood, under fire, in addition to which a battery of four guns was seen on the heights beyond Friedrichshall, accompanied by Infantry and Cavalry, as far as could be seen, consisting of two battalions and two squadrons.

The Colonel spread out his troops in company columns ; the 9th and 12th Companies occupied the skirts of the wood on the right bank of the Saale ; the 11th Company was thrown out in the direction of Kissingen to cover the right flank ; the 10th was despatched towards Hausen as protection for the left flank against the enemy stationed there. Both companies fired on the flanks of the enemy's position at Friedrichshall. The 8th Company was posted as support of the 10th ; the 5th, 6th, and 7th remained in reserve.

The fire was kept up briskly on both sides till about half-past 11, at which time General Manteuffel arrived on the spot with a squadron of the 6th Dragoons and the 4th 4-pounder Battery. The General had been informed that Colonel Goltz was engaged with only two battalions against superior forces. He therefore hastened the advance of his corps, and rode on a-head with the above-mentioned troops to Claushof. The ground was so confined that only one gun could be planted on the high-road, which fired some shots on the enemy's Cavalry, forcing it to withdraw, but without otherwise changing the course of the action. It was necessary to wait for Infantry reinforcements.

At a quarter before 2 General Von Freyhold arrived at

Claushof with the 59th Infantry Regiment, a squadron of the 6th Dragoons, and a 6-pounder Battery, and received orders from General Von Manteuffel to advance on Hausen, where the ground was more favourable for attacking the enemy.

Four guns of the 4-pounder Battery were attached to these troops; two remained with Colonel Von der Goltz. The two batteries first opened fire upon some hostile columns which seemed to be marching from Hausen to Friedrichshall, and then upon the enemy's artillery (twelve guns), which returned the fire. After a short time General Freyhold ordered his Infantry to attack. The enemy did not wait for the charge, but ceased firing and retreated. General Freyhold then occupied Hausen, and established his outposts in connection with those of General Goeben's Division.

Colonel Goltz assumed the offensive simultaneously with the occupation of Hausen. He increased his line of skirmishers by the 5th Company, and led the 6th and 7th in compact order against the passage over the river at Friedrichshall. The guns fired on the saltworks, against which the 12th Company advanced along the banks of the river. The skirmishers advanced with the column, and the enemy evacuated Friedrichshall, but had to pass the fire of the Prussian Artillery whilst retreating over the heights.

An immediate pursuit was impossible, because the only bridge over the river was destroyed. Two musketeers swam across and brought back a boat that was fastened at the other side. Some men were ferried over by this means, who forthwith occupied the village and began to repair the bridge with ladders, &c. By the time this work was finished a considerable number of men had crossed over on pontoons of the light field bridge train, which was brought up to the spot, but the enemy had made good his retreat in the meantime.

## 4. ACTION AT WALDASCHACH.*

Whilst General Manteuffel's corps was marching on Kissingen, the Commandant of the main body, Colonel Von Hanstein, was informed by a Dragoon patrol that Waldaschach was occupied by the enemy. The Fusilier Battalion of the 25th Regiment was therefore sent forward by way of Stralsbach towards this place, to cover the left flank of the corps.

Lieut.-Colonel Von Cranach sent the 9th Company on a-head as advanced guard, followed with the 10th and 12th as main body, and with the 11th as reserve. The foremost patrols were fired on from the west entrance of Waldaschach. Whilst the 9th Company commenced a skirmishing fire and gradually drew near the village, the 10th Company approached from the north, and a peloton of the 12th from the south, so as to surround the

* *Vide* Appendix XXX.

village. It was in all probability the latter movement which induced the enemy to fall back on Münnerstadt, because it threatened the bridge over the Saale. The battalion rapidly closed in on all sides, and took thirty-one prisoners, besides four dead and six wounded found in the village. The Prussians only lost two wounded.

Lieut.-Colonel Von Cranach halted at Waldaschach, opened communications with General Von Freyhold at Hausen, and watched the country in the direction of Bocklet.

The losses in the actions at Kissingen and higher up the river were considerable on both sides, particularly those of the Prussian troops engaged in the evening combat at Winkels. They amounted to—

|  | Prussians. | | Bavarians. | |
|---|---|---|---|---|
|  | Officers. | Men. | Officers. | Men. |
| Killed .. .. .. .. | 10 | 133 | 11 | 82 |
| Wounded .. .. .. | 25 | 673 | 33 | 540 |
| Missing and prisoners.. .. | 1 | 57 | 6 | 549 |
| Total .. .. | 36 | 863 | 50 | 1,171 |

A great part of those included among the Bavarian "missing" fell into the hands of the Prussians without wound.

In the meantime, according to orders, the main body and reserve of General Manteuffel's Corps continued its march to Kissingen, where it arrived towards evening, and then partly bivouacked, partly cantoned close behind General Goeben's Division.

In the course of the evening a telegram arrived at Kissingen from His Majesty's head-quarters in answer to a previous inquiry, in which stress was again laid on the necessity of obtaining a victory over the Bavarians. It contained the words, "The districts north of the Maine will fall into our "power without our entering them." The same day General Von Falckenstein sent in his report on the successful actions which had just taken place on the Saale, and added, in conclusion, "To-morrow I march on Schweinfurth."

We have already stated that the Bavarian Army was taken by surprise on this day. It had not yet reached the position in which it intended to accept a decisive action. The greater part of the Army was still at Münnerstadt, and as far off as Neustadt. The Saale was occupied as far down as Hammelburg to cover the march of the Army. The forces employed for this purpose were considerable, if all that was intended was to obtain intelligence of the enemy's approach, and to impede his advance whilst the Army waited in a central position further to the rear; but they were insufficient, if the passage of the river was to be disputed. As soon as the line of the Saale was once attacked at Hammelburg and Kissingen, reinforcements from Münnerstadt and Neustadt must necessarily arrive too late; and it would have been productive of far greater results if three divisions had assumed the offensive from the two last-named spots, crossing the river at Waldaschach.

Instead of so doing, the troops were successively brought into action at Kissingen, and were beaten in detail. At first only the 5th Brigade was engaged there; after noon the greater part of General Feder's Division and some battalions of General Hartmann's Division came up by degrees; General Stephan's Division did not arrive from Neustadt till evening. The latter was at Münnerstadt as early as 11 o'clock, but was not ordered up to Nüdlingen until 1 P.M., and was delayed on its march thither in a narrow defile by the troops retreating from the Saale, as well as by their trains and wounded. General Hartmann's Division, lastly, advanced from Poppenhausen towards Euerdorf to guard this crossing also. Although repeatedly desired to march to Kissingen, still, by reason of a series of misunderstandings, the division did not appear on the scene of action at all.

On the evening of this day the Divisions Stephan and Feder, the 5th Brigade, the Light Cavalry Brigade, and the Reserve Artillery, bivouacked southward of Münnerstadt on the road to Schweinfurth. General Hartmann's Division had retreated by the same road as far as Poppenhausen. The 6th Brigade and the Reserve Cavalry, which had fought at Hammelburg, fell back on Arnstein in the direction of Würzburg. At Münnerstadt only a detachment was left to protect the departure of the trains, and to cover the retreat of those troops that had been stationed further northward on the Saale.

The reports on these actions, which reached the Bavarian head-quarters from different directions, left no doubt but what the enemy had arrived at the Saale with his whole force. It was not thought feasible to resume the contest at this spot, because the corps was not assembled, and the line of retreat to Schweinfurth seemed in danger, now that Hammelburg was lost.

The Army commenced its retreat very early on the morning 11th July. of the 11th, and made some considerable detours from fear of a flank attack from Kissingen.

General Feder's Division, the 2nd Brigade of General Stephan's Division, and the Reserve Artillery thus marched eastward over Lauringen to Hassfurth on the Maine, where a bridge had been thrown over the river as early as the 8th. These troops reached the neighbourhood of Aidhausen and Hofheim the same evening.

General Hartmann's Division remained for some hours as rear guard at Poppenhausen, and then retreated to Schweinfurth.

The 6th Brigade and the Reserve Cavalry marched on this day towards Würzburg.

Instead of concentrating its forces, the Army thus effected an eccentric retreat. Four and twenty hours after the actions on the Saale it extended over a line of seven miles in length.

The greater part of the new-formed Reserve Brigade, which was on its march to join the Army, had reached Schweinfurth, and Prince Charles took up a position with about two and a half divisions on the heights on the right bank of the Maine, close to the town, with the defiles immediately in his rear. He was determined, and indeed had no other alternative, to fight to the last man on this spot.

The divergent and rapid retreat of the Bavarians had, however, the result of raising doubts in the Prussian camp as to which direction the Army had taken. It was not known whether the enemy's main force had retreated on Münnerstadt or on Schweinfurth, nor what degree of order prevailed in the Army.

Wishing to assure himself on this head before making further dispositions, General Von Falckenstein gave orders to General Von Manteuffel to advance from Kissingen in the direction of Schweinfurth as far as the Münnerstadt-Schweinfurth road, and to obtain more precise information. General Beyer's Division was also despatched, by way of Euerdorf and Ramsthal, to the same road. General Goeben's Division remained for the present at Kissingen.

About 11 o'clock General Manteuffel came upon the rear guard of General Hartmann's Division (only two companies) near Oerlenbach. The Bavarians occupied the village and the adjoining wood, but retreated on Schweinfurth after a brief skirmish. One officer and 33 men were taken prisoners, and their statements proved that the greater part of the Bavarian Army had retreated to Schweinfurth very early in the morning; this was immediately reported to head-quarters at Kissingen.

Before any further instructions arrived, the Cavalry, which had advanced beyond Poppenhausen, reported that the enemy was advancing; and General Manteuffel, whose troops had already finished their dinners, immediately started for Schweinfurth, but soon received orders which altered his route.

When Prussia's enemies were being forced back from the Werra to the Maine, the Prussian main Army was uninterruptedly advancing towards the Danube. There was a prospect of peace conferences very soon taking place, and in all probability the time for military operations would be but short. Under these circumstances the political situation rendered it neither necessary nor advisable that an important action should be fought in the west. Even a fresh victory would not materially alter the result of the campaign, and reverses, which were always within the bounds of possibility, might render negotiations with the South German States difficult. At the request of the Prime

Minister, therefore, a telegram was despatched to General Von Falckenstein, stating,—

> " . . . It is now of political importance to be in
> " actual possession of the district north of the Maine, for
> " the sake of negotiations which will probably take place
> " on the *statu quo* basis."

Without doubt the correct military step was to advance on Schweinfurth, but in the beginning and at the end of campaigns military considerations must give way before political ones.

General Falckenstein received these instructions at 1 in the afternoon at Kissingen, and then ordered the Army to march to the right on Gemünden. Orders were sent to General Manteuffel to start in the same direction, provided he were not engaged with the enemy. General Beyer's Division halted for the present, in case General Manteuffel needed support, but General Goeben's Division set off immediately for Hammelburg.

General Manteuffel received this order after 5 o'clock, at Maibach, which village his advanced guard had reached without meeting with any resistance. The rumoured advance of the enemy from Schweinfurth was not confirmed, but the position of part of his forces immediately in front of the town had been reconnoitred, and it was determined to attack them. Not being actually engaged with the enemy, but, on the contrary, 4½ miles off from his position, General Manteuffel was now obliged to relinquish his intention ; moreover the distance of General Beyer's troops and the lateness of the day left no chance of fighting out any considerable engagement. General Manteuffel therefore marched to the right by way of Poppenhausen to Gressthal, and pushed forward his advanced guard towards Geldersheim to cover the movement.

General Beyer's Division bivouacked at the road-side, between Arnshausen and Oerlenbach.

During the following days the Prussian Army continued its march towards the Lower Maine. General Goeben's Division was pushed far on a-head as advanced guard, in order to gain the western *débouchée* of the main road through the " Spessart " to Aschaffenburg as soon as possible. The division reached Lohr on the 12th, and was to occupy Laufach on the 13th. 12th and 13th July.

General Manteuffel followed General Goeben, but General Beyer took the road to Hanau through the valleys of the Sinn and the Kinzig, in order that the whole Army might not march on one single road. The former arrived at Gemünden on the 13th, the latter at Rieneck on the Sinn.

The Bavarian troops at Schweinfurth retreated on the 12th to the neighbourhood of Schwebheim and Grettstadt on the left bank of the Maine. The rear guard still occupied Schweinfurth.

For the moment the dreaded attack of the Prussian Army was averted, it was even reported to have withdrawn. Time was thus gained in forming new plans, and the troops remained in their cantonments on the 13th. The detachments which marched to Hassfurth crossed the Maine there on the 12th and 13th.

We now return to the course of events at the VIIIth Corps, which reached the Lower Maine on the 9th, and was stationed as follows :—

The Hessian and the Austrian-Nassau Divisions stood close round about Frankfort; the former at Bergen, the latter at Bockenheim, the Reserve Artillery on the left bank of the Maine from Offenbach to Niederrad. A bridge was thrown over the river at Oberrad to facilitate the communication. All three brigades of the Würtemberg Division were pushed forward eastwards between Hanau and Gelnhausen. The Division of Baden held the line of the Nidda from Gronau to Heddernheim. The Reserve Cavalry was posted in front of the latter division in the neighbourhood of Assenheim. Head-quarters of the corps were at Bornbeim.

During the following days the corps was occupied in completing some field-works which had been thrown up on the north side of Frankfort at the commencement of the campaign, and in detaching larger or smaller bodies of troops in different directions.

At the earnest request of the Duke of Nassau the Nassau Brigade was despatched to Wiesbaden on the 11th for the protection of the Duchy. There was indeed now greater cause for alarm in this direction than there had previously been. By order of the Military Governor of the Rhenish Provinces and Westphalia, Prince of Hohenzollern, General Von Roeder had entered Nassau from Coblentz on the 7th, with the five garrison battalions Jülich, Malmedy, Siegburg, Treves I and Treves II, the garrison squadron of Coblentz, four rifled 4-pounders of the Reserve Division of the 8th Artillery Regiment, and four smooth-bore 12-pounders, on the whole amounting to about 4,000 men, and had occupied Ems and Nassau on the Lahn, and despatched detachments to Limburg, Katzenellenbogen, Nastätten, &c. On the 10th these troops marched to Holzhausen, and took up their quarters round about Diethardt on the 12th.

On the 12th the Nassau Brigade advanced as far as Kemel, and the 1st Regiment and two guns, under Lieutenant-Colonel Schwab, were pushed forward towards Zorn, intelligence having been received of the occupation of this village by the Prussians. The outposts of the Landwehr Battalion Treves II, which was quartered there, were unexpectedly attacked in the course of the afternoon, and driven in, after a short fight, with a loss of eight wounded.

On the 13th General Roeder, whose object had been to induce the VIIIth Corps to detach troops from the Maine northward, retired to Coblentz on the 13th. In consequence of the reiterated orders of the Commander-in-Chief to disengage the Bavarian Army by advancing on Schlüchtern, the Prince of Hesse pushed the Würtemberg Division somewhat further up the valley of the Kinzig on the 11th. One brigade reached Sallmunster; patrols scoured the country as far as Schlüchtern and Brückenau. Some prisoners were brought back, but of course no signs of the enemy were discovered.

On the 11th the advance of the Prussians beyond the Saale and the retreat of the Bavarians behind the Maine became known in Frankfort. It now seemed impossible to remain any longer in front of the latter river. It was feared that the enemy would fall on the VIIIth Corps with his whole force as long as it was in its isolated position on the Lower Maine. Under these circumstances the Prince of Hesse eagerly took up the idea of joining the Bavarians, a plan of which he had hitherto had no great opinion. Joint requests from Würtemberg, Baden, and Hesse, if possible not to abandon the line of the Maine before the approaching truce should be concluded, were now disregarded, and on the 12th the Prince not only repeated his proposition of effecting a junction of both corps on the Maine—this time at Würzburg—but sent the Hessian brigade the same day per railway from Hanau to Aschaffenburg, in order to make sure of this important passage over the Maine.

On the forenoon of the 13th the other Hessian brigade followed to the same place, and the Würtemburg Division was again moved nearer to Hanau. Its brigades were stationed in Gelnhausen, Langenselbold, and Rückingen on the 13th.

Intelligence obtained by spies stated as early as the 12th that hostile troops had appeared in the Spessart, but it was hoped that the route to Würzburg would still be found free. The Hessian brigade Frey was ordered to reconnoitre the Prussian troops, which were said to be advancing from Lohr, next day, but not to become involved in a serious engagement.

---

## ACTION AT LAUFACH ON THE 13th OF JULY.

In the forenoon of the 13th General Frey started from Aschaffenburg, taking the road to Laufach with his main body. A battalion of the 2nd Regiment and a division of Cavalry were detached from Eisenhammer over Weiberhöfe and Unter-Bessenbach towards Wald-Aschaff to cover the right flank.

The advanced guard, consisting of the other battalion of the 2nd Regiment, three-quarters of a squadron and two rifled guns, met the advanced troops of General Goeben's division about 2 o'clock, just as it was debouching from Laufach. We have already heard that the latter's division was to reach Laufach on this day. General Wrangel's brigade was to bivouac near the place, General Kummer's brigade was to advance on the road leading further southward to Wald-Aschaff, so that both brigades might not be confined to one single road whilst crossing the "Spessart."

The leading detachment of General Wrangel's advanced guard consisted of the 1st Squadron of the 8th Hussar Regiment. It was accompanied by General Goeben himself.

The Hessian Infantry opened fire on the Hussars, and the latter retreated through Hain to behind the high railway embankment, under which the Lohr-Aschaffenburg road runs through a tunnel.

The Hessian Cavalry followed as far as the embankment, which was for the moment only defended by the carbine-fire of the Hussars. It was not long before the Fusilier Battalion of the 55th Regiment, which had laid down its knapsacks, came up at a run, passed the embankment without opposition, then formed columns of companies, and drove the enemy back over Laufach and Frohnhofen to Eisenhammer and Weiberhöfe. The latter offered but slight resistance.

At these places General Frey had taken up a position with his main body, the 1st Regiment of Infantry, the Homburg Rifle Company, a squadron and four rifled guns, and now covered the retreat of his advanced guard. His right Flank detachment, which had met the head of General Kummer's brigade near Wald-Aschaff at about 3 o'clock, and had retreated to Weiberhöfe after a trifling skirmish, rejoined General Frey in this position.

General Goeben left Lieutenant-Colonel Von Rex with his Fusilier Battalion in front of the enemy's position, but gave orders that the troops should go into their bivouacs, as the object of the day's march was attained. General Kummer remained at Waldaschaff, and threw forward a line of outposts beyond Weiler towards Keilberg and Unter-Bessenbach. General Von Wrangel bivouacked near Laufach, and placed his outposts in an advantageous position at Frohnhofen. They consisted of the Fusilier Battalion of the 15th Regiment and a squadron of Hussars.

Whilst the outposts were taking up their ground and the troops were still occupied in arranging their bivouac, considerable columns of the enemy were seen advancing. The day had been uncommonly hot, and the troops were excessively fatigued after crossing the Spessart, which they did in one forced march. General Wrangel determined, therefore, to meet the coming attack on the spot without advancing to meet it.

Lieut.-Colonel Von Rex immediately threw the 9th and 10th Companies of his battalion into the ground northward of Frohn-hofen, occupied the village with the 11th Company, and posted half of the 12th Company in the road southward of the railway embankment, and the other half as reserve eastward of the village. At the same time General Wrangel had sent the 10th and 11th Companies of the 15th Regiment to Frohnhofen, the 9th northward, and the 12th southward of the high-road. These troops were followed by the 1st and 2nd Battalions of the 15th Regiment, which were posted in support of both wings of the position. All these detachments, however, only came up successively, one after the other, and did not reach their destination until the midst of the action. At the first moment the Hessian attack could only be met by the fire of some weak detachment of skirmishers that had established themselves in the enclosure of the village as well as they could, each detachment fighting for itself without the whole being under one united command.

The Hessians commenced the action by the fire of a rifled battery planted on the Geissen-Berg, after which the 1st Infantry Regiment advanced against Frohnhofen in three columns, and preceded by a dense swarm of skirmishers. The 1st Battalion marched on and close by the side of the high-road, one company of the 2nd Battalion on the railway embankment, and the three others on the north side of the high-road. In the meantime four guns of the battery advanced within closer range to a position immediately on the north of Eisenhammer.

At first the Hessian Infantry advanced with bands playing in excellent order and with great bravery, in spite of the destructive fire of the needle-gun. They came within 140 paces of the Prussian position, but then the attacking columns wavered, then turned, and retreated to Weiberhöfe.

A second attack of the same troops ended in like manner, although some detachments, actually pressed close up to and even into the enclosure of the village, but only held their ground for a moment.

In the meantime General Stockhausen arrived on the field with the 2nd Hessian Brigade, and led it forwards for a fresh attack about 7 P.M., whilst the 2nd Regiment remained at Weiberhöfe and Eisenhammer in support, and the beaten 1st Regiment re-formed under cover of the latter.

By this time, however, General Wrangel had brought up the 1st and 2nd Battalions of the 55th Regiment and the 3rd 12-pounder Battery to Wendelstein in support of the troops of his brigade that were already engaged. The whose reserves eastward of the railway station now consisted of the Lippe Fusilier Battalion and the 3rd 4-pounder Battery.

The 2nd Hessian Brigade now advanced in two *échelons* against the position at Frohnhofen, the 3rd Regiment on the high-road, the 4th Regiment, somewhat behind it, and northwards of the road.

When but 300 paces off, and therefore within full range of the Infantry fire of the Prussian position, the Hessians formed columns of companies with very small intervals and skirmishers in the latter, and then rushed with loud cheers upon the skirts

of the village. The Prussians having held back their fire until
their adversaries were within point-blank range, the greater
part of the attacking party were driven back by it, but part of
them nevertheless succeeded in reaching the foremost buildings, and in holding their ground there for some time. Particularly fierce and sanguinary was the struggle for a skittle
ground occupied by Fusiliers of the 15th Regiment. At this
spot fell Captain Königer, of the Hessians, a well known military
historian. In the meantime the Prussian reserves stationed at
Wendelstein joined in the fight. Five companies and the
12-pounder Battery advanced northward, one company southward of the high-road. A bayonet charge now cleared the
village of all the Hessians who had gained a footing there. On
the extreme right some Prussian Infantry detachments crept up
to the enemy's battery, and drove the guns off by their fire.
The Prussian 12-pounder Battery then came into action. Under
cover of its fire Colonel Goltz made a bold dash with the troops
of the right wing and a squadron of Hussars, and decided the
combat by forcing the enemy to retreat beyond Eisenhammer
and Weiberhöfe.

The troops fighting in and southward of the village broke
forth in pursuit, and the Hessians hastily fell back on Aschaffenburg, abandoning almost the whole of their knapsacks, which
they had laid off.

Night was closing in, so that further pursuit beyond Eisenhammer was not advisable. The outposts were, therefore,
again thrown out, and the troops returned to their previous
bivouacs at Laufach.

With the exception of the last period of the engagement
the Prussians had fought in sheltered, defensive positions, and
suffered but very trifling losses. Those of the Hessians who
repeatedly advanced over the open country in the face of a most
effective cross-fire were beyond all proportion heavy. The
great efficiency of the Prussian needle-gun for defensive warfare
was proved beyond all doubt.

The casualties were as follows :—

|  | Prussians. | | Hessians. | |
| --- | --- | --- | --- | --- |
|  | Officers. | Men. | Officers. | Men. |
| Killed .. .. .. .. | .. | 5 | 6 | 73 |
| Wounded .. .. .. | 1 | 57 | 24 | 360 |
| Missing.. .. .. .. | .. | 3 | 2 | 312 |
| Total .. .. | 1 | 65 | 32 | 745 |

Most of the Hessian wounded fell into the hands of the
Prussians.

The Prince of Hesse received the first intelligence of the
enemy being met at Laufach in the course of the same after-

noon. This news left no room for doubt but that a considerable force was advancing on Aschaffenburg. It was before all things necessary to strengthen this important post, and the first battalions of General Hahn's brigade (Austrians) left Frankfort by rail for Aschaffenburg as early as 4 o'clock. The Würtemberg Brigade, which was at Gelnhausen, was ordered to march there early on the 14th. The Baden Division was summoned to Frankfort, in order to be despatched per rail to Aschaffenburg next morning, in company with some batteries.

## ACTION AT ASCHAFFENBURG, JULY 14TH.*

The very same evening of the 13th the first-arrived detachments of General Hahn's brigade, the Rifle Battalion and a battalion of the 21st Regiment (Reischach), relieved the Hessian outposts near Goldbach.

The remainder of the Austrian Brigade reached Aschaffenburg by 5 A.M. of the 14th, and formed line of battle about a 14th July. mile eastward of the town à cheval of the railway and the high-road.

The first line consisted of a battalion of the 16th Regiment (Wernhardt) on the right wing, where it occupied the pheasantry (Fasanerie), and was afterwards joined by the battalion of the Regiment Reischach on its return from the outposts ; a battalion of the 74th Regiment (Nobili) and the 35th Rifle Battalion in the centre, and a battalion of the 49th Regiment (Hesse) on the left wing. Between the latter and the Rifle Battalion the Hessian Rifled Battery was posted, under cover of the two Hesse-Darmstadt squadrons.

Lieutenant Field-Marshal Count Neipperg formed his second line of a battalion of the Wernhardt Regiment on the extreme right, where it afterwards joined the troops in the Fasanerie ; and the 1st Hessian Regiment in the centre and on the left wing. Detachments of the latter regiment occupied the Pfaffenmühle, the Haselmühle, and the village of Damm.

The Austrian Artillery did not arrive on the field until shortly after the commencement of the action. The 4-pounder Battery first took up a position at the railway station, and then by the side of the Hessian Battery, from whence the whole fore-ground could be kept under a very effective fire. The two Hesse-Cassel squadrons attached to Count Neipperg's division were stationed behind the second line near the Austrian battery.

The 3rd Battalion of the "Wernhardt" Regiment and the 8-pounder Battery stopped behind at the bridge over the Maine at Aschaffenburg. The railway station was occupied by the

---

* *Vide* Appendix XXXII.

Hessian Rifle Battalion. The other troops of the Hessian division retired to Stockstadt at the commencement of the engagement, without any regard to it, and crossed to the left bank of the Maine by the railway-bridge at this place.

On the morning of the 14th General Goeben assembled his division for the purpose of marching on Aschaffenburg. At 7 A.M. the troops stood as follows :—

General Kummer's brigade at Weiberhöfe, General Wrangel's at Eisenhammer, Colonel Tresckow's Cavalry brigade was close behind the latter.

General Kummer was to advance by the railway, General Wrangel along the high-road. The troops started about 8 o'clock. The 1st Battalion of the 13th Regiment marched along the railway embankment, the Fusilier Battalion over the wooded heights on the south side of the line, and the 2nd Battalion midway between both, somewhat further to the rear. The 53rd Regiment with the 3rd 6-pounder and 3rd 4-pounder batteries followed in second line.

General Wrangel's brigade kept to the high-road, but detached Colonel Von der Goltz with the 1st Battalion and the 6th, 7th, 9th, 10th, and 11th Companies of the 15th Regiment, and the 4th Squadron of the 8th Hussars in the wooded country on the right flank in order to operate against the left flank of the enemy's position.

The patrols thrown out by the Cavalry reported Hoesbach to be occupied by the enemy, but the latter fell back from the village on the approach of the first Prussian troops, and then quitted Goldbach also without making any resistance. As soon as Hoesbach was passed, General Goeben brought forward his whole Cavalry (three squadrons of the 4th Cuirassiers and four squadrons of the 8th Hussars), with the Horse Artillery Battery, and deployed them on the north side of the high-road. They then advanced on a line with General Wrangel's brigade.

Even before the head of General Kummer's brigade got on a level with Goldbach it was heavily shelled by the enemy. In consequence, both batteries of the brigade were brought forward to a position à cheval of the railway between the Aschaff and the "Kugelberg." From here they kept up a lively fire against the hostile Artillery, under cover of which the Infantry continued to advance.

By this time General Wrangel's brigade had passed Goldbach, and encountered the enemy westward of the village at the spot where the high-road crosses the Aschaff. A dense line of hostile skirmishers held the bushes on the banks of the brook. The three leading companies (5th, 8th, and 12th) of the 15th Regiment forced the passage of the stream, and then advanced in the direction of the "Aumühle."

The two batteries of General Wrangel's brigade followed under cover of this movement, and proceeded to the wooded heights northward of "Holzhof." They were not, however, able to find a position from which they could fire on the enemy's artillery with any advantage.

The main body of the brigade had found a tolerably sheltered position near Holzhof, but any further advance against the front of the enemy's line led across the perfectly open country, and must necessarily expose the troops to heavy losses from the hostile Artillery. For some time, therefore, the action came to a standstill on the right wing. The three companies of the 15th Regiment, which had advanced towards the "Aumühle," and part of the Fusilier Battalion of the 55th Regiment, which had followed in the same direction, soon, however, succeeded in gaining possession of the knoll to the south of the Aumühle. Pressing on further from this spot their flanking fire forced one by one the hostile batteries to withdraw.

In the meantime, on the left wing, General Von Kummer proceeded to attack the Fasanerie, a movement which had been prepared beforehand, and was assisted during its execution by the fire of his two batteries. A simultaneous concentric attack was directed against the north-east corner of this wood, the 1st Battalion of the 13th Regiment advancing from the north, the 2nd from the east, and the Fusiliers from the south-east. The skirts were soon carried, and by degrees the wood also. In many parts, particularly at a shooting lodge in the interior, the enemy did not yield until after a stout resistance. Some Prussian detachments soon reached the further end of the wood, and thus cut off several of the small groups of their opponents that were still fighting in the interior. The greater part of the latter were taken prisoners.

The Infantry of the Austrian centre, which retreated across the open country after quitting the Fasanerie, suffered very severely from the effective file-firing of the foremost detachments of the 13th Regiment.

Whilst the Prussian battalions, that had become somewhat scattered during the combat in the wood, were being re-formed at the western end of the Fasanerie, General Kummer brought up the 53rd Regiment, and personally leading it through the faubourgs of Aschaffenburg, which were still occupied by the enemy, proceeded to storm the south-eastern entrance of the inner town. The attack in which the nearest companies of the 13th Regiment joined was in every way successful, and the leading troops of both regiments irresistibly fought their way along the streets and through the houses, by the different routes, which lead to the bridge over the Maine, numerous prisoners falling into the hands of the detachments that followed them.

As soon as the enemy's artillery withdrew, General Wrangel's division also advanced to the attack along its whole line. Three companies of the 15th and the Fusilier Battalion of the 55th Regiment marched on the railway station; the 9th Battalion of the 55th and the 1st Company of the 13th Regiment (the latter was detached by General Kummer to keep up the communica-

2 F

tions between both brigades) advanced along the high-road against the north-eastern gate of the town. The "Lippe" Fusilier Battalion followed on the high-road in support. The 2nd Battalion of the 55th Regiment remained on the right wing as escort of the artillery, the batteries of both brigades having taken up positions further forward.

The Austrian 35th Rifle Battalion defended the railway station with great bravery, but it was eventually carried after a severe struggle, and the north-eastern gate stormed; the troops of General Wrangel's brigade then poured into the town also.

The loss of the Fasanerie and the withdrawal of the artillery from the left wing had compelled the Austrian Infantry in the centre of the line to effect a hasty retreat into the town. Count Neipperg now sent forward the two Hesse Cassel squadrons to cover the retreat of his Infantry, but finding nothing to charge, and getting into a heavy cross-fire, they hastily fell back through the town, and only escaped being taken prisoners by the Prussian troops that were already close to the bridge over the Maine, because the latter mistook them for Hussars of their own army on account of the similarity of the uniform. Captain Von Bastineller with the 5th and 7th Companies of the 53rd Regiment was the first to reach the bridge, and compelled a hostile detachment, consisting of a staff officer, five other officers, and about 200 men of various regiments, which attempted to cross the river by boats somewhat lower down, to lay down their arms. A party of skirmishers pressed on over the bridge and forced an 8-pounder battery, which was firing with grape on the bridge, to withdraw with a loss of one ammunition wagon.

The Prussians were thus in complete possession of the town, and the 13th Regiment was posted beyond the bridge.

General Goeben occupied the railway bridge over the Maine at Stockstadt, over which part of the Federal troops had retreated, with the 15th Regiment, two squadrons of Hussars, and the 3rd 4-pounder Battery under the command of Colonel Goltz.

The latter officer had reached Damm with his right flank detachment, when the main part of the action was over. Only the 4th Squadron of the 8th Hussars, which headed the column, had an opportunity of attacking the enemy's riflemen as they retreated from the railway station. A small square was ridden down, and 40 prisoners taken.

The remaining Cavalry of the division took no part in the action. As has been already mentioned, it followed the advance of the division on the extreme right, for the purpose of covering this flank against any hostile detachment that might be advancing from Hanau, as well as of taking up the pursuit of the enemy, in case he should retreat in this direction. It reached the Maine below Damm in the course of the afternoon, and the Horse Artillery fired a few shots at a column marching on the other side of the river. The latter soon withdrew out of range, but some hostile guns returned the fire for about half-an-hour. At Aschaffenburg itself there was thus no Cavalry at hand which could follow in immediate pursuit of the enemy beyond the Maine, but General Von Falckenstein, who was present during the action, despatched his personal escort, the 1st Squadron of the 4th Cuirassiers, for this purpose. The squadron brought back 175 prisoners in the course of the afternoon.

According to official statements the losses on both sides were as follows :—

|  | Prussians. | | VIIIth Federal Corps. | |
|---|---|---|---|---|
|  | Officers. | Men. | Officers. | Men. |
| Killed .. .. .. .. | 5 | 22 | 3 | 223 |
| Wounded .. .. .. | 12 | 132 | 20 | 464 |
| Missing and prisoners.. .. | .. | 9 | 21 | 1,738 |
| Total .. .. | 17 | 163 | 44 | 2,425 |

By far the greater part of the losses of the VIIIth Federal Corps was borne by the Austrian Brigade Hahn, as but few troops of the Hesse Darmstadt and Hesse Cassel contingents were engaged.

It may be remarked in reference to the Austrian statements that not only did 1,700 unwounded prisoners fall into the hands of the Prussians, but that, in addition to numerous dead, nearly 800 wounded were left on the battle-field.

The number of the prisoners may be partly accounted for by the nature of the ground, the course which the action took, and the timely occupation of the bridge over the Maine. It must, however, also be taken into consideration that the Italians of the "Wernhardt" Regiment, who fought bravely at the commencement of the action, did not make much exertion to cut their way through as soon as affairs took an unfavourable turn, and in many cases yielded themselves prisoners without much resistance.

This was the third time during this short campaign that the rapidity of General Falckenstein's movements thwarted the plans of the Allies.

At Aschaffenburg as well as at Dermbach, it was General Goeben's Division alone which threw itself in the way of the enemy. After the action at Laufach the other detachments of the army were not brought up to the front, and whilst General Goeben attacked the enemy on the Lower Maine, they were halting at the Sinn river, above 32 miles further to the rear. Nevertheless, the admirable manner in which the whole action was conducted, the timely co-operation of all Commanding Officers, and the bravery of the Westphalian battalions gained possession of the important post Aschaffenburg at a very trifling cost.

2 F 2

The possibility of the Allies effecting their junction at Würzburg had now become very doubtful. The bold manner in which their opponents debouched from the Spessart mountains and so recklessly advanced against such strong positions led them to conjecture that they were in face of the whole Prussian force. This impression, the heavy loss sustained and the state of feeling among the troops were by no means inducements to attempt to reconquer Aschaffenburg, thereby covering the flank of the VIIIth Corps, which was now so immediately menaced during its march to the appointed rendezvous.

The 1st Würtemberg Brigade, which the Prince of Hesse had ordered to march on Aschaffenburg, had left Gelnhausen for this purpose. Had it appeared on the field during the action it might have had a very unfavourable influence on the Prussian attack. Hearing, however, at Alzenau already of the unfavourable course of the action, the brigade turned back and crossed over to the left bank of the Maine at Steinheim.

The retreat of the troops from Aschaffenburg was covered by a brigade of Baden posted at the wood eastward of Stockstadt; this brigade had left Frankfort by rail immediately after the Austrians, and had disembarked at Babenhausen.

Within the space of seven days General Goeben's Division had marched about 90 miles without a single day's rest, had crossed the Rhön and the Spessart mountains, and fought three victorious actions. As we have heard already, sufficient forces were not at hand at this moment to carry on operations beyond the Maine, where the whole VIIIth Corps would probably be encountered.

As the Prussians did not pursue the enemy succeeded in somewhat restoring order amongst his beaten troops. It was necessary to give up the line of the Lower Maine, and all detachments were withdrawn from there to Dieburg, in order in the first place to concentrate the corps. Under these circumstances, the Assembly, which still demeaned itself as the German Diet, took its departure from Frankfort and moved to Augsburg as a quieter spot.

By the evening of the 14th, the Baden Division and one Hessian Brigade with the Reserve Artillery, were at Babenhausen, the Austrian Brigade close behind them at Hergertshausen; the Würtemberg Division and a Hessian Brigade southward of Hanau at Steinheim-Weisskirchen, and Froschhausen. The Reserve Cavalry marched on the Frankfort-Darmstadt road as far as Langen. Head-quarters were moved to Dieburg.

The whole corps, therefore, might well have been assembled in this neighbourhood within one day, but there was not any intention of profiting by this circumstance. On the contrary, according to all accounts, confusion and helplessness seem to have prevailed to a great extent at the Federal head-quarters.

In the meantime Prince Charles's answer to the Prince of

Hesse's proposals for uniting both Federal corps arrived. At the moment when it was despatched the actions of Laufach and Aschaffenburg were not yet known of at the Bavarian head-quarters. But even if the difficulties of the situation had not been thus increased, still the direct march from Aschaffenburg to Würzburg would only have been possible if assisted by an advance of the VIIth Corps on Gemünden. The corps was, however, not capable of this movement, both on account of the state of its troops and the manner in which they were dispersed after the 11th. It could not be concentrated at Würzburg before the 16th.

Prince Charles, therefore, very rightly pointed out the danger with which the Prussian forces on the right bank of the Maine would menace the march of the VIIIth Corps across the Spessart mountains, as well as the difficulty of provisioning the troops. He proposed the neighbourhood of Uffenheim as the spot to which the VIIIth Corps was to march by way of Milten-berg and Tauberbischofsheim.

The point of assembly was thus transferred to Central Franconia. In this case the Bavarian Army would keep in its own country, and would have but a few miles to march from the neighbourhood of Schweinfurth to Uffenheim, covered by the Maine. From the VIIIth Corps, on the other hand, a march of 90 miles was expected, even reckoning it as commencing from its present place of concentration, southward of Frankfort.

The 20th of July was appointed as the time for effecting this junction; great activity was therefore required of the VIIIth Corps. Added to this the enemy, who was known to be in the Spessart, was just as near to Miltenberg and Tauber-bischofsheim as the latter corps which had to pass these places.

On the 14th of July Prince Charles despatched a flag of truce to General Falckenstein, proposing an armistice of eight days in consideration of the negotiations for a truce then already pending between Prussia and Austria. The Prussian Commander was willing to agree to an armistice with the VIIth but not with the VIIIth Corps, and the negotiations were broken off for the present.

On the 15th already the VIIIth Corps commenced its south-ward march on the three roads leading through the Odenwald, 15th and 16th July. by way of Obernburg, Höchst, and Reinheim.

By the first of these roads the Austrian Brigade reached Miltenberg and Klein-Heubach on the 16th, the Baden Division, Trennfurt and Wörth; by the second one, the Würtemberg Division König, Mömlinggrumbach, and Umstadt; the Hessians, Mömlinggrumbach and Höchst, whilst the Nassau Brigade and the Reserve Artillery reached Fränkisch-Grumbach and Gross-Bieberau by the last-named route.

Head-quarters were at Castle Fürstenau, near Michelstadt, whither they had moved as early as the night of the 15th, because of alarming reports that the enemy was advancing.

On the Prussian side General Goeben's Division halted at

Aschaffenburg on the 15th, General Manteuffell's Corps followed across the Spessart mountains as far as Rechtenbach; General Beyer's Division took the direction of Gelnhausan and reached the neighbourhood of Orb.

On the 16th General Wrangel's Brigade marched to Hanau, and on information being received here that the enemy had totally evacuated Frankfort, was conveyed there by railway, together with General Falckenstein's head-quarters, in the course of the same afternoon. General Kummer kept possession of Aschaffenburg until General Manteuffel's Corps came up, and then followed to Kahl, 4½ miles south of Hanau. General Beyer's Division reached Gelnhausen.

17th to 20th July.

On the 17th General Kummer's Brigade entered Frankfort also; General Beyer marched to Hanau, and the Prussian Army of the Maine remained without any alteration at the three points, Frankfort, Hanau, and Aschaffenburg, until the 21st.

During this time General Falckenstein regulated the administration of the newly occupied territories, Nassau, Upper Hesse, and Frankfort, opened the lines of railway in his rear, and provided the means of bringing up reinforcements for the Army of the Maine. When at Gemünden he had already despatched a request to the Prince of Hohenzollern to make a demonstration against Frankfort with all his available forces. In consequence mixed detachments were again formed along the Lahn out of the Rhenish garrison and depôt troops, and were moved towards the Maine. Up to the 19th General Von Roeder marched from Ems to Wiesbaden; Lieut.-Colonel Von Fischer from Weilburg and Wetzlar to Homburg. These detachments consisted of four Landwehr Battalions, the Fusileer Battalions of Schwarzburg-Rudolstadt and Waldeck, a depôt squadron, eight guns, and some detachments from the different depôts. They mustered about 5,000 men, and remained from this time upward at the disposal of the Army of the Maine.

Another considerable detachment was on the march from Cassel. General Falckenstein had been obliged to leave troops behind to occupy Hanover and Hesse Cassel; now, however, one battalion each of the 30th and 70th Infantry, two battalions of the 17th Landwehr Regiment, and three squadrons of the 10th Landwehr Hussars became available for other purposes. In addition to these three newly-formed fourth battalions, four rifled guns, a company of Pioneers, and a light field bridge train were in readiness to reinforce the Army of the Maine. All these troops had assembled at Cassel and were despatched from thence under the command of Colonel Von Kortzfleisch, at first in the direction of Meiningen, but when the line of operations was changed they proceeded to Gelnhausen, where they arrived on the 17th of July.

Lastly, the Oldenburg-Hanseatic Brigade—as yet only four battalions, three squadrons, and two batteries—and a few days later the newly-formed 9th Prussian Rifle Battalion and two more fourth battalions joined the Army.

On the 17th the VIIIth Federal Corps had a day's rest, with the exception of the Würtemberg troops which left Helmstadt and occupied Zell instead.

The march toward the Tauber was continued during the following days. On the 20th the foremost *échelons* reached this river, viz., the 1st Baden Brigade at Wertheim, the Würtemberg Division at Tauberbischofsheim, and the Austrian Brigade at Gerlachsheim.

The second line consisted of the 2nd Baden Brigade at Hundheim; the Hessian Division between Miltenberg and Hardheim, the Reserve Cavalry and Artillery in the neighbourhood of Walldürn, and the Nassau Brigade at Buchen.

Head-quarters were established at Tauberbischofsheim.

From the 14th to the 16th the Bavarian Army had concentrated between Würzburg, Dettelbach and Kitzingen, and began moving troops to the left bank, in the direction of Markt Heidenfeld, on the 17th.

The following were its positions on the 20th :—

> Division Hartmann at Marktheidenfeld.
> Division Stephan at Remlingen.
> Division Prince Luitpold at Hettstadt.
> The remainder of the army in and round about Würzburg.

The march of the 15th and 16th of July was executed with unwonted activity and led the VIIIth Corps past the heads of the Prussian Army at a moment, it is true, when the latter was just on the point of taking the contrary direction down the course of Maine. The course then marched through the Odenwald without being disturbed, and although the Bavarian Army only made 40 miles in six days, still the connection between the two halves of the Federal Army was established at the Tauber on the 20th of July. It seemed also that no further obstacle could now be opposed to their completing their junction.

Very little alteration took place in the position of the 21st and 22nd Bavarian Army on the 21st and 22nd of July, but the VIIIth July. Corps moved completely up to the line of the Tauber where it occupied the following positions.

> The Baden Division at Wertheim, Reichholzheim, and Niclashausen.
> The Würtemberg Division at Bischofsheim, Werbachhausen, and Grünsfeld.
> The Austrian-Nassau Division at Gerlachsheim.
> The Reserve Artillery at Zimmern.
> The Reserve Cavalry alone was left further forward, between Hardheim and Hundheim.

On the 19th already a conference had been held at Tauberbischofsheim between Prince Charles and the Prince of Hesse to arrange the plan of further operations.

Under the impression that the Prussian Army would content itself with the possession of the Lower Maine, and would not attempt fresh offensive operations against the united and numerically far superior Federal Army, it was determined that the latter should advance to the attack of its opponent.

· There was a great difference of opinion with regard to the route by which this was to be done. The Bavarians wished to advance on the left bank of the Maine, straight across the Odenwald to Frankfort, thereby seeking to re-establish communications with Mayence. The Chief of the Staff of the VIIIth Corps, on the other hand, proposed to march through the Spessart, remarking that it was not to be expected that the Corps should now retrace its steps along the toilsome route by which it had just crossed the Odenwald.

It cannot be well denied but what the plan of operating on the left bank of the Maine was the most correct one, and that the best way of ensuring its success would have been for the VIIth Corps, which was assembled at Würzburg by the 17th, to have advanced to meet the VIIIth as far as Miltenberg by the 20th; for this there was ample time. But during the whole course of the campaign the only way in which the junction of the two Corps was attempted was by the VIIIth Corps marching to meet the Bavarians, whilst the latter never moved further eastward than the line Wertheim-Eisenach.

For the moment, the two adverse opinions could not be reconciled, and a fresh conference took place at Würzburg on the 21st. In order that something might be done, Prince Charles gave his consent to the precarious route through the wooded country on the right bank of the Maine. The VIIth Corps was to advance over Lohr, the VIIIth by way of Marktheidenfeld on Aschaffenburg, and the operations were to commence on the 24th. After having already lost two days by reason of the divergent opinions, two more were now deemed necessary for preparation.

The enemy, however, forestalled these combinations in a most unexpected manner.

---

The continually increasing difficulty of providing supplies for the large mass of troops in Moravia rendered it necessary to make use of the resources of districts in rear of the Army. It was also equally urgent to secure the line on which the operations of the main army were based, and which ran for 225 miles through the enemy's territory.

It was of primary importance to re-establish a well regulated state of administration in Bohemia and to re-organize this country which all former authorities had forsaken.

This important and difficult task was entrusted to the firm hands of General Von Falckenstein.

General Von Manteuffel received the command of the Army of the Maine, and was replaced at the head of his corps by General Von Flies.

Although the South German contingents had been defeated wherever they had shown themselves, still the South German Army was in perfect fighting order, and was now for the first time united. The States of the principal allied Powers had been as yet but partially occupied, Prussian troops had only entered a small portion of Bavaria and none of the territories of either Würtemberg or Baden. The time for military action could now only last but a few days longer, and for this reason, although totally unprepared for undertaking the command of the Army, General Von Manteuffel did not hesitate to resume active operations immediately.

He reached Frankfort at midday of the 20th, and made all necessary arrangements the very same day. (The Appendix shows the order of battle of the Army from this time on.)

The occupation of Nassau, Upper Hesse, and Frankfort, the collecting of the contributions levied in the latter town, and the observation of Mayence were entrusted to General Von Roeder. A detachment of about 10,000 men was left with him for this purpose. With all remaining forces, about 50,000 men and 121 guns, General Von Manteuffel left Frankfort on the 21st in pursuit of the enemy who, in spite of all losses, had so raised his strength by bringing up reinforcements, that his forces amounted to above 80,000 men and 286 guns. It was known that the Bavarians were in the neighbourhood of Würzburg; Cavalry patrols which had followed the VIIIth Corps, reported it to have retreated in the direction of Miltenberg. General Manteuffel determined to advance in this direction. The moral ascendency which all troops gain by a series of successes justifies the selection of a line of operations, which was not without danger to the communications of the Prussian Army, although it menaced those of the enemy in a still higher degree.

Whilst the allied Generals were deliberating at the Bavarian head-quarters on offensive operations on the right bank of the Maine, the Prussian Army was already advancing on the left bank, viz., General Goeben's Division by Darmstadt and Dieburg, the Divisions Flies and Beyer, along the Maine itself. On the 22nd General Goeben was at König, General Flies at Laudenbach, General Beyer at Wallstadt.

The latter detached a battalion and a squadron from Aschaffenburg towards Heidenfeld to obtain more positive intelligence respecting the movements of the Bavarians. This detachment, which encountered Bavarian troops at Esselbach, discovered Marktheidenfeld to be occupied by the enemy in force and rejoined the division at Miltenberg, caused the Bavarians to turn their attention continually in this direction.

The first information of the real advance of the Prussians was received by Prince William of Baden in the course of the 22nd, whereupon he pushed forward small detachments of Infantry on the main road to Freudenberg and Eichenbühl the same evening, and occupied Hundheim with Infantry.

On the forenoon of the 23rd he advanced to the latter place, where the Brigade Laroche took up a position for action; Brigade Neubronn was stationed somewhat behind it, in and round about Steinbach.

Two Companies of Rifles and one squadron remained at Wertheim to keep up the connection with the Bavarian Corps.

At midday, intelligence arriving of the advance of strong Prussian columns by way of Miltenberg, two companies and two guns were thrown into the wood at Tiefenthaler-Hof, half a company was sent to Sonderried, and somewhat after 4 P.M., General Von Laroche made a reconnaissance in the direction of Nassig with the 5th Regiment of Infantry, the 2nd Battalion of the Grenadier Regiment and a battery.

The Prussian Army had marched from Frankfort through the Odenwald toward the Tauber in three days—a distance which the VIIIth Federal Corps had taken six days to complete.

General Flies's Division was instructed to advance to Nassig on the 23rd. It was to guard the road along the Maine on the left flank and to occupy Hundheim on the right. On the other side of Miltenberg the scouting parties of the Cavalry met the advanced troops of the enemy at several points, and a slight encounter took place, at Burgstadt, in which Lieutenant Von Eisenhardt, of the 5th Dragoons, was mortally wounded. The enemy hastily retreated at all points, and General Flies's Division continued its advance after resting for several hours near Miltenberg. The advanced guard passed Freudenfeld and reached Mondfeld without opposition; the main body and the reserve took the direction of Neukirchen. Hostile Cavalry was seen beyond this place towards Hundheim, and some strong detachments were discovered marching from Sonderried to the latter village.

These detachments were the troops of General Laroche, who had pushed his reconnaissance as far as Sonderried, but retreated as General Flies's Division advanced.

## ACTION OF HUNDHEIM.

### 23RD OF JULY.

Whilst General Flies continued his march on Nassig, driving the enemy out of Sonderried on his way thither, Colonel Fabeck received orders to advance on Hundheim with the Coburg-Gotha Regiment, two guns of the 3rd 12-pounder battery of the 6th Field Artillery Regiment, half the 1st and half the 3rd Squadron of the 6th Dragoons. The leading files of the Cavalry, which was at the head of the detachment, came upon Baden Infantry in the wood immediately to the east of the Tiefenthaler-Hof; the latter fell back towards Birkhof after a few shots. Colonel Fabeck now formed his 1st Battalion in columns of companies, and sent it from Tiefenthaler-Hof through the wood, the 1st Company advancing on the right wing towards Birkhof, the 3rd on the left against the wood "Hintere-Stauden," the 2nd Company midway between both; the 4th following in second line. The Fusileer Battalion, the Artillery, and half of the 3rd Squadron remained on the high-road in reserve; the half of the 1st Squadron drew up at the outlet of the wood fronting Hundheim, so as to cover the right flank. The "Birkhof" and the adjoining wood was found to have been evacuated by the enemy, and the wood Hintere-Stauden was also reached without meeting with any resistance; but on advancing still further in the latter wood a very sharp Infantry fire soon commenced.

The Prussian detachment very seriously menaced General Laroche's retreat, for the head of this General's column, consisting of the Grenadier Battalion and the Artillery, was already drawing near Hundheim, whilst his last troops, the 1st Battalion of the 5th Regiment, was still very far to the rear. The 2nd Battalion, therefore, which was in the neighbourhood of the Staudener wood, immediately fronted towards the latter. Two companies were thrown out as skirmishers, the two others followed in support of them.

Both parties met in the part of the wood which lies in the direction of Stauden. The Coburg-Gotha companies pressed the Baden skirmishers back, repulsed an attack of the supporting companies, and drove their adversaries over the high-road in the direction of Ernsthof, thus forcing them into the fire of the two 12-pounder guns which had come into action about 500 paces eastward of Birkhof.

Captain Von Pfeffer, who was near Birkhof with the half 1st Squadron of the 6th Dragoons, took advantage of this moment to charge the battalion, which was retreating across the plain in some disorder.

In the meantime, however, the 1st Battalion of the 5th Baden Regiment had arrived, and drew up in front of Ernsthof to cover the retreat of the 2nd Battalion. All troops of the 1st Baden Brigade that were at Hundheim likewise advanced.

At a distance of 80 paces the Dragoons received the fire of strong detachments of Infantry—viz., of the 1st Battalion of the 5th Regiment, a company of Rifles, and one of Grenadiers, which troops had been hitherto completely concealed by the undulations of the ground. In addition to these, two battalions, two squadrons and a battery debouched from Hundheim on the right flank of the Dragoons. The Prussian half squadron therefore fell back to its previous station at the wood. The two guns were also ordered to return to this spot, a whole battery of the enemy having come into action against them. The companies of the right wing, which had in the meantime advanced on the high-road towards Hundheim, were likewise recalled thither.

We have heard already that the flank detachment which General Flies had sent towards Hundheim only consisted of two battalions, one squadron, and two guns. Perceiving that he was opposed to far superior numbers, Colonel Fabeck confined himself to holding the ground he had gained; he therefore assembled his detachment at Tiefenthaler Hof, and posted a line of outposts along the eastern skirt of the wood on both sides of the high-road, and facing Hundheim.

⊂ The Baden Brigade did not attempt any further attack, and only shelled the wood for some time. When darkness set in the brigade was concentrated round about Hundheim, with outposts on the roads to Neukirchen and to Wertheim.

The Prussian loss in this slight encounter was very trifling. It amounted to—

|  | Killed. | Wounded. |
|---|---|---|
| 1st Battalion, Saxe-Coburg Gotha Regiment.. | 4 | 12 |
| 6th Regiment of Dragoons .. .. .. | 1 | 3 |
| Total .. .. .. .. | 5 | 15 |

In addition to which the latter regiment lost 10 killed and 5 wounded horses.

The losses of the Baden troops were more considerable, viz. :—

|  | Officers. | Men. |
|---|---|---|
| Killed .. .. .. .. .. .. | 3 | 10 |
| Wounded .. .. .. .. .. | 3 | 53 |
| Missing .. .. .. .. .. .. | .. | 23 |
| Total .. .. .. .. | 6 | 86 |

Only one of these was taken prisoner without wounds, so that all the other missing were left dead or wounded on the field.

The evening of the next day the Prussian Army stood as follows :—Division Flies at Neukirchen, Division Beyer round about Miltenberg, Division Goeben at Amorbach. The advanced guard of the latter had been sent in the direction of Walldürn, and was approaching the town when a squadron of the Baden "Leib" Dragoon Regiment debouched from it. Major Krug Von Nidda immediately charged with the 1st and 4th Squadrons of the 8th Hussars, and drove the enemy, in hand-to-hand combat, through the streets of the town towards Königheim, with a loss of 2 men killed, 1 officer, 30 men, and 21 horses wounded and missing. The Prussian Hussars had only a few men and horses slightly wounded.

When the Prussian advance by way of Miltenberg was reported on the 23rd, the Prince of Hesse concentrated the Hessian Division between Königheim and Schweinberg, and pushed forward the 3rd Würtemberg Brigade from Bischofheim to Wolferstetten, where the Reserve Cavalry was also assembled. Towards evening news arrived here of the action at Hundheim, accompanied by a request of the Baden Division for support. The Prince, however, did not afford the assistance demanded of him, because further intelligence arrived that strong forces of the enemy were advancing by way of Walldürn also. The sound of firing at Hundheim, moreover, soon ceased, and orders were despatched the same night to the Baden Division to retreat to Külsheim. The detachment which was left at Wertheim was also recalled to the division.

General Flies occupied Wertheim with a battalion in the course of the night, and Colonel Fabeck advanced to Hundheim before daybreak, on hearing that the enemy had evacuated the place.

Although it was known at Bavarian head-quarters that hostile forces were advancing on the left bank of the Maine, still it was deemed impossible that the main force of the Prussian Army should have taken this direction. Troops of the latter had been seen in the Spessart, and it may have appeared dangerous to execute a general march to the left to the assistance of the VIIIth Corps, thereby exposing the road from Aschaffenburg to Würzburg.

Thus, at the same time that the advanced troops of the VIIIth Corps were being driven in along their whole line on the left bank of the Maine, the VIIth Corps commenced its projected advance on the right bank of the river.

A brigade of General Hartmann's Division marched from Heidenfeld to Lohr, and the whole of General Feder's Division was conveyed per rail from Würzburg to Gemünden and Karlstadt. To cover this movement detachments of General Stephan's Division were despatched to Wertheim in the left flank.

The line of the allied Army thus extended from Gemünden to Gerlachsheim, 36 miles, on the evening of this day; and the junction of both corps, which had been successfully effected, was broken up again at the very moment when the enemy drew near to their immediate neighbourhood.

At all events the VIIIth Corps could not expect any assistance 24th July. from the VIIth in front of the Tauber on the 24th of July, and the Prince of Hesse therefore withdrew all his detachments behind the river. His orders issued on this occasion state this to have been done " for the purpose either of opposing the " enemy, who was advancing between Walldürn and Milten- " berg, or of operating against his flank." For this reason the following positions were taken by midday :—

The Baden Division between Werbach and Werbachhausen the Würtemberg. Division at Impfingen and Bischofsheim, the Hessians at Gross-Rinderfeld, the Austrian-Nassau Division between Paimar and Grünsfeld, the Reserve Cavalry at Gerchsheim, Ober and Unter Altertheim, the Reserve Artillery at Schönfeld and Ilmspan.

The above-mentioned orders then proceed to state,—

" In this position on the right bank of the Tauber " the 1st (Würtemberg) Division will be considered as " advanced guard, the 2nd (Baden) and 4th (Austrian- " Nassau) as *corps de bataille*, the 3rd (Hessian) as re- " serve."

The corps was thus distributed over an extent of nearly 7 miles in breadth, and of 9 miles in depth. The different divisions were not even in themselves closely concentrated. The Cavalry and Artillery, the latter of which was so important for defending the line of the Tauber, were half way to Würzburg, in a country where long and deep sunken ravines not only made it difficult to bring them up again to the front, but also impeded all movements in the highest degree.

Although, therefore, the Prince of Hesse's dispositions express a determination not only to dispute his ground, but also to undertake offensive operations, still the distribution of his forces was such that their positions could only be a stage on his retreat to Würzburg, in which it may at the most have been intended to fight a rear-guard action at the Tauber.

On the other hand, taking into consideration the force which the enemy had shown at Hundheim, the Prussians must necessarily be prepared to meet the whole strength of their adversaries next day, even before reaching the Tauber. It was therefore decided that the Army should first of all close up on the 24th.

Whilst General Flies's Division was concentrated at Nassig General Beyer's Division advanced to Neukirchen and Hundheim by 10 A.M., General Goeben to Hundheim and Wolferstetten.

The enemy having, however, in the meantime retreated behind the Tauber, the Divisions of Generals Beyer and Goeben, which had executed a long march already, received orders to go into cantonments, but General Flies's Division crossed the river and advanced as far as the heights southward of Urphar, where it stood between the two hostile corps.

---

## ACTIONS ON THE TAUBER.

### 1. Action at Tauberbischofsheim.*

General Goeben was engaged in arranging the quarters of his troops when he received intelligence that Bischofsheim and the neighbouring passages over the Tauber were either not at all or only very slightly occupied by the enemy. He therefore determined to put himself in possession of these important points.

Brigades Weltzien and Wrangel were at Wolferstetten. The latter had already detached the 1st and Fusilier Battalions of the 15th Regiment, a squadron and two rifled guns under command of Colonel Von der Goltz from Hardheim over Schweinberg towards Königheim, to cover the right flank. The remainder of the brigade was now despatched towards Bischofsheim, Brigade Weltzien towards Hochhausen and Werbach;

---

* *Vide* Appendix XXXV.

Brigades Kummer and Tresckow, which had only reached Hardheim, were ordered up to Eiersheim as supports.

As General Von Wrangel drew near Bischofsheim the Hussar patrols that were thrown out in advance reported that the place was occupied by the enemy, notwithstanding which he immediately proceeded to attack it at about 2 P.M.

At this time the Würtemberg Division held the following position :—

The 2nd Brigade stood in Bischofsheim and Impfingen. The former town, situated on the left bank, in itself very defensible, but completely commanded by the heights in its immediate neighbourhood, was occupied by the 2nd Regiment of Infantry. Seven companies forming a line of skirmishers, with supports behind them, held the enclosure of the town. The right wing of this line of defence rested on the churchyard northward, the left wing on the high railway embankment southward of the place. A company was posted at the bridge over the Tauber ; two others were stationed as reserves behind it. Higher up on the right bank of the river, two guns, covered by a squadron, had taken up a position on the high-road to Dittigheim. The remainder of the brigade—three battalions, one squadron, and six guns, under General Fischer—was at Impfingen. The 1st and 3rd Brigades stood on the further slope of the heights, 1,000 paces eastward of Bischofsheim, where they were completely hidden from view. The right wing of this reserve—the 1st Brigade—reached as far as the Würzburg high-road, on the north side of which the Horse Artillery Battery Marchthaler was planted ; the left wing was supported by the Field Battery Faber. Neither of these batteries was more than 1,500 paces distant from the town, and both are so advantageously placed that the muzzles of the guns only just rose over the crest of the hill. Seven squadrons were drawn up behind this line in a perfectly sheltered hollow near the Würzburg road.

General Wrangel commenced his attack on Bischofsheim by the fire of the 3rd 4-pounder Battery (Captain Coester), which took up a position on the Immberg near the upper chapel, and opened fire on the only detachments of the enemy that were visible in and near the town. After this preparatory cannonade the 5th Company of the 15th Regiment of Infantry advanced in skirmishing order against the west skirts of the town. It was followed by the 1st Battalion of the 55th Regiment in columns of companies. The main body of the brigade remained concealed behind the Immberg. The 6th and 7th Companies of the 15th Regiment were detached towards Hochhausen to cover the left flank, and to keep up communication with the Brigade Weltzien.

It does not seen to have been the intention of the Würtemberg Commander to make any obstinate defence at Bischofsheim ; indeed the possession of the town was only of importance in case it was intended to assume the offensive at this spot. After a brief skirmish the defenders began to quit the town, and to retreat to the right bank of the Tauber. The Prussian troops entered the place, and immediately occupied the eastern skirts. An officer and 27 men, besides several wounded, were taken prisoners.

The troops that were dislodged from Bischofsheim had to ascend the opposite heights under the fire of the Prussian skirmishers and of the 4-pounder battery, at the side of which the 3rd 12-pounder battery had also unlimbered. Although severely shelled by both Würtemberg batteries, the Prussian guns continued to fire on the enemy's Infantry as long as it was within range, and then engaged the Artillery.

The Würtemberg companies soon found some shelter in the neighbouring vineyards, from which dense masses of skirmishers fired on the town.

A park of about thirty Commissariat wagons, which were obliged to put on extra horses for their transport, stuck fast in the steep road, where it ascends the hill in a deep cutting, and got into the fire of the Prussian Infantry and Artillery. It suffered severely, and, being forsaken by its drivers, almost completely blocked up the road with its dead and wounded horses during the whole time the action lasted, thus obstructing both advance and retreat of the Würtemberg troops. The two guns and the squadron that had been stationed on the right bank of the Tauber close to Bischofsheim had the greatest difficulty in passing this obstacle. They then took up a position on the right wing of the Horse Artillery Battery Marchthaler.

The enemy had thus now eighteen guns in action, to which the Prussians could only oppose the fire of the five guns of Captain Coester's Battery, as the distance was too great for the 12-pounder Battery Eynatten to be of any effect, now that the troops had made good their retreat from Bischofsheim. As the battery would only have suffered unnecessary loss by remaining under fire, it was withdrawn.

As soon as Lieut.-Colonel Böcking was in possession of Bischofsheim he occupied the town with the 1st Battalion of the 55th Regiment.

One company was posted at the bridge and in the neighbouring houses, one company occupied the skirts of the town on the right, and one on the left of the former ; the fourth remained as reserve on the market-place. The 5th Company of the 15th Regiment, and later in the day the skirmishing division of the 8th Company, were also sent into the town. The latter company had been hitherto employed in covering the Artillery.

It might have been expected that the enemy would now have confined himself to defending the very strong position he held, and to preventing any attempt on the part of the Prussians to debouch from Bischofsheim ; instead of which he undertook a series of attacks with the object of retaking a place which a short time before he himself had for very good reasons given up after a very slight resistance. To be sure the weakness of the Prussian Brigade, opposed as it was to a whole division, may now have been discovered, besides which numerous reinforcements were drawing near. Between half-past 2 and 5 P.M., at intervals of from a quarter to half an hour, repeated attempts were made to retake Bischofsheim; though undertaken with great bravery, they all of them failed from want of unity of action on the part of all available forces. In these attacks the 1st Brigade advanced northward, the 3rd southward of the sheltering heights; but they were only made by single battalions, joined by the numerous detachments which had ensconced themselves, after their previous failures, among the vineyards and ravines on the face of the hill: thus at last all troops, detachments of different battalions and brigades, became mingled together. In general these attacks were made by columns of companies preceded by a cloud of skirmishers. The troops advanced with great courage, in spite of the great loss they suffered whilst descending the face of the hill. The nearer they approached the Prussian position, the more their losses increased, until the foremost troops began to halt at the Rector's Kapelle, the brick-kilns (Ziegelei), or the Lorenz Kapelle, and were then compelled to retreat. Each attack ended with the same unfortunate result, and with very heavy losses.

Lieut.-Colonel Von Böcking had scarcely made the necessary preparations for defending his position when the first of these partial attacks ensued. It was met by the file-fire of the companies which lined the outskirts of the town, and by volleys from the 4th Company, which was posted at the bridge. The latter could only attain the breadth of half a division: the first rank therefore knelt down, so as to be able to deliver a fire of four ranks deep. This fire was of very great effect, as had been the case at Podol also.

A second attack was repulsed in like manner, but Lieut.-Colonel Böcking was now obliged to request reinforcements, as his ammunition was beginning to fail. The Fusilier Battalion of the 55th Regiment was sent to his assistance, and its head just reached Bischofsheim as the Würtemberg troops renewed their attack on the bridge.

Colonel Goltz led the 9th and 10th Companies to the spot in person, relieved the detachments posted there, and stationed them as reserves on the market-place.

The 11th and 12th Companies were already on the latter spot, but were soon brought forward to the bridge; the 2nd Battalion arriving at the same took their former place. The "Lippe" Battalion was now the only reserve behind the town.

As the enemy's attacks on Bischofsheim now increased in number and in the energy of their execution, Colonel Goltz advanced over the bridge with the 5th and 6th Companies, *tambour battant*. This offensive movement was joined by the greater part of the 11th and 12th Companies, and was flanked on both sides by the fire of the 9th and 10th Companies. The enemy's storming columns were soon driven back, and the Colonel now occupied the houses and gardens on the right bank

2 G

of the Tauber, which could not be done before on account of the insufficiency of the forces at hand. At the same time the detachments of the 1st Battalion, which were stationed higher up the river, partly waded and partly swam over the stream and then assumed the offensive also. By about 5 o'clock they had established themselves at the Lorenz Kapelle, from whence they kept up an effective flank-fire on the foremost detachments of the enemy.

During the Infantry combat that has been just described the Artillery was continually in action on both sides. Although under the fire of eighteen hostile pieces of artillery, Captain Coester's five guns played upon the storming columns of the enemy's Infantry as often as possible. The batteries of the latter were in such excellent positions that it was impossible to do them any harm; and at half-past 4 the Prussian battery was obliged to cease firing for some time, one gun having been dismounted. The Würtemberg Artillery immediately advanced within 1,200 paces range, and opened a severe cross-fire from four different points on the skirts of the town, the bridge, and the buildings on the right bank of the river. The buildings soon caught fire, and the wounded Würtemberg soldiers that had been left there were only with great difficulty removed and carried to a place of safety.

By 2 o'clock already Lieut.-General Hartmann's report that the division was attacked at Bischofsheim reached Prince Alexander of Hesse in his head-quarters at Gross Rinderfeld. The Prince immediately set off himself for the scene of action, and ordered first two batteries, three quarters of an hour afterwards the whole reserve Artillery, and somewhat later the 4th (Austrian-Nassau) Division, to proceed there likewise. A Hessian Horse Artillery Battery of six guns came up about 5 o'clock, and was posted at the high-road near the two Würtemberg battalions that were held in reserve. A Baden rifled battery which followed behind the former battery could not make its way to the front on the high-road, and remained with the whole of the reserve Artillery further to the rear without coming into action; but the two rifled Austrian batteries, which arrived shortly afterwards, were placed on either side of the Hessian battery. Four smooth-bore guns of the latter withdrew, but still eighteen Würtemberg and twenty-two Hessian, Austrian, and Nassau guns played upon Bischofsheim.

In the meantime the fire between the Prussians that had crossed to the right bank of the Tauber and the Würtemberg detachments in the vineyards, &c., continued without interruption. Ammunition soon became scarce among the former. The concentrated fire of the enemy's artillery made it impossible to cross the bridge, and from this time till the end of the engagement the supplies of ammunition had to be carried through the Tauber to the foremost troops. The water reached up to the breasts of the men employed in this duty.

About 6 o'clock Prince Alexander gave orders for all Würtemberg detachments engaged to retreat that had not done so already. The Austrian-Nassau Division, which had arrived by this time, was to cover their retreat.

The division advanced with the Austrian Brigade in its first and the Nassau Brigade in second line. The latter extended somewhat beyond the left wing of the first line, and took the direction of the extreme right of the Prussian line at the Lorenz Kapelle, where the detachments were in a somewhat exposed position.

In support of this menaced point General Von Wrangel sent forward his last reserves, the "Lippe" Battalion, through the Tauber.

This renewed attack was made with more order, but with less energy than the previous ones. It was not pushed far, and obtained no result. As we have already heard, the Würtemberg troops were very much mixed together. This prevented their quickly executing the order to assemble and to retreat gradually, besides which they wished to bear off their numerous wounded in safety.

It had been intended to relieve the Würtemberg division by the 4th Division, but this did not in reality take place; indeed some of the Würtemberg detachments, in particular the 3rd Rifle Battalion, did not quit the vineyards opposite Bischofsheim, until after the Austrian-Nassau Division. The troops retreating from the engagement was not rallied until "im Forst," on the Würzburg high-road; from thence they were led to bivouacs near Gross-Rinderfeld.

For some time after the failure of this last attack the fire of the enemy's artillery on the skirts of the town was kept up with its previous intensity, but was well returned by Captain Coester's battery, which had repaired damages in the meantime. One by one the hostile batteries gradually withdrew, and the artillery fire ceased when darkness set in.

It had not been General Goeben's intention to advance beyond Bischofsheim; he therefore contented himself with having gained possession of the passage over the Tauber. As soon as patrols sent after the enemy proved the latter to have completely retreated, General Kummer's brigade, which had arrived about 8 P.M., formed the outposts of the division.

At the very first intelligence of an action taking place at Bischofsheim, Colonel Von der Goltz had hastened there, but did not arrive until the engagement was over. Brigade Wrangel was thus again complete, and bivouacked in and near the town.

The Würtemberg Commissariat wagons, which, as we have heard, were so roughly handled by the Prussian Artillery whilst passing a ravine eastward of Bischofsheim fell into the hands of the Prussians after the action; their contents were most welcome. Several horses that were still fit for service replaced the losses of Captain Coester's battery.

The Würtemberg troops that were engaged for the first time on this day showed great bravery, but little skill. The division

2 G 2

did not know how to make use of its very great numerical superiority, but exhausted its strength in a series of attempts to storm Bischofsheim, a place difficult of attack, and defended by the Prussian needle-gun. The forces opposed to each other in this defile must always meet on equal terms as to the number actually engaged, and the superior weapon of the Prussian Infantry came into full play.

General Wrangel had held his ground against the overwhelming numbers of his opponents, but it was only by dint of great skill and determination on the part of Colonel Goltz, the judicious co-operation of all officers and the bravery of the men that this post was held during a struggle of several hours, towards the end of which no less than 40 pieces of artillery concentrated their fire on the defenders.

In all previous actions, with the exception of Laufach and Bischofsheim, the Prussians had taken the offensive, the list of casualties in these two engagements shows how admirably the needle-gun is adapted for defensive warfare—that is to say, when in the hands of well-practised troops.

The losses at Bischofsheim were—

|  | Prussians. | | Würtemberg Troops. | |
|---|---|---|---|---|
|  | Officers. | Men. | Officers. | Men. |
| Killed .. .. .. .. | .. | 16 | 6 | 39 |
| Wounded .. .. .. | 10 | 97 | 24 | 509 |
| Prisoners and missing.. .. | .. | 3 | 1 | 91 |
| Total .. .. | 10 | 116 | 31 | 639 |

All the leaders of companies in the Fusilier Battalion of the 55th Regiment were disabled.

From the above-mentioned losses of the Würtemberg troops, three killed and 18 wounded must be deducted as belonging to troops that were stationed at Impfingen. About 100 wounded were taken prisoners. Only the smaller half of the missing were captured without wounds. The losses of the Austrian-Nassau Division are said to have amounted to 1 man killed, 1 officer and 2 men wounded, 1 man missing.

## 2. Action at Werbach.*

The Baden Division had taken up a position at the passages over the Tauber at Werbach and Hochhausen ever since midday.

Here also the debouché on the left bank of the river was occupied at the commencement of the action. Two companies of the 2nd Regiment were stationed in Hochhausen.

---

* *Vide* Appendix XXXV.

The bridge over the deep railway cutting in front of the village was destroyed, and a small bridge for the passage of Infantry thrown over the river. The 3rd Regiment was at Werbach, and faced the river. The bridge there was barricaded. The 6-pounder Battery Hoffmann and a squadron of the 2nd Regiment of Dragoons were drawn up immediately behind the village. The remaining 2½ battalions of the 2nd Brigade, the 6-pounder Battery Dinger, and eight squadrons of the 2nd Regiment of Dragoons were held in reserve at Werbachhausen; the 1st Brigade and the 6-pounder Battery Deimling were encamped still further to the rear at Brunnthal.

About half-past 1 P.M. the head of the Oldenburg-Hanseatic Brigade reached the heights opposite Hochhausen. Major-General Von Weltzien first brought forward the 6-pounder Battery Nieber, and planted it on the heights south-westward of Hochhausen, near the two chapels. The battery was immediately opened upon by six guns of the Würtemberg Battery Roschmann, which came into action northward of Impfingen, but the former returned their fire from its more advantageous position with so much effect that its adversaries very soon withdrew. Captain Nieber then brought his fire to bear exclusively on the Baden Battery Hoffmann, which had arrived northward of Werbach.

In the meantime General Von Weltzein brought forward the 12-pounder Battery Baumbach, and directed it to a position opposite Werbach. His artillery now concentrated its fire against the reserves of the Baden Brigade that were to be seen advancing from Werbachhausen along the valley of the Welzbach, and caused them some loss, although the distance was very great. The Battery Dinger trotted on in advance, and took up a position near the Battery Hoffmann, at the cemetery of Werbach. Both batteries, however, suffered so severely from the cross-fire of the Oldenburg batteries, which were placed in commanding and more advantageous positions, that they were soon obliged to withdraw from their position with the loss of one dismounted gun, and to quit the battle-field altogether.

During this artillery combat General Von Weltzein had formed his Infantry for action in the wood called the "Grossholz," which covers the summit of the hills running along the left bank of the Tauber. The first line consisted of the 1st Oldenburg Battalion on the right wing, in front of Hochhausen, the 2nd Battalion in the centre, in front of Werbach, and the "Bremer" Battalion on the left wing, opposite the north entrance of the latter village. The 3rd Oldenburg Battalion remained in the wood as reserve. At 3 o'clock the three battalions of the first line began to advance in company column formation. Whilst they with much difficulty descended the steep face of the hill, which afforded no shelter, the attacking companies were sharply fired on by the enemy's Infantry. They continued their advance, however, without either wavering or returning the fire, and gained possession of the line of the railway at the first onset, and then of the village of Hochhausen, which their adversaries quitted after very slight resistance. The enemy now withdrew his right wing also from the line of the Tauber, and retreated to the right bank of the Welzbach, but kept up a brisk skirmishing fire from the skirts of Werbach.

The advanced guard of General Beyer's division was proceeding to its allotted cantonments when the sound of artillery announced the commencement of the action at Hochhausen. Hastening its march as much as possible, the leading battalion, Fusileers of the 70th Regiment, came up in time to take part in the capture of Hochhausen, which they attacked from the south-west. The 4-pounder Battery Schmidt likewise came into action in a position near Battery Nieber, and engaged the Baden Artillery at Werbach, thereby assisting in preparing for the attack on this part of the enemy's position, which now took place.

Werbach was attacked from three sides simultaneously at 4 o'clock.

Having made the Tauber bridge passable, the 2nd Oldenburg Battalion crossed it, and advanced against the front, the detachment which occupied Hochhausen against the left wing of the enemy's position. The Bremer Battalion forded the river below the bridge, and advanced against the enemy's right bank. The Baden troops brought up a battalion from the reserve to reinforce the garrison at Werbach, and fought with great bravery, in spite of which the skirts of the village were carried. Almost at the same moment the 9th Company of the 70th, the 5th and 7th Companies of the Oldenburg Regiment, and detachments of the Bremer Battalion forced their way into the village. The enemy retreated up the Welzbach Valley under the fire of the Prussian-Oldenburg batteries, and with a loss of some prisoners and of the above-mentioned dismounted gun.

At this moment the Würtemburg Battery Roschmann, which had taken up a fresh position near Impfingen, re-opened on Hochhausen, and set the village on fire. The Battery Schmidt moved to another position north-westward of Hochhausen, and engaged the Würtemberg guns, assisted by the fire of the Prussian 6-pounder Battery Wasserfuhr, which just arrived on the hill at the chapels from General Beyer's division.

The fire of these two batteries soon silenced the Würtemberg guns, and forced them to withdraw. Battery Wasserfuhr then took up a position exactly opposite Impfingen, and tried to fire at a very long range on the Würtemberg artillery beyond Bischosheim. In company with Battery Schmidt it afterwards directed its fire on the Würtemberg Infantry that retreated from Impfingen in the evening after having remained there during the whole afternoon without taking much part in the action.

At the end of the day the Oldenburg Battery Nieber

advanced to a position opposite Impfingen and likewise joined in the fire.

The losses were—

|  | Officers. | Men. |
|---|---|---|
| BADEN DIVISION. | | |
| Killed .. .. .. .. | 1 | 6 |
| Wounded .. .. .. | 1 | 59 |
| Missing .. .. .. | .. | 16 |
| Total .. .. | 2 | 81 |

In addition to the gun above mentioned the division abandoned two ambulances, the horses of which had been killed.

|  | Officers. | Men. |
|---|---|---|
| GEN. WELTZEIN'S BRIGADE. | | |
| Killed .. .. .. .. | 2 | 9 |
| Wounded .. .. .. | 4 | 33 |
| Total .. .. | 6 | 42 |
| FUSILIER BATTALION 70TH REGIMENT. | | |
| Killed .. .. .. .. | .. | 1 |
| Wounded .. .. .. | 1 | 21 |
| Total .. .. | 1 | 22 |

Brigade Weltzein went into cantonments behind the Tauber, the advanced guard of Division Beyer planted the outposts beyond Werbach. A company followed the enemy as far as Werbachhausen. The Baden Division continued its retreat without intermission as far as Unter-Altertheim, only leaving a rear-guard at Steinbach.

This movement seriously exposed the Prince of Hesse's right flank. Late the same evening, therefore, he ordered the Hessian Division to advance from Gross-Rinderfeld to Wenkheim. The division bivouacked on the heights southward of Wenkheim, and occupied the village itself with a battalion.

Early on the 24th Prince Charles of Bavaria moved his head-quarters to Remlingen, where he at first received only intelligence of the action of the 23rd at Hundheim and of the occupation of Wertheim by the enemy.

This news gave rise to apprehensions lest the Prussians should again push in between both halves of the Federal Army. It now became evident that the offensive movement through the Spessart was a false step. If it were continued the VIIIth Corps would be opposed alone to the whole force of the enemy, who would be between the allies and their own country if another action were lost. It would be risking all if the movement were not countermanded.

It was therefore determined to concentrate the Bavarian Army immediately in the neighbourhood of Rossbrunn.

Prince Luitpold's division advanced thither from Hettstadt, the reserves assembled between Grusenheim and Waldbüttelbrunn. Division Fedar returned per railway to Zell, near Würzburg, where it was to cross the Maine on a pontoon bridge, and then proceed to Rossbrunn likewise.

Division Stephan had been pushed forward towards Wertheim, and stood round about Uettingen, Helmstadt, and Holzkirchen, with advanced troops in Neubrunn, Kembach, and Dertingen. General Hartmann's division remained at Markt-Heidenfeld and Lohr, because the arrival of the small flank detachment of General Beyer's division in the Spessart still caused apprehensions, lest the enemy should advance by way of Aschaffenburg on Würzburg. Division Fedar therefore left three battalions in Gemünden.

By the evening the VIIIth Corps received intelligence of the movements which the Bavarian divisions had executed in the course of the day, and at the same time orders to open communications with the nearest division (Stephan).

It has already been mentioned that General Manteuffel had already pushed General Flies' division over the Tauber on this day. It had been his intention to cross the river with the two other divisions next day, and to fall on the right flank of the VIIIth Corps, which would probably have separated it from the VIIth Corps. The action which had unexpectedly taken place at Bischofsheim, at the extreme right of the Prussian Army, induced the Prince of Hesse to evacuate the line of the Tauber, and to draw nearest to the Bavarians with all his troops.

25th July. Early in the morning of the 25th of July an officer who had been sent to the Prince of Hesse returned to head-quarters of the Bavarian Army at Remlingen. He brought news of the actions at the Tauber on the previous day and of the retreat of the VIIIth Corps to the neighbourhood of Gross-Rinderfeld. In consequence an attack might be expected from at least part of the Prussian forces from the direction of Bischofsheim, and the dispositions for the Bavarian Corps were therefore so far modified that it was to approach nearer to the VIIIth Corps.

Division Stephan received orders to leave its outposts in front of the enemy, and to march to Unter-Altertheim. Prince Luitpold's division, which had in the meantime been instructed to advance on Helmstadt, was now ordered to Ober-Altertheim, Division Fedar to Waldbrunn.

These divisions only had to march upon an average $4\frac{1}{2}$ miles to reach their destinations, where they would have been at hand to support the right wing of the VIIIth Corps. The reserves, however, and Division Hartmann, which was ordered to march to Rossbrunn, still remained on the Aschaffenburg road.

At 9 A.M. orders were despatched to the VIIIth Corps totally ignoring the reported fact that the line of the Tauber had been evacuated ever since yesterday. They were as follows :—

> "The line of the Tauber is to be held with all avail-
> "able forces, whilst the VIIth Corps is concentrating by
> "way of Ober-Altertheim and Waldbrunn, on the Bis-
> . "chofsheim-Würzburg road, for the purpose of supporting
> "the VIIIth Corps."

By 10 o'clock official information arrived that the VIIIth Corps intended to retreat still further towards Gerchsheim, and it was at the same time proposed to Prince Charles to disengage it from the enemy's pursuit by an offensive movement of the VIIth Corps on Wertheim.

The Commander-in-Chief, however, merely repeated his previous orders.

The letter alluded to stated :—

> "Lieutenant-Colonel Werner, of the Nassau contin-
> "gent, has brought intelligence here that the position at
> "the Tauber was evacuated by the troops of the VIIIth
> "Corps yesterday afternoon, and that it is intended to
> "retreat slowly still further on Gerchsheim.
> "The orders which Major Von Massenbach bore to
> "the VIIIth Corps this morning, instructing the
> "corps to hold the line of the Tauber to the utmost,
> "whilst the Bavarian Corps at the same time effects its
> "concentration on the Würzburg-Tauberbischofsheim
> "road, remain unaltered, because it is only by thus de-
> "fending the line of the Tauber at Bischofsheim that the
> "enemy can be successfully opposed. A retreat on our
> "part to Würzburg or Ochsenfurt is in no way necessary
> "or justified, either by the general proportions of the
> "forces on both sides, or by the number of those that
> "are opposed to the VIIIth Corps.
> "The Commander-in-Chief, therefore, orders the VIIIth
> "Corps to hold out firmly at the Tauber with its whole
> "force, whilst the Bavarian Corps is hastening up to its
> "support.
> "An offensive movement of the Bavarian Corps in the
> "direction of Wertheim, with a view to relieve the VIIIth
> "Corps from the pressure of the enemy, would not have the
> "desired result, and would only lead to a division of the
> "forces, which must be disadvantageous.
> "(Signed)        "CHARLES, Prince of Bavaria,
>                               "Fieldmarshal."

It is difficult to surmise on what motives these renewed orders may have been founded, unless indeed it was intended that the VIIIth Corps, which had not been able to defend the line of the Tauber yesterday, was to re-conquer it to-day, and that without any direct assistance from the VIIth Corps.

If, on the other hand, the VIIth Corps covered the Prince of Hesse's retreat at Gerchsheim, the latter would come in direct connexion with the left wing of the Bavarians at Altertheim, Waldbrunn, and Kist, and then, supposing the short left flank movement of the VIIth Corps to be executed in due time, offensive operations could have commenced next day with the united army against the Prussian divisions advancing from the Tauber.

Moreover, the Prince of Hesse had already commenced his retreat on Gerchsheim at 11 A.M., before even the first of these orders reached him. The advance of hostile columns along his whole line led him to expect a fresh attack, and his position, Wenkheim-Gross-Rinderfeld, seemed too extensive for his corps.

The trifling Bavarian detachments, which were as far forward as the right wing of the VIIIth Corps, did not afford the latter any security, and as the enemy was seen advancing against the left wing likewise, apprehensions arose that the corps might even be cut off from Würzburg.

By retreating on Gerchsheim the Prince of Hesse was enabled to draw his columns close together. The Hessian and Würtemberg divisions marched northward of the high-road; the Austrian-Nassau division and the Reserve Artillery on the road itself. The Baden division advanced early in the morning to Steinbach, and remained there for the present. A Cavalry regiment was despatched to Neubrunn to establish communications with the Bavarians.

At 10 A.M. of the 25th General Goeben's division was assembled at Bischofsheim, General Beyer's at Werbach, and the division of General Flies at Urphar. The enemy was known still to occupy Wenkheim and Gross-Rinderfeld, and it was intended to turn his right flank, in order, if possible, to cut him off from retreating to Würzburg. General Beyer's division was therefore despatched to Neubrunn with orders to advance from thence on Unter-Altertheim, in case the enemy should hold his ground, whilst General Von Goeben was instructed to advance along the high-road direct to Gross-Rinderfeld. The latter was not to set off until half-past 12, so as to give General Beyer sufficient start. General Flies' division was ordered for the present only to advance as far as Dertingen. Up to midday of the 24th only weak detachments of the enemy had been at the latter place. Nothing was known respecting the bulk of the Bavarian Army, but it was supposed to be on the left flank of to-day's march, and it therefore seemed necessary to have a compact body of troops available in this direction. The division was instructed to push detachments forward towards Lengfurt and Remlingen in order to obtain more information.

## 1. Action at Helmstadt.[*]

General Beyer's division set off for Neubrunn in two columns about 11 A.M.; the advanced guard, under Colonel Von Woyna, marching on the right by way of Böttigheim, followed by the reserve. The Fusileer Battalion of the 30th Regiment and the 4th Squadron of the 9th Hussars were despatched up the Welzbach Valley to cover the right flank and to reconnoitre the enemy; the 1st Battalion of the 30th Regiment was left as garrison in Werbach. General Glümer marched with the main body more to the left, by way of Niclashausen.

The head of the Prussian advanced guard came upon Bavarian Chevauxlegers at Böttigheim already, but they fell back without resistance. The heads of the two principal columns arrived in front of Neubrunn almost simultaneously about half-past 1, and found the village and the neighbouring woods occupied by the 1st Battalion of the 8th Bavarian Regiment, which General Stephan had sent there with a squadron of the 3rd Chevauxleger Regiment.

The 6-pounder battery Wasserfuhr of the main body and the 4-pounder battery Schmidt of the advanced guard were brought forward. A few shots of the Artillery and the determined advance of the Infantry sufficed to cause the enemy's retreat, which he effected by different routes, keeping, however, in general the direction of Helmstadt. General Glümer followed through Neubrunn to the lesser "Ameisenberg;" Colonel Woyna passed the south side of the village towards the Klettenberg and the wooded heights "Forstgrund."

This encounter with the Bavarians was unexpected; they were supposed to be still further northward. If the march were continued according to the previous orders on Altertheim they would remain on the left flank of the division, besides which no news had been yet received of General Goeben's progress. General Beyer, therefore, determined to wait for the present at Neubrunn. The enemy, however, kept up so severe a fire, although at a long range, on the foremost Prussian troops from the skirts of the road on the Sesselberg that it was deemed advisable to dislodge him at least from this position.

General Von Glümer stationed the 32nd Regiment and the 12-pounder battery Richter as reserve in front of Neubrunn, and sent forward the 20th Regiment over and westward of the Ameisenberg. After some fighting, the leading Fusileer Battalion drove the enemy out of the wood on the Sesselberg, and threw him back towards Helmstadt.

During its advance the regiment was sharply shelled by a Bavarian battery which unmasked on the south-west slope of the "Lange Höhe," eastward of Helmstadt, from whence it commanded the whole of the foreground. The Prussian battery Wasserfuhr took up a position on the south-eastern slope of the

---

[*] *Vide* Appendix **XXXVI.**

Mausberg and returned the fire. Colonel Von Woyna had in the meantime stationed his detachment northward of the " Forstgrund," in a hollow, where it was sheltered from the enemy's fire.

For a short time it seemed possible to break off the engagement, but the Bavarians soon brought more forces into action and obliged the Prussians to continue the fight. The detachments which retreated to Helmstadt found reinforcements there that opened a very sharp fire against the eastern skirts of the Sesselberg, where General Glümer's skirmishers had established themselves.

A second Bavarian battery came into action on the "Katzenbuckel," still nearer to the Prussian line, and Infantry issued from the Hausacker wood and advanced through the wood on the "Lerchen-Berg" against the "Alters-Berg."

These troops were Prince Luitpold's Division, of which we have already heard that it was on the march from Rossbrunn to Helmstadt. At the same time with the news of the Prussian advance it now received the above-mentioned orders to proceed to Ober-Altertheim. Under the present circumstances this was not possible, but, in order to conform to the orders of the Commander-in-Chief, Prince Luitpold drew up his division on the flat hill northward of the "Geisboden," *à cheval* of the road to Altertheim, a position in which he exposed his flank to the enemy who was advancing from Neubrunn.

Whilst Captain Wasserfuhr's battery occupied the attention of the enemy's Artillery, General Glümer advanced from the Sessel-Berg, and Colonel Woyna from the south and proceeded to attack Helmstadt. The 32nd Regiment that had been hitherto held in reserve, was sent into the wood to cover the right flank against Prince Luitpold's Division.

The enemy did not make a long stand at Helmstadt, his batteries withdrew, and the place was evacuated as the storming columns approached it. The garrison retreated to Uettingen, followed by the Fusiliers of the 20th Regiment. The two musketeer battalions of the regiment halted at Helmstadt and were joined southward of this place by Colonel Woyna's battalions.

Assisted by the fire of the 12-pounder battery Richter, the 32nd Regiment had in the meantime carried the skirts of the wood on the "Altersberg," and was slowly but steadily gaining ground eastward in a sanguinary and obstinate wood fight, the enemy disputing every inch of the ground.

Meanwhile the two Prussian batteries, afterwards joined by the 12-pounder battery Hoffbauer, had taken up a position on the Katzenbuckel. From there they fired on the Bavarian Artillery, which had taken a new position on the heights south-westward of the "Ziegelhütte."

Several battalions now advancing on both sides of the Bavarian batteries, both from the "Ziegelhütte," and from the direction of the "Giesboden," Colonel Von Woyna proceeded to attack them. This bold advance and the Prussian Artillery fire first forced the Bavarian Infantry to leave the open country and to seek shelter in the neighbouring woods, and then the enemy's batteries were also obliged to withdraw by the fire of the Prussian skirmishers.

General Manteuffel, who viewed the engagement from the "Katzenbuckel," now gave orders to his head-quarters' escort, the 3rd Squadron of the 9th Hussars, to join in the action whenever an opportunity occurred.

Advancing along a small dell which extends eastward from Helmstadt, Captain Klaatsch was on the point of charging the Bavarian Infantry which was just then commencing its retreat, when two squadrons of the 2nd Chevauxlegers Regiment came forward to meet him. He charged them immediately, and both lines met on the summit of a small hillock south-westward of "Ziegelhütte." The Chevauxlegers fell back in a north-easterly direction after a sharp hand-to-hand combat, Captain Klaatsch followed for a few hundred paces, and then rallied his squadron in the hollow immediately southward of "Ziegelhütte."

Whilst he was still engaged in reforming his squadron two other Bavarian squadrons were seen descending the face of the hill called the Platte. They were accompanied by the Commander of the Chevauxleger Regiment, who had already led the first charge.

Though scarcely formed, the squadron advanced to meet them, and the Commander of the 9th Hussars, Major Von Cosel, coming up at the same moment with three sub-divisions of the 5th Squadron, fell on the flank of the enemy's Cavalry. This time also the Chevauxlegers were completely worsted and pursued as far as the wood, where the Hussars were received by a severe skirmishing fire. In this second charge the Commander of the Bavarian Regiment, Lieutenant-Colonel Röhder and Captain Prince Taxis—the latter severely wounded—were taken prisoners.

Pressing on northward of "Ziegelhutte," the Fusileer Battalion of the 70th Regiment had in the meantime entered the "Heergrund-Wald," and now forced the enemy back in the direction of Müdelhofen. Colonel Von Woyna's remaining troops, the Cavalry, and those batteries that were not engaged assembled in the dell between the "Lange Höhe" and the "Ziegelhutte."

The engagement had not taken so rapid a course on the right wing of the Prussian line. Each step it gained in advance, the 32nd Regiment met with more vehement and more obstinate resistance, so that about the time the second Cavalry charge took place, General Manteuffel sent the 39th Fusileer Regiment, which had come up as far as Geisboden, to support and, if necessary, to relieve the first-named regiment. The Fusileers set off about half-past 5 P.M., with the 3rd Battalion in company columns at the head of the regiment, passed through the skirmishers of the 32nd Regiment which had by this time reached the east skirts of the wood on the Lerchen-Berg and carried the west skirts of the Hausacker-Holz at the first onset without firing a shot. Battery Richter had been for some time already firing on these skirts. Detachments of all three battalions of the 32nd Regiment joined in this charge. The four skirmishing pelotons and the 11th Company of the 39th Regiment followed the enemy, who retreated in the direction of Wald-brunn, as far as the east border of the extensive wood, the remainder of the regiment stopped in the interior of the Hausacker Holz, and the 32nd Regiment was rallied northward of the Lerchen-Berg.

Prince Luitpold had sent a request for assistance to the Baden Division which he knew to be the troops nearest to him. Prince William of Baden was, however, not able to afford it without further orders, because, as we shall presently see, the VIIIth Corps, of which he formed the right wing, was in the meantime itself attacked.

As there was no time to wait for the Prince of Hesse's decision, Prince Luitpold determined to retreat.

It was past 6 o'clock and the engagement seemed at an end. The firing even in the wood in front of Walbrunn gradually ceased. General Beyer's Division was resting near the Ziegel-hutte, with its front towards the east, when all of a sudden heavy columns of the enemy appeared on the crest of the hill between the "Uettinger-Gemeinde-Wald" and the Hohenroth-Wald, in rear of its left wing.

It was at first not known whether these forces belonged to friend or foe, but General Beyer, immediately changed his front and the Fusileer Battalion and the 2nd and 3rd Companies of the 70th Regiment advanced to meet them through the "Heer-grund" and the Hohenroth-Wald; the 1st and 4th Companies of the 70th and the 2nd Battalion of the 30th Regiment further to the left.

The approaching columns were General Stephan's Division, which had taken a long time to assemble from its widely-scattered cantonments, and had not started from Uettingen until towards evening. It was now marching on Unter-Altertheim.

Although the outposts of this division had been driven back from Neubrunn over Helmstadt towards Uettingen earlier in the day, still the Bavarian Commander, not being aware of the momentary position of affairs, was also doubtful what troops those were which he now perceived in the low ground before him.

On advancing somewhat further both parties discovered themselves to be in the face of the enemy. Two Bavarian batteries forthwith opened a very fierce fire, in consequence of which the Prussian left column drew nearer to the woods on both sides, so as not to be exposed to the heavy loss which it would have suffered in crossing the open plain.

Bavarian Infantry was advancing over the Frohnberg towards the "Ober-Holz," but the Fusileer Battalion of the 20th Regiment was stationed there and advanced to meet it with such energy that it was driven back again into the Uettinger-Germeinde-Wald. General Glümer led forward the two musketeer battalions of the regiment, one to the left of the Uettingen high-road, the other further to the right over the "Lange Höhe," against the enemy's artillery. The high corn enabled these troops to get near to the latter without much loss. In the Heergrund-Wald the enemy was also forced so far back that the foremost Prussian skirmishers got within range of his artillery. The Bavarian batteries being now taken *en écharpe* by Captain Hoffbauer's battery from a position at the north-west corner of the Heergrund-Wald, and at the same time menaced by the Prussian Infantry in front and flank, were obliged to withdraw to Uettingen about half an hour after they first opened fire.

The two musketeer battalions of the 30th Regiment which had been joined by the 1st and 4th Companies of the 70th Regiment now wheeled to the left towards the Uettingen-Gemeinde-Wald to assist the Fusileer Battalion of the 20th Regiment, whose further progress was checked by the determined resistance of a superior force of Bavarian Infantry. The Prussians now carried the skirts of the wood by storm and drove the enemy out of the wood in spite of his brave defence. Hand-to-hand combats ensued in many places, in particular with detachments of the 2nd Bavarian Rifle Battalions which were almost totally destroyed. By degrees Colonel Woyna's Infantry likewise gained possession of the Hohenroth and the Schlehrberg woods.

A soon as the advance of the Infantry on both wings permitted it to be done, the Prussian batteries were sent forward to the position which the Bavarians had quitted on the lofty ridge northwards of the "Lange Höhe" so as to be able to fire on the retreating troops of the enemy. This movement, however, again produced a fierce struggle between the Artillery on both sides, as the Bavarian batteries had taken up a position on the heights northwards of Uettingen in greater force.

On the Prussian side the 6-pounder batteries Brosent and Wasserfuhr, and the 4-pounder battery Schmidt came successively into action here. The fire of the 12-pounder batteries could not reach the enemy's position, and they were therefore withdrawn to avoid unnecessary loss. Although the Bavarian shells flew as far as the Lange Höhe, this whole cannonade produced but little effect. Darkness (it was past 8 o'clock) and the very evident retreat of the enemy at last put an end to the combat. The Prussian detachments that had become much scattered by the fighting in the woods, were rallied on both wings. The 39th Regiment was now moved up to Helmstadt, where the 32nd had already previously gone, and the division bivouacked in the immediate vicinity of the hamlet. Outposts were stationed along the north skirts of the Uettingen-Gemeinde-Wald and at the Heergrund-Wald. The right flank detachment that had been sent from Werbach up the Welzbach valley rejoined the division from Unter-Altertheim without having met with the enemy.

The two Bavarian divisions had started on the short march to their point of assembly late in the day and at different times. It thus came that they found their opponent, coming from the Tauber, already on their line of march, and that General Von Beyer had driven back one division before the other arrived on the field, so that in spite of their numerical superiority, both were decidedly defeated. They retreated by divergent routes—Division Prince Luitpold by way of Waldbrunn, Division Stephan by Uettingen, to Rossbrunn, from whence they had both come.

The Prussian losses were:—

|  | Officers. | Men. |
|---|---|---|
| Killed .. .. .. .. .. .. | 1 | 30 |
| Wounded .. .. .. .. .. | 12 | 273 |
| Missing .. .. .. .. .. .. | .. | 37 |
| Total .. .. .. .. | 13 | 340 |

With very few exceptions, all the missing were dead, left lying in the woods. The greatest loss was sustained by the 32nd, and next to it by the 39th Regiment.

The casualties among the Bavarian troops cannot be given, as all official lists which have as yet been published only give them jointly with the next day's losses at Rossbrunn.* They must have been at least as numerous as those of the Prussians. About 60 Bavarians were taken prisoners without wounds.

### ACTION AT GERCHSHEIM.†

The unexpected encounter with the Bavarians had drawn General Beyer's Division away from its originally appointed line of march. In the course of the action it had reached Helmstadt instead of Unter-Altertheim, and could not, therefore, carry out the previous intention of directly co-operating with General Goeben's Division.

According to its orders, the latter had commenced its march on the high-road towards Würzburg about 1 o'clock. Brigade Kummer formed the advance guard; it was followed first by Brigade Weltzein and then by Brigade Tresckow as reserve. Brigade Wrangel marched by way of Grunsfeldhausen and Ilmspan to cover the right flank.

---

* An official Bavarian account of the campaign which has been since published gives the following numbers of their losses at Helmstadt:—

|  | Officers. | Men. | Horses. |
|---|---|---|---|
| Killed .. .. .. .. | 6 | 37 | 14 |
| Wounded .. .. .. | 24 | 384 | 15 |
| Missing and prisoners .. .. | 6 | 273 | 53 |
| Total .. .. .. | 36 | 694 | 82 |

† *Vide* Appendix XXXVII.

About this time Prince Alexander assembled the VIIIth Federal Corps at Gerchsheim, where it took up the following positions :—

The Austrian-Nassau Division stood as advanced guard between Gerchsheim and the "Sandrain," fronting southward, with the Nassau Brigade in the first and the Austrian Brigade in the second line. The Reserve Cavalry was drawn up on the left of the former division in the open country between Gerchsheim and the "Jägerholz." The actual line-of-battle position, about a mile further to the rear, was occupied by the Baden Division on the right wing, between Ober-Altertheim and the Rinderfeld forest. The division had retreated there from Steinbach when General Beyer's advance menaced its right flank. The artillery of the division was planted on the Scheinberg, where the whole reserve artillery of the corps was also stationed. The centre of the line, extending on both sides of the high-road south-westward of the "Forsthaus-Irtenberg," was held by the 2nd Würtemberg Brigade on the right and the Hessian Division on the left wing. The 1st and 3rd Würtemberg Brigades were in reserve at Kist beyond the Rinderfeld Forest.

As the foremost troops of General Kummer's Brigade debouched from the Hachtel wood midway between Gross-Rinderfeld and Gerchsheim, considerable forces of the enemy were perceived in position on the heights near Gerchsheim. This was immediately reported to General Goeben, who at about 4 P.M., ordered the brigade to form for action in the wood, and sent instructions to General Von Wrangel to march from Ilmspan on Gerchsheim, and to turn the enemy's left flank.

General Kummer lined the skirts of the wood facing the enemy with the 13th Regiment and the Fusileer Battalion of the 53rd Regiment. The two musketeer battalions of the latter regiment remained alongside of the high-road as reserves. The 3rd 6-pounder and 4th 4-pounder batteries unlimbered immediately in front of the wood, eastward of the high-road ; the four squadrons of the 8th Hussars attached to General Kummer's Brigade drew up in a dell to the right of the artillery.

As soon as the Prussian batteries began to debouch from the wood, they were fired upon at a distance of from 2,500 to 3,000 paces by two Austrian and one Nassau battery, numbering together 24 guns, and suffered not only losses of men and horses, but several guns were also seriously damaged. Added to this, the enemy's fire was very soon still further increased by the arrival of two Würtemberg batteries. The Prussian batteries could not possibly hold their ground for any length of time against such far superior numbers, and were withdrawn behind the wood to repair damages after a combat of about three quarters of an hour.

The enemy now kept up a fierce fire of shells and shrapnels against the wood preparatory to attacking it with his Infantry. When, however, the Nassau Brigade advanced for this purpose, it was met by a rapid file-fire of the Prussian skirmishers

2 H

and by vollies from their supports which advanced to the edge of the wood for this purpose. After advancing to within about 400 paces of the wood the enemy's columns turned and retreated to their former position.

The action in front of the position was now for some time only sustained by the fire of the enemy's artillery on the skirts of the wood occupied by the Prussians.

Prince Alexander had the intention of resuming the attack, and sent orders to the Würtemberg and the Hessian Divisions to advance. Both of them, however, were of opinion that their troops were too fatigued to do so, besides which the 1st and 3rd Würtemberg Brigades had already been sent further to the rear to Kist. The Prince could therefore now only defend his own position.

Even before General Goeben's orders reached him, General Wrangel had hastened his march as much as possible on hearing the sound of the firing proceeding from the direction of Gerchsheim. About 7 o'clock the head of the brigade, which was already formed for action, debouched from Schönfeld, and, throwing forward the 4-pounder battery Coester to a position between Heuberg and Jägerhölzle, commenced the engagement by opening a flank-fire on the enemy's artillery at Gerchsheim.

To cover the battery, the 1st Battalion of the 15th Regiment occupied the copses near Heuberg on the left wing; on the right Colonel Von der Goltz advanced with the Fusileer Battalion, followed by the 2nd Battalion as support, through the Jägerhölzle, and gradually gained ground in the direction of Forsthaus-Irtenberg, driving back the Hessian skirmishers that he encountered in the wood. The 5th Squadron of the 8th Hussars advanced on his right flank, keeping on a line with the 2nd Battalion outside of the wood.

General Wrangel remained for the present with the main-body of his brigade—55th Regiment, "Lippe," Fusileer Battalion, and 3rd 12-pounder battery—in the low ground on the right rear of Captain Coester's battery.

The arrival of General Wrangel's Brigade compelled Prince Alexander to face to this direction with the left wing of his line, and the greater part of his artillery immediately turned its guns on this new adversary. General Goeben, however, now also advanced to attack him in front.

In the meantime General Kummer's two batteries had repaired their damages and the Oldenburg rifled battery had arrived upon the field. These three batteries now debouched from the wood and opened fire on the Austrian-Nassau Division which was stationed in the foremost line of the enemy's position near Gerchsheim. This time they obtained better results.

Brigade Kummer, followed by Brigade Weltzien, now advanced against the heights westward of Gerchsheim. The enemy did not withstand this attack, but fell back in the direction of Irtenberg, which Prince Alexander had already determined to do as soon as Colonel Goltz's energetic advance seriously endangered his line of retreat. The continually increasing quantity of Bavarian military train and stragglers streaming back from Helmstadt showed but too plainly that the action at this place had taken an unfortunate turn, and the VIIIth Corps was in danger of the high-road being completely blocked up by the fugitives. It was therefore decided that the Austrian-Nassau Division should begin the retreat under cover of the Reserve Artillery, which was planted on the Scheinberg. All the smooth-bore batteries of the latter were then very soon withdrawn and the Reserve Cavalry followed them. Only two Baden, half an Austrian, one Würtemberg, and one Hessian battery still remained at the margin of the wood.

The Hessian Division and the 2nd Würtemberg Brigade were to cover the general retreat.

At first this retreat proceeded very regularly, but when the troops were in the interior of the wood the order in their ranks diminished every minute. The Commanders of the divisions and the brigades had partly received no instructions in what succession they were to follow each other, partly such orders, when given, were not adhered to. The active pursuit on the part of the enemy forced one battery after the other to withdraw, which had the effect of hastening the steps of the retreating Infantry. Everyone strove to reach the end of the defile, which ran for nearly 2½ miles through the wood, if possible, before darkness set in. Troops of all the divisions thus became mingled together, and numerous stoppages occurred on the high-road, on some parts of which three different columns were pressing on alongside of each other. Fortunately for the corps, its adversaries could not perceive the increasing confusion in the interior of the wood ; all the troops visible were those outside the wood, and they were apparently in good order.

Only the Fusileers and 2nd Battalion of the 15th Regiment had at the last a somewhat sharp encounter near Forsthaus Irtenberg with parts of the Hessian Rifle Battalion, of the 1st Battalion of the 2nd Würtemberg Regiment, and of the 2nd Baden Grenadier Battalion, who made a stand here, led by General Von Fischer in person. Total darkness at last ended this fight, and further pursuit through the wood at about 9 o'clock.

Thus the VIIIth Federal Corps had on two succeeding days failed in resisting the advance of General Von Goeben's Division, although the corps had more than twice as much Infantry, three times as much Cavalry, and four times as many rifled guns as the division.

General Von Goeben bivouacked and cantoned with his division in and close to Gerchsheim.

The VIIIth Federal Corps was rallied and re-formed in the course of the night near Kist. The Reserve Cavalry was sent back as far as Höchberg, the Reserve Artillery to Reichenberg.

The loss of the Prussians in this action amounted to—

|  | Officers. | Men. |
|---|---|---|
| Killed .. .. .. .. .. .. | .. | 8 |
| Wounded .. .. .. .. .. | 3 | 48 |
| Missing .. .. .. .. .. .. | .. | 1 |
| Total .. .. .. .. | 3 | 57 |

As far as they are known the losses of the enemy were—

|  | Würtemberg. | | Nassau. | |
|---|---|---|---|---|
|  | Officers. | Men. | Officers. | Men. |
| Killed .. .. .. .. | 1 | .. | .. | 4 |
| Wounded .. .. .. .. | .. | 11 | .. | 25 |
| Prisoners and missing .. .. | 1 | 5 | .. | 13 |
| Total .. .. | 2 | 16 | .. | 42 |

The lists of the losses of the Austrian, Hesse, and Baden troops are either incomplete or do not exist at all.

In addition to the wounded that fell into the hands of the Prussians, the latter took about 100 prisoners.

We now turn to the Prussian left wing. On the morning of the 25th General Von Flies had already driven back the detachments of the enemy posted at Dertingen and Kembach. The division then advanced without opposition, in the course of the afternoon, from Urphar to Dertingen, and sent detachments against Homburg and Holzkirchhausen, which were occupied by the enemy. The Bavarians evacuated the former place without resistance, but a sharp skirmish ensued at Holzkirchhausen between two companies of the 36th Regiment and a superior force of the enemy, which cost the former one officer killed and five men wounded.

Whilst the action at Helmstadt was still going on, General Manteuffel had already directed General Flies to send troops to the assistance of General Beyer's Division. General Von Korth advanced with the main body of the former to Uettingen, where he arrived about 9 o'clock. Somewhat later Colonel Von Krug proceeded to Helmstadt with three squadrons of the 6th Dragoons and the 4th 4-pounder Battery. The remainder of General Flies's Division bivouacked at Dertingen and Wüstenzell.

Judging by the actions at Helmstadt and Gerchsheim, the Prussians naturally expected to encounter the united Federal Army in advancing still further next day. General Flies was therefore ordered to push on to Uettingen next morning with his whole force; he was to receive further instructions on arriving there.

Till this took place, the divisions of General Beyer and General Goeben were to remain in their present positions.

The Bavarian Army took up the following positions in the course of the night:—

The Divisions Feder and Hartmann (one brigade of the latter did not arrive from the neighbourhood of Marktheidenfeld until midnight), the Reserve Infantry Brigade, and part of the Reserve Artillery at Rossbrunn, the remainder of the Army between Hettstadt and Waldbrunn.

The Army was thus concentrated in front of Würzburg, but with the steep and deep sunken valley of the Maine immediately in its rear. The passages over the latter, at all times difficult of access, were now blocked up by the trains of both corps to a most dangerous degree. If further retreat became necessary, the corps might be placed in a most critical situation, and Prince Charles of Bavaria perceived that offensive operations would be the best way to avoid this danger. He therefore determined to attack his adversaries on the 26th. The necessary details were already settled in a council of war held at Hettstadt during the night, when the news arrived that the VIIIth Corps had retreated to Kist.

The position of the two corps was now more favourable to a simultaneous offensive of both than it was before, but the condition of the troops of the VIIIth Corps prevented its execution. Before daybreak intelligence was received that the corps had continued its retreat to Würzburg.

Under these circumstances Prince Charles also relinquished his idea of assuming the offensive; and as an attack on the part of the enemy might be expected as certain, it was ultimately resolved to assemble the Bavarian Army on the plateau of Waldbüttelbrünn, and orders were sent to the VIIIth Corps to take up a position on the Nicolausberg immediately in front of Würzburg, so as to cover the retreat of the Army over the Maine in case it should be necessary.

These dispositions were scarcely made before the thunder of cannon was heard from the direction of Rossbrunn.

---

## ACTION AT ROSSBRUNN ON THE 26th OF JULY.*

We have heard that General Von Korth had reached Uettingen late on the preceding evening. Finding the village full of Bavarian wounded, but otherwise abandoned by the enemy, he occupied it by the two musketeer battalion of the 59th Regiment. A detachment was sent to the Obere-Mühle eastward of the village, but no further precautions could be taken in the darkness.

26th July.

---

* *Vide* Appendix XXXVIII.

The Fusileer Battalion of the 59th Regiment, the 11th Regiment, the 1st and 2nd Squadrons of the 5th Dragoons, and the 3rd 6-pounder Battery bivouacked together immediately to the west of the village. General Korth thus faced eastward, and was in front of General Beyer's Division and its outposts on the northern border of the Uettingen-Gemeinde-Wald. General Flies, who inspected this rather exposed situation the same evening, started as early as 3 A.M. of the 26th with the remaining troops of his division to support General Korth. Hastening on ahead of them he received the intelligence that the enemy was already advancing, and forthwith gave orders that the Kirchberg should before all things be immediately occupied, as this had not been able to be done during the night.

One battalion each of the 11th and 59th Regiments immediately set off for the hill.

As we know, two Bavarian divisions and part of the Reserve Artillery were stationed at Rossbrunn, little more than one mile in front of General Korth's Brigade. The enemy was also fully aware of the importance of the heights which come close up to the north and south of Uettingen. On the right, detachments of General Hartmann's Division were already in full march towards the Hessnert and the Kirchberg, and reached and occupied the latter hill shortly before the Prussians arrived. On the left, a brigade of General Feder's Division was advancing towards the Brunschlag and the Leite, so that Uettingen was now in danger of being completely surrounded.

Until the remaining troops of his division had time to come up, General Flies could only strive to hold this part of his position by mere passive resistance, but the two battalions that were detached to the Kirchsberg, and were followed in second line by the 1st Battalion of the 11th Regiment, immediately proceeded to attack the enemy. The fatiguing ascent of the steep hill cost them much loss, but they soon gained possession of the vineyards in front of the wood, and carried the skirts of the latter at their first onset. After a brief but sanguinary struggle the Bavarian 8th Rifle Battalion was driven back beyond the Würzburg-Aschaffenburg high-road to the "Hessnert," where other troops were stationed to support it.

The Prussian battalions followed close upon the Rifles, which brought them into a heavy fire of Infantry and Artillery, particularly from a battery which was stationed on their flank near Greusenheim. Nevertheless, the wooded hill Hessnert was also carried, and its defenders now fell back in an easterly direction beyond the "Mühlbach," on the heights beyond which General Hartmann's Division was drawn up.

The margin of the wood on the Hessnert was immediately occupied in force, and the battalions, having got somewhat mingled together during the fight, were reformed under its shelter, so as to be in readiness for a further advance. Numerous dead and wounded, as well as 1 officer and 100 men, fell into the hands of the Prussians.

In the meantime the other detachments of General Flies's Division had reached Uettingen.

The enemy opened a heavy fire on this village from his artillery position at the Rossbrunn post-house, and set several buildings on fire. The fire of the Bavarian Infantry prevented the Prussian batteries from taking up positions northward of Uettingen, in which they could have returned the fire of the Artillery, as long as the enemy was in possession of the Kirchberg; but General Von Freyhold was ordered to debouch southward of the village, and to take the heights on this side.

About 5 A.M. the 2nd Battalion of the 36th Regiment, followed by the 3rd 4-pounder Battery, reached the open country southward of Uettingen, upon which a hostile battery was unmasked at the north-east corner of the wood on the Schlehrberg, but withdrew after firing a few shots. The Prussian battery came into action at the "Taubenheerd," and was joined about a quarter of an hour later by the 3rd 6-pounder Battery. Both batteries directed their fire against some masses of the enemy that were seen on the face of the hill "Leite," and did not return the fire of the Bavarian batteries at the Posthaus, which had played upon them without intermission, until the former had retreated out of sight.

The enemy's position on the "Leite" was very difficult of access from Uettingen. The wood on these heights only reaches half way down the face of the hill, and the country in front of it was perfectly open. The only shelter within 1,200 paces of the road was to be found in the low meadow ground between the Brunschlag hill and Uettingen. This latter height was, however, also in the hands of the Bavarians, and their fire from thence enfiladed the meadows. The wood on the Brunschlag projected far out, and afforded an opportunity of bringing an effective flank-fire to bear on any troops that approached the Leite. For this reason the first object to be attacked was naturally the Brunschlag hill. The face of this hill was not only less steep, but the wood came down to the foot of the hill, and could be reached from the side of the Schlehrberg, which the enemy had already quitted, without exposing the attacking troops to a cross-fire. The head of a Prussian column (2nd Battalion of the 36th Regiment) advanced in this direction against the left flank of the enemy's position. The 3rd Battalion was the next one to debouch from Uettingen, and was ordered to attack the Leite. The 10th and 11th Companies advanced as skirmishers, and were followed by the 9th and 12th in compact order. They were met by a murderous fire in front and flank, and were shelled by a battery posted on the Vogelberg, so that the men instinctively leaned more to the right towards the Brunschlag, the west corner of which was already entered by the companies of the 2nd Battalion.

As his line was thus extended very far to the right, General Von Freyhold thought it necessary to gain possession of the Leite without any further delay, the hill being very dangerously near to Uettingen, and preventing the development of the troops. He therefore gave orders to attack the enemy in front with compact columns.

Colonel Von Thile now formed the last remaining battalion (the 1st) of his regiment in two half battalions, with skirmishers thrown out in advance, and proceeded to storm the enemy's position with fixed bayonets and *tambour battant,* but without firing a shot. General Freyhold and Colonel Thile placed themselves at the head of the attacking troops. The losses were very considerable.

The enemy concentrated a most withering fire on the battalion. The horses of both above-named officers fell, the Commander of the battalion was killed, and a great number of officers and men were disabled. Nevertheless, the battalion followed the example of its leaders, and pressed on without stopping until it reached the strip of meadow land, where a short pause was made to give the men time to regain their breath.

At the same time the 2nd and 3rd Battalions were gaining ground in the Brunschlag wood, and thus relieved their comrades from the galling flank-fire which they suffered from this direction. After this the general advance of all parts of the regiment, both within and without the wood, was resumed, in which the two divisions of the 59th Regiment joined that had been on outpost duty at the Ober-Mühle during the night.

Not without suffering severe losses, but in compact order, the Magdeburg Fusileers now threw themselves upon the skirts of the wood, which the enemy occupied in force, and carried them at the first charge. An obstinate and sanguinary fight then ensued in the interior, which resulted in the enemy being driven out of the wood. The battery on the Vogelberg was forced to retreat in haste. By 7 o'clock the Bavarians had lost this important position.

Whilst they were climbing up the steep hill, and during the fight in the wood, the Prussians could make but little use of their firearms, and consequently lost far more men than their opponents. Now, however, that the latter had to retreat across the open country, the tables were turned. In addition to this the Bavarians made several attempts to retake the wood. Their attacks were principally directed against the right wing of the position, but were all of them repulsed. In like manner several attempts of the Prussians to debouch from the wood failed, on account of the severe fire of the Bavarian Artillery.

Whilst this severe Infantry fight was going on on both wings of General Flies's Division, the action in the centre of the line was confined to a cannonade between the batteries on both sides. The Bavarian Artillery at the post-house had hitherto prevented any advance being made from Uettingen in the valley of the Aalbach, but gave up its position at about 6 o'clock, whereupon both Prussian rifled batteries passed through the village and took up a position to the north of it, where the 3rd 12-pounder Battery had already been engaged some time before. About 7 o'clock the 4th 4-pounder Battery arrived at the same spot from Helmstadt, and a very brisk cannonade again commenced.

At the same time the three remaining battalions assumed the offensive. The Fusileer Battalion of the 59th Regiment (followed first by the 1st Battalion of the same, and then by the Fusileers of the 11th Regiment) crossed the meadows and the Aalbach, and advanced against the northern face of the Leite hill. They drove back the last detachments of the enemy that still lingered there. Whilst assistance was thus afforded to the left wing of the 36th Regiment, the troops of General Beyer pressed forward on the right wing. As soon as the latter heard the heavy firing of the action at Uettingen early in the morning, he speedily turned out his division, and started to join and assist General Flies's troops. The 20th Regiment, which had bivouacked during the night in the Uettingen-Gemeinde-Wald, and General Woyna's detachment at the Heergrund-Wald, were sent in the direction of Rossbrunn. All other troops, and three squadrons and a battery of General Flies's Division, which had arrived during the night, were pushed forward to the heights eastward of the Gemeinde-Wald, so as to have them at hand for any contingency. By the time they reached this spot the Leite had just been stormed by the 36th Regiment. This regiment, which had suffered so severely, was withdrawn from the action about 8 o'clock.

General Beyer sent Colonel Woyna, who had reached Platten, against Mädelhofen, the 20th Regiment more to the left, and followed the latter with his main body and reserves.

Batteries Wasserfuhr and Schmidt took up positions on the Vogelberg and at Platten.

The Bavarians had already commenced their retreat. First, Division Hartmann retreated in the direction of Hettstadt, whilst the Reserve Infantry Brigade deployed on the heights between Greusenheim and Rossbrunn, behind the Mühlbach. The brigade of General Feder's division, which had fought at the Leite and the Vogelberg, then followed and fell back on the 2nd Brigade of the division at the Himmelreich-Wald. Five batteries were in position on the open plateau between this wood and Greusenheim.

About 8 o'clock both wings and the centre of the Prussians advanced almost simultaneously against the position of the enemy behind the Mühl-Bach and the Pfatzer-Bach.

On the extreme left the troops on the Hessnert, which had been re-formed, in the meantime advanced on Greusenheim, headed by the 2nd Battalion of the 59th Regiment, in column of companies. The Bavarian Reserve Brigade did not offer much resistance, but soon by degrees evacuated the high copses, the vineyards, and Greusenheim, and followed General Hartmann's division to Hettstadt. The Prussian detachment halted in the low ground south-eastward of Greusenheim, where it was joined by the two squadrons of the 5th Dragoons.

As soon as the battalions of the Prussian centre had been re-formed under cover of the Leite wood, they advanced against Rossbrunn, and took possession of the village, the post-house, and the heights to the north of it. The 9th Rifle Battalion, which had been brought up from the Reserve to the left wing of the main body, took part in this attack. The resistance of the enemy's Infantry at this point was also but slight, and the Artillery, which had severely shelled the attacking columns at a long range, fell back likewise on Hettstadt as they drew nearer. General Flies' reserves were brought up to the Rossbrunn post-house.

On the right wing, lastly, the 20th Regiment descended from the Brunschlag into the Pfatzer-Bach Valley. At the same time Colonel Woyna led his detachment against Mädel-hofen. The 2nd Battalion of the 30th and the 1st of the 70th Regiments carried the village at the first onset, and the enemy retreated to the Himmelreich-Wald. After the wood had been for some time shelled, the detachments of Colonel Woyna, General Flies, and the 20th Regiment entered it together at three different points, drove the enemy out, and occupied the skirts on the further side. The enemy's artillery, which was drawn up in great force near Hettstadt, prevented any further advance at this point. The 3rd 4-pounder battery Blottnitz tried to hold a position on the heights to the north of the Himmel-reich-Wald, but was forced to give up the attempt.

The Prussian Infantry now established itself in the position it had conquered, the fire of the enemy's artillery gradually ceased, and the action along the front of the line was at an end, but a sharp Cavalry fight took place between 11 and 12 o'clock beyond Hettstadt.

Colonel Krug Von Nidda had assembled three squadrons of the 6th Dragoons, two of the 10th Landwehr Hussars, one of the 9th Hussars, and the 4th Horse Artillery Battery (König) near Uettingen, and advanced against the enemy's right flank by way of Greusenheim, where he was joined by the two squadrons of the 5th Dragoons, under the command of Major Von Westphal.

This combined brigade had taken up a position about one mile from Hettstadt, where a small dell hid it from the enemy's sight, and protected it from his fire. Two hostile batteries of 12 guns each were seen near the Hettstädt farm-houses, fronting to the north-west, and supported by the bulk of the Bavarian Cavalry, which Prince Charles had posted behind these batteries to cover his extreme right flank. The enemy's skir-mishers were driven back, but had discovered the presence of their adversaries. A heavy fire was very soon opened in this direc-tion, but produced but little effect, as all the shells flew too high. Hereupon the 6th Chevauxlegers Regiment advanced towards the heights which sheltered the Prussian Cavalry, and charged with the two flank squadrons. Colonel Von Krug sent forward the 2nd Squadron of the 6th Dragoons and the 3rd Squadron of the 10th Landwehr Hussars to meet them. The Prussian squadrons overthrew the Chevauxlegers, but got into the fire of the enemy's artillery, and were obliged to fall back again. The two centre squadrons of the Chevauxlegers advanced to the charge. They were also driven back by the two remaining squadrons of Prussian Hussars, but a whole brigade of Bavarian Cuirassiers then advanced to cover their retreat. The two Dragoon squadrons that had not yet been engaged charged the right flank, and such of the other squadrons as had had time to re-form the front of the Cuirassiers, but the numbers of the latter were too overwhelming. The mass of pursuers and pursued rolled back in a sharp running hand-to-hand fight in the direction of Captain König's battery. Not being able to engage the enemy's rifled guns by reason of the distance, the latter had hitherto remained behind the Cavalry, and now hastily unlimbered. The commander of the battery feeling the danger of being surrounded by the overwhelming force of the enemy's Cavalry, sent back his limbers and teams to take shelter in a neighbouring wood, and then turning his guns in different directions received the Cuirassiers, who were advancing from several sides, with such a hail of grape-shot at a very close range that their career was checked. At the same moment Major Westphal's two squadrons of the 5th Dragoons threw themselves with the utmost vehemence upon the enemy's line. The men of the other Prussian squadrons, again facing to the front and joining in the charge, the hostile brigade was compelled to retreat.

The pursuit very soon again brought the Prussian Cavalry within range of the enemy's batteries, besides which, a fresh brigade of Bavarian Cavalry, consisting of a Cuirassier and a Lancer Regiment, appeared on Colonel Krug's left flank, and forced him to fall back on his battery, which had in the meantime taken up a position further to the rear.

The Bavarian Cuirassier Regiment, followed by the Lancers as support, now advanced against the battery, but were repulsed by a discharge of grape.

Colonel Krug drew his squadrons out of range of his opponents' artillery, and re-formed them; being much too weak seriously to harrass the enemy's retreat, he then re-joined General Flies' main body. We have already heard that the latter had already dislodged the Bavarians from their position near Rossbrunn by 10 o'clock.

The VIIIth Federal Corps had been assembled on the Nicolaus Berg and the Hexen Berg* as early as 4 A.M. The reserves, however, then immediately retreated to the other bank of the Maine, and the other detachments of the corps soon followed, some through Würzburg and some by way of Heidingsfeld. The

---

* Two hills westward of Würzburg, close to the town.

Austrian-Nassau division bivouacked near the latter place, the Würtemberg division at Gerbrunn, the remainder of the corps at Rottendorf, Prince Alexander's head-quarters were at Würzburg.

Thus the Bavarian Corps was now alone on the left bank, with the defiles of the Maine immediately in its rear. A renewed attack on the part of the Prussian main forces would necessarily have forced it to a struggle for life and death.

The political situation of affairs showed no reason for bringing on so desperate a combat. The only object henceforth was to occupy as much territory of the allies as possible, in order to facilitate peace negotiations with them, and manœuvring against the enemy's left flank, would oblige him to retreat without any hard struggle.

The retreat of the VIIIth Corps behind the Maine was not known at Prussian head-quarters. General Goeben's division was still at Gerchsheim, the ammunition of the army far spent, and the troops were excessively fatigued.

In the course of the afternoon Division Flies took up its bivouac at Rossbrunn, Division Beyer at Mädelhofen. Outposts were placed in front of Hettstadt and Waldbrunn, and communications opened with General Goeben's division by means of patrols.

By 1 P.M. the Bavarian Army had carried out its intended concentration on the plateau of Waldbüttelbrunn. Scarcely, however, was this position taken up according to Prince Charles's disposition, when its evacuation and the further retreat of the army commenced.

Bridges were thrown over the Maine at Veitshöchheim and Mittel-Zell, and Divisions Stephan and Hartmann, taking advantage of the pause which had ensued in the action, crossed the river partly over them and partly through Würzburg, and retreated, the former to Gerbrunn, the latter to Versbach. One brigade of General Feder's division still held Veitshöchheim, the other marched to Rottendorf. The Reserve Cavalry and Artillery, Prince Luitpold's division, and Prince Charles's head-quarters likewise proceeded to the latter place, the Reserve Infantry Brigade to Dürrbach.

For the first time in the course of the campaign the allied forces were now assembled behind a strong position, ready for immediate action.

The Prussian losses on the 26th of June amounted to—

|  | Officers. | Men. |
|---|---|---|
| Killed .. .. .. .. | 4 | 97 |
| Wounded .. .. .. | 35 | 680 |
| Missing .. .. .. .. | .. | 40 |
| Total .. .. | 39 | 817 |

all of whom, with the exception of six officers and about 100 men, belonged to General Flies' division.

The share of these losses which was borne by the 36th Regiment alone amounted to 22 officers, 436 men.

The Bavarians lost in the two actions of Helmstadt and Rossbrunn :—

|  | Officers. | Men. |
|---|---|---|
| Killed .. .. .. .. | 22 | 110 |
| Wounded .. .. .. | 47 | 898 |
| Missing and prisoners .. .. | 6 | 507 |
| Total .. .. | 75 | 1,515* |

About half the missing may be counted as killed or wounded, for in both actions together only about 200 men were taken prisoners by the Prussians without wounds.

Early on the 27th the Prussians advanced on Würzburg, 27th July. viz., Division Flies to the Hettstädter Höfe, Division Beyer to Waldbüttelbrunn, Division Goeben to Höchberg. The latter covered the right flank by sending a detachment of two battalions, two squadrons, and two guns, under Colonel Stoltz, by way of Reichenberg, towards Heidingsfeld.

---

## ARTILLERY COMBAT NEAR WÜRZBURG ON THE 27TH OF JULY.

The advanced guard of General Goeben's division, Brigade Kummer, found Höchberg unoccupied by the enemy, but was fired upon by heavy artillery from the Marienberg on advancing still further. General Von Kummer threw forward skirmishers on the Hexenberg and the northern slope of the Nicolausberg, and drew up his brigade in a position north-eastward of Höchberg, where it was sheltered from the enemy's fire; General Wrangel's brigade deployed on the Nicolausberg, to the right of the former, in an equally sheltered position; Brigade Weltzein remained in reserve further to the rear. Some trifling detachments of the enemy that were stationed here and there outside the fortress fell back to the Marienberg without fighting as the Prussian skirmishers advanced. Before doing so they fired the powder-magazine on the Hexenberg, after having previously removed its contents.

Detachments of Brigades Kummer and Wrangel took possession of this point and of an unfinished work on the Nicolausberg.

A reconnaissance proved the Marienberg and the entrench-

---

* If we deduct the losses at Helmstadt, as stated in the note to page 76, we find the Bavarian loss at Rossbrunn to have been 39 officers, 821 men.

ments leading from thence to the Maine on the north to be armed with a considerable quantity of heavy artillery. Although fired upon from the fortress whenever the men came either within range or even within sight, the Prussian Infantry managed to take up its positions without much loss, as the undulations of the ground afforded much shelter. Considerable bodies of troops were seen on the works of the Marienberg and on the walls and upon open places of the town, more particularly beyond the latter. Entrenchments for field batteries were visible on the heights on the right bank of the Maine.

The fire from the citadel continued without intermission and induced General Goeben to bring up his Artillery about eleven o'clock, in order to demonstrate against the fortress. The 3rd 6-pounder and 4th 4-pounder batteries unlimbered on the south-east face of the Hexenberg, the 3rd 4-pounder and the Oldenburg 6-pounder batteries on the north-west slope of the Nicolausberg—1,600 to 1,800 paces from the works of the place. They opened fire simultaneously between 12 and 1 o'clock.

As soon as they came into action, the enemy increased his fire from Marienberg by that of the artillery in the entrenchments on the other side of the river, where two Austrian, one Nassau, and one Würtemberg rifled battery commenced a sharp and partly flanking fire on the Prussian Artillery.

The latter was, however, very advantageously posted and sheltered by the nature of the ground, besides which, the distance from the last-named batteries ranging between 3,500 and 5,000 paces, their fire had but little effect. On the other hand, however, the guns on the Marienberg were scarcely visible and partly placed in casemates, so that little advantage was to be expected by firing on them. General Goeben therefore ordered his batteries to bring their fire to bear more on the buildings, and especially on the arsenal of the citadel. The Oldenburg 12-pounder battery was also brought up to the Nicolausberg, and in about a quarter of an hour the arsenal was in flames. The latter battery was then withdrawn, as it could not find sufficient shelter.

General Manteuffel rode in the meantime with a squadron of Hussars to the plateau in front of Ober-Zell to reconnoitre the enemy's position. Some shots were, fired on his suite from the town, and a Bavarian battery at the ruin of "Schenkenschloss" opened a very severe fire, which was by degrees extended to the very utmost range of its guns. As a cannonade would have produced no result, General Manteuffel did not allow this fire to be returned, and sent orders to General Goeben to cease firing on the fortress likewise. By degrees the batteries were withdrawn, and the troops went into bivouac—Division Flies at Hettstadt, Division Beyer at Waldbüttelbrünn, Division Goeben at Höchberg; head-quarters were established at Eisingen. The fire which the enemy kept up on the outposts from the Marienberg until the evening was not returned.

His Royal Highness the Grand Duke of Oldenburg, who had

joined the army the day before, was present with his batteries during the action.

The losses of General Goeben's Division were 5 men killed, 2 officers and 17 men wounded, in addition to which 1 officer of General Manteuffel's suit was mortally wounded and 2 horses killed. •

The Bavarian losses are not known.

During the advance of the Prussians, part of the troops of the Federal Army were stationed along the Maine, so as to be in readiness to dispute the passage of the river in case it should be attempted. The Prince of Bavaria must, however, very soon have become convinced that it was by no means General Manteuffel's intention to force the passage of the river at so unfavourable a spot.

The Federal Army and the Prussian Army, both with their whole force, were here opposed to each other in almost impregnable positions. That of General Manteuffel, however, completely intercepted the communications of the Allies with the territories of Hesse, Baden, and Würtemberg, and even endangered their communication with Bavaria, at a moment when the Prussian 2nd Reserve Corps was already menacing Bayreuth in rear of the Wurzburg position. The formation of this corps (*Vide* Appendix No. II.) had only been decreed by an order of the King, of the 3rd of July. It had not yet attained its full complement of 25,000 men, because some detachments, such as the Landwehr Cavalry, some batteries and the intendance, the mobilization of which was not decreed until the 8th and 14th of the month, had not joined the corps, the latter having commenced its operations with the first available troops without any loss of time.

His Royal Highness the Grand Duke of Mecklenburg, who was entrusted with the command of this corps, arrived at Leipzig on the 18th, and the Prussian-Mecklenburg troops commenced operations on the 20th. They advanced by the Werdau and Zwickau roads and were joined at Altenburg by the two battalions of this duchy. The Leipzig-Hof Railway having been speedily repaired, the advanced guard of the corps— Fusileer battalion of the 4th Guard Regiment, one company of Rifles, one squadron and two guns—were sent on by rail, and reached Plauen on the 22nd, from whence a night march brought it early on the 23rd to Hof. At this place it surprised two Bavarian companies, took an outpost detachment of 65 men prisoners, and fired some shells at a railway train that was just leaving with troops and stores.

The next day the Bavarians were dislodged from Müncheberg also, and on the 27th the 2nd Company of Mecklenburg Rifles appeared unexpectedly before Culmbach. The garrison of the Plassenburg was disarmed and this strong post occupied, which protected the Bayreuth Railway against any attempt to destroy it that might be made from Bamberg. The main body of the Reserve Corps reached Hof on the 27th.

The position of the Bavarian Army at Würzburg had now become untenable; it could only extricate itself from its present situation either by assuming the offensive against the Prussian Army—which was scarcely possible at this point—or by a retrograde movement up the Maine, so as to face the army to the north and re-establish its basis on the Bavarian territory in its rear.

For the latter purpose the Baden Division started for Ochsenfurt on the 27th to secure this important passage over the Maine, whilst Bavarian detachments occupied Kitzingen. The same evening a flag of truce brought a letter from Field-marshal Prince Charles to General Manteuffel at Eisingen, in which the former in the first place laid stress on Würzburg, being an open town, and demanded in the name of international right that it should be spared in case hostilities recommenced. This was followed by the communication of a despatch sent by the Bavarian Minister Von der Pfordten to Prince Charles stating that an armistice had been signed by Austria and Prussia, and that hostilities had ceased between these two Powers. The despatch stated at the same time that a similar treaty was to be expected between Prussia and Bavaria. Prince Charles, in consequence, repeated the request for a week's suspension of hostilities which he had already made on the 14th. This flag of truce was soon followed by a second one, producing despatches which had arrived from His Majesty the King of Bavaria and his Government. They stated that an armistice had been concluded with Bavaria also, and that it was already stipulated that hostilities should cease until it became valid.

These statements, not having been communicated to him by his own Government, could not of course have any weight with General Manteuffel; nevertheless, taking into consideration the peculiar nature of the situation, he thought it right to enter into preliminary negotiations on the subject. In the answer he returned on the evening of the 27th, he pointed out that it had been evident that the fire of his batteries had only been directed against the fortress Marienberg, which was occupied and defended by the enemy, besides which a town, the immediate neighbourhood of which was entrenched and crowned with batteries, must be considered as a military occupied position, and could not therefore be spared the unavoidable consequences of war. Würzburg would be saved by surrendering the town, and, if this basis of negotiations were agreed to, the Commanding General would be willing to treat for a week's truce. An answer was requested by 7 A.M. next morning.

In order, if necessary, to give greater force to these negotiations, orders were issued the same evening to throw up entrenched batteries for the Artillery, and that all three divisions should be ready for action in their bivouacs by daybreak the next morning.

28th July The moment fixed for receiving the answer had not arrived when Lieut.-General Von der Tann, Chief of the Bavarian

Staff, appeared in Eisingen early in the morning for the purpose of further conference. In the course of the morning he returned to the Bavarian Head-Quarters, accompanied by Colonel Von Kraatz-Koschlau, Chief of the Prussian Staff. The conferences that were then held at the Bavarian Head-Quarters proceeded very rapidly at first, and in a manner favourable to the Prussian demands, for Prince Charles expressed himself willing to surrender Würzburg, with the exception of the fortress Marienberg, if his Sovereign should give his assent, which was to be requested by telegram. In this case Marienberg was to be declared neutral. A written treaty to this effect was already drawn up when Prince Charles received a telegram containing the positive assurance not only that an armistice had been signed with Bavaria at Nikolsburg, but also that hostilities were to be suspended until the 2nd of August.

This assertion was not founded on fact. Hostilities were suspended between the Prussian and the Austrian-Saxon armies, and were, as a matter of course, to remain so until the impending armistice commenced. At the Maine, on the other hand, the state of war still prevailed to its full extent; nor was it in the least intended to make any alteration in this state of affairs by suspending hostilities.

The telegram forwarded by the Bavarian Minister was accompanied by a cypher despatch for General Manteuffel, which was to be sent on to the Prussian Head-Quarters. Prince Charles did not doubt but what this despatch contained the official Prussian ratification of an armistice, and was, in consequence, no longer inclined to make any concessions whatever; he therefore broke off the negotiation for evacuating Würzburg.

Colonel Kraatz returned with the above-mentioned cypher despatch, which could only be deciphered at the Prussian Head-Quarters.

This telegram was dated July 28th, 5.40 a.m., and contained the following:—

> "Peace preliminaries with Austria signed on the "24th. Truce with Bavaria agreed to; to commence on "the 2nd August. Telegram by way of Berlin, and "courier *en route* since yesterday.
>
> (Signed) "VON MOLTKE."

Although the above did not contain any mention of a truce previous to the 2nd August, General Manteuffel still felt himself bound to await the promised written orders before taking any further measures. He sent off a cypher telegram explaining his position, and requesting information regarding the truce, which telegram was forwarded by the Bavarian Head-Quarters in order to save time. It was settled with the Bavarian Commanding General that both parties should abstain from hostilities until further news arrived, and the work at the entrenched batteries was suspended. A warning of twenty-four hours was to be given on either side before hostilities were recommenced.

2 I

As bad weather had set in, both Commanding Generals sent their troops into close cantonments on the 29th, which they covered by a slight line of outposts. An attempt was also made to fix a line of demarcation for the cantonments of both armies, but no definite agreement was made, in spite of much parleying on both sides.

Bavarian Head-Quarters had been already moved to Kitzingen on the 28th; those of the Prussian Army went on the 29th to Marktheidenfeld, in order to be nearer to railway and telegraphic communication.

The region in which the Prussian troops were quartered was bounded as follows:—

The quarters of General Flies's Division by the villages Zellingen, Holzkirchen, Zell, and by the Maine.

Those of General Beyer's Division by Waldbüttelbrünn, Mädelhofen, Helmstadt, Neubronn, Steinbach, Kist.

Those of General Goeben's Division by Heidingsfeld, Hochberg, Gross-Rinderfeld, Winterhausen, and the Maine.

The Bavarian Army, which had been previously *écheloned* on the line Veitshöchheim-Würsburg-Rottendorf, now spread out its cantonments along the Maine, northward as far as Karlstadt, and south-eastward to Kitzingen.

The VIIIth Federal Corps left only the Austrian-Nassau Division on the right bank of the Maine at Eibelstadt, and moved the remainder of the corps to the left bank to the rayon Gossmannsdorf-Euerhausen-Martinsheim-Marktbreit.

Whilst Prussian Head-Quarters were still at Eisingen, flags of truce had been already sent thither by the Würtemberg, Hessian, and Nassau contingents, demanding a cessation of hostilities in the names of their respective Governments. General Manteuffel not having received any instructions on this subject, simply refused their demands, without entering into any discussion whatever.

Telegraphic communication between Moravia and the Army of the Maine was at this period very slow and uncertain, as it had to pass over Berlin, and the Head-Quarters of the Army were often moved. Soon after reaching Marletheidenfeld, General Manteuffel received a telegram from General Moltke, but it was dated on the 26th, and was therefore of earlier date than that which had arrived the day before. It contained the news that a truce had been signed with Austria and Saxony for four and with Bavaria for three weeks, to commence on the 2nd August, and authorised General Manteuffel to grant similar conditions to Baden, Würtemberg, and Darmstadt, if asked for by them, but not to the North German States. It was then added that it was advisable to occupy as much territory as possible for the purpose of facilitating future negotiations on the *statu quo* basis, but that this was, if possible, to be effected without any great action. Another telegram which arrived in the course of the forenoon of the 30th brought more precise orders, stating that Würtemberg territory was also to be occupied.

In neither of these despatches was any mention made of a cessation of hostilities previous to the 2nd August.

In expectation of the repeatedly announced written despatches, the negotiations respecting a line of demarcation were concluded the same evening at Kitzingen, and General Manteuffel improved the occasion to gain possession of the Heidingsfeld-Giebelstadt-Mergentheim road, which was granted without any difficulty. This road was important for the purpose of entering Würtemberg.

The line of demarcation was drawn from the Würtemberg frontier eastward of Stalldorf, Sächsenheim, and Wolkshausen to Gossmannsdorf on the Maine, and then followed the course of this river to Gemünden, leaving the rayon of the fortress Marienberg on the left bank in the hands of the Bavarians. Beyond Gemünden the rivers Sinn and Saale formed the boundaries on either side, the district between both rivers remaining neutral. Besides this, the Convention permitted the Prussian Army to make use of the stations of Gemünden and Karlstadt on the Frankfort-Würzburg Railway, in order to facilitating the provisioning of the troops.

It was repeatedly pointed out on the Prussian part, that all these negotiations respecting an armistice only bore reference to the Bavarian Army, and not to the other hostile contingents. Hostilities against the latter only ceased *de facto*, and not by virtue of any treaty; they could therefore be resumed at any moment without further warning. Although the Prussian Commander-in-Chief was now authorised to treat with these contingents also, still as yet none of them had made any fresh overtures. In order, therefore, to avoid useless provocation or conflicts with General Goeben's Division, which was immediately in front of these contingents, it was settled that the troops of the VIIIth Federal Corps should be withdrawn, and only Bavarian troops stationed along the whole line of demarcation in front of the Prussian outposts.

Whilst on the Lower Maine a *de facto* truce thus now prevailed, the Prussian Reserve Corps still continued its advance on the Upper Maine, in spite of repeated protests founded on the pretence of an existing armistice. After having, as we have already heard, reached Hof with its main-body, the advanced guard of the corps occupied Schorgast and Berneck on the 28th, where intelligence arrived at noon of the same day that General Von Fuchs was advancing from Regensburg, and had reached Kemnast and Weiden.

A Bavarian flag of truce again claimed an armistice, and stated that the Bavarians intended occupying Beyreuth. To prevent this a company of Fusiliers in country carts, accompanied by a squadron of Dragoons, was sent from Berneck to Bayreuth, under command of Major Von Loos.

This detachment reached the south entrance of the town at 3 P.M. at the same time that Bavarian Infantry, which had been conveyed thither from Kemnat per rail, arrived there. The

Bavarian officer protested against the Prussians occupying the town, as a breach of international law, and it was agreed to defer hostilities until the decision of the Grand Duke could be obtained. In the meantime reinforcements arrived, and at 9 P.M. notice was given that the momentary truce was at an end, whereupon Captain Von Zülow advanced at 10 P.M. against the Bavarians, who were stationed between Conneisreuth and Colmdorf.

The 1st Mecklenburg Rifle Company, followed by three companies of the 4th Guards, skirmished with the Bavarians in the moonlight until 1 A.M., when the latter slowly retreated.

Early on the 29th the advanced guard marched on the road to Creussen to reconnoitre, leaving five companies as garrison in Beyreuth. Intelligence coming in that the enemy was seen at Seubottenreut, Colonel Von Lützow started off with two Dragoon squadrons in this directions, after giving orders to the 11th Company of the 4th Guards to follow as quickly as possible.

A Bavarian battalion which, as it seems, was marching to Creussen evacuated Seubottenreut on the approach of the Cavalry, and fell back northward towards the Doberschütz moor, whilst its advanced guard endeavoured to retreat southward by way of the Pötzel mill to the "Birkenwald." Captain Von Boddien passed this defile in spite of the fire of the Bavarian skirmishers which lined its bushy banks, rode down a company that had formed square, and took it prisoner.

Whilst the Dragoons and the 11th Company were returning to the main-body of the advanced guard at Lehen they were fired on by the Bavarian battalion, which now began to advance again from the Doberschütz moor. When the latter crossed the high-road the 11th Company opened fire on its left flank, and the Dragoons charged and rode down its skirmishers, whereupon the battalion retreated to a railway cutting. On the other side the 10th and 12th Companies of the 4th Guard Regiment now came up, and two guns opened upon the Bavarian battalion, which defended itself obstinately in the deep cutting, and then, after suffering much loss, tried to make good its retreat to Weiden, but being met there by Captain Von Zülow with the 1st Rifle Company, 4 officers and 210 men were taken prisoners. The two Dragoon squadrons had lost 1 officer and 14 men wounded, 17 horses killed, and 27 wounded.

At midday the troops went into cantonments at Lehen and Stockau in a pouring rain. The main-body of the corps and the Grand Duke's Head-Quarters reached Bayreuth. Intelligence was received here of the successful actions of the Army of the Maine, and of the retreat of the Federal Army behind the Maine at Würzburg. The Grand Duke decided, in consequence of this news, to march on Nürnberg—a movement which he commenced on the 30th.

On this day the first step was taken towards the breaking up of the VIIIth Federal Corps. In the course of the forenoon a flag of true arrived at the Prussian Head-Quarters at Markt-heidenfeld with a letter from Prince William of Baden, stating that direct negotiations, which His Royal Highness the Grand Duke of Baden had entered into with His Majesty the King of Prussia, had resulted in the latter granting permission to the Baden troops to return unmolested to their homes; that, in consequence, these troops would quit the VIIIth Federal Corps the same day, and would commence their march to the Baden territory immediately in three *échelons*, by way of Ochsenfurt, Giebelatadt Graubüttelbrünn, and Wittighausen, ·and that the first *échelon* had already started.

General Manteuffel had not received any instructions on this subject, nevertheless, in consideration of the peculiarity of existing circumstances, he sanctioned the march of the Baden troops, under the condition that they kept to a route prescribed by him, viz., Berolsheim-Schefflenz-Sinsheim-Bruchsal, and that, pending further arrangements, no Baden troops should be stationed northward of Carlsruhe.

At the same time that the above-mentioned line of demarcation was settled at Kitzingen on the evening of the 30th, a cypher telegram from General Moltke arrived at Marktheiden-feld in answer to General Manteuffel's inquiry of the 28th. It contained the words, "Full freedom of action until the 2nd August."

The Prussian Army was thus again placed in the same position it was in when the evacuation of Würzburg was demanded on the 28th—a demand which would in all probability have been acceded to had it not been that Minister Von der Pfordten's despatch of contrary purport had·induced Prince Charles of Bavaria to break off the negotiations. General Manteuffel now determined to renew his original demand immediately, and despatched his Chief of the Staff to the Bavarian Head-Quarters the same evening.

General Manteuffel returned to Eisingen early on the 31st, 31st July. and issued orders to the troops to take up their former positions in front of Würzburg by 5 A.M. of the 1st August. A small detachment of General Flies's Division was sent to Lohr to protect the railway and telegraphic communication. There was then still twenty-four hours' time for further action.

Colonel Von Kraatz reached Kitzingen by 3 A.M. of the 31st, and gave notice that the armistice would cease at 6 A.M. of the 1st August, but that General Manteuffel would agree to prolong it if Würzburg were surrendered to him under the conditions which had been formerly stipulated. Prince Charles did not consider himself authorized to decide this question, but promised to apply to Munich immediately, and to send an answer to Eisingen by midday. This answer arrived in due time, and was favourable to the Prussian demands, so that a final arrangement was agreed to in the course of the 31st. The Marienberg and the Maine quarter of the town were declared neutral, but the town itself was to be evacuated by the Bavarians early on the 2nd August, and to be occupied by Prussian troops as long as the armistice lasted.

Hitherto it had been necessary to keep the Army well concentrated, in readiness for any eventualities, but on the evening of the 30th General Manteuffel had already sent orders to the Commandant of Frankfort to send part of the troops stationed there southward as expeditiously as possible, so as to occupy Darmstadt, Heidelburg, and Mannheim, by the evening of the 1st August. These troops were to be replaced in Frankfort by two battalions of General Flies's Division, which were sent thither in forced marches by way of Heidenfeld and Aschaffenburg. This could now be safely done, as two battalions and two squadrons of the Hamburg contingent, and one battalion of the Lubeck contingent, had joined the Army since hostilities had ceased. On the 31st General Goeben was ordered to start with his division in the direction of Mergentheim, and to occupy Wurtemburg territory; he was to effect this by forced marches and with the help of country carts. All other troops were sent back to their former cantonments.

1st August. On the 1st August the Grand Duke of Mecklenburg entered Nürnberg with the Reserve Corps, and hoisted the Prussian flag on the old castle of the Hohenzollers. His advanced guard had arrived the day before, after encountering a small hostile detachment at Eschenau, where 4 officers and 164 men of the 12th Bavarian regiment surrendered to a detachment of Dragoons. The Bavarian garrison of Nurnberg had left a short time before, and the Landwehr that was left to mount guard in the town laid down its arms.

In 12 days the Reserve Corps had marched 180 miles. During its march it had by degrees attained nearly its full complement, and, thanks to the circumspection and activity of its Intendant Engelhardt, was provided with all branches of the administration, hospitals, &c. A park of 300 wagons and a Mecklenburg provision train had afforded the means of providing the corps with the necessary supplies, in spite of its rapid march through a poor and mountainous district.

Now that Nürnberg, Erlangen, Fürth, and Schwabach were in his hands, the Grand Duke agreed to an armistice, the more so as a truce with Bavaria was to commence on the 2nd August, and General Manteuffel had granted a three weeks' armistice, commencing on the same day, to Würtemberg and Hesse-Darmstadt also. In the treaty with Würtemberg a clause was inserted that this Power was to evacuate the Hohenzoller Principalities immediately.

2nd August. On the 2nd August General Manteuffel entered Würzburg. The line of demarcation during the term of the armistice corresponded in the main with that settled on the 30th July, with the addition, in favour of the Prussians, of a rayon of about $2\frac{1}{2}$ miles round about Würzburg, and free use of the railway as far as this town.

All necessary arrangements for the Reserve Corps were

settled between Colonel Veith, Chief of the Staff of this Corps, and the Bavarian General Von Hartmann.

The terms of the truces granted by General Manteuffel and the Grand Duke are given in Appendix No. IV.

According to these conventions, a line drawn from the frontier of Bohemia to the Rhine, and passing by Amberg, Hall, and Mannheim, marked the boundary of that part of South Germany which was occupied by the Prussian troops.

All troops received the acknowledgments of their services from their respective Sovereigns. The King expressed his especial thanks to the Grand Duke of Mecklenburg for those of the IInd Reserve Corps.

The following orders which His Majesty had issued some time before, but which only now reached the Army of the Maine per telegram, were published to the Army by General Manteuffel as a reward for its services :—

> " I commission you to express to the troops of the
> " Army of the Maine my full satisfaction with the
> " bravery and devotion they have shown. I give my
> " royal thanks to all Generals, officers, and men. The
> " troops of the Army in Bohemia, Moravia, and Austria
> " join with me in sending a comrade's greeting and
> " congratulations to their Prussian and German comrades
> " of the Army of the Maine.
>
> (Signed)     " WILHELM."

If we look back to the commencement of this campaign, we find on the western theatre of war, as well as on the eastern, the Prussian forces assembled in three distinct groups at Wetzlar, Minden, and Hamburg, on a line of 225 miles. Their junction could only be effected by operations against the enemy. In contrast to the compact unity of the Austrian Army in the East, we find in the West the contingents of eight Sovereign States spread over the district between the Leine and the Danube, all more or less in a state of unreadiness, their sole bond of union being their hostility to Prussia. Neither one of them was alone able to resist this Power, and yet only the direst need induced them so far to forget their own particular interests that six of them were united towards the end of the campaign. It thus became possible for the Prussian Army to assume the offensive with 47,000 men against 100,000, and to advance from the Elbe to the Iaxt (340 miles) in 47 days.

The mere passage of the Army through Electoral Hesse suffices for the occupation of this country ; the cadres of its contingent, not being yet assembled, save themselves by retreating beyond the Maine. The Hanoverian Army, on the other hand, succeeds in assembling at Göttingen, ready to take the field. At that moment, in the direction of South Germany, there was only one Prussian Division on the flank of the Hanoverian Army, and nothing but a few slight detachments on its direct line of march through Thüringer Wald,

However, through its irresolute wavering, the Hanoverian leaders let slip this opportunity of forcing their way through. On the other hand, the undecided marches and countermarches of their adversaries made it difficult for the Prussians to find and surround their foe, and yet it was of the utmost importance to disarm this enemy in their rear before turning to meet the other enemy in their front. The most unwelcome contingency would have been if the Hanoverian Army had turned back to its own territory, as this would have compelled the Prussians to follow it in a direction contrary to the line of operations against South Germany.

It was therefore strategically correct that General Flies, with his 8,000 men, attacked an enemy 20,000 strong at Langensalza, as he thereby brought the latter to a stand at a moment whem overwhelming forces were coming up on all sides, and thus caused the capitulation. Painful as the loss was which this action cost, still the two foes had met in a well-fought strife, and the mutual respect which this produced formed the best foundation for their future reconciliation.

Two days after the action we find the Prussian divisions advancing against the South Germans, who were about twice their number, and had appointed to meet at Hersfeld.

It is true, the further forward the Allies united their forces, the more effectually would they afford protection to the territories and promote the interests of all concerned, which was the best method of securing unity of action. This plan of operations, however, did not take into consideration the celerity with which General Falkenstein was wont to conduct his movements. Moreover, Prince Charles of Bavaria had already advanced in the direction of the Thüringer Wald with the intention of coming to the assistance of the Hanoverians, whilst the contingents of Prince Alexander of Hesse's Corps were still assembling at the Maine. This had increased the distance between the VIIth and VIIIth Corps.

During its flank march to the appointed rendezvous, the Bavarian Army meets the heads of the Prussian Army. This produces the unsuccessful engagement at Dermbach and the panic of the Bavarian Cavalry. Being thus compelled to renounce the idea of forcibly effecting the junction of both corps towards his front, the Field Marshal now seeks to unite them further to the rear. The Prussian Army does not follow him, but pushes in between both corps on the Fulda road.

When the overwhelming news of the Austrian disaster at Königgrätz arrives, the separate interests of each allied State again prevail, and, instead of marching to join its ally on the Sinn, the VIIIth Corps retreats to the Maine, in order to cover its own special territories. This exposes the flank of the VIIIth Corps during its march to Poppenhausen, which, however, would not have been the case had this march not been executed so slowly. By means of a cleverly arranged march General Falkenstein concentrates his whole force at Brücknau, and on the 10th July wrests from his adversary all those defiles of the Franconian Saale which should have afforded protection to the Bavarian Corps during its concentration. On the 17th, after an excentric retreat, Prince Charles takes up a position in front of the whole Prussian Army with little more than half of his troops, and with the Maine immediately in his rear.

In the meantime, however, politics prevailed over military considerations with the Prussian Army also. Although the mere advance of the latter to the Maine would have compelled the enemy to evacuate Upper Hesse, Nassau, Frankfort, and part of Bavaria, still, as the general fate of the war was now decided, and peace conferences on the *uti possedetis* basis might very soon be expected, actual military occupation of these districts was deemed advisable. The march on Schweinfurt is therefore relinquished, and the Army moves towards Frankfort.

The failures which had hitherto attended their undertakings have proved to the Allies how absolutely necessary it is to unite their whole force if they wish to hold their ground against the enemy. The point of concentration which they had originally sought towards Thüringen is now laid 90 miles further southward in Central Franconia, but even now it is not proposed to effect this concentration by the mutual approach of both corps to each other, but by bringing up the VIIIth Corps to join the VIIth.

Prince Alexander, perceiving that the only way to cover his difficult flank march is by retaining the command of the Maine from Hanau to Miltenberg, pushes a detachment forward on the important Spessart road. General Goeben is, however, already approaching on this same road; he drives the Hessian Division back at Laufach on the 13th, and on the 14th wrests from the Austrian Division the important defile of Aschaffenburg, past which the imperfectly assembled VIIIth Corps has to march. In spite of this, Prince Charles's march is performed, because the Army of the Maine takes the direction of Frankfort, and his junction with the Bavarians in front of Würzburg is effected on the Tauber by the 20th July. Thinking that the Prussians have attained their object, and will not undertake further operations, the Allies now determine to assume the offensive, and to cross the Spessart. Were the Prussians to wait for this movement to be carried into effect, their Army might be cut off from its communication with the east of the monarchy, and might be forced back upon the Rhine by one unsuccessful engagement.

In the very moment, however, when the Allies, after again wasting time, commence this movement with their right wing, General Manteuffel, after a brief repose, appears with his whole Army in front of their left. After some slight engagements the Prince of Hesse concentrates his corps behind the Tauber, but on the 24th July General Weltzien's Brigade of General Goeben's Division takes the passage at Werbach from the Baden Division, and General Wrangel's Brigade Bischofsheim from the Würtemberg troops, in spite of the reinforcements that they receive during the action. The very next day the last-named brigade again attacks the enemy at Gerchsheim, thereby endangering the retreat of the VIIIth Corps to Würzburg. This bold advance would have driven the corps back in the direction of its junction with the Bavarians if the latter had but been assembled in due time to support it, but the separate Bavarian detachments being met on their road by General Beyer's Division at Helmstadt, are forced to change the direction of their march. On the 26th General Flies arrives also; the fight is continued at Uettingen and Rossbrunn, and the Field Marshal is for the second time compelled to stand alone, and with the defiles of the Maine immediately behind his rear. The VIIIth Corps, which should form the left wing of his line of battle, is already in full retreat behind the river, in consequence of its unsuccessful actions of the preceding days.

To overcome the Bavarians in their precarious situation it would have been necessary to bring up General Goeben's Division, which halted for the day at Gerchsheim, after a period of incessant marching and fighting. The attack, therefore, did not take place; and on the 27th July the whole force of the Allies, though much weakened by the previous mishaps, was assembled in a position at Würzburg, the front of which was perfectly unassailable. Facing the Federal Army stood the Prussian Army of the Maine, interposing between the contingents of the VIIIth Corps and their homes, and in a position to menace the communications of the Bavarians also by a simple march to the right. Besides this, the Grand Duke of Mecklenburg was coming rapidly up to Bayreuth in their rear with the IInd Reserve Corps.

These were the circumstances under which the armistice was concluded which eventually ended in peace.

At the end of this campaign Prussia was thus in actual possession of either the whole or a considerable part of the territories of all her enemies, and thereby in a position to dictate the terms of peace. This object had been attained on the western theatre of war, not by a grand decisive battle, but by a series of engagements fought right and left.

Unity of leadership and unceasing activity had counterbalanced the numerical superiority of the enemy.

# THE PEACE CONFERENCES AND HOMEWARD MARCH OF THE PRUSSIAN ARMY.

Immediately after the battle of Königgrätz the Emperor of Austria, as is well known, ceded Venetia to Emperor Napoleon, and declared himself willing to accept the mediation of the latter, in order to put an end to the war in Germany and Italy. This was communicated by Emperor Napoleon to King William by a telegram which reached Head-Quarters at Horsitz during the night of the 4th. In this telegram the Emperor said that the events produced by the great and rapid success of the Prussian arms forced him to lay aside the complete reserve he had hitherto maintained, but that he was too well acquainted with the high-minded feelings of the King not to feel assured that the latter would look favourably on his attempt to restore peace, and that an armistice would pave the way to peace conferences.

This produced a fresh and very important change in the political situation.

Ever since the attempt to settle amicably the dispute between Austria and Prussia by Congress had failed by reason of Austria's disinclination, France had held herself aloof from all participation in the strife, and had maintained the attitude of an observant spectatress. Now that Austria requested her mediation, she proffered it to Prussia and Italy.

The nature of the circumstances and the King of Prussia's love of peace prevented this offer of mediation from being summarily refused. It is very difficult to calculate what effect such a refusal might have on France's future attitude, because the course of regular negotiation and diplomatic correspondence could not keep pace with the course of events, and France's intervention had been immediately made so public that its result was watched by the whole French nation.

It was very possible that France might become the friend and well-wisher of that side which had called forth her intervention, and placed in her hands the forfeit which the misfortunes of war had compelled it to yield. As soon as the evening "Moniteur" of the 4th had announced this sudden change, numerous and influential voices were raised in France, urgently demanding that Emperor Napoleon should accept the office of mediator. The task of Prussia's policy now was to ward off the danger which lay in the public opinion of a great part of the French nation, and to assist the wisdom of the Imperial Government in forming a calm judgment of the circumstances.

The military situation and Prussia's relations to Italy absolutely forbade any standstill in the operations. Both these Powers had bound themselves that, when war had once commenced, neither should conclude either peace or armistice without the consent of the other.

His Majesty the King decided, therefore, to accept France's mediation in principle, and to endeavour to obtain Italy's consent, but at the same time to continue military operations with full vigour.

On the 5th already a telegram was despatched from Horsitz to the Emperor of the French, stating that Prussia accepted his proposals, and was willing to discuss the means for restoring peace. At the same time the Prussian Ambassador at Paris was instructed to lay before the Emperor the conditions under which Prussia's duty to Italy and military position would render an armistice possible. The Italian Government was informed of the state of affairs by the Prussian Ambassador in Florence, and through the medium of Count d'Avet, the Italian Military Attaché at the Prussian Head-Quarters. Meanwhile the Army continued its march, and the political problem had to be solved whilst the work of war proceeded.

On the 7th July Major Prince Henry VII of Reuss, formerly Prussian Ambassador at Munich, was despatched from Pardubitz with an autograph letter from the King to Emperor Napoleon, and with instructions for the Prussian Ambassador at Paris.

These instructions again expressed the King's willingness to negotiate, but also the necessity of obtaining Italy's assent, and at the same time pointed out that the military situation did not admit of an armistice without some guarantee as to what the terms of the coming peace would be. In the question of peace, as indeed in the whole of his previous policy, His Majesty took his stand on the perfect similarity between the interests of Germany and Prussia. Germany needed the development of her interests on the basis and in the spirit of the national wishes, the complete and clear realization of which had, as long as the former confederation existed, been prevented mainly by the pressure exerted by Austria, a power whose principal component parts were foreign to Germany. Prussia's interest demanded the consolidation and strengthening of the monarchy within the natural sphere of its influence in North Germany, i.e. direct and actual connection between the disconnected parts of the monarchy and the leadership in North Germany, based on a firm confederacy of the several States. Both these objects, so immediately connected with each other, were pointed out to the Prussian Ambassador at Paris as always to be borne in mind when discussing the basis of mediation with the Imperial Government.

In the course of the night of the 11th July the French Ambassador, M. Benedetti, arrived at His Majesty's Head-Quarters; he was commissioned to negotiate a suspension of hostilities.

In conformity with the instructions sent to the Prussian Ambassador at Paris, he was informed that this could not be done without Italy's consent, and without some guarantee for the future peace conditions. M. Benedetti had no authority to treat on the latter subject, but France thought that she could hold out the prospect of Italy's consent, because the Emperor, being in possession of Venetia, was able to assure to that Power the real object for which it had gone to war. However, this mere prospect could not be accepted as an equivalent for the direct expression of Italy's consent. The Italian Military Attaché was without either instructions or power to treat, and it even seemed for some time as if the Florence Government was not inclined to accept Venetia as a gift. Under these circumstances an armistice was impossible; nevertheless, as the repeated interruption of telegraphic communication threw great difficulties in the way of direct correspondence and caused much delay, the King declared that his troops would not attack the Austrian forces for three days, if the latter would evacuate the region northward of the Thaya.

With these proposals the French Ambassador despatched his Secretary on the 12th from Czernahora to the Austrian Head-Quarters.

On the 14th Austrian counter-proposals arrived at Brünn, which saddled the proposed cessation of hostilities with conditions which would have enabled Austria to bring up reinforcements from the south in the meantime, thereby totally changing the military situation. The documents concerning the failure of these negotiations were communicated to the French Government.

In the meantime Emperor Napoleon had drawn up his programme for the basis of the peace conference, and sent it to Austria and Prussia. It arrived at Brünn on the 16th per telegram, and contained the following clauses:—

> " Maintenance of Austria's integrity, but withdrawal
> " of this Power from Germany, which State was to be
> " re-organized; establishment of a North German Union
> " under the military supremacy of Prussia; right of the
> " South German States to form an independent. union,
> " but a bond of nationality to exist between North and
> " South Germany, to be regulated by free and mutual
> " agreement between the German States."

This was the basis, on the acceptance of which at Vienna and Brünn all future negotiation, and the possibility of speedily ending the war, depended.

Austria had to decide whether she would save the integrity of the empire, which the continuation of the war might endanger, by renouncing all participation in the re-organization of Germany, and acknowledging the undoubted supremacy of Prussia in this State. It was most certainly a very serious demand to make of Austria's Imperial house.

But in the Prussian Head-Quarters the acceptance of this preliminary basis required very setious consideration also.

The question arose, whether the two conditions contained in the above-mentioned instructions sent to the Prussian Ambassador at Paris—viz., national development of Germany and consolidation of Prussia's power—were sufficiently guaranteed.

The programme set up at Paris, although it contained important guarantees for preventing any foreign interference in the national development of Germany, was nevertheless deficient in the offers held forth to Prussia, especially after such signal success, and in contrast with what Prussia had risked and what her adversaries would have demanded from her had affairs taken a different turn.

The French Government must therefore have esteemed it a proof of great love of peace on the part of the King that an answer was sent per telegram from Brünn to Paris on the 18th, to the effect—

> " That the programme could not be acknowledged as
> " a sufficient basis for a definite peace, because a decided
> " increase of Prussia's power, by enlarging her territory
> " at the expense of the hostile North German States,
> " was a necessity demanded by the events of the war
> " and the feelings of the nation, but that the programme
> " would, if agreed to by Italy, and accepted by Austria,
> " afford sufficient ground to conclude an armistice for the
> " purpose of negotiating a definite peace. In order to
> " afford an opportunity for ascertaining Austria's inten-
> " tions, the King would agree to suspend hostilities for
> " five days. If Austria should accept the programme
> " before the expiration of this term, an armistice would
> " then be concluded, and peace conferences commence as
> " soon as Italy acquiesced. The negotiations would only
> " be conducted between Prussia and Austria; all other
> " belligerent States would have to treat independently.
> " If Austria should not accept the programme within the
> " given time, the war would be continued.

This interchange of opinions between Brünn and Paris was attended with much difficulty. In spite of the efficiency of the telegraph department, telegraphic communication was often delayed and often totally interrupted, on account of the damage clandestinely done to the wires, and important despatches did not reach their destination for several days, sometimes even not at all. It became, however, evident that the incorporation of dominions of all those North German States which had waged war against Prussia could not be effected by her without risking fresh complications, but that, in addition to other western territories, possession might be obtained either of part of Saxony, on condition of giving up a corresponding portion of Hanover, or of the whole of Hanover, without calling forth France's intervention.

In order to facilitate the negotiations, and to be in direct telegraphic communication with Paris, M. Benedetti went to

Vienna. In the meantime Count Barral, the Italian Ambassador at Berlin, had arrived at the Prussian Head-Quarters, so that negotiations could now be carried on with the concurrence of Italy.

On the 18th the King's Head-Quarters were moved to Nikolsburg, whilst the Army continued its march towards the Danube and Vienna.

Early on the 19th M. Benedetti returned from Vienna to Nikolsburg. He announced verbally that Austria was willing to accept the basis as proposed by France, and to conclude an armistice, so that peace preliminaries might commence. As soon as this was corroborated by an official despatch from the Duc de Grammont, French Ambassador at Vienna, Prussia declared herself willing to suspend hostilities for five days.

Generals from both sides then met at Eibesbrunn, and drew up the Convention as given in Book the Second, page 382, by virtue of which hostilities ceased along the whole line.

On the evening of the 21st Count Karoly, formerly Austrian Ambassador at Berlin, the former Minister of War, Count Degenfeld, and Baron Brenner, formerly Austrian Ambassador, arrived at Nikolsburg, as Austrian Plenipotentiaries to discuss the preliminaries of peace. The conferences began the very next day, and were conducted on the part of Prussia by Prime Minister Count Bismarck, on the part of Austria by Count Karoly and Baron Brenner, whilst at the same time General Baron Moltke and Fieldmarshal Count Degenfeld drew up a military convention respecting the armistice. (*Vide* Book the Second, page 382.)

It was Prussia's intention that they should join in these conferences, and Count Barral, who had accompanied Head-Quarters to Nikolsburg, was invited to take part in them, but declined on the plea that he was neither provided with instructions, nor authorised to do so. It was therefore agreed upon that the Prussian Commissioners should inform him of the result of the conferences, and thus enable him to keep his Government acquainted with the progress of affairs and in a position to make whatever suggestions it might deem necessary. Italy's assent to the eventual result of the conference may, moreover, be said to have been given beforehand, as she had bound herself not to refuse her consent to the conclusion of peace if the possession of Venetia were secured to her.

The conferences lasted from the 23rd to the 26th July.

Although they had been brought about by France's intervention, still the Emperor did not intend to play the part of a formal mediator; his Ambassador, therefore, was not present at the discussions. These discussions were of course based on the peace programme proposed to both parties by the French Government, the general outlines of which were—the independent national development of Germany without the co-operation of Austria, the recognition of the closest confederation in North Germany; the privilege of the South German

States of forming an independent federal union and the maintenance of a national connection between all States of Germany.

The integrity of Austria, with the exception of Venetia, was also agreed to in principle. The next point upon which the Austrian Commissioners were instructed to insist was the maintenance of the territorial integrity of Saxony, as that one of the Allies that had fought on the same battle-fields with Austria. On both these points Prussia could well meet Austria's wishes as soon as her own position in North and West Germany, where her interests were most at stake, was sufficiently guaranteed for the future. The position which France took with regard to the question of territorial change, has been already alluded to; she backed Austria's wishes with respect to Saxony, because she wished a speedy end of the war, and earnestly desired to facilitate the conclusion of peace for the sake of Austria. Added to this, Saxony, as a member of the North German Union, would be a firm and true ally of Prussia, whose value the King fully appreciated.

It was neither necessary, nor indeed feasible, that the terms of this peace should fix the exact limits of that additional territory which Prussia's interests demanded. All other German States—Saxony not even excepted—took no part in the conferences; it was their own affair to settle the conditions under which they would make peace with Prussia. Austria, as a matter of course, could not dispose of their territories, she could only give her assent in advance to whatever changes Prussia might make, and when the latter promised that none of them should affect Saxony, Austria promised to consent to all the rest.

Other questions afforded less difficulty; for instance, the transfer to Prussia of Austria's rights in Schleswig-Holstein, which was now a matter of course; the settlement of the sum to be paid towards the costs of the war, &c. The peace preliminaries were therefore drawn up.

The question now submitted to the King's decision was a serious and important one, similar to that upon which depended the commencement of the war.

Was war to be continued in the hope of obtaining still greater results? The Army stood in sight of Vienna; Pressburg had already been well nigh in the hands of the Prussian forces. No anxiety was felt with regard to the fate of a second battle, should one become necessary, and an entry into Vienna without too heavy a loss was within the bounds of possibility.

Prussia's military position was for the moment favourable, and, viewed in this light, the wish to push the victory to the utmost, and to give free development to the well-tried power of the Prussian Army was a natural one. The enemy's capital—a goal which Napoleon I. had never refrained from reaching—was temptingly near; its spires were within sight of the Prussian outposts. On the other hand, it had to be taken into consideration that Austria, even after the loss of Vienna, would not be forced to make peace. Her Army could retreat to Hungary and bide its time in anticipation of fresh complications in European politics.

If peace were not concluded on the basis proposed by Emperor Napoleon, and so publicly made known, it would wound both the interests and the dignity of France.

A great object was already gained; was it worth while to call upon the Prussian nation for fresh sacrifices and still further exertions for the purpose of gaining more, and perhaps risk what was already won?

The aim of a wise policy is not regulated by that which is desirable, but by that which is necessary. Germany's development under Prussia's supremacy was secured by the proffered peace; further plans of conquest, such as many would attribute to Prussia, lay not in the intention of the Government.

Monarch and people might well say that they had acted up to the duty which high vocation imposes upon States as well as upon individuals; they must recognize the fact that nothing further was imperiously necessary either for the security or the national development of Prussia and Germany. Prussia had good reason to hope that the increase of territory and power which she was on the point of winning would ere long be completely and firmly knitted in one mutual organism with the former elements of the State.

The conditions offered by Austria did not preclude the possibility of in the future re-establishing friendly relations with the old allies. Neither had Austria's honour nor her might been so wounded that irreconcileable enmity between both States must necessarily ensue. If more were demanded, if a successful continuation of the war were to extort more then a sting would remain behind that no lapse of time would remove. It was in the interest neither of Germany nor of Prussia to perpetuate the breach between Austria and Prussia.

We have only been able to glance cursorily at the general outlines of the considerations which influenced His Majesty the King and his Council in the momentous question of peace or war during the decisive days at Nikolsburg. To exhibit them unreservedly must be the task of future historians.

His Majesty decided for peace.

On the 26th July the preliminaries were signed, and ratifications exchanged on the 28th.

The King's decision was joyfully welcomed by an Army and a nation who, in the midst of a successful and glorious campaign, had not learnt to underrate the blessings of peace.

Neither the Ambassador, Count Barral nor General Govone, who had arrived at Nikolsburg on the 26th from King Victor Emmanuel's Head-Quarters, were furnished with authority to declare Italy's consent to an armistice; this assent, therefore, was entered as a proviso in the VIth Article of the preliminaries, under the condition of the acquisition of Venetia. In order that the representatives of the Italian Government might have time to obtain the assent of the latter, the commencement of the armistice was fixed for the 2nd August, and the suspension of hostilities prolonged till then. On the 29th July M. Benedetti announced officially and in writing that the cessation of Venetia to Italy was guaranteed, and on the 30th the Italian Ambassador, Count Barral, was able to proclaim the assent of his Government to the armistice.

From the moment that the ratifications were exchanged all military dispositions were regulated in accordance with the new state of affairs. The very same day orders were sent to the armies to exchange the crowded quarters, in which they had been in front of Vienna ever since hostilities had ceased, for the more extensive cantonments in Bohemia and Moravia accorded to them in virtue of paragraph 1 of the Truce Convention.

When this rayon was allotted to the three Armies care was taken so to distribute the cantonments to the different corps, that none might have to make any detour when their march and railway transport homewards commenced.

To the Ist Army, therefore, the centre of the whole region was given, bounded on the east by the Lundenburg-Brünn-Zwittau Railway and the Bohemian-Moravian frontier, on the west by the Tabor-Prague-Melnik-Böhmisch Leipa-Rumburg-road.

Eastwards of this district lay the cantonments of the Ist, Vth, and VIth Army Corps of the IInd Army, whilst the Corps of Guards was quartered in the tract of country which extends on both sides of the Prague-Bodenbach Railway as far westwards as Laun and Teplitz.

The north-western part of the whole region was occupied by the Army of the Elbe, jointly with the 1st Reserve Corps.

In order to avoid the crossing of the different columns and crowding of the troops during their march to their new cantonments, the routes, for the first few days, were fixed by the King's Head-Quarters. The troops commenced their march from their crowded cantonments as follows :—

The IInd Army on the 30th July ;
The Army of the Elbe on the 31st ;
The Ist Army on the 1st of August ;
The IInd Army Corps on the 30th July.

After reviewing the Army of the Elbe at Ladendorf on the 30th and three divisions of the Ist Army at Schönlau on the 31st, His Majesty the King moved his Head-Quarters from Nikolsburg to Brünn on the 1st August. From here he reviewed the Vth Army Corps near Wischau on the 2nd, and then returned to Berlin by way of Prague and Görlitz, on the 3rd and 4th, accompanied by His Royal Highness the Crown Prince.

The march of the Prussian troops was so arranged that their last detachments crossed the Thaya on the 7th August, and then went into their wide-spread quarters as each detachment reached its destined cantonments. Some of the routes being long, the last detachment (14th Infantry Division) did not reach its quarters before the 27th August.

The Head-Quarters, around which the different corps and divisions were distributed, were as follows :—

Ist Army, Head-Quarters, Prague.
    5th Infantry Division, Iglau (8th Regiment, Prague).
    6th Infantry Division, Kuttenberg (3rd Rifle Battalion, Prague).
    7th Infantry Division, Namiest.
    8th Infantry Division, Eichborn, near Bitischka.
    IInd Army Corps, Prague.
        3rd Infantry Division, Weisswasser.
        4th Infantry Division, Reichenberg.
    Reserve Artillery of the Army.
        Head-Quarters, Kunstadt.
        Reserve Artillery of the IIIrd Corps with the 5th and 6th Divisions.
        Reserve Artillery of the IVth Corps with the 7th and 8th Divisions.
    Head-Quarters of the Cavalry Corps were at Prague.
    Head-Quarters of the 1st Cavalry Division at Bistrau.
    Head-Quarters of the 2nd Cavalry Division at Prague.
    (The brigades of the Cavalry Corps were attached to the 4th Infantry Division and the IInd Army Corps, in order to facilitate the providing of quarters for them.)

IInd Army, Head-Quarters, Brünn (from the 16th August upwards, Prague).
    Corps of Guards, Prague.
        1st Division of Guards, Rauduitz.
        2nd Division of Guards, Prague.
        (The 3rd Infantry Brigade of the Guards was moved per rail, to Dresden on the 20th and 21st, and placed at the disposal of the Gôvernor-General of Saxony.)
    Ist Army Corps, Napagedl.
        1st Infantry Division, Wagstadt.
        2nd Infantry Division, Koritschau.
    Vth Army Corps, Chatzen.
        9th Infantry Division, Pardubitz.
        10th Infantry Division, Hohenmauth.
    VIth Army Corps, Brünn.
        11th Infantry Division, Brünn.
        12th Infantry Division, Zöbtau.
    Cavalry Division, Prague.
        (The regiments of the Cavalry Division were attached to the Vth and VIth Army Corps.)
    General Knobelsdorff's detachment joined the VIth Corps.

Army of the Elbe, Head-Quarters, Horowic.
    14th Infantry Division, Carlsbad.
    15th Infantry Division, Liten.
    Ist Reserve Army Corps.
        Division of Guard Landwehr, Caatz.
        Combined Landwehr Division, Commotau.
        Cavalry Division, Bilin.

A combined brigade of the corps remained at Prague until the troops of the Corps of Guards arrived there.

As soon as the armies reached their destinations they occupied the lines of communication in their respective districts, thus relieving the unmobilized troops which had been so long employed for this purpose.

Immediately after the commencement of the armistice it was twice broken by the Austrians on the eastern theatre of war; in the first place by a sortie from Theresienstadt, and secondly, by a brief occupation of Znaym.

The Kralup-Turnau Railway was guarded on both banks of the Elbe by a detachment of General Bentheim's Landwehr Division, consisting of two companies of the 15th Landwehr Regiment and a sub-division of Dragoons quartered in the neighbourhood. Trusting to the armistice, the detachment had omitted to take any precautions, and at daybreak of the 28th was surprised by a detachment from the fortress Theresienstadt, consisting of about a battalion and a sub-division of Hussars. The Prussian detachment lost 4 men killed, 1 officer 7 men wounded, and 4 officers 148 men taken prisoners, besides which the enemy blew up one pier of the bridge over the Elbe at Neratowitz. The prisoners were not released until the 31st.

On the same day that this sortie took place an Austrian detachment which had arrived westward of the Znaym-Stockerau road during the armistice, took possession of Znaym, the 86 Prussian soldiers stationed there made good their retreat in the direction of Brünn, and succeeded in carrying with them also the sick that could be moved. The King forbade the brigade of the Army of the Elbe, which had been stationed at Jetzelsdorf since the 27th, to attack Znaym, so that the Austrians retired without being molested. These irregularities were caused by delay in sending official information of the armistice, which had then existed for six days, to the officers in command at these points.

In the meantime the state of affairs at the western theatre of war now also admitted of extending the cantonments of the troops.

Simultaneously with the truce with Austria a Convention suspending hostilities with Bavaria also was signed on the 28th at Nikolsburg, where the Würtemberg Minister, Baron Von Varnbüler, and the Minister of Hesse Darmstadt, Baron Von Dalwigk, arrived on the 29th, for the purpose of entering into negotiations. Baden had previously requested a truce, and now gave notice that her troops were already on their road home.

Under such circumstances, the Commander-in-Chief of the Army of the Maine was now authorised to grant a truce to these States also.

By the 2nd August the necessary conferences had so far progressed that the troops of the Army of the Maine could take up their quarters in rear of the line of demarcation settled by the different Conventions. The districts allotted to them were—

General Goeben's Division:

Head-Quarters, Würzburg; the division in those parts of Bavaria, Baden and Würtemberg which extend from this town to the Neckar.

General Flies's Division:

Head-Quarters, Frankfort on the Maine; the division in those parts of Bavaria, Electoral Hesse, and Frankfort which extended eastward and south-eastward of this town, as well as in that tract of the Duchy of Nassau which lay southward of the Taunus.

General Beyer's Division:

Head-Quarters, Darmstadt: the division in those parts of Hesse and Baden between the Maine and the Neckar.

Head-quarters of the Army of the Maine were moved to Frankfort on the Maine.

The unmobilized troops of occupation that had been pushed forward by the Governor-General of the Rhenish Provinces and Westphalia could now be successively withdrawn. To replace them a combined brigade was formed, by order of His Majesty, out of troops of General Beyer's Division, and placed at the disposal of General Von Werder, Governor-General of Electoral Hesse. The brigade started for Cassel on the 10th August.

On the 5th August the IInd Reserve Corps began to spread out in the rayon behind the line of demarcation; Head-Quarters of the Corps and of both divisions were stationed at Nürnberg; the Mecklenburg Division cantoned in the district eastward of the Gräfenberg-Nürnberg-Schwabach road; one brigade of the Prussian Division westward of this road, the other in Bayreuth and neighbourhood.

Peace had already been concluded on the 13th August with Würtemberg, on the 17th with Baden, and on the 22nd with Bavaria, when that with Austria was ratified on the 30th at Prague.

In this treaty Austria recognised the dissolution of the German Confederation as it heretofore existed, and accepted the new organisation of Germany without the participation of Austria.

The treaty then declares Austria's consent to all new arrangements and territorial changes effected by Prussia, provided the latter Power bind itself to allow the kingdom of Saxony to retain its present territorial limits.

The Emperor also transferred to the King of Prussia all the rights which he had acquired by the treaty of Vienna over the Duchies of Schleswig and Holstein, with the reservation that the question of a re-union with Denmark should be eventually put to the vote in the northern districts.

Besides this, Austria gave her consent to the union of Venetia to the kingdom of Italy.

These were the objects which the preliminaries of peace had in view. The remaining German States (Hesse on the 3rd September, Saxony on the 21st October) gave their assent to these conditions, in particular as far as they regarded the future organization of Germany.

The Zollverein Treaty of the year 1865 came immediately again into force in these States, and formed, from the very first moment, a tie of national connection between the South and the North of Germany. Hesse Darmstadt entered the newly-formed North German Confederation with all territories north of the Maine, Saxony with the whole kingdom.

Besides the annexation of Hanover, Electoral Hesse, Nassau, and the former free town, Frankfort on the Maine, and the incorporation of Schleswig and Holstein, the different treaties ceded the following districts to Prussia:—Hesse Darmstadt gave up the Landgraviate of Hesse Homburg and the districts of Biedenkopf and Vöhl, as well as some small enclaves which lay within Prussian territory; in lieu of these Hesse Darmstadt received some districts which hitherto belonged to Electoral Hesse, Nassau, and Frankfort, but lay within the province of Upper Hesse.

Bavaria ceded the districts of Gersfeld and Orb and the enclave Caulsdorf.

Besides this, each State paid Prussia a stipulated sum as indemnity for the cost of the war.

Of these sums were to be paid:—by Austria 40,000,000 dollars, from which, however, 20,000,000 for war expenses incurred in the Schleswig-Holstein campaign, and for the provisioning the Prussian Army during the armistice, were deducted; by Saxony, 10,000,000 dollars; by Bavaria, 30,000,000 florins; by Würtemburg, 8,000,000; by Baden, 6,000,000; and by Hesse-Darmstadt, 3,000,000 florins.

A supplementary convention with reference to Articles III and XII of the Treaty with Austria was added to the latter, in which the evacuation of the Austrian territory was stipulated as follows:—

Within the stipulated period of three weeks after the exchange of the ratifications of the treaty the Prussian troops were to evacuate the district south of the line Napajedl-Brünn-Iglau-Tabor by the seventh day; all countries southward of the Pilsen-Prague-Littau Railway, and of a line drawn from thence to the mouth of the Oppa by the fifteenth day.

The Austrian troops were bound to remain $12\frac{3}{4}$ miles distant from the rear of the Prussian columns, and Prussia undertook all the cost of provisioning her own troops from the day after the ratification of the treaty.

Regarding the release of all prisoners of war, it was settled that their transport should commence the third day after the ratification of the treaty, and should take place in daily échelons, not exceeding 6,000 men each day, by way of Oderberg.

In accordance with these arrangements, the evacuation of Austrian territory occupied by Prussian troops now commenced. The necessary orders were issued on the 25th August, and the withdrawal of the Prussian troops was regulated in the following manner :—

## ARMIES IN BOHEMIA AND MORAVIA.

### *1st Army.*

The IInd Army Corps took the route to Görlitz, so as to commence its railway transport by way of Frankfort-Berlin, and of Kreuz to Pomerania, on the 4th September,

The 5th and 6th Infantry Divisions and the Brandenburg Reserve Artillery marched on foot to Saxony.

The 7th and 8th Infantry Divisions and the Magdeburg Reserve Artillery were concentrated round about Brünn, Trübau, and Pardubitz, at which places they were to embark and proceed by rail to their home garrisons.

The regiments of the Cavalry Corps rejoined the divisions to which they belonged in times of peace.

### *IInd Army.*

The Corps of Guards marched in two columns over Dresden and Bautzen to Berlin.

The Ist Army Corps was concentrated at Oderberg, from whence its railway transport over Breslau and Posen to Prussia Proper was to commence on the 4th September.

The Vth and VIth Army Corps marched home on foot; on crossing the frontier the latter corps left a detachment of two battalions and four squadrons in Troppau to occupy this part of Austrian Silesia until the 20th September, on which day the last instalment of the war indemnity of 20,000,000 dollars stipulated by the treaty of peace was paid.

### *Army of the Elbe.*

The 14th Division marched to Zeitz, where it embarked in the railway; the Cavalry and Artillery of the Division then proceeded, per rail, by way of Erfurt and Cassel to their former garrisons, whilst the Infantry and the combined Fusileer Brigade of the 16th Division were conveyed to Hanover.

The VIIIth Army Corps embarked on the 5th at Prague and Pilsen and were conveyed by rail over Nürnberg and Aschaffenburg to the Rhenish Provinces.

The 1st Reserve Corps marched to Dresden and Röderau, and then proceeded by rail to the stations where the different troops had been formed.

The Austrian territory was thus evacuated by the 20th September.

At the Army of the Maine orders for evacuating the territory of Baden, Würtemberg, and Bavaria, in accordance with the terms of the different treaties, were issued respectively on the 24th and 28th August and the 5th September. Possession was taken of the fortress of Mayence on the 26th August, and the home transport of the 15th Infantry Division then took place between the 13th and 17th September, on the line Frankfort-Giessen-Hamm.

Peace was not concluded with Hesse-Darmstadt until the 3rd September, and on the 17th orders were given to evacuate the country, in conformity with which the divisions of Generals Beyer and Flies and the Oldenburg-Hanseatic Brigade returned to their respective garrisons between the 18th and 24th September, by means of the Rhenish and the Hessian-Hanoverian lines of railway.

Of the troops of these two divisions only the Fusileer Regiments Nos. 36, 39, and 40 remained for a time in a state of mobilization in the neighbourhood of Frankfort, and by a Royal command of the 6th September, the 13th Infantry Regiment of General Goeben's Division was billeted in the Duchy of Saxe-Meiningen until further orders; it reached these quarters on the 19th by foot march.

The home transport of the IInd Reserve Corps commenced on the 5th, partly direct from Nürnberg and partly from Hof; but the two Prussian Regiments of the Guard only made use of the railway as far as Hof and Eisenach and then marched to their garrisons.

On the 10th September the last troops quitted the Bavarian territory.

---

The feelings which inspired the Prussian nation at home equalled those of the soldier on the battlefield. The soldier had exchanged the exciting peril of the strife for the sufferings and privations of a life in cantonments in a district devastated by war, and in addition ravaged by epidemic disease. For six trying weeks—twice the length of time that it had taken him to conquer the enemy's country—had he to hold out before he could be permitted to return home.

Already, however, numerous committees of help, under the patronage of Her Majesty the Queen, and also called forth by private impulse, had been formed to furnish supplies to the troops, and all ranks of society vied with each other in their voluntary contributions. The grandeur of the moment settled all internal dissensions; drew together the different political parties, and united all in a feeling of gratitude to the Army. Was it not, indeed, the flower, the pride, the future hope of the nation, the armed youth of the land, that was to be succoured, and how few families either in castle or cottage were there that had not a son, a brother, or a friend in its ranks?

Protestant, as well as Roman Catholic Sisters of Mercy nursed the wounded without regard to the religion they professed, heedless whether they were friends or foes. The order of the Knights of St. John still pursued its extensive work on the battlefield and in the hospital. Gifts of love flowed in from all quarters, not only from Prussia, but also from the whole of North Germany, from Bremen, and in such profusion that it was at times impossible to convey them to their destination. Such spontaneous help given by a nation to its army, side by side of that provided by the care of the Government had never yet been witnessed before this campaign. It was, however, proved here also that the fearful sufferings which war inflicts can only be insufficiently alleviated, and that no human arrangements can fully provide for the wants of an Army immediately after a great battle.

At last the day for returning home arrived.

In one unbroken stream the troops crossed the frontier, and from the moment their foot touched the soil of the Fatherland their march became a continual festival. In the capital the King headed the proud procession, leading it to his palace between a continuous twofold row of troops, and accompanied by the cheers of a countless multitude. Not the less touching was the soldier's reception in his distant village, even though its cottages were only adorned with a simple branch of fir.

Many a one, however, returned no more; the sacrifice had been great and bitter; 4,450 sons of the Fatherland had bought the victory at the cost of their lives, 6,427 had fallen victims to cholera or other diseases, and 16,177 bore honourable wounds.

Still these losses are considerably smaller than those of other wars, and never yet had Prussia fought a campaign of such short duration and attended with such important results.

The increase of territory and inhabitants alone amounted to more than 1,300 square miles (German), with above 4,000,000 inhabitants, but of far greater value was it that Prussia had proved anew and gained confidence in her own strength, and had reasserted her importance. Above all things, however, a position had been gained in which the words spoken by King William to his people at the commencement of the war could now be fully carried out.

> "If God should grant us victory we shall be strong
> "enough to renew, under a firmer and more beneficial
> "form, those frail ties which have hitherto held the
> "German districts together, more by name than in
> "reality."

# APPENDIX.

## TABLE OF CONTENTS.

# APPENDIX I.

THE railway transport for the mobilization and movement of the Prussian main army in 1866 was managed by an Executive Commission at Berlin, consisting of Major Count Wartensleben and Mr. Weishaupt, of the Ministry of Trade. Under their orders were the Executive Commissions which administered the different lines, and of which mention will be made hereafter. The whole progress of the transport can be divided into four sections, which, indeed, partly, in time, overlap each other, but still form four sufficiently distinct periods.

In the first of these sections, that is, in the first half of May, though, indeed, extending also into the second half of the month, the railways were principally employed in the transport of augmentations of men and horses; they served also to accelerate the preparation and mobilization decreed in successive orders. In this administrative period falls also the partial transport of Landwehr battalions to the fortresses or the provinces of Saxony and Silesia, through which the troops mobilized there could be removed; also the transport of every kind of matériel of war to fortresses, garrisons, and magazines. It would be tedious to detail the daily transport for these objects; sufficient to say that this transport was more spasmodic than maturely planned. At that time operations of a considerable nature could not be expected from the railways, as experience shows that they require from eight to ten days to make their preparations for great exertions. To such belong the collection of rolling stock, the preparations for loading and unloading trains, &c. We can only in general state that even during this normal period of preparation all transport required for the mobilization of the field troops, and the garrisoning of the fortresses was effected by the railway companies.

The second period includes the march and railway transport of the Vth, VIth, IIIrd, and IVth Corps to Silesia and Lusatia. This practically took place between the 16th and 23rd May, although a portion of the special arms and trains arrived a few days later. The concentration of these corps depended upon the political situation. Prussia had been anticipated in preparation by Austria and Saxony, and, in case of a not improbable declaration of war, it had become necessary to place the troops first prepared—which were these corps—in the frontier districts, where they could directly cover Berlin and Breslau. This was a purely defensive measure.

The VIth Corps, almost entirely, was concentrated by means of marching at Niesse and Frankenstein. Only three trains in all were used between the 17th and 21st May on the Upper Silesian Railways, for some Staffs and a hospital. The last train of the corps reached Neisse on the 21st.

The whole Vth Corps was, between the 17th and 20th May, transported on the line Kreuz-Posen-Breslau-Königszelt. Its last park arrived on the 30th. A joint railway commission, composed of a Staff officer and a civilian, arranged the transport of both these corps.

Only six Infantry and four Cavalry regiments of the IIIrd Corps were

transported by rail; the rest of the corps marched to its rendezvous at
Drebkau. The railway transport was arranged by a similar commission;
it lasted from the 17th to the 22nd May on the lines—

Brandenburg ⎫
Wittenberge ⎬ Berlin .. Frankfort-on-the-Oder-Guben.
Angermünde ⎭
Landsberg-on-the-Warthe.

Besides these some trains of the corps was moved by rail on the 27th
and 30th May to Guben.

A similar separate railway commission was established for the IVth
Corps. It acted within the Province of Saxony, and on the lines leading
to Bitterfeld and Herzburg, through Thuringia. On these the whole
troops of the corps were forwarded to Bitterfeld, between the 16th and
19th May; the last train reached Herzburg on the 24th May. While
the corps was thus concentrated on both banks of the Elbe, at Torgau
and Herzburg, trains of Landwehr went at the same time to Erfurt and
Wittenberg.

In this section is also included the transport between the 16th and
20th May, of four Infantry and one Cavalry regiment of the VIIIth
Corps, from Trier and Saarbrücken to Coblenz, which was connected
with the originally intended assembly of this corps at Wetzlar.

During these purely defensive measures, the political situation had
from day to day grown more hazardous, and it had been determined to
make the other corps, which had been in the meanwhile mobilized, ready
to act. Herewith commenced the third period of transport, in which
the greatest exertions of the railways were made, by which the Field
Army was reinforced between the 23rd May and the 5th June, by the
daily arrival of about 40 trains of troops. As at the commencement of this
period the transport of the Vth Corps was not yet complete, the through
lines available were—for the Ist (Prussian proper) Corps, destined for
Görlitz, to strengthen either the Ist or IInd Army, the line Königsberg-
Kreuz-Frankfort-on-the-Oder-Görlitz; for the IInd (Pomeranian) Corps,
destined to reinforce the Ist Army, the line from Pomerania to Herzberg,
by Berlin; for the VIIth Corps, the lines from Düsseldorf and Münster
by way of Cassel-Eisenach to Zeitz; for the VIIIth Corps, the lines from
Coblenz by Cologne-Minden-Magdeburg to Halle.

A special Railway Committee was in charge of each of these lines.

Although the lines allotted to the eight Corps during the 2nd and
3rd period could be worked independently of each other, still, to prevent
collisions, the military control of the transport on the right of the Elbe
was in the hands of one, that on the left in those of another, Officer of
the General Staff.

The transport of the four last-named corps was as follows:—

Of the Ist Corps eight troop trains were daily despatched; of these
the first left Königsberg on the 24th May. The last division of troops
reached Görlitz on the 2nd June; the last park entered Kohlfurt on
the 6th June. In this transport that of the 3rd Regiment of Guards
from Dantzig to Berlin, and also five trains of troops for the IInd Corps
from Bromberg to Nakel, were included.

The IInd Corps similarly was forwarded by eight trains daily, between
the 23rd May and 5th June, to Herzberg. On the 1st June all the troops
of the corps had arrived.

Of the VIIth Corps, the 13th Division and two Cavalry regiments,
and a division of Artillery, were retained in Westphalia on account of
Hanoverian affairs. The 14th Division, with the bulk of the Artillery
and the trains of the corps, reached Corbetha, in eight trains daily,

between the 27th May and 5th June. The first train arrived on the 28th May, the last portion of troops on the 2nd June, the last park on the 5th June.

Of the VIIIth Corps, between the 19th and 26th May, two Infantry and one Cavalry regiment, and two batteries, ordered to join Beyer's Division, were transported to Wetzlar. The great portion of the corps was, however, on the double line, transported in 12 trains a-day to Halle, in the short space between the 27th May and 5th June.

With only a few exceptions of slight delay, the trains arrived at their destinations at the arranged hour.

By the 5th June the work of the railways for the assembly of the Army was practically concluded ; their work in the following 4th period was not so considerable as in the 3rd. The following transport of troops still took place :—

The transport of the VIIIth Corps was immediately followed by the transport, on the 5th and 6th June, of the 16th and 17th Regiments of Landwehr from Westphalia by Hanover to Lauenburg. Also, between the 6th and 11th June, 24 battalions, 24 squadrons, 9 batteries of Landwehr were concentrated at Berlin out of different provinces, and formed into the Reserve Corps. By far the greatest part of these troops were sent by rail, for which the lines Cologne-Minden-Berlin, Königsberg-Kreuz-Berlin, Cöslin-Stettin-Berlin, were principally used. Some delay occurred in the formation of these troops ; and as meanwhile the delaration of war against Saxony drew the Ist Army to Dresden, and it was desirable to support it with the Reserve Corps, the troops coming from the west were diverted by way of Magdeburg, and those from Berlin transported to the Saxon frontier.

Lastly, we must notice the transport of the Guards. Of these a great part of the Infantry had been retained at Berlin and Potsdam; the rest had marched in the direction of Cottbus. In the middle of June it was desirable to attach the Guards to the IInd Army ; and between the 15th and 21st June, this corps, with the exception of four regiments of Cavalry and two horse batteries attached to the Cavalry Corps of the Ist Army, was transported direct, in 12 trains daily, from Berlin and Potsdam, and from Guben and Sorau to Brieg. Here the last troops arrived on the 19th, the last park on the 22nd.

Later railway transports, such as that of the 4th Guards and Flies' detachments to Eisenach and Gotha, and the transports of reinforcements, provisions, and other requirements of the Army need not be included in this sketch.

# APPENDIX II.

---

## ORDER OF BATTLE OF THE PRUSSIAN ARMY.

| | |
|---|---|
| Commander-in-Chief .. .. | His Majesty the King. |
| Chief of the Staff .. .. | General Von Moltke. |
| Inspector-General of Artillery .. | Lieut.-Gen. Von Hindersin. |
| Inspector-General of Engineers .. | „ Von Wasserschleben. |

### FIRST ARMY.

| | |
|---|---|
| Commander-in-Chief .. .. | H.R.H. Prince Frederick Charles, General of Cavalry. |
| Chief of the Staff .. .. .. | Lieut.-Gen. Von Voigt-Rhetz. |
| Quartermaster-General .. .. | Major-General Von Stülpnagel. |
| Commandant of Artillery .. .. | ,, Von Lengsfeld. |
| „ Pioneers .. .. | ,, Keiser. |

#### *Second Corps d'Armée.*

| | |
|---|---|
| General Commanding .. .. | Lieut.-General Von Schmidt. |
| Chief of the Staff .. .. .. | Major-General Von Kameke. |
| Commandant of Artillery .. .. | „ Hurrelbrink. |
| „ Pioneers .. .. | Lieut.-Colonel Leuthaus. |
| „ 3rd Division .. | Lieut.-General Von Werder. |
| „ 5th Brigade .. | Major-Gen. Von Januschowsky, (2nd and 42nd Regiments, of three battalions each). |
| „ 6th Brigade .. | Major-General Von Winterfeld (14th and 54th Regiments, of three battalions each). |

Pomeranian Rifle Battalion, No. 2.
Blucher Hussars, No. 5.
Pioneer Battalion, No. 2.
Four Batteries.
One Light Field Hospital.
Section of Krankenträgers.

| | |
|---|---|
| Commandant of 4th Division .. | Lieut.-General Von Herwarth. |
| „ 7th Brigade .. | Major-Gen. Von Schlabrendorf (9th and 49th Regiments). |
| „ 8th Brigade .. | Major-General Von Hanneken (21st and 61st Regiments). |

Pomeranian Uhlans, No. 4.
Four batteries.
Light Field Hospital.
Section of Krankenträgers.
Reserve Artillery of 2nd Corps d'Armée.
Four Batteries.

#### *Third Corps d'Armée.*

| | |
|---|---|
| General Commanding .. .. | None. |
| Commandant of 5th Division .. | Lieut.-General Von Tümpling. |

Commandant of 9th Brigade    ..    Major-Gen. Von Schimmelmann
(8th and 48th Regiments.)

,,        10th Brigade    ..    Major-General Von Kamiensky
(12th and 18th Regiments).

1st Brandenburg Uhlans, No. 3.
3rd Battalion Pioneers.
Four Batteries.
Light Field Hospital.
Section of Krankenträgers.

,,        6th Division    ..    Lieut.-General Von Manstein.

,,        11th Brigade    ..    Major-General Von Gersdorf
(35th and 60th Regiments).

,,        12th Brigade    ..    Major-General Von Kotze
(24th and 64th Regiments).

Brandenburg Dragoons, No. 2.
3rd Jäger Battalion.
Four Batteries.
Light Field Hospital.
Two Sections of Krankenträgers.

*Fourth Corps d'Armée.*

General Commanding    ..    ..    None.

Commandant of 7th Division    ..    Lieut.-General Von Fransecky.

,,        13th Brigade    ..    Major-General Von Schwarzhoff
(26th and 66th Regiments).

,,        14th Brigade    ..    Major-General Von Gordon
(27th and 67th Regiments.)

4th Pioneer Battalion.
Magdeburg Hussars, No. 10.
Four Batteries.
Field Hospital.
Section of Krankenträgers.

,,        8th Division    ..    Lieut.-General Von Horn.

,,        15th Brigade    ..    Major-General Von Bose
(31st and 71st Regiments).

,,        16th Brigade    ..    Major-General Von Schmidt
(72nd Regiment).

4th Jäger Battalion.
Thuringian Uhlans, No. 6.
Four Batteries.
Light Field Hospital.
Section of Krankenträgers.

*Cavalry Corps of the First Army.*

H.R.H. Prince Albrecht, General of Cavalry.

Commandant of 1st Cavalry Division,    Major-General Von Alvensleben.

,,    *1st Heavy Brigade, Major-Gen. H.R.H. Prince Albrecht.
Garde du Corps.
Cuirassiers of the Guard.

,,    2nd Heavy Brigade,    Major-General Von Pfuel.
Brandenburg Cuirassiers, No. 6.
Magdeburg Cuirassiers, No. 7.

,,    1st Light Brigade    ..    Major-General Von Rheinbaben.

---

* The 1st Heavy Brigade with horse battery was attached to the Guards Corps of the IInd Army.

1st Dragoons of the Guard.
1st Uhlans      ,,      ,,
2nd      ,,      ,,      ,,
Two Horse Batteries.
Light Field Hospital.
Section of Krankenträgers.

Commandant of 2nd Cavalry Division, Major-Gen. Hann Von Weyhern.
,,      2nd Light Brigade. .   Major-General Duke William of
Mecklenburg-Schwerin.
2nd Dragoons of the Guard.
Brandenburg Hussars, No. 3.
2nd Brandenburg Uhlans, No. 11.
,,      3rd Light Brigade. .   Major-General Count Groeben.
Neumark Dragoons, No. 3.
Thuringian Hussars, No. 12.
,,      *3rd Heavy Brigade. .  Major-General Von der Goltz.
Queen's Own Cuirassiers, No. 2.
2nd Pomeranian Uhlans, No. 9.
Two Horse Batteries.
Reserve Artillery of Cavalry Corps, one Horse Battery.
Reserve Artillery of 1st Army, sixteen Batteries.


### SECOND ARMY.

| | | |
|---|---|---|
| Commander-in-Chief | .. .. | H.R.H. the Crown Prince. |
| Chief of the Staff .. | .. .. | Major-General Von Blumenthal. |
| Quartermaster-General | .. .. | ,,      Von Stosch. |
| Commandant of Artillery .. | .. | ,,      Von Jacobi. |
| ,,      Engineers .. | .. | ,,      Von Schweinitz. |

*First Corps d'Armée.*

General Von Bonin.

| | | |
|---|---|---|
| Chief of Staff.. | .. .. .. | Colonel Von Borries. |
| Commandant of Artillery .. | .. | Colonel Knothe. |
| ,,      Engineers .. | .. | Colonel Weber. |
| ,,      1st Division | .. | Lieut.-General Von Grossman. |
| ,,      1st Brigade | .. | Major-General Von Pape |
| | | (1st and 41st Regiments). |
| ,,      2nd Brigade | .. | Major-General Von Barnekow |
| | | (3rd and 43rd Regiments). |

Lithuanian Dragoons, No. 1.
1st Jäger Battalion.
Four Batteries.
Field Hospital.
Section of Krankenträgers.

| | | |
|---|---|---|
| ,,      2nd Division | .. | Lieut.-General Von Clausewitz. |
| ,,      3rd Brigade | .. | Major-General Von Malotki |
| | | (4th and 44th Regiments). |
| ,,      4th Brigade | .. | Major-General Von Buddenbrock |
| | | (5th and 45th Regiments). |

1st Royal Hussars, No. 1.
1st Pioneer Battalion.
Four Batteries.

---

* The 3rd Heavy Brigade with horse battery was attached to the IInd Corps d'Armée,

Field Hospital.
Section of Krankenträgers.

Commandant of Reserve Brigade } Colonel Von Bredow.
of Cavalry of First Corps

East Prussian Cuirassiers, No. 3.
East Prussian Uhlans, No. 8.
Lithuanian Uhlans, No. 12.
One Horse Battery.
Reserve Artillery of Ist Corps d'Armée, seven Batteries.

### Fifth Corps d'Armée.

| | | |
|---|---|---|
| General Commanding .. .. | | General Von Steinmetz. |
| Chief of the Staff .. .. .. | | Colonel Von Wittich. |
| Commandant of Artillery .. .. | | ,, Von Kraewel. |
| ,, Engineers.. .. | | ,, Von Kleist. |
| ,, 9th Division .. | | Major-General Von Löwenfeld |
| ,, 17th Brigade .. | | ,, Von Ollech. |

(37th and 58th Regiments).

,, 18th Brigade .. Major-General Von Horn
(7th Regiment, 5th Jäger Battalion)
1st Silesian Dragoons, No. 4.
Four Batteries.
Field Hospital.
Section of Krankenträgers.

,, 10th Division .. Major-General Von Kirchbach.
,, 19th Brigade .. ,, Von Tiedemann.
(6th and 46th Regiments).
,, 20th Brigade .. Major-General Wittich
(47th and 52nd Regiments)
5th Pioneer Battalion.
West Prussian Uhlans, No. 1.
Four Batteries.
Field Hospital.
Section of Krankenträgers.
Reserve Artillery of Vth Corps d'Armée, seven Batteries.

### Sixth Corps d'Armée.

General Commanding .. .. General Von Mutius.
Chief of the Staff .. .. .. Colonel Von Sperling.
Commandant of Artillery .. .. Major-General Herkt.
,, Engineers.. .. Colonel Schulz.
,, 11th Division .. Lieut.-General Von Zastrow.
,, 21st Brigade .. Major-General Von Hanenfeldt
(10th and 50th Regiments)
,, 22nd Brigade .. Major-General Von Hoffmann
(38th and 51st Regiments).
Silesian Pioneer Battalion.
2nd Silesian Dragoons, No. 8.
Three Batteries.
Field Hospital.
Section of Krankenträgers.
,, 12th Division .. Lieut.-General Von Prondzinsky.
,, Combined Brigade Major-General Von Kranach
(22nd and 23rd Regiments
from 23rd and 24th Brigades).

2nd Silesian Hussars, No. 6.
6th Jäger Battalion.
Two Batteries.
Light Field Hospital.
Reserve Cavalry.
1st Silesian Hussars.
Reserve Artillery of VIth Corps, five Batteries.

N.B.—Two Infantry regiments of the 12th Division were detached, the 63rd to garrison Neisse, the 62nd to the command of General Von Knobelsdorf, who protected Silesia at Ratibor, and to whom the Silesian Uhlans and one battery were attached. Three batteries were with General Manteuffel.

### Guard Corps.

| | |
|---|---|
| General Commanding .. .. | Prince August of Würtemberg. |
| Chief of the Staff .. .. .. | Colonel Von Dannenberg. |
| Commandant of Artillery .. .. | Major-General Von Colomier. |
| ,,      Engineer .. .. | Colonel Biehler. |
| ,,      1st Div. of the Guard | Lieut.-Gen.HillerVonGärtringen. |
| ,,      1st Brigade .. | Colonel Von Obernitz (1st and 3rd Guards). |
| ,,      2nd Brigade .. | Major-General Von Alvensleben (2nd Grds. and Grd. Fusiliers). |

Hussars of the Guard.
Jägers of the Guard.
Four Batteries.
Field Hospital.
Section of Krankenträgers.

| | | |
|---|---|---|
| ,, | 2nd Div. of the Guard. | Lieut.-Gen. Von Plonski. |
| ,, | 3rd Brigade .. | Major-General Von Budritzki (Grenadiers of Kaiser Alexander, and 3rd Grenadiers of the Guard). |
| ,, | 4th Brigade .. | Major-General Von Loen (Grenadiers of Kaiser Franz, and 4th Grenadiers of the Guard). |

3rd Uhlans of the Guard.
Sharpshooter Battalion of the Guard.
Four Batteries.
Field Hospital.
Section of Krankenträgers.
Reserve Artillery of Guard Corps, five Batteries.

N.B.—The 4th Regiment of the Guard was retained at Berlin, and sent later to the Second Reserve Corps.

### Reserve Cavalry of the Second Army.

| | |
|---|---|
| Divisional Commander .. .. | Major-General Von Hartmann. |

1st Line.

Commandant of Cuirassier Brigade  Major-General Von Schoen
(West Prussian Cuirassiers, No. 5.
Silesian Cuirassiers, No. 1).

2nd Line.
Commander Major-General Von Borstell.
Commandant of Light Brigade .. Major-General Von Witzleben
(Posen Uhlans, No. 10.
2nd Royal Hussars No. 2).
 ,,     Landwehr Brigade .. Major-General Von Frankenberg.
2nd Landwehr Hussars.
1st Landwehr Uhlans.
Two Horse Batteries.


## ARMY OF THE ELBE.

Commander in-Chief    ..    ..  General Von Herwarth.
Chief of the Staff  ..    ..    ..  Colonel Von Schlotheim.
Commandant of Artillery  ..    ..    ,,   Von Rozynski.
Commandant of Engineers ..    ..  Lieut.-Colonel Von Forell.
 ,,     14th Division    ..  Lieut.-General Count Münster.
 ,,     27th Brigade    ..  Major-Gen. Von Scwarzkoppen
(16th and 56th Regiments).
 ,,     28th Brigade    ..  Major-General Von Hiller
(17th and 57th Regiments).
Westphalian Dragoons, No. 7.
7th Jäger Battalion.
Two Companies of 7th Pioneer Battalion.
Four Batteries.
Light Field Hospital.
Section of Krankenträgers.
 ,,     15th Division    ..  Lieut.-General Von Canstein.
 ,,     29th Brigade    ..  Major-General Von Stückradt
(40th and 65th Regiments).
 ,,     30th Brigade    ..  Major-General Von Glasenapp
(28th and 68th Regiments).
Royal Hussars, No. 7.
8th Pioneer Battalion.
Four Batteries.
Light Field Hospital.
Section of Krankenträgers.
 ,,     16th Division    ..  Lieut.-General Von Etzel.
 ,,     31st Brigade    ..  Major-General Von Schöler
(29th and 69th Regiments).
 ,,     Fusilier  ,,    ..  Colonel Wegerer (33rd and
34th Regiments).
8th Jäger Battalion.
Two Batteries.
Light Field Hospital.
Section of Krankenträgers.
Commandant of 14th Cavalry Brigade, Major-General Count Goltz.
Westphalian Uhlans, No. 5.
2nd Westphalian Hussars, No. 11.
Commandant of Reserve Cavalry Brigade, Major-General Von Kotze.
Rhenish Cuirassiers, No. 8.
Rhenish Uhlans, No. 7.
Pomeranian Landwehr Reiter Regiment.
One Horse Battery.
Reserve Artillery VIIth Corps, six Batteries.
 ,,     ,,    VIIIth  ,,  seven Batteries.

*First Reserve Corps.*

Lieutenant-General Von der Mülbe.

*Landwehr Division of the Guard.*—General Von Rosenberg.

1st Brigade of Guard Landwehr (1st and 2nd Guard Landwehr
Regiments).
2nd Brigade of Guard Landwehr (1st and 2nd Guard Grenadier
Landwehr Regiments).

*Combined Landwehr Division.*—General Von Bentheim.

1st Landwehr Brigade (9th and 21st Landwehr Regiments).
2nd   ,,    ,,   (13th and 15th   ,,      ,,   ).

*Landwehr Cavalry Division.*—Major-General Count Dohna.

Six Landwehr Cavalry Regiments.
Reserve Artillery Regiment.
Nine Reserve Batteries.

## ARMY OF THE MAINE.

Commander-in Chief      ..      ..      General Vogel Von Falckenstein.
Chief of the Staff    ..      ..      ..      Colonel Von Kraatz-Koschlau.

*A.*—13*th Division.*—Lieut.-General Von Goeben.

Commandant of 25th Brigade    ..    Major-General Von Kummer
                                                      (13th and 53rd Regiments).
    ,,        26th     ,,      ..    Major-General Von Wrangel
                                                      (15th and 55th Regiment).
Two Companies of 7th Pioneer Battalion.
13th Cavalry Brigade   { Westphalian Cuirassiers, No. 4.
                          { 1st Westphalian Hussars, No. 8.
Six Batteries.
Light Field Hospital.

*B.*—*Combined Division.*—Major-General Von Beyer.

19th, 20th, 30th, 32nd, 39th, and 70th Regiments.
N.B.—The 30th and 70th were detached to garrison Hesse Cassel.
2nd Rhenish Hussars, No. 9.
Three Batteries.
Light Field Hospital.

*C.*—*Combined Division (formerly in Holstein).*

Major-General Von Manteuffel.

Commandant of 1st Combined Brigade, Major-General Von Freyhold
                                             (25th and 36th Regiments).
    ,,        2nd     ,,    ,,   ..   Major-General Von Korth
                                             (11th and 59th Regiments).
   ,      Cavalry Brigade   ..   Major-General Von Flies
                                         (Rhenish Dragoons, No. 5;
                                         Magdeburg Dragoons, No. 6).
Two Battalions of Coburg-Gotha.
One Battalion of Lippe.
Five Fourth Battalions.
9th Jäger Battalion.

Three newly-raised Regiments of Landwehr Cavalry.
Oldenburg, Hanseatic Brigade (nine Battalions, three Squadrons,
two Batteries).


*Second Reserve Corps.*

Commander-in-Chief.—His Royal Highness the Duke of Mecklenburg-
Schwerin.
*a.* Mecklenburg Division (five Battalions, four Squadrons, two Batteries).
*b.* Combined Prussian Division (sixteen Battalions).
*c.* Two Anhalt Battalions.
Two Reserve Regiments of Landwehr Cavalry.
Eight Batteries.

---

## ORDER OF BATTLE OF THE IMPERIAL AUSTRIAN ARMY OF THE NORTH.

| | |
|---|---|
| General-in-Chief | Feldzeugmeister Ritter Von Benedek. |
| Chief of the Staff | Lieutenant-Field-Marshal Von Henikstein. |
| Director of Artillery | Lieut.-Field-Marshal Archduke William. |
| „ Engineers | Colonel Von Pidoll. |

*First Corps d'Armée.*

| | |
|---|---|
| General Commanding | General of Cavalry, Count Clam-Gallas. |
| Assistant | General Count Gondrecourt. |
| Chief of the Staff | Colonel Von Litzelhofen. |

Commandant of Brigade.—Major-General Poschacher.
18th Field Jäger Battalion.
30th Infantry Regiment (Martini).
34th Infantry (King William of Prussia).

Commandant of Brigade.—Colonel Count Leiningen.
32nd Field Jäger Battalion.
30th Infantry Regiment (Giulay).
38th Infantry Regiment (Haugwitz).

Commandant of Brigade.—Major-General Piret.
29th Field Jäger Battalion.
18th Infantry Regiment (Constantin).
45th „ „ (Sigismund).

Commandant of Brigade.—Major-General Ringelsheim.
26th Jäger Battalion.
42nd Infantry Regiment (Hanover).
73rd „ „ (Duke William of Würtemburg).

To each Brigade, one squadron of the Nikolaus Regiment of Hussars (No. 2), and one 4-pounder Field Battery were attached.

N B.—To the Corps were besides attached one Sanitary Company, one Field Ambulance, one Company of Pioneers, two 4-pounder and two 8-pounder Field Batteries, two Horse Artillery Batteries, and one Rocket Battery.

## Second Corps d Armée.

| | | |
|---|---|---|
| General Commanding | .. .. | Lieut. Field-Marshal Count Thun-Hohenstadt. |
| Assistant .. .. | .. .. | Major-General Von Philippowich. |
| Chief of the Staff .. | .. .. | Colonel Von Döpfner. |

Commandant of Brigade.—Colonel Thom.
2nd Field Jäger Battalion.
40th Infantry Regiment (Rossbach).
69th „ „ (Jellachich).

Commandant of Brigade.—Major-General Henriquez.
9th Field Jäger Battalion.
14th Infantry Regiment (Hesse).
27th „ „ (Belgium).

Commandant of Brigade —Major-General Von Saffran.
11th Field Jäger Battalion.
64th Infantry Regiment (Saxe-Weimar).
80th „ „ (Holstein).

Commandant of Brigade.—Major-General Duke Würtemburg.
20th Field Jäger Battalion.
47th Infantry Regiment (Hartung).
57th „ „ (Mecklenburg).

To each Brigade one Squadron of the Imperial Uhlans (No. 6), and one 4-pounder Field Battery were attached.
To this Corps were attached the same as to the First Corps.

## Third Corps d'Armée.

| | | |
|---|---|---|
| General Commanding | .. .. | Lieutenant-Field-Marshal Arch-Duke Ernst. |
| Assistant .. .. | .. .. | Major-General Von Baumgarten. |
| Chief of the Staff .. | .. .. | Colonel Von Catty. |

Commandant of Brigade.—Major-General Kalik, afterwards Colonel Von Abele.
22nd Field Jäger Battalion.
35th Infantry Regiment (Khevenhüller).
72nd „ „ (Ramming).

N.B —This brigade, which had garrisoned Holstein on the outbreak of hostilities, was attached to the first Corps d'Armée.

Commandant of Brigade.—Major-General Appiano.
4th Field Jäger Battalion.
46th Infantry Regiment (Meiningen).
62nd „ „ (Archduke Henry).

Commandant of Brigade.—Colonel Benedek.
1st Field Jäger Battalion.
52nd Infantry Regiment (Archduke Franz Karl).
78th        ,,              ,,        (Sokcevics).

Commandant of Brigade.—Colonel Kirchsberg).
3rd Field Jäger Battalion.
44th Infantry Regiment (Archduke Albrecht).
49th        ,,              ,,        (Hess).

Commandant of Brigade.—Colonel Prohaska.
13th Border Infantry Regiment.
4th Battalion of the 55th Regiment (Gondrecourt).
,,           ,,      56th      ,,        (Gorizutti).
33rd Jäger Battalion.
34th        ,,              ,,

To each brigade were attached one squadron of the Count Mensdorf
Uhlans (No. 9), and one 4-pounder field battery.
To this Corps were attached the same as to the First Corps.

### Fourth Corps d'Armée.

| | | |
|---|---|---|
| General Commanding | .. .. | Lieutenant Field-Marshal Count Festitics. |
| Assistant .. .. | .. .. | Major-General Von Mollinary. |
| Chief of the Staff .. | .. .. | Colonel Von Görz. |

Commandant of Brigade.—Major-General Von Brandenstein.
27th Field Jäger Battalion.
12th Infantry Regiment (Archduke William).
26th        ,,              ,,        (Michael).

Commandant of Brigade.—Colonel Fleischhacker.
13th Field Jäger Battalion.
6th Infantry Regiment (Coronini).
61st        ,,              ,,        (Cesarewitsch of Russia).

Commandant of Brigade.—Colonel Poeckh.
8th Field Jäger Battalion.
37th Infantry Regiment (Archduke Joseph).
51st        ,,              ,        (Archduke Charles Ferdinand).

Commandant of Brigade.—Major-General Archduke Joseph.
30th Field Jäger Battalion.
67th Infantry Regiment (Schmerling).
68th        ,,              ,,        (Steininger).

To each brigade one squadron of the 7th Hussars and one 4-pounder
Field Battery were attached.

To this Corps the same were attached as to the First Corps.

### Sixth Corps d'Armée.

| | | |
|---|---|---|
| General Commanding | .. .. | Lieutenant-Field-Marshal Baron Ramming. |
| Assistant .. .. | .. .. | Major-General Von Kochmeister. |
| Chief of the Staff .. | .. .. | Colonel Frölich. |

Commandant of Brigade.—Colonel Von Waldstätten.
6th Field Jäger Battalion.
6th Infantry Regiment (Hartmann).
79th    ,,     ,,    (Frank).

Commandant of Brigade.—Colonel Hertwegh.
25th Field Jäger Battalion.
41st Infantry Regiment (Kellner).
56th    ,,     ,,    (Gorizutti).

Commandant of Brigade.—Major-General Rosenweig.
17th Field Jäger Battalion.
4th Infantry Regiment (Deutschmeister).
55th    ,,     ,,    (Gondrecourt).

Commandant of Brigade.—Colonel Jonak.
14th Field Jäger Battalion.
20th Infantry Regiment (Crown Prince of Prussia).
60th    ,,     ,,    (Wasa).

To each brigade one squadron of the 10th Uhlans, and one 4-pounder Field Battery were attached.

Besides were attached to the Corps one Sanitary Company, one Field Ambulance, one Company of Pioneers, one 4-pounder and two 8-pounder Field Batteries, two 4-pounder Batteries of Horse Artillery, and a Rocket Battery.

### *Eighth Corps d'Armée.*

General Commanding   ..   ..    Archduke Leopold.
Assistant   ..   ..   ..   ..    Major-General Weber.
Chief of the Staff   ..   ..   ..    Lieutenant-Colonel Von Majnone.

Commandant of Brigade.—Colonel Fragnern.
5th Field Jäger Battalion.
15th Infantry Regiment (Nassau).
77th    ,,     ,,    (Archduke of Tuscany).

Commandant of Brigade.—Major-General Von Kreyssern.
31st Field Jäger Battalion.
8th Infantry Regiment (Gerstner).
74th    ,,     ,,    (Nobili).

Commandant of Brigade.—General Count Rothkirch.
25th Infantry Regiment (Mamula).
71st    ,,     ,,    (Leopold of Tuscany).

Commandant of Brigade.—Colonel Von Roth.
24th Field Jäger Battalion.
21st Infantry Regiment (Reischach).
32nd    ,,     ,,    (Este).

To each brigade one squadron of the Archduke Charles's Uhlans (No. 3), and one 4-pounder Battery were attached.

Besides were attached to the Corps the same as to the Sixth Corps.

### *Tenth Corps d'Armée.*

General Commanding   ..   ..    Lieutenant-Field-Marshal Von Gablenz.
Assistant   ..   ..   ..   ..    Baron Koller.
Chief of the Staff   ..   ..   ..    Colonel Bourgignone.

Commandant of Brigade.—Colonel Mondl.
12th Field Jäger Battalion.
10th Infantry Regiment (Mazuchelli).
24th ,, ,, (Parma).

Commandant of Brigade.—Colonel Grivicics.
16th Field Jäger Battalion.
2nd Infantry Regiment (Alexander).
23rd ,, ,, (Airoldi).

Commandant of Brigade.—Major-General Von Knebel.
28th Field Jäger Battalion.
1st Infantry Regiment (Emperor Francis Joseph).
3rd ,, ,, (Archduke Charles).

Commandant of Brigade.—Major-General Wimpffen.
13th Infantry Regiment (Bamberg).
58th ,, ,, (Archduke Stephen, four Battalions).

To each brigade were attached one squadron of the 1st Uhlans, and
one 4-pounder Field Battery.

The same were attached to the Corps as to the First Corps, except
that this Corps had only one 4-pounder Field Battery.


*First Light Cavalry Division.*—Major-General Baron Edelsheim.

Chief of the Staff.—Major Waldstätten.

Commandant of Brigade.—Colonel Appel.
2nd Dragoons (Windischgrätz).
9th Hussars (Liechtenstein).

Commandant of Brigade.—Colonel Wallis.
1st Dragoons (Savoy).
10th Hussars (King of Prussia).

Commandant of Brigade.—Colonel Fratricievics.
5th Hussars (Radetzky).
8th ,, (Hesse-Cassel).


*Second Light Cavalry Division.*—Major-General Prince Thurn and Taxis.

Chief of the Staff.—Major Rodakovsky.

Commandant of Brigade.—Colonel Count Bellegarde.
4th Hussars (Cseh).
12th ,, (Haller).

Commandant of Brigade.—Major-General Westphalen.
6th Hussars (Würtemberg).
11th ,, (Palffy).


*First Reserve Division of Cavalry.*—Lieutenant-Field-Marshal Prince
Schleswig-Holstein.

Commandant of Brigade.—Major-General Prince Solms.
4th Cuirass Regiment (Ferdinand).
6th ,, ,, (Hesse).
8th Uhlans (Emperor Max).

Commandant of Brigade.—Major-General Schindlöcker.
    9th Cuirass Regiment (Stadion).
    11th    ,,    ,,    (Emperor Francis Joseph).
    4th Uhlans    ,,    ,,    ,,

*Second Reserve Division of Cavalry.*—Major-General Von Zaitsek.

Commandant of Brigade.—Major-General Boxberg.
    3rd Cuirass Regiment (Saxony).
    7th    ,,    ,,    (Brunswick).
    2nd Uhlans (Schwarzenberg).

Commandant of Brigade.—General Count Soltyk.
    1st Cuirass Regiment (Emperor Francis Joseph).
    5th    ,,    ,,    (Nicolas).
    5th Uhlans (Walmoden).

*Third Reserve Division of Cavalry.*—Major-General Count Coudenhove.

Commandant of Brigade.—Major-General Prince Windischgrätz.
    2nd Cuirass Regiment (Wrangel).
    8th    ,,    ,,    (Prince Charles of Prussia).
    7th Uhlans (Archduke Charles Louis).

Commandant of Brigade.—Major-General Von Mengen.
    10th Cuirass Regiment (Bavaria).
    12th    ,,    ,,    (Neipperg).
    11th Uhlans (Alexander).
To each Cavalry brigade was attached one battery of Horse Artillery.

*Reserve Artillery of the Army.*
16 Batteries.

---

## ORDER OF BATTLE OF THE ROYAL SAXON ARMY CORPS.

| | | |
|---|---|---|
| General Commanding | .. .. | General Crown Prince of Saxony. |
| Chief of Staff | .. .. .. | Major-General Von Fabrice. |
| Adjutant-General .. | .. .. | ,,    Von Thielau. |
| Commander of Artillery | .. .. | ,,    Schmalz. |
| 1st Infantry Division | .. .. | Lieut.-General Von Schimpff. |
| 2nd Infantry Brigade | .. .. | Major-General Von Carlowitz. |
| | | (5th, 6th, 7th, 8th Infantry, and 2nd Rifle Battalions). |
| 3rd Infantry Brigade | .. .. | Colonel Von Hake |
| | | (9th, 10th, 11th, 12th, and 3rd Rifle Battalions). |

Divisional Cavalry :
Two Squadrons of 2nd and 3rd "Reiter" Regiments.
Divisional Artillery :
12-pounder Battery "Von der Pforte."
6    ,,    ,,    "Leonhardi."

| | | |
|---|---|---|
| 2nd Infantry Division | .. .. | Lieutenant-General Von Stieglitz. |
| 1st Infantry Brigade | .. .. | Colonel Von Boxberg |

                                     (1st, 2nd, 3rd, 4th Infantry, and 1st Rifle Battalions).

4th Infantry ("Leib") Brigade .. Colonel Von Hausen
                                     (13th, 14th, 15th, 16th Infantry, and 4th Rifle Battalions).

Divisional Cavalry:
Two Squadrons of the Guard and 1st " Reiter" Regiments.
Divisional Artillery:
12-pounder Battery " Hering-Göppingen."
6   ,,   ,,   " Richter."

| | | |
|---|---|---|
| Cavalry Division | .. .. .. | Lieutenant-General Von Fritsch. |
| 1st Cavalry Brigade .. | .. .. | ,,   ,,   Prince George |

                             of Saxony
                             (Guard "Reiter" and 1st "Reiter" Regiments).

2nd Cavalry Brigade .. .. Major-General Von Biedermann
                             (2nd and 3rd "Reiter" Regiments).

12-pounder Horse Artillery Battery, "Zenker."

Reserve Artillery .. .. .. Colonel Köhler.
Three 12-pounder Batteries, "Lengnick," "Westmann," and "Hoch."
Two 6   ,,   ,,   " Heidenreich" and "Walter."
Two Companies of Pioneers and Pontoon Detachment.
Total of Saxon Corps:
16 Battalions of Infantry; 4 Battalions of Rifles; 16 Squadrons;
58 guns; 2 Companies Pioneers.

---

## ORDER OF BATTLE OF THE ROYAL HANOVERIAN ARMY, ON 18th JUNE.

| | | |
|---|---|---|
| Commanding General | .. .. | Lieut.-Gen. Von Ahrentsschildt. |
| Chief of Staff.. .. | .. .. | Colonel Cordemann. |
| Adjutant-General .. | .. .. | ,,   Dammers. |
| Commander of Artillery | .. .. | ,,   Von Stolzenberg. |
| Commander of Engineers | .. .. | Lieutenant-Colonel Oppermann. |
| 1st Brigade .. | .. .. .. | Major-Gen. Von dem Knesebeck. |

            Guard Regiment, 1st ("Leib") Regiment.
               Battalion of Guard Rifles.
               Queen's Hussar Regiment.
               12-pounder Battery " Meyer."

2nd Brigade .. .. .. .. Colonel de Vaux.
               2nd Infantry Regiment.
               3rd Infantry Regiment.
               1st Battalion of Rifles.
          Duke of Cambridge Dragoon Regiment.
             6-pounder Battery " Laves."

3rd Brigade .. .. .. .. Colonel Von Bülow Stolle.
4th Infantry Regiment.
5th  „        „
2nd Battalion of Rifles.
Crown Prince Dragoon Regiment.
6 pounder Battery " Eggers."

4th Brigade .. ., .. .. Major-General Von Bothmer.
6th Infantry Regiment.
7th  „        „
3rd Battalion of Rifles.
Guard Hussar Regiment.
6-pounder Battery " Müller."
Horse Artillery Battery " Mertens."

Reserve Cavalry .. .. .. Lieutenant-Colonel Von Geyso.
Guard du Corps Regiment.
Guard Cuirassier Regiment.
Horse Artillery Battery " Böttiger."

Reserve Artillery .. .. .. Major Hartmann.
6-pounder Battery " Blumenbach."
24  „    Howitzer Battery "Hartmann."
Total of Royal Hanoverian Army :
16 Battalions of Infantry; 4 Battalions of Rifles; 24 Squadrons;
24 Guns; besides 10 Guns incompletely horsed.

---

## ORDER OF BATTLE OF THE ELECTORAL HESSIAN DIVISION.

Commanding General .. .. Major-General Von Lossberg.
Chief of Staff .. .. .. Major Darapsky.
Commander of Artillery .. .. Major-Gen. Von Kochenhausen.
1st Infantry Division .. .. Major-General Von Buttlar.
Guard Regiment.
1st Infantry Regiment.
Rifle Battalion.
Sharpshooter Battalion.

2nd Infantry Division .. .. Colonel Von Osterhausen.
2nd Infantry Regiment.
3rd  „        „

Cavalry Brigade .. .. .. Major-General Von Bardeleben.
1st Hussar Regiment.
2nd  „        „
Two Squadrons of the Guard du Corps Regiment.

Artillery :
One 4-pounder and three 6-pounder Batteries; besides four 6-pounder
and eight 4-pounder Guns, not yet horsed.
One Company of Pioneers, with Bridge Equipage.

Total of Electoral Hessian Division :
8 Battalions of Infantry; 2 Battalions of Rifles; 8 Squadrons; 16 guns
and 1 Company of Pioneers.

N.B.—Two Squadrons were detached to the combined Austrian-
Nassau Division and will be accounted for there.

ORDER OF BATTLE OF THE ROYAL BAVARIAN ARMY.

| | |
|---|---|
| Commander-in-Chief .. .. | H.R.H. Field-Marshal Prince Charles of Bavaria. |
| Chief of the Staff .. .. .. | Lieut.-Gen. Baron Von der Tann. |
| Director of Field Artillery .. .. | Lieut.-General Von Brodesser. |
| Director of Engineers .. .. | Lieutenant-Colonel Limbach. |

Attached to Head-Quarters Staff.
5th Sharpshooter Company of 7th Infantry Regiment.
Half a Company of Engineers.

| | |
|---|---|
| 1st Infantry Division .. .. | Lieutenant-Colonel Stephan. |
| 1st Infantry Brigade .. .. | Major-General Von Steinle ("Leib" and 1st Infantry Regiments and 2nd Rifle Battalion). |
| 2nd Infantry Brigade .. .. | Major-General Von Wetsch (2nd and 8th Infantry Regiments). |

3rd Regiment of Chevauxlegers.
One 6-pounder and one 12-pounder Battery.
1st Sanitary Company.
Two Field Hospitals.

| | |
|---|---|
| 2nd Infantry Division .. .. | Lieutenant-General Von Feder. |
| 3rd Infantry Brigade .. .. | Major-General Schumacher (3rd and 12th Infantry Regiments and 7th Rifle Battalion). |
| 4th Infantry Brigade .. .. | Major-General Von Hauer (7th and 10th Infantry Regiments and 3rd Rifle Battalion). |

4th Regiment of Chevauxlegers.
One 6-pounder and one 12-pounder Battery.
4th Sanitary Company.
Two Field Hospitals.

| | |
|---|---|
| 3rd Infantry Division .. .. | Lieutenant-General Von Zoller. |
| 5th Infantry Brigade .. .. | Major-General Ribeaupierre (11th and 15th Infantry Regiments and 5th Rifle Battalion). |
| 6th Infantry Brigade .. .. | Colonel Schweitzer (6th and 14th Infantry Regiments and 1st Rifle Battalion). |

2nd Regiment of Chevauxlegers.
One 6-pounder and one 12-pounder Battery.
3rd Sanitary Company.
Two Field Hospitals.

| | |
|---|---|
| 4th Infantry Division .. .. | Lieut.-Gen. Von Hartmann. |
| 7th Infantry Brigade .. .. | Major-General Faust (5th and 13th Infantry Regiments and 8th Rifle Battalion). |
| 8th Infantry Brigade .. .. | Major-General Cella (4th and 9th Infantry Regiments and 6th Rifle Battalion). |

6th Regiment of Chevauxlegers.
One 6-pounder and one 12-pounder Battery.
2nd Sanitary Company.
Two Field Hospitals.

Reserve Cavalry Corps .. .. Lieut.-General Prince Taxis.
Heavy Cavalry Brigade .. .. Major-General Von Rummel
(1st, 2nd, and 3rd Regiments
of Cuirassiers).

1st Light Cavalry Brigade .. .. Major-General Duke Ludwig of
Bavaria
(1st and 2nd Regiments of
Lancers).

2nd Light Cavalry Brigade.. .. Major-Gen. Count Pappenheim
(5th Regiment of Chevaux-
legers and 3rd Regiment of
Lancers).

Two 12-pounder Batteries.

Artillery Reserve:
Six 12-pounder and two 6-pounder Batteries.
Two Engineer Companies.
Four Field Hospitals.
Total of Bavarian Army:
38 Battalions of Infantry; 7 Battalions of Rifles; 44 Squadrons; 144
Guns and 3 Companies of Engineers.

---

## ORDER OF BATTLE OF THE VIIITH FEDERAL CORPS D'ARMEÉ, ON 9TH JULY.

Commander-in-Chief .. .. Prince Alexander of Hesse.
Chief of Staff, Würtemberg . .. Lieutenant-General Von Baur.
Second Chief, Baden.. .. .. Major-General Kraus.
Director of Artillery, Baden .. Lieutenant-General Von Faber.
„ Engineers, Würtemberg Colonel Niethammer.

1st Division, Würtemberg .. .. Lieut.-General Von Hardegg.
Chief of Staff .. .. .. Major-General Von Callee.
1st Brigade .. .. .. .. Major-General Von Baumbach
(1st and 5th Regiments of In-
fantry and 3rd Rifle Battalion).

2nd Brigade .. .. .. .. Major-General Von Fischer
(2nd and 7th Regiments of In-
fantry and 2nd Rifle Battalion).

3rd Brigade .. .. .. .. Major-General Hegelmeier
(3rd and 8th Regiments of In-
fantry and 1st Rifle Battalion).

Cavalry Brigade .. .. .. Major-Gen. Count Von Scheler
(1st and 4th Cavalry Regi-
ments).

N.B.—A third Regiment with the Reserve Cavalry of the Corps.

Artillery .. .. .. .. Colonel Von Leube
(Three 6-pounder Batteries).

N.B.—Three Batteries were with the Reserve of the Corps.

2nd Division, Baden.. .. .. Lieut.-Gen. Prince William of
Baden.

Commander of Infantry .. .. Lieutenant-General Waag.
Chief of Staff .. .. .. Colonel Keller.
1st Brigade .. .. .. .. Major-General Von Laroche
("Lieb" Grenadiers Regi-
ment, 5th Infantry Regiment,
and Rifle Battalion).

2nd Brigade ..    ..    ..    ..    Colonel Von Neubronn
(2nd and 3rd Infantry Regiments and 2nd Fusilier Battalion).

Cavalry Brigade:
Two Regiments of Dragoons.

N.B.—A third Regiment with the Reserves of the Corps.

Artillery    ..    ..    ..    ..    Colonel Count Sponeck.

Three 6-pounder Batteries.

N.B.—Two Batteries with the Reserves of the Corps.

3rd Division, Hesse-Darmstadt    ..    Lieutenant-General Von Perglas
Chief of Staff    ..    ..    ..    Colonel Becker.
1st Brigade ..    ..    ..    ..    Major-General Frey
(1st and 2nd Infantry Regiments, Company of Rifles).
2nd Brigade ..    ..    ..    ..    Major-General Von Stockhausen
(3rd and 4th Infantry Regiments, Company of Rifles).

Battalion of Sharpshooters.

Cavalry Brigade    ..    ..    ..    Major-General Prince Ludwig of
Hesse.

One Chevauxlegers Regiment.

N.B.—A second Regiment with the Reserves of the Corps.

Artillery:
Two 6-pounder Batteries.

4th Division, Austria, Nassau, } Lieutenant Field-Marshal Count
   Electoral Hesse.                Neipperg.
Austrian Brigade    ..    ..    ..    Major-General Von Hahn.

16th Infantry Regiments (Wernhardt).
4th Battalions of the 21st and 49th Regiments (Reischach and Hess).
35th Field Jäger Battalion.
4-pounder Battery.

N.B.—One 8-pounder Battery with the Reserves of the Corps.

Nassau Brigade    ..    ..    ..    Major-General Roth.

1st and 2nd Infantry Regiments and Rifle Battalion.
Two Half Batteries (6-pounder).

N.B.—One 6-pounder Battery with the Reserves of the Corps.

Two Squadrons of Electoral Hessian Hussars.

Reserves of the Corps:

Cavalry    ..    ..    ..    ..    Lieutenant-General Von Entress
(Würtemberg).

One Würtemberg, one Baden, and one Hessian Regiment.
One Würtemberg Horse Artillery Battery.

Artillery    ..    Two 12-pounder Batteries, Würtemberg.
               One 12    ,,       ,,    Hesse.
               One  6    ,,       ,,       ,,
               One  5    ,,       ,,    Nassau.
               One  5    ,,       ,,    Baden.
               One  6    ,,       ,,       ,,
               One  8    ,,       ,,    Austria.

Total of VIIIth Federal Corps:
39 Battalions of Infantry; 7½ Battalions of Rifles; 36 Squadrons;
134 Guns.

2 M

# APPENDIX III.

Summary of the Armies of all the States allied against Prussia.

## I. On the Eastern Theatre of War.

| | Battalions of Infantry. | Battalions of Rifles. | Squadrons of Cavalry. | Guns. | Rocket Batteries. | Companies of Pioneers. |
|---|---|---|---|---|---|---|
| 1. Austrian Army of the North | 178 | 28 | 163 | 752 | 6 | .. |
| 2. Saxon Corps d'Armée.. | 16 | 4 | 16 | 58 | .. | 2 |
| Total of I. .. | 194 | 32 | 179 | 810 | 6 | 2 |

## II. On the Western Theatre of War.

| | Battalions of Infantry. | Battalions of Rifles. | Squadrons of Cavalry. | Guns. | Rocket Batteries. | Companies of Pioneers. |
|---|---|---|---|---|---|---|
| 1. Hanoverian Army | 16 | 4 | 24 | 52 | .. | .. |
| 2. Electoral Hessian Division .. | 8 | 2 | 8 | 16 | .. | 1 |
| 3. Bavarian Army | 38 | 7 | 4 | 144 | .. | 3 |
| 4. VIIIth Federal Corps d'Armée | 39 | 7½ | 36 | 134 | .. | .. |
| Total of II. .. | 101 | 20½ | 112 | 346 | .. | 4 |
| Total of I. .. | 194 | 32 | 179 | 810 | 6 | 2 |
| Total of I. and II... | 295 | 52½ | 291 | 1,156 | 6 | 6 |

## APPENDIX IV.

His Majesty the King has added the following additions to the capitulation agreed upon between General Falckenstein and General Arentschildt, commanding the Royal Hanoverian Army, this morning. Above all things, his Majesty has ordered me to express his very high recognition of the courageous behaviour of the Royal Hanoverian troops.

The following points are put forward :—

1. The King of Hanover can, with the Crown Prince and any suite he chooses to select, have a free choice of residence anywhere without the Kingdom of Hanover. His Majesty's private property is to be reserved for his own use.

2. The officers and officials of the Hanoverian Army give their parole nôt to serve against Prussia, and retain their arms, baggage, and horses, as well as pay and allowances, and enter upon the Prussian administration of Hanover with the same rights and claims as they would have had on the Hanoverian Government.

3. Non-commissioned officers and soldiers of the Hanoverian Army give up arms, horses, and ammunition to officers appointed by the King of Hanover, and betake themselves, in parties to be told off by Prussia, by rail, to their homes, promising not to serve against Prussia.

4. The arms, horses, and matériel of war of the Hanoverian Army are to be handed over by the above-mentioned officers to Prussian Commissioners.

5. By the special desire of General Arentschildt, the retention of the pay of Non-Commissioned Officers of the Hanoverian Army is agreed to.

(Signed)     Von Arentschildt,
*Lieut.-General Commanding of the Hanoverian Army.*

(Signed)     Baron Von Manteuffel,
*Governor in the Elbe Duchies, Lieut.-Gen. and Adjt.-Gen. of His Majesty the King of Prussia.*

*Langensalza, June 29th, 1866.*

# APPENDIX V.

Order of Battle of the Detachment of General Von Flies in the Action of Langensalza, 27th June, 1866.

General Commanding .. .. .. Major-General Von Flies.
Commander of Artillery.. .. .. Major Petzel.

| | Battalions of Infantry. | Battalions of Rifles. | Squadrons. | Guns. | Battalions of Pioneers. |
|---|---|---|---|---|---|
| **ADVANCED GUARD.** | | | | | |
| Colonel Von Fabeck, Commanding Saxe-Coburg-Gotha Regiment. | | | | | |
| Saxe-Coburg-Gotha Infantry Regiment, Lieut.-Colonel Von Westernhagen : | | | | | |
| 1st Battalion, Captain Von Bassewitz.. .. | } 2 | .. | .. | .. | .. |
| Fusilier Battalion, Major Von Gerstein .. | | | | | |
| "Merseburg" Garrison Squadron of 12th Landwehr Hussar Regiment, Lieutenant Schmitz .. .. .. .. .. .. | .. | .. | 1 | .. | .. |
| Half of a Sully Battery of the 4th Artillery Brigade, Captain Caspary .. .. .. .. .. | .. | .. | .. | 2 | .. |
| Third 4-pounder Battery of 6th Field Artillery Regiment, Captain Bloch Von Blottnitz .. | .. | .. | .. | 6 | .. |
| Total Advanced Guard .. .. | 2 | .. | 1 | 8 | .. |
| **MAIN BODY.** | | | | | |
| Colonel Baron Von Hanstein, Commanding 25th Regiment. | | | | | |
| 25th Regiment of Infantry : | | | | | |
| 1st Battalion, Major Von Loebell .. .. | } 2 | .. | .. | .. | .. |
| Fusilier Battalion, Major Bassenge .. .. | | | | | |
| 2nd (Torgau) Battalion of 32nd Landwehr Regiment | 1 | .. | .. | .. | .. |
| 11th Regiment of Grenadiers, Colonel Von Zglinitzki : | | | | | |
| 1st Battalion, Lieutenant-Colonel des Barres.. | } 3 | .. | .. | .. | .. |
| 2nd Battalion, Major Von Bonin .. .. | | | | | |
| Fusilier Battalion, Major Von Busse .. .. | | | | | |
| Depôt Squadron of 10th Hussar Regiment, Lieut. Von Kemnitz .. .. .. .. .. | .. | .. | 1 | .. | .. |
| 4th Horse Artillery Battery of 7th Field Artillery Regiment, Captain König.. .. .. .. | .. | .. | .. | 6 | .. |
| Total Main Body .. .. | 6 | .. | 1 | 6 | .. |

## APPENDIX V.—*continued.*

| | Battalions of Infantry. | Battalions of Rifles. | Squadrons. | Guns. | Battalions of Pioneers. |
|---|---|---|---|---|---|
| **RESERVE.** | | | | | |
| Major-General Von Seckendorff. | | | | | |
| 1st Line, Colonel Von Hellmuth, Commanding Landwehr Battalion (Aschersleben): | | | | | |
| 3rd (Naumburg) Battalion of 32nd Landwehr Regiment, Major Von Oettinger .. .. | 2 | .. | .. | .. | .. |
| 3rd (Aschersleben) Battalion of 27th Landwehr Regiment (Colonel Von Hellmuth) .. | | | | | |
| 2nd Line, Major Baron Von Wintzingerode, Commanding Depôt Battalion 71st Regiment: | | | | | |
| 3rd Battalion (Potsdam) 20th Landwehr Regiment, Captain Von Kirschy .. .. | | | | | |
| 2nd Battalion (Treuenbrietzen) 20th Landwehr Regiment, Major Küntzel .. .. .. | 2¾ | .. | .. | .. | .. |
| 3 Companies of Depôt Battalion 71st Regiment, Captain von Breitenbauch .. .. .. | | | | | |
| "Stendal" Garrison Squadron .. .. .. | .. | .. | 1 | .. | .. |
| Two guns of Sally Battery of 4th Artillery Brigade, Lieutenant Hupfield : .. .. | .. | .. | .. | 2 | .. |
| 3rd Horse Artillery Battery of 7th Field Artillery Regiment, Captain Metting .. .. .. | .. | .. | .. | 6 | .. |
| Total Reserve .. .. | 4¾ | .. | 1 | 8 | .. |

### SUMMARY.

| | Battalions. | Squadrons. | Guns. |
|---|---|---|---|
| Advanced Guard .. .. | 2 | 1 | 8 |
| Main Body .. .. .. | 6 | 1 | 6 |
| Reserve .. .. .. | 4¾ | 1 | 8 |
| Total .. .. | 12¼ | 3 | 22 |

Absent as escort of baggage : 4th Company of the Depôt Battalion of the 71st Regiment.

# APPENDIX VI.

STATE of the Hanoverian Troops in the Action of Langensalza, 27th June, 1866, according to Hanoverian accounts.

| | Battalions. | Squadrons. | Guns. | Men, Infantry. | Men, Cavalry. | Men, Artillery. | Total. |
|---|---|---|---|---|---|---|---|
| | | | | Present on the Field. | | | |
| 1st Brigade .. .. .. | 5 | 4 | 6 | 3,519 | 290 | 167 | 4,006 |
| 2nd Brigade .. .. .. | 5 | 3⅓ | 6 | 4,024 | 276 | 138 | 4,456 |
| 3rd Brigade .. .. .. | 5 | 4 | 6 | 2,864 | 328 | 149 | 3,341 |
| 4th Brigade .. .. .. | 5 | 2⅔ | 8 | 2,935 | 222 | 215 | 3,372 |
| Reserve Cavalry .. .. .. | .. | 7 | 4 | .. | 615 | 100 | 715 |
| Reserve Artillery .. .. .. | .. | .. | 12 | .. | .. | 287 | 287 |
| Total Present in the Field .. | 20 | 21 | 42 | 13,390 | 1,731 | 1,056 | 16,177 |
| *Besides not Engaged in the Action .. .. .. .. | .. | 3 | 10 | 2,294 | 657 | 1,441 | 4,382 |
| Total .. .. .. | 20 | 24 | 52 | 15,684 | 2,388 | 2,497 | 20,559 |

\* N.B.—The latter include Body Guard of Head-Quarters, men not yet armed and mounted, recruits not yet enrolled, baggage escorts, entrenching parties, engineers, sanitary companies, and Army Train.

## APPENDIX VII.

### TO MY PEOPLES.

In the midst of the work of peace, which I had undertaken for the purpose of laying the foundation of a Constitution which was to strengthen the unity and power of the Empire, and at the same time secure to my several countries and peoples their free internal development, my duties of a Sovereign have compelled me to call all my forces to arms.

On the frontiers of my Empire, in the south and in the north, stand the armies of two enemies, who have allied with the intention of breaking the power of Austria as a European State.

To neither of these enemies have I given cause for war. I call on an Omniscient God to bear witness that I have always considered it one of my first and most sacred duties as a Sovereign to secure for my peoples the blessings of peace : a duty I have always striven to fulfil.

One of the two hostile Powers requires no pretence. Having a longing to deprive me of parts of my empire, the favourable opportunity is his reason for going to war.

Allied with the Prussian troops, which are now up in arms against us, a part of my faithful and valorous army went two years ago to the shores of the North Sea. I entered into that alliance with Prussia for the purpose of upholding rights guaranteed by treaties, to protect an imperilled German race, to confine the miseries of an unavoidable war within the narrowest possible limits, and by means of an intimate connection between the two central European Powers, whose principal study is to maintain the peace of Europe, to obtain a lasting guarantee for the peace of my Empire, of Germany, and of Europe.

I have never sought for conquests; I did not, in the Vienna Treaty of Peace, seek to obtain any advantage for myself. Austria is not to blame for the sad series of unfortunate complications, which could never had arisen had Prussia been equally disinterested, and which might instantly have been solved had she been equally faithful to the Confederation. Those complications were brought about for the furtherance of selfish purposes, and consequently could not be done away with by my Government in a peaceful way.

Thus the state of affairs became more and more serious.

Even when it was notorious that the two hostile States were making preparations for war, and it became evident that an understanding existed between them, which could only be based on an intention of making a joint attack on my empire, I, mindful of my duties as a Sovereign, remained in a state of profound peace, as I was willing to make any concessions that were compatible with the honour and welfare of my peoples. But, when I saw that further delay would render it difficult to ward off hostile attacks, and would imperil the safety of the monarchy, I was obliged to resolve on making those heavy sacrifices which are inseparable from preparations for war. The assurances given by my Government of my love of peace, and the repeated declarations which were made of my readiness to disarm at the same time with Prussia, were replied to by counter propositions from that Power, which could not be accepted without sacrificing the honour and safety of my empire.

Prussia insisted on the full and previous disarmament not only of those troops near her own frontiers, but also of those in Italy, where the army of an enemy was standing on the confines of my empire, for whose love of peace no guarantee either was or could be given.

All negotiations with Prussia, in respect to the question of the Elbe Duchies, have more and more proved the fact that such a settlement as would be compatible with the dignity of Austria, and with the rights and interests of Germany and the Duchies, cannot be brought about by an understanding with Prussia, whose line of policy is evidently one of violence and conquest. The negotiations were therefore broken off, the whole affair was referred to the decision of the Diet, and at the same time the legal representatives of Holstein were convoked.

The imminent prospect of war induced the three Powers—France, England, and Russia—to invite my Government to participate in general conferences, the object of which was to be the preservation of peace. My Government, in accordance with my views, if possible to maintain peace for my peoples, did not refuse to share in the conferences, but made their acceptance dependent on the decided supposition that the public law of Europe and the existing treaties were to form the basis of these attempts at mediation, and that the Powers joining in them would not promote any interests that were prejudicial to the balance of power in Europe and to the rights of Austria. The fact that the mere attempt at peace discussions failed because these natural suppositions were made, is a proof that the discussions themselves could not have led to the maintenance and strengthening of peace.

Recent events prove undeniably that Prussia now substitutes open violence for right.

The rights and the honour of Austria, the rights and the honour of the whole German nation, were no longer regarded by Prussia as a barrier to her fatally increased ambition. Prussian troops have entered Holstein; the Estates convoked by the Imperial Stadtholder have been violently dissolved; the government of Holstein, which the Treaty of Vienna gives to Austria and Prussia in common, has been claimed for Prussia alone, and the Austrian garrison has been forced to give way before a force ten times as strong as itself.

When the German Diet, which saw in these measures an arbitrary infraction of the Federal laws, accepted the Austrian proposition, and decreed the mobilization of the Federal troops, Prussia, who prides herself on being the defender of the interests of Germany, pursued still further the fatal course she had already commenced. Violently severing the tie which unites the German races, she announced her secession from the Confederation, required from the German Governments the acceptance of a so-called project of reform, which in reality is a division of Germany, and employed military force against those Sovereigns who have faithfully discharged their Federal duties.

The most pernicious of wars, a war of Germans against Germans, has thus become inevitable.

I summon before the tribunal of history, before the tribunal of Eternal Almighty God, those who have been the cause of it, to answer for all the misery that it will bring on individuals, families, districts, and countries.

I begin the war with confidence arising from the justness of my cause, with the consciousness of the power that lies in a great empire, where Prince and people have the same conviction of the good rights of Austria, with joyful perfect courage at the sight of my gallant and well-appointed army, that forms a bulwark against which the force of the enemies of Austria will be broken, and of my faithful peoples, who look up to me in unity, confidence, and self-devotion.

The pure fire of patriotic devotion burns with equal strength in all parts of my vast empire; joyfully do all, who are called in, hasten to take their places in the ranks of the army, numerous volunteers offer themselves for active service, the whole able-bodied population of some of the most exposed districts are preparing to take the field, and the noblest sacrifices are willingly made to alleviate distress, and to provide for the wants of the army.

One and the same feeling pervades all the inhabitants of my kingdoms and countries—the feeling that they belong to one and the same empire, the feeling of the power that lies in their unity, the feeling of indignation at so gross a violation of justice.

It is doubly painful to me that the settlement of the questions relative to the internal constitution of the empire has not yet made so much progress, that I can assemble around my throne the representatives of all my peoples at this grave but inspiring moment. The present want of this support renders my duty as a Sovereign the more evident to me, and strengthens my determination to secure it to my empire for the future.

We shall not stand alone in the ensuing struggle.

Princes and people of Germany are fully aware of the danger which menaces their liberty and independence from a power, whose conduct is only influenced by the selfish dictates of a reckless craving after aggrandizement; they know what a guardian of their welfare Austria is, what a stay for the power and integrity of the united German Fatherland.

As we have taken up arms for the most precious rights that nations have to defend, so our German brethren also. We have been forced to do so. Be it so. Now that we are armed, we will not disarm again until the free internal development of my empire, and of the German States allied with it, has been secured, and their power and influence in Europe strengthened anew.

Our confidence and our hopes must, however, not rest on our unity and our power alone; I put my trust, at the same time on an Almighty and just God, whom my house has served from its very foundation, and who never forsakes those who righteously put their trust in him.

To him I pray for assistance and victory, and I call on my peoples to join me in that prayer.

Given at my residence, and metropolis of Vienna on this 17th of June, 1866.

(Signed)     FRANCIS JOSEPH.

## APPENDIX VIII.

## TO MY PEOPLE.

AT this moment, when Prussia's army is going forth to war, I feel myself constrained to address my people, the sons and grandsons of those brave fathers to whom my father, of blessed memory, spoke unforgotten words, " the Fatherland is in danger."

Austria and a great part of Germany have taken up arms against us.

Not many years have passed since I proffered the hand of friendship to the Emperor of Austria, of my own free will and forgetful of former injuries, when it became necessary to free a German country from a foreign dominion. I was in hopes that a brotherhood of arms would spring out of the blood that we shed in common, a brotherhood that would lead, not only to firm alliance, based on mutual respect and esteem, but also to such united action as would render Germany prosperous at home and influential abroad ; but my hopes have been disappointed. Austria will not forget that her sovereigns once ruled over Germany ; she will not consider Prussia, which, though a younger State, is increasing in strength and vigour, as her natural ally, but only as a hostile rival. According to her opinion, all aims and efforts of Prussia must be opposed, for Prussia's gain is Austria's loss. The flames of old and fatal rivalry blaze up anew ; Prussia is to be enfeebled, crushed, dishonoured. Under this view of the question no treaties are of any avail. German Princes are not only called upon to oppose Prussia, they are even persuaded to break the Federal laws. Look where we will in Germany, we are surrounded by enemies whose war cry is " Down with Prussia."

But, in my people, the good spirit of 1813 prevails. Who will wrest a foot's breadth of Prussian soil from us if we are firmly resolved to defend the prize our fathers gained ; if King and people, united more firmly than ever by the country's danger, esteem it as their highest and holiest duty to sacrifice life and fortune for their country's honour ?

In careful anticipation of what has now come to pass, I have for years deemed it my first duty as a Sovereign to prepare Prussia's able-bodied population for placing a considerable army in the field. With me, all Prussians will view the forces which guard our frontier with satisfaction and confidence. With her Sovereign at her head, Prussia will feel herself a veritable nation in arms. Our adversaries deceive themselves if they imagine Prussia's power to be lamed by internal dispute. In face of an enemy, those opposed to each other agree, and hold together through good and evil.

I have done my utmost to spare Prussia the burden and sacrifices of war ; that my people knows—that God knows, who proves the hearts. In company with France, England, and Russia, I have both sought an amicable arrangement and have been open to one up to the very last moment. Austria would not agree, and other German States have openly espoused her cause. So be it. The fault is not mine if my people have to fight a hard fight, and have, perhaps, to endure grievous affliction ; but no choice is left to us. We must fight for our existence : we must commence a struggle for life and death against those who would thrust the Prussia of the Great Elector and of Frederick the Great—Prussia as she issued from the wars of freedom*— from the position she has attained by the genius and might of her rulers, the bravery, devotion, and civilization of her people.

Let us pray to the Almighty, the ruler of nations, the Lord of the battle-field, to bless our arms.

If God should grant us victory we shall be strong enough to renew, under a firmer and more beneficial form, those frail ties which have hitherto held the German districts together more by name than in reality, and which have now been severed by those who dread the right and the might of the national spirit.

God with us,

(Signed)    WILHELM.

*Berlin, the 18th of June, 1866.*

---

* The " wars of freedom " is the term used for the campaigns 1813, 1814, and 1815.

## APPENDIX IX.

Special Order of Battle of the Advanced Guard of the Army of the Elbe in the Action of Hühnerwasser, on the 26th of June, 1866.

Major-General Von Schoeler.
Commandant of the Infantry, Colonel Von Gerstein-Hohenstein.
(Commanding 28th Regiment.)

### 1st Line.

40th Regiment of Fusiliers, Lieut.-Colonel Von Zimmermann.

| | | |
|---|---|---|
| 1st Battalion | .. .. .. | Lieut.-Colonel Von Conrady. |
| 2nd Battalion | .. .. .. | Major Von Hemming. |
| 3rd Battalion | .. .. .. | Major Junk. |

### 2nd Line.

| | | |
|---|---|---|
| Fusilier Battalion of the 28th Regiment of Infantry .. .. .. | | Major Mettler. |
| 2nd Battalion of the 33rd Regiment of Fusiliers .. .. .. | | Lieut.-Colonel Von Marschall. |
| Fusilier Battalion of the 69th Regiment of Infantry.. .. .. | | Major Von Sulicki. |

8th Battalion of Rifles, Major Zierold.

7th Regiment of Hussars, Colonel Von Lindern.

3rd Horse Artillery Battery of 8th Field Artillery Regiment, Captain Von Fuchsius.

4th 4-pounder Battery of the 8th Field Artillery Regiment, Captain Wolf.

Detachment of the 8th Battalion of Pioneers.

Section of " Krankenträger."

### Total.

| | |
|---|---|
| Battalions of Infantry .. .. .. .. | 6 |
| Battalion of Rifles .. .. .. .. | 1 |
| Squadrons .. .. .. .. .. | 5 |
| Guns .. .. .. .. .. .. | 16 |
| Detachment of Pioneers .. .. .. | 1 |

N.B.—The 2nd and 3rd Battalions of the 40th Regiment joined the Advanced Guard at midday of the 26th.

# APPENDIX X.

SPECIAL Order of Battle of the Troops of the Ist Army, which was engaged in the Action of Podol on the 26th of June, 1866.

| | Battalions of Infantry. | Battalions of Rifles. |
|---|---|---|
| 4th Battalion of Rifles, 2nd Company, Captain Mertens .. | .. | ¼ |
| „ „ 4th Company, Captain Von Michalowsky .. .. .. .. | .. | ¼ |
| 72nd Regiment of Infantry, Fusilier Battalion, Major Von Flotow .. .. .. .. .. .. | 1 | .. |
| Major-General Von Bose, Commander of the 15th Brigade. | | |
| 31st Regiment of Infantry, 2nd Battalion, Major Von Hagen.. .. .. .. .. .. .. .. | 1 | .. |
| 71st Regiment of Infantry, 2nd Battalion, Major Von Bothmer .. .. .. .. .. .. .. | 1 | .. |
| Colonel Von Avemann, Commander of the 71st Regiment. | | |
| 31st Regiment of Infantry, Fusilier Battalion, Lieut.-Colonel Von Drygalski .. .. .. .. .. | 1 | .. |
| 71st Regiment of Infantry, Fusilier Battalion, Lieut.-Colonel Von Valentini .. .. .. .. .. | 1 | .. |
| | 5 | ½ |

# APPENDIX XI.

Special Order of Battle of the 1st Corps d'Armée in the Action of Trautenau, June the 27th, 1866.

General Commanding   ..  General of Infantry Von Bonin
Chief of Staff   ..   ..  Colonel Von Borries.
Commandant of Artillery..  Colonel Knothe.

| | Battalions of Infantry. | Battalions of Rifles. | Squadrons. | Guns. | Battalions of Pioneers. |
|---|---|---|---|---|---|
| RIGHT FLANK COLUMN. | | | | | |
| *Advanced Guard of the Corps.* | | | | | |
| Lieutenant-General Von Grossmann, Commanding 1st Division of Infantry. | | | | | |
| General Staff Officer, Major Meydam. | | | | | |
| *Vanguard.* | | | | | |
| Colonel Von Beeren, Commanding 1st Regiment of Grenadiers. | | | | | |
| 3rd and 5th Squadrons of the 1st Dragoon Regiment.. .. .. .. .. .. .. | .. | .. | 2 | .. | .. |
| 1st Regiment of Grenadiers : | | | | | |
| 1st Battalion, Lieut.-Colonel Von Schlichting.. | 1 | .. | .. | .. | .. |
| 2nd Battalion, Major Scheuermann .. .. | 1 | .. | .. | .. | .. |
| 1st 4-pounder Battery, Captain Magnus .. .. | .. | .. | .. | 6 | .. |
| Detachment of Pioneers, Lieutenant Volkmann | | | | | |
| *Main Body of the Advanced Guard.* | | | | | |
| Major-General Von Pape, Commanding 1st Infantry Brigade. | | | | | |
| 1st Battalion of Rifles, Major Von Sommerfeld : | | | | | |
| 1st Company, Captain Reuter .. .. .. | .. | } ¾ | .. | .. | .. |
| 2nd   ,,   Captain Medem .. .. .. | .. | | .. | .. | .. |
| 3rd   ,,   Captain Von Oheimb .. | .. | | | | |
| Fusilier Battalion of the 1st Regiment, Major Von Blumenthal.. .. .. .. .. .. | 1 | .. | .. | .. | .. |
| Fusilier Battalion of the 41st Regiment, Major Kulenkamp .. .. .. .. .. .. | 1 | .. | .. | .. | .. |
| 5th 4-pounder Battery, Captain Gerhards .. .. | .. | .. | .. | 4 | .. |
| 1st Horse Artillery Battery, Captain Preinitzer .. | .. | .. | .. | 6 | .. |
| 2nd and 4th Squadrons of the 1st Dragoons, Col. Von Bernhardi .. .. .. .. .. | .. | .. | 2 | .. | .. |
| 3½ Squadrons of the 8th Lancers, Lieut.-Colonel Von Below .. .. .. .. .. .. | .. | .. | 3½ | .. | .. |
| 1st Company of the 1st Pioneer Battalion .. .. | .. | .. | 3½ | .. | ¼ |
| Total of Advanced Guard .. .. | 4 | ¾ | 7½ | 16 | ¼ |

## APPENDIX XI—*continued.*

|  | Battalions of Infantry. | Battalions of Infantry. | Squadrons. | Guns. | Battalions of Pioneers. |
|---|---|---|---|---|---|
| RIGHT FLANK COLUMN—*cont.* |  |  |  |  |  |
| *Reserve Infantry of the Corps ( following right flank column).* |  |  |  |  |  |
| Major-General Von Barnekow, Commanding 2nd Infantry Brigade. |  |  |  |  |  |
| 43rd Regiment of Infantry, Colonel Von Tresckow: |  |  |  |  |  |
|   1st Battalion, Major Von Hüllesheim .. .. |  |  |  |  |  |
|   Fusilier Battalion, Major Koehn Von Jaski .. | } 2 | .. | .. | .. | .. |
| 3rd Regiment of Grenadiers, Colonel Von Blumenthal: |  |  |  |  |  |
|   1st and 3rd Companies, Lieutenant-Colonel Weese .. .. .. .. .. |  |  |  |  |  |
|   2nd Battalion, Major Von Franckenberg-Ludwigsdorff .. .. .. .. |  |  |  |  |  |
|   Fusilier Battalion, Lieutenant-Colonel Von Wedell .. .. .. .. .. | } 2½ | .. | .. | .. | .. |
| 4th 12-pounder Battery, Captain Wittich ... .. | .. | .. | .. | 6 | .. |
| ½ Squadron of the 8th Lancers .. .. .. | .. | .. | ½ | .. | .. |
|       Total of Reserve Infantry .. .. | 4½ | .. | ½ | 6 | .. |
| *Right Flank Detachment ( from the Advanced Guard)* |  |  |  |  |  |
| Colonel Von Koblinski, Commanding 41st Regiment. |  |  |  |  |  |
| 1st Squadron of the 1st Dragoons, Captain Hagen | .. | .. | 1 | .. | .. |
| 41st Regiment of Infantry: |  |  |  |  |  |
|   1st Battalion, Major Von Schirmeister .. |  |  |  |  |  |
|   2nd Battalion, Major Schroeder .. .. | } 2 | .. | .. | .. | .. |
| 4th Company of the 1st Rifle Battalion, Captain Von Ziegler .. .. .. .. .. .. | .. | ¼ | .. | .. | .. |
| Two guns of 5th 4-pounder Battery, Lieut. Schmidt | .. | .. | .. | 2 | .. |
|       Total of Right Flank Detachment .. | 2 | ¼ | 1 | 2 | .. |
| LEFT FLANK COLUMN. |  |  |  |  |  |
| *Main Body of the Corps d'Armée.* |  |  |  |  |  |
| Lieutenant-General Von Clausewitz, Commanding 2nd Division. |  |  |  |  |  |
| General Staff Officer, Major Von Stosch. |  |  |  |  |  |
| *3rd Brigade of Infantry.* |  |  |  |  |  |
| Major-General Malotki Von Trzebiatowski. |  |  |  |  |  |
| 44th Regiment of Infantry, Col. Von La Chevallerie. |  |  |  |  |  |
|   1st Battalion, Lieutenant-Colonel Von Etzel .. |  |  |  |  |  |
|   2nd Battalion, Major Koch .. .. .. |  |  |  |  |  |
|   Fusilier Battalion, Lieut.-Colonel Von Behr .. | } 3 | .. | .. | .. | .. |
| 4th Regiment of Grenadiers, Colonel Von Wedell. |  |  |  |  |  |
|   1st Battalion, Major Von Nordenflycht .. |  |  |  |  |  |
|   2nd Battalion, Major Mansard.. .. .. |  |  |  |  |  |
|   Fusilier Battalion, Lieutenant-Colonel Von Pannwitz .. .. .. .. | } 3 | .. | .. | .. | .. |
|       Total of 3rd Brigade .. .. .. | 6 | .. | .. | .. | .. |

APPENDIX XI—*continued.*

| | Battalions of Infantry. | Battalions of Rifles. | Squadrons. | Guns. | Battalions of Pioneers. |
|---|---|---|---|---|---|
| LEFT FLANK COLUMN—*cont.* | | | | | |
| *4th Brigade of Infantry.* Major-General Baron Von Buddenbrock. | | | | | |
| 45th Regiment of Infantry, Colonel Von Boswell. | | | | | |
| 1st Battalion, Major Shoenemann | | | | | |
| 2nd Battalion, Major Von Kamecke | 3 | .. | .. | .. | .. |
| Fusilier Battalion, Lieutenant-Colonel Von Schmeling | | | | | |
| 5th Regiment of Grenadiers, Colonel Von Memerty. | | | | | |
| 1st Battalion, Major Baron Von Hüllessem | | | | | |
| 2nd Battalion, Lieut.-Col. Von Franckenberg.. | 3 | .. | .. | .. | .. |
| Fusilier Battalion, Lieutenant-Colonel Von Busse | | | | | |
| 1st Regiment of Hussars, Lieutenant-Colonel Von Kehler.. | .. | .. | 4 | .. | .. |
| 3rd Field Division of the 1st Field Artillery Regiment, Major Noack : | | | | | |
| 4th 4-pounder Battery, Captain Boehncke | .. | .. | .. | 6 | .. |
| 3rd 4-pounder Battery, Captain Kaunhoven .. | .. | .. | .. | 6 | .. |
| 3rd 6-pounder Battery, Captain Niehr.. | .. | .. | .. | 6 | .. |
| 2nd 12-pounder Battery, Captain Werner | .. | .. | .. | 6 | .. |
| Total of Main Body of Corps .. | 12 | .. | 4 | 24 | .. |
| *Reserve Cavalry of the Corps (following left flank column).* | | | | | |
| Colonel Von Bredow, Commanding 1st Cavalry Brigade. | | | | | |
| 3rd Regiment of Cuirassiers, Colonel Count Dohna | .. | .. | 4 | .. | .. |
| 12th Regiment of Lancers, Lieutenant-Colonel Von Kehler | .. | .. | 4 | .. | .. |
| 3rd Horse Artillery Battery, Captain Körber | .. | .. | .. | 6 | .. |
| Total of Reserve Cavalry .. | .. | .. | 8 | 6 | .. |
| *Reserve Artillery of the Corps.* | | | | | |
| Colonel Von Oertzen, Commanding 1st Field Artillery Regiment. | | | | | |
| Horse Artillery Division, Major Von Leslie : | | | | | |
| 2nd Horse Artillery Battery, Captain Kaunhoven | .. | .. | .. | 6 | .. |
| 4th Horse Artillery Battery, Captain Iwentz.. | .. | .. | .. | 6 | .. |
| First Field Artillery Division : | | | | | |
| 1st 6-pounder Battery, Captain Von Napolski | .. | .. | .. | 6 | .. |
| 2nd Field Division, Major Wiesing : | | | | | |
| 2nd 6-pounder Battery, Captain Rosenzweig .. | .. | .. | .. | 6 | .. |
| 4th 6-pounder Battery, Captain Matthiass | .. | .. | .. | 6 | .. |
| 2nd 4-pounder Battery, Captain Schmidt | .. | .. | .. | 6 | .. |
| 6th 4-pounder Battery, Captain Dollmann | .. | .. | .. | 6 | .. |
| 1st Battalion of Pioneers, Major Cramer : | | | | | |
| 2nd, 3rd, and 4th Companies .. | .. | .. | .. | .. | $\frac{3}{4}$ |
| Escorting the Reserve Artillery : | | | | | |
| 2nd Battalion of 43rd Regiment, Major Von Loebell.. | 1 | .. | .. | .. | .. |
| | 1 | .. | .. | 42 | $\frac{3}{4}$ |

APPENDIX XI—*continued*.

SUMMARY.

| | Battalions of Infantry. | Battalions of Rifles. | Squadrons. | Guns. | Battalions of Pioneers. |
|---|---|---|---|---|---|
| Advanced Guard .. | 4 | $\frac{3}{4}$ | $7\frac{1}{2}$ | 16 | $\frac{1}{4}$ |
| Right Flank Detachment .. .. | 2 | $\frac{1}{4}$ | 1 | 2 | .. |
| Main Body .. .. | 12 | .. | 4 | 24 | .. |
| Reserve Infantry .. | $4\frac{1}{2}$ | .. | $\frac{1}{2}$ | 6 | .. |
| Reserve Cavalry .. | .. | .. | 8 | 6 | .. |
| Reserve Artillery .. | 1 | .. | .. | 42 | $\frac{3}{4}$ |
| | $23\frac{1}{2}$ | 1 | 21 | 96 | 1 |

Absent as escort of baggage :
2nd and 4th Companies of the 43rd Regiment.

# APPENDIX XII.

SPECIAL Order of Battle of the Vth Corps d'Armée in the Action of Nachod, June the 27th, 1866.

General Commanding    ..    General of Infantry, Von Steinmetz.
Chief of Staff    ..    ..    Colonel Von Wittich.
Commandant of Artillery ..    Colonel Von Kraewell.

| | Battalions of Infantry. | Battalions of Rifles. | Squadrons. | Guns. | Battalions of Pioneers. |
|---|---|---|---|---|---|
| **ADVANCED GUARD.** | | | | | |
| Major-General Von Loewenfeld, Commanding 9th Division. | | | | | |
| General Staff Officer, Lieut.-Colonel Von Ziemietzki. | | | | | |
| Commandant of Artillery, Major Meissner. | | | | | |
| *Vanguard.* | | | | | |
| Colonel Von Below, Commanding 37th Regiment of Fusiliers. | | | | | |
| 37th Regiment of Fusiliers : | | | | | |
|   2nd Battalion, Lieutenant-Colonel Baron Von Eberstein  ..  ..  .. | | | | | |
|   ½ Battalion, Captain Von Schimonski, 5th and 7th Companies .  ..  .. | | | | | |
|     ,,    Captain Braun, 6th and 8th Companies ..  ..  ..  .. | 2 | | | | |
|   3rd Battalion, Major Von Plötz  ..  .. | | | | | |
|   ½ Battalion, Captain Von Kurowski, 9th and 12th Companies  ..  .. | | | | | |
|     ,,    Captain Von Bojan, 10th and 11th Companies  ..  .. | | | | | |
| 5th Battalion of Rifles : | | | | | |
|   1st Company, Captain Von Klass  ..  .. | | | | | |
|   4th Company, Captain Von Sobbe  ..  .. | .. | ½ | .. | .. | .. |
| 4th Regiment of Dragoons : | | | | | |
|   1st Squadron, Captain de Claer  ..  .. | | | | | |
|   2nd Squadron, Lieutenant Count Roedern  .. | .. | .. | 2 | .. | .. |
| 5th 4-pounder Battery of 5th Artillery Regiment Captain Schmidt..  ..  .. | .. | .. | .. | 6 | .. |
| *Main Body of the Advanced Guard.* | | | | | |
| Major-General Von Ollech, Commanding 17th Brigade. | | | | | |
| 37th Regiment of Fusiliers : | | | | | |
|   1st Battalion, Major Von Lemmers  ..  .. | | | | | |
|   ½ Battalion, Captain Von Winterfeld, 1st and 4th Companies..  ..  .. | 1 | .. | .. | .. | .. |
|     ,,    Captain Vogelsang, 2nd and 3rd Companies  ..  ..  .. | | | | | |

APPENDIX XII—*continued.*

| | Battalions of Infantry. | Battalions of Rifles. | Squadrons. | Guns. | Battalions of Pioneers. |
|---|---|---|---|---|---|
| ADVANCED GUARD— | | | | | |
| 58th Regiment of Infantry, Colonel Von François : | | | | | |
| 1st Battalion, Major Von Eberhardt .. .. | | | | | |
| ½ Battalion, Captain Schreiner, 1st and 4th Companies .. .. .. | | | | | |
| „ Captain Von Gfug, 2nd and 3rd Companies .. .. .. | | | | | |
| 2nd Battalion, Major Von Haugwitz .. .. | | | | | |
| ½ Battalion, Captain Wernecke, 5th and 8th Companies .. .. .. | 2½ | .. | .. | .. | .. |
| Fusilier Battalion, Major du Plessis .. .. | | | | | |
| ½ Battalion, Captain Von Gronefeld, 9th and 12th Companies .. .. | | | | | |
| „ Captain Von Suchodoletz, 10th and 11th Companies .. .. | | | | | |
| 5th Battalion of Rifles, Lieutenant-Colonel Von Wedell, 2nd and 3rd Companies .. .. .. .. | .. | ½ | .. | .. | .. |
| 4th Regiment of Dragoons, Major Von Mayer, 3rd, 4th, and 5th Squadrons.. .. .. | .. | .. | 3 | .. | .. |
| 1st 4-pounder Battery of the 5th Artillery Regiment, Captain Michaelis .. .. .. | .. | .. | .. | 6 | .. |
| 5th Battalion of Pioneers, 2nd Company, Captain Mentzel .. .. .. .. .. | .. | .. | .. | .. | ½ |
| Total of Advanced Guard .. .. | 5½ | 1 | 5 | 12 | ½ |
| Absent as Escort of Baggage : | | | | | |
| ½ Battalion, Von der Horst, 6th and 7th Companies of the 58th Regiment of Infantry. | | | | | |
| MAIN BODY OF THE CORPS. | | | | | |
| Lieutenant-General Von Kirchbach, Commanding 10th Division. | | | | | |
| Officer of General Staff, Major Von Grolmann. | | | | | |
| Commandant of Artillery, Lieut-Colonel Elten. | | | | | |
| Combined Brigade of Cavalry : | | | | | |
| Major-General Von Wnuck. | | | | | |
| 1st Regiment of Lancers, Colonel Von Tresckow .. | .. | .. | 4 | .. | .. |
| 8th Regiment of Dragoons, Lieutenant-Colonel Von Wichmann .. .. .. .. .. | .. | .. | 4 | .. | .. |
| 1st Horse Artillery Battery of 5th Artillery Regiment, Captain Von Manteuffel .. .. .. | .. | .. | .. | 6 | .. |

APPENDIX XII—*continued.*

| | Battalions of Infantry. | Battalions of Rifles. | Squadrons. | Guns. | Battalions of Pioneers. |
|---|---|---|---|---|---|
| MAIN BODY OF THE CORPS—*cont.* | | | | | |
| *19th Brigade of Infantry.* | | | | | |
| Major-General Von Tiedemann. | | | | | |
| 46th Regiment of Infantry, Colonel Von Walther: 1st Line, Lieut.-Colonel Von Schkopp: ½ Battalion, Captain Von Gallwitz, 6th and 7th Companies .. ..     „   Captain Von Müllenheim, 5th and 8th Companies .. ..     „   Captain Priebsch, 10th and 11th Companies .. .. 2nd Line, Lieut.-Colonel Von Manteuffel: ½ Battalion, Captain Von Stocki, 1st and 4th Companies .. ..     „   Major Von Bessel, 2nd and 3rd Companies .. ..     „   Captain Von Goessnitz, 9th and 12th Companies .. .. | 3 | .. | .. | .. | .. |
| 6th Regiment of Grenadiers, Lieut.-Colonel Von Scheffler. 1st Line, Major Von Wnuck: ½ Battalion, Captain Von Thadden, 1st and 3rd Companies .. ..     „   Captain Von Bronikowski, 2nd and 4th Companies .. ..     „   Major Von Webern, 6th and 8th Companies .. .. 2nd Line, Lieut.-Colonel Von Gottberg: ½ Battalion, Major Von Nitsche, 10th and 11th Companies .. ..     „   Captain Fischer, 9th and 12th Companies.     „   Captain Von Heugel, 5th and 7th Companies. | 3 | .. | .. | .. | .. |
| *20th Brigade of Infantry.* | | | | | |
| Major-General Wittich. | | | | | |
| 52nd Regiment of Infantry, Col. Von Blumenthal. 1st Line, Major Von Blumröder: ½ Battalion, Major Bendler, 1st and 3rd Companies .. .. ..     „   Captain Von Runckel, 2nd and 4th Companies .. ..     „   Captain Bilefeldt, 9th and 11th Companies. 2nd Line, Major Von Karger: ½ Battalion, Captain Von Bünau, 5th and 7th Companies .. ..     „   Captain Pappritz, 6th and 8th Companies .. ..     „   Captain Blumenthal, 10th and 12th Companies .. .. | 3 | .. | .. | .. | .. |

APPENDIX XII—*continued.*

| | Battalions of Infantry. | Battalions of Rifles. | Squadrons. | Guns. | Battalions of Pioneers. |
|---|---|---|---|---|---|
| MAIN BODY OF THE CORPS—*cont.* | | | | | |
| 47th Regiment of Infantry, Colonel Von Massow. | | | | | |
| 1st Line, Major Von Brandenstein : | | | | | |
| ½ Battalion, Captain Von Vietinghoff, 9th and 12th Companies .. .. | | | | | |
| „ Captain Von Tschirschky, 10th and 11th Companies .. .. | | | | | |
| „ Captain Vellay, 2nd and 3rd Companies .. .. | | | | | |
| 2nd Line, Major Von Heinemann : | 3 | .. | .. | .. | .. |
| ½ Battalion, Captain Von Schachtmeyer, 5th and 8th Companies .. | | | | | |
| „ Captain Von Sydow, 6th and 7th Companies .. .. | | | | | |
| „ Captain Masuch, 1st and 4th Companies .. .. | | | | | |
| 3rd Field Division of 5th Field Artillery Regiment, Lieut.-Colonel Elten. | | | | | |
| 3rd 4-pounder Battery, Captain Philipp | .. | .. | .. | 6 | .. |
| 4th 4-pounder, Captain Habelmann .. | .. | .. | .. | 6 | .. |
| 3rd 6-pounder, Captain Aust .. | .. | .. | .. | 6 | .. |
| 3rd 12-pounder, Captain Von Schultzendorff | .. | .. | .. | 6 | .. |
| 5th Battalion of Pioneers, Major Von Tiedemann. | | | | | |
| 3rd Company, Lieutenant Schulz .. .. | .. | .. | .. | .. | ½ |
| 4th Company, Captain Hepke .. .. .. | | | | | |
| Total of Main Body .. .. .. | 12 | .. | 8 | 30 | ½ |
| RESERVES. | | | | | |
| *Infantry.* | | | | | |
| Major-Gen. Von Horn, Commanding 18th Brigade. | | | | | |
| 7th Regiment of Grenadiers, Colonel Von Voigts Rhetz. | | | | | |
| 1st Line, Lieut.-Colonel Von Werder : | | | | | |
| ½ Battalion, Captain Von Kamptz, 9th and 12th Companies .. .. | | | | | |
| „ Captain Von Kaisenberg, 6th and 7th Companies .. .. | | | | | |
| „ Captain Von Natzmer, 5th and 8th Companies .. .. | 3 | .. | .. | .. | .. |
| 2nd Line, Lieut.-Colonel Von Quedenfeldt : | | | | | |
| ½ Battalion, Captain Von der Mülbe, 10th and 11th Companies .. | | | | | |
| „ Captain Von Unruhe, 1st and 4th Companies .. .. | | | | | |
| „ Captain Von Necker, 2nd and 3rd Companies .. .. | | | | | |
| 4th 12-pounder Battery, Captain Von Sowinsky .. | .. | .. | .. | 6 | .. |
| 1st 6-pounder Battery, Captain Von Troilo .. | .. | .. | .. | 6 | .. |

APPENDIX XII—*continued.*

| | Battalions of Infantry. | Battalions of Rifles. | Squadrons. | Guns. | Battalions of Pioneers. |
|---|---|---|---|---|---|
| RESERVES—*cont.* | | | | | |
| *Artillery.* | | | | | |
| Lieut.-Colonel Von Kameke : | | | | | |
| 2nd Field Division, Lieut.-Colonel Dalitz. | | | | | |
| 4th 6-pounder Battery, Captain Von Willich | .. | .. | .. | 6 | .. |
| 2nd 6-pounder Battery, Captain Caspari .. | .. | .. | .. | 6 | .. |
| 6th 4-pounder Battery, Captain Von Treuenfels | .. | .. | .. | 6 | .. |
| 2nd 4-pounder Battery, Captain Wilhelmi .. | .. | .. | .. | 6 | .. |
| Horse Artillery Division : | | | | | |
| 2nd Horse Artillery Battery, Captain Von Zakrzewski .. .. .. .. .. | } .. | .. | .. | 6 | .. |
| 4th Horse Artillery Battery, Captain Von Ohnesorge .. .. .. .. .. | } .. | .. | .. | 6 | .. |
| 1 Company of Pioneers, with Bridge Train, Captain Scheibert .. .. .. .. .. | } .. | .. | .. | .. | ¼ |
| Total of Reserves .. .. .. | 3 | .. | .. | 48 | ¼ |

SUMMARY.

| | Battalions of Infantry. | Battalions of Rifles. | Squadrons. | Guns. | Battalions of Pioneers. |
|---|---|---|---|---|---|
| Advanced Guard .. | 5½ | 1 | 5 | 12 | ¼ |
| Main Body .. .. | 12 | .. | 8 | 30 | ½ |
| Reserves .. .. | 3 | .. | .. | 48 | ¼ |
| Total .. | 20¼ | 1 | 13 | 90 | 1 |

## APPENDIX XIII.

SPECIAL Order of Battle of the Detachment of Major-General Count Stolberg in the Action of Oswiecim, June 27th, 1866.

Commanding General, Major-General Count Stolberg.
General Staff Officer, Lieutenant Von Müller, 4th Regiment of Foot Guards, doing duty as General Staff Officer.

| | Battalions of Infantry. | Battalions of Rifles. | Squadrons. | Guns. |
|---|---|---|---|---|
| ADVANCED GUARD. | | | | |
| Major Von der Osten Sacken. | | | | |
| ½ Company of Rifles, Lieutenant Von Montbach .. .. | .. | ⅛ | .. | .. |
| 11th Company of 62nd Regiment of Infantry, Captain Von Massow .. .. .. .. .. .. | ¼ | .. | .. | .. |
| 2 Companies of the Landwehr Battalion, Von der Osten.. | ½ | .. | .. | .. |
| 1 Peloton of the 2nd Regiment of Landwehr Lancers .. | .. | .. | ¼ | .. |
| 2 Guns of the 1st 6-pounder Battery of the 6th Field Artillery Regiment, Lieutenant Von Mechow .. .. | .. | .. | .. | 2 |
| Total of Advanced Guard .. .. | ¾ | ⅛ | ¼ | 2 |
| MAIN BODY. | | | | |
| Major-General Von Gillhausen. | | | | |
| 10th Company of the 62nd Regiment of Infantry, Captain Count Königsdorf .. .. .. .. | ¼ | .. | .. | .. |
| 2 Companies of the 2nd Landwehr Battalion } Major Von | }1 | .. | .. | .. |
| 2 ,, ,, 5th ,, ,, } Bessel. | | | | |
| 6th Landwehr Battalion, Major Von Kleist .. .. | 1 | .. | .. | .. |
| 4th Landwehr Battalion, Lieut.-Colonel Von Schmidt .. | 1 | .. | .. | .. |
| Bridge Train, Lieutenant Priem. | | | | |
| Total of Main Body .. .. | 3¼ | .. | .. | .. |
| RESERVES. | | | | |
| Major Von Busse. | | | | |
| ½ Company of Rifles, Lieutenant Baron Von Troschke .. | .. | ⅛ | .. | .. |
| 2 Companies of the 2nd Landwehr Battalion, Captain Von Studnitz .. .. .. .. .. .. .. | ½ | .. | .. | .. |
| 2nd Landwehr Lancer Regiment .. .. .. .. | .. | .. | 3¾ | .. |
| Total of Reserves .. .. .. | ½ | ⅛ | 3¾ | .. |

### SUMMARY.

| | Battalions of Infantry. | Battalions of Rifles. | Squadrons. | Guns. |
|---|---|---|---|---|
| Advanced guard .. .. | ¾ | ⅛ | ¼ | 2 |
| Main body .. .. | 3¼ | .. | .. | .. |
| Reserves .. .. .. | ½ | ⅛ | 3¾ | .. |
| Total .. .. | 4½ | ¼ | 4 | 2 |

## APPENDIX XIV.

SPECIAL Order of Battle of all the Troops of the 1st Army and the Army of the Elbe which were in readiness to take part in the Action of Münchengrätz, June 28th, 1866.

| | Battalions of Infantry. | Battalions of Rifles. | Squadrons. | Guns. | Battalions of Pioneers. |
|---|---|---|---|---|---|
| **TROOPS OF THE 1st ARMY.** | | | | | |
| 7TH DIVISION OF INFANTRY. | | | | | |
| Lieutenant-General Von Fransecky. | | | | | |
| General Staff Officer, Major Von Krenski. | | | | | |
| Commandant of Artillery, Lieut.-Colonel Weigelt. | | | | | |
| *Advanced Guard.* | | | | | |
| Major-General Von Gordon. | | | | | |
| 27th Regiment of Infantry, Colonel Von Zychlinski: | | | | | |
| 1st Battalion, Lieut.-Colonel Von Sommerfeld | | | | | |
| 2nd Battalion, Major Von Busse .. .. | 3 | .. | .. | .. | .. |
| Fusilier Battalion, Lieut.-Colonel Von Zedtwitz | | | | | |
| 67th Regiment of Infantry: | | | | | |
| Fusilier Battalion, Lieut.-Col. Baron Von Buttlar | 1 | .. | .. | .. | .. |
| 10th Regiment of Hussars, Colonel Von Besser .. | .. | .. | 4 | .. | .. |
| 1st 4-pounder Battery of the 4th Artillery Regiment, Captain Von Raussendorff .. .. .. | .. | .. | .. | 6 | .. |
| 2nd Company of Pioneers, with Light Bridge Train | .. | .. | .. | .. | ¼ |
| *Main Body.* | | | | | |
| Major-General Von Schwarzhoff. | | | | | |
| 26th Regiment of Infantry, Lieut.-Colonel Baron Von Medem: | | | | | |
| 1st Battalion, Major Paucke .. .. .. | | | | | |
| 2nd Battalion, Major Von Gilsa .. .. | 3 | .. | .. | .. | .. |
| Fusilier Battalion, Major Von Schönholz | | | | | |
| *66th Regiment of Infantry, Col. Von Blankensee: | | | | | |
| 2nd Battalion, Major Von Wiedner .. .. | | | | | |
| Fusilier Battalion, Major Von Schmeling .. | 2 | .. | .. | .. | .. |
| 1st 6-pounder Battery of the 4th Artillery Regiment, Captain Kühne .. .. .. .. .. | .. | .. | .. | 6 | .. |
| *Reserves.* | | | | | |
| Colonel Von Bothmer. | | | | | |
| 1st Battalion of the 67th Infantry Regiment, Lieut.-Colonel Von Hochstetter .. .. .. | | | | | |
| 2nd Battalion of the 67th Infantry Regiment, Major Von Zedtwitz .. .. .. .. | 2 | .. | .. | .. | .. |
| 5th 4-pounder Battery of 4th Artillery Regiment, Captain Baron Nordeck .. .. .. | .. | .. | .. | 6 | .. |
| 4th 12-pounder Battery of 4th Artillery Regiment, Captain Von Notz .. .. .. .. | .. | .. | .. | 6 | .. |
| 1st Company of 4th Battalion of Pioneers.. .. | .. | .. | .. | .. | ¼ |
| Total of 7th Division .. .. | 11 | .. | 4 | 24 | ½ |

* The 1st Battalion of the 66th Regiment remained at Turnau.

|  | Battalions of Infantry. | Battalions of Rifles. | Squadrons. | Guns. | Battalions of Pioneers. |
|---|---|---|---|---|---|
| **8TH DIVISION OF INFANTRY.** |  |  |  |  |  |
| Lieutenant-General Von Horn. |  |  |  |  |  |
| General Staff Officer, Major Von Massow. |  |  |  |  |  |
| Commandant of Artillery, Major Heinrich. |  |  |  |  |  |
| *Advanced Guard.* |  |  |  |  |  |
| Colonel Von Avemann, |  |  |  |  |  |
| 1st Battalion of 71st Regiment of Infantry, Major Von Hagen .. .. .. .. .. | 2 | .. | .. | .. | .. |
| 2nd Battalion of 71st Regiment of Infantry, Lieut.-Colonel Von Bothmer .. .. .. |  |  |  |  |  |
| 2nd Squadron of the 6th Lancers .. .. .. | .. | .. | 1 | .. | .. |
| 4th 4-pounder Battery of the 4th Field Artillery Regiment, Captain Von Schlotheim .. .. | .. | .. | .. | 6 | .. |
| *Main Body.* |  |  |  |  |  |
| Major-General Von Bose. |  |  |  |  |  |
| 31st Regiment of Infantry, Colonel Von Wedell. |  |  |  |  |  |
| 1st Battalion, Lieut.-Colonel Heinemann .. |  |  |  |  |  |
| 2nd Battalion, Major Von Hagen .. | 3 | .. | .. | .. | .. |
| Fusilier Battalion, Major Von Petery .. |  |  |  |  |  |
| 72nd Regiment of Infantry, Colonel Count Gneisenau. |  |  |  |  |  |
| 1st Battalion, Major Hensel .. .. |  |  |  |  |  |
| 2nd Battalion, Captain Von Gilsa .. | 3 | .. | .. | .. | .. |
| Fusilier Battalion, Major Von Flotow .. |  |  |  |  |  |
| 4th Battalion of Rifles, Lieut.-Colonel Von Colomb. | .. | 1 | .. | .. | .. |
| 1st, 3rd, and 4th Squadrons of the 6th Lancers, Lieut.-Colonel Baron Von Langermann .. | .. | .. | 3 | .. | .. |
| 3rd 4-pounder Battery of the 4th Field Artillery Regiment, Captain Kipping .. .. .. | .. | .. | .. | 6 | .. |
| 3rd 6-pounder Battery, Captain Anton .. | .. | .. | .. | 6 | .. |
| *Reserve.* |  |  |  |  |  |
| Fusilier Battalion of the 71st Regiment, Lieut.-Colonel Von Valentini .. .. .. | 1 | .. | .. | .. | .. |
| 3rd 12-pounder Battery of the 4th Field Artillery Regiment, Captain Von Seebach .. .. | .. | .. | .. | 6 | .. |
| 3rd Company of the 4th Battalion of Pioneers, Capt. Von Wasserschleben .. .. .. | .. | .. | .. | .. | ¼ |
| Total of 8th Division .. .. | 9 | 1 | 4 | 24 | ¼ |
| **TROOPS OF THE ARMY OF THE ELBE.** |  |  |  |  |  |
| ADVANCED GUARD OF THE ARMY OF THE ELBE. |  |  |  |  |  |
| Major-General Von Schoeler. |  |  |  |  |  |
| Commandant of the Infantry, Colonel Von Gerstein-Hohenstein, Commanding the 28th Regiment. |  |  |  |  |  |
| 40th Regt. of Fusiliers, Lieut.-Col. Von Zimmermann. |  |  |  |  |  |
| 1st Battalion, Lieut.-Colonel Von Conrady .. |  |  |  |  |  |
| 2nd Battalion, Major Von Henning .. | 3 | .. | .. | .. | .. |
| 3rd Battalion, Major Junk .. .. |  |  |  |  |  |

APPENDIX XIV—*continued.*

| | Battalions of Infantry. | Battalions of Rifles. | Squadrons. | Guns. | Battalions of Pioneers. |
|---|---|---|---|---|---|
| **ADVANCED GUARD—*cont.*** | | | | | |
| Fusilier Battalion of the 28th Regiment of Infantry, Major Mettler .. .. .. .. .. | 1 | .. | .. | .. | .. |
| 2nd Battalion of the 33rd Regiment of Fusiliers, Lieut.-Colonel Von Marschall .. .. .. | 1 | .. | .. | .. | .. |
| Fusilier Battalion of the 69th Regiment of Infantry, Major Von Sulicki.. .. .. .. .. | 1 | .. | .. | .. | .. |
| 8th Battalion of Rifles, Major Zierold .. .. | .. | 1 | .. | .. | .. |
| 7th Regiment of Hussars, Colonel Von Lindern .. | .. | .. | 5 | .. | .. |
| 3rd Horse Artillery Battery of the 8th Field Artillery Regiment, Captain Von Fuchsius .. .. | .. | .. | .. | 6 | .. |
| 4th 4-pounder Battery, Captain Wolf .. .. | .. | .. | .. | 6 | .. |
| Detachment of 8th Pioneer Battalion. | | | | | |
| Section of " Krankenträger." | | | | | |
| Total of Advanced Guard .. | 6 | 1 | 5 | 12 | .. |
| **14TH DIVISION OF INFANTRY.** | | | | | |
| Lieut.-General Count Münster-Meinhoevel. | | | | | |
| General Staff Officer, Major Von Thile. | | | | | |
| Commandant of Artillery, Major Von | | | | | |
| Schimmelpfennig. | | | | | |
| *Advanced Guard.* | | | | | |
| Major-General Von der Goltz. | | | | | |
| 56th Regiment of Infantry, Colonel Von Dorpowski. | | | | | |
| 1st Battalion, Major Von Hymmen .. .. | | | | | |
| 2nd Battalion, Major Von Thielau .. .. } | 3 | .. | .. | .. | .. |
| Fusilier Battalion, Lieut.-Colonel Von Busse.. | | | | | |
| 7th Battalion of Rifles, Lieutenant-Colonel Baron Von Sell .. .. .. .. .. .. | .. | 1 | .. | .. | .. |
| 7th Regiment of Dragoons, Colonel Von Ribbeck.. | .. | .. | 4 | .. | .. |
| 5th 4-pounder Battery of the 7th Field Artillery Regiment, Captain Trautmann .. .. .. | .. | .. | .. | 6 | .. |
| 3rd Company of the 7th Pioneer Battalion, Lieut. Von Fedkowiez .. .. .. .. .. | .. | .. | .. | .. | ¼ |
| *Main Body.* | | | | | |
| Major-General Von Schwarzkoppen. | | | | | |
| 16th Regiment of Infantry, Colonel Von Schwarz. | | | | | |
| 1st Battalion, Lieut.-Colonel Von Reichenbach | | | | | |
| 2nd Battalion, Major Von Grevenitz .. .. } | 3 | .. | .. | .. | .. |
| Fusilier Battalion, Major Von Horn .. | | | | | |
| 2nd Battalion of the 17th Regiment of Infantry, Major Von Bieberstein .. .. .. .. | 1 | .. | .. | .. | .. |
| 1st 6-pounder Battery of the 7th Field Artillery Regiment, Captain Von Fragstein .. .. | .. | .. | .. | 6 | .. |
| 1st 4-pounder Battery, Captain Pilgrim .. .. | .. | .. | .. | 6 | .. |

APPENDIX XIV.—*continued.*

|  | Battalions of Infantry. | Battalions of Rifles. | Squadrons. | Guns. | Battalions of Pioneers. |
|---|---|---|---|---|---|
| **14TH DIVISION**—*cont.* | | | | | |
| *Reserve.* | | | | | |
| Major-General Von Hiller. | | | | | |
| 57th Regiment of Infantry, Colonel Von der Osten. | | | | | |
| 1st Battalion, Lieut.-Colonel Von Schoening.. | | | | | |
| 2nd Battalion, Major Von Roell ..    .. | 3 | .. | .. | .. | .. |
| Fusilier Battalion, Lieut.-Colonel Grolman .. | | | | | |
| 5th Regiment of Lancers, Col. Baron Von Richthofen | .. | .. | 4 | .. | .. |
| 4th 12-pounder Battery, Captain Schmelzer    .. | .. | .. | .. | 6 | .. |
| 2nd Company of the 7th Pioneer Battalion, Major Von Rohrscheidt ..    ..    ..    ..    .. | .. | .. | .. | .. | ¼ |
| Total of 14th Division ..    .. | 10 | 1 | 8 | 2½ | ¼ |

## SUMMARY.

|  | Battalions of Infantry. | Battalions of Rifles. | Squadrons. | Guns. | Battalions of Pioneers. |
|---|---|---|---|---|---|
| Advanced Guard of the Army of the Elbe   .. | 6 | 1 | 5 | 12 | .. |
| 14th Division of Infantry | 10 | 1 | 8 | 2½ | ¼ |
| 8th    „    „ | 9 | 1 | 4 | 24 | ¼ |
| 7th    „    „ | 11 | .. | 4 | 24 | ¼ |
| Total    ..    .. | 36 | 3 | 21 | 84 | 1¼ |

## APPENDIX XV.

SPECIAL Order of Battle of the Corps of Guards in the Action of
Soor, June 28th, 1866.

Commanding-General ..    General of Cavalry, Prince Augustus of
Würtemberg.
Chief of Staff   ..    ..    Colonel Von Dannenberg.
Commandant of Artillery    Major-General Von Colomier.

| | Battalions of Infantry. | Battalions of Rifles. | Squadrons. | Guns. | Battalions of Pioneers. |
|---|---|---|---|---|---|
| **1ST DIVISION OF GUARD INFANTRY.** | | | | | |
| Lieutenant-General Baron Hiller Von Gärtringen. General Staff Officer, Major Von Kameke. Commandant of Artillery, Major Bychelberg. | | | | | |
| *Advanced Guard.* Colonel Von Kessel. | | | | | |
| Fusilier Battalion of 3rd Regiment of Foot Guards, Major Von Tempsky .. .. .. .. | 1 | .. | .. | .. | .. |
| Fusilier Battalion of 1st Regiment of Foot Guards, Lieutenant-Colonel Von Helldorf .. .. | 1 | .. | .. | .. | .. |
| Fusilier Battalion of 2nd Regiment of Foot Guards, Major Erckert .. .. .. .. .. | $\frac{3}{4}$ | .. | .. | .. | .. |
| 3rd Battalion of Guard Fusiliers, Lieutenant-Colonel Count Waldersee .. .. .. | 1 | .. | .. | .. | .. |
| 1st Company of Guard Rifles, Captain Count Carmer | .. | $\frac{1}{4}$ | .. | .. | .. |
| 4th Squadron of Guard Hussars, Captain Count Von der Groeben .. .. .. .. .. | .. | .. | 1 | .. | .. |
| 1st 4-pounder Battery of the Guard Artillery, Lieut. Witte .. .. .. .. .. .. | .. | .. | .. | 6 | .. |
| 1st Light Field Hospital, $\frac{1}{2}$ Company of " Krankenträger " .. .. .. .. .. .. | .. | .. | .. | .. | .. |
| 2nd Company, Captain Berger, and 4th Company, Captain Von Adler, of the Guard Pioneer Battalion | .. | .. | .. | .. | $\frac{1}{2}$ |
| Total Advanced Guard .. | $3\frac{3}{4}$ | $\frac{1}{4}$ | 1 | 6 | $\frac{1}{2}$ |
| *Main Body.* | | | | | |
| Major-General Von Alvensleben. | | | | | |
| 2nd Brigade of Guard Infantry, Colonel Von Pape : Regiment of Guard Fusiliers, Colonel Von Werder 1st Battalion, Major Von Tietzen .. .. 2nd Battalion, Lieutenant-Colonel Von der Knesebeck .. .. .. .. .. | 2 | .. | .. | .. | .. |
| 2nd Regiment of Foot Guards, Lieutenant-Colonel Von Neumann. 1st Battalion, Major Von Petery .. .. 2nd   ,,    Major Von Reuss .. .. | 2 | .. | ... | .. | .. |
| 2nd Company of Guard Rifles, Capt. Count Pourtales | . | $\frac{1}{4}$ | .. | .. | .. |
| 1st 6-pounder Battery, Captain Braun .. | .. | .. | .. | 6 | .. |
| 1st Squadron of the Guard Hussars, Captain Von Stralendorff.. .. .. .. .. .. | .. | .. | 1 | .. | .. |
| Total of Main Body .. | 4 | $\frac{1}{4}$ | 1 | 6 | .. |

APPENDIX XV—*continued.*

| | Battalions of Infantry. | Battalions of Rifles. | Squadrons. | Guns. | Battalions of Pioneers. |
|---|---|---|---|---|---|
| **1st Division of Guard Infantry**—*cont.* | | | | | |
| *Reserve.* | | | | | |
| 1st Brigade of Guard Infantry, Colonel Von Obernitz | | | | | |
| 3rd Regiment of Foot Guards : | | | | | |
| 1st Battalion, Major Von Plehwe | } 2 | .. | .. | .. | .. |
| 2nd Battalion, Major Von Barby | | | | | |
| 1st Battalion of 1st Foot Guards, Major Von Kleist | 1 | .. | .. | .. | .. |
| 5th 4-pounder Battery, Captain Von Eltester .. | .. | .. | .. | 6 | .. |
| 4th 12-pounder Battery, Captain Von Schmeling | .. | .. | .. | 6 | .. |
| 2nd Squadron of Guard Hussars, Captain Von Rundstedt | } .. | .. | 2 | .. | .. |
| 3rd Squadron of Guard Hussars, Captain Von Meyerinck | | | | | |
| Total of Reserve .. .. | 3 | .. | 2 | 12 | .. |

Total of 1st Guard Infantry Division, 10¾ battalions of Infantry, ¼ battalion of Rifles, 4 squadrons, 24 guns, ¼ battalion of Pioneers.

### ABSENT ON OTHER DUTY.

12th Company of the 2nd Foot Guards, escorting baggage of the division.

4th Company of Guard Fusiliers, escorting 1st 6-pounder Battery.

2nd Battalion of the 1st Foot Guards, escorting Reserve Artillery on the march from Braunau to Kosteletz.

3rd and 4th Companies of the Guard Rifles, escorting the baggage of the division.

1st Company of the Guard Pioneers was with the Pontoon Train.

| | Battalions of Infantry. | Battalions of Rifles. | Squadrons. | Guns. | Battalions of Pioneers. |
|---|---|---|---|---|---|
| **2nd Division of Guard Infantry.** | | | | | |
| Lieutenant-General Von Plonski. | | | | | |
| General Staff Officer, Lieutenant-Colonel Von Voigts-Rhetz. | | | | | |
| Commandant of Artillery, Major Baron Von der Goltz | | | | | |
| *Advanced Guard.* | | | | | |
| Colonel Von Fabeck. | | | | | |
| 2nd Regiment of Guard Grenadiers : | | | | | |
| 2nd Battalion, Lieutenant-Colonel Von Gaudy | } 3 | .. | .. | .. | .. |
| 1st Battalion, Major Von Böhn | | | | | |
| Fusilier Battalion, Major Von Delitz | | | | | |
| 4th 4-pounder Battery, Captain Von Schmeling .. | .. | .. | .. | 6 | .. |
| 1st Squadron of the 3rd Guard Lancers, Captain Von Berge and Herrendorff | } .. | .. | 2 | .. | .. |
| 4th Squadron of the 3rd Guard Lancers, Captain Zimmermann | | | | | .. |
| 3rd Company of Guard Pioneers, Captain Owstein | .. | .. | .. | .. | ¼ |
| Total of Advanced Guard .. | 3 | .. | 2 | 6 | ¼ |

APPENDIX XV—*continued.*

| | Battalions of Infantry. | Battalions of Rifles. | Squadrons. | Guns. | Battalions of Pioneers. |
|---|---|---|---|---|---|
| **2ND DIVISION OF GUARD INFANTRY**—*cont.* | | | | | |
| *Main Body.* | | | | | |
| Major-General Baron Von Loen. | | | | | |
| 4th Regiment Guard Grenadiers, Col. Von Strubberg: | | | | | |
| 1st Battalion, Major Von der Osten .. .. | | | | | |
| 2nd Battalion, Major Von Gliscynski.. .. } | 3 | .. | .. | .. | .. |
| Fusilier Battalion, Major Von L'Estocq .. | | | | | |
| Fusilier Battalion of the 1st Guard Grenadiers, Major Von Rauchhaupt .. .. .. .. .. | 1 | .. | .. | .. | .. |
| Fusilier Battalion of the 3rd Guard Grenadiers, Major Von Polczynski .. .. .. .. | 1 | .. | .. | .. | .. |
| Battalion of Guard Skirmishers, Major Von Besser | .. | 1 | .. | .. | .. |
| 3rd 12-pounder Battery, Captain Hein .. .. | .. | .. | .. | 6 | .. |
| 3rd 6-pounder Battery, Captain Deibel .. .. | .. | .. | .. | 6 | .. |
| 2nd Squadron of 3rd Guard Lancers, Captain Baron Von Heintze .. .. .. .. .. | | | | | |
| 3rd Squadron of 3rd Guard Lancers, Captain Baron Senfft Von Pilsach.. .. .. .. } | .. | .. | 2 | .. | .. |
| 2nd Light Field Hospital .. .. .. .. | | | | | |
| **Total of Main Body ..** | **5** | **1** | **2** | **12** | **..** |
| *Reserve.* | | | | | |
| Colonel Von Pritzelwitz. | | | | | |
| 3rd Regiment of Guard Grenadiers: | | | | | |
| ¼ of 1st Battalion, Major Von Zaluskowski .. } | 1¾ | .. | .. | .. | .. |
| 2nd Battalion, Captain Von Fabeck .. .. | | | | | |
| 1st Regiment of Guard Grenadiers: | | | | | |
| ¼ of 1st Battalion, Lieutenant-Colonel Von Brandenstein .. .. .. .. .. } | 1¾ | .. | .. | .. | .. |
| 2nd Battalion, Major Von Brixen .. .. | | | | | |
| 3rd 4-pounder Battery, Captain Von Hirschfeld | .. | .. | .. | 6 | .. |
| **Total of Reserves.. ..** | **3½** | **..** | **..** | **6** | **..** |

Total of 2nd Guard Infantry Division, 11½ battalions of Infantry, 1 battalion of Rifles, 4 squadrons, 24 guns, ¼ battalion of Pioneers.

ABSENT ON OTHER DUTY.

7th Company 4th Guard Grenadiers, escorting 3rd 6-pounder Battery.

10th and 11th Companies 3rd Guard Grenadiers, detached to Gross-Schwadenitz to cover the flank of the division.

2nd Company of 3rd Guard Grenadiers escorting baggage.

3rd Company 1st Guard Grenadiers head-quarter escort of the Crown Prince.

Total of Corps of Guards, 22½ battalions of Infantry, 1½ battalion Rifles, 8 squadrons, 64 guns, ¼ battalion of Pioneers.

N.B.—During the action, about half-past 1, the 2nd Guard Infantry Division was formed as follows :—

| Brigade of Colonel Von Strubberg. | Brigade of Colonel Von Fabeck. |
|---|---|
| Fusilier Battalion of 2nd Guard Grenadiers. | Battalion of Guard Skirmishers. |
| 4th Regiment of Guard Grenadiers. | 1st Regiment of Guard Grenadiers. |
| 3rd 12-pounder Battery. | 3rd 6-pounder Battery. |

Reserves.

1½ Battalion of 3rd Guard Grenadiers.
3rd 4-pounder Battery.

## APPENDIX XVI.

Special Order of Battle of the Vth Corps d'Armée, with the 22nd Brigade of Infantry and the Heavy Brigade of Guard Cavalry, in the Action of Skalitz, June 28th, 1866.

| | |
|---|---|
| General Commanding .. | General of Infantry, Von Steinmetz. |
| Chief of Staff .. .. | Colonel Von Wittich. |
| Commandant of Artillery | Colonel Von Kræwell. |

| | Battalions of Infantry. | Battalions of Rifles. | Squadrons. | Guns. | Battalions of Pioneers. |
|---|---|---|---|---|---|
| **Advanced Guard.** | | | | | |
| Colonel Von Voigts Rhetz. | | | | | |
| 7th Regiment of Grenadiers, Lieut.-Col. Von Werder. | | | | | |
| 1st Line, Lieutenant-Colonel Von Kalkstein : | | | | | |
| ½ Battalion, Captain Von Natzmer, 5th and 8th Companies .. .. .. | | | | | |
| „ Captain Von Kaisenberg, 6th and 7th Companies .. .. .. | | | | | |
| „ Capt. Von Kamptz, 9th & 12th Comp. | | | | | |
| 2nd Line, Lieutenant-Colonel Quedenfeldt : | 3 | .. | .. | .. | .. |
| ¼ Battalion, Captain Von der Mülbe, 10th and 11th Companies .. .. .. | | | | | |
| „ Capt. Von. Necker, 2nd & 3rd Comp. | | | | | |
| „ Capt. Von. Unruh, 1st & 4th Comp. | | | | | |
| 5th Battalion of Rifles, Lieutenant-Colonel Von Weller, 2nd and 3rd Companies .. .. | .. | ½ | .. | .. | .. |
| 1st Horse Artillery Battery of 5th Field Artillery Regiment, Captain Von Manteuffel .. | .. | .. | .. | 6 | .. |
| 1st 6-pounder Battery, Captain Von Troilo .. | .. | .. | .. | 6 | .. |
| 4th Regiment of Dragoons, Major Von Mayer .. | .. | .. | 4 | .. | .. |
| 3rd Company of 5th Pioneer Battalion, Capt. Schulz | .. | .. | .. | .. | ¼ |
| Total of Advanced Guard .. | 3 | ½ | 4 | 12 | ¼ |
| **Main Body.** | | | | | |
| Lieutenant-General Von Kirchbach. | | | | | |
| General Staff Officer, Major Von Grolmann. | | | | | |
| *19th Infantry Brigade.* | | | | | |
| Major-General Von Tiedemann. | | | | | |
| 6th Regt. of Grenadiers, Lieut.-Col. Von Scheffler. | | | | | |
| 1st Line, Lieutenant-Colonel Von Gottberg : | | | | | |
| ½ Battalion, Major Von Webern, 6th & 8th Comps. | | | | | |
| „ Captain Von Heugel, 5th and 7th Companies .. .. .. .. | | | | | |
| „ Major Von Nitsche, 10th and 11th Companies .. .. .. .. | | | | | |
| 2nd Line, Major Von Wnuck : | 3 | .. | .. | .. | .. |
| ¼ Battalion, Captain Von Bronikowski, 2nd and 4th Companies .. .. .. | | | | | |
| „ Captain Von Thadden, 1st and 3rd Companies .. .. .. | | | | | |
| „ Capt. Fischer, 9th & 12th Companies | | | | | |

| | Battalions of Infantry. | Battalions of Rifles. | Squadrons. | Guns. | Battalions of Infantry. |
|---|---|---|---|---|---|
| **MAIN BODY—*cont.*** | | | | | |
| **46th Regiment of Infantry, Colonel Von Walther.** 1st Line, Lieutenant-Colonel Von Schkopp: ‡ Battalion, Captain Von Müllenheim, 5th and 8th Companies .. .. .. .. „ Captain Von Gallwitz, 6th and 7th Companies .. .. .. .. „ Captain Priebsch, 10th and 11th Companies .. .. .. .. 2nd Line, Lieutenant-Colonel Von Manteuffel: ‡ Battalion, Major Von Bessel, 2nd and 3rd Companies .. .. .. .. „ Captain Von Stocki, 1st and 4th Companies .. .. .. .. „ Captain Von Goessnitz, 9th and 12th Companies .. .. .. .. | 3 | .. | .. | .. | .. |
| *20th Infantry Brigade.* | | | | | |
| Major-General Wittich. | | | | | |
| **52nd Regiment of Infantry, Colonel Von Blumenthal.** 1st Line, Major Von Karger: ‡ Battalion, Captain Pappritz, 6th and 8th Companies .. .. .. .. „ Captain Von Bünau, 5th and 7th Companies .. .. .. .. „ Captain Von Bielefeldt, 9th and 11th Companies .. .. .. .. 2nd Line, Major Von Blum-öder: ‡ Battalion, Captain Von Runkel, 2nd and 4th Companies .. .. .. .. „ Captain Von Wuthenow, 1st and 3rd Companies .. .. .. .. „ Captain Blumenthal, 10th and 12th Companies .. .. .. .. | 3 | .. | .. | .. | .. |
| **47th Regiment of Infantry, Colonel Von Massow.** 1st Line, Major Von Brandenstein: ‡ Battalion, Captain Von Vietinghoff, 9th and 12th Companies .. .. .. .. „ Captain Vellay, 2nd and 3rd Companies .. .. .. .. „ Captain Masuch, 1st and 4th Companies . .. .. 2nd Line, Major Von Heinemann: ‡ Battalion, Captain Von Tschirschky, 10th and 11th Companies .. .. „ Captain Von Sydow, 6th and 7th Companies .. .. .. .. „ Captain Von Schachtmeyer, 5th and 8th Companies .. .. | 3 | .. | .. | .. | .. |
| 1st Regiment of Lancers, Captain Von Bernhardi | .. | .. | 4 | .. | .. |

| | Battalions of Infantry. | Battalions of Rifles. | Squadrons. | Guns. | Battalions of Pioneers. |
|---|---|---|---|---|---|
| MAIN BODY—*cont.* | | | | | |
| 3rd Field Division of 5th Field Arti'lery Regiment, Lieutenant-Colonel Elten : | | | | | |
|    3rd 4-pounder Battery, Captain Philipp  .. | .. | .. | .. | 6 | .. |
|    4th 4-pounder Battery, Captain Habelmann.. | .. | .. | .. | 6 | .. |
|    3rd 6-pounder Battery, Captain Aust..  .. | .. | .. | .. | 6 | .. |
|    3rd 12-pounder Battery, Capt. Von Schultzendorff  ..  ..  ..  ..  .. | .. | .. | .. | 6 | .. |
| 2nd and 4th Companies of 5th Pioneer Battalions, Captain Hepke  ..  ..  .. | .. | .. | .. | .. | ½ |
| Total of Main Body  .. | 12 | .. | 4 | 24 | ½ |
| RIGHT FLANK DETACHMENT. | | | | | |
| Major-General Von Loewenfeld. General Staff Officer, Lieutenant-Colonel Von Ziemietzky. | | | | | |
| *17th Infantry Brigade.* | | | | | |
| Colonel Von Below. | | | | | |
| 37th Regiment of Fusiliers, Lieutenant-Col. Von Eberstein : | | | | | |
|   ½ Battalion, Captain Von Bojan, 10th and 11th Companies  ..  .. | | | | | |
|     ,,    Captain Von Kurowski, 9th and 12th Compauies..  ..  .. | | | | | |
|     ,,    Captain Braun, 6th and 7th Companies  ..  .. | 3 | .. | .. | .. | .. |
|     ,,    Captain Von Loewenstern, 2nd and 3rd Companies  .. | | | | | |
|     ,,    Captain Von Winterfeld, 1st and 4th Companies  ..  .. | | | | | |
|     ,,    Lieutenant Kupfer, 5th and 8th Companies  ..  .. | | | | | |
| 58th Regiment of Infautry, Colonel Von François : | | | | | |
|   ½ Battalion, Captain Von Gfug, 2nd and 3rd Companies  ..  .. | | | | | |
|     ,,    Captain Schreiner, 1st and 4th Companies  ..  .. | 2 | .. | .. | .. | .. |
|     ,,    Captain Von der Horst, 6th and 7th Companies  .. | | | | | |
|     ,,    Captain Wernecke, 5th and 8th Companies  ..  .. | | | | | |
| 1st and 4th Companies of 5th Rifle Battalion, Capt. Von Klass  ..  ..  ..  .. | .. | ½ | .. | .. | .. |
| 4th Squadron of 4th Dragoons, Lieutenant Von Mas-ow  ..  ..  ..  .. | .. | .. | 1 | .. | .. |
| 1st F.eld Division of 5th Field Artillery Regiment, Major Meissner : | | | | | |
|    1st 4 pounder Battery, Captain Michaelis  .. | .. | .. | .. | 6 | .. |
|    5th 4-pounder Battery, Captain Schmidt  .. | .. | .. | .. | 6 | .. |
|    4th 12-pounder Battery, Captain Von Sowinski | .. | .. | .. | 6 | .. |
| Total of Right Flank Detachment  .. | 5 | ½ | 1 | 18 | .. |

APPENDIX XVI—*continued.*

|  | Battalions of Infantry. | Battalions of Rifles. | Squadrons. | Guns. | Battalions of Pioneers. |
|---|---|---|---|---|---|
| **RESERVE ARTILLERY.** | | | | | |
| Lieutenant-Colonel Von Kameke. | | | | | |
| 2nd Field Division of 5th Field Artillery Regiment, Lieutenant-Colonel Von Dalitz : | | | | | |
|    2nd 6-pounder Battery, Captain Caspari | .. | .. | .. | 6 | .. |
|    2nd 4-pounder Battery, Captain Wilhelmi | .. | .. | .. | 6 | .. |
|    4th 6-pounder Battery, Captain Von Willich | .. | .. | .. | 6 | .. |
|    6th 4-pounder, Captain Voh Treuenfels | .. | .. | .. | 6 | .. |
| 2nd Horse Artillery Battery, Captain Zakrzewski.. | .. | .. | .. | 6 | .. |
| 4th Horse Artillery Battery, Captain Von Ohnesorge | .. | .. | .. | 6 | .. |
| Total of Reserve Artillery .. | .. | .. | .. | 36 | .. |
| Detached as Escorts of Baggage and Trains : | | | | | |
|    Fusilier Battalion of the 58th Regiment, Major du Plessis. | | | | | |
|    1st Company of the 5th Battalion of Pioneers. | | | | | |
| **RESERVE.** | | | | | |
| (Detachment of the VIth Corps d'Armée.) | | | | | |
| *22nd Brigade of Infantry.* | | | | | |
| Major-General Von Hoffman. | | | | | |
| 38th Regiment of Fusiliers, Colonel Von Witzleben : | | | | | |
|    1st Line : | | | | | |
|    1st Battalion, Lieutenant-Colonel Von Knobels-dorff | | | | | |
|    2nd Battalion, Lieutenant-Colonel Von Wenck-stern | 3 | .. | .. | .. | .. |
|    3rd Battalion, Major Count Trenk | | | | | |
|    2nd Line : | | | | | |
| 51st Regiment of Infantry, Colonel Paris : | | | | | |
|    1st Battalion, Major Von Haine | | | | | |
|    2nd Battalion, Major Von Ostrowski.. | 3 | .. | .. | .. | .. |
|    Fusilier Battalions, Lieut.-Colonel Von Kontzki | | | | | |
| 8th Regiment of Dragoons, Lieutenant-Colonel Von Wichmann .. | .. | .. | 4 | .. | .. |
| 6th Field Artillery Regiment : | | | | | |
|    2nd 4-pounder Battery, Captain Von Wahlen-Jürgass.. | .. | .. | .. | 6 | .. |
|    2nd 6-pounder Battery, Capt. Von Schweinichen | .. | .. | .. | 6 | .. |
| Total of Reserve .. | 6 | .. | 4 | 12 | .. |
| **HEAVY BRIGADE OF GUARD CAVALRY.** | | | | | |
| H.R.H. Prince Albrecht of Prussia, Junior. | | | | | |
| Regiment of Garde du Corps, Colonel Count Brandenburg | .. | .. | 4 | .. | .. |
| Regiment of Guard Cuirassiers, Colonel Von Lüderitz | .. | .. | 4 | .. | .. |
| 3rd Horse Artillery Battery of the Garde Artillery, Captain Von Buddenbrock | .. | .. | .. | 6 | .. |
| Total Brigade of Guard Cavalry .. | .. | .. | 8 | 6 | .. |

APPENDIX XVI—*continued*.

## SUMMARY.

| — | Battalions of Infantry. | Battalions of Rifles. | Squadrons. | Guns. | Battalions of Pioneers. |
|---|---|---|---|---|---|
| Advanced Guard .. | 3 | $\frac{1}{2}$ | 4 | 12 | $\frac{1}{4}$ |
| Main Body .. .. | 12 | .. | 4 | 24 | $\frac{1}{2}$ |
| Right Flank Detachment .. .. | 5 | $\frac{1}{2}$ | 1 | 18 | .. |
| Reserve Artillery .. | .. | .. | .. | 36 | .. |
| Reserve .. .. | 6 | .. | 4 | 12 | .. |
| Brigade of Guard Cavalry .. .. | .. | .. | 8 | 6 | .. |
| Total .. .. | 26 | 1 | 21 | 108 | $\frac{3}{4}$ |

## APPENDIX XVII.

SPECIAL Order of Battle and of March of the 5th Infantry Division in the Action of Gitschin, June 29th, 1866.

General Commanding    ..    Lieut.-General Von Tümpling.
General Staff Officer    ..    Lieut.-Colonel Von Hertzberg.
Commandant of Artillery ..   Major Rüstow.

| | Battalions of Infantry. | Battalions of Rifles. | Squadrons. | Guns. | Battalions of Pioneers. |
|---|---|---|---|---|---|
| **ADVANCED GUARD.** | | | | | |
| Lieut.-Colonel Von Gaudy, 8th Regiment. | | | | | |
| 2nd Squadron of the 3rd Lancers, Captain Von Eckartsberg .. .. .. .. .. | .. | .. | 1 | .. | .. |
| Fusilier Battalion of the 8th Regiment, Maj. Unruhe | ¾ | .. | .. | .. | .. |
| 5th 4-pounder Battery of 3rd Field Artillery Regiment, Captain Munk .. .. .. .. | .. | .. | .. | 6 | .. |
| 1st 4-pounder Battery of 3rd Field Artillery Regiment, Captain Griess .. .. .. .. | .. | .. | .. | 6 | .. |
| Fusilier Battalion of the 48th Regiment, Major Von Zglinitzki .. .. .. .. .. .. | 1 | .. | .. | .. | .. |
| Fusilier Battalion of the 12th Regt., Maj. des Barres | 1 | .. | .. | .. | .. |
| **MAIN BODY.** | | | | | |
| *9th Infantry Brigade.* | | | | | |
| Major-General Von Schimmelmann. | | | | | |
| 48th Regiment of Infantry, Lieut.-Colonel Von Dieringshofen : | | | | | |
| 1st Battalion, Major Spieker .. .. } 2 | 2 | .. | .. | .. | .. |
| 2nd Battalion, Lieut.-Colonel Von Wulffen .. } | | | | | |
| 8th Regiment of Grenadiers, Colonel Von Berger : | | | | | |
| 1st Battalion, Major Von Rheinbaben .. } 2 | 2 | .. | .. | .. | .. |
| 2nd Battalion, Major Michelmann .. } | | | | | |
| 1st 6-pounder Battery of 3rd Field Artillery Regiment, Captain Baron Von der Goltz .. .. | .. | .. | .. | 6 | .. |
| 4th 12-pounder Battery of 3rd Field Artillery Regiment, Captain Hübener .. .. .. .. | .. | .. | .. | 6 | .. |
| 1st, 3rd, and 4th Squadrons of the 3rd Lancers, Lieut.-Colonel Von Tresckow .. .. .. | .. | .. | 3 | .. | .. |
| *10th Infantry Brigade.* | | | | | |
| Major-General Von Kamienski. | | | | | |
| 18th Regiment of Infantry, Colonel Von Kettler : | | | | | |
| 1st Battalion, Lieut.-Colonel Von Auer .. } | 3 | .. | .. | .. | .. |
| 2nd Battalion, Major Von Witten .. } 3 | | | | | |
| Fusilier Battalion, Major Count Finckenstein } | | | | | |
| 12th Regiment of Grenadiers, Col. Von Debschitz : | | | | | |
| 1st Battalion, Major Von Kalinowski.. .. } 2 | 2 | .. | .. | .. | .. |
| 2nd Battalion, Major Von der Heyde .. } | | | | | |
| Total of 5th Division .. | 11¾ | .. | 4 | 24 | .. |
| Absent as baggage escort, 1 company of the 8th Regt. | | | | | |

## APPENDIX XVIII.

Special Order of Battle and of March of the 3rd Infantry Division in the Action of Gitschin, June 29th, 1866.

General Commanding .. Lieut.-General Von Werder.
General Staff Officer .. Major Von Quistorp.
Commandant of Artillery .. Major Heubes.

| | Battalions of Infantry. | Battalions of Rifles. | Squadrons. | Guns. | Battalions of Pioneers. |
|---|---|---|---|---|---|
| **ADVANCED GUARD.** | | | | | |
| Colonel Von Borcke, Commanding 42nd Regiment. | | | | | |
| 1½ Squadrons of the 5th Hussars, Captain Von Knobelsdorff .. .. .. .. .. | .. | .. | 1½ | .. | .. |
| 2 Companies of 2nd Rifle Battalion, Captains Von der Dollen and Von Reibnitz .. .. | .. | ½ | .. | .. | .. |
| 2 Companies of the 14th Regiment, Major Von Stegmann .. .. .. .. .. .. | ½ | .. | .. | .. | .. |
| Fusilier Battalion of 42nd Regiment, Major Von Malotki .. .. .. .. .. | 1 | .. | .. | .. | .. |
| 5th 4-pounder Battery of 2nd Field Artillery Regiment, Captain Gallus .. .. .. .. | .. | .. | .. | 6 | .. |
| 2½ Squadrons of 5th Hussars, Col. Von Flemming | .. | .. | 2½ | .. | .. |
| **MAIN BODY.** | | | | | |
| *5th Brigade of Infantry.* | | | | | |
| Major-General Von Januchowsky. | | | | | |
| 2nd Regiment of Grenadiers, Col. Von Reichenbach: | | | | | |
| 1st Battalion, Major Von Briesen .. .. | } 3 | .. | .. | .. | .. |
| 2nd Battalion, Major Von der Osten .. .. | | | | | |
| Fusilier Battalion, Major Von Stölting .. | | | | | |
| 42nd Regiment of Infantry, Colonel Von Borcke: | | | | | |
| 1st Battalion, Major Von Olszewsky .. .. | } 2 | .. | .. | .. | .. |
| 2nd Battalion, Lieut.-Colonel Von Kortzfleisch | | | | | |
| 1st 4-pounder Battery of 2nd Field Artillery Regiment, Captain Von Eckensteen .. .. | .. | .. | .. | 6 | .. |
| 4th 6-pounder Battery of 2nd Field Artillery Regiment, Captain Von Dewitz .. .. .. | .. | .. | .. | 6 | .. |
| 4th 12-pounder Battery of 2nd Field Artillery Regiment, Captain Crüger .. .. .. | .. | .. | .. | 6 | .. |
| *6th Brigade of Infantry.* | | | | | |
| Major-General Von Winterfeld. | | | | | |
| 14th Regiment of Infantry, Colonel Von Stahr: | | | | | |
| 1st Battalion, Major Von Wittgenstein .. | } 2 | .. | .. | .. | .. |
| Fusilier Battalion, Lieut.-Col. Von Zaborowsky | | | | | |
| 54th Regiment of Infantry, Lieut.-Colonel Baron Von Buddenbrock: | | | | | |
| 1st Battalion, Major Von Wedell .. .. | } 3 | .. | .. | .. | .. |
| 2nd Battalion, Major Von Voss .. .. | | | | | |
| Fusilier Battalion, Captain Von Pestel .. | | | | | |
| 2 Companies of 2nd Rifle Batt., Major Von Garrelts | .. | ½ | .. | .. | .. |
| 2nd Battalion of Pioneers, Major Von Bonin .. | .. | .. | .. | .. | 1 |
| Total of 3rd Division .. .. | 11½ | 1 | 4 | 24 | 1 |

N.B—The 5th Company of 14th Regiment was detached as escort of Field Hospitals. The 8th Company was left as garrison in Zittau.

# APPENDIX XIX.

ORDER of Battle of the Advanced Guard Brigade of the 1st Division of Guard Infantry in the Action of Königinhof, June 29th, 1866.

Commander of Advanced Guard, Colonel Von Kessel.

| | Battalions of Infantry. | Battalions of Rifles. | Squadrons. | Guns. | Battalions of Pioneers. |
|---|---|---|---|---|---|
| **VANGUARD.** | | | | | |
| Lieut.-Col. Count Waldersee. | | | | | |
| 1st and 3rd Squadrons of Guard Hussars, Captains Von Stralendorff and Von Rundstedt .. .. | .. | .. | 2 | .. | .. |
| 3rd Battalion of Guard Fusiliers .. .. .. | 1 | .. | .. | .. | .. |
| 3 Companies of Guard Rifles .. .. .. | .. | ½ | .. | .. | .. |
| **MAIN BODY.** | | | | | |
| Fusilier Battalion of 1st Foot Guards, Lieut.-Colonel Von Helldorff .. .. .. .. | 1 | .. | .. | .. | .. |
| 3 Companies of 2nd Foot Guards, Major Von Erckert | ¾ | .. | .. | .. | .. |
| 5th 4-pounder Battery of Guard Artillery, Captain Von Eltester .. .. . . .. .. | .. | .. | .. | 6 | .. |
| 1 6-pounder Battery of Guard Artillery, Captain Braun .. .. . .. .. | .. | .. | .. | 6 | .. |
| Fusilier Battalion of 3rd Foot Guards, Major Von Holleben .. .. .. .. .. .. | 1 | .. | .. | .. | .. |
| 4th Company of Guard Pioneers, Captain Von Adler .. .. .. .. .. .. | .. | .. | .. | .. | ¼ |
| 1 Light Field Hospital. | | | | | |
| Total .. .. .. .. | 3¾ | ½ | 2 | 12 | ¼ |

N.B.—The 12 Company of the 2nd Foot Guards was detached as baggage escort.
The 2nd Squadron of Guard Hussars was detached to open communication with the Ist Corps d'Armée.
The 4th Squadron of Guard Hussars was detached to open communication with the Vth Corps d'Armée.

## APPENDIX XX.

SPECIAL Order of Battle of the Vth Corps d'Armée, the 22nd Brigade of Infantry, and the Heavy Cavalry Brigade of the Guards in the Action of Schweinschadel, June 29th, 1866,

General Commanding .. .. General of Infantry, Von Steinmetz.
Chief of Staff .. .. .. Colonel Von Wittich.
Commandant of Artillery .. Colonel Von Kræwell.

| | Battalions of Infantry. | Battalions of Rifles. | Squadrons. | Guns. | Battalions of Pioneers. |
|---|---|---|---|---|---|
| **ADVANCED GUARD.** | | | | | |
| Lieut.-General Von Kirchbach. | | | | | |
| General Staff Officer, Major Von Grolmann. | | | | | |
| *19th Infantry Brigade.* | | | | | |
| Major-General Von Tiedemann. | | | | | |
| 6th Regiment of Grenadiers, Lieut.-Colonel Von Scheffler: | | | | | |
| 1st Line, Lieutenant-Colonel Von Gottberg: | | | | | |
| ½ Battalion, Captain Von Heugel, 5th and 7th Companies .. .. .. | | | | | |
| „ Major Von Webern, 6th and 8th Companies | | | | | |
| „ Captain Fischer, 9th and 12th Companies .. .. .. | | | | | |
| 2nd Line, Major Von Wnuck: | 3 | .. | .. | .. | .. |
| ½ Battalion, Captain Von Bronikowski, 2nd and 4th Companies .. .. .. | | | | | |
| „ Captain Von Thadden, 1st and 3rd Companies .. .. .. | | | | | |
| „ Major Von Nitsche, 10th and 11th Companies .. .. .. | | | | | |
| 46th Regiment of Infantry, Col. Von Walther. | | | | | |
| 1st Line, Lieut.-Colonel Von Schkopp: | | | | | |
| ½ Battalion, Captain Priebsch, 10th and 11th Companies .. .. .. | | | | | |
| „ Captain Von Gallwitz, 6th and 7th Companies .. .. .. | | | | | |
| „ Captain Von Müllenheim, 5th and 8th Companies .. .. | | | | | |
| 2nd Line, Lieut.-Colonel Von Manteuffel: | 3 | .. | .. | .. | .. |
| ½ Battalion, Captain Von Goessnitz, 9th and 12th Companies .. .. .. | | | | | |
| „ Captain Von Stocki, 1st and 4th Companies .. .. .. | | | | | |
| „ Major Von Bessel, 2nd and 3rd Companies .. .. .. | | | | | |
| 5th Battalion of Rifles, Lieut.-Colonel Von Weller, 2 Companies .. .. .. .. | .. | ½ | .. | .. | .. |
| 3rd 4-pounder Battery of the 5th Field Artillery Regiment, Captain Philipp .. .. .. | .. | .. | .. | 6 | .. |
| 4th 4-pounder Battery of the 5th Field Artillery Regiment, Captain Habelmann .. .. .. | .. | .. | .. | 6 | .. |
| 1st Regiment of Lancers, Captain Von Bernhardi.. | .. | .. | 4 | .. | .. |
| Total of Advanced Guard .. .. | 6 | ½ | 4 | 12 | .. |

APPENDIX XX—*continued.*

| | Battalions of Infantry. | Battalions of Rifles. | Squadrons. | Guns. | Battalions of Pioneers. |
|---|---|---|---|---|---|
| **MAIN BODY.** | | | | | |
| Major-General Von Loewenfeld.<br>General Staff Officer, Lieut.-Col. Von Ziemietzki. | | | | | |
| *17th Infantry Brigade.* | | | | | |
| Colonel Von Below. | | | | | |
| 37th Regiment of Fusiliers, Lt.-Col. Von Eberstein :<br>1st Battalion, Major Von Lemmers<br>2nd Battalion, Major Von Gabain<br>3rd Battalion, Major Von Plötz | } 3 | .. | .. | .. | .. |
| 58th Regiment of Infantry, Colonel Von François :<br>1st Battalion, Major Von Eberhardt<br>2nd Battalion, Major Von Glasenapp..<br>Fusilier Battalion, Major du Plessis .. | } 3 | .. | .. | .. | .. |
| *18th Infantry Brigade.* | | | | | |
| Major-General Von Horn. | | | | | |
| 7th Regiment of Grenadiers, Col. Von Voigts Rhetz:<br>1st Battalion, Lieut.-Colonel Von Werder ..<br>2nd Battalion, Lieut.-Colonel Quedenfeldt ..<br>Fusilier Battalion, Lieut.-Col. Von Kalkstein.. | } 3 | .. | .. | .. | .. |
| *1st Field Division of 5th Field Artillery Regiment.* | | | | | |
| Major Meissner. | | | | | |
| 1st 4-pounder Battery, Captain Michaelis .. | .. | .. | .. | 5 | .. |
| 5th 4-pounder Battery, Captain Schmidt .. | .. | .. | .. | 6 | .. |
| 1st 6-pounder Battery, Captain Von Troilo .. | .. | .. | .. | 6 | .. |
| 4th 12-pounder Battery, Captain Von Sowinski | .. | .. | .. | 6 | .. |
| *Heavy Brigade of Guard Cavalry.* | | | | | |
| His Royal Highness Major-General Prince Albrecht,<br>junior. | | | | | |
| Regiment of Garde du Corps, Colonel Count Brandenburg | .. | .. | 4 | .. | .. |
| Regiment of Guard Cuirassiers, Lieut.-Col. Von Lüderitz | .. | .. | 4 | .. | .. |
| 2nd Horse Artillery Battery of Guard Artillery,<br>Captain Von Buddenbrock | .. | .. | .. | 6 | .. |
| Total of Main Body .. | 9 | .. | 8 | 30 | .. |
| **LEFT FLANK DETACHMENT.** | | | | | |
| *20th Infantry Brigade.* | | | | | |
| Major-General Wittich. | | | | | |
| 52nd Regiment of Infantry, Col. Von Blumenthal :<br>1st Battalion, Major Bendler ..<br>2nd Battalion, Major Von Karger<br>3rd Battalion, Major Von Blumröder., | } 3 | .. | .. | .. | .. |

| | Battalions of Infantry. | Battalions of Rifles. | Squadrons. | Guns. | Battalions of Pioneers. |
|---|---|---|---|---|---|
| LEFT FLANK DETACHMENT—*cont.* | | | | | |
| 47th Regiment of Infantry, Colonel Von Massow: | | | | | |
| 1st Battalion, Major Von Haeseler .. .. | | | | | |
| 2nd Battalion, Major Von Heinemann .. | 3 | .. | .. | .. | .. |
| Fusilier Battalion, Major Von Brandenstein.. | | | | | |
| 3rd 6-pounder Battery of 5th Field Artillery Regiment, Captain Aust .. .. .. .. | .. | .. | .. | 6 | .. |
| 3rd 12-pounder Battery of 5th Field Artillery Regiment, Captain Von Schultzendorff .. .. | .. | .. | .. | 6 | .. |
| *Combined Brigade of Cavalry.* | | | | | |
| Major-General Von Wnuck. | | | | | |
| 4th Regiment of Dragoons, Major Von Mayer .. | .. | .. | 5 | .. | .. |
| 8th Regiment of Dragoons, Lieut.-Col. Von Wichmann .. .. .. .. .. .. | .. | .. | 4 | .. | .. |
| 1st Horse Artillery Battery of 5th Field Artillery Regiment, Captain Von Manteuffel .. .. | .. | .. | .. | 6 | .. |
| Total of Left Flank Detachment.. .. | 6 | .. | 9 | 18 | .. |
| RESERVES. | | | | | |
| *22nd Brigade of Infantry.* | | | | | |
| Major-General Von Hoffmann. | | | | | |
| 38th Regiment of Fusiliers, Lieut.-Colonel Von Knobelsdorff: | | | | | |
| 1st Battalion, Captain Count Hertzberg .. | | | | | |
| 2nd Battalion, Captain Weber.. .. .. | 3 | .. | .. | .. | .. |
| 3rd Battalion, Captain Count Von der Trenk.. | | | | | |
| 51st Regiment of Infantry, Colonel Paris: | | | | | |
| 1st Battalion, Major Von Haine .. .. | | | | | |
| 2nd Battalion, Major Von Ostrowski .. .. | 3 | .. | .. | .. | .. |
| Fusilier Battalion, Lieut.-Colonel Von Kontzki | | | | | |
| 2nd 6-pounder Battery of 6th Field Artillery Regiment, Captain Von Schweinichen .. .. | .. | .. | .. | 6 | .. |
| 2nd 4-pounder Battery of 6th Field Artillery Regiment, Captain Von Wahlen-Jürgass .. | .. | .. | .. | 6 | .. |
| *Reserve Artillery.* | | | | | |
| Lieut.-Colonel Von Kameke. | | | | | |
| 2nd Field Division of 5th Field Artillery Regiment, Lieut.-Colonel Von Dalitz: | | | | | |
| 2nd 6-pounder Battery, Captain Caspari .. | .. | .. | .. | 6 | .. |
| 4th 6-pounder Battery, Captain Von Willich.. | .. | .. | .. | 6 | .. |
| 2nd 4-pounder Battery, Captain Wilhelmi .. | .. | .. | .. | 6 | .. |
| 6th 4-pounder Battery, Captain Von Treuenfels | .. | .. | .. | 6 | .. |

| | Battalions of Infantry. | Battalions of Rifles. | Squadrons. | Guns. | Battalions of Pioneers. |
|---|---|---|---|---|---|
| RESERVES, &c.—*cont.* | | | | | |
| Horse Artillery of 5th Field Artillery Regiment : | | | | | |
| 2nd Horse Artillery Batt. Capt. Von Zakrzewski | .. | .. | .. | 6 | .. |
| 4th Horse Artillery Batt. Capt. Von Ohnesorge | .. | .. | .. | 6 | .. |
| Total of Reserves .. .. .. | 6 | .. | .. | 48 | .. |

Detached as escort of baggage, 2 companies of 5th Rifle Battalion.

## SUMMARY.

| | Battalions of Infantry. | Battalions of Rifles. | Squadrons. | Guns. |
|---|---|---|---|---|
| Advanced Guard .. .. | 6 | ½ | 4 | 12 |
| Main Body .. .. .. | 9 | .. | 8 | 30 |
| Left Flank Detachment .. | 6 | .. | 9 | 18 |
| Reserves .. .. .. | 6 | .. | .. | 48 |
| Total.. .. .. | 27 | ½ | 21 | 108 |

# APPENDIX XXI.

ORDER of Battle of the Royal Prussian Armies in the Battle of Königgrätz, July 3rd, 1866.

## HIS MAJESTY KING WILLIAM.

### *Head-Quarters of His Majesty.*

Chief of Staff .. .. General of Infantry, Baron Von Moltke.
Quartermaster-General Major-General Von Podbielski.
Inspector-General of
  Artillery .. .. Lieutenant-General Von Hindersin.
Inspector-General of
  Engineers .. .. Lieutenant-General Von Wasserschleben.

### 1ST ARMY AND ARMY OF THE ELBE.

Commander-in-Chief, His Royal Highness Prince Frederick Charles of Prussia.
Chief of Staff, Lieutenant General Von Voigts-Rhetz.
Quartermaster, Major-General Von Stülpnagel.
Commandant of Artillery, Major-General Von Lengsfeld.
First Engineer Officer, Major General Keiser.

| | Present on the Field. | | | | | Absent on other Duties. | | |
|---|---|---|---|---|---|---|---|---|
| | Infantry Battalions. | Rifle Battalions. | Cavalry Squadrons. | Artillery Batteries. | Pioneer Companies. | Infantry Battalions. | Cavalry Squadrons. | Pioneer Companies. |
| IInd Corps d'Armée, Lieutenant-Gen. Von Schmidt.. .. .. .. | 21½ | 1 | 16 | 13 | 2 | 2½ | .. | 2 |
| 5th Division of Infantry, under the command of Lieutenant-General Von Manstein .. .. .. | | | | | | | | |
| 6th Division of Infantry, under the command of Lieutenant-General Von Manstein .. .. .. | 20¾ | 1 | .. | 8 | 2 | ¼ | .. | 2 |
| 7th Division of Infantry, Lieut.-General Von Fransecky .. .. .. | 11¾ | .. | 4 | 4 | 2 | ¼ | .. | 1 |
| 8th Division of Infantry, Lieut.-General Von Horn .. .. .. .. | 9 | 1 | 4 | 4 | 1 | .. | .. | .. |
| Cavalry Corps, H.R.H. Prince Albrecht, senior .. .. .. .. .. | .. | .. | 41 | 5 | .. | .. | .. | .. |
| Combined Cavalry Brigade, Major-General Count Bismarck Bohlen .. | .. | .. | 9 | .. | .. | .. | .. | .. |
| Reserve Artillery, Major-General Schwarz .. .. .. .. .. | .. | .. | .. | 16 | .. | .. | .. | .. |
| Army of the Elbe, General of Infantry, Herwarth Von Bittenfeld .. .. | 34¼ | 2 | 29 | 24 | 3 | 1¼ | 1 | 5 |
| Total of 1st Army and Army of the Elbe .. .. .. | 100¾ | 5 | 103 | 74 | 80 | 4½ | 1 | 5 |

(N.B.—For further details *see* Appendix XXII*a*, *b*, *c*, and *d*.)

### Appendix XXI—*continued*.

### IInd Army.

Commander-in-Chief, H.R.H. The Crown Prince of Prussia.
Chief of Staff, Major-General Von Blumenthal.
Quartermaster, Major-General Von Stosch.
Commandant of Artillery, Major-General Von Jacobi.
First Officer of Engineers, Major-General Von Schweinitz.

| | Present on the Field. | | | | | Absent on other Duty. | | |
|---|---|---|---|---|---|---|---|---|
| | Infantry Battalions. | Rifle battalions. | Squadrons of Cavalry. | Artillery Batteries. | Pioneer Companies. | Infantry Battalions. | Cavalry Squadrons. | Pioneer Companies. |
| Corps of Guards, General of Cavalry, Prince Augustus of Wurtemberg .. | 21¾ | 2 | 16 | 13 | 3 | 2¼ | .. | 1 |
| 1st Corps d'Armée, General of Infantry, Von Bonin .. .. .. .. | 22¾ | 1 | 21 | 16 | 4 | 1¼ | .. | .. |
| VIth Corps d'Armée, General of Cavalry, Von Mutius .. .. .. | 16 | 1 | 11 | 16 | 2 | 2 | 1 | 2 |
| Vth Corps d'Armée, General of Infantry, Von Steinmetz .. .. | 20 | 1 | 9 | 15 | .. | .. | .. | 4 |
| Cavalry Division, Major-General Von Hartmann .. .. .. .. | .. | .. | 24 | 2 | .. | .. | .. | .. |
| Total or IInd Army .. .. | 80½ | 5 | 81 | 56 | 9 | 5½ | 1 | 7 |

(N.B.—For further details *see* Appendix XXII*e, f, g*, and *h*.)

### SUMMARY.

| | Present on the Field. | | | | | Absent on other Duty. | | |
|---|---|---|---|---|---|---|---|---|
| | Infantry Battalions. | Rifle Battalions. | Cavalry Squadrons. | Artillery Batteries. | Pioneer Companies. | Infantry Battalions. | Cavalry Squadrons. | Pioneer Companies. |
| 1st Army and Army of the Elbe .. | 100¾ | 5 | 103 | 74 | 10 | 4¼ | 1 | 10 |
| IInd Army .. .. .. .. | 80½ | 5 | 81 | 56 | 9 | 5½ | 1 | 7 |
| Total of all three Armies .. | 181¼ | 10 | 184 | 130 | 19 | 9¾ | 2 | 17 |
| The Division of Guard Landwehr .. | 11½ | .. | 3 | 2 | .. | ½ | 1 | .. |

(N.B.—Under the head of "Absent" only such troops are included as did not reach
the field by the evening of the day of battle.)

# APPENDIX XXII*a*.

## IIND CORPS D'ARMÉE.

| | | |
|---|---|---|
| General Commanding.. | .. | Lieutenant-General Von Schmidt. |
| Chief of Staff .. .. | .. | Major-General Von Kameke. |
| Commandant of Artillery | .. | Major-General Von Hurrelbrink. |
| First Officer of Engineers | .. | Lieutenant-Colonel Leuthaus. |

| | Battalions of Infantry. | Battalions of Rifles. | Squadrons. | Guns. | Battalions of Pioneers. |
|---|---|---|---|---|---|
| | | | Present on the Field. | | |
| **3RD INFANTRY DIVISION.** | | | | | |
| Lieutenant-General Von Werder. General Staff Officer, Major Von Quistorp. Commandant of Artillery, Major Heubes. | | | | | |
| *Advanced Guard.* | | | | | |
| Lieutenant-Colonel Baron Von Buddenbrock, 54th Regiment. | | | | | |
| Fusilier Battalion of 42nd Regiment, Captain Von Wilde .. .. .. .. .. | 1 | .. | .. | .. | .. |
| Fusilier Battalion of 54th Regiment, Captain Von Pestel .. .. .. .. .. | 1 | .. | .. | .. | .. |
| Two Companies of 2nd Rifle Battalion, Captain Von der Dollen .. .. .. | .. | ½ | .. | .. | .. |
| 5th Regiment of Hussars, Colonel Von Flemming.. | .. | .. | 4 | .. | .. |
| *Main Body.* | | | | | |
| 5th Brigade of Infantry, Major-General Von Januschowsky. | | | | | |
| 42nd Regiment of Infantry, Colonel Von Borcke : 1st Battalion, Major Von Olszewski .. .. 2nd Battalion, Lieutenant-Colonel Von Kortzfleisch .. .. .. .. .. | 2 | .. | .. | .. | .. |
| 2nd Regiment of Grenadiers, Colonel Von Reichenbach : 1st Battalion, Major Von Briesen .. .. ½ of 2nd Battalion, Captain Count Schlippenbach .. .. .. .. .. Fusilier Battalion, Major Von Stoelting .. | 2½ | .. | .. | .. | .. |
| Two Companies of 2nd Rifle Battalion, Major Von Garrelts .. .. .. .. | .. | ½ | .. | .. | .. |
| 1st 4-pounder Battery of 2nd Regiment, Captain Von Ekensteen .. .. .. .. | .. | .. | .. | 6 | .. |
| 5th 4-pounder Battery of 2nd Regiment, Captain Gallus .. .. .. .. .. | .. | .. | .. | 6 | .. |
| 2 Companies of 2nd Pioneer Battalion, Captain Hilgert .. .. .. .. .. | .. | .. | .. | .. | ½ |

APPENDIX XXIIa—*continued.*

|  | Battalions of Infantry. | Battalions of Rifles. | Squadrons. | Guns. | Battalions of Pioneers. |
|---|---|---|---|---|---|
|  | Present on the Field. | | | | |
| **3RD INFANTRY DIVISION**—*cont.* | | | | | |
| 6th Infantry Brigade, Major-Gen. Von Winterfeld. | | | | | |
| 54th Regiment of Infantry: | | | | | |
|   1st Battalion, Major Von Wedell | } 2 | .. | .. | .. | .. |
|   2nd Battalion, Major Von Voss | | | | | |
| 14th Regiment of Infantry, Colonel Von Stahr: | | | | | |
|   1st Battalion, Major Von Wittgenstein | } 2¾ | .. | .. | .. | .. |
|   3 Companies of 2nd Battalion, Major Von Stegmann | | | | | |
|   Fusilier Battalion, Lieutenant-Colonel Von Zaborowski | | | | | |
| 4th 12-pounder Battery of 2nd Regiment, Captain Crüger | .. | .. | .. | 6 | .. |
| 1st 6-pounder Battery of 2nd Regiment, Captain Von Dewitz .. | .. | .. | .. | 6 | .. |
| **Total of 3rd Infantry Division..** | 11¼ | 1 | 4 | 24 | ¼ |
| **4TH INFANTRY DIVISION.** | | | | | |
| Lieut.-General Herwarth Von Bittenfeld. | | | | | |
| General Staff Officer, Captain Von Saldern. | | | | | |
| Commandant of Artillery, Major Von Wasielewski. | | | | | |
| *Advanced Guard.* | | | | | |
| Colonel Von Wietersheim, Commanding 49th Regiment. | | | | | |
| 49th Regiment of Infantry: | | | | | |
|   1st Battalion, Major Von Salpius | } 2¾ | .. | .. | .. | .. |
|   2nd Bn., Maj. Von Tiedewitz, three companies | | | | | |
|   Fusilier Battalion, Major Von Rechenberg | | | | | |
| 4th Regiment of Lancers, Colonel Von Kleist .. | .. | .. | 4 | .. | |
| 3rd 4-pounder Battery of 2nd Field Artillery Regiment, Captain Leo .. | .. | .. | .. | 6 | .. |
| *Main Body.* | | | | | |
| Major-General Von Hanneken, Commanding 8th Brigade. | | | | | |
| 61st Regiment of Infantry, Colonel Von Michaelis: | | | | | |
|   1st Battalion, Lieut.-Colonel Von Beckedorff.. | } 2¼ | .. | .. | .. | .. |
|   Two companies of 2nd Battalion, Lieutenant Colonel Von Haas | | | | | |
|   Fusilier Battalion, Captain Von Below | | | | | |
| 21st Regiment of Infantry, Colonel Von Krane: | | | | | |
|   1st Battalion, Captain Von Bagensky .. | } 3 | .. | .. | .. | .. |
|   2nd Battalion, Major Von Roell | | | | | |
|   Fusilier Battalion, Lieutenant-Colonel Von Goetzen | | | | | |
| 4th 4-pounder Battery, Captain Von Schmeling .. | .. | .. | .. | 6 | .. |

| | Battalions of Infantry. | Battalions of Rifles. | Squadrons. | Guns. | Battalions of Pioneers. |
|---|---|---|---|---|---|
| | Present on the Field. | | | | |

### 4TH INFANTRY DIVISION—*cont.*
*Reserve.*

Major-General Von Schlabrendroff, Commanding 7th Brigade.

| | Battalions of Infantry. | Battalions of Rifles. | Squadrons. | Guns. | Battalions of Pioneers. |
|---|---|---|---|---|---|
| 9th Regiment of Grenadiers, Colonel Von Sandrart : | | | | | |
| 1st Battalion, Major Von Massenbach.. | } 2 | .. | .. | .. | .. |
| Fusilier Battalion, Major Von Normann | | | | | |
| 3rd 12-pounder Battery, Captain Roehl | .. | .. | .. | 6 | .. |
| 3rd 6-pounder Battery, Captain Zoellner .. | .. | .. | .. | 6 | .. |
| Total of the 4th Infantry Division .. | 10½ | .. | 4 | 24 | .. |

### ABSENT ON OTHER DUTY.

The 7th and 8th Companies of the 2nd Regiment, as garrison at Gitschin.

The 1st and 4th Companies of the 2nd Pioneer Battalion, at the disposal of the Commandant of Reichenberg.

The 8th Company of the 14th Regiment, as garrison in Zittau.

The 5th Company of the 49th Regiment in Reichenberg.

The 5th and 8th Companies of the 61st Regiment, escorting ammunition parks.

The 2nd Battalion of the 9th Regiment, guarding the line of communication.

### RESERVE CAVALRY.

*3rd Heavy Cavalry Brigade of Cavalry Corps.*
Major-General Baron Von der Goltz.

| | Battalions of Infantry. | Battalions of Rifles. | Squadrons. | Guns. | Battalions of Pioneers. |
|---|---|---|---|---|---|
| 2nd Regiment of Curassiers, Colonel Von Schaevenbach | .. | .. | 4 | .. | .. |
| 9th Regiment of Lancers, Colonel Baron Von Diepenbroick Grüter | .. | .. | 4 | .. | .. |
| 2nd Horse Artillery Battery of 2nd Field Artillery Regiment, Captain Von Heusch .. | .. | .. | .. | 6 | .. |
| Reserve Cavalry .. | .. | .. | 8 | 6 | .. |

### RESERVE ARTILLERY.

Colonel Baron Von Puttkamer.

*2nd Field Division of 2nd Fie'd Artillery Regimen'.*
Lieutenant-Colonel Wohlgemuth.

| | Battalions of Infantry. | Battalions of Rifles. | Squadrons. | Guns. | Battalions of Pioneers. |
|---|---|---|---|---|---|
| 2nd 6-pounder Battery, Captain Rautenberg .. | .. | .. | .. | 6 | .. |
| 4th 6-pounder Battery, Captain Moewes .. | .. | .. | .. | 6 | .. |
| 2nd 4-pounder Battery, Captain Bode.. .. | .. | .. | .. | 6 | .. |
| 6th 4-pounder Battery, Captain Von der Dollen | .. | .. | .. | 6 | .. |
| Reserve Artillery .. .. | .. | .. | .. | 24 | .. |

### SUMMARY.

|  | | Present on the Field. | | | | | Absent on other Duty. | | |
|---|---|---|---|---|---|---|---|---|---|
|  | | Battalions of Infantry. | Battalions of Rifles. | Squadrons. | Guns. | Battalions of Pioneers. | Companies of Infantry. | Squadrons of Cavalry. | Companies of Pioneers. |
| 3rd Infantry Division | .. | 11¼ | 1 | 4 | 24 | ½ | 3 | .. | 2 |
| 4th Infantry Division | .. | 10¼ | .. | 4 | 24 | .. | 7 | .. | .. |
| Reserve Artillery | .. | .. | .. | .. | 24 | .. | .. | .. | .. |
| Reserve Cavalry | .. | .. | .. | 8 | 6 | .. | .. | .. | .. |
| Total | .. | 21½ | 1 | 16 | 78 | ½ | 10 | .. | 2 |

## APPENDIX XXII*b*.

### 5th, 6th, 7th, and 8th Divisions of Infantry.

(5th and 6th Divisions under Command of Lieut.-General Von Manstein.)

| | Battalions of Infantry. | Battalions of Rifles. | Squadrons. | Guns. | Battalions of Pioneers. |
|---|---|---|---|---|---|
| | | | Present on the Field. | | |
| **5TH DIVISION OF INFANTRY.** | | | | | |
| Major-General Von Kamienski. | | | | | |
| General Staff Officer, Lieut.-Colonel Von Hertzberg. | | | | | |
| Commandant of Artillery, Major Rüstow. | | | | | |
| *9th Brigade of Infantry.* | | | | | |
| Major-General Von Schimmelmann. | | | | | |
| 48th Regiment of Infantry, Colonel Von Diringshofen: | | | | | |
| 1st Battalion, Captain Kassner.. | | | | | |
| 2nd Battalion, Lieut.-Colonel Von Wulffen .. | 3 | .. | .. | .. | .. |
| Fusilier Battalion, Major Von Zglinicki | | | | | |
| 8th Regiment of Grenadiers, Colonel Von Berger : | | | | | |
| 1st Battalion, Major Von Unruhe | | | | | |
| 2nd Battalion, Major Michelmann .. | 3 | .. | .. | .. | .. |
| Fusilier Battalion, Captain Von Wussow .. | | | | | |
| *10th Brigade of Infantry.* | | | | | |
| Colonel Von Debschitz, commanding 12th Regiment. | | | | | |
| 18th Regiment of Infantry, Colonel Von Kettler : | | | | | |
| 1st Battalion, Lieut.-Colonel Von Auer .. | | | | | |
| 2nd Battalion, Major Von Witten (3 Companies) | 2¾ | .. | .. | .. | .. |
| Fusilier Battalion, Major Count Finck Von Finkenstein .. .. .. : | | | | | |
| 12th Regiment of Grenadiers, Major des Barres : | | | | | |
| 1st Battalion, Major Von Kalinowski.. | | | | | |
| 2nd Battalion, Captain Von Zitzewitz .. | 3 | .. | .. | .. | .. |
| Fusilier Battalion, Captain Von Wedell .. | | | | | |
| 1st Field Division of 3rd Field Artillery Regiment : | | | | | |
| 4th 12-pounder Battery, Captain Hübner .. | .. | .. | .. | 6 | .. |
| 1st 6-pounder Battery, Captain Baron Von der Goltz .. .. .. .. | .. | .. | .. | 6 | .. |
| 1st 4-pounder Battery, Captain Griess .. | .. | .. | .. | 6 | .. |
| 5th 4-pounder Battery, Captain Munk! .. | .. | .. | .. | 6 | .. |
| 2nd Company of 3rd Pioneer Battalion .. | .. | .. | .. | .. | ¼ |
| Total of 5th Infantry Division .. | 11¾ | .. | .. | 24 | ¼ |

Absent on other duty :
　The 3rd Lancer Regiment, attached to the Cavalry Brigade of Count Bismarck-Bohlen.
　The 8th Company of the 18th Regiment, escorting the baggage of the division.

2 P

APPENDIX XXIIb—*continued.*

| | Present on the Field. | | | | |
|---|---|---|---|---|---|
| | Battalions of Infantry. | Battalions of Rifles. | Squadrons. | Guns. | Battalions of Pioneers. |
| **6TH DIVISION OF INFANTRY.** | | | | | |
| Lieutenant-General Von Manstein. | | | | | |
| General Staff Officer, Captain Von Rauch, | | | | | |
| 6th Cuirassiers. | | | | | |
| Commandant of Artillery, Major Roeckner. | | | | | |
| | | | | | |
| *Advanced Guard.* | | | | | |
| Major-General Von Gersdorf, Commanding | | | | | |
| 11th Brigade. | | | | | |
| 35th Regiment of Fusiliers, Colonel Von Rothmaler: | | | | | |
| 1st Battalion, Major Von Koethen   .. | | | | | |
| 2nd Battalion, Lieut.-Colonel Von Fragstein.. } | 3 | .. | .. | .. | .. |
| 3rd Battalion, Major Von Papstein   .. | | | | | |
| 3rd Battalion of Rifles, Captain Von Paczenski .. | .. | 1 | .. | .. | .. |
| 4th 4-pounder Battery of the 3rd Field Artillery | | | | | |
| Regiment, Captain Hirschberg  ..   ..   .. | .. | .. | .. | 6 | .. |
| 3rd Company of 3rd Pioneer Battalion, Captain | | | | | |
| Thelemann ..   ..   ..   ..   ..   .. | .. | .. | .. | .. | ¼ |
| Light Field Hospital. | | | | | |
| | | | | | |
| *Main Body.* | | | | | |
| Major-General Von Kotze, Commanding | | | | | |
| 12th Brigade. | | | | | |
| 64th Regiment of Infantry, Colonel Von Goetz: | | | | | |
| 1st Battalion, Lieut.-Colonel Von Hüner   .. | | | | | |
| 2nd Battalion, Major Von Cramer   ..   .. } | 3 | .. | .. | .. | .. |
| Fusilier Battalion, Major Von Wunsch   .. | | | | | |
| 24th Regiment of Infantry, Colonel Count Hacke: | | | | | |
| 1st Battalion, Major Funck   ..   ..   .. | | | | | |
| 2nd Battalion, Major Von Unruhe   ..   .. } | 3 | .. | .. | .. | .. |
| Fusilier Battalion, Lieut.-Colonel Von Krohn | | | | | |
| 3rd 4-pounder Battery of 3rd Field Artillery Regi- | | | | | |
| ment, Captain Schäffer   ..   ..   ..   .. | .. | .. | .. | 6 | .. |
| | | | | | |
| *Reserve.* | | | | | |
| Colonel Von Hartmann, Commanding | | | | | |
| 60th Regiment. | | | | | |
| 60th Regiment of Infantry: | | | | | |
| 1st Battalion, Major Von Kettler   ..   .. | | | | | |
| 2nd Battalion, Major Baron Von Kittlitz   .. } | 3 | .. | .. | .. | .. |
| Fusilier Battalion, Major Von Cranach   .. | | | | | |
| 3rd 12-pounder Battery of 3rd Field Artillery Regi- | | | | | |
| ment, Captain Gülle   ..   ..   ..   .. | .. | .. | .. | 6 | .. |
| 3rd 6-pounder Battery of 3rd Field Artillery Regi- | | | | | |
| ment, Captain Gräfe   ..   ..   ..   .. | .. | .. | .. | 6 | .. |
| Total of 6th Infantry Division   .. | 12 | 1 | .. | 24 | ¼ |

Absent on other duty:

2nd Dragoon Regiment, attached to the Cavalry Brigade of Count Bismarck-Bohlen.

1st Company of 3rd Pioneer Battalion, with Pontoon Train in Roederau-Riesa.

4th Company of 3rd Pioneer Battalion in Reichenberg.

| | Battalions of Infantry. | Battalions of Rifles. | Squadrons. | Guns. | Battalions of Pioneers. |
|---|---|---|---|---|---|
| | | | Present on the Field. | | |
| **7TH DIVISION OF INFANTRY.** | | | | | |
| Lieutenant-General Von Fransecky. | | | | | |
| General Staff Officer, Major Von Krenski. | | | | | |
| Commandant of Artillery, Lieut.-Colonel Weigelt. | | | | | |
| *Advanced Guard.* | | | | | |
| Major-General Von Gordon, Commanding 14th Brigade. | | | | | |
| 27th Regiment of Infantry, Colonel Von Zychlinski : | | | | | |
| 1st Battalion, Lieut.-Colonel Von Summerfeld. | | | | | |
| 2nd Battalion, Major Von Busse .. .. | 3 | .. | .. | .. | .. |
| Fusilier Battalion, Lieut.-Colonel Von Zedtwitz | | | | | |
| Fusilier Battalion of 67th Regiment, Lieut.-Colonel Baron Von Buttlar .. .. .. .. | 1 | .. | .. | .. | .. |
| 10th Regiment of Hussars, Colonel Von Besser ... | .. | .. | 4 | .. | .. |
| 1st 4-pounder Battery of 4th Field Artillery Regiment, Captain Von Raussendorf .. .. | .. | .. | .. | 6 | .. |
| ¼ of the 2nd Company of the 4th Pioneer Battalion, Captain Hutier .. .. .. .. .. | .. | .. | .. | .. | ¼ |
| *Main Body.* | | | | | |
| Major-General Gross Von Schwarzhoff, Commanding 13th Brigade. | | | | | |
| 66th Regiment of Infantry, Colonel Von Blankensee : | | | | | |
| 1st Battalion, Major Schwager.. | | | | | |
| 2nd Battalion, Major Von Wiedner .. .. | 3 | .. | .. | .. | .. |
| Fusilier Battalion, Major Von Schmeling .. | | | | | |
| 26th Regiment of Infantry, Col. Baron Von Medem : | | | | | |
| 1st Battalion, Major Paucke .. .. | | | | | |
| 2nd Battalion, Major Von Gilsa .. .. | 3 | .. | .. | .. | .. |
| Fusilier Battalion, Major Loewenberger Von Schoenholtz .. .. .. .. | | | | | |
| 1st 6-pounder Battery of the 4th Field Artillery Regiment, Captain Kühne .. .. .. .. | .. | .. | .. | 6 | .. |
| *Reserve.* | | | | | |
| Colonel Von Bothmer, Commanding 67th Regiment. | | | | | |
| 66th Regiment of Infantry : | | | | | |
| 1st Battalion, Lieut.-Colonel Von Hochstetter | | | | | |
| 2nd Battalion, Major Von Zedtwitz (3 Comps.) | 1¾ | .. | .. | .. | .. |
| 4th 12-pounder Battery or 4th Field Artillery Regiment, Captain Von Notz .. .. .. | .. | .. | .. | 6 | .. |
| 5th 4-pounder Battery of 4th Field Artillery Regiment, Captain Von Nordeck .. .. .. | .. | .. | .. | 6 | .. |
| 1½ Companies of 4th Pioneer Battalion with Light Bridge Train, Major Eltester .. .. .. | .. | .. | .. | .. | ⅜ |
| Light Field Hospital. | | | | | |
| Total of 7th Infantry Division .. | 11¾ | .. | 4 | 24 | ½ |

Absent on other duty :
    5th Company of 67th Regiment, escorting baggage.
    4th Company of 4th Pioneer Battalion, in Reichenberg.

APPENDIX XXIIb—*continued.*

| | Present on the Field. | | | | |
|---|---|---|---|---|---|
| | Battalions of Infantry. | Battalions of Rifles. | Squadrons. | Guns. | Battalions of Pioneers. |
| **8TH DIVISION OF INFANTRY.** | | | | | |
| Lieutenant-General Von Horn. General Staff Officer, Major Von Massow. Commandant of Artillery, Major Heinrich. | | | | | |
| *Advanced Guard.* | | | | | |
| Lieut.-Colonel Von Valentini, Commanding Fusilier Battalion 71st Regiment. | | | | | |
| Fusilier Battalion of 71st Regiment | 1 | .. | .. | .. | .. |
| Fusilier Battalion of 31st Regiment, Capt. Von Braun | 1 | .. | .. | .. | .. |
| 4th Squadron of the 6th Lancers, Lieut. Krüger .. | .. | .. | 1 | .. | .. |
| 3rd 4-pounder Battery of 4th Field Artillery Regiment, Captain Kipping | .. | .. | .. | 6 | .. |
| 3rd Company of 4th Pioneer Battalion, Captain Von Wasserschleben | .. | .. | .. | .. | 1 |
| *Main Body.* | | | | | |
| Major-General Von Bose, Commanding 15th Brigade. | | | | | |
| 71st Regiment of Infantry, Colonel Von Avemann : 1st Battalion, Major Von Hagen 2nd Battalion, Lieut.-Colonel Von Bothmer .. | } 2 | .. | .. | .. | .. |
| 31st Regiment of Infantry, Colonel Von Wedell : 1st Battalion, Lieut.-Colonel Von Heinemann 2nd Battalion, Major Von Hagen | } 2 | .. | .. | .. | .. |
| 6th Regiment of Lancers, Lieutenant-Colonel Baron Langermann (3 Squadrons) | .. | .. | 3 | .. | .. |
| 4th 4-pounder Battery of 4th Field Artillery Regiment, Captain Von Schlotheim .. | .. | .. | .. | 6 | .. |
| 3rd 6-pounder Battery of 4th Field Artillery Regiment, Captain Anton | .. | .. | .. | 6 | .. |
| *Reserve.* | | | | | |
| Major-General Von Schmidt, Commanding 16th Brigade. | | | | | |
| 72nd Regiment of Infantry, Col. Count Gneisenau : 1st Battalion, Major Hensel 2nd Battalion, Captain Von Gilsa Fusilier Battalion, Major Von Flotow.. | } 3 | .. | .. | .. | .. |
| 4th Battalion of Rifles, Lieut.-Colonel Von Colomb | .. | 1 | .. | .. | ... |
| 3rd 12-pounder Battery of 4th Field Artillery Regiment, Captain Von Seebach | .. | .. | .. | 6 | .. |
| Total of 8th Infantry Division .. | 9 | 1 | 4 | 24 | 1 |

## APPENDIX XXIIc.

CAVALRY Corps, Combined Cavalry Brigade of Major-General Count Bismarck-Bohlen, and Reserve Artillery of the 1st Army.

| | Present on the Field. | | | | |
|---|---|---|---|---|---|
| | Battalions of Infantry. | Battalions of Rifles. | Squadrons. | Guns. | Pioneers. |
| **CAVALRY CORPS.** | | | | | |
| General of Cavalry, Prince Albrecht of Prussia, senior. | | | | | |
| Chief of Staff, Lieut.-Colonel Von Witzendorff. | | | | | |
| Commandant of Artillery, Lieut.-Colonel Von der Becke. | | | | | |
| **1ST DIVISION OF CAVALRY.** | | | | | |
| Major-General Von Alvensleben. | | | | | |
| General Staff Officer, Major Baron Von Eller-Eberstein. | | | | | |
| *1st Light Cavalry Brigade.* | | | | | |
| Major-General Von Rheinbaben. | | | | | |
| 1st Regiment of Guard Dragoons, Lieut.-Colonel Von Barner .. | .. | .. | 4 | .. | .. |
| 1st Regiment of Guard Lancers, Col. Von Colomb .. | .. | .. | 4 | .. | .. |
| 2nd Regiment of Guard Lancers, Colonel Count Brandenburg | .. | .. | 4 | .. | .. |
| 2nd Horse Artillery Battery of Guard Artillery, Captain Von Gregory | .. | .. | .. | 6 | .. |
| *2nd Heavy Cavalry Brigade.* | | | | | |
| Major-General Von Pfuel. | | | | | |
| 6th Regiment of Cuirassiers, Colonel Von Rauch .. | .. | .. | 4 | .. | .. |
| 7th Regiment of Cuirassiers, Colonel Von Hontheim | .. | .. | 4 | .. | .. |
| 1st Horse Artillery Battery of Guard Artillery, Captain Von Krieger | .. | .. | .. | 6 | .. |
| *Reserve Battery.* | | | | | |
| th Horse Artillery Battery of 2nd Field Artillery Regiment, Captain Von Roehl .. | .. | .. | 6 | .. | .. |
| **2ND DIVISION OF CAVALRY.** | | | | | |
| Major-General Hann Von Weyhern. | | | | | |
| General Staff Officer, Captain Von Schönfels. | | | | | |
| *3rd Light Cavalry Brigade.* | | | | | |
| Major-General Count Groeben. | | | | | |
| 3rd Regiment of Dragoons, Lieut.-Col. Von Willisen | .. | .. | 5 | .. | .. |
| 12th Regiment of Hussars, Col. Baron Von Barnekow | .. | .. | 4 | .. | .. |

APPENDIX XXIIc—*continued.*

| | | Present on the Field. | | | |
|---|:---:|:---:|:---:|:---:|:---:|
| | Battalions of Infantry. | Battalions of Rifles. | Squadrons. | Guns. | Pioneers. |
| 2ND DIVISION OF CAVALRY—*cont.* | | | | | |
| 3rd Horse Artillery Battery of 2nd Field Artillery Regiment, Captain Von Gayl .. .. .. | .. | .. | .. | 6 | .. |
| *2nd Light Cavalry Brigade.* | | | | | |
| Major-General Duke of Mecklenburg. | | | | | |
| 3rd Regiment of Hussars, Lieutenant-Colonel Von Kalkreuth .. .. .. | .. | .. | 4 | .. | |
| 11th Regiment of Lancers, Lieut.-Colonel Prince Hohenlohe .. .. .. .. .. .. | .. | .. | 4 | .. | .. |
| 2nd Regiment of Guard Dragoons, Colonel Von Redern .. .. .. .. .. .. | .. | .. | 4 | .. | .. |
| 1st Horse Artillery Battery of 2nd Field Artillery Regiment, Captain Von Ekensteen .. .. | .. | .. | .. | 6 | .. |
| Total Cavalry Corps .. | .. | .. | 41 | 30 | .. |
| Absent on other duty : | | | | | |
| 1st Heavy Cavalry Brigade and 1 Battery, attached to Corps of Guards. | | | | | |
| 3rd Heavy Cavalry Brigade and 1 Battery, attached to IInd Corps. | | | | | |
| COMBINED CAVALRY BRIGADE. | | | | | |
| (Formed out of the Divisional Cavalry of the 5th and 6th Divisions.) | | | | | |
| Major-General Count Bismarck-Bohlen. | | | | | |
| 3rd Regiment of Lancers, Lieut.-Col. Von Tresckow | .. | .. | 4 | .. | .. |
| 2nd Regiment of Dragoons, Lieut.-Col. Heinichen.. | .. | .. | 5 | .. | .. |
| Total of Combined Brigade .. | .. | .. | 9 | .. | .. |
| RESERVE ARTILLERY OF THE 1ST ARMY. | | | | | |
| Major-General Schwarz. | | | | | |
| *Brandenburg Reserve Artillery, No. 3.* | | | | | |
| Lieut.-Col. Von Ramm. | | | | | |
| 2nd Field Division of 3rd Field Artillery Regiment, Major Von Held : | | | | | |
| 2nd 6-pounder Battery, Captain Benecke .. | .. | .. | .. | 6 | .. |
| 4th 6-pounder Battery, Captain Burbach .. | .. | .. | .. | 6 | .. |
| 2nd 4-pounder Battery, Captain Eunicke .. | .. | .. | .. | 6 | .. |
| 6th 4-pounder Battery, Captain Müller .. | .. | .. | .. | 6 | .. |
| Horse Artillery Division of 3rd Field Artillery Regiment, Lieut.-Col. Von Lilienthal : | | | | | |
| 1st Horse Artillery Battery, Captain Kreyher.. | .. | .. | .. | 6 | .. |
| 2nd Horse Artillery Battery, Capt. Schüssler.. | .. | .. | .. | 6 | .. |
| 3rd Horse Artillery Battery, Captain Corsep .. | .. | .. | .. | 6 | .. |
| 4th Horse Artillery Battery, Captain Sterzel .. | .. | .. | .. | 6 | .. |

APPENDIX XXIIc--*continued.*

| | Present on the Field. | | | | |
|---|---|---|---|---|---|
| | Battalions of Infantry. | Battalions of Rifles. | Squadrons. | Guns. | Battalions of Pioneers. |
| RESERVE ARTILLERY OF 1ST ARMY—*cont.* | | | | | |
| *Magdeburg Reserve Artillery, No. 4.* | | | | | |
| Colonel Roth. | | | | | |
| 2nd Field Division of 4th Field Artillery Regiment, Lieutenant-Colonel Von Scherbening : | | | | | |
| 2nd 6-pounder Battery, Captain Von Schaper | .. | .. | .. | 6 | .. |
| 4th 6-pounder Battery, Captain Meisner .. | .. | .. | .. | 6 | .. |
| 2nd 4-pounder Battery, Captain Reinhardt .. | .. | .. | .. | 6 | .. |
| 6th 4-pounder Battery, Lieutenant Philippi .. | .. | .. | .. | 6 | .. |
| Horse Artillery Division of 4th Field Artillery Regiment, Lieut.-Colonel Von Iagemann : | | | | | |
| 1st Horse Artillery Battery, Captain Sylvius .. | .. | .. | .. | 6 | .. |
| 2nd Horse Artillery Battery, Captain Siber .. | .. | .. | .. | 6 | .. |
| 3rd Horse Artillery Battery, Capt. Von der Burg | .. | .. | .. | 6 | .. |
| 4th Horse Artillery Battery, Captain Bode .. | .. | .. | .. | 6 | .. |
| Total of Reserve Artillery .. | .. | .. | .. | 96 | .. |

## APPENDIX XXIId.

### ARMY OF THE ELBE.

| | |
|---|---|
| Commander-in-Chief .. .. | General of Infantry, Herwarth Von Bittenfeld. |
| Chief of Staff .. .. .. | Colonel Von Schlotheim. |
| Commandant of Artillery .. | Colonel Von Rozynski-Manger. |
| First Officer of Engineers .. | Lieutenant-Colonel Von Forell. |

| | Present on the Field. | | | | |
|---|---|---|---|---|---|
| | Battalions of Infantry. | Battalions of Rifles. | Squadrons. | Guns. | Battalions of Pioneers. |
| **ADVANCED GUARD.** | | | | | |
| Major-General Von Schoeler, Commanding 31st Brigade. | | | | | |
| Commander of the Infantry, Colonel Von Gerstein Hohenstein, 28th Regiment. | | | | | |
| Fusilier Battalion of the 17th Regiment, Lieut.-Colonel Von Koblinski .. .. .. .. | 1 | .. | .. | .. | .. |
| Fusilier Battalion of the 28th Regiment, Major Mettler .. .. .. .. .. | 1 | .. | .. | .. | .. |
| 2nd Battalion of the 33rd Regiment, Lieut.-Col. Von Marschall .. .. .. .. .. | 1 | .. | .. | .. | .. |
| 1st Battalion of the 40th Regiment, Lieut.-Colonel Von Conrady .. .. .. .. | 1 | .. | .. | .. | .. |
| 2nd Battalion of the 56th Regiment, Major Von Thielau .. .. .. .. .. | 1 | .. | .. | .. | .. |
| Fusilier Battalion of the 69th Regiment, Lieut.-Colonel Marschall Von Sulicki .. .. .. | 1 | .. | .. | .. | .. |
| 8th Battalion of Rifles, Major Zierold .. .. | .. | 1 | .. | .. | .. |
| 4th 4-pounder Battery of 8th Field Artillery Regiment, Captain Wolf .. .. .. | .. | .. | .. | 6 | .. |
| 1st 4-pounder Battery of 7th Field Artillery Regiment, Captain Pilgrim .. .. .. | .. | .. | .. | 6 | .. |
| Detachment of 8th Pioneer Battalion, Lieutenant Vopelius. | | | | | |
| *Cavalry Brigade.* | | | | | |
| Major-General Count Von der Goltz. | | | | | |
| 7th Regiment of Hussars, Colonel Von Lindern .. | .. | .. | 5 | .. | .. |
| 11th Regiment of Hussars, Colonel Von Rauch .. | .. | .. | 5 | .. | .. |
| 3rd Horse Artillery Battery of 8th Field Artillery Regiment, Captain Von Fuchsius.. .. .. | .. | .. | .. | 6 | .. |
| Total of Advanced Guard .. | 6 | 1 | 10 | 18 | .. |

APPENDIX XXII*d—continued.*

| | Present on the Field. | | | | |
|---|---|---|---|---|---|
| | Battalions of Infantry. | Battalions of Rifles. | Squadrons. | Guns. | Battalions of Pioneers. |
| **14TH DIVISION OF INFANTRY.** | | | | | |
| Lieutenant-General Count Münster.<br>General Staff Officer, Major Von Thile.<br>Commandant of Artillery, Major Schimmelfennig<br>Von der Oye. | | | | | |
| *27th Brigade of Infantry.* | | | | | |
| Major-General Von Schwarzkoppen. | | | | | |
| 16th Regiment of Infantry, Colonel Schwartz :<br>1st Battalion, Lieut.-Colonel Von Reichenbach.<br>2nd Battalion, Major Von Grevenitz .. ..<br>Fusilier Battalion, Major Von Horn .. .. | 3 | .. | .. | .. | .. |
| 56th Regiment of Infantry, Colonel Von Dorpowski :<br>1st Battalion, Major Von Hymmen .. ..<br>Fusilier Battalion, Lieut.-Colonel Von Busse | 2 | .. | .. | .. | .. |
| 7th Battalion of Rifles, Lieut.-Colonel Von Sell .. | .. | 1 | .. | .. | .. |
| *28th Brigade of Infantry.* | | | | | |
| Major-General Von Hiller. | | | | | |
| 57th Regiment of Infantry, Colonel Von der Osten :<br>1st Battalion, Lieut.-Colonel Von Schoening..<br>Fusilier Battalion, Lieut.-Colonel Grolmann | 2 | .. | .. | .. | .. |
| 17th Regiment of Infantry, Col. Baron Von Kottwitz :<br>1st Battalion, Major Von Rex .. .. ..<br>2nd Battalion, Major Von Bieberstein .. | 2 | .. | .. | .. | .. |
| 5th Regiment of Lancers, Colonel Baron Von<br>Richthofen .. .. .. .. .. | .. | .. | 4 | .. | .. |
| 1st Field Division of 7th Field Artillery Regiment :<br>1st 6-pounder Battery, Captain Von Fragstein | .. | .. | .. | 6 | .. |
| 5th 4-pounder Battery, Captain Trautmann .. | .. | .. | .. | 6 | .. |
| 4th 12-pounder Battery, Captain Schmelzer .. | .. | .. | .. | 6 | .. |
| 2 Companies of 7th Pioneer Battalion, with Light<br>Field Bridge Train, Major Von Rohrscheidt .. | .. | .. | .. | .. | ⅓ |
| Total of 14th Division of Infantry.. | 9 | 1 | 4 | 18 | ⅓ |
| Absent on other duty : Two companies of 7th Pioneer<br>Battalion in Dresden. | | | | | |
| **15TH DIVISION OF INFANTRY.** | | | | | |
| Lieut.-General Baron Von Canstein.<br>General Staff Officer, Major Von der Esch.<br>Commandant of Artillery, Major Bechtold Von<br>Ehrenschwerdt. | | | | | |
| *29th Brigade of Infantry.* | | | | | |
| Major-General Von Stueckradt. | | | | | |
| 65th Regiment of Infantry, Colonel du Trossel :<br>2nd Battalion, Lieut.-Colonel Leonhardt ..<br>Fusilier Battalion, Major Stawitzki .. .. | 2 | .. | .. | .. | .. |

## APPENDIX XXII*d*—*continued*.

| | Present on the Field. | | | | |
|---|:---:|:---:|:---:|:---:|:---:|
| | Battalions of Infantry. | Battalions of Rifles. | Squadrons. | Guns. | Battalions of Pioneers. |
| **15TH DIVISION OF INFANTRY**—*cont.* | | | | | |
| 40th Regiment of Fusiliers, Col. Von Zimmermann: | | | | | |
| 2nd Battalion, Major Von Henning .. .. } | 2 | .. | .. | .. | .. |
| 3rd Battalion, Major Von Slupecki .. .. | | | | | |
| *30th Brigade of Infantry.* | | | | | |
| Major-General Von Glasenapp. | | | | | |
| 68th Regiment of Infantry, Lieut.-Colonel Von Gayl: | | | | | |
| 1st Battalion, Major Von Schramm .. .. | | | | | |
| 2nd Battalion, Major Zwenger.. .. .. } | 3 | .. | .. | .. | .. |
| Fusilier Battalion, Major Schartow .. | | | | | |
| 28th Regiment of Infantry, Major Von Brauchitsch: | | | | | |
| 1st Battalion, Major Von Brauchitsch (commanding regiment) .. .. .. .. } | 2 | .. | .. | .. | .. |
| 2nd Battalion, Major Von Cosel .. | | | | | |
| 7th Regiment of Dragoons, Colonel Von Ribbeck .. | .. | .. | 4 | .. | .. |
| 3rd Field Division of 8th Field Artillery Regiment: | | | | | |
| 3rd 12-pounder Battery, Captain Theiler .. | .. | .. | .. | 6 | .. |
| 3rd 6-pounder Battery, Captain Fastnagel .. | .. | .. | .. | 6 | .. |
| 3rd 4-pounder Battery, Captain Bausch .. | .. | .. | .. | 6 | .. |
| Total of 15th Division .. | 9 | .. | 4 | 18 | .. |
| **RESERVE BRIGADE OF CAVALRY.** | | | | | |
| Major-General Von Kotze. | | | | | |
| 8th Regt. of Cuirassiers, Lieut.-Col. Count Roedern | .. | .. | 4 | .. | .. |
| Pomeranian Heavy Landwehr "Reiter" Regiment, | | | | | |
| Major Count Schwerin, 3 Squadrons .. .. | .. | .. | 3 | .. | .. |
| Total of Reserve Cavalry .. | .. | .. | 7 | .. | .. |
| Absent on other duty: | | | | | |
| The 1st Battalion of 65th stopped at Neu Bidsow until the Guard Landwehr Division came up. | | | | | |
| The 4th Squadron of the Landwehr "Reiter" Regiment was in Rumburg. | | | | | |
| **16TH DIVISION OF INFANTRY.** | | | | | |
| Lieut.-General Von Etzel. | | | | | |
| General Staff Officer, Major Baron Von Doernberg. | | | | | |
| *31st Brigade of Infantry.* | | | | | |
| Colonel Schuler Von Senden, 29th Regiment. | | | | | |
| 29th Regiment of Infantry: | | | | | |
| 1st Battalion, Lieut.-Colonel Von Foerster (3 Companies) .. .. .. .. | | | | | |
| 2nd Battalion, Lieut.-Col. Baron Von der Osten } | 2¼ | .. | .. | .. | .. |
| Fusilier Battalion, Lieut.-Colonel Modrach .. | | | | | |

APPENDIX XXIId—*continued.*

| | Present on the Field. | | | | |
|---|---|---|---|---|---|
| — | Battalions of Infantry. | Battalions of Rifles. | Squadrons. | Guns. | Battalions of Pioneers. |
| 16TH DIVISION OF INFANTRY—*cont.* | | | | | |
| 69th Regiment of Infantry, Colonel Von Beyer : | | | | | |
| 1st Battalion, Lieut.-Colonel Von Linsingen .. | } 2 | .. | .. | .. | .. |
| 2nd Battalion, Major Von Legat .. .. | | | | | |
| *Fusilier Brigade.* | | | | | |
| Colonel Von Wegerer, 33rd Regiment. | | | | | |
| 33rd Regiment of Fusiliers : | | | | | |
| 1st Battalion, Major Fragstein Von Niemsdorff | } 2 | .. | .. | .. | .. |
| 3rd Battalion, Major Hahn Von Dorsche .. | | | | | |
| 34th Regiment of Fusiliers, Colonel Von Schmeling : | | | | | |
| 1st Battalion, Lieut.-Colonel Wahlert.. .. | | | | | |
| 2nd Battalion, Major Von Usedom .. .. | } 3 | .. | .. | .. | .. |
| 3rd Battalion, Captain Von Westernhagen .. | | | | | |
| 7th Regt. of Lancers, Lieut.-Col. Stein Von Kaminski | .. | .. | 4 | .. | .. |
| 1st Horse Artillery Battery of 8th Field Artillery Regiment, Captain Caspari .. .. .. | .. | .. | .. | 6 | .. |
| 5th 4-pounder Battery of 8th Field Artillery Regiment, Captain Baron Von Eynatten .. .. | .. | .. | .. | 6 | .. |
| 1st 6-pounder Battery of 8th Field Artillery Regiment, Captain Bastian .. .. .. | .. | .. | .. | 6 | .. |
| 2nd Company of 8th Pioneer Battalion, with Light Bridge Train, Captain Bliesener .. .. .. | .. | .. | .. | .. | ¼ |
| Total of 16th Division .. | 9¾ | .. | 4 | 18 | ¼ |
| Absent on other duty : | | | | | |
| 1st Company of 29th Regiment, in Hoch Wesely. 1st, 3rd, and 4th Companies of 8th Pioneer Battalion, in Dresden. | | | | | |
| COMBINED RESERVE ARTILLERY. | | | | | |
| Of the VIIth Corps, Colonel Von Buelow. | | | | | |
| 2nd Field Division, Major Erdmann : | | | | | |
| 2nd 4-pounder Battery, Captain Lancelle .. | .. | .. | .. | 6 | .. |
| 6th 4-pounder Battery, Captain Grabe .. | .. | .. | .. | 6 | .. |
| 2nd 6-pounder Battery, Captain Sack .. .. | .. | .. | .. | 6 | .. |
| 4th 6-pounder Battery, Captain Huebner .. | .. | .. | .. | 6 | .. |
| 1st Horse Artillery Battery, Captain Overdyck | .. | .. | .. | 6 | .. |
| 2nd Horse Artillery Battery, Capt. Von Gontard | .. | .. | .. | 6 | .. |
| Of the VIIIth Corps, Colonel Hausmann. | | | | | |
| 2nd Field Division, Captain Waltsgott : | | | | | |
| 2nd 6-pounder Battery, Lieut. Kaulbach .. | .. | .. | .. | 6 | .. |
| 4th 6-pounder Battery, Captain Pahlke .. | .. | .. | .. | 6 | .. |
| 2nd 4-pounder Battery, Captain Von Zglinitzki | .. | .. | .. | 6 | .. |
| 6th 4-pounder Battery, Captain Sabel .. .. | .. | .. | .. | 6 | .. |
| 2nd Horse Art. Battery, Capt. Count Seyssel d'Aix | .. | .. | .. | 6 | .. |
| 4th Horse Artillery Battery, Lieut. Kleine .. | .. | .. | .. | 6 | .. |
| Escort of Artillery : | | | | | |
| 2nd Battalion of 57th Regt., Major Von Roell | 1 | .. | .. | .. | .. |
| Total of Reserve Artillery .. | 1 | .. | .. | 72 | .. |

APPENDIX XXII*d—continued.*

## SUMMARY OF ARMY OF THE ELBE.

| | Present on the Field. | | | | | Absent on other Duty. | | |
|---|---|---|---|---|---|---|---|---|
| — | Infantry Battalions. | Rifle Battalions. | Cavalry Squadrons. | Artillery Guns. | Pioneer Companies. | Infantry Battalions. | Cavalry Squadrons. | Pioneer Companies. |
| Advanced Guard .. | 6 | 1 | · 10 | 18 | .. | .. | .. | 2 |
| 14th Division .. .. | 9 | 1 | 4 | 18 | 2 | .. | .. | .. |
| 15th Division .. .. | 9 | .. | 4 | 18 | .. | 1 | .. | .. |
| 16th Division .. .. | 9¾ | .. | 4 | 18 | 1 | ¼ | .. | 3 |
| Combined Cavalry Brig. | .. | .. | 7 | .. | .. | .. | 1 | .. |
| Reserve Artillery .. | 1 | .. | .. | 72 | .. | .. | .. | .. |
| Total .. .. | 34¾ | 2 | 29 | 144 | 3 | 1¼ | 1 | 5 |

APPENDIX XXIId—*continued.*

| | Battalions of Infantry. | Battalions of Rifles. | Squadrons. | Guns. | Battalions of Pioneers. |
|---|---|---|---|---|---|
| DIVISION OF GUARD LANDWEHR. | | | | | |
| (Arrived on the Field the evening of the Battle.) | | | | | |
| General Commanding, Major-General Von Rosenberg Gruszczynski. | | | | | |
| 2nd Regiment of Guard Landwehr Infantry, Colonel Frohnhoèfer : | | | | | |
| 1st Battalion (Berlin), Major Count Finck Von Finckenstein .. .. .. .. .. | 3 | .. | .. | .. | .. |
| 2nd Battalion (Magdeburg), Maj. Von Wolffradt | | | | | |
| 3rd Battalion (Cottbus), Major Von Schickfuss | | | | | |
| 1st Regiment of Guard Landwehr Infantry, Lieut.-Colonel Ranisch : | | | | | |
| 3rd Battalion (Graudenz), Major Jancke .. | 2¾ | .. | .. | .. | .. |
| 2nd Battalion (Stettin), Major Baron Von der Horst .. .. .. .. .. | | | | | |
| 1st Battalion (Koenigsberg), Lieut.-Colonel Genée, 3 Companies .. .. .. .. | | | | | |
| 2nd Regiment of Guard Landwehr Grenadiers, Colonel Baron Gans Edler Von Puttlitz : | | | | | |
| 1st Battalion (Hamm), Major Baron Von Steinaecker .. .. .. .. .. | 3 | .. | .. | .. | .. |
| 2nd Battalion (Coblenz), Major Von L'Estocq | | | | | |
| 3rd Battalion (Duesseldorf), Major Von Doering | | | | | |
| 1st Regiment of Guard Landwehr Grenadiers, Lieut.-Colonel Von Roehl : | | | | | |
| 1st Battalion (Goerlitz), Major Von Loos .. | 2¾ | .. | .. | .. | .. |
| 2nd Battalion (Breslau), Major Von Bernhardi, 3 Companies .. .. .. .. | | | | | |
| 3rd Battalion (Polnisch Lissa), Major Von Zacha .. .. .. .. .. | | | | | |
| 5th Regiment of Landwehr Hussars, Lieut.-Colonel Von Oppen, 3 Squadrons .. .. .. .. | .. | .. | 3 | .. | .. |
| 1st Reserve Battery, Captain Von Helden Sarnowski: | .. | .. | .. | 6 | .. |
| 3rd Reserve Battery, Captain Von Gilsa .. .. | .. | .. | .. | 6 | .. |
| Total of Guard Landwehr Division | 11½ | .. | 3 | 12 | .. |

Absent on other duty :
    The 7th Company of 1st Guard Landwehr Grenadiers, in Jung Bunzlau.
    The 2nd Company of the 1st Regiment of Guard Landwehr Infantry, as escort of the baggage.
    The 4th Squadron of the 5th Landwehr Hussars, in Gabel.

## APPENDIX XXII*e*.

### CORPS OF GUARDS.

| | |
|---|---|
| General Commanding .. | Prince Augustus of Würtemberg. |
| Chief of Staff .. .. | Colonel Von Dannenberg. |
| Commandant of Artillery .. | Major-General Von Colomier. |
| First Officer of Engineers .. | Colonel Biehler. |

| | Present on the Field. | | | | |
|---|---|---|---|---|---|
| | Battalions of Infantry. | Battalions of Rifles. | Squadrons. | Guns. | Battalions of Pioneers. |
| **1ST DIVISION OF GUARD INFANTRY.** Lieutenant-General Baron Hiller Von Gärtringen. General Staff Officer, Major Von Kameke. Commandant of Artillery, Major Bychelberg. | | | | | |
| *Advanced Guard.* Major-General Von Alvensleben. | | | | | |
| 2nd Brigade of Guard Infantry, Colonel Von Pape (2nd Foot Guards). 2nd Regiment of Foot Guards: 1st Battalion, Major Von Petery .. .. 2nd Battalion, Major Von Reuss, 3 companies | } 1¾ | .. | .. | .. | .. |
| 2 Companies of Guard Rifles, Lieut.-Colonel Von Roeder .. .. .. .. .. | .. | ½ | .. | .. | .. |
| Regiment of Guard Fusiliers, Col. Von Werder: 1st Battalion, Major Von Tietzen .. .. 2nd Battalion, Lieut.-Col. Von der Knesebeck, 3 Companies .. .. .. .. | } 1¾ | .. | .. | .. | .. |
| 2 Squadrons of Guard Hussars, Captains Count Groeben and Von Stralendorff .. .. .. | .. | .. | 2 | .. | .. |
| 5th 4-pounder Battery of Guard Artillery, Captain Von Eltester .. .. .. .. | .. | .. | .. | 6 | .. |
| 1st 6-pounder Battery of Guard Artillery, Capt. Braun | .. | .. | .. | 6 | .. |
| Escort of Artillery, 6th Company 2nd Foot Guards 7th Company Guard Fusiliers.. | } ½ | .. | .. | .. | .. |
| *Main Body.* Colonel Von Obernitz. | | | | | |
| 1st Brigade of Guard Infantry, Colonel Knappe Von Knappstädt, 3rd Foot Guards. 3rd Regiment of Foot Guards: 1st Battalion, Major Von Plehwe .. .. 2nd Battalion, Major Von Barby .. .. | } 2 | .. | .. | .. | .. |
| 1st Regiment of Foot Guards: 1st Battalion, Major Von Kleist .. .. 2nd Battalion, Colonl Von Block .. .. | } 2 | .. | .. | .. | .. |

## Appendix XXIIe—*continued.*

| | Present on the Field. | | | | |
|---|---|---|---|---|---|
| | Battalions of Infantry. | Battalions of Rifles. | Squadrons. | Guns. | Battalions of Pioneers. |
| **1st Division of Guard Infantry**—*cont.* | | | | | |
| *Combined Brigade of Fusiliers.* | | | | | |
| Colonel Von Kessel, 1st Foot Guards. | | | | | |
| Fusilier Battalion of 1st Foot Guards, Lieut.-Col. Von Helldorff .. .. .. .. .. | 1 | .. | .. | .. | .. |
| Fusilier Battalion of 2nd Foot Guards, Major Von Erckert .. .. .. .. .. | 1 | .. | .. | .. | .. |
| 3rd Battalion of Guard Fusiliers, Lieut.-Colonel Count Waldersee .. .. .. .. .. | 1 | .. | .. | .. | .. |
| 2 Companies of Guard Rifles, Captains Count Pourtales and Count Carmer .. .. .. | .. | ½ | .. | .. | .. |
| 2 Squadrons of Guard Hussars, Captains Von Meyerinck and Von Rundstedt .. .. .. | .. | .. | 2 | .. | .. |
| 1st 4-pounder Battery of Guard Artillery, Lieut. Witte .. .. .. .. .. | .. | .. | .. | 6 | .. |
| 4th 12-pounder Battery of Guard Artillery, Captain Von Schmeling .. .. .. .. .. | .. | .. | .. | 6 | .. |
| 2 Companies of Guard Pioneers, Captains Von Adler and Von Bergen .. .. .. .. | .. | .. | .. | .. | ½ |
| Total of 1st Division of Guard Infantry .. | 11 | 1 | 4 | 24 | ½ |
| **2nd Division of Guard Infantry.** | | | | | |
| Lieut.-General Von Plonski. | | | | | |
| General Staff Officer, Lieut.-Col. Von Voigts Rhetz. Commandant of Artillery, Major Baron Von der Goltz. | | | | | |
| *Advanced Guard.* | | | | | |
| Colonel Von Pritzelwitz, 3rd Guard Grenadiers. | | | | | |
| Battalion of Guard Skirmishers, Major Von Besser | .. | 1 | .. | .. | .. |
| Fusilier Battalion of 1st Guard Grenadiers, Major Von Rauchhaupt .. .. .. .. | 1 | .. | .. | .. | .. |
| Fusilier Battalion of 2nd Guard Grenadiers, Major Von Delitz .. .. .. .. .. | 1 | .. | .. | .. | .. |
| 3rd Regiment of Guard Lancers, Colonel Mirus .. | .. | .. | 4 | .. | .. |
| 3rd 4-pounder Battery of Guard Artillery, Captain Von Hirschfeld .. .. .. .. .. | .. | .. | .. | 6 | .. |
| 3rd Company of Guard Pioneers, Capt. Von Owstien | .. | .. | .. | .. | ¼ |
| *Main Body.* | | | | | |
| Major-General Von Budritzki. | | | | | |
| 3rd Guard Infantry Brigade. | | | | | |
| 1st Regiment of Guard Grenadiers, Colonel Von Knappe :<br>  1st Battalion, Lieut.-Colonel Von Brandenstein<br>  2nd Battalion, Major Von Brixen .. .. | } 2 | .. | .. | .. | .. |

APPENDIX XXII*e—continued.*

| | Present on the Field. | | | | |
|---|---|---|---|---|---|
| | Battalions of Infantry. | Battalions of Rifles. | Squadrons. | Guns. | Battalions of Pioneers. |
| **2ND DIVISION OF GUARD INFANTRY—*cont.*** | | | | | |
| 3rd Regiment of Guard Grenadiers, Lieut.-Colonel Von Pannewitz : | | | | | |
|     1st Battalion, Major Von Zaluskowski.. | | | | | |
|     2nd Battalion, Captain Von Fabeck | 3 | .. | .. | .. | .. |
|     Fusilier Battalion, Major Von Polcznski | | | | | |
| 3rd 12-pounder Batt. of Guard Artillery, Capt. Hein | .. | .. | .. | 6 | .. |
| 2nd Light Field Hospital. | | | | | |
| *Reserve.* | | | | | |
|     Major-General Baron Von Loen. | | | | | |
|     4th Brigade of Guard Infantry. | | | | | |
| 4th Regiment of Guard Grenadiers, Colonel Von Strubberg : | | | | | |
|     ¼ of 1st Battalion, Major Von der Osten | | | | | |
|     2nd Battalion, Major Von Gliszoynski.. | 1¼ | .. | .. | .. | .. |
|     12th Company, Lieutenant Von Seydlitz | | | | | |
| 2nd Regiment of Guard Grenadiers, Colonel Von Fabeck : | | | | | |
|     1st Battalion, Major Von Boehn | 2 | .. | .. | .. | .. |
|     2nd Battalion, Captain Von Bentivegni | | | | | |
| 4th 4-pounder Battery of Guard Artillery, Captain Von Schmeling | .. | .. | .. | 6 | .. |
| 3rd 6-pr. Battery of Guard Artillery, Capt. Deibel.. | .. | .. | .. | 6 | .. |
|     Total of 2nd Division of Guards .. | 10¾ | 1 | 4 | 24 | ¼ |
| *Reserve Cavalry.* | | | | | |
| 1st Heavy Cavalry Brigade, Major-General Prince Albrecht, junior. | | | | | |
| Regiment Garde du Corps, Colonel Count Brandenburg | .. | .. | 4 | .. | .. |
| Regiment of Guard Cuirassiers, Col. Von Lüderitz | .. | .. | 4 | .. | .. |
| 3rd Horse Artillery Battery of Guard Artillery, Captain Von Buddenbrock | .. | .. | .. | 6 | .. |
|     Total of Reserve Cavalry .. | .. | .. | 8 | 6 | .. |
| *Reserve Artillery.* | | | | | |
|     Colonel Prince Hohenlohe-Ingelfingen. | | | | | |
| 2nd Field Division, Lieut.-Col. Von Miesitscheck : | | | | | |
|     2nd 6-pounder Battery, Capt. Von Heineccius | .. | .. | .. | 6 | .. |
|     4th 6-pounder Battery, Captain Von Werder.. | .. | .. | .. | 6 | .. |
|     2nd 4-pounder Battery, Captain Von Mutius.. | .. | .. | .. | 6 | .. |
|     6th 4-pounder Battery, Capt. Von Schweinichen | .. | .. | .. | 6 | .. |
| Horse Artillery Division, Major Von Langen : | | | | | |
| 4th Horse Artillery Battery, Captain Von Prittwitz | .. | .. | .. | 6 | .. |
|     Total of Reserve Artillery.. | .. | .. | .. | 30 | .. |

APPENDIX XXIIe—*continued.*

| | Present on the Field. | | | | | Absent on other Duty. | | |
|---|---|---|---|---|---|---|---|---|
| | Infantry Battalions. | Rifle Battalions. | Cavalry Squadrons. | Artillery Guns. | Pioneer Battalions. | Infantry Companies. | Cavalry Squadrons. | Pioneer Companies. |
| 1st Division of Guard Infantry .. .. | 11 | 1 | 4 | 24 | ½ | 4 | .. | 1 |
| 2nd Division of Guard Infantry .. .. | 10¾ | 1 | 4 | 24 | ¼ | 5 | .. | .. |
| Reserve Cavalry Brigade | .. | .. | 8 | 6 | .. | .. | .. | .. |
| Reserve Artillery .. | .. | .. | .. | 30 | .. | .. | .. | .. |
| Total .. .. | 21¾ | 2 | 16 | 84 | ¾ | 9 | .. | 1 |

ABSENT ON OTHER DUTY.

Fusilier Battalion of 3rd Foot Guards at Koeniginhof.
3 Companies of 4th Guard Grenadiers, at Trautenau and escorting prisoners.
2 Companies 4th Guard Grenadiers, escorting baggage.
1 Company of Pioneers with the Pontoon Train.

# APPENDIX XXII*f*.

## 1st Corps d'Armée.

General Commanding      ..      General of Infantry, Von Bonin.
Chief of Staff      ..      ..      Colonel Von Borries.
Commandant of Artillery ..      Colonel Knothe.
First Officer of Engineers ..      Colonel Weber.

| | Present on the Field. | | | | |
| --- | :---: | :---: | :---: | :---: | :---: |
| | Battalions of Infantry. | Battalions of Rifles. | Squadrons. | Guns. | Battalions of Pioneers. |
| **ADVANCED GUARD.** <br> Lieut.-General Von Grossmann. <br> General Staff Officer, Major Meydam. <br> Commander of Artillery, Lieut.-Colonel Rohde. | | | | | |
| *1st Brigade of Infantry.* <br> Major-General Von Pape. | | | | | |
| 41st Regiment of Infantry, Colonel Von Koblinski: <br> 1st Battalion, Major Von Schirmeister    .. <br> 2nd Battalion, Major Schroeder    ..    .. <br> Fusilier Battalion, Major Kulenkamp..    .. | 3 | .. | .. | .. | .. |
| 1st Regiment of Grenadiers, Colonel Von Beeren: <br> 1st Battalion, Lieut.-Colonel Von Schlichting.. <br> 2nd Battalion, Major Scheuermann    ..    .. <br> Fusilier Battalion, Major Von Blumenthal    .. | 3 | .. | .. | .. | .. |
| 1st Battalion of Rifles, Major Von Sommerfeld    .. | .. | 1 | .. | .. | .. |
| *Combined Brigade of Cavalry.* | | | | | |
| 1st Regiment of Dragoons, Col. Von Bernhardi    .. | .. | .. | 5 | .. | .. |
| 3 Squadrons of 8th Lancers, Col. Von Below    .. | .. | .. | 3 | .. | .. |
| 1st 4-pounder Battery of 1st Field Artillery Regiment, Captain Magnus    ..    ..    .. | .. | .. | .. | 6 | .. |
| 5th 4-pounder Battery of 1st Field Artillery Regiment, Captain Gerhardts ..    ..    ..    .. | .. | .. | .. | 6 | .. |
| 1st Horse Artillery Battery of 1st Field Artillery Regiment, Captain Preinitzer    ..    .. | .. | .. | .. | 6 | .. |
| 1st Company of 1st Pioneer Battalion, with Light Field Bridge Train, Captain Schütze    ..    .. | .. | .. | .. | .. | ¼ |
| 1 Light Field Hospital. | | | | | |
| Total of Advanced Guard    .. | 6 | 1 | 8 | 18 | ¼ |

| | Battalions of Infantry. | Battalions of Rifles. | Squadrons. | Guns. | Battalions of Pioneers. |
|---|---|---|---|---|---|
| | | Present on the Field. | | | |

**MAIN BODY.**

*2nd Division of Infantry.*
Lieut.-General Von Clausewitz.
General Staff Officer, Major Von Stosch.
Commandant of Artillery, Major Noack.

*3rd Brigade of Infantry.*
Major-General Von Malotki.

| | Battalions of Infantry. | Battalions of Rifles. | Squadrons. | Guns. | Battalions of Pioneers. |
|---|---|---|---|---|---|
| 44th Regiment of Infantry, Col. Von La Chevallerie: 2nd Battalion, Major Koch; Fusilier Battalion, Lieut.-Colonel Von Behr | 2 | .. | .. | .. | .. |
| 4th Regiment of Grenadiers, Colonel Von Wedell: 1st Battalion, Captain Von Schmeling; 2nd Battalion, Major Mansard; Fusilier Battalion, Lieut.-Col. Von Pannwitz | 3 | .. | .. | .. | .. |
| *4th Brigade of Infantry.* Major-General Von Buddenbrock. 45th Regiment of Infantry, Colonel Von Boswell: 1st Battalion, Major Schoenemann; 2nd Battalion, Major Von Kamecke; Fusilier Battalion, Lieut.-Col. Von Schmeling | 3 | .. | .. | .. | .. |
| 5th Regiment of Grenadiers, Colonel Von Memerty: 1st Battalion, Major Baron Von Huellessem; 2nd Battalion, Captain Von Boetticher | 2 | .. | .. | .. | .. |
| 1st Regiment of Hussars, Lieut.-Col. Von Kehler | .. | .. | 4 | .. | .. |
| 3rd Field Division of 1st Field Artillery Regiment: 3rd 12-pounder Battery, Captain Werner | .. | .. | .. | 6 | .. |
| 3rd 6-pounder Battery, Captain Niehr | .. | .. | .. | 6 | .. |
| 3rd 4-pounder Battery, Captain Kaunhofen | .. | .. | .. | 6 | .. |
| 4th 4-pounder Battery, Captain Boehncke | .. | .. | .. | 6 | .. |
| Total of Main Body | 10 | .. | 4 | 24 | .. |
| **RESERVE CAVALRY.** Colonel Von Bredow. | | | | | |
| 3rd Regiment of Cuirassiers, Colonel Count Dohna | .. | .. | 4 | .. | .. |
| 12th Regiment of Lancers, Lieut.-Col. Von Kehler | .. | .. | 4 | .. | .. |
| 3rd Horse Artillery Battery of 1st Field Artillery Regiment, Captain Körber | .. | .. | .. | 6 | .. |
| Total of Reserve Cavalry | .. | .. | 8 | 6 | .. |
| **RESERVE INFANTRY.** *2nd Brigade of Infantry.* Major-General Von Barnekow. 3rd Regiment of Grenadiers, Col. Von Blumenthal: 1st Battalion, Lieut.-Colonel Weese; 2nd Battalion, Major Von Franckenberg-Ludwigsdorff (3 Companies); Fusilier Battalion, Lieut.-Colonel Von Wedell | 2¾ | .. | .. | .. | .. |

APPENDIX XXII*f*—*continued.*

| | Present on the Field. | | | | |
|---|:---:|:---:|:---:|:---:|:---:|
| | Battalions of Infantry. | Battalions of Rifles. | Squadrons. | Guns. | Battalions of Pioneers. |
| **RESERVE INFANTRY**—*cont.* | | | | | |
| 43rd Regiment of Infantry, Colonel Von Tresckow : | | | | | |
| 1st Battalion, Captain Von Deutsch .. .. | 3 | .. | .. | .. | .. |
| 2nd Battalion, Major Von Loebell .. .. | | | | | |
| Fusilier Battalion, Major Koehn Von Jaski .. | | | | | |
| 1st Squadron of 8th Lancers .. .. .. .. | .. | .. | 1 | .. | .. |
| 4th 12-pounder Battery of 1st Field Artillery Regiment, Captain Wittich .. .. .. .. | .. | .. | .. | 6 | .. |
| Total of Reserve Infantry .. | 5¾ | .. | 1 | 6 | .. |
| **RESERVE ARTILLERY.** | | | | | |
| Colonel Von Oertzen. | | | | | |
| Horse Artillery Division, Major Von Leslie : | | | | | |
| 2nd Horse Artillery Battery, Capt. Kaunhofen | .. | .. | .. | 6 | .. |
| 4th Horse Artillery Battery, Captain Iwentz .. | .. | .. | .. | 6 | .. |
| 2nd Field Division, Major Wiesing : | | | | | |
| 2nd 6-pounder Battery, Capt. Von Rosenzweig | .. | .. | .. | 6 | .. |
| 4th 6 pounder Battery, Captain Matthiass .. | .. | .. | .. | 6 | .. |
| 2nd 4-pounder Battery, Captain Schmidt .. | .. | .. | .. | 6 | .. |
| 6th 4-pounder Battery, Captain Dollmann .. | .. | .. | .. | 6 | .. |
| 1st Field Division : | | | | | |
| 1st 6-pounder Battery, Captain Von Napolski . | .. | .. | .. | 6 | .. |
| Escort of Artillery, 1st Battalion of 44th Regiment, Lieut.-Colonel Von Etzel .. .. .. .. | 1 | .. | .. | .. | .. |
| 1st Battalion of Pioneers, Major Cramer (3 Cos.) .. | .. | .. | .. | .. | ¾ |
| Total of Reserve Artillery .. | 1 | .. | . | 42 | ¾ |

## SUMMARY.

| | Present on the Field. | | | | | Absent on other Duty. | | |
|---|:---:|:---:|:---:|:---:|:---:|:---:|:---:|:---:|
| | Infantry Battalions. | Rifle Battalions. | Cavalry Squadrons. | Artillery Guns. | Pioneer Battalions. | Infantry Companies. | Cavalry Squadrons. | Pioneer Companies. |
| Advanced Guard .. | 6 | 1 | 8 | 18 | ¼ | .. | .. | .. |
| Main Body .. | 10 | .. | 4 | 24 | .. | 4 | .. | .. |
| Reserve Infantry .. | 5¾ | .. | 1 | 6 | .. | 1 | .. | .. |
| Reserve Cavalry .. | .. | .. | 8 | 6 | .. | .. | .. | .. |
| Reserve Artillery .. | 1 | .. | .. | 42 | ¾ | .. | .. | .. |
| Total .. | 22¾ | 1 | 21 | 96 | 1 | 5 | .. | .. |

Absent on other duty : Fusilier Battalion of 5th Regiment, as escort of Light Field Hospital. 7th Company of 3rd Regiment, as escort of baggage.

# APPENDIX XXII*g*.

## VIth Corps d'Armee.

| | |
|---|---|
| General Commanding .. | General of Cavalry, Von Mutius. |
| Chief of Staff .. .. | Colonel Von Sperling. |
| Commandant of Artillery .. | Major-General Herkt. |
| First Officer of Engineers .. | Colonel Schulz. |

| | Present on the Field. | | | | |
|---|---|---|---|---|---|
| | Battalions of Infantry. | Battalions of Rifles. | Squadrons. | Guns. | Battalions of Pioneers. |
| **11th Division of Infantry.** | | | | | |
| Lieutenant-General Von Zastrow. | | | | | |
| General Staff Officer, Major Baron Von Falkenhausen. Commandant of Artillery, Major Broecker. | | | | | |
| *21st Brigade of Infantry.* | | | | | |
| Major-General Von Hanenfeldt. | | | | | |
| 50th Regiment of Infantry, Colonel Von Natzmer : 1st Battalion, Major Von Sperling .. .. 2nd Battalion, Major Von Berken .. .. Fusilier Battalion, Major Von Salisch | 3 | .. | .. | .. | .. |
| 10th Regiment of Grenadiers, Colonel Baron Von Falkenstein : 1st Battalion, Major Von Kalinowsky .. 2nd Battalion, Major Baumeister .. .. Fusilier Battalion, Major Von Neumann | 3 | .. | .. | .. | .. |
| *22nd Brigade of Infantry.* | | | | | |
| Major-General Von Hoffmann. | | | | | |
| 38th Regiment of Fusiliers, Lieut.-Colonel Von Knobelsdorff : 1st Battalion, Captain Count Herzberg .. 2nd Battalion, Captain Weber.. .. Fusilier Battalion, Major Count Trenck | 3 | .. | .. | .. | .. |
| 51st Regiment of Infantry, Colonel Paris : 1st Battalion, Major Von Haine .. .. 2nd Battalion, Major Von Ostrowski .. .. Fusilier Battalion, Lieut.-Colonel Von Kontzki | 3 | .. | .. | .. | .. |
| *2nd Field Division of 6th Field Artillery Regt.* | | | | | |
| 4th 6-pounder Battery, Captain Von Windheim .. | .. | .. | .. | 6 | .. |
| 2nd 6-pounder Battery, Captain Von Schweinichen | .. | .. | .. | 6 | .. |
| 2nd 4-pounder Battery, Captain Von Wahlen .. | .. | .. | .. | 6 | .. |
| 6th 4-pounder Battery, Captain Von Garczynski .. | .. | .. | .. | 6 | .. |
| Total of 11th Infantry Division .. | 12 | .. | .. | 24 | .. |

|  | Present on the Field. | | | | |
|---|:---:|:---:|:---:|:---:|:---:|
|  | Battalions of Infantry. | Battalions of Rifles. | Squadrons. | Guns. | Battalions of Pioneers. |
| **11TH DIVISION OF INFANTRY**--*continued.* | | | | | |
| *Combined Cavalry Brigade.* | | | | | |
| Lieut.-Colonel Von Wichmann. | | | | | |
| 4th Regt. of Hussars, Lieut.-Col. Von Buddenbrock | .. | .. | 4 | .. | .. |
| 8th Regt. of Dragoons, Major Von Paczensky .. | .. | .. | 4 | .. | .. |
| Total of combined Cavalry Brigade .. | .. | .. | 8 | .. | .. |
| **12TH DIVISION OF INFANTRY.** | | | | | |
| Lieutenant-General Von Prondzynski. | | | | | |
| General Staff Officer, Captain Von Leczynski. | | | | | |
| Commandant of Artillery, Major Forst. | | | | | |
| *Combined Brigade of Infantry.* | | | | | |
| Major-General Von Cranach. | | | | | |
| 22nd Regiment of Infantry, Colonel Von Ruville : | | | | | |
| Fusilier Battalion, Major Von Lyncker .. | 1 | .. | .. | .. | .. |
| 23rd Regiment of Infantry, Col. Stein Von Kaminski: | | | | | |
| 1st Battalion, Captain Tschirsky— | | | | | |
| ¼ Battalion, Captain Himpe (4th and 2nd Companies) .. | | | | | |
| ½ Battalion, Captain Von Tschirsky (3rd and 1st Companies) .. | | | | | |
| 2nd Battalion, Lieut.-Col. Von Fehrentheil— | | | | | |
| ¼ Battalion, Lieut.-Col. Von. Fehrentheil (8th and 6th Companies) .. | 3 | .. | .. | .. | .. |
| ¼ Battalion, Captain Von Elpons (7th and 5th Battalions) .. | | | | | |
| Fusilier Battalion. Lieut.-Col. Von Chamier— | | | | | |
| ¼ Battalion, Captain Von Tresckow (9th and 12th Companies) .. | | | | | |
| ¼ Battalion, Captain Von Tschischwitz (10th and 11th Companies) .. | | | | | |
| 6th Battalion of Rifles, Lieut.-Col. Count Dohna : | | | | | |
| ¼ Battalion, Captain Müller (2nd and 3rd Companies) .. | .. | 1 | .. | .. | .. |
| ½ Battalion, Captain Von Minckwitz (1st and 4th Companies) .. | | | | | |
| 6th Regiment of Hussars, Colonel Von Trotha (3 squadrons) .. | .. | .. | 3 | .. | .. |
| 1st 4-pounder Battery of 6th Field Artillery Regiment, Captain Stoeckel .. | .. | .. | .. | 6 | .. |
| 5th 4-pounder Battery of 6th Field Artillery Regiment, Captain Pilet .. | .. | .. | .. | 6 | .. |
| 2nd Company of 6th Pioneer Battalion, Capt. Guhl | .. | .. | .. | .. | ¼ |
| Total of 12th Division .. .. | 4 | 1 | 3 | 12 | ¼ |

## Appendix XXII*g*—*continued*.

| | Present in the Field. | | | | |
|---|---|---|---|---|---|
| | Battalions of Infantry. | Battalions of Rifles. | Squadrons. | Guns. | Battalions of Pioneers. |
| **Reserve Artillery.** | | | | | |
| Colonel Von Scherbening. | | | | | |
| *Horse Artillery Division of 6th Field Artillery Regiment.* | | | | | |
| Major Arnold. | | | | | |
| 1st Horse Artillery Battery, Capt. Von Luettwitz.. | .. | .. | .. | 6 | .. |
| 3rd Horse Artillery Battery, Captain Weltz .. | .. | .. | .. | 6 | .. |
| 4th Horse Artillery Battery, Capt. Von Rheinbaben | .. | .. | .. | 6 | .. |
| *1st Field Division.* | | | | | |
| 4th 12-pounder Battery, Captain Ulrich .. .. | .. | .. | .. | 6 | .. |
| 1st Company of 6th Pioneer Battalion with Pontoon Train, Captain Klefecker .. .. .. .. | .. | .. | .. | .. | ¼ |
| Total of Reserve Artillery .. .. | .. | .. | .. | 24 | ¼ |

## SUMMARY.

| | Present on the Field. | | | | | Absent on other Duty. | | |
|---|---|---|---|---|---|---|---|---|
| | Infantry Battalions. | Rifle Battalions. | Cavalry Squadrons. | Artillery Guns. | Pioneer Battalions. | Infantry Companies. | Cavalry Squadrons. | Pioneer Companies. |
| 11th Division of Infantry .. .. | 12 | .. | .. | 24 | .. | .. | .. | .. |
| 12th Division of Infantry .. .. | 4 | 1 | 3 | 12 | ¼ | 8 | 1 | 2 |
| Combined Cavalry Brigade .. .. .. | .. | .. | 8 | .. | .. | .. | .. | .. |
| Reserve Artillery .. | .. | .. | .. | 24 | ¼ | .. | .. | .. |
| Total .. .. | 16 | 1 | 11 | 60 | ½ | 8 | 1 | 2 |

### Absent on other Duty.

1st Battalion of 22nd Regiment, in front of Josephstadt.
2nd Battalion of 22nd Regiment, at Nachod and Kuku, to guard line of communication and passage over the Elbe.
2nd Squadron of 6th Hussars, in front of Josephstadt.
3rd Company of 6th Pioneers, at Kukus.
4th Company of 6th Pioneers, in Schweidnitz.

# APPENDIX XXII*h.*

## Vth Corps.

| | |
|---|---|
| General Commanding .. .. | { General of Infantry, Von Steinmetz. |
| Chief of Staff .. .. | .. Colonel Von Wittich. |
| Commandant of Artillery | .. Colonel Von Kraewel. |
| First Officer of Engineers | .. Major-General Von Kleist. |

| | Present on the Field. | | | | |
|---|:---:|:---:|:---:|:---:|:---:|
| | Battalions of Infantry. | Battalions of Rifles. | Squadrons. | Guns. | Battalions of Pioneers. |
| **9TH DIVISION OF INFANTRY.** | | | | | |
| Major-General Von Loewenfeld. | | | | | |
| General Staff Officer, Lieut.-Col. Von Ziemietzky. Commandant of Artillery, Major Meissner. | | | | | |
| *17th Brigade of Infantry.* | | | | | |
| Colonel Von Below, 37th Regiment. | | | | | |
| 58th Regiment of Infantry, Colonel Von François: | | | | | |
| 1st Battalion, Major Von Eberhardt .. .. | | | | | |
| 2nd Battalion, Captain Von Gronefeld .. } | 3 | .. | .. | .. | .. |
| Fusilier Battalion, Major du Plessis .. .. | | | | | |
| 37th Regiment of Fusiliers, Lieut.-Colonel Baron Von Eberstein: | | | | | |
| 1st Battalion, Major Von Lemmers Danforth.. | | | | | |
| 2nd Battalion, Captain Von Bojan .. .. } | 3 | .. | .. | .. | .. |
| 3rd Battalion, Major Von Ploetz .. .. | | | | | |
| *18th Brigade of Infantry.* | | | | | |
| Major-General Von Horn. | | | | | |
| 7th Regiment of Grenadiers, Colonel Von Voigts-Rhetz: | | | | | |
| 1st Battalion, Lieut.-Colonel Quedenfeldt .. | | | | | |
| 2nd Battalion, Lieut.-Colonel Von Werder .. } | 3 | .. | .. | .. | .. |
| Fusilier Battalion, Lieut.-Col. Von Kalckstein. | | | | | |
| 5th Battalion of Rifles, Lieut.-Colonel Von Weller. | .. | 1 | .. | .. | .. |
| 4th 12-pounder Battery of 5th Field Artillery Regiment, Captain Sowinski .. .. | .. | .. | .. | 6 | .. |
| 1st 6-pounder Battery of 5th Field Artillery Regiment, Captain Baron Von Troilo .. .. | .. | .. | .. | 6 | .. |
| 1st 4-pounder Battery of 5th Field Artillery Regiment, Captain Michaelis .. .. .. | .. | .. | .. | 6 | .. |
| 5th 4-pounder Battery of 5th Field Artillery Regiment, Captain Schmidt .. .. .. | .. | .. | .. | 6 | .. |
| Total of 9th Division .. .. .. | 9 | 1 | .. | 24 | .. |

APPENDIX XXII*h—continued.*

| | Battalions of Infantry. | Battalions of Rifles. | Squadrons. | Guns. | Battalions of Pioneers. |
|---|---|---|---|---|---|
| | | | Present on the Field. | | |

COMBINED CAVALRY BRIGADE.

(Formed out of the Cavalry of the 9th and 10th Divisions.)

Major-General Von Wnuck.

| | | | | | |
|---|---|---|---|---|---|
| 4th Regiment of Dragoons, Major Von Mayer .. | .. | .. | 5 | .. | .. |
| 1st Regiment of Lancers, Captain Von Bernhardi .. | .. | .. | 4 | .. | .. |
| 2nd Horse Artillery Battery, Capt. Von Zakrzewski | .. | .. | | 6 | .. |
| 4th Horse Artillery Battery, Capt. Von Ohnesorge.. | .. | .. | .. | 6 | .. |
| Total of Combined Cavalry Brigade .. | .. | .. | 9 | 12 | .. |

10TH DIVISION OF INFANTRY.

Lieutenant-General Von Kirchbach.

General Staff Officer, Captain Von Grolmann.
Commandant of Artillery, Lieut.-Colonel Elten.

*19th Brigade of Infantry.*

Major-General Von Tiedemann.

| | | | | | |
|---|---|---|---|---|---|
| 46th Regiment of Infantry, Colonel Walther Von Monbary : 1st Battalion, Major Von Bessel .. .. 2nd Battalion, Captain Von Gallwitz .. .. Fusilier Battalion, Lieutenant-Colonel Von Manteuffel .. .. .. .. .. | 3 | .. | .. | .. | .. |
| 6th Regiment of Grenadiers, Lieutenant-Colonel Von Scheffler: 1st Battalion, Major Von Wnuck .. .. 2nd Battalion, Major Von Nitsche .. .. Fusilier Battalion, Lieut.-Col. Von Gottberg .. | 3 | .. | .. | .. | .. |

*20th Brigade of Infantry.*

Major-General Wittich.

| | | | | | |
|---|---|---|---|---|---|
| 47th Regiment of Infantry, Colonel Von Massow : 1st Battalion, Major Von Haeseler .. .. 2nd Battalion, Major Von Heinemann.. .. Fusilier Battalion, Major Von Brandenstein .. | 3 | .. | .. | .. | .. |
| 52nd Regiment of Infantry, Col. Von Blumenthal : 1st Battalion, Major Bendler .. .. 2nd Battalion, Major Von Karger .. Fusilier Battalion, Major Von Blumroeder .. | 3 | .. | .. | .. | |
| 3rd 12-pounder Battery of 5th Field Artillery Regiment, Captain Von Schultzendorff .. .. | .. | .. | .. | 6 | .. |
| 3rd 6-pounder Battery of 5th Field Artillery Regiment, Captain Aust.. .. .. .. .. | .. | .. | .. | 6 | .. |
| 3rd 4-pounder Battery of 5th Field Artillery Regiment, Captain Reiche .. .. .. | .. | .. | .. | 6 | .. |

APPENDIX XXII*h—continued.*

| | Present on the Field. | | | | |
|---|---|---|---|---|---|
| — | Battalions of Infantry. | Battalions of Rifles. | Squadrons. | Guns. | Battalions of Pioneers. |
| 10TH DIVISION OF INFANTRY—*cont.* | | | | | |
| 4th 4-pounder Battery of 5th Field Artillery Regiment, Captain Habelmann.. .. .. .. | .. | .. | .. | 6 | .. |
| Total of 10th Division .. .. | 12 | .. | .. | 24 | .. |
| RESERVE ARTILLERY. | | | | | |
| Colonel Von Kameke. | | | | | |
| 2nd Field Division of 5th Field Artillery Regiment, Lieutenant-Colonel Von Dalitz : | | | | | |
| 2nd 6-pounder Battery, Captain Caspari .. | .. | .. | .. | 6 | .. |
| 4th 6-pounder Battery, Captain Von Willich .. | .. | .. | .. | 6 | .. |
| 2nd 4-pounder Battery, Captain Wilhelmi .. | .. | .. | .. | 6 | .. |
| 6th 4-pounder Battery, Capt. Von Treuenfels.. | .. | .. | .. | 6 | .. |
| 1st Horse Artillery Battery, Captain Von Manteuffel .. .. .. .. .. | .. | .. | .. | 6 | .. |
| Total of Reserve Artillery .. .. | .. | .. | .. | 30 | .. |

| | Present on the Field. | | | | | Absent on other Duty. | | |
|---|---|---|---|---|---|---|---|---|
| | Infantry Battalions. | Rifle Battalions. | Cavalry Squadrons. | Artillery Guns. | Pioneer Battalions. | Infantry Companies. | Cavalry Squadrons. | Pioneer Companies. |
| 9th Division of Infantry | 9 | 1 | .. | 24 | .. | .. | .. | 4 |
| Combined Cavalry Brigade .. ♥. | .. | .. | 9 | 12 | .. | .. | .. | .. |
| 10th Division of Infantry | 12 | .. | .. | 24 | .. | .. | .. | .. |
| Reserve Artillery .. | .. | .. | .. | 30 | .. | .. | .. | .. |
| | 21 | 1 | 9 | 90 | .. | .. | .. | 4 |

ABSENT ON OTHER DUTY.

1st Company 5th Pioneer Battalion, guarding bridge at Burg.
2nd Company 5th Pioneer Battalion, guarding bridge at Schurz.
3rd Company 5th Pioneer Battalion, escorting ammunition park.
4th Company 5th Pioneer Battalion, escorting baggage.

APPENDIX XXII*h*—*continued.*

|  | Present on the Field. | | | | |
|---|---|---|---|---|---|
| — | Battalions of Infantry. | Battalions of Rifles. | Squadrons. | Guns. | Battalions of Pioneers. |
| **CAVALRY DIVISION OF IIND ARMY.** | | | | | |
| General Commanding, Major-Gen. Von Hartmann. | | | | | |
| General Staff Officer, Captain Von Versen. | | | | | |
| Commandant of Artillery, Major Count Wengersky. | | | | | |
| *Advanced Guard.* | | | | | |
| Major-General Von Witzeleben. | | | | | |
| 2nd Regiment of Hussars, Lieutenant-Colonel Von Schauroth .. .. .. .. .. .. | .. | .. | 4 | .. | .. |
| 10th Regiment of Lancers, Lt.-Col. Von Barnekow | .. | .. | 4 | .. | .. |
| 2nd Horse Artillery Battery of 6th Field Artillery Regiment, Captain Le Bauld de Nans .. .. | .. | .. | .. | 6 | .. |
| 3rd Horse Artillery Battery of 5th Field Artillery Regiment, Captain Lenz .. .. .. .. | .. | .. | .. | 6 | .. |
| *Main Body.* | | | | | |
| Major-General Von Borstel. | | | | | |
| Cuirassier Brigade, Major-General Von Schoen : | | | | | |
| 1st Regiment of Cuirassiers, Colonel Von Barby | .. | .. | 4 | .. | .. |
| 5th Regiment of Cuirassiers, Lieutenant-Colonel Von Bredow .. .. .. .. .. | .. | .. | 4 | .. | .. |
| Landwehr Cavalry Brigade, Colonel Von Franckenberg : | | | | | |
| 2nd Regiment of Landwehr Hussars, Colonel Von Glasenapp .. .. .. .. | .. | .. | 4 | .. | .. |
| 1st Regiment of Landwehr Lancers, Major Von Kock .. .. .. .. .. .. | .. | .. | 4 | .. | .. |
| Total of Cavalry Division .. .. | .. | .. | 24 | 12 | .. |

## APPENDIX XXIII.

Losses of the Prussian Armies in the Battle of Koeniggraetz, July 3rd, 1866.

| | Killed. | | Wounded | | Missing. | | Total. | | |
|---|---|---|---|---|---|---|---|---|---|
| | Officers. | Men. | Officers. | Men. | Officers. | Men. | Officers. | Men. | Horses. |
| **A. LOSS OF THE IST ARMY.** | | | | | | | | | |
| *a. IInd Corps.* | | | | | | | | | |
| 3rd Division of Infantry : | | | | | | | | | |
| 42nd Regiment of Infantry .. .. | .. | 7 | .. | 56 | .. | 2 | .. | 65 | .. |
| 2nd " " .. .. | .. | 3 | 1 | 7 | .. | .. | 1 | 10 | .. |
| 54th " " .. .. | .. | 36 | 4 | 154 | .. | 2 | 4 | 192 | .. |
| 14th " " .. .. | 1 | 17 | 1 | 81 | .. | 8 | 2 | 106 | .. |
| 2nd Battalion of Rifles .. | .. | 1 | .. | 1 | .. | .. | .. | 2 | .. |
| 5th Regiment of Hussars .. | .. | 1 | 1 | 9 | .. | .. | 1 | 10 | 4 |
| Total loss of 3rd Division .. | 1 | 65 | 7 | 308 | .. | 12 | 8 | 385 | 4 |
| 4th Division of Infantry : | | | | | | | | | |
| 49th Regiment of Infantry .. | 2 | 84 | 3 | 240 | .. | 3 | 5 | 327 | .. |
| 9th " " .. | .. | 4 | 2 | 18 | .. | .. | 2 | 22 | 4 |
| 61st " " .. | 4 | 64 | 6 | 295 | .. | 11 | 10 | 370 | .. |
| 21st " " .. | 1 | 17 | 3 | 68 | .. | .. | 4 | 85 | .. |
| 4th Regiment of Lancers .. | .. | 7 | 5 | 22 | .. | 2 | 5 | 31 | 40 |
| Total loss of 4th Division .. | 7 | 176 | 19 | 643 | .. | 16 | 26 | 835 | 44 |
| 3rd Heavy Cavalry Brigade : | | | | | | | | | |
| 2nd Regiment of Cuirassiers .. | .. | .. | .. | 1 | .. | .. | .. | 1 | 11 |
| 9th Regiment of Lancers .. | .. | .. | .. | 1 | .. | .. | .. | 1 | .. |
| Total loss of 3rd Heavy Cavalry Brigade .. | .. | .. | .. | 2 | .. | .. | .. | 2 | 11 |
| Total loss of IInd Corps de Armée, including 3rd Heavy Cavalry Brigade } | 8 | 241 | 26 | 953 | .. | 28 | 34 | 1222 | 59 |
| N.B. The losses of the Divisional and the Reserve Artillery will be found under the head of the different Field Artillery Regiments. | | | | | | | | | |
| *b. Loss of the 5th and 6th Divisions of Infantry.* | | | | | | | | | |
| 5th Division of Infantry : | | | | | | | | | |
| 48th Regiment of Infantry .. | .. | 19 | 3 | 65 | .. | .. | 3 | 84 | 1 |
| 8th " " .. | .. | .. | .. | 16 | .. | .. | .. | 16 | .. |
| 18th " " .. | .. | 11 | 1 | 95 | .. | 1 | 1 | 107 | 2 |
| 12th " " .. | .. | 10 | 2 | 18 | .. | .. | 2 | 28 | .. |
| 3rd Regiment of Lancers .. | .. | 3 | 1 | 5 | .. | .. | 1 | 8 | 7 |
| Total of 5th and 6th Divisions .. | .. | 43 | 7 | 199 | .. | 1 | 7 | 243 | 10 |

APPENDIX XXIII—*continued.*

| | Killed. | | Wounded | | Missing. | | Total. | | |
|---|---|---|---|---|---|---|---|---|---|
| | Officers. | Men. | Officers. | Men. | Officers. | Men. | Officers. | Men. | Horses. |
| **A. LOSSES OF THE 1ST ARMY**—*cont.* | | | | | | | | | |
| 6th Division of Infantry : | | | | | | | | | |
| 63th Regiment of Infantry | 1 | 21 | 2 | 81 | .. | .. | 3 | 102 | .. |
| 35th ,, ,, | .. | 19 | 2 | 95 | .. | .. | 2 | 114 | .. |
| 64th ,, ,, | .. | 3 | .. | 1 | .. | .. | .. | 4 | 1 |
| 24th ,, ,, | .. | 1 | 2 | 4 | .. | .. | 2 | 5 | .. |
| 3rd Battalion of Rifles .. | .. | 3 | .. | 18 | .. | .. | .. | 21 | .. |
| 2nd Regiment of Dragoons | 2 | 11 | 2 | 14 | .. | .. | 4 | 25 | 37 |
| Total of 6th Division of Infantry | 3 | 58 | 8 | 213 | .. | .. | 11 | 271 | 38 |
| Total loss of 5th and 6th Divisions of Infantry .. .. .. | } 3 | 101 | 15 | 412 | .. | 1 | 18 | 514 | 48 |
| *c. Loss of 7th and 8th Divisions of Infantry.* | | | | | | | | | |
| 7th Division of Infantry : | | | | | | | | | |
| Staff of 13th Brigade .. .. | 1 | .. | .. | .. | .. | .. | 1 | .. | 2 |
| 66th Regiment of Infantry | 3 | 92 | 10 | 357 | .. | 27 | 13 | 476 | 1 |
| 26th ,, ,, | 5 | 164 | 21 | 541 | .. | 4 | 26 | 709 | 13 |
| 67th ,, ,, | 9 | 90 | 8 | 297 | .. | 13 | 17 | 400 | 4 |
| 27th ,, ,, | 11 | 88 | 14 | 352 | .. | 4 | 25 | 444 | 4 |
| 4th Battalion of Pioneers | .. | 1 | 1 | 5 | .. | .. | 1 | 6 | .. |
| 10th Regiment of Hussars .. | 1 | 1 | .. | .. | .. | .. | 1 | 1 | 8 |
| Total of 7th Division of Infantry | 30 | 436 | 54 | 1552 | .. | 48 | 84 | 2036 | 32 |
| 8th Division of Infantry : | | | | | | | | | |
| 71st Regiment of Infantry .. | 1 | 83 | 8 | 195 | .. | 13 | 9 | 291 | 1 |
| 31st ,, ,, | 1 | 29 | 9 | 167 | .. | 11 | 10 | 207 | 1 |
| 72nd ,, ,, | 1 | 29 | 6 | 94 | .. | 12 | 7 | 135 | .. |
| 4th Battalion of Rifles .. | 1 | 16 | 2 | 68 | .. | 1 | 3 | 85 | .. |
| 6th Regiment of Lancers | .. | 1 | .. | 3 | .. | .. | .. | 4 | 9 |
| Total loss of 8th Division | 4 | 158 | 25 | 527 | .. | 37 | 29 | 722 | 11 |
| Total loss of 7th and 8th Divisions | 34 | 594 | 79 | 2072 | .. | 85 | 113 | 2758 | 43 |
| *d. Loss of the Artillery of the 1st Army.* | | | | | | | | | |
| 2nd Regiment of Field Artillery .. | 2 | 11 | 5 | 56 | .. | 1 | 7 | 68 | 114 |
| 3rd ,, ,, | 1 | 3 | 4 | 50 | .. | .. | 5 | 53 | 44 |
| 4th ,, ,, | .. | 11 | .. | 39 | .. | .. | .. | 50 | 35 |
| Total .. .. | 3 | 25 | 9 | 145 | .. | 1 | 12 | 171 | 193 |
| *e. Loss of the Cavalry Corps of the 1st Army.* | | | | | | | | | |
| Staff of Corps .. .. .. .. | .. | .. | 1 | .. | .. | .. | 1 | .. | 1 |
| 1st Cavalry Division : | | | | | | | | | |
| 6th Regiment of Cuirassiers .. | .. | 2 | .. | 10 | .. | .. | .. | 12 | 9 |
| 7th ,, ,, .. | .. | .. | .. | 1 | .. | .. | .. | 1 | 1 |

APPENDIX XXIII—*continued.*

| | Killed. | | Wounded | | Missing. | | Total. | | |
|---|---|---|---|---|---|---|---|---|---|
| | Officers. | Men. | Officers. | Men. | Officers. | Men. | Officers. | Men. | Horses. |
| **A. LOSSES OF THE 1ST ARMY**—*cont.* | | | | | | | | | |
| 1st Light Cavalry Brigade: | | | | | | | | | |
| 2nd Guard Lancer Regiment .. | .. | 1 | .. | .. | .. | .. | .. | 1 | 1 |
| 1st Guard Dragoon Regiment .. | 1 | 12 | 3 | 62 | .. | .. | 4 | 74 | 19 |
| 1st Guard Lancer Regiment .. | .. | .. | .. | 2 | .. | 1 | .. | 3 | 1 |
| Total loss of 1st Cavalry Division | 1 | 15 | 4 | 75 | .. | 1 | 5 | 91 | 32 |
| *2nd Cavalry Division.* | | | | | | | | | |
| 2nd Light Cavalry Brigade: | | | | | | | | | |
| 2nd Guard Dragoon Regiment .. | .. | .. | .. | 1 | .. | .. | .. | 1 | 5 |
| 3rd Regiment of Hussars .. | 1 | 1 | 3 | 21 | .. | .. | 4 | 25 | 7 |
| 11th Regiment of Lancers .. | .. | 4 | 3 | 31 | .. | 1 | 3 | 36 | 28 |
| 3rd Light Cavalry Brigade: | | | | | | | | | |
| Staff of Brigade .. | .. | .. | 1 | 1 | .. | .. | 1 | 1 | .. |
| 3rd Regiment of Dragoons .. | 2 | 25 | 10 | 162 | .. | 2 | 12 | 189 | 87 |
| 12th Regiment of Hussars .. | .. | 7 | 4 | 38 | .. | 1 | 4 | 46 | 59 |
| Total loss of 2nd Cavalry Division | 3 | 37 | 21 | 257 | .. | 4 | 24 | 298 | 116 |
| Total losses of 1st Corps of Cavalry | 4 | 52 | 25 | 332 | .. | 5 | 29 | 389 | 218 |

## SUMMARY OF LOSSES OF THE 1ST ARMY.

| | Killed. | | Wounded | | Missing. | | Total. | | |
|---|---|---|---|---|---|---|---|---|---|
| | Officers. | Men. | Officers. | Men. | Officers. | Men. | Officers. | Men. | Horses. |
| *a.* Total loss of IInd Corps, including the 3rd Heavy Cavalry Brigade.. | 8 | 241 | 26 | 953 | .. | 28 | 34 | 1222 | 59 |
| *b.* Total loss of 5th and 6th Divisions | 3 | 101 | 15 | 412 | .. | 1 | 18 | 514 | 48 |
| *c.* Total loss of 7th and 8th Divisions | 34 | 594 | 79 | 2079 | .. | 85 | 113 | 2758 | 43 |
| *d.* Total loss of the Artillery of the 1st Army .. .. | 3 | 25 | 9 | 145 | .. | 1 | 12 | 171 | 193 |
| *e.* Total loss of the Cavalry Corps of the 1st Army .. .. .. | 4 | 52 | 25 | 332 | .. | 5 | 29 | 389 | 218 |
| Total losses of the 1st Army | 52 | 1013 | 154 | 3921 | .. | 120 | 206 | 5051 | 561 |
| **B. LOSSES OF THE ARMY OF THE ELBE.** | | | | | | | | | |
| *a. Loss of the 14th Division of Infantry.* | | | | | | | | | |
| Staff of the Division .. .. .. | .. | .. | .. | .. | .. | .. | .. | .. | 1 |
| 56th Regiment of Infantry .. .. | 6 | 78 | 8 | 248 | .. | 15 | 14 | 341 | 2 |
| 16th ,, ,, .. .. | 2 | 21 | 3 | 65 | .. | .. | 5 | 86 | 3 |
| 57th ,, ,, .. .. | 2 | 23 | 6 | 76 | .. | .. | 8 | 99 | 3 |
| 17th ,, ,, .. .. | 4 | 31 | 3 | 147 | .. | 2 | 7 | 180 | 3 |
| Total loss of 14th Division | 14 | 153 | 20 | 536 | .. | 17 | 34 | 706 | 12 |

| | Killed. | | Wounded | | Missing. | | Total. | | |
|---|---|---|---|---|---|---|---|---|---|
| | Officers. | Men. | Officers. | Men. | Officers. | Men. | Officers. | Men. | Horses. |
| **B. LOSSES OF THE ARMY OF THE ELBE**—*cont.* | | | | | | | | | |
| *b. Loss of 15th Division of Infantry.* | | | | | | | | | |
| 65th Regiment of Infantry .. .. | 1 | 32 | 7 | 124 | .. | 7 | 8 | 163 | 1 |
| 40th Regiment of Fusiliers .. .. | 1 | 18 | 4 | 45 | .. | 11 | 5 | 74 | .. |
| Staff of 30th Brigade .. .. .. | .. | .. | .. | .. | .. | .. | .. | .. | 2 |
| 68th Regiment of Infantry .. .. | 1 | 27 | 3 | 136 | .. | 13 | 4 | 176 | 3 |
| 28th ,, ,, .. .. | 3 | 49 | 9 | 163 | .. | 1 | 12 | 213 | .. |
| Total loss of 15th Division .. | 6 | 126 | 23 | 468 | .. | 32 | 29 | 626 | 6 |
| *c. Loss of 16th Division of Infantry.* | | | | | | | | | |
| 69th Regiment of Infantry .. .. | .. | 1 | .. | 21 | .. | .. | .. | 22 | .. |
| 29th ,, ,, .. .. | .. | 9 | .. | 30 | .. | .. | .. | 39 | .. |
| 33rd Regiment of Fusiliers .. .. | 1 | 21 | 2 | 52 | .. | 6 | 3 | 79 | .. |
| 8th Battalion of Rifles .. .. | .. | 3 | 1 | 2 | .. | .. | .. | 1 | 5 |
| Total loss of 16th Division .. | 1 | 34 | 3 | 105 | .. | 6 | 4 | 145 | .. |
| N.B. The losses of the detachments of the advanced guard are included among the losses of their respective regiments. | | | | | | | | | |
| *d. Loss of the 14th Cavalry Brigade.* | | | | | | | | | |
| 5th Regiment of Lancers .. | .. | .. | .. | 3 | .. | .. | .. | 3 | 7 |
| 7th Regiment of Dragoons .. | .. | .. | 2 | 12 | .. | .. | 2 | 12 | 32 |
| Total .. .. .. | .. | .. | 2 | 15 | .. | .. | 2 | 15 | 39 |
| *e. Loss of the 15th Cavalry Brigade.* | | | | | | | | | |
| 8th Regiment of Cuirassiers .. | .. | 3 | .. | 11 | .. | .. | .. | 14 | 28 |
| 7th Regiment of Lancers .. | .. | .. | .. | 3 | .. | .. | .. | 3 | 11 |
| 2nd Landwehr Regiment .. | 1 | 5 | .. | 11 | .. | 2 | 1 | 18 | 30 |
| Total .. .. .. | 1 | 8 | .. | 25 | .. | 2 | 1 | 35 | 69 |
| N.B. The Cavalry Brigade of Count Goltz suffered no loss. | | | | | | | | | |
| *f. Loss of the Artillery of the Army of the Elbe.* | | | | | | | | | |
| 7th Regiment of Field Artillery .. | .. | 1 | .. | 16 | .. | .. | .. | 17 | 18 |
| 8th ,, ,, ,, | 1 | 11 | 1 | 20 | .. | .. | 2 | 31 | 30 |
| Total .. .. .. | 1 | 12 | 1 | 36 | .. | .. | 2 | 48 | 48 |

APPENDIX XXIII—*continued.*

SUMMARY OF THE LOSSES OF THE ARMY OF THE ELBE.

| | Killed. | | Wounded | | Missing. | | Total. | | |
|---|---|---|---|---|---|---|---|---|---|
| | Officers. | Men. | Officers. | Men. | Officers. | Men. | Officers. | Men. | Horses. |
| **B. LOSSES OF THE ELBE ARMY**—*cont.* | | | | | | | | | |
| *a.* Loss of 14th Division of Infantry | 14 | 153 | 20 | 536 | .. | 17 | 34 | 706 | 12 |
| *b.* Loss of 15th Division of Infantry | 6 | 126 | 23 | 463 | .. | 32 | 29 | 626 | 6 |
| *c.* Loss of 16th Division of Infantry | 1 | 34 | 3 | 105 | .. | 6 | 4 | 145 | .. |
| *d.* Loss of 14th Cavalry Brigade .. | .. | .. | 2 | 15 | .. | .. | 2 | 15 | 39 |
| *e.* Loss of 15th Cavalry Brigade .. | 1 | 8 | .. | 25 | .. | 2 | 1 | 35 | 69 |
| *f.* Loss of Artillery .. .. .. | 1 | 12 | 1 | 36 | .. | .. | 2 | 48 | 48 |
| Total losses of the Army of the Elbe | 23 | 333 | 49 | 1185 | .. | 57 | 72 | 1575 | 174 |
| **C. LOSSES OF THE IIND ARMY.** | | | | | | | | | |
| *a. Loss of the Corps of Guards.* | | | | | | | | | |
| 1st Division of Guard Infantry : | | | | | | | | | |
| Staff of the Division .. .. | 2 | .. | .. | .. | .. | .. | 2 | .. | 1 |
| Staff of 1st Brigade .. .. | .. | .. | 2 | .. | .. | .. | 2 | .. | 1 |
| 3rd Regiment of Foot Guards .. | .. | 41 | 4 | 186 | .. | 19 | 4 | 246 | 3 |
| 1st ,, ,, .. | 4 | 115 | 9 | 247 | .. | 18 | 13 | 380 | 8 |
| Guard Fusilier Regiment .. | 2 | 32 | 3 | 82 | .. | 1 | 5 | 115 | 2 |
| 2nd Regiment of Foot Guards .. | 4 | 55 | 6 | 166 | .. | 30 | 10 | 251 | 1 |
| Battalion of Guard Rifles .. | .. | 4 | .. | 23 | .. | .. | .. | 27 | .. |
| Regiment of Guard Hussars .. | .. | 1 | 2 | 2 | .. | .. | 2 | 3 | 4 |
| Total of 1st Division of Guards .. | 12 | 248 | 26 | 706 | .. | 68 | 38 | 1022 | 20 |
| 2nd Division of Guard Infantry : | | | | | | | | | |
| 3rd Regiment Grenadier Guards | 2 | .. | 2 | 3 | .. | .. | 4 | 3 | .. |
| 1st ,, ,, ,, | .. | 8 | .. | 61 | .. | .. | .. | 69 | 3 |
| 4th ,, ,, ,, | .. | .. | 1 | 7 | .. | .. | 1 | 7 | .. |
| 2nd ,, ,, ,, | 2 | 7 | 1 | 41 | .. | .. | 3 | 48 | 1 |
| Battalion of Guard Skirmishers | 2 | 9 | .. | 58 | .. | .. | 2 | 67 | 1 |
| 3rd Regiment of Guard Lancers | .. | 1 | 1 | 1 | .. | .. | 1 | 2 | .. |
| Battalion of Guard Pioneers .. | .. | .. | .. | 2 | .. | .. | .. | 2 | .. |
| Total of 2nd Division of Guards .. | 6 | 25 | 5 | 173 | .. | .. | 11 | 198 | 5 |
| Field Artillery Regiment of Guards | .. | 17 | 3 | 38 | .. | 1 | 3 | 56 | 56 |
| 1st Heavy Cavalry Brigade : | | | | | | | | | |
| Regiment of Guards du Corps .. | 1 | 4 | 1 | 4 | .. | .. | 2 | 8 | 3 |
| Total of Corps of Guards, including the 1st Heavy Cavalry Brigade .. | 19 | 294 | 35 | 921 | .. | 69 | 54 | 1284 | 84 |
| *b. Loss of the 1st Corps d'Armée.* | | | | | | | | | |
| 1st Division of Infantry : | | | | | | | | | |
| 41st Regiment of Infantry .. | 1 | 9 | 5 | 54 | .. | 3 | 6 | 66 | 3 |
| 1st Regiment of Grenadiers .. | .. | 16 | 1 | 62 | .. | 6 | 1 | 84 | .. |
| 1st Battalion of Rifles .. .. | 2 | 15 | 2 | 37 | .. | .. | 4 | 52 | .. |
| 1st Regiment of Dragoons .. | .. | 3 | 1 | 14 | .. | .. | 1 | 17 | 21 |
| Total of 1st Division .. | 3 | 43 | 9 | 167 | .. | 9 | 12 | 219 | 24 |

APPENDIX XXIII—*continued.*

| | | Killed. | | Wounded | | Missing. | | Total. | | |
|---|---|---|---|---|---|---|---|---|---|---|
| | | Officers. | Men. | Officers. | Men. | Officers. | Men. | Officers. | Men. | Horses. |
| LOSSES OF THE IIND ARMY—*cont.* | | | | | | | | | | |
| 2nd Division of Infantry: | | | | | | | | | | |
| 44th Regiment of Infantry | .. | .. | .. | .. | 2 | .. | .. | .. | 2 | .. |
| 4th Regiment of Grenadiers | .. | .. | .. | .. | 3 | .. | .. | .. | 3 | .. |
| 5th    „       „ | .. | .. | 6 | .. | 12 | .. | .. | .. | 18 | .. |
| 1st Battalion of Pioneers | .. | .. | 1 | .. | 3 | .. | .. | .. | 4 | .. |
| 1st Regiment of Hussars | .. | .. | 1 | .. | 4 | .. | .. | .. | 5 | 7 |
| Total of 2nd Division | .. | .. | 8 | .. | 24 | .. | .. | .. | 32 | 7 |
| | | | | | | | | | | |
| Reserve Brigade of Cavalry: | | | | | | | | | | |
| 3rd Regiment of Cuirassiers | .. | .. | .. | .. | 2 | .. | .. | .. | 2 | 4 |
| 12th Regiment of Lancers | .. | .. | 2 | .. | 3 | .. | .. | .. | 5 | 8 |
| Total.. | .. | .. | 2 | .. | 5 | .. | .. | .. | 7 | 12 |
| 1st Field Artillery Regiment.. | .. | .. | .. | .. | 6 | .. | .. | .. | 6 | 3 |
| Total losses of Ist Corps | .. | 3 | 53 | 9 | 202 | .. | 9 | 12 | 264 | 46 |
| | | | | | | | | | | |
| *c. Loss of the VIth Corps d'Armée.* | | | | | | | | | | |
| 11th Division of Infantry: | | | | | | | | | | |
| Staff of 21st Brigade | .. | .. | .. | .. | .. | .. | .. | .. | .. | 1 |
| 50th Regiment of Infantry | .. | 1 | 43 | 2 | 128 | .. | 4 | 3 | 175 | 3 |
| 10th Regiment of Grenadiers | .. | 2 | 33 | 2 | 118 | .. | 4 | 4 | 155 | 1 |
| 51st Regiment of Infantry | .. | .. | 23 | 4 | 86 | .. | 3 | 4 | 112 | .. |
| 38th Regiment of Fusiliers | .. | .. | 1 | .. | 15 | .. | .. | .. | 16 | .. |
| 8th Regiment of Dragoons | .. | .. | 2 | .. | .. | .. | .. | .. | 2 | 3 |
| Total of 11th Division | .. | 3 | 102 | 8 | 347 | .. | 11 | 11 | 460 | 8 |
| | | | | | | | | | | |
| 12th Division of Infantry: | | | | | | | | | | |
| 22nd Regiment of Infantry | .. | .. | 6 | 1 | 26 | .. | 4 | 1 | 36 | 3 |
| 23rd Regiment of Infantry | .. | .. | 15 | 1 | 38 | .. | 3 | 1 | 56 | .. |
| 6th Battalion of Rifles .. | .. | .. | 1 | .. | 8 | .. | 1 | .. | 10 | 1 |
| 6th Regiment of Hussars | .. | .. | 3 | .. | 3 | .. | 1 | .. | 7 | 3 |
| Total of 12th Division | .. | .. | 25 | 2 | 75 | .. | 9 | 2 | 109 | 7 |
| | | | | | | | | | | |
| Reserve Cavalry: | | | | | | | | | | |
| 4th Regiment of Hussars | .. | .. | 9 | 2 | 38 | .. | 3 | 2 | 50 | 50 |
| 6th Field Artillery Regiment | .. | .. | 6 | 1 | 10 | .. | .. | 1 | 16 | 7 |
| Total losses of VIth Corps d'Armée.. | | 3 | 142 | 13 | 470 | .. | 23 | 16 | 635 | 72 |

APPENDIX XXIII—*continued.*

SUMMARY OF THE LOSSES OF THE IIND ARMY.

| | Killed. | | Wounded | | Missing. | | Total. | | |
|---|---|---|---|---|---|---|---|---|---|
| | Officers. | Men. | Officers. | Men. | Officers. | Men. | Officers. | Men. | Horses. |
| *a.* Loss of the Corps of Guards, including the 1st Heavy Cavalry Brigade .. .. .. .. | 19 | 294 | 35 | 921 | .. | 69 | 54 | 1284 | 84 |
| *b.* Loss of the Ist Corps d'Armée .. | 3 | 53 | 9 | 202 | .. | 9 | 12 | 264 | 46 |
| *c.* Loss of the VIth Corps d'Armée .. | 3 | 142 | 13 | 470 | .. | 23 | 16 | 635 | 72 |
| Total losses of IInd Army .. | 25 | 489 | 57 | 1593 | .. | 101 | 82 | 2183 | 202 |

N.B. The Vth Corps d'Armée and the Cavalry Division of the IInd Army suffered no loss.

LOSSES OF THE PRUSSIAN ARMIES IN THE BATTLE OF KÖNIGGRATZ, JULY 3RD, 1866.

| | Killed. | | Wounded | | Missing. | | Total. | | |
|---|---|---|---|---|---|---|---|---|---|
| | Officers. | Men. | Officers. | Men. | Officers. | Men. | Officers. | Men. | Horses. |
| A. Losses of the 1st Army .. .. | 52 | 1013 | 154 | 3921 | .. | 120 | 206 | 5054 | 563 |
| B. Losses of the Army of the Elbe .. | 23 | 333 | 49 | 1185 | .. | 57 | 72 | 1575 | 174 |
| C. Losses of the IInd Army .. .. | 25 | 489 | 57 | 1593 | .. | 101 | 82 | 2183 | 202 |
| Total Prussian loss .. .. | 100 | 1835 | 260 | 6699 | .. | 278 | 360 | 8812 | 939 |

# APPENDIX XXIV.

### Losses of the Austrian-Saxon Army in the Battle of Königgratz, July 3rd, 1866.

We do not as yet know the exact amount of the Austrian losses. The following lists are compiled from the statements in the Austrian military journals "Streffleur" and "Kamerad," they differ somewhat from those given in "Hirtenfeld's Calendar":—

A. Losses of the IInd Corps d'Armée, according to "Streffleur" and "Kamerad."

| Killed. | | | Wounded. | | | Prisoners. | | Missing. | | | Total. | | |
|---|---|---|---|---|---|---|---|---|---|---|---|---|---|
| Officers. | Men. | Horses. | Officers. | Men. | Horses. | Officers. | Men. | Officers. | Men. | Horses. | Officers. | Men. | Horses. |
| 45 | 827 | 47 | 100 | 2,578 | 29 | 3 | 122 | 12 | 2,451 | 36 | 160 | 5,978 | 112 |
| 872 | | | 2,678 | | | 125 | | 2,463 | | | 6,138 | | |
| | | | | | | | 2,588 | | | | | | |

B. Losses of the IVth Corps d'Armée, according to "Streffleur" and "Kamerad."

| Killed. | | | Wounded. | | | Missing. | | | Total. | | |
|---|---|---|---|---|---|---|---|---|---|---|---|
| Officers. | Men. | Horses. | Officers. | Men. | Horses. | Officers. | Men. | Horses. | Officers. | Men. | Horses. |
| 66 | 1,204 | 116 | 171 | 2,990 | 41 | 49 | 6,165 | 505 | 286 | 10,359 | 662 |
| 1,270 | | | 3,161 | | | 6,214 | | | 10,645 | | |

According to official reports made up to the end of May, 1867, but not including the 13th Rifle Battalion and the 51st Regiment, the death of 72 officers and 944 men of this corps was proved; 10 officers and 1,300 men are stated to be missing, and probably killed, making a total of killed, 82 officers and 2,244 rank and file.

## Appendix XXIV—continued.

| | Killed. | | Wounded. | | Missing. | | Total. | |
|---|---|---|---|---|---|---|---|---|
| | Officers. | Men. | Officers. | Men. | Officers. | Men. | Officers. | Men. |
| **C. Losses of the Royal Saxon Army.** | | | | | | | | |
| Staffs of the 1st and 2nd Infantry Divisions, and the 3rd Infantry Brigade | 2 | .. | 2 | .. | .. | .. | 4 | .. |
| 1st Brigade of Infantry | 2 | 11 | 4 | 98 | .. | 46 | 6 | 155 |
| " Leib " Brigade of Infantry | 4 | 17 | 4 | 171 | .. | 110 | 8 | 298 |
| 2nd Brigade of Infantry | 4 | 39 | 18 | 327 | .. | 179 | 22 | 545 |
| 3rd Brigade of Infantry | 3 | 39 | 12 | 270 | .. | 78 | 15 | 387 |
| Cavalry | .. | 7 | .. | 16 | .. | 6 | .. | 29 |
| Artillery | .. | 7 | .. | 17 | .. | 3 | .. | 27 |
| Sanitary Troops | .. | .. | .. | 1 | .. | 4 | .. | 5 |
| Total | 15 | 120 | 40 | 900 | .. | 426 | 55 | 1,446 |

" Hirtenfeld's Calendar " states the losses of the other Austrian Corps to be as follows :—

| | Killed. | Wounded. | Missing. | Total. |
|---|---|---|---|---|
| **D. Ist Corps d'Armee.** | | | | |
| a. Brigade Poschacher | 2 | 3 | 19 | 24 |
| b. Brigade Leininge | 314 | 552 | 1,602 | 2,468 |
| c. Brigade Piret | 185 | 593 | 1,032 | 1,810 |
| d. Brigade Ringelsheim* | .. | .. | .. | .. |
| e. Brigade Abele | 102 | 209 | 607 | 918 |
| 1st Regiment of Artillery | 18 | 92 | 186 | 296 |
| 2nd Regiment of Hussars | .. | .. | 1 | 1 |
| Total, exclusive of Brigade Ringelsheim | } 621 | 1,449 | 3,447 | 5,517 |
| **E. IIIrd Corps d'Armee.** | | | | |
| a. Brigade Appiano† | 110 | 202 | 1,969 | 2,281 |
| b. Brigade Benedek | 356 | 935 | 844 | 2,135 |
| c. Brigade Kirschberg | 225 | 879 | 377 | 1,481 |
| d. Brigade Prohaska | 26 | 66 | 156 | 248 |
| 8th Artillery Regiment | 20 | 73 | 81 | 174 |
| 9th Regiment of Lancers | 18 | 40 | 62 | 120 |
| Total of IIIrd Corps | 755 | 2,195 | 3,489 | 6,439 |

\* The considerable losses of General Ringelsheim's Brigade are not yet known. The Brigade consisted of the 42nd Regiment (King of Hanover), the 73rd Regiment (Duke of Würtemberg No. 73), and 26th Battalion of Rifles.

† Exclusive of the 4th Rifle Battalion, the losses of which are not yet known.

APPENDIX XXIV—*continued.*

| | Killed. | Wounded. | Missing. | Total. |
|---|---|---|---|---|
| **LOSSES OF THE AUSTRIAN ARMY**—*cont.* | | | | |
| **F. VITH CORPS D'ARMEE.** | | | | |
| *a.* Brigade Waldstätten | 35 | 29 | 382 | 446 |
| *b.* Brigade Hertwegh | 26 | 125 | 947 | 1,098 |
| *c.* Brigade Rosenzweig | 212 | 544 | 692 | 1,448 |
| *d.* Brigade Jonak | 77 | 122 | 1,568 | 1,767 |
| 10th Artillery Regiment | 2 | 19 | 25 | 46 |
| Total of VIth Corps | 352 | 839 | 3,614 | 4,805 |
| **G. VIIITH CORPS D'ARMEE.** | | | | |
| *a.* Brigade Woeber | 65 | 66 | 223 | 354 |
| *b.* Brigade Schulz | 168 | 433 | 866 | 1,467 |
| *c.* Brigade Roth | 48 | 117 | 616 | 781 |
| 9th Artillery Regiment | 6 | 12 | 19 | 37 |
| 3rd Regiment of Lancers | 2 | .. | 13 | 15 |
| Total of VIIIth Corps | 289 | 628 | 1,737 | 2,654 |
| **H. XTH CORPS D'ARMEE.** | | | | |
| *a.* Brigade Moudl | 63 | 175 | 363 | 601 |
| *b.* Brigade Fabry | 157 | 468 | 1,122 | 1,747 |
| *c.* Brigade Knebel | 19 | 122 | 246 | 387 |
| *d.* Brigade Wimpfen | 89 | 767 | 640 | 1,496 |
| 3rd Artillery Regiment | 24 | 64 | 28 | 116 |
| Total of Xth Corps | 352 | 1,596 | 2,399 | 4,347 |
| **J. THE CAVALRY DIVISIONS.** | | | | |
| *a.* 1st Light Cavalry Division | 6 | 9 | 51 | 66 |
| *b.* 2nd Light Cavalry Division | 15 | 25 | 114 | 154 |
| *c.* 1st Reserve Cavalry Division | 57 | 137 | 426 | 620 |
| *d.* 2nd Reserve Cavalry Division | 22 | 20 | 58 | 100 |
| *e.* 3rd Reserve Cavalry Division | 38 | 106 | 494 | 638 |
| Total of Cavalry Divisions | 138 | 297 | 1,143 | 1,578 |
| **K. ARTILLERY OF THE CAVALRY DIVISIONS AND THE RESERVE ARTILLERY OF THE ARMY.** | | | | |
| 6th Artillery Regiment | 34 | 70 | 57 | 161 |
| 11th Artillery Regiment | 6 | 20 | 20 | 46 |
| 12th Artillery Regiment | 36 | 40 | 151 | 227 |
| Total of Artillery | 76 | 130 | 228 | 434 |
| **L. PIONEERS, SANITARY TROOPS, &c.** | | | | |
| *a.* 2nd, 5th, and 6th Pioneer Battalions | .. | 3 | 20 | 23 |
| *b.* 1st, 2nd, 3rd, 4th, 9th, and 10th Sanitary Companies | 1 | 2 | 63 | 66 |
| *c.* Military Train | .. | 2 | 51 | 53 |
| Total of Pioneers, &c. | 1 | 7 | 134 | 142 |

APPENDIX XXIV—*continued.*

SUMMARY OF THE LOSSES OF THE AUSTRIAN ARMY IN THE BATTLE OF KOENIGGRAETZ.

| | Killed. | Wounded. | Missing. | Total. |
|---|---|---|---|---|
| A. Total loss of the IInd Corps d'Armée.. | 872 | 2,678 | 2,588 | 6,138 |
| B. Total loss of the IVth Corps d'Armée | 1,270 | 3,161 | 6,214 | 10,645 |
| C. Total loss of the Saxon Army .. .. | 135 | 940 | 426 | 1,501 |
| D. Total loss of the 1st Corps, exclusive of Brigade Ringelsheim .. .. | 621 | 1,449 | 3,447 | 5,517 |
| E. Total loss of the IIIrd Corps d'Armée, exclusive of the 4th Rifle Battalion .. | 755 | 2,195 | 3,489 | 6,439 |
| F. Total loss of the VIth Corps d'Armée | 352 | 839 | 2,614 | 4,805 |
| G. Total loss of VIIIth Corps d'Armée .. | 289 | 628 | 1,737 | 2,654 |
| H. Total loss of the Xth Corps d'Armée.. | 352 | 1,596 | 2,399 | 4,347 |
| J. Total loss of the Cavalry Divisions .. | 138 | 297 | 1,143 | 1,578 |
| K. Total loss of the Artillery of the Cavalry Divisions and the Reserve Artillery .. .. .. .. | 76 | 130 | 228 | 434 |
| L. Total loss of Pioneers, &c. .. .. | 1 | 7 | 134 | 142 |
| Total Austrian loss, exclusive of the troops specified above .. .. } | 4,861 | 13,920 | 29,419 | 44,200 |

Of the above total 19,800 men were taken as prisoners.

# APPENDIX XXV.

SPECIAL Order of Battle of the Troops engaged in the Action of Tobitschau and Rokeinitz, July 15th, 1866.

General Commanding..      ..      General of Infantry Von Bonin.
Chief of Staff ..      ..      ..      Colonel Von Borries.

| | Battalions of Infantry. | Battalions of Rifles. | Squadrons. | Guns. | Companies of Pioneers. |
|---|---|---|---|---|---|
| **ADVANCED GUARD OF THE 1ST CORPS ON THE 15TH OF JULY.** | | | | | |
| Lieutenant-General Von Grossmann. General Staff Officer, Major Meydam. Commandant of Artillery, Major Noack. | | | | | |
| *2nd Brigade of Infantry.* | | | | | |
| Major-General Von Barnekow. | | | | | |
| 3rd Regiment of Grenadiers, Col. Von Blumenthal: 1st Battalion, Lieutenant-Colonel Weese .. 2nd Battalion, Major Von Frankenberg .. Fusilier Battalion, Lieutenant-Colonel Von Wedell .. .. .. .. .. .. | 3 | .. | .. | .. | .. |
| 43rd Regiment of Infantry, Colonel Von Tresckow: 1st Battalion, Captain Von Deutsch .. 2nd Battalion, Major Von Loebell .. .. Fusilier Battalion, Major Koehn Von Jaski .. | 3 | .. | .. | .. | .. |
| 1st Battalion of Rifles, Major Von Sommerfeld .. | .. | 1 | .. | .. | .. |
| 1st Regiment of Dragoons, Colonel Von Bernhardi | .. | .. | 5 | .. | .. |
| 8th Regiment of Lancers, Lieutenant-Colonel Von Below .. .. .. .. .. .. | .. | .. | 4 | .. | .. |
| 4th 4-pounder Battery of 1st Field Artillery Regiment, Captain Boehncke .. .. .. | .. | .. | .. | 6 | .. |
| 3rd 6-pounder Battery of 1st Field Artillery Regiment, Captain Niehr .. .. .. .. | .. | .. | .. | 6 | .. |
| 4th Horse Artillery Battery of 1st Field Artillery Regiment, Captain Iwentz.. .. .. .. | .. | .. | .. | 6 | .. |
| 1st Company of 1st Pioneer Batln., Captain Schütze | .. | .. | .. | .. | 1 |
| Total of Advanced Guard of 1st Corps.. | 6 | 1 | 9 | 18 | 1 |
| (N.B.—The advanced guard of the 1st Corps did not arrive upon the field until the afternoon of the 15th.) | | | | | |
| **DETACHMENT OF MAJOR-GENERAL VON MALOTKI.** | | | | | |
| *3rd Brigade of Infantry.* | | | | | |
| Major-General Von Malotki. | | | | | |
| 4th Squadron of 10th Lancers, Lieut. Von Lieres.. | .. | .. | 1 | .. | .. |

APPENDIX XXV—*continued.*

| | Battalions of Infantry. | Battalions of Rifles. | Squadrons. | Guns. | Battalions of Pioneers. |
|---|---|---|---|---|---|
| DETACHMENT OF MAJOR-GENERAL VON MALOTKI—*cont.* | | | | | |
| 44th Regiment of Infantry, Colonel Von La Chevallerie: 1st Battalion, Lieutenant-Colonel Von Etzel.. 2nd Battalion, Major Koch .. .. .. Fusilier Battalion, Lieutenant-Colonel Von Behr .. .. .. .. .. | 3 | .. | .. | .. | .. |
| 4th Regiment of Grenadiers, Colonel Von Wedell: 1st Battalion, Captain Von Schmeling .. 2nd Battalion, Major Mansard.. .. .. Fusilier Battalion, Lieutenant-Colonel Von Pannwitz .. .. .. .. .. | 3 | .. | .. | .. | .. |
| 1st 4-pounder Battery of 1st Field Artillery Regiment, Captain Magnus .. .. .. .. | .. | .. | .. | 6 | .. |
| Total of Detachment of General Malotki .. | 6 | .. | 1 | 6 | .. |
| CAVALRY DIVISION OF THE IIND ARMY. | | | | | |
| Major-General Von Hartmann. General Staff Officer, Captain Von Versen. Commandant of Artillery, Major Count Wengersky. | | | | | |
| *Light Brigade.* | | | | | |
| Major-General Von Witzleben. | | | | | |
| 2nd Regiment of Hussars, Lieutenant-Colonel Von Schauroth .. .. .. .. .. .. | .. | .. | 3 | .. | .. |
| *Cuirassier Brigade.* | | | | | |
| Major-General Von Borstell. | | | | | |
| 1st Regiment of Cuirassiers, Colonel Von Barby .. | .. | .. | 4 | .. | .. |
| 5th Regiment of Cuirassiers, Lieutenant-Colonel Von Bredow .. .. .. .. .. | .. | .. | 4 | .. | .. |
| *Landwehr Cavalry Brigade.* | | | | | |
| Colonel Von Frankenberg. | | | | | |
| 1st Regiment of Landwehr Lancers, Lieutenant-Colonel Von Kock .. .. .. .. .. | .. | .. | 4 | .. | .. |
| 2nd Regiment of Landwehr Hussars, Colonel Von Glasenapp .. .. .. .. .. .. | .. | .. | 4 | .. | .. |
| 2nd Horse Artillery Battery of 6th Field Artillery Regiment, Captain Le Bauld de Nans .. .. | .. | .. | .. | 6 | .. |
| 3rd Horse Artillery Battery of 5th Field Artillery Regiment, Captain Lentz .. .. .. .. | .. | .. | .. | 6 | .. |
| Total of Cavalry Division .. .. | .. | .. | 19 | 12 | .. |

Of the above the following were engaged in the action of Rokeinitz :—
   The 4th Squadron of the 10th Lancers.
   The 2nd Landwehr Hussar Regiment.
   Three Squadrons of the 2nd Hussar Regiment.
   The 2nd Horse Artillery Battery.
     Total, 8 squadrons and 6 guns.

APPENDIX XXV—*continued.*

## SUMMARY.

| — | Battalions of Infantry. | Battalions of Rifles. | Squadrons. | Guns. | Companies of Pioneers. |
|---|---|---|---|---|---|
| Detachment of General Von Malotki     ..    ..    .. | 6 | .. | 1 | 6 | .. |
| Cavalry Division, Hartmann | .. | .. | 19 | 12 | .. |
| | 6 | .. | 20 | 18 | .. |
| Advanced Guard of 1st Corps | 6 | 1 | 9 | 18 | 1 |
| Total    ..    .. | 12 | 1 | 29 | 36 | 1 |

# APPENDIX XXVI.

SPECIAL Order of Battle of the Troops under the command of Lieutenant-General Von Fransecky, on the 22nd of July, 1866, at Blumenau.

General Commanding .. Lieut.-General Von Fransecky.
General Staff Officer .. Major Von Krenski.

| | Battalions of Infantry. | Battalions of Rifles. | Squadrons. | Guns. | Battalions of Pioneers. |
|---|---|---|---|---|---|
| **7TH DIVISION OF INFANTRY.** | | | | | |
| *Advanced Guard.* | | | | | |
| Major-General Von Gordon. Commandant of Infantry, Colonel Von Bothmer. | | | | | |
| Fusilier Battalion of the 27th Regiment, Lieut.-Colonel Von Zedtwitz .. .. .. .. | 1 | .. | .. | .. | .. |
| Fusilier Battalion of the 67th Regiment, Captain Liebenciner.. .. .. .. .. .. | 1 | .. | .. | .. | .. |
| 67th Regiment of Infantry, Lieut.-Colonel Baron Von Buttlar : 1st Battalion, Captain Von Drygalski.. .. 2nd Battalion, Major Von Zedtwitz .. .. | } 2 | .. | .. | .. | .. |
| 10th Regiment of Hussars, Colonel Von Besser, 3 squadrons .. .. .. .. .. .. | .. | .. | 3 | .. | .. |
| 1st 4-pounder Battery of 4th Field Artillery Regiment, Captain Von Raussendorf .. .. .. | .. | .. | .. | 6 | .. |
| 4th Company of 4th Pioneer Battalion, Capt. Giese | .. | .. | .. | .. | ¼ |
| *Main Body.* | | | | | |
| Major-General Von Schwartzhoff. | | | | | |
| 3 companies of— 1st Battalion of 27th Regiment, Major Hildebrandt | ¾ | | | | |
| 26th Regiment of Infantry, Col. Baron Von Medem : 1st Battalion, Major Paucke .. .. .. Fusilier Battalion, Major Von Boltenstern .. | } 2 | .. | .. | .. | .. |
| 66th Regiment of Infantry, Colonel Von Blankensee : 1st Battalion, Major Sehwager : 2nd Battalion, Major Von Wiedner .. .. Fusilier Battalion, Major Von Schmeling .. | } 3 | .. | .. | .. | .. |
| 1st 6 pounder Battery of 4th Field Artillery Regiment, Captain Kuehne .. .. .. .. | .. | .. | .. | 6 | .. |
| 5th 4-pounder Battery of 4th Field Artillery Regiment, Captain Baron Nordeck .. .. .. | .. | .. | .. | 6 | .. |
| 4th 12-pounder Battery of 4th Field Artillery Regiment, Captain Von Notz .. .. .. .. | .. | .. | .. | 6 | .. |
| Total of 7th Division of Infantry.. | 9¾ | .. | 3 | 24 | ¼ |

N.B. The 1st Squadron of the 10th Hussars was absent, escorting prisoners.
The 2nd Battalion of the 27th Regiment was in Horsitz.
The 3rd Company of the 27th Regiment was absent, escorting the baggage of the division.
The 2nd Battalion of the 26th Regiment was in Bruenn.

## Appendix XXVI—*continued.*

| | Battalions of Infantry. | Battalions of Rifles. | Squadrons. | Guns. | Battalions of Pioneers. |
|---|---|---|---|---|---|
| **8th Division of Infantry.** | | | | | |
| Major-General Von Bose. | | | | | |
| General Staff Officer, Major Von Massow. | | | | | |
| Commandant of Artillery, Major Heinrich. | | | | | |
| *15th Brigade of Infantry.* | | | | | |
| 31st Regiment of Infantry, Colonel Von Wedell : | | | | | |
| 1st Battalion, Lieut.-Colonel Von Heinemann | | | | | |
| 2nd Battalion, Major Von Hagen | 3 | .. | .. | .. | .. |
| Fusilier Battalion, Major Von Petery.. | | | | | |
| 71st Regiment of Infantry, Colonel Von Avemann : | | | | | |
| 1st Battalion, Major Von Hagen | | | | | |
| 2nd Battalion, Captain Von der Oelsnitz | 3 | .. | .. | .. | .. |
| Fusilier Battalion, Captain Von Hagen | | | | | |
| *16th Brigade of Infantry.* | | | | | |
| Major-General Von Schmidt. | | | | | |
| 72nd Regiment of Infantry, Colonel Count Gniesenau | | | | | |
| 1st Battalion, Major Hensel, 2 Companies | | | | | |
| 2nd Battalion, Captain Von Gilsa | 2½ | .. | .. | .. | .. |
| Fusilier Battalion, Major Von Flotow.. | | | | | |
| 6th Regiment of Lancers, Lieut.-Colonel Baron Von Langermann | .. | .. | 4 | .. | .. |
| 3rd Field Division of 4th Field Artillery Regiment : | | | | | |
| 3rd 12-pounder Battery, Captain Von Seebach | .. | .. | .. | 6 | .. |
| 3rd 6-pounder Battery, Captain Anton | .. | .. | .. | 6 | .. |
| 3rd 4-pounder Battery, Captain Kipping | .. | .. | .. | 6 | .. |
| 4th 4-pounder Battery, Captain Von Schlotheim | .. | .. | .. | 6 | .. |
| 3rd Company of 4th Pioneer Battalion, Capt. Von Wasserschleben | .. | .. | .. | .. | ¼ |
| Total of 8th Division of Infantry | 8½ | .. | 4 | 24 | ¼ |

N.B. The 4th Rifle Battalion was attached to the advanced guard of the 1st Army.

The 2nd and 3rd Companies of the 72nd Regiment were escorting the baggage.

### Reserves.

| | | | | | |
|---|---|---|---|---|---|
| *2nd Cavalry Division.* | | | | | |
| Major-General Hann Von Weyhern. | | | | | |
| General Staff Officer, Captain Von Schoenfels. | | | | | |
| 3rd Heavy Cavalry Brigade, Major-General Baron Von der Goltz : | | | | | |
| 2nd Regiment of Cuirassiers, Colonel Von Schœvenbach .. | .. | .. | .. | 4 | .. |
| 9th Regiment of Lancers, Colonel Von Diepenbroick Grueter | .. | .. | .. | 4 | .. |

APPENDIX XXVI—*continued.*

| | Battalions of Infantry. | Battalions of Rifles. | Squadrons. | Guns. | Battalions of Rifles. |
|---|---|---|---|---|---|
| RESERVES—*cont.* | | | | | |
| 3rd Light Cavalry Brigade, Major-General Count Bismarck-Bohlen : | | | | | |
|   3rd Regiment of Dragoons, Lieut.-Colonel Von Willisen .. .. .. .. .. | .. | .. | 5 | .. | .. |
|   12th Regiment of Hussars, Col. Von Barnekow | .. | .. | 4 | .. | .. |
|   2nd Horse Artillery Battery of 2nd Field Artillery Regiment, Captain Von Heusch .. | .. | .. | .. | 6 | .. |
| 2nd Field Division of 4th Field Artillery Regiment, Lieut-Colonel Von Scherbening : | | | | | |
|   2nd 6-pounder Battery, Captain Von Schaper | .. | .. | .. | 6 | .. |
|   4th 6-pounder Battery, Captain Meisner .. | .. | .. | .. | 6 | .. |
|   2nd 4-pounder Battery, Captain Reinhardt .. | .. | .. | .. | 6 | .. |
|   6th 4-pounder Battery, Lieutenant Philippi .. | .. | .. | .. | 6 | .. |
|          Total of Reserves .. | .. | .. | 17 | 30 | .. |

## SUMMARY.

| | Battalions of Infantry. | Squadrons. | Guns. | Companies of Pioneers. |
|---|---|---|---|---|
| 7th Division of Infantry .. | $9\frac{3}{4}$ | 3 | 24 | 1 |
| 8th Division of Infantry .. | $8\frac{1}{2}$ | 4 | 24 | 1 |
| Reserves .. .. .. .. | .. | 17 | 30 | .. |
|     Total .. .. .. | $18\frac{1}{4}$ | 24 | 78 | 2 |

## APPENDIX XXVII.

### ORDER OF BATTLE OF THE WEST GERMAN FEDERAL ARMY DURING THE CAMPAIGN 1866.

Commander-in Chief .. .. H.R.H. Fieldmarschal Prince Charles of Bavaria (commanding VIIth Federal Corps.)

Chief of Staff .. .. .. Lieut.-General Baron Von der Tann.

Assistant Chief of Staff .. .. Major-General Von Schintling.

Director of Field Artillery .. .. Lieut.-General Von Brodesser.

Director of Engineers .. .. Lieut.-Colonel Limbach.

First Adjutant .. .. .. Colonel Struntz.

---

### VIITH FEDERAL ARMY CORPS.
#### (FROM 26TH MAY TO 20TH JUNE).

1st Infantry Division .. .. Major-General Stephan.
1st Infantry Brigade .. .. Major-General Von Steinle.
"Leib" Infantry Regiment, 2nd and 3rd Battalions.
1st (King's) Infantry Regiment, 2nd and 3rd Battalions.
2nd Rifle Battalion.

2nd Infantry Brigade .. .. Major-General Von Welsch.
2nd (Crown Prince) Infantry Regiment, 2nd and 3rd Battalions.
8th (Seckendorff) Infantry Regiment, 1st and 3rd Battalions.
4th Rifle Battalion.
3rd (Duke Max) Chevauxleger Regiment.
6-pounder Battery (Hutten).
12-pounder Battery (Mussinan).

2nd Infantry Division .. .. Lieut.-General Von Feder.
3rd Infantry Brigade .. .. Major-General Schumacher.
3rd (Prince Charles) Infantry Regiment, 1st and 2nd Battalions.
12th (King Otto of Greece) Infantry Regiment, 1st and 2nd Battalions.
7th Rifle Battalion.
4th Infantry Brigade .. .. Major-General Von Hauser.
7th (Hohenhausen) Infantry Regiment, 1st and 2nd Battalions.
10th (Albert Pappenheim) Infantry Regiment, 1st and 3rd Battalions.
3rd Rifle Battalion.
4th (King's) Chevauxleger Regiment.
6-pounder Battery (Zeller).
12-pounder Battery (Kirchhoffer).

3rd Infantry Division .. .. Lieut.-General Baron Von Zoller.
5th Infantry Brigade .. .. Major-General Von Ribeaupierre.
11th (Ysenburg) Infantry Regiment, 2nd and 3rd Battalions.
15th (King John of Saxony) Infantry Regiment, 1st and 3rd Battalions.
5th Rifle Battalion.

6th Infantry Brigade .. .. Colonel Schweitzer.
6th (Prince William of Prussia) Infantry Regiment, 1st and 3rd
Battalions.
14th (Zandt) Infantry Regiment, 1st and 2nd Battalions.
1st Rifle Battalion.
2nd (Taxis) Chevauxleger Regiment.
6-pounder Battery (Lottersberg).
12-pounder Battery (Schuster).

4th Infantry Division .. .. Lieut.-General Von Hartmann.
7th Infantry Brigade .. .. Major-General Faust.
5th (Grand Duke of Hesse) Infantry Regiment, 1st and 3rd Battalions.
13th (Emperor Francis Joseph of Austria) Infantry Regiment.
1st and 2nd Battalions.
8th Rifle Battalion.
8th Infantry Brigade .. .. Major-General Cella.
4th (Gumppenberg) Infantry Regiment, 2nd and 3rd Battalions.
6th (Wrede) Infantry Regiment, 1st and 2nd Battalions.
6th Rifle Battalion.
6th (Duke of Leuchtenberg) Chevauxleger Regiment.
6-pounder Battery (Kœniger).
12-pounder Battery (Hang).

N.B.—Each division had besides:—One sanitary company, two field
hospitals, and one commissariat division.

The following reinforcements joined the divisions between the 20th
June and 15th July :—

1st Division : the 1st Battalion of the 2nd, and the 2nd of the
8th Infantry Regiment.
2nd Division : the 3rd Battalion of the 3rd, and the 3rd of the
7th Infantry Regiment.
3rd Division : the 1st Battalion of the 11th, and the 2nd of the
15th Infantry Regiment.
4th Division : the 2nd Battalion of the 5th, and the 3rd of the
9th Infantry Regiment.

Reserve Infantry Brigade .. .. Colonel Baron Von Pranckh.
(Did not join till after the action of Kissingen.)
1st Battalion of the 4th Infantry Regiment.
2nd Battalion of the 10th Infantry Regiment.
2nd Battalion of the 6th Infantry Regiment.
3rd Battalion of the 13th Infantry Regiment.
3rd Battalion of the 12th Infantry Regiment.
3rd Battalion of the 14th Infantry Regiment.
2nd and 3rd Squadrons of the 1st Chevauxlegers Regiment.
6-pounder Battery (Kriebel).
Sanitary Detachment.

Cavalry Reserve Corps .. .. General of Cavalry : Prince Taxis.
Heavy Cavalry Brigade .. .. Major-Gen. Baron Von. Rummel.
1st (Prince Charles) Cuirassier Regiment.
2nd (Prince Adalbert) Cuirassier Regiment.
3rd (Grand Duke Constantine) Cuirassier Regiment.

1st Light Cavalry Brigade..    ..    Major-General Duke Ludwig of
            Bavaria.
     1st (Cesarewitsch) Lancer Regiment.
     2nd (King's) Lancer Regiment.

2nd Light Cavalry Brigade    ..    Major-Gen. Count Pappenheim.
     5th (Leiningen) Chevauxlegers Regiment.
     3rd Lancer Regiment.
     12-pounder Horse Artillery Battery (Massenbach).
     12-pounder Horse Artillery Battery (La Roche).
     Commissariat Division, No. 6.

Artillery Reserve    ..    ..    ..    Major-General Count Bothmer.
     1st Division : Two Horse Artillery Batteries (12-pounders).
         "Lepel" and "Hellingrath."
   2nd Division : Two 6-pounder Batteries "Redenbacher" and "Girl."
   3rd Division : Two 12-pounder Batteries "Cöster" and "Gramich."
   4th Division : Two 12-pounder Batteries "Minges" and "Mehler."

## Summary of VIIth Federal Corps.

|  | Battalions of Infantry. | Battalions of Rifles. | Squadrons. | Guns. |
|---|---|---|---|---|
| 1st Infantry Division on 15th July .. .. .. | 10 | 2 | 4 | 16 |
| 2nd Infantry Division on 15th July .. .. .. | 10 | 2 | 4 | 16 |
| 3rd Infantry Division on 15th July .. .. .. | 10 | 2 | 4 | 16 |
| 4th Infantry Division on 15th July .. .. .. | 10 | 2 | 4 | 16 |
| Reserve Infantry Brigade on 15th July .. .. | 6 | .. | 2 | 8 |
| Cavalry Reserve Corps on 15th July .. .. | .. | .. | 28 | 12 |
| Artillery Reserve .. .. | .. | .. | .. | 60 |
| Total.. .. .. | 46 | 8 | 46 | 144 |

## VIIIth FEDERAL ARMY CORPS.

General Commanding    ..    ..    General of Infantry : Prince Alex-
            ander of Hesse.
Chief of the Staff    ..    ..    ..    Würtemberg : Lieutenant-Gene-
            ral Von Baur.
Assistant Chief of Staff    ..    ..    Baden : Major Kraus.
Director of Artillery    ..    ..    Baden : Lieutenant-General Von
            Faber.
Director of Engineers    ..    ..    Austrian : Major Von Orelli.
1st Division ..    ..    ..    ..    Würtemberg : Lieut. - General
            Von Hardegg.
Chief of the Staff    ..    ..    ..    Major-General Von Kallée.

1st Brigade .. .. .. .. Major-General Von Baumbach.

1st (Queen Olga) Infantry Regiment .. .. .. .. } Colonel Von Starkloff.

5th (King Charles) Infantry Regiment .. .. .. } Colonel Von Hügel.

3rd Rifle Battalion .. .. Major Von Starkloff.

2nd Brigade .. .. .. .. Major-General Von Fischer.

2nd Infantry Regiment .. Colonel Von Glaser.
7th Infantry Regiment .. Colonel Von Hügel.
2nd Rifle Battalion .. .. Major Von Hayn.

3rd Brigade .. .. .. Major-General Von Hegelmaier.

8th Infantry Regiment .. Colonel Von Reitzenstein.
3rd Infantry Regiment .. Colonel Von Lipp.
1st Rifle Battalion .. .. Major Rampacher.

1st 6-pounder Horse Artillery Battery Captain Von Marchthaler.
6th 6-pounder Battery .. .. Captain Roschmann.
7th 6-pounder Battery .. .. Captain Faber du Faur.

Three Sanitary Divisions.

Cavalry Brigade .. .. .. Major-General Count Scheler.

4th (Queen Olga) "Reiter" Regiment .. .. .. } Colonel Von Gukelen.

1st (King Charles) "Reiter" Regiment .. .. .. } Colonel Von Harling.

Detachment of Pioneers.

Total of 1st Division:—12 Battalions of Infantry, 3 Battalions, 9 Squadrons, 24 guns.

2nd Division (Baden) .. .. Lieut.-General Prince William of Baden.
Chief of the Staff .. .. .. Colonel Keller.
Commander of Infantry .. .. Lieut.-General Waag.

1st Brigade .. .. .. .. Maj.-Gen. Baron Von La Roche.

1st (Leib) Regiment of Grenadiers .. .. .. .. } Colonel Von Degenfeld.

5th Infantry Regiment .. Colonel Keller.
Rifle Battalion .. .. .. Lieut.-Colonel Von Peternell.

2nd Brigade .. .. .. .. Colonel Baron Von Neubronn.

2nd (King of Prussia) Infantry Regiment .. .. .. } Colonel Hofmann.

3rd Infantry Regiment .. Colonel Von Villiez.
2nd Fusilier Battalion .. .. Lieut.-Colonel Bauer.

2nd (Markgrave Maximilian) Regiment of Dragoons .. .. } Lieut.-Colonel Wirth.

1st 6-pounder Battery .. .. Captain Dienger.
2nd 6-pounder Battery .. .. Captain Deimling.
5th 6-pounder Battery .. .. Captain Hofmann.

Sanitary Company.

Total of 2nd Division :—9 battalions of Infantry, 1 battalion of Rifles, 4 squadrons, 18 guns.

| | |
|---|---|
| 3rd Division (Hessian) .. .. | Lieut.-General Von Perglas. |
| 1st Brigade .. .. .. .. | Major-General Frey. |
| 1st ("Leib Garde") Regiment of Infantry .. .. .. } | Colonel Von Grolmann. |
| 2nd (Grand Duke) Regiment of Infantry .. .. .. } | Colonel Wiikens. |

1st Homburg Company of Rifles.

| | |
|---|---|
| 2nd Brigade .. .. .. .. | Major-General Von Stockhausen. |
| 2rd (Leib) Regiment of Infantry | Colonel Von Ochsenstein. |
| 4th (Prince Charles) Regiment of Infantry .. .. .. } | Colonel Schenck. |

2nd Homburg Rifle Company.

| | |
|---|---|
| Sharpshooter Corps .. | Lieut.-Colonel Von Grolmann. |
| 2nd 6-pounder Battery .. .. | Captain Von Herget. |
| 3rd 6-pounder Battery .. .. | Captain Hallwachs. |
| Cavalry Brigade .. .. | Colonel Prince Ludwig of Hesse. |
| 1st Regiment of Guard "Reiters" | Lieut.-Colonel Riedesel Baron Von Eisenbach. |

Detachment of Pioneers.

Total of 2nd Division :—8 battalions of Infantry, 1½ battalions of Rifles, 4 squadrons, 12 guns.

| | |
|---|---|
| 4th Division (combined Austrian-Nassau .. .. .. .. } | Lieutenant Field-Marshal Count Neipperg. |
| Chief of the Staff .. .. .. | Captain Rathschiller. |
| Imperial Austrian Brigade .. .. | Major-General Von Hahn. |
| 16th (Wernhardt) Infantry Regiment .. .. .. } | Colonel Glückselig. |
| 4th Battalion of 21st (Reisch-ach) Infantry Regiment .. } | Major Eckhardt. |
| 4th Battalion of 49th (Hess) Infantry Regiment .. .. } | Major Kleinweyern. |
| 4th Battalion of 79th (Nobili) Infantry Regiment .. .. } | Lieut.-Colonel Baron Sterneck. |
| 35th Field "Jäger" Battalion | Major Mathalitzky. |
| 4-pounder Battery .. .. | Captain Klopetz. |
| Ducal Nassau Brigade .. .. | Major-General Roth. |
| 1st Infantry Regiment .. | Colonel Neuendorff. |
| 2nd Infantry Regiment .. | Colonel Von Arnoldi. |
| Rifle Battalion .. .. .. | Major Baron Von Hadeln. |

6-pounder Battery.
Pioneer Detachment.
Sanitary Detachment.
Two Squadrons of Electoral Hessian Hussars.

Total of 4th Division :—10 battalions of Infantry, 2 battalions of Rifles, 2 squadrons, 16 guns.

| | |
|---|---|
| Reserve Cavalry (Würtemberg) .. | Lieutenant-General Von Entress-Fürsteneck. |
| Würtemberg 3rd (King Wil-liam) "Reiter" Regiment .. } | Colonel Von Falkenstein. |

Baden "Leib" Dragoon Regiment .. .. .. .. } Colonel Von Degenfeldt.

Baden 3rd (Prince Charles) Dragoon Regiment .. .. } Colonel Baron Von Laroche.

Hessian 2nd Reiter Regiment — Lieut.-Col. Baron Von Jungenfeld.

Würtemberg 4-pounder Battery .. Captain Von Wagner.

Total of Reserve Cavalry :—17 squadrons, 8 guns.

Reserve Artillery (Hessian) .. Colonel Seederer.

Two Würtemberg 12-pounder Batteries .. .. .. } Captains Lenz and Brenkmann.

Austrian 8-pounder Battery .. Captain Burger.

Two Baden 6-pounder Batteries — Captains Chelius and Baron Von Gemmingen.

Two Hessian Batteries (12- and 6-pounders) .. .. .. } Captains Von Lynker and Reh.

One Nassau 6-pounder Battery — Captain Kleinschmidt.

Total of Reserve Artillery :—56 guns.

Würtemberg, Baden, and Hessian Field Hospitals.

|  | Battalions of Infantry. | Battalions of Rifles. | Squadrons. | Guns. |
|---|---|---|---|---|
| Total of VIIIth Federal Corps | 39 | 7½ | 36 | 134 |
| „ VIIth Corps .. .. | 46 | 8 | 46 | 144 |
| Total of West German Federal Army .. .. .. } | 85 | 15½ | 82 | 278 |

# APPENDIX XXVIII.

SPECIAL Order of Battle of the Prussian Troops engaged at Dermbach, 4th July, 1866.

| | Battalions of Infantry. | Battalions of Rifles. | Squadrons. | Guns. | Battalions of Pioneers. |
|---|---|---|---|---|---|
| **13TH INFANTRY DIVISION.** | | | | | |
| Lieut.-General Von Goeben. General Staff Officer, Captain Von Jena. Commander of Artillery, Major Von Drabich-Wächter. | | | | | |
| RIGHT FLANK DETACHMENT. | | | | | |
| *25th Infantry Brigade.* | | | | | |
| Major-General Von Kummer. | | | | | |
| 53rd Infantry Regiment, Colonel Von Tresckow : 1st Battalion, Major Von Frankenberg 2nd Battalion, Major Von Gontard Fusilier Battalion, Major Von Rosenzweig | 3 | .. | .. | .. | .. |
| Fusilier Battalion of 13th Infantry Regiment, Major Von Brause . | 1 | .. | .. | .. | .. |
| 4th and 5th Squadrons of 8th Hussar Regiment .. | .. | .. | 2 | .. | .. |
| 3rd 6-pounder Battery of 7th Field Artillery Regiment, Captain Von Eynatten (I).. | .. | .. | .. | 6 | .. |
| Total of 25th Infantry Brigade | 4 | .. | 2 | 6 | .. |
| LEFT FLANK DETACHMENT. | | | | | |
| *26th Infantry Brigade.* | | | | | |
| Major-General Baron Von Wrangel. | | | | | |
| 2nd Battalion of 15th Infantry Regiment, Major Rüstow | 1 | .. | .. | .. | .. |
| 13th Infantry Regiment, Colonel Von Gellhorn : 1st Battalion, Lieut.-Colonel Von Borries 2nd Battalion, Lieut.-Colonel Von Dürre | 2 | .. | .. | .. | .. |
| 55th Infantry Regiment, Colonel Stoltz : 1st Battalion, Lieut.-Colonel Von Böcking 2nd Battalion, Major Von Getzkow .. | 2 | .. | .. | .. | .. |
| Three Squadrons of 8th Hussar Regiment, Colonel Von Rantzau | .. | .. | 3 | .. | .. |
| 3rd 12-pounder Battery of 7th Field Artillery Regiment, Captain Von Eynatten (II) | .. | .. | .. | 6 | .. |
| 3rd 4-pounder Battery of 7th Field Artillery Regiment, Captain Cöster | .. | .. | .. | 7 | .. |
| Total of 26th Infantry Brigade | 5 | .. | 3 | 13 | .. |

2 s 2

## APPENDIX XXVIII—*continued.*

| | Battalions of Infantry. | Battalions of Rifles. | Squadrons. | Guns. | Battalions of Pioneers. |
|---|---|---|---|---|---|
| **13TH INFANTRY DIVISION—***continued.* | | | | | |
| SPECIAL RESERVE. | | | | | |
| Colonel Baron Von der Goltz, commanding 15th Infantry Regiment. | | | | | |
| 15th Infantry Regiment: | | | | | |
| 1st Battalion, Major Von Kaweczynski | } 2 | .. | .. | .. | .. |
| Fusilier Battalion, Major Baron Von Boningk | | | | | |
| Fusilier Battalion of 55th Infantry Regiment, L'eut.-Colonel Von Rex | 1 | .. | .. | .. | .. |
| 4th 4-pounder Battery of 7th Field Artillery Regiment, Captain Weigelt | .. | .. | .. | 6 | .. |
| Total of Special Reserve | 3 | .. | .. | 6 | .. |
| RESERVE BRIGADE. | | | | | |
| Major-General Von Tresckow. | | | | | |
| 19th Infantry Regiment, Lieutenant-Colonel Von Henning: | | | | | |
| 2nd Battalion, Major Von Wangenheim | } 2 | .. | .. | .. | .. |
| Fusilier Battalion, Major Kühne | | | | | |
| 4th Cuirassier Regiment, Colonel Von Schmidt | .. | .. | 4 | .. | .. |
| 3rd Horse Artillery Battery of 7th Field Artillery Regiment, Captain Melting | .. | .. | .. | 6 | .. |
| Total of Reserve Brigade | 2 | .. | 4 | 6 | '.. |

Absent as escort of baggage :—1st Battalion of 19th Regiment.

## SUMMARY.

| | Battalions. | Squadrons. | Guns. |
|---|---|---|---|
| Total of 25th Infantry Brigade | 4 | 2 | 6 |
| „ 26th Infantry Brigade | 5 | 3 | 13 |
| „ Special Reserve | 3 | .. | 6 |
| „ Reserve Brigade | 2 | 4 | 6 |
| Total | 14 | 7 | 31 |

## APPENDIX XXIX.

SPECIAL Order of Battle of the Prussian Troops engaged in the Action of Hammelburg, 10th July, 1866.

| Combined Infantry Division | .. | .. | Major-General Von Beyer. |
|---|---|---|---|
| Combined Staff Officer | .. | .. | Major Von Zeuner. |
| Commander of Artillery | .. | .. | Major Stumpff. |

| | Battalions of Infantry. | Battalions of Rifles. | Squadrons. | Guns. | Battalions of Pioneers. |
|---|---|---|---|---|---|
| **ADVANCED GUARD.** | | | | | |
| Major-General Von Schachtmeyer, Commanding 32nd Infantry Brigade. | | | | | |
| 39th Fusilier Regiment, Colonel Von Woyna (II.): | | | | | |
| 1st Battalion, Major Von Cederstolpe.. | | | | | |
| 2nd Battalion, Major Kruse .. | 3 | .. | .. | .. | .. |
| 3rd Battalion, Major Kurth .. | | | | | |
| 4th Squadron of 9th Hussar Regiment, Captain Von Lücken . | .. | .. | 1 | .. | .. |
| 1st 4-pounder Battery of 8th Field Artillery Regiment, Captain Schmidts .. | .. | .. | .. | 6 | .. |
| Total of Advanced Guard .. | 3 | .. | 1 | 6 | .. |
| **MAIN BODY.** | | | | | |
| Major-General Von Glümer. | | | | | |
| 32nd Infantry Regiment, Colonel Von Schwerin: | | | | | |
| 1st Battalion, Lieut.-Colonel Von Donat | | | | | |
| 2nd Battalion, Lieut.-Colonel Von der Lundt | 3 | .. | .. | .. | .. |
| Fusilier Battalion, Lieutenant-Colonel Von Wülcknitz .. | | | | | |
| 20th Infantry Regiment, Colonel Von der Wense: | | | | | |
| 1st Battalion, Major Eskens .. | | | | | |
| 2nd Battalion, Major Baron Von Herzberg .. | 3 | .. | .. | .. | .. |
| Fusilier Battalion, Major Brüggemann .. | | | | | |
| 2nd Squadron of 9th Hussar Regiment, Captain Von Rommel .. | .. | .. | 1 | .. | .. |
| 1st 12-pounder Battery of 8th Field Artillery Regiment, Captain Richter .. | .. | .. | .. | 6 | .. |
| 12th 12-pounder Battery of Reserve Field Artillery Regiment, Lieutenant Hoffbauer.. | .. | .. | .. | 6 | .. |
| Total of Main Body .. | 6 | .. | 1 | 12 | .. |

APPENDIX XXIX—*continued.*

| | Battalions of Infantry. | Battalions of Rifles. | Squadrons. | Guns. | Battalions of Pioneers. |
|---|---|---|---|---|---|
| **RESERVE.** | | | | | |
| Colonel Von Selchow, Commanding 30th Infantry Regiment. | | | | | |
| 2nd Battalion of 30th Infantry Regiment, Major Von Schnehen | | | | | |
| Fusilier Battalion of 30th Infantry Regiment, Major Von Frankenberg | 1¾ | .. | .. | .. | .. |
| 70th Infantry Regiment, Colonel Von Woyna (I.): | | | | | |
| 1st Battalion, Major Von Mützschepfahl | | | | | |
| Fusilier Battalion, Major de L'Espinol | 2 | .. | .. | .. | .. |
| 3 Squadrons of 9th Hussar Regiment, Major Von Cosel | .. | .. | 3 | .. | .. |
| 10th and 11th Reserve 12-pounder Batteries, Captains Von Horn and Von Bastineller | .. | .. | .. | 12 | .. |
| Total of Reserve | 3¾ | .. | 3 | 12 | .. |

SUMMARY.

| | Battalions. | Squadrons. | Guns. |
|---|---|---|---|
| Advanced Guard | 3 | 1 | 6 |
| Main Body | 6 | 1 | 12 |
| Reserve | 3¾ | 3 | 12 |
| Total | 12¾ | 5 | 30 |

Absent on other Duty :—
    1st Battalion of 30th and 2nd Battalion of 70th Regiment as Garrison in Cassel.
Five Companies of 30th Regiment as escort of baggage.

# APPENDIX XXX.

SPECIAL Order of Battle of the Prussian Troops engaged in the Actions of Friedrichshall, Hausen, Waldaschach, and Kissingen, 10th July, 1866.

## FRIEDRICHSHALL, HAUSEN, WALDASCHACH.

Corps of Lieutenant-General Baron Von Manteuffel.
Chief of the Staff, Colonel Von Strantz.
Commander of Artillery, Major Von Seel.

| | Battalions of Infantry. | Battalions of Rifles. | Squadrons. | Guns. | Battalions of Pioneers. |
|---|---|---|---|---|---|
| **ADVANCED GUARD.** | | | | | |
| Major-General Von Freyhold. | | | | | |
| 59th Infantry Regiment, Colonel Von Kessler: | | | | | |
| 1st Battalion, Major Haack .. .. .. | | | | | |
| 2nd Battalion, Major des Barres .. .. | 3 | .. | .. | .. | .. |
| Fusilier Battalion, Lieutenant-Colonel Von Köppen.. .. .. .. .. .. | | | | | |
| 1st Squadron of 6th Dragoon Regiment .. .. | .. | .. | 1 | .. | .. |
| 4th 4-pounder Battery of the 6th Field Artillery Regiment, Captain Von Tempsky .. .. | .. | .. | .. | 6 | .. |
| Total of Advanced Guard .. .. | 3 | .. | 1 | 6 | .. |
| **MAIN BODY.** | | | | | |
| Colonel Baron Von Hanstein, Commanding 25th Infantry Regiment. | | | | | |
| 36th Fusilier Regiment, Colonel Von Thile: | | | | | |
| 1st Battalion, Major Von Lupinsky .. .. | | | | | |
| 2nd Battalion, Major Baron Von Keyserlingk | 3 | .. | .. | .. | .. |
| 3rd Battalion, Major Liebeskind .. .. | | | | | |
| Saxe-Coburg Gotha Infantry Regiment, Colonel Von Fabeck: | | | | | |
| 1st Battalion, Captain Von Bassewitz .. | 2 | .. | .. | .. | .. |
| Fusilier Battalion, Major Von Gerstein .. | | | | | |
| 3rd and 4th Squadrons of 6th Dragoon Regiment, Colonel Krug Von Nidda .. .. .. | .. | .. | 2 | .. | .. |
| 6-pounder Battery from Stade, Lieutenant Loose.. | .. | .. | .. | 6 | .. |
| Left Flank Detachment against Waldaschach Fusilier Battalion of 25th Infantry Regiment, Lieutenant-Colonel Von Cranach.. .. .. | 1 | .. | .. | .. | .. |
| Total of Main Body .. .. .. | 6 | .. | 2 | 6 | .. |

| | Battalions of Infantry. | Battalions of Rifles. | Squadrons. | Guns. | Battalions of Pioneers. |
|---|---|---|---|---|---|
| **RESERVE.** | | | | | |
| Major-General Von Flies. | | | | | |
| 11th Grenadier Regiment, Colonel Von Zglinitzki : | | | | | |
| 1st Battalion, Lieutenant-Colonel des Barres.. | | | | | |
| 2nd Battalion, Major Von Bonin    ..    .. | 3 | .. | .. | .. | .. |
| Fusilier Battalion, Major Von Busse ..    .. | | | | | |
| 1st Battalion of 25th Infantry Regiment, Major Von Loebell..    ..    ..    ..    .. | | | | | |
| 2nd Battalion of 25th Infantry Regiment, Major Bassenge    ..    ..    ..    .. | $1\frac{3}{4}$ | .. | .. | .. | .. |
| 1st and 2nd Squadrons of 5th Dragoons Regiment, Colonel Von Wedell | .. | .. | 2 | .. | .. |
| 4, 12, and 6-pounder Batteries of 6th Field Artillery Regiment, Captain Von Biottnitz, Captain Von der Goltz, and Captain Gaertner..    ..    .. | .. | .. | .. | 24 | .. |
| Total of Reserve    ..    .. | $4\frac{3}{4}$ | .. | 2 | 24 | .. |

Absent on other Duties :—
    4th Company of 25th Regiment as garrison at Brückenau.
    3rd Squadron of 5th Dragoons as escort of baggage.
    4th Squadron of 5th Dragoons as escort of foraging party at Brückenau.
    2nd Squadron of 6th Dragoons as head-quarters escort.

## SUMMARY OF CORPS MANTEUFFEL.

| | Battalions. | Squadrons. | Guns. |
|---|---|---|---|
| Advanced Guard    ..    .. | 3 | 1 | 6 |
| Main Body    ..    ..    .. | 6 | 2 | 6 |
| Reserve    ..    ..    .. | $4\frac{3}{4}$ | 2 | 24 |
| Total    ..    .. | $13\frac{1}{4}$ | 5 | 36 |

## APPENDIX XXX—*continued*,

## AT KISSINGEN,

| | Battalions of Infantry. | Battalions of Rifles. | Squadrons. | Guns. | Battalions of Pioneers. |
|---|---|---|---|---|---|
| **13TH INFANTRY DIVISION.** | | | | | |
| Lieutenant-General Von Goeben. | | | | | |
| ADVANCED GUARD. | | | | | |
| *25th Infantry Brigade.* | | | | | |
| Major-General Von Kummer. | | | | | |
| 53rd Infantry Regiment, Colonel Von Tresckow: | | | | | |
| 1st Battalion, Captain Von Grabow .. .. | | | | | |
| 2nd Battalion, Captain Von Bastineller .. } 3 | 3 | .. | .. | .. | .. |
| Fusilier Battalion, Major Von Rosenzweig .. | | | | | |
| 13th Infantry Regiment, Colonel Von Gellhorn: | | | | | |
| 2nd Battalion, Captain Von Kerssenbrock .. } 2 | 2 | .. | .. | .. | .. |
| Fusilier Battalion, Captain Von Wichmann .. | | | | | |
| 2nd Squadron of 8th Hussar Regiment .. .. | .. | .. | 1 | .. | .. |
| 4 and 6-pounder Batteries of 7th Field Artillery Regiment, Captains Weigelt and Von Eynatten (I.) .. .. .. .. .. | .. | .. | .. | 12 | .. |
| Total of Advanced Guard .. .. | 5 | .. | 1 | 12 | .. |
| **MAIN BODY.** | | | | | |
| *26th Infantry Brigade.* | | | | | |
| Major-General Baron Von Wrangel. | | | | | |
| 1st Battalion of 15th Infantry Regiment, Major Von Kaweczynski .. .. .. .. .. | 1 | .. | .. | .. | .. |
| Lippe Fusilier Battalion, Major Rohdewald .. | 1 | .. | .. | .. | .. |
| 55th Infantry Regiment, Colonel Stoltz: | | | | | |
| 1st Battalion, Lieutenant-Colonel Von Böck-ing .. .. .. .. .. | | | | | |
| 2nd Battalion, Major Von Gotzkow .. .. } 3 | 3 | .. | .. | .. | .. |
| Fusilier Battalion, Lieutenant-Colonel Von Rex .. .. .. .. .. | | | | | |
| 4 Squadrons of 8th Hussar Regiment, Colonel Von Rantzau .. .. .. .. | .. | .. | 4 | .. | .. |
| 3rd 4-pounder Battery of 7th Field Artillery Regiment, Captain Cöster .. .. .. | .. | .. | .. | 7 | .. |
| 3rd 12-pounder Battery of 7th Field Artillery Regiment, Captain Von Eynatten (II.) .. .. | .. | .. | .. | 6 | .. |
| *Left Flank Detachment.* | | | | | |
| Colonel Baron Von der Goltz. | | | | | |
| 2nd Battalion of 15th Infantry Regiment, Captain Von Hattorf .. .. .. .. .. | 1 | .. | .. | .. | .. |
| Fusilier Battalion of 15th Infantry Regiment, Major Baron Von Böningk .. .. .. | 1 | .. | .. | .. | .. |
| Total of Main Body .. .. | 7 | .. | 4 | 13 | .. |

APPENDIX XXX—*continued.*

| | Battalions of Infantry. | Battalions of Rifles. | Squadrons. | Guns. | Battalions of Pioneers. |
|---|---|---|---|---|---|
| 13TH INFANTRY DIVISION—*continued.* | | | | | |
| RESERVE. | | | | | |
| Major-General Von Tresckow. | | | | | |
| 19th Infantry Regiment, Lieutenant-Colonel Von Henning : | | | | | |
| 1st Battalion, Major Von Drigalsky .. .. | } 3 | .. | .. | .. | .. |
| 2nd Battalion, Major Von Wangenheim .. | | | | | |
| Fusilier Battalion, Major Kühne .. .. | | | | | |
| 4th Cuirassier Regiment, Colonel Schmidt .. .. | .. | .. | 4 | .. | .. |
| 3rd Horse Artillery Battery of 7th Field Artillery Regiment, Captain Metting .. .. .. | .. | .. | .. | 6 | .. |
| Total of Reserve .. .. .. | 3 | .. | 4 | 6 | .. |

Absent on other Duty :—1st Battalion of 13th Regiment detached to Aura.

## SUMMARY OF DIVISION GOEBEN.

| | Battalions. | Squadrons. | Guns. |
|---|---|---|---|
| Advanced Guard .. .. | 5 | 1 | 12 |
| Main Body .. .. .. | 7 | 4 | 13 |
| Reserve .. ., .. | 3 | 4 | 6 |
| Total .. .. | 15 | 9 | 31 |

# APPENDIX XXXI.

SPECIAL Order of Battle of the Prussian Troops engaged in the action of Laufach, 13th July, 1866.

General Commanding ..    ..    Lieut.-General Von Goeben.
General Staff Officer  ..       Captain Von Jena.
Commander of Artillery    ..    Major Von Drabich-Wächter.

| | Battalions of Infantry. | Battalions of Rifles. | Squadrons. | Guns. | Battalions of Pioneers. |
|---|---|---|---|---|---|
| **25th Infantry Brigade.** | | | | | |
| Major-General Von Kummer. | | | | | |
| 53rd Infantry Regiment, Colonel Von Tresckow: | | | | | |
| 1st Battalion, Captain Von Bastineller | | | | | |
| 2nd Battalion, Captain Von Grabow .. | 3 | .. | .. | .. | .. |
| Fusilier Battalion, Major Von Rosenzweig .. | | | | | |
| 13th Infantry Regiment, Cologel Von Gellhorn: | | | | | |
| 1st Battalion, Lieut.-Colonel Von Borries | | | | | |
| 2nd Battalion, Captain Von Kerssenbrock .. | 3 | .. | .. | .. | .. |
| Fusilier Battalion, Captain Von Wichmann .. | | | | | |
| 3rd and 5th Squadrons of 8th Hussar Regiment, Major Krug Von Nidda .. .. .. .. | .. | .. | 2 | .. | .. |
| 3rd 4-pounder Battery of 7th Field Artillery Regiment, Captain Weiglet .. .. .. .. | .. | .. | .. | 6 | .. |
| 3rd 6-pounder Battery of 7th Field Artillery Regiment, Captain Von Eynatten (I).. .. .. | .. | .. | .. | 6 | .. |
| **26th Infantry Brigade.** | | | | | |
| Major-General Von Baron Von Wrangel. | | | | | |
| 55th Infantry Regiment, Colonel Stoltz: | | | | | |
| 1st Battalion, Lieut.-Colonel Von Böcking .. | | | | | |
| 2nd Battalion, Major Von Gotzkow .. .. | 3 | .. | .. | .. | .. |
| Fusilier Battalion, Lieut.-Colonel Von Rex .. | | | | | |
| 15th Infantry Regiment, Colonel Baron Von der Goltz: | | | | | |
| 1st Battalion, Major Von Kaweczynski .. | | | | | |
| 2nd Battalion, Captain Von Hattorf .. .. | 3 | .. | .. | .. | .. |
| Fusilier Battalion, Major Baron Von Böningk | | | | | |
| Lippe Fusilier Battalion, Captain Kellner .. .. | 1 | .. | .. | .. | .. |
| Three Squadrons of 8th Hussar Regiment, Colonel Von Rantzau .. .. .. .. .. | .. | .. | 3 | .. | .. |
| Two Batteries of 7th Field Artillery Regiment, Captains Coster and Von Eynatten (II.) .. | .. | .. | .. | 13 | .. |

APPENDIX XXXI—*continued.*

| | Battalions of Infantry. | Battalions of Rifles. | Squadrons. | Guns. | Battalions of Pioneers. |
|---|---|---|---|---|---|
| *Reserve Brigade.* | | | | | |
| Major-General Von Tresckow. | | | | | |
| 19th Infantry Regiment, Lieutenant-Colonel Von Henning: | | | | | |
| 1st Battalion, Captain Von Skrbensky.. | } 3 | .. | .. | .. | .. |
| 2nd Battalion, Major Von Wangenheim | | | | | |
| Fusilier Battalion, Captain Von Wlosto | | | | | |
| Three Squadrons of 4th Cuirassier Regiment, Colonel Von Schmidt .. .. .. .. | .. | .. | 3 | .. | .. |
| 3rd Horse Artillery Battery of 7th Field Artillery Regiment, Captain Metting .. .. .. | .. | .. | .. | 6 | .. |
| Total .. .. .. | 16 | .. | 8 | 31 | .. |

N.B.—The 1st Squadron of the 4th Cuirassier Regiment did duty as head-quarters' escort.

## APPENDIX XXXII.

ORDER of Battle of the Prussian Troops engaged in the action of Aschaffenburg, 14th July, 1866.

| | Battalions of Infantry. | Battalions of Rifles. | Squadrons. | Guns. | Battalions of Pioneers. |
|---|---|---|---|---|---|
| **13TH INFANTRY DIVISION.** | | | | | |
| Lieutenant-General Von Goeben. | | | | | |
| General Staff Officer, Captain Von Jena. | | | | | |
| *25th Infantry Brigade.* | | | | | |
| Major General Von Kummer. | | | | | |
| 13th Infantry Regiment, Colonel Von Bellhorn : | | | | | |
| 1st Battalion, Lieut.-Colonel Von Borries .. | | | | | |
| 2nd Battalion, Captain Von Kerssenbrock .. | 3 | .. | .. | .. | .. |
| Fusilier Battalion, Captain Von Wichmann .. | | | | | |
| 53rd Infantry Regiment, Colonel Von Tresckow : | | | | | |
| 1st Battalion, Captain Von Grabow .. | | | | | |
| 2nd Battalion, Captain Von Bastineller .. | 2¾ | .. | .. | .. | .. |
| Fusilier Battalion, Major Von Rosenzweig .. | | | | | |
| Two batteries of 7th Field Artillery Regiment, | | | | | |
| Captains Weigelt and Von Eynatten (I) .. | .. | .. | | | .. |
| *26th Infantry Brigade.* | | | | | |
| Major-General Baron Von Wrangel. | | | | | |
| 15th Infantry Regiment, Col. Baron Von der Goltz : | | | | | |
| 1st Battalion, Major Von Kaweczynski .. | | | | | |
| 2nd Battalion, Captain Von Hattorf .. .. | 3 | .. | .. | .. | .. |
| Fusilier Battalion, Major Baron Von Böningk | | | | | |
| 55th Infantry Regiment, Colonel Stoltz : | | | | | |
| 1st Battalion, Lieut.-Colonel Von Böcking .. | | | | | |
| 2nd Battalion, Major Von Gotzkow .. .. | 3 | .. | .. | .. | .. |
| Fusilier Battalion, Lieut.-Co'onel Von Rex .. | | | | | |
| Lippe Fusilier Battalion, Captain Kellner.. | 1 | .. | .. | .. | .. |
| 4th Squadron of 8th Hussar Regt., Capt. Von Grodzki | .. | .. | 1 | .. | .. |
| Two batteries of 7th Field Artillery Regiment, | | | | | |
| Captains Cöster and Von Eynatten (II).. .. | .. | .. | .. | 13 | .. |
| *Reserve Brigade.* | | | | | |
| Major-General Von Tresckow. | | | | | |
| 19th Infantry Regiment : | | | | | |
| 1st Battalion, Captain Von Skrbensky.. .. | 2 | .. | .. | .. | .. |
| Fusilier Battalion, Captain Von Wlosto .. | | | | | |
| Four Squadrons 8th Hussar Regt., Col. Von Rantzau | .. | .. | 4 | .. | .. |
| Three Squadrons of 4th Cuirassier Regiment, | | | | | |
| Colonel Von Schmidt .. .. .. .. | .. | .. | 3 | .. | .. |
| 3rd Horse Artillery Battery of 7th Field Artillery | | | | | |
| Regiment, Captain Metting .. .. .. | .. | .. | .. | 6 | .. |
| Total .. .. .. | 14¾ | .. | 8 | 31 | .. |

N.B.—The 2nd Battalion of the 19th Regiment was absent escorting prisoners; the 1st Squadron of the 4th Cuirassiers did duty as head-quarters' escort: the 6th Company of the 53rd Regiment as escort of baggage.

## APPENDIX XXXIII.

ORDER OF BATTLE OF THE PRUSSIAN ARMY OF THE
MAINE, DURING THE PERIOD FROM THE 20th JULY
TILL THE ARMISTICE.

| | |
|---|---|
| Commander-in-Chief.. | Lieutenant-General Baron Von Manteuffel. |
| Chief of the Staff | Colonel Von Kraatz Koschlau. |
| Quartermaster-General | Colonel Von Strautz. |
| Commander of Artillery | Colonel Von Decker. |
| First Engineer Officer | Colonel Schulz. |
| 13th Infantry Division | Lieut.-General Von Goeben. |
| General Staff Officer.. | Captain Von Jena. |
| 25th Infantry Brigade | Major-General Von Kummer. |
| 53rd Infantry Regiment | Lieut.-Colonel Von Manteuffel. |
| 13th Infantry Regiment | Colonel Von Gellhorn. |
| 26th Infantry Brigade | Major-Gen. Baron Von Wrangel. |
| 55th Infantry Regiment | Colonel Stoltz. |
| 15th Infantry Regiment | Colonel Baron Von der Goltz. |
| Lippe Detmold Fusilier Battalion | Captain Kellner. |
| 8th Regiment of Hussars .. | Colonel Von Rantzau. |
| Four batteries of 7th Field Artillery Regiment .. | Major Von Drabich-Wächter. |
| Combined Reserve Brigade.. | Major-General Von Tresckow. |
| 19th Infantry Regiment | Lieut.-Colonel Von Henning. |
| 4th Cuirassier Regiment | Colonel Von Schmidt. |

3rd Horse Artillery Battery of 7th Field Artillery Regiment.
4th Company of 7th Pioneer Battalion.
Light Field Hospital.

Total of the three Prussian Brigades :—16 battalions, 9 squadrons,
31 guns, 1 company of Pioneers.

| | |
|---|---|
| Oldenburg Hanseatic Brigade | Major-General Von Weltzien. |
| General Staff Officer .. | Major Becker. |
| Oldenburg Infantry Regiment | Colonel Lehmann. |
| Lübeck Battalion of Light Infantry | Major Von Bültzingslöwen (joined on 26th July). |
| Bremen Fusilier Battalion .. | Lieut.-Colonel Niebour. |
| Hamburg Infantry Regiment.. | Colonel Bess. |
| Two squadrons of Hamburg Dragoons .. | Major Heinsen (joined on 29th July). |
| Oldenburg "Reiter" Regiment | Colonel Beseke. |
| Two Oldenburg batteries | Lieut.-Colonel Rüder. |

Oldenburg Light Field Hospital.

Total of Oldenburg Hanseatic Brigade :—7, battalions, 5 squadrons,
12 guns.
Total of 13th Infantry Division:—23 battalions, 14 squadrons, 43 guns,
1 company of Pioneers.

*Combined Division of Major-General Von Beyer.*

| | |
|---|---|
| General Staff Officer.. .. .. | Major Von Zeuner. |
| 32nd Infantry Brigade .. .. | Colonel Von Woyna (I), commanding 70th Infantry Regiment. |
| 70th Infantry Regiment. | |
| 30th Infantry Regiment .. | Lieut.-Colonel Von Koblinski. |
| Combined Infantry Brigade .. | Major-General Von Glümer. |
| 20th Infantry Regiment .. .. | Colonel Von der Wense. |
| 32nd Infantry Regiment .. .. | Colonel Von Schwerin. |
| 39th Fusilier Regiment .. .. | Colonel Von Woyna (II). |
| 9th Hussar Regiment .. .. .. | Major Von Cosel. |
| Two Squadrons of 10th Landwehr Hussar Regiment.. .. .. | Major Von Kuylenstierna (joined on 21st July). |
| Three batteries .. .. .. | Major Stumpff (one battery joined on 22nd July). |
| Reserve Artillery .. .. .. | Major Petzel (formed on 22nd July). |

Four Reserve Batteries.
One Company of Pioneers.
Light Field Hospital.

Total of Division Beyer:—15 battalions, 7 squadrons, 42 guns, 1 company of Pioneers.

N.B.—2nd Battalion 70th Regiment and 1st Battalion 30th Regiment had been left as garrison in Cassel, and re-joined on 21st July. Two squadrons of 10th Hussars were in Frankfort and Hanover.

*Combined Division of Major-General Flies.*

| | |
|---|---|
| General Staff Officer .. .. | Major Von Gottberg. |
| 1st Combined Infantry Brigade .. | Major-General Von Freyhold. |
| 36th Fusilier Regiment .. | Colonel Von Thile. |
| 25th Infantry Regiment .. | Colonel Baron Von Hanstein. |
| 9th Rifle Battalion .. | Captain Von Medem (joined on 22nd July). |
| 2nd Combined Infantry Brigade .. | Major-General Von Korth. |
| 59th Infantry Regiment .. | Colonel Von Kessler. |
| 11th Grenadier Regiment .. | Colonel Von Zglinitzki. |
| Saxe-Coburg-Gotha Infantry Regiment .. .. .. | Colonel Von Fabeck. |
| Five batteries .. .. .. | Major Von Seel. |
| Combined Cavalry Brigade.. .. | Major-General Von Below (took command 30th July). |
| 5th Regiment of Dragoons .. | Colonel Von Wedell. |
| 6th Regiment of Dragoons .. | Colonel Krug Von Nidda. |

4th Horse Artillery Battery of 7th Field Artillery Regiment.
Light Field Hospital.

Total of Division Flies:—15 battalions, 8 squadrons, 36 guns.
Total of Army of the Maine:—53 battalions, 29 squadrons, 121 guns, 2 companies of Pioneers.

## APPENDIX XXXIV.

### FORMATION OF THOSE TROOPS WHICH WERE STATIONED AT AND NEAR FRANKFORT-ON-THE-MAINE, FROM 20TH JULY TO THE ARMISTICE.

General Commanding .. .. { Major-General Von Roeder, Commandant of Frankfort-on-the Maine.

A. TROOPS which formed the garrison of Frankfort-on-the-Maine, under the command of Colonel Von Kortzfleisch, commanding 7th Landwehr Regiment:—

17th Landwehr Regiment:

The 4th Battalion of the 30th Infantry Regiment.

The 4th Battalion of the 32nd Infantry Regiment (arrived at Frankfort on 29th July).

The 4th Battalion of the 36th Fusilier Regiment (detached as garrison of Aschaffenburg).

The 4th Battalion of the 39th Fusilier Regiment.

The 4th Battalion of the 70th Infantry Regiment.

One Squadron of the 10th Landwehr Hussar Regiment.

One Depôt Battery of 7th Field Artillery Regiment.

Total:—8 battalions, 1 squadron, 4 guns.

B. TROOPS which occupied Wiesbaden and neighbourhood, and observed the Fortress of Mayence, under the command of Lieut.-Colonel Von Fischer Treuenfeld:—

Infantry:

Waldeck Fusilier Battalion.

Schwarzburg Rudolstadt Fusilier Battalion.

2nd (Jülich) and 3rd (Malmedy) Garrison Battalions of 25th Landwehr Regiment.

3rd (Siegburg) Garrison Battalion of 28th Landwehr Regiment.

1st (Treves) Garrison Battalion of 30th Landwehr Regiment.

Two Companies of the Depôt Battalion of the 56th Regiment (returned to Cologne on 24th July).

One Combined Battalion of Rifles.

Cavalry:

One Garrison Squadron from Coblenz.

One Combined Squadron (7th and 11th Hussars).

Detachment of the Depôt Squadron of the 8th Cuirassier Regiment.

Artillery:

One 4-pounder Battery (four guns) of the Depôt Division of 8th Field Artillery Regiment.

Half a Sally Battery from Coblenz (four guns).

Pioneers:

A Detachment of Pioneers.

Total:—6½ battalions, 1 company of Rifles, 2 squadrons, 8 guns.

Detachment of Pioneers.

# APPENDIX XXXV.

SPECIAL Order of Battle of the Prussian Troops engaged at Tauberbischofsheim, Hochhausen, and Werbach, on 24th July, 1866.

| | Battalions of Infantry. | Battalions of Rifles. | Squadrons. | Guns. | Battalions of Pioneers. |
|---|---|---|---|---|---|
| **13TH INFANTRY DIVISION.** | | | | | |
| Lieut.-General Von Goeben. | | | | | |
| General Staff Officer, Captain Von Jena. | | | | | |
| Commander of Artillery, Major Von Drabich-Wächter. | | | | | |
| **ADVANCED GUARD.** | | | | | |
| Major-General Baron Von Wrangel. | | | | | |
| *26th Infantry Brigade.* | | | | | |
| 55th Infantry Regiment, Colonel Stoltz : | | | | | |
| 1st Battalion, Lieut.-Colonel Von Böcking .. | | | | | |
| 2nd Battalion, Major Von Gotzkow .. .. | 3 | .. | .. | .. | .. |
| Fusilier Battalion, Captain Von Arnim .. | | | | | |
| 2nd Battalion of 15th Regiment, Captain Von Hattorf .. .. .. .. .. .. | 1 | .. | .. | .. | .. |
| Lippe Fusilier Battalion, Captain Kellner.. .. | 1 | .. | .. | .. | .. |
| Three Squadrons of 8th Hussar Regiment, Colonel Von Rantzau .. .. .. .. .. | .. | .. | 3 | .. | .. |
| Two Batteries of 7th Field Artillery Regiment, Captains Coster and Von Eynatten (II).. .. | .. | .. | .. | 11 | .. |
| **MAIN BODY.** | | | | | |
| *25th Infantry Brigade.* | | | | | |
| Major-General Von Kummer. | | | | | |
| 53rd Infantry Regiment, Lieut.-Colonel Von Manteuffel : | | | | | |
| 1st Battalion, Captain Von Grabow .. .. | | | | | |
| 2nd Battalion, Captain Von Bastineller .. | 3 | .. | .. | .. | .. |
| Fusilier Battalion, Major Von Rosenzweig ·.. | | | | | |
| 13th Infantry Regiment, Colonel Von Gellhorn : | | | | | |
| 1st Battalion, Lieut.-Colonel Von Borries .. | | | | | |
| 2nd Battalion, Captain Von Kerssenbrock .. | 3 | .. | .. | .. | .. |
| Fusilier Battalion, Captain Von Wichmann .. | | | | | |
| 2nd Squadron of 8th Hussar Regiment .. .. | .. | .. | 1 | .. | .. |
| Two batteries of 7th Field Artillery Regiment, Captains Weigelt and Von Eynatten (I).. .. | .. | .. | .. | 12 | .. |
| *Reserve Brigade.* | | | | | |
| Major-General Von Tresckow. | | | | | |
| 19th Infantry Regiment, Lieutenant-Colonel Von Henning : | | | | | |
| 1st Battalion, Captain Von Skrbensky .. | | | | | |
| 2nd Battalion, Major Von Wangenheim .. | 2¾ | .. | .. | .. | .. |
| Fusilier Battalion, Captain Von Wlosto .. | | | | | |
| 4th Cuirassier Regiment, Colonel Von Schmidt .. | .. | .. | 4 | .. | .. |
| 3rd Horse Artillery Battery of 7th Field Artillery Regiment, Captain Metting .. .. .. | .. | .. | .. | 6 | .. |

2 T

APPENDIX XXXV—*continued.*

| | Battalions of Infantry. | Battalions of Rifles. | Squadrons. | Guns. | Battalions of Pioneers. |
|---|---|---|---|---|---|
| **13TH INFANTRY DIVISION**—*continued.* | | | | | |
| LEFT FLANK COLUMN. | | | | | |
| *Oldenburg Hanseatic Brigade.* | | | | | |
| Major-General Von Welzien. | | | | | |
| Oldenburg Infantry Regiment, Colonel Lehmann : | | | | | |
| 1st Battalion, Major.Von Beaulieu-Marconnáy | | | | | |
| 2nd Battalion, Lieut.-Colonel Lamping | 3 | .. | .. | .. | .. |
| 3rd Battalion, Lieut.-Colonel Kellner .. | | | | | |
| Bremen Battalion, Lieut.-Colonel Niebour.. | 1 | .. | .. | .. | .. |
| Oldenburg " Reiter " Regiment, Colonel Besecke .. | .. | .. | 3 | .. | .. |
| Two Oldenburg Batteries, Major Nieber and Capt. Von Baumbach | .. | .. | .. | 12 | .. |
| *Detachment* of Colonel Baron Von der Goltz, commanding 15th Infantry Regiment : | | | | | |
| 1st Battalion of 15th Infantry Regiment, Major Von Kaweczynski | 1 | .. | .. | .. | .. |
| Fusilier Battalion of 15th Infantry Regiment, Major Baron Von Böningk | 1 | .. | .. | .. | .. |
| 3rd Squadron of 8th Hussar Regiment | .. | .. | 1 | .. | .. |
| Two guns of 3rd 4-pounder Battery of 7th Field Artillery Regiment.. | .. | .. | .. | 2 | .. |
| Total of 13th Infantry Divion | 19¾ | .. | 12 | 43 | .. |

N.B.—The 4th Company of 19th Regiment was engaged as escort of baggage.

SUMMARY.

| | Battalions. | Squadrons. | Guns. |
|---|---|---|---|
| Advanced Guard : 26th Brigade .. | 5 | 3 | 11 |
| Main Body : 25th Brigade.. | 6 | 1 | 12 |
| Reserve Brigade | 2¾ | 4 | 6 |
| Oldenburg Hanseatic Brigade | 4 | 3 | 12 |
| Detachment of Von der Goltz | 2 | 1 | 2 |
| Total .. | 19¾ | 12 | 43 |

# APPENDIX XXXVI.

Special Order of Battle of the Prussian Troops engaged in the Action of Helmstadt, 25th July, 1866.

| | Battalions of Infantry. | Battalions of Rifles. | Squadrons. | Guns. | Battalions of Pioneers. |
|---|---|---|---|---|---|
| **Combined Infantry Division.** | | | | | |
| Major-General Von Beyer. | | | | | |
| General Staff Officer, Major Von Zeuner. | | | | | |
| *Advanced Guard.* | | | | | |
| Colonel Von Woyna (I) commanding 70th Infantry Regiment: | | | | | |
| 1st Battalion 30th Infantry Regiment, Major Von Mützschefahl | 1 | .. | .. | .. | .. |
| 2nd Battalion 30th Infantry Regiment, Major Von Schnehen | 1 | .. | .. | .. | .. |
| Fusilier Battalion 70th Infantry Regiment, Major de l'Espinol.. | 1 | .. | .. | .. | .. |
| 5th Squadron 9th Hussar Regiment, Captain Von Bötticher | . | .. | 1 | .. | .. |
| 1st 4-pounder Battery of 8th Field Artillery Regiment, Captain Schmidts | .. | .. | .. | 6 | .. |
| *Main Body.* | | | | | |
| Major-General Von Glümer. | | | | | |
| Commander of Infantry, Colonel Von der Wense, commanding 20th Infantry Regiment. | | | | | |
| 20th Infantry Regiment, *ad interim* Major Baron Von Hertzberg: | | | | | |
| 1st Battalion, Major Eskens | | | | | |
| 2nd Battalion, Captain Von Wichmann | 3 | .. | .. | .. | .. |
| Fusilier Battalion, Major Brüggemann | | | | | |
| 32nd Regiment, *ad interim* Lieut.-Colonel Von der Lundt: | | | | | |
| 1st Battalion, Lieut.-Colonel Von Donat | | | | | |
| 2nd Battalion, Captain Redies.. | 3 | .. | .. | .. | .. |
| Fusilier Battalion, Lieut.-Colonel Von Wülcknitz | | | | | |
| 2nd Squadron of 9th Hussar Regiment, Captain Von Rommel | .. | .. | 1 | .. | .. |
| 1st 12-pounder Battery of 8th Field Artillery Regiment, Captain Richter | .. | .. | .. | 6 | .. |
| 2nd 6-pounder Reserve Battery, Lieut. Wasserfuhr | .. | .. | .. | 6 | .. |
| *Reserve.* | | | | | |
| Colonel Von Schwerin, commanding 32nd Regiment. | | | | | |
| 39th Fusilier Regiment, Colonel Von Woyna (II): | | | | | |
| 1st Battalion, Major Von Cederstolpe.. | | | | | |
| 2nd Battalion, Major Kruse | 3 | .. | .. | .. | .. |
| 3rd Battalion, Major Kurth | | | | | |

APPENDIX XXXVI—*continued.*

| | Battalions of Infantry. | Battalions of Rifles. | Squadrons. | Guns. | Battalions of Pioneers. |
|---|---|---|---|---|---|
| COMBINED INFANTRY DIVISION—*continued.* | | | | | |
| Two Squadrons of 10th Landwehr Hussar Regiment, Major Von Kuylenstierna .. .. .. | .. | .. | 2 | .. | .. |
| *Reserve Artillery.* | | | | | |
| Major Petzel. | | | | | |
| 1st 6-pounder Reserve Battery, Lieut. Brosent .. | .. | .. | .. | 6 | .. |
| 10th, 11th, and 12th 12-pounder Reserve Batteries, Captains Von Horn and Von Bastineller, and Lieut. Hoffbauer .. .. .. .. .. | .. | .. | .. | 18 | .. |
| Total of Combined Infantry Division | 12 | .. | 4 | 42 | .. |

N.B.—2nd Battalion 70th Regiment and 1 squadron 9th Hussars were detached to Marktheidenfeld ; 3rd Squadron 9th Hussars was head-quarters' escort, but joined in the action ; 1st Battalion 30th Regiment was employed as garrison of Werbach and escort of baggage ; 4th Squadron 9th Hussars was detached to Altertheim to cover the right flank.

## APPENDIX XXXVII.

SPECIAL Order of Battle of the Prussian Troops engaged in the action of Gerchsheim, 25th July, 1866.

|  | Battalions of Infantry. | Battalions of Rifles. | Squadrons. | Guns. | Battalions of Pioneers. |
|---|---|---|---|---|---|
| **13TH INFANTRY BRIGADE.** |  |  |  |  |  |
| Lieut.-General Von Goeben. |  |  |  |  |  |
| General Staff Officer, Captain Von Jena. |  |  |  |  |  |
| **ADVANCED GUARD.** |  |  |  |  |  |
| *25th Infantry Brigade.* |  |  |  |  |  |
| Major-Gen. Von Kummer. |  |  |  |  |  |
| 53rd Infantry Regiment, Lieut.-Colonel Von Mauteuffel : |  |  |  |  |  |
|   1st Battalion, Captain Von Grabow .. .. | 3 | .. | .. | .. | .. |
|   2nd Battalion, Captain Von Bastineller .. |  |  |  |  |  |
|   Fusilier Battalion, Major Von Rosenzweig .. |  |  |  |  |  |
| 13th Infantry Regiment, Colonel Von Bellhorn : |  |  |  |  |  |
|   1st Battalion, Lieut.-Colonel Von Borries .. | 3 | .. | .. | .. | .. |
|   2nd Battalion, Captain Von Kerssenbrock .. |  |  |  |  |  |
|   Fusilier Battalion, Captain Von Wichmann .. |  |  |  |  |  |
| 8th Hussar Regiment, Colonel Von Rantzau .. | .. | .. | 4 | .. | .. |
| 4th 4-pounder Battery, Captain Weigelt .. .. | .. | .. | .. | 6 | .. |
| 3rd 6-pounder Battery, Captain Von Eynatten (I).. | .. | .. | .. | 6 | .. |
| **RIGHT FLANK COLUMN.** |  |  |  |  |  |
| *26th Infantry Brigade.* |  |  |  |  |  |
| Major-General Baron Von Wrangel. |  |  |  |  |  |
| 15th Infantry Regiment, Colonel Baron Von der Goltz : |  |  |  |  |  |
|   1st Battalion, Major Von Kaweczynski .. | 3 | .. | .. | .. | .. |
|   2nd Battalion, Captain Von Hattorf .. .. |  |  |  |  |  |
|   Fusilier Battalion, Major Baron Böningk .. |  |  |  |  |  |
| 55th Infantry Regiment, Colonel Stoltz : |  |  |  |  |  |
|   1st Battalion, Lieut.-Colonel Von Böcking .. | 3 | .. | .. | .. | .. |
|   2nd Battalion, Major Von Gotzkow .. .. |  |  |  |  |  |
|   Fusilier Battalion, Captain Von Arnim .. |  |  |  |  |  |
| Lippe Fusilier Battalion, Captain Kellner.. | 1 | .. | .. | .. | .. |
| 5th Squadron of 8th Hussar Regiment .. .. | .. | .. | 1 | .. | .. |
| 3rd 4-pounder Battery, Captain Cöster .. .. | .. | .. | .. | 7 | .. |
| 3rd 12-pounder Battery, Captain Von Eynatten (II) .. | .. | .. | .. | 6 | .. |
| **MAIN BODY.** |  |  |  |  |  |
| *Oldenburg Hanseatic Brigade.* |  |  |  |  |  |
| Major-General Von Weltzien. |  |  |  |  |  |
| Oldenburg Infantry Regiment, Colonel Lehmann : |  |  |  |  |  |
|   1st Battalion, Major Von Beaulieu Marconnay | 3 | .. | .. | .. | .. |
|   2nd Battalion, Lieut.-Colonel Lamping .. |  |  |  |  |  |
|   3rd Battalion, Lieut.-Colonel Kellner.. |  |  |  |  |  |

APPENDIX XXXVII—*continued.*

| | Battalions of Infantry. | Battalions of Rifles. | Squadrons. | Guns. | Battalions of Pioneers. |
|---|---|---|---|---|---|
| 13TH INFANTRY DIVISION—*continued.* | | | | | |
| Bremen Battalion, Lieut.-Colonel Niebour .. .. | 1 | .. | .. | .. | .. |
| Oldenburg Dragoon Regiment, Colonel Beseke .. | .. | .. | 3 | .. | .. |
| Two Oldenburg batteries, Major Nieber and Capt. Von Baumbach .. .. .. .. .. | .. | .. | .. | 12 | .. |
| *Reserve Brigade.* | | | | | |
| Major-General Von Tresckow. | | | | | |
| 19th Infantry Regiment, Lieutenant-Colonel Von Henning: | | | | | |
|   1st Battalion, Captain Von Skrbensky .. .. | | | | | |
|   2nd Battalion, Major Von Wangenheim .. | 2¾ | .. | .. | .. | .. |
|   Fusilier Battalion, Captain Von Wlosto .. | | | | | |
| 4th Cuirassier Regiment, Colonel Von Schmidt .. | .. | .. | 4 | .. | .. |
| 3rd Horse Artillery Battery, Captain Metting .. | .. | .. | .. | 6 | .. |
| Total of 13th Infantry Division | 19¾ | .. | 12 | 43 | .. |

N.B.—4th Company 19th Regiment employed as escort of baggage.

# APPENDIX XXXVIII.

Special Order of Battle of the Prussian Troops engaged in the Action of Rossbrun, 26th July, 1866.

Commander-in-Chief .. .. Lieut.-Gen. Baron Von Manteuffel.
Chief of the Staff.. .. .. Colonel Von Kraatz-Koschlau.
Quartermaster-General .. .. Colonel Von Strantz.

| | Battalions of Infantry. | Battalions of Rifles. | Squadrons. | Guns. | Battalions of Pioneers. |
|---|---|---|---|---|---|
| **COMBINED DIVISION OF MAJOR-GENERAL VON BEYER.** | | | | | |
| General Staff Officer, Major Von Zeuner. | | | | | |
| *Advanced Guard.* | | | | | |
| Colonel Von Woyna (I.), Commanding 70th Infantry Regiment. | | | | | |
| 1st Battalion of 70th Regiment, Major Von Mützchefahl | 2 | .. | .. | .. | .. |
| Fusilier Battalion of 70th Infantry Regiment, Major de L'Espinol | | | | | |
| 2nd Battalion of 30th Infantry Regiment, Major Von Schnehen | 1 | .. | .. | .. | .. |
| 1st Battalion of 39th Fusilier Regiment, Major Von Cederstople | 1 | .. | .. | .. | .. |
| 5th Squadron of 9th Hussar Regiment, Captain Von Bötticher | .. | .. | 1 | .. | .. |
| 1st 4-pounder Battery of 8th Field Artillery Regiment, Captain Schmidts | .. | .. | .. | 6 | .. |
| *Main Body.* | | | | | |
| Major-General Von Glümer. | | | | | |
| 20th Infantry Regiment, Colonel Von der Wense : | | | | | |
| 1st Battalion, Major Eskens | 3 | .. | .. | .. | .. |
| 2nd Battalion, Major Baron Von Hertzberg.. | | | | | |
| Fusilier Battalion, Major Brüggemann | | | | | |
| 32nd Infantry Regiment, *ad interim* Lieutenant-Colonel Von der Lundt : | | | | | |
| 1st Battalion, Lieutenant-Colonel Von Donat | 2 | .. | .. | .. | .. |
| Fusilier Battalion, Lieutenant-Colonel Von Wülcknitz | | | | | |
| 2nd Squadron of 9th Hussar Regiment, Captain Von Rommel | .. | .. | 1 | .. | .. |
| 2nd 6-pounder Reserve Battery, Lieutenant Wasserfuhr .. | .. | .. | .. | 6 | .. |

APPENDIX XXXVIII—*continued.*

|  | Battalions of Infantry. | Battalions of Rifles. | Squadrons. | Guns. | Battalions of Pioneers. |
|---|---|---|---|---|---|
| COMBINED DIVISION—*continued.* | | | | | |
| *Reserve.* | | | | | |
| Colonel Von Schwerin, Commanding 32nd Infantry Regiment. | | | | | |
| 39th Fusilier Regiment, Colonel Von Woyna (II.) : 2nd Battalion, Major Kruse 3rd Battalion, Major Kurth | 2 | .. | .. | .. | .. |
| 2nd Battalion of 32nd Infantry Regiment, Captain Redies | 1 | .. | .. | .. | .. |
| 1st 12-pounder Battery of 8th Field Artillery Regiment, Captain Richter | .. | .. | .. | 6 | .. |
| *Reserve Artillery.* | | | | | |
| Major Petzel. | | | | | |
| One 6-pounder and two 12-pounder Batteries, Lieutenant Brosent, Captains Von Bastineller, and Von Horn | .. | .. | .. | 18 | .. |
| *Special Reserve* held at the disposal of Lieutenant General Von Manteuffel : Fusilier Battalion of 30th Infantry Regiment, Major Von Frankenberg | $\frac{3}{4}$ | .. | .. | .. | .. |
| 1st Squadron of 9th Hussar Regiment, Captain Reuter | .. | .. | 1 | .. | .. |
| 12th 12-pounder Reserve Battery, Lieutenant Hoffbauer | .. | .. | .. | 6 | .. |
| Total of Major-General Von Beyer's Combined Division.. | $12\frac{3}{4}$ | .. | 3 | 42 | .. |
| COMBINED DIVISION OF MAJOR-GENERAL VON FLIES. | | | | | |
| General Staff Officer, Captain Von Gottberg. | | | | | |
| *Advanced Guard.* | | | | | |
| Major-General Von Freyhold. | | | | | |
| 36th Fusilier Regiment, Colonel Von Thile : 1st Battalion, Major Von Lupinski 2nd Battalion, Major Baron Von Kayserlingk 3rd Battalion, Major Liebeskind | 3 | .. | .. | .. | .. |
| 3rd and 4th Squadrons of 5th Dragoon Regiment, Colonel Von Wedell | .. | .. | 2 | .. | .. |
| 3rd 4-pounder Battery of 6th Field Artillery Regiment, Captain Von Blottnitz | .. | .. | .. | 6 | .. |
| *Main Body.* | | | | | |
| Major-General Von Korth. | | | | | |
| 59th Infantry Regiment, Colonel Von Kessler : 1st Battalion, Major Haack 2nd Battalion, Major des Barres Fusilier Battalion, Lieutenant-Colonel Von Köppen | 3 | .. | .. | .. | .. |

## Appendix XXXVIII—*continued.*

|  | Battalions of Infantry. | Battalions of Rifles. | Squadrons. | Guns. | Battalions of Pioneers. |
|---|---|---|---|---|---|
| **Combined Division**—*continued.* |  |  |  |  |  |
| 11th Grenadier Regiment, Colonel Von Zglinitzki : | | | | | |
|   1st Battalion, Lieutenant-Colonel des Barres.. | | | | | |
|   2nd Battalion, Major Von Bonin | 3 | .. | .. | .. | .. |
|   Fusilier Battalion, Major Von Busse .. | | | | | |
| 1st and 2nd Squadrons of 5th Dragoon Regiment, Major Von Wesphal | .. | .. | 2 | .. | .. |
| 3rd 6-pounder Battery of 6th Field Artillery Regiment, Captain Von der Goltz | .. | .. | .. | 6 | .. |
| *Reserve.* | | | | | |
| Colonel Baron Von Haustein, Commanding 25th Infantry Regiment. | | | | | |
| 25th Infantry Regiment : | | | | | |
|   1st Battalion, Major Von Loebell | | | | | |
|   2nd Battalion, Major Bassenge | 3 | .. | .. | .. | .. |
|   Fusilier Battalion, Lieutenant-Colonel Von Cranach | | | | | |
| 9th Battalion of Rifles, Captain Von Medem | 1 | .. | .. | .. | .. |
| 4th Squadron of 6th Dragoon Regiment .. | .. | .. | 1 | .. | .. |
| Stader 6-pounder Battery, Lieutenant Loose | .. | .. | .. | 6 | .. |
| 4-pounder and 12-pounder Battery of 6th Field Artillery Regiment, Captains Von Tempsky and Von Gärtner | .. | .. | .. | 12 | .. |
| Total of General Flies' Division | 13 | .. | 5 | 30 | .. |
| **Combined Cavalry Brigade.** | | | | | |
| Colonel Krug Von Nidda, Commanding 6th Dragoon Regiment. | | | | | |
| Three Squadrons of 6th Dragoon Regiment, Major Von Hanstein | .. | .. | 3 | .. | .. |
| Two Squadrons of 12th Landwehr Hussar Regiment, Major Von Kuylenstierna .. | .. | .. | 1¾ | .. | .. |
| 4th Squadron of 9th Hussar Regiment | .. | .. | 1 | .. | .. |
| 4th Horse Artillery Battery of 7th Field Artillery Regiment, Captain König .. | .. | .. | .. | 6 | .. |
| Total of Combined Cavalry Brigade .. | .. | .. | 5¾ | 6 | .. |

N.B.—The 2nd Battalion of 70th Infantry Regiment, which was detached to Heidenfeld, did not rejoin the Regiment until after the action.

The 1st Battalion of 30th Infantry Regiment was detached as escort of baggage.

The 11th Company   „      „      „      „

The 4th Squadron of 9th Hussars was head-quarters' escort.

A Subdivision of the 10th Landwehr Hussars was employed in reconnoitring on the left bank of the Maine.

The 1st Battalion of the Saxe-Coburg Regiment was detached as escort of baggage; the Fusilier Battalion occupied the passage over the Maine at Wertheim.

Appendix XXXVIII—*continued.*

## SUMMARY.

|  | Battalions. | Squadrons. | Guns. |
|---|---|---|---|
| Combined Division of— | | | |
| General Von Beyer .. | 12¾ | 3 | 42 |
| General Von Flies .. | 13 | 5 | 30 |
| Combined Cavalry Brigade | .. | 5¾ | 6 |
| Total .. .. | 25¾ | 13¾ | 78 |

# APPENDIX XXXIX.

ORDER OF BATTLE of the IInd Reserve Army Corps.

General Commanding  ..  ..  H.R.H. Frederick Francis, Grand
Duke of Mecklenburg-Schwerin.
Chief of Staff  ..  ..  ..  Lieut.-Colonel Veith.
Commander of Artillery  ..  ..  Colonel Von Müller.
First Engineer Officer  ..  ..  Lieut.-Colonel Schmidt.

|  | Battalions of Infantry. | Battalions of Rifles. | Squadrons. | Guns. | Battalions of Pioneers. |
|---|---|---|---|---|---|
| PRUSSIAN DIVISION. <br> Lieut.-General Von Horn. |  |  |  |  |  |
| *Combined Brigade of Guard Infantry.* <br> Colonel Von Tresckow. |  |  |  |  |  |
| 4th Regiment of Foot Guards, Colonel Baron Von Osten-Sacken  ..  ..  ..  ..  .. | 4 | .. | .. | .. | .. |
| Combined Guard Reserve Infantry Regiment, Lieut.-Colonel Beyer Von Karger  ..  .. | 4 | .. | .. | .. | .. |
| *Combined Brigade of Infantry.* <br> Colonel Von Schkopp. |  |  |  |  |  |
| The 4th Battalions of the 2nd and 9th Grenadier, and the 14th, 42nd, and 61st Infantry Regiments | 5 | .. | .. | .. | .. |
| *Contingent of the Duchy of Anhalt.* |  |  |  |  |  |
| Fusilier Regiment, Colonel Baron Von Heimrod .. | 2 | .. | .. | .. | .. |
| *Cavalry.* |  |  |  |  |  |
| 1st Reserve Landwehr Hussar Regiment, Lieut.-Colonel Ursin Von Baer ..  ..  ..  .. | .. | .. | 4 | .. | .. |
| 1st Reserve Landwehr Lancer Regiment, Lieut.-Colonel Von Tiedemann ..  ..  ..  .. | .. | .. | 4 | .. | .. |
| *Artillery.* <br> Major Collmann. |  |  |  |  |  |
| 1st and 5th 4-pounder Batteries of 2nd Reserve Field Artillery Regiment ..  ..  ..  .. | .. | .. | .. | 12 | .. |
| 2nd Reserve Field Artillery Regiment, Lieutenant-Colonel Von Lilienthal : <br> Six batteries  ..  ..  ..  .. | .. | .. | .. | 36 | .. |
| Two light field hospitals. |  |  |  |  |  |
| Total of Prussian Division  .. | 15 | .. | 8 | 48 | ... |

APPENDIX XXXIX—*continued.*

| | Battalions of Infantry. | Battalions of Rifles. | Squadrons. | Guns. | Detachment of Pioneers. |
|---|---|---|---|---|---|
| COMBINED MECKLENBURG-SCHWERIN DIVISION. | | | | | |
| Major-General Von Bilgner.<br>General Staff Officer, Major Von Koppelow. | | | | | |
| *Mecklenburg Brigade.* | | | | | |
| Colonel Von Jasmund. | | | | | |
| 1st Mecklenburg Infantry Regiment, Lieut.-Colonel Von Lützow.. | 2 | .. | .. | .. | .. |
| 2nd Mecklenburg Infantry Regiment, Lieut.-Colonel Meklenburg.. | 2 | .. | .. | .. | .. |
| *Brunswick-Saxe-Altenburg Brigade.* | | | | | |
| Colonel Von Girsewald. | | | | | |
| Brunswick Infantry Regiment, Lieut.-Colonel Von Dedekind .. | 2 | .. | .. | .. | .. |
| Saxe-Altenburg Infantry Regiment, Colonel Von Wartenberg .. | 2 | .. | .. | .. | .. |
| Mecklenburg Rifle Battalion, Major Von Klein .. | 1 | .. | .. | .. | .. |
| Mecklenburg Dragoon Regiment, Maj. Von Kahlden | .. | .. | 4 | .. | .. |
| Brunswick Hussar Regiment, Major Von Strombeck | .. | .. | 2 | .. | .. |
| Artillery : Two Mecklenburgh and half Brunswick batteries .. | .. | .. | .. | 16 | .. |
| Combined Mecklenburg and Brunswick Pioneer detachment. | | | | | |
| Brunswick Sanitary Company. | | | | | |
| Mecklenburg field hospital. | | | | | |
| Total of Mecklenburg Division, and Pioneer Detachment .. } | 9 | .. | 6 | 16 | .. |

## SUMMARY.

| | Battalions of Infantry. | Squadrons. | Guns. | Detachment of Pioneers. |
|---|---|---|---|---|
| Prussian Division .. .. | 15 | 8 | 48 | .. |
| Combined Mecklenburg Division | 9 | 6 | 16 | .. |
| Pioneer Detachment .. .. | .. | .. | .. | 1 |
| Total .. .. | 24 | 14 | 64 | 1 |

N.B.—The two Landwehr Cavalry Regiments and two of the Prussian Reserve Batteries did not join until after the corps reached Nürnberg.

(Wt. 3161 2000 6 | 07—H & S 1430)